D0544697

Paul Philip
Chief executive
of the Solicitors
Regulation Authority
(SRA)

Andrew Walker QC
Chair of the Bar

It gives me great pleasure to welcome you to The LawCareers.Net Handbook.

The standing of the legal profession in England and Wales is one of the highest in the world. Solicitors, representing 85% of regulated legal service providers, clearly contribute greatly to this international reputation. We are therefore proud to play our part in making sure all would-be solicitors have reached the high standards expected of them before entering the profession.

You will be aware that to continue achieving this, we are introducing the Solicitors Qualifying Examination (SQE). This will make sure that, regardless of the training route potential entrants choose, everyone meets a consistent, high standard.

So, what does this mean for you? There are no immediate changes and the SQE will not be introduced until September 2020 at the earliest. Still, you might want to consider it as part of your plans.

Regardless of whether you are looking at a training contract or pupillage, I wish you all the best in your training.

A career at the Bar offers both challenge and excitement. The Bar is the specialist advocacy profession in England and Wales, and barristers' work focuses on advocacy and legal advice. The Bar's reputation for excellence, professionalism and legal acumen is recognised and respected around the world. It is a profession which offers real fulfilment to those who succeed.

The attraction of a career at the Bar means that applying for pupillage remains a highly competitive process and it is more important than ever that we attract and encourage the best candidates from the widest pool of talent possible, regardless of background, ethnicity or gender.

Pupillage is an important stepping stone to becoming a barrister, providing pupils with the skills and experience required to practise at the Bar. This handbook will help you with your application for pupillage and guide you through the various stages. It contains a comprehensive account of the training required for a career at the Bar, as well as information to help you decide to which area of practice you may be most suited.

Further information about pupillage and the Bar can be found at www.pupillagegateway.com and www.barcouncil.org.uk. For more information about a career at the Bar, please visit: www.barcouncil.org.uk/careers.
I wish you all good luck with your pupillage applications and in your future careers.

Managing director	Sinead Dineen	sdineen@GlobeBMG.com
Senior content manager	Antonio Ignatius	aignatius@GlobeBMG.com
Content and events coordinator	Bethany Wren	bwren@GlobeBMG.com
Digital communications assistant	Beth Hawling	bhawling@GlobeBMG.com
Consultant editor	Isla Grant	igrant@GlobeBMG.com
Senior editor	Josh Richman	jrichman@GlobeBMG.com
Editorial services director	Jo Moore	
Business development director	Matthew Broadbent	mbroadbent@GlobeBMG.com
Studio manager	Alpa Pattni	apattni@GlobeBMG.com
Design & production	Matthew Snow	
	Eliza Wasilik	
Printer	Stephens & George Print Group, Merthyr Tydfil	

Published by	Globe Business Media Group
	New Hibernia House, Winchester Walk, London SE1 9AG
Tel	020 7234 0606
Email	info@lawcareers.net

	Copyright © Globe Business Media Group
	All rights reserved

ISBN	978-1-911432-15-9
ISSN	2631-4932

While every attempt has been made to ensure the accuracy of this publication, the publishers cannot accept responsibility for any errors, omissions, mis-statements or mistakes.

Further copies of this book can be ordered at handbook.lawcareers.net

Becoming a lawyer

How to use this book

The *LawCareers.Net Handbook* (LCNH) is designed to be your companion and adviser throughout your journey to becoming a solicitor or barrister. It is important that you use it correctly to get the maximum benefit. You are embarking on a learning process: learning what lawyers do and the different types of law that they practise; learning about the different types of organisation involved in law; learning how to become a lawyer and – possibly most importantly – learning about yourself, what you have to offer the profession and how to sell your skills and personality to employers.

We advise you to divide your research and planning into stages. If you complete each one in order, you should have the knowledge and understanding required to make an impact when it comes to recruitment and selection. You should also remember that you need to continually top up your expertise – it's much easier to learn steadily and gradually than try to cram in everything at the last minute.

Stage 1: The basics

A solid base of knowledge is important. Without this, your appreciation of your choices and opportunities will be severely diminished. The "Becoming a lawyer" section of the handbook introduces you to the core challenges ahead of you, while the "Solicitors" and "Barristers" sections explore the two main branches of the profession in more detail. Once you have done this preparatory reading, you should be able to answer the following questions with confidence:

- What are the differences between a solicitor and a barrister?
- Are there other types of lawyer?
- What are the different types of law firm and who do they serve?
- What are the different types of practice area?
- How is a set of chambers organised?

- What is the timetable for becoming a solicitor/barrister?
- Which postgraduate courses will you have to take?
- Which bodies regulate and represent lawyers?
- Why are vacation schemes/placements and mini-pupillages so important?

Stage 2: Getting up to speed

Once you have clearly established what needs to be done, you need to maintain an upward learning curve by regularly immersing yourself in the legal world and behaving, in effect, like a 'mini lawyer'. Read information provided specifically for aspiring lawyers such as LawCareers.Net's newsletter, LCN Weekly, but also the professional legal press (eg, *The Lawyer* and *Legal Week*), the national and international business press (eg, the *FT* and *The Economist*) and specialist websites such as LegalFutures.com. In doing so, you should begin to recognise the key news, themes and debates within the profession, see how the different parts of the law relate to each other and identify leading figures and organisations. Check out "The legal scene" in the handbook as a jumping-off point; your goal is to be sufficiently well informed that you could hold your own in a conversation among lawyers.

- What are the major developments in the legal profession over the last year?
- Have there been any major mergers recently?
- What do you know about high-street legal brands?

Stage 3: Analyse yourself

Your investigations into the basics of the law and ongoing contact with the profession should already have given you a good idea of the attributes that employers are looking for. The exact skill set may vary, but you can rest assured that you will be expected to be intelligent and able to communicate well, show determination, possess close attention to detail and operate well as part of a team. You need to review your experiences to pull out as many examples of these skills as possible and work out how to present them in the best possible light – employers like to see examples of go-getting, passionate, motivated people doing something constructive and interesting with their time. Read "Application technique" and "Interview technique" for more advice, and use LawCareers.Net's MyLCN functionality to build up your record of achievements and activities.

- Can you give a dozen detailed examples of activities you have participated in that demonstrate skills relevant to working in the legal profession?
- Can you explain why you want to be a lawyer?
- What are the weaknesses in your CV that you hope employers won't spot and what are you doing to address them?
- What is your USP?

Stage 4: Narrowing the field
We are only now getting to the stage of differentiating between employers. LCNH offers comprehensive listings of over 800 firms and nearly 200 chambers offering training contracts or pupillages. You can't apply to them all, so you need to refine your search – read "Types of law firm", "Types of chambers" and "Choosing where to apply" as a start. Use the indexing pages to identify firms/chambers by size, practice areas and location. Ideally, you should be able to identify a market sector you are interested in (eg, leading commercial firms in Northwest England) and work out which firms/chambers fall into this classification. Their directory entries in LCNH are your springboard for further research. You then need to look at organisations' own websites, explore legal press archives and do some Google-based digging.

- What are their main work areas?
- Who are their clients?

- How do they make money?
- What is their ethos?
- Who are their competitors?
- Where have they come from and where are they going (ie, history v ambition)?

What now?
The rest of LCNH expands on many of these themes. The sooner you start using it in earnest – understanding the challenge ahead, making a plan and acting on it – the better your chances. Most candidates who are unsuccessful fail because they have not followed the rules of the game. Do so and you'll be okay!

As ever, we wish you all the very best with your legal career and hope that the handbook can help you along the way.

Remember that you don't need to read this book cover to cover to get maximum benefit from it – it all depends on what path you choose, either before you open LCNH or as you read it. This diagram illustrates the basic process of using LCNH, from initial research to applying for a job – although don't forget that any specific information you need that is not covered by the chapters mentioned elsewhere in the diagram is likely to be in the more specialist chapters of the book. The colour scheme is the same as the colours used to separate each section of LCNH.

First steps
Learn about the legal profession and identify the career you want:

- Solicitor v barrister (p10)
- Alternative careers (p46)
- The legal scene (p14)
- Becoming a solicitor (p150)
- The Chartered Institute of Legal Executives (p147)
- Becoming a barrister (p480)

Research
Find out more about the qualifications and work experience you will need for your chosen profession, and learn about different careers available within it:

- Career timetable (p13)
- Work experience (whole section)
- Postgraduate training (whole section)
- Solicitor practice areas (p157)
- Types of law firm (p155)
- Bar practice areas (p489)
- Types of chambers (p486)

Launching your career
Use LCNH for details of how to apply for the right training contract or pupillage for you:

- Choosing where to apply (p25)
- Application technique (p34)
- Interview technique (p39)
- Getting the best careers advice (p19)
- Training contract directory (whole section)
- Pupillage directory (whole section)

Solicitor v barrister

One of the most fundamental questions you must address when considering a career in the law is whether to become a solicitor or a barrister. Simply put, a barrister appears in court, while a solicitor works in a law firm.

However, the differences are much more complex. Some say that it comes down to whether you are an individualist (barrister) or a team player (solicitor). While it is true that a barrister is almost always self-employed and bound to other barristers only by convenience, and a solicitor may be just one worker in a law firm of thousands of people, in reality the situation is less black and white. Barristers are often involved in teamwork and some solicitors may spend many hours on their own drafting documents.

Here's a general guide to some factors which may help you to decide.

Academic performance
Fantastic academic results are the ideal underpinnings of every legal career. You will generally find a pretty close correlation between the best academic scores and the best (or at least the best-paying) jobs in the legal profession. This may be slightly more important for the Bar, as it is smaller and consequently even more selective. The Bar is also probably rather more weighted towards the traditional universities, to which the Oxbridge-heavy tenant lists at many chambers attest (although the Bar is working to address this bias).

Positions of responsibility
Again, having been the head prefect is an impressive achievement whichever strand you choose. However, positions of responsibility are often concerned with keeping hierarchies in order and thus could be described as management training. For this reason, they may be more highly valued by firms of solicitors.

Sports
Participating in sport implies drive, teamwork and organisational skills, which are ideal for both solicitors and barristers.

Acting/performing
These are highly relevant skills for both branches of the profession. Whether you are a solicitor or barrister, you will be in the business of persuading people, and conveying information and ideas. However, the courtroom side of a barrister's work is a direct application of these attributes, so the Bar may value them slightly higher.

Commercial/business knowledge
Whatever you do in the law, you will at some level be involved in running a business – be it as part of a huge firm or as a self-employed person in sole practice or at the Bar. Furthermore, you will often be working to assist the businesses of others. Firms of solicitors no longer provide purely legal advice, but are employed as business advisers with an eye on overall strategy. Barristers are more typically 'hired hands' for advocacy or for preparing highly specific legal opinions, but those at the commercial Bar must still appreciate and prioritise the business interests of their clients when preparing to advocate on their behalf.

Legal work experience
At trainee or pupil level, nobody expects you to know the law inside out. What they do expect is for you to have a relatively sophisticated grasp of the profession, its activities and its rhythms, as a way of showing that you have thought sensibly about why you want to become a lawyer. One of the best ways of doing this is to find a law (or law-related) environment in which you can learn what it's all about.

Eloquence
As we saw above, the ability to communicate is the fundamental tool of the trade. The

better you are at communicating, the better a lawyer you will be. Again, the fact that a barrister must regularly stand up and talk in court means that this skill is more important at the Bar.

Sociability
The law is a sociable profession in which you can expect to meet large numbers of people from all walks of life. Crucially, you must be able to get on with your clients and other lawyers with whom you work. The legal community is intimate and occasionally incestuous; it helps to be able to fit in and get on. Yes, there are legendary curmudgeons floating around (particularly at the Bar), but don't think it's advisable to become one of them.

Self-reliance
You'll need a fair amount of self-reliance and self-belief whatever you do in law. Solicitors generally have a more definite career structure, but after a certain point it's dog eat dog. As a barrister, though, you are literally on your own: it's your career and you've got to make it happen, make the most of it and deal with the quiet times. If you need more structure, then think again.

Intellectual curiosity
In reality, the area of law in which you end up will be the greatest driver of the intellectual content of your work. However, if you want to be a really serious analyst and provider of opinions on heavyweight points of law, then the Bar may be for you.

Finances
Quite clearly, it is right and proper that a career in the law should be available to all.

That said, the relevant tuition fees (especially at postgraduate level) mean that it is not uncommon for individuals to end up with debts of well over £45,000. Before you rack up this kind of bill, be realistic about your job prospects.

Enthusiasm for dressing up
Do you like wearing gowns and wigs? Do you feel that panto should be staged all year round? The Bar values tradition above virtually any calling and the outfits reflect this. Solicitors' dress is, by contrast, dull, dull, dull (even on Fridays).

Commitment to social justice
There remain many commendable organisations and individuals in the legal profession who work tirelessly to overturn injustice and ensure that right prevails. Many will be involved in something socially useful (ie, pro bono).

Further reading
Solicitors – www.lawcareers.net/solicitors
Barristers – www.lawcareers.net/barristers

Reality check: The decision as to which strand suits you best rests on a number of factors concerning your abilities, temperament and – dare we say it – financial circumstances. Choose wisely.

This table illustrates some of the differences between the two branches of the profession, including as they relate to demographics, working environments, career progression and salary.

Solicitors	Barristers
As of July 2017, there were 139,624 practising solicitors. The total number of solicitors on the roll was 181,968.	As of 2017, 80% of barristers (ie, 13,076) were self-employed (not including those in dual practice, registered European lawyers or second six pupils). There were a total of 16,435 practising barristers.
Women make up just over 50% of the profession. However, many fewer women than men are currently at partner level – an average split in private practice is 67% male partners compared to 33% female.	Around 37% of all practising barristers are women (ie, 6,022 women compared to 10,380 men).
BAME individuals make up 16.5% of all solicitors.	BAME individuals make up 9.5% of all practising barristers (ie, 1,569).
Mostly employed in private law firms, so receive regular monthly salary.	Mostly self-employed, so receive irregular (but often substantial) fees.
Work mainly with individuals, companies and barristers.	Work mainly with solicitors and other barristers.
Office-based. Engage more in ongoing advisory and one-to-one client work.	Chambers and court-based. Engage more in one-off advocacy (ie, court cases).
Aspire to become partner (ie, part ownership of firm and entitlement to a percentage of its profits).	Aspire to become Queen's Counsel (QC) (ie, a top barrister, normally instructed in very serious and complex cases).
While there is no longer a minimum annual trainee salary, the average UK salary for a first-year trainee is around £27,000, while City firms pay considerably more – anywhere from £35,000 upwards.	The Bar Standards Board requires that all pupils be paid no less than £12,000 per annum. Many earn much more – upwards of £60,000 in some cases.

Career timetable

Confused about the career path to becoming a lawyer? With the simple career timetable below, there's no need to be!

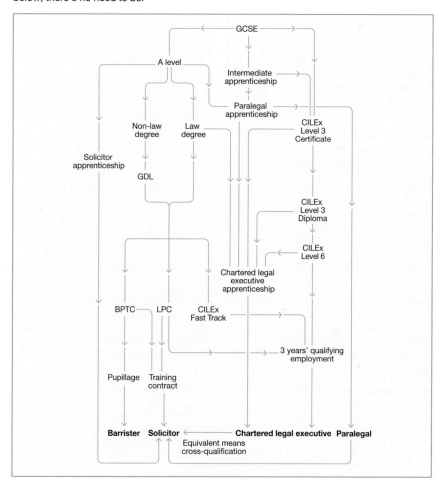

Further reading
For more on the solicitors' career timetable, see p152.
For more on the barristers' career timetable, see p482.
For more on the chartered legal executive timetable, see p147.
For more on legal apprenticeships, pick up a copy of *The Law Apprenticeships Guide 2019*.

The legal scene

As you start out in your career, it is vital to know the issues affecting the profession you are entering. You are bound to be asked your opinion in an interview, of course, but deepening your understanding of this vast conglomeration of different areas of law and divergent career paths is about more than securing a training contract or vacation scheme place. You need to be aware of the issues that will affect your future beyond the final recruitment hurdle, too.

And the law is facing change on multiple fronts. In the City, solicitors and barristers are trying to read the runes of Brexit to discern what Britain's break from the European Union could mean for London's status as a hub for international legal services, while at the same time scrambling to keep up with new technologies and their impact. Meanwhile, firms and educators are bracing for major changes to the way that solicitors train and qualify, due in the next couple of years.

But elsewhere, away from the glass-fronted bubble of the Square Mile, lawyers working in the areas of criminal and family law are facing a public funding crisis that has become so severe that courts have slowed to a crawl, while access to justice has been stripped away from the vast majority of UK citizens who are not wealthy enough to afford legal fees. The strain has been so severe that this year, crime and family barristers took the unprecedented step of striking in protest at unviable fees and a justice system hanging on by its fingernails.

However, let's begin our overview with another milestone – and one of the biggest issues currently facing the profession.

An unequal profession
For the first time ever there are now more women solicitors than men, and this is a trend that looks set to continue – 64% of new trainees were women in 2017. However, the high numbers of talented women at the junior end of the profession have not led to women being promoted to senior roles in equal numbers to men or earning as much as their male colleagues. Many top law firms refused to include partners in their mandatory gender pay gap reporting this year, but one that did – magic circle giant Clifford Chance – reported that men at the firm are paid on average 66% more than women, while the partnership on its own has a 27% pay gap in favour of men. Meanwhile, data from fellow magic circle firm Linklaters revealed that the average male employee is paid 60% more than the average female employee.

The senior echelons of the profession remain male dominated, as are the lists of partner promotions reported by the legal press every year – some firms still feel that aiming for a 30% female partnership by a certain date is a worth a 'good news' press release. In reality, many women still drop out of the profession before they are promoted to senior roles. In an international survey of over 7,500 women lawyers conducted by the Law Society, the top three barriers to women's career progression were reported to be unconscious bias on the part of senior colleagues (52% of respondents), an unacceptable work/life balance (48%), and a belief that the traditional networks and routes to promotion in law are male orientated (46%).

The lack of gender equality in the legal profession is structural. Male-governed workplaces and career paths mean that the men at the top tend to promote in their own image, according to their own set of values, which fail to appreciate qualities and skills outside of their own narrow experience. The result is that women earn less on average than men, access fewer opportunities for advancement and are expected to shoulder disproportionate levels of parenting responsibilities compared to male parents, often at the cost of career progression.

And structural inequality also creates the conditions for workplace cultures in which it is possible to perpetrate and get away with harassment; a male-dominated managerial class rarely questioning a shared set of assumptions, beliefs and behaviours, that polices itself as it sees fit. Two-thirds of women respondents to a survey conducted by *Legal Week* in late 2017 reported experiencing sexual harassment at work, with 51% reporting that they have experienced such behaviour on more than one occasion.

Of course, disproportionate hoarding of seniority and power among a small, homogenous group cannot be laid solely at the feet of lawyers – the practice is ubiquitous wherever money and hierarchies are found. Research by the Fawcett Society shows that in politics, women make up only 32% of MPs, 26% of peers in the House of Lords and just 26% of cabinet ministers (although the shadow cabinet is made up of 50% women). In business, a mere 6% of FTSE 100 chief executives are women, while in the charity sector this rises to a still-unbalanced 28%.

How can structural inequality be addressed so that women are competing for senior jobs on a level playing field with men? The Fawcett Society has called for a "time-limited use of quotas across public bodies and the boards of large corporate organisations enabled by law" – essentially forcing organisations to ensure that a certain proportion of their promotions go to women.

The subject of quotas is controversial and few powerful voices in the profession have been willing to champion the policy, beyond the honourable exceptions of Shadow Attorney General Shami Chakrabarti and barrister and feminist campaigner Charlotte Proudman. Indeed, the idea of quotas has been heavily criticised by those who believe that under such a system, women would be promoted just to make up the numbers, rather than on merit. However, critics fail to acknowledge that with clear evidence of structural barriers to

women's advancement, there are many highly skilled women in the profession who deserve promotions but are not accessing them. To ignore structural inequality ultimately leads to the conclusion that women are being promoted in far lower numbers than men because they are not good enough, which is demonstrably false.

Speaking at a Westminster Legal Policy Forum in March 2018, Law Society vice-president Christina Blacklaws set out a number of best practice measures to support women:
- making access to flexible working for women and men mainstream in all workplaces;
- providing women with access to mentoring and sponsorship from senior staff and peers;
- networking opportunities;
- engaging men in the equality debate; and
- ensuring that there are women role models in senior positions.

The crisis in public funding
The term 'crisis' is perhaps overused, but it is an entirely accurate way to describe the dire situation faced by people who need legal advice but are not wealthy, and the lawyers who have dedicated their careers not to material gain, but to doing the kind of work that is vital for a fair and democratic society.

Many law centres have been forced to close due to successive cuts to legal aid provision, leaving entire communities without access to legal advice, unless those in need of help are able to travel great distances to another centre – which some simply cannot afford to do.

Meanwhile at the Bar, many barristers are leaving publicly funded work because they cannot make ends meet doing these kinds of cases. Those that have stayed took action that effectively amounted to a mass strike this year, in which over 50 chambers stopped taking on new publicly funded cases in protest at changes to the Advocates Graduated Fee Scheme, under which barristers are routinely forced to choose between working for days on end for free, or not preparing for cases properly. Admirably, barristers chose the former, but the situation was untenable. The government finally bowed to pressure from the Bar and promised a limited amount of extra resources to go into the system, ending the strike, but the deal has not resolved the wider problem because it falls way short of what the justice system needs to keep going long term.

The strike was also about much more than fees. It was a protest at the shambolic state of the wider justice system, from court closures and the difficulties defendants face in getting to their own hearings; to prisoners not being transported to court at the right time or at all; to disclosure problems at the Crown Prosecution Service which have caused dozens of rape trials to collapse, with the idea of justice nowhere in sight.

After years of ignoring these problems, the government is finally conducting a review into the effects of legal aid cuts introduced by The Legal Aid, Sentencing and Punishment of Offenders Act 2012. However, the government's continued commitment to its austerity agenda, as well as the high turnover and small-state ideological beliefs of the ministers tasked with overseeing the justice system, have led some lawyers to hold out little hope that improvements are on the horizon.

Robot lawyers?
The ever-increasing automation of tasks such as due diligence and document checking is changing how law firms work, but the first to feel the impact of technological advancement could be trainee solicitors.

Over the next few years, law firms will be confronted with the problem of balancing the commercial imperatives of technology with training new lawyers. Technology is taking over the roles that trainees have historically started out with to aid their development, and the fact

that AI is able to complete tasks more cheaply than trainees gives firms no choice but to adopt it regardless of the effect on training, or lose their competitive edge.

Some firms are responding by introducing dedicated technologist trainee roles. Addleshaw Goddard, meanwhile, has gone a step further and created a new legal technology associate role, while also enabling trainees to do a seat in the firm's innovation and legal technology department.

More change for trainees: the Solicitors Qualifying Exam
The route to qualifying as a solicitor is changing, as the Graduate Diploma in Law (GDL) and Legal Practice Course (LPC) give way to the Solicitors Qualifying Exam (SQE). Under the new system, prospective solicitors will no longer need a law degree or law conversion. Instead, applicants will need any undergraduate degree or equivalent (eg, a degree-level apprenticeship) before completing SQE stages one and two, which will test legal skills and knowledge through a mix of multiple-choice and practical tests.

The requirement for two years' qualifying work experience remains in place from the current route, but instead of a training contract, under SQE that experience can be with up to four different legal employers (and could include appropriate pro bono experience). Candidates will be able to do this during, before or after completing SQE assessments, although it is expected that in most cases applicants will have successfully completed at least SQE stage one before starting their main period of work experience.

The new process is due to be put in place in 2020 "at the earliest", according to the Solicitors Regulation Authority, but as that language indicates, the introduction of SQE could be delayed. Regardless of when it comes in, though, there will be a long transitional period (from the launch of SQE until 2031) for those at the law degree, GDL and LPC stages to complete the current route.

The future of barrister training

The Bar's review of how it trains barristers is ongoing. Progress appears to be glacial, but at least there is now some evidence that regulators are serious about addressing how close the Bar has become to being a closed profession for all but the privileged few. Starting out in an area such as criminal or family law without an alternative source of income or parental support is unviable, so it is good to see that the Bar Standards Board intends to include an increase to the minimum pupillage award that will be raised yearly in line with the recommendations of the Living Wage Foundation. If the award were to have been made on this basis in 2018, it would have increased from £12,000 to £17,212 in London, and £14,765 outside London.

It has also been confirmed that joining an inn of court will continue to be a compulsory part of the process of becoming a barrister, while the Bar Professional Training Course will remain as it is "for the immediate future".

Recent mergers

The last year has been much quieter for law firm mergers than 2017. By far the biggest was that of City firm Berwin Leighton Paisner and US-based Bryan Cave in April. Now operating under the name Bryan Cave Leighton Paisner, the merged firm has increased international reach with 32 offices in 11 countries, employing some 1,600 lawyers.

Elsewhere, DLA Piper's Chilean arm merged with Noguera, Larraín & Dulanto. The new offering, DLA Piper BAZ NLD comprises some 60 lawyers. Meanwhile, partners and staff at sports specialist Couchmans joined Charles Russell Speechlys in January, creating a "new model for legal services in sport" offering "agile specialists with global reach".

Legal developments – talking points

- Appalling disclosure failures caused the collapse of 47 rape and sexual assault cases in the first six weeks of 2018 alone, but the true number of affected cases is likely to be far higher. The Crown Prosecution Service (CPS) failed to meet its obligation to share potential evidence with defence lawyers (even in situations where this undermines the prosecution's case) on dozens of occasions. Director of Public Prosecutions Alison Saunders told MPs that problems at the CPS were systemic and that high volumes of digital evidence, particularly on social media, present a huge challenge.

- Research has revealed that over half (52%) of all training contract vacancies in England and Wales are based in London. Law Society statistics show that of the 5,719 training contracts that started in 2016-17, 1,923 were based in the City alone, where firms hire large trainee intakes, while a further 1,002 were in "the rest of London".

- Trainee solicitors' average pay has decreased since the SRA abolished its minimum salary rule, according to the regulator's impact survey of 33,000 trainees between 2011 and 2016. The average fall in trainee earnings since the minimum salary was scrapped amounts to £560, with most of that decrease borne by trainees at the lowest-paying 2% of firms, where the maximum salary is £13,104. The minimum salary was £17,268 when it was stopped in 2014. The deregulation has had a disproportionate effect on trainees from BAME backgrounds, who are statistically more likely to work at lower-paying firms. The pay gap between women and men trainees has also widened, with women now paid £460 a year less on average than their male counterparts. The discrepancy has increased by £128 since the minimum salary was abolished. In addition, the survey showed that state-schooled trainees are less likely to earn high salaries than those who are privately educated.

Major cases

- The public inquiry into the Grenfell Tower fire, which killed 72 people on 14 June 2017, is ongoing. There was protest at the government's decision to appoint white middle class retired judge Sir Martin Moore-Bick to lead the inquiry by lawyers acting on behalf of the victims' families. They and the MP for Kensington, Emma Dent Coad, called for him to stand down, arguing that the hundreds of people bereaved and/or made homeless by the fire needed someone who could relate to their lives as well as look at the detail. The government defended Moore-Bick's appointment and the inquiry began hearing evidence in June 2018. It aims to cover the immediate cause of the fire, the design and construction of Grenfell Tower, the scope of regulations and compliance, the response of firefighters, and the response of the government and the local council to the fire's aftermath.
- The government's mass data surveillance legislation, set out in the Investigatory Powers Act, was found to be incompatible with EU law by the High Court in April. The legal challenge to the so-called 'snooper's charter' was brought by human rights organisation Liberty. The government has until November 2018 to rewrite its surveillance laws.
- A judicial review brought by The Children's Society led the government to U-turn on its decision to deny legal aid to unaccompanied migrant children in July. The government was forced to admit that its policy may have denied access to justice to 150,000 vulnerable children, and even put some at risk of exploitation. The Children's Society, supported by other civil society organisations, conducted a five-year legal challenge on behalf of the separated and unaccompanied children, who have faced a punishing system of legal aid cuts and increasing Home Office fees since 2013. Some of the children deliberately denied legal aid by the Home Office have been through horrific ordeals, including being trafficked by criminals, while only a small number have received the legal aid they need through 'exceptional case' funding.
- US taxi app Uber was granted a short-term licence to operate in London following a two-day hearing at Westminster Magistrates' Court in June. Transport for London had refused to renew Uber's licence in September 2017, saying that it was not "fit and proper" to operate because of its gung-ho determination to grow at any cost – as evidenced by its woeful record on reporting criminal activity and scant regard for the safety of its passengers and drivers. Uber initially responded aggressively, but struck an apologetic tone during the hearing and promised that it had changed the way it operates. The company is now on probation, having been granted a 15-month licence to prove that it has taken concerns on board.
- The government has set up a public inquiry into why NHS patients were given infected blood or blood products over a sustained period, resulting in the deaths of at least 1,250 people.
- Veteran singer Sir Cliff Richard won a landmark case against the BBC after the broadcaster filmed police searching his home without him having been charged or arrested. The police were investigating historical sexual abuse allegations but found no evidence with which they could charge Richard. The case established that individuals, including high-profile ones, have the right to privacy before they have been charged with a suspected crime. However, other media outlets have defended the corporation, arguing that the ruling will have a chilling affect on the media's ability to accurately report criminal investigations.

Getting the best careers advice

They say that forewarned is forearmed, and this is never truer than when you are considering a career in law. You will need the best advice you can get, given that competition for the legal profession is fierce and the outlay is high in terms of both time and money.

It's never too early to seek careers advice. You really do need it from the very beginning in order to be in the know about careers fairs, open days, campus presentations and crucial work placement scheme/mini-pupillage deadlines. Mirrick Koh, former head of graduate recruitment and graduate development at CMS, has the following advice: "All the careers advisers I speak to are incredibly committed people with the best interests of the students at heart; but for whatever reason, some students do not use them as effectively as they could."

Available help

We suggest that you use every resource on offer at your university/college careers service in order to be as informed as possible. Usually, resources include:
- details of law fairs with visiting firms of solicitors and postgraduate course providers, and law firm open days;
- a programme of campus visits by firms;
- workshops on applications/CVs and interview technique;
- names of people in the profession who are willing to talk to you (eg, former students who are now practising law);
- up-to-date files on employers;
- information leaflets and brochures;
- recruitment literature for firms and prospectuses for postgraduate courses; and
- copies of the trade press and *The LawCareersNet Handbook* to keep you abreast of the legal scene.

Your adviser should also be able to give you some individual help with improving your CV,

written applications and interview technique (eg, assisting with mock interviews). Careers advisers may also be able to help organise work experience.

Diana Spoudeas, graduate recruitment and development manager at Jones Day, thinks that a career adviser performs a vital role, including offering "practical assistance to help students secure jobs - some great careers services provide one-to-one specialist advice, job opportunities, employer visits and specialist sector knowledge". She does advise, however, against "step-by-step instructions on how to fill in an application form or answer interview questions – too much rehearsal can kill individuality and prevent your true personality from shining through at interview".

Claire Leslie, senior careers consultant at the University of Warwick, has this to say: "Your careers service should usually be able to offer you the following: one-to-one advice to help you decide the direction you should take and when things need to be done; practical help and advice on applications and interviews; and opportunities to meet recruiters. If you are away from campus, you can usually get advice from your careers service by email, telephone or Skype. Use the extensive information available to you – it's never too early to plan your legal career."

Puneet Tahim, senior recruitment coordinator at Latham & Watkins, advises playing to your university's strengths: "If a university has a particularly active student law society that manages the recruitment events calendar and has an up-to-date website with information about firms and deadlines, you should become a member. Alternatively, you might attend a university where the careers service manages the events and have all of that information readily available."

Meanwhile, Andrew Pearson, a barrister at 7 King's Bench Walk, advises trying to get help from those already in the legal profession: "Contacts are perhaps the most difficult, but the most useful people to talk to. When you've worked out the basics, ask your careers service whether they can put you in touch with someone who works in a field which interests you. The better the careers service, the more likely they are to be able to do so. This person will be able to give you very useful, focused advice. Make the most of it by working out what you want to know and by following up any help that you get with an appreciative email or note. That way they'll be keen to help you again, or even to put you in touch with other people who might be able to give you advice or assistance."

A significant minority of students don't come to the profession straight out of full-time education. In the first instance, they should contact their local university and see whether they can get careers advice under the mutual aid scheme. Most universities are happy to provide any graduate with a period of assistance – in some cases, up to three years. They may find the careers service particularly useful in terms of obtaining tailored advice on ways to present previous experience to the greatest effect.

Last, but by no means least, if you have a problem that's keeping you awake at night, simply log on to www.LawCareers.Net and click on "The Oracle". As its name suggests, this section of the website is the bearer of advice and wisdom. Check out the Oracle's back catalogue of questions (chances are, someone has been troubled by the same issue), and see whether the answers apply to you. If you have an original question, feel free to email us for individual careers advice. Click on "Ask the Oracle" or email oracle@lawcareers.net.

Common advice
Dates and deadlines
Stay clued-up about on-campus events and application deadlines. Laura Newton,

a barrister at Brick Court Chambers, says: "Use your university/law school website as a first port of call. You will be able to stay on top of events and deadlines by setting up a Twitter account and following those who provide an active Twitter feed such as LawCareers.Net, Pupillage Blog, your career advice centres and the sets or firms you are interested in."

Puneet says: "It's pretty simple these days to keep on top of deadlines and events, as most firms will heavily publicise these on their own websites as well as on the university careers websites."

Don't rush
Dick Lidwell, freelance careers adviser and former careers adviser at the University of Oxford, advises against panicking if you are still uncertain as to which legal path to take: "If you're not sure whether it's a barrister or solicitor you want to be, don't rush into it. Take the time to explore; you can always come into the system a bit later. There's no point applying until you know, and this is where your careers service comes in. We can help and guide you right from the beginning – don't think that you can only go and see an adviser if you already know what you want to do! Obviously, we're also there to help at the next stage of actually applying: targeting, CVs/forms and interview technique." Dick's top tips are as follow: "Not only make sure that your writing is clear and grammatically correct in your application, but also provide actual evidence for your statements, be yourself at interview and be honest at all times."

Got what it takes?
Above all, what you want most from a careers adviser can be summed up in one word – honesty. One London barrister agrees on its importance: "Students should think about whether they stand a realistic chance of obtaining pupillage and forging a career at

the Bar. If not, they should seriously consider whether it is worth undertaking the BPTC, with its attendant costs." Any careers adviser worth his or her salt should make it clear that you must have the following qualities and skills (without which you will find getting a training contract or pupillage much more difficult):

- Academic ability – the job is intellectually rigorous and demands that you be capable of clear and lucid thought, and able to process and assimilate large swathes of information. Most top-paying employers require at least a 2.1 degree and excellent A-level grades.
- Interpersonal skills – it is vital that you can interact with colleagues and clients alike to engender confidence, form lasting relationships and clearly explain complex situations.
- Written and oral communication skills – we know that lawyers are famed for their ability to use 20 words when five would suffice, but that is changing. Lawyers spend a large amount of their time talking to clients and drafting documents. The use of clear and succinct language is appreciated by all.
- Personal responsibility and integrity – be true to yourself.

As an example of what firms are looking for in their prospective trainees, Sarah Stockley, international talent manager and former senior associate at Vinson & Elkins RLLP, says it is all about "good academics, an ability to present well and show knowledge about the firm and the sectors we practise in, and have a personality". On the Bar side of things, Laura highlights the following desirable attributes: "Intellectual ability, written presentational and advocacy skills are key. We will also try to gauge the applicant's motivation to become a barrister and their ability to build a successful practice in our chambers. As we operate in a highly competitive, client-focused industry, commercial awareness and interpersonal skills are crucial to success at the Bar: academic ability alone is not enough."

This brings us to that most crucial of assets: commercial awareness. Almost every recruiter we talked to mentioned this as vital. It is not enough just to know about strict legal principles; you have to be able to apply them to the commercial context within which your clients operate. It may also be important to have a sense of regional commercial issues.

Reality check: If you don't have all of the above qualities and you are considering doing the GDL/LPC/BPTC without the security net of a training contract or pupillage, think very carefully. For some postgraduate institutions, money is the bottom line. Putting it bluntly, they sometimes offer places to students who don't have the remotest chance of getting a training contract/pupillage. As one recruiter said: "Many institutions consider their course a licence to print money, forcing candidates into debt. They allow in students who are unlikely ever to get an interview, let alone pupillage."

ƧƧ aspiringsolicitors

"Committed to increasing diversity
in the legal profession."

Are you:
- Socially mobile?*
- Black, Asian or minority ethnic?
- A member of the LGBT+ community?
- Disabled and/or have a long term health condition?

**If the answer to any of those is yes, register as a
member of Aspiring Solicitors today to access free:**
- Mentoring and coaching
- Legal work experience at industry leading organisations
- Bespoke employability programmes
- Specialist events at leading City firms

Register today with the UK's largest legal diversity platform:
www.aspiringsolicitors.co.uk/register

*State school educated, from a low income family or first generation to go to university

Diversity in the legal profession

No one will be surprised to learn that the senior ranks of law firms, barristers' chambers and the judiciary are still overwhelmingly dominated by one particular group of people: white, upper-class men, predominantly public school and Oxbridge educated. Although this is widely acknowledged as a problem for the profession and many firms are attempting to redress the balance, doubts remain as to whether much progress is being made.

The vast majority of law firms have a diversity policy in place to guide their recruitment and promotion behaviours and many use affinity groups, targets and mentors to increase diversity and inclusion. The Bar is likewise making an effort, with its 'No Bar to the Bar' initiative, and with stats confirming that around 19% of first-six pupils in 2016-17 were from a black and minority ethnic (BAME) background. The representation of women on both sides of the profession is also improving, with around 50% of pupils and trainees female. However, while there seems to be no problem attracting women to the law, retaining them is another matter and partners, QCs and judges are still mostly men.

A number of organisations have been set up to help students from underrepresented groups, including Aspiring Solicitors, Pathways to Law, PRIME, RARE, the Sutton Trust and SEO London. Many firms are also committed to making a change; all recognise the benefits to their firms of a diverse workforce. Below are some examples of best practices among firms keen to address the disparities in opportunity.

Gender
Baker McKenzie was the first major global law firm to appoint a female head when Christine Lagarde became 'madame chairman'. It runs many affinity groups, including BakerWomen.

Disability
Twice winner of the Commendation for Diversity at the LawCareers.Net (LCN) Awards, Shoosmiths has been focusing on disability

access, solidifying its commitment to being a government-backed 'Two Ticks' employer, which means interviewing all candidates with a disability who meet the minimum requirements. "We were doing it already, but hadn't been effectively communicating that to students, so made an effort to proactively talk about it," explains Samantha Hope, Shoosmiths' graduate recruitment manager.

Social mobility
Another former winner of the LCN Commendation for Diversity, Hogan Lovells uses a Contextual Recruitment System (CRS) for its vacation scheme and training contract applicants. The CRS tool hardwires social mobility metrics into the firm's existing recruitment system, allowing recruiters to quantitatively and consistently measure applicants' social mobility characteristics.

BAME
As well as setting up a number of ethnicity-specific affinity groups, Latham & Watkins has partnered with RARE, working directly with students from underrepresented minority ethnic groups on their applications. The firm also uses a CRS system to ensure that it "understands the context in which all candidates' experiences have been gained, ensuring that disadvantaged or underprivileged students are not ruled out for reasons of background rather than aptitude and skill".

Aspiring Solicitors: increasing diversity through opportunities
Since 2014, Aspiring Solicitors (AS) has helped diverse candidates secure over 1,400 training contracts and vacation schemes. These candidates include individuals who are:
- black, Asian and minority ethnic;
- socially mobile (eg, from low-income families, state school comprehensives or the first generation in their family to go to university);
- disabled or with long-term health conditions; or
- LGBT+.

2S aspiringsolicitors

Historically, these successes have resulted from free one-to-one coaching and mentoring, events and bespoke legal careers guidance. With a focus on boosting confidence and competencies, the employability team at AS works with candidates to strengthen applications, excel at interview and find the firm that's right for them. Today, AS is also able to offer a wide range of additional opportunities, including events in partnership with law firms, work experience placements at industry-leading commercial organisations and UK-wide employability workshops.

AS continues to provide bespoke careers coaching through its Aspire programme, which also offers access to law firm specific open days and bespoke coaching from partner law firms and legal teams. For all AS members, the annual Commercial Awareness Competition is not only an effective means of improving commercial acumen, but also of thoroughly preparing candidates for law firm assessments. The Grand Final takes place at Barclays HQ in Canary Wharf and winners are awarded five weeks' work experience at sponsoring firms and Barclays Legal.

A series of annual diversity events including AS Pride, AS Ability, AS Social Mobility and AS Culture are hosted throughout the academic year. In attendance are panels of diverse professionals who share their experiences of overcoming perceived and actual barriers on their road to success.

Members seeking work experience can apply for placements with our partner organisations with in-house legal teams including ASOS, Barclays, Bank of America Merrill Lynch, the Government Legal Service, Royal Mail, Network Rail, Siemens, Shell and Virgin Money. For those with ambitions of a career in private practice, experiencing life as an in-house lawyer can be highly beneficial, especially since City lawyers regularly advise client in-house teams.

On campus, the employability and universities teams deliver a series of workshops and presentations at over 50 Russell and non-Russell Group universities each academic year, including future trainee talks about their journeys to acquiring a training contract. The HeadStart Programme, run in conjunction with BPP Law School, combines advice from graduate recruiters, future trainees and qualified solicitors on how to successfully navigate vacation schemes and applications to law firms. From February 2019, first-year law and second-year non-law students will be able to participate in AS First to find out what a career in law can offer, as well as participate in an assessed group exercise.

The Professional Ambassador Network allows AS members to contact legal professionals directly via the AS website. Over 450 ambassadors representing 110 firms are extending their hand back down the ladder to provide insight and advice within this network. Finally, for those members who have started their training contracts, the newly launched Alumni Network ensures continued support throughout their careers. AS is committed to increasing diversity in the legal profession and if you're a talented aspiring solicitor from an underrepresented group, we hope you'll be able to benefit from our coaching, programmes, events and other opportunities.

Go to aspiringsolicitors.co.uk or follow AS on Instagram or Twitter to find out more about all AS opportunities. Applications for Aspire 2019-20 open in Summer 2019.

Further reading:
- Diversity access schemes - www. lawcareers.net/MoreLaw/ DiversityAccessSchemes
- Gender diversity - www.lawcareers.net/ Information/Features/06062017-Feminist-lawyers-the-fight-for-gender-equality-in-the-legal-profession

Choosing where to apply

Don't even think about applying to a law firm or set of chambers until you have figured out your own criteria for applying and done the relevant homework. The trick isn't to apply to loads of firms aimlessly in the hope that you will strike lucky with one. Similarly, don't follow the herd. Rather, identify the sort of organisation that you want to work for and then target those that fit the bill. Lucie Rees, graduate manager at Watson Farley & Williams LLP, advises the following: "Think about the opportunities you want during your training contract – for example, practice areas, client exposure and international seats. Many firms will offer you what you want, so one key thing to look at to help you narrow down your shortlist is the culture of the firm – is it somewhere you see yourself enjoying your time at work?"

What type of law?

Many firms and chambers specialise in one or more areas of law (eg, family, banking or media). They are pretty proud of this fact and a pet peeve is when applicants fail to mention the specialism or, worse, get it entirely wrong. In other words, don't write to a firm that is known for its family law expertise saying that you want to be a banking lawyer. The head of graduate recruitment at one City firm says: "What drives me insane is when applicants talk about a practice area we don't have - for example, 'your thriving media practice'. It comes across as sloppy and badly researched." So it pays to match your comments to the firm – achievable only by doing your research.

Meanwhile, Natalie Connor, a barrister at 11KBW, has this advice for those hoping to join the Bar: "Apply to places where members practise in the areas you are interested in. Many sets will advertise themselves as full service, when in reality they deal almost exclusively in one or two specialist areas. A good way of finding

out what those areas are is to look at the 'news' and 'recent cases' section of each chambers' website to get an idea of the high-profile cases members are involved in."

Think about what broad sort of lawyer you want to be: do you see yourself as a human rights barrister? A commercial solicitor? A criminal lawyer spending lots of time in police stations? Or something else altogether? As an example, let's say that you want to be a human rights barrister – the best way of going about the application process is as follows:

- First, find out which sets specialise in human rights law (a search of www. LawCareers.Net and the legal directories at your careers centre will give you this info).
- Next, notice what is particularly special or exciting about the set and what separates it from its rivals (so look on its website to see whether there is a particular line of cases or a niche area of law that its tenants are developing).
- Finally, see whether you match the criteria that the set asks for from applicants. Be realistic – if it asks for applicants with a first, you are not going to get in with a 2.2.

If you meet all the criteria and the set has grabbed your interest, you should apply. Otherwise, keep looking, using the same step-by-step guide. This approach applies equally to other sets, law firms and practice areas.

However, it is generally important to keep an open mind about the exact area into which you will ultimately qualify. You won't know what you truly enjoy until you actually get some experience under your belt as a trainee or pupil, so don't narrow your focus too early, especially in your applications. If you have no idea about what you want your specialism to be, focus on getting into a firm or set that offers a well-rounded training contract/pupillage. Also, focus on firms and sets that offer a variety of seats and experience, and that have a good reputation generally (so scan the trade press for positive/negative coverage as well as looking at the glossy recruitment literature).

Where do I want to work?

Once you have figured out the sort of firm or set you want to target, you need to consider whether you'll be happy with the location. It's no use applying to a firm in the City if you don't like London; your heart won't be in it and this will be apparent at interview.

Often, regional firms prefer applicants with local connections. This is because they will be investing a lot of money in their trainees and, not unreasonably, they want to see a good return on their investment. In asking whether an applicant has local connections, they figure that those with ties to an area are less likely to leave for greener pastures after the training contract ends.

Also, regional firms want to be sure that you are not applying to them just because the London firms have passed you over. As one partner of a Yorkshire firm explains: "Does a candidate who has attended a prep school in Sussex, attended the University of Sussex and always lived in Sussex seriously expect us to believe that he or she wishes to move to Scunthorpe? There's clearly no long-term commitment and we've received the application for a training contract only because the candidate has been rejected by every practice in the Southeast."

What sort of working environment?

Many students find it difficult to distinguish between the different types of firm. However, many recruiters also talk about the need for students to have some idea of the culture of a firm, and whether it will match their needs and personalities. Puneet Tahim, senior recruitment coordinator at Latham & Watkins, says: "It can be challenging for students to differentiate between firms, as many offer high-quality work. Students

should therefore consider which other factors will influence their experience as a trainee. These may include the size of the firm; if you are interested in multi-jurisdictional work, secondments or using any additional language skills, then a firm with offices in many jurisdictions could be for you."

Martha Jeacle, legal recruiting and associate development manager at Davis Polk & Wardwell London LLP, makes this point: "It is important to look at the size of the trainee intake. Being one of 100 as opposed to one of four will offer a very different experience, and each individual needs to decide what will work best for them. I also suggest that students find out what kind of training programme is in place for trainees, as a comprehensive formal training programme will ensure a more well-rounded period of training."

However, it is possible to generalise broadly about firms and chambers. For example, types of firm might broadly be categorised as international/City, national/regional and legal aid/general practice. For an in-depth explanation of what trainee life at each of these might be like, see "Types of firm" on page 155.

As for barristers' chambers, they can broadly be split into those that are in Central London and specialise by practice area – such as commercial, public law, common law and crime – and those in the regions, including the 'supersets'. Brian Lee, practice development and marketing director at 7 King's Bench Walk, says: "Students should make sure that the pupillage being offered is constructive and properly managed. A pupil supervisor should not only manage the workload for the pupil, in terms of who the pupil works for and when, but should also act as mentor. The pupil supervisor should also ensure that the pupil is not overworked. It is incumbent on all chambers to ensure that the pupil provides their best work for those they work for so that informed decisions can be made when a vote on tenancy is taken. Students should make sure they know what is being provided before they apply."

Matthew Parker, barrister at 3 Verulam Buildings, says: "Bear in mind the differences in day-to-day practice at different parts of the Bar. For some kinds of barrister, the emphasis is on regular court work; for others, the volume of paperwork is much larger. And choose an area of law in which you have a genuine interest."

Sarah Stockley, international talent manager and former senior associate at Vinson & Elkins RLLP, urges students not to be swayed by the decisions of their contemporaries: "Students should ignore where their peers are looking to apply – what suits one person will not necessarily suit another." Laura Newton, a barrister at Brick Court Chambers, says: "Try to get a feel for different sets yourself, rather than relying solely on their reputation or word of mouth. You may find that a day or a week in chambers gives a completely different impression of a set from your preconception." For an in-depth explanation of what a pupil's life at each of these might be like, see "Types of chambers" on page 486.

What other factors are important?

When considering applying for a training contract or pupillage, you might also want to bear in mind the following factors:
- the nature of the training programme or pupillage;
- the way you will be treated as a trainee/pupil;
- the firm or set's overall reputation in the legal market;
- any awards received (www.LawCareers. Net has a list of firms recognised for training and recruitment);
- any impending changes such as mergers that may affect the firm or set's future;
- any financial help offered during postgraduate training;
- trainee/pupil retention rates;
- the firm or set's client base;
- the salary on offer and any benefits; and

- future opportunities and remuneration.

Caroline Lindner, senior manager global communications and engagement, and former trainee recruitment manager, at Norton Rose Fulbright, suggests not being too swayed by the much-touted "work-life balance" factor: "All lawyers work very hard and you will work long hours at times, so you need to accept this. Some firms, however, are better at encouraging their trainees to get involved with pro bono, social activities, sports teams and so on, so you should look at this aspect if it's important to you." Equally, don't be entirely swayed by salary, as Fiona Medlock, former graduate recruitment manager at Mills & Reeve LLP, wisely urges: "A higher salary might be attractive but look at the long-term prospects and quality of training too."

Many firms and chambers will hold events at your university/college campus, such as workshops or seminars and/or social occasions at which you can learn about their working culture. You can also view graduate recruitment videos, browse their websites, attend open days and go on work placement schemes and mini-pupillages.

Michelle Ruddle, recruitment marketing manager at Hogan Lovells, explains that your first step must be to seriously analyse and think carefully about what you want from your career: "Ask yourself questions, such as: 'Why do I want to be a lawyer?'; 'What kind of work environment suits me?'; 'What motivates me?'; and 'What appeals to me about international, regional or niche firms?'"

With that in mind, let's leave you with a quick-fire checklist for easy reference:
- Type – commercial or high street?
- Size – law factory or local firm?
- Focus – highly specialised or a wide range of clients/practice areas?
- Location – London or regional?
- 'Feel' – pressured or relaxed?

Key competencies

Most legal recruiters want broadly the same thing – to hire excellent lawyers – and all look for key competencies when hiring to help identify who those potential recruits might be. It follows, therefore, that the trick to landing a training contract or pupillage is showing recruiters that you have as many of those key skills as possible.

So what does a successful lawyer look like? Different roles within the profession will place varying emphasis on the following skills, but you can be confident that all are extremely desirable when you are being assessed for suitability. Here, we take a look at the many ways you can sell yourself to recruiters and demonstrate that there are plenty of ways to identify the attributes that you have and that employers want.

Academic ability

Lawyers are involved daily with challenging material and work that stretches their intellectual capabilities. They need to have the mental capacity to process complicated information, draw inferences and form conclusions. Inevitably, your academic results are used by recruiters as the main indicator of your intellect; having impressive A levels and being on track for at least a 2:1 is a great first step (although be aware that this alone is no longer enough to distinguish you from the thousands of others who have also done well).

How to demonstrate: The obvious answer is your school and university performance – it is likely to be the first thing that a prospective employer looks at. Your results need to be good; don't shy away from highlighting the grades that show you off in the best possible light. For career changers, whose exam results are far in the past and don't necessarily reflect their current skills and experience, evidence of professional achievements and qualifications is valuable. Another way to prove your brainpower is to talk coherently about current affairs, showing that you have background knowledge, can understand context and draw rational conclusions.

Determination

Getting a job in the legal profession is much tougher than it used to be and a healthy dose of ambition is crucial to success. But securing a training contract or pupillage is just the beginning – the hard work and pressure really begin at that point, so you have to be able to show that you're the type of person who is determined to make it as a successful lawyer and can take the sustained heat.

How to demonstrate: Achievements of the highest order, ideally involving physical discomfort (eg, fell running, open water swimming, tractor pulling or playing the bagpipes) or tenacious perseverance. If there is anything you've done in the past that you can't quite believe you managed to do, mention it.

Attention to detail

A slipshod lawyer is a bad lawyer. Legal professionals must work accurately and concisely, spot and resolve mistakes, and go over everything with a fine-tooth comb. Proofreading is something that comes naturally to lawyers, as almost every element of the job involves accurate written work.

How to demonstrate: The best way to prove your eagle-eyed credentials is to produce a flawless and typo-free application form. Check, check and check again! Within your form, you could describe a computer program that you have written featuring thousands of lines of code, any one of which could have stopped it working; or discuss your organisation of a football league, including fixtures, results, pitch allocation and player registration. These are just two examples though – plenty of things require organisation and attention to detail, from managing the till behind a bar to taking a stock check.

Communication

Legal work is all about conveying advice. You need to prove that you can listen to what others say and ask of you, and communicate your thoughts and opinions effectively. After all, there's no point in being a genius if you can't express legal concepts to colleagues and clients.

How to demonstrate: We all communicate, all the time, so you should not be short of examples, but look for those where your communication skills made a material difference to a situation. These might include running a campaign (eg, student elections) involving written and oral communication, examples of journalism in which you present complicated ideas simply, or debating and mooting.

Teamwork and leadership

In the law, teams are everything – while there is much solo work to be done, even the lone wolves (eg, top barristers) perform within the context of a team in which everyone contributes to the whole. You must be committed to working this way and, again, you've probably done more of this than you think – teamwork is how society functions.

How to demonstrate: Remember that we are talking about teamwork and leadership; show where you have led, but also show where you have bowed to the will of the group. Sports teams are the obvious examples, but any communal activity where different tasks contribute towards a shared goal can be used: orchestras and bands, clubs, Duke of Edinburgh, science projects or team debating.

Commercial awareness

Commercial awareness boils down to understanding individuals' or businesses' motives for acting in the way that they do. If you cannot understand your clients' motivations, goals and constraints, your advice on how they should act will be worthless. Furthermore, the place you will practise law is a business, be it a multinational corporation or a high-street firm. Your role within it will have a direct relationship to it achieving its goals.

How to demonstrate: Experience in the working world will come in handy here, as you are likely to have worked for a company of some sort and experienced how it functions from the inside. Talk about real-life business scenarios in which you have been involved, no matter how junior or peripheral you were. Demonstrate that you have followed commercial and business stories in the press over a protracted period and can comment on why a business or sector is expanding/contracting/changing.

Chances are, you will already have many of the above skills and the tough part may be coming up with the evidence to support your claims. Most of the examples above are drawn from the academic and extracurricular field. However, the richest pickings may well come from the work and work experience you have encountered. So, determine your goal (finding a career in law); take a body of material (you and your life); analyse it against a set of criteria (the skills that employers seek); and present your findings clearly and economically (make an application). Within your LawCareers.Net MyLCN account, the MySelf tool allows you to do this in a systematic fashion. The same applies to other activities; break them down and look for the nuggets of achievement and insight that demonstrate and have developed your skills.

Commercial awareness

Commercial awareness is one of the key skills that law firms look for in future trainees. It means understanding the environment in which the firm and its clients operate, and then using your legal expertise to help both achieve their goals. To succeed in the law, you will need to demonstrate that you can think in this way.

To persuade a recruiter of your commercial awareness, you need to develop a genuine interest in the business world. Without this, you are unlikely to enjoy a career in commercial law or properly understand what your clients want to achieve. Even if you intend to train as a private client lawyer, you need to be able to speak the language of clients who are themselves business owners. You need to show recruiters that you can be trusted to represent the firm to a client and that you have the potential to develop new client relationships, and perhaps even new legal products and services further down the line. Firms invest in candidates in whom they have confidence.

What is it?

Commercial awareness means understanding your clients' businesses and being able to use your legal knowledge to help them achieve their objectives. Commercially aware candidates also appreciate that the law firms they are applying to are also commercial enterprises. Whichever area of law you decide to go into, you will need to demonstrate that you can help drive your firm's business forward, beyond just securing your training contract.

You will need to show that you understand the importance of client relationships and the need for businesses to be cost effective. Make a habit of reading the business and politics sections of a high-quality news source to improve your grasp of the issues. With this in mind, you will need to show that you can:
- manage your time effectively;

- demonstrate initiative;
- work well within a team;
- develop strong client relationships; and
- demonstrate a good understanding of current economic conditions and in-depth legal knowledge.

Learning more

To this end, it is important to focus on the word 'awareness', and not mistake it for the word 'knowledge'. Remember that you are going to be a trainee and are not expected to know everything about the law firm or its clients' businesses from day one.

As we know, commercial awareness for a future lawyer is split into two categories: factors that relate to law firms as businesses themselves and factors that affect the clients for which they work. In the first category, prospective trainees should have at least a basic understanding of the purpose of the Legal Services Act 2007 and a general understanding of what a partnership is and how law firms are traditionally structured. A sense of how legal work and clients are sourced and charged is also helpful. For those keen to work at international law firms, learning about the firm's network of offices and why it is shaped in this way is essential. This is easier if you have a reasonable grasp of the global economic landscape. What are the BRICS? What is an emerging market? What have been the consequences of the 2008 financial crisis for economies, businesses and regulators? What caused that financial crisis? Why has austerity been the watchword of the decade in the United Kingdom? Has it been an effective response compared to the approaches taken in other countries? And what about Brexit – with negotiations now underway, will it be possible for the United Kingdom to introduce stricter immigration controls and still access the single market? These topics are covered extensively in the mainstream media, often in great detail.

Radio: BBC R4 and the World Service	
Today programme	Today is the most influential news programme in the United Kingdom and sets the political agenda each morning. If you want to quickly build awareness of current affairs in politics, business and society, then listen to this.
The World Tonight	Broad coverage of international news and business.
The Bottom Line	Evan Davis's roundtable interviews get to the heart of business thinking.
Peter Day's World of Business	Veteran business journalist Peter Day's show includes on-the-ground stories from around the world.
Today in Parliament	Learn how decisions in Parliament affect and are affected by the wider economy and the Overton window (look it up).
World Business Report	Daily stories from around the globe.
PM	A probing look at the day's issues - excellent analysis and interviews with leading figures.
The World at One	One of BBC R4's main flagship news and current affairs programmes, along with Today and PM. Presented by leading interviewer Sarah Montague.

TV	
Channel 4 News	The hour-long show allows time for special reports to explain issues more deeply – by far the best news journalism on British TV.
Bloomberg TV	Bloomberg West is a tech-focused one-hour show, bringing all the news from Silicon Valley.

BBCs 1 and 2	The BBC's business and economics team contributes regularly to BBC News and also has blogs and stories on the BBC website. Look out for reports and blogs from Kamal Ahmed, and follow him on Twitter. Tune in to The Andrew Marr Show for interviews with leading figures from politics and business (or its ITV rival, Peston on Sunday). The Beeb also makes some good one-off documentaries/short series about world economics and business.

Press	
The Economist	Try a discounted trial or student subscription for full access, or choose your limited free reads carefully. The app is free to download.
The Telegraph	Partial paywall. Home to many leading Conservative voices, including star columnist Boris Johnson.
The Times	Behind a pay wall. The Times law supplement is published on Thursdays.
Financial Times	Paywall (can read some material free). Good international features and interesting opinion pieces.
Guardian	No paywall, yet. The Guardian law section has been reduced, but good overall news reporting and home to left-leaning voices such as economics journalist Aditya Chakrabortti.
Reuters	Heavy on the financial markets and good for fast news reports.
Wall Street Journal	Interesting to read about European issues from another perspective.
BBC News website	Pitches many stories at the non-expert, but this can be really helpful.

However, a last-minute skim of the *Financial Times* before your interview will be of limited use. You should set yourself a routine and stick to it, so that you can develop a genuine interest and a knack for spotting themes and trends. You will eventually be able to see things from a businessperson's perspective and develop a bigger-picture understanding of the impact of events. In short, you will adopt the media habits of a good legal professional before you become one.

On the previous page are some recommendations of good places to start learning.

Past experiences

Another way of assessing your commercial awareness is to think about what you already know. Consider your employment history and see whether you can identify any previous examples of commercial work experience. For example, have you worked in a service environment, interacting with customers or clients? Did you gain insight into how the business you was run? Have you ever undertaken a project or devised a solution to a business problem? Was there a challenge that you had to overcome?

It is not only your employment history that counts as commercial work experience. Positions of responsibility can also demonstrate the necessary skills. Did you belong to any societies at university and if so, what was your role? For example, if you were the treasurer of a sports club, this can be used to demonstrate your ability to manage finances and budgets.

Not-for-profit work can also be used to demonstrate commercial awareness as, depending on your role, you may have been involved in promoting events or persuading companies to sponsor you or provide free products. These activities help to show that you have an understanding of basic business

processes. Working in the family business or setting up and managing your own business (including online) can all point to commercial nous, as there is no better way to understand the fundamentals of a business than by running one yourself.

New experiences

In addition to looking at what you have done already, you may want to increase your commercial awareness by undertaking some useful employment while you study or after you have finished your degree or Legal Practice Course. The first step is to assess yourself. Consider the area of law that you wish to practise, the type of firm you want to work in and any skills which you may be lacking. Next, work out where you could gain the skills that may be relevant to your firm of choice. For example, if you are interested in banking or corporate finance, then consider gaining experience in a corporate setting (eg, an accountancy firm or tax office).

Commercial thinking can be developed in any employment setting, particularly if your role allows you access to the rationale for decisions made by your employer. For example, in the publishing industry, you might learn about the challenges faced by print media in light of the growth of online journalism. If you work in retail, logistics or warehousing during your holidays, you could develop an understanding of, say, the seasonality of demand or just-in-time purchasing principles.

Another option is to consider the types of client that you might be dealing with in a corporate law firm and try to gain some experience with those (eg, in a bank or financial institution). If you can gain insight into how potential clients run their businesses, this will be a strong selling point at interview. Alternatively, think about how a corporate firm is run and the skills you would need to work there (ie, working on large, complex deals as part of a large team). Use this basic idea to think laterally about other organisations which would allow you to work in the same way (eg, insurers or finance houses).

Ultimately, what matters is that you learn about and understand the environments in which you work. Even positions which appear very low level can produce great commercial insight. It just depends how you look at it and how well you can explain your understanding to a potential recruiter.

For more on developing commercial awareness, head to LawCareers.Net for weekly commercial news roundups, in-depth features and tailored advice from its Oracle email service. In particular, make sure you bookmark LCN's Commercial Question

section, where each week solicitors from a different commercial or corporate firm analyse a topical issue from a commercial-legal perspective. Commercial Questions examine everything from intellectual property, to trends in international M&A, to the employment law implications of the gig economy, so reading them will help you to start thinking like a lawyer on a whole range of matters.

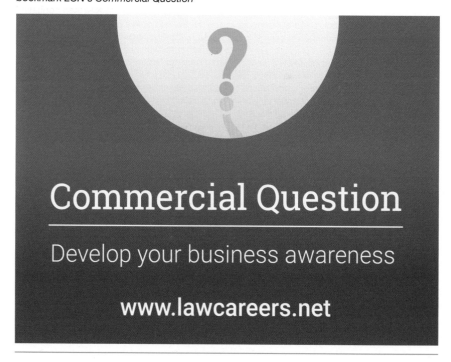

Commercial Question

Develop your business awareness

www.lawcareers.net

Application technique

By the time it comes to applying, you should have thoroughly researched the profession and know where it is that you want to apply. Wherever that is, mention why you are attracted to the firm or chambers in question (ie, the special/exciting things that you've found out about it after following our advice in the previous chapter), and how your skills and qualities match what they are looking for.

Andrew Campbell, a barrister at Queen Elizabeth Building and heavily involved with the chambers pupillage committee, explains why your application is such a crucial step in the process: "An application form is in many ways a form of written advocacy. The case the candidate is presenting is why they should be offered a pupillage or mini-pupillage. Every question must be seen as an opportunity to impress, rather than a hurdle to overcome. The best answers will be like any good argument in court and will support the case with strong evidence."

Bear in mind the need to apply to a manageable number of firms or chambers. Ten well-researched and considered applications will serve you far better than 100 randomly fired-off CVs. Read on for targeted advice that will help you to create just such an application.

What's in a name?

Quite a lot, actually. Imagine how peeved you would be if you received a letter from a firm offering a training contract to someone else. Firms and chambers take offence when you get their name wrong. One graduate recruitment partner at a regional firm recalls a student who "sent an application and covering letter for a training contract stating that 'I would love to work at Withers.' Wrong firm!" Don't make this amateurish mistake. And don't take it upon yourself to change the name of the firm by shortening it – Caroline Lindner, global communications and engagement senior manager and former trainee recruitment manager at Norton Rose Fulbright, says: "Along with spelling and grammatical errors, abbreviating the name of the firm should be avoided at all costs." Equally, don't be the applicant who admitted to one City firm, on being called for interview, that "she couldn't remember applying to us – we were not impressed!". Keep a handle on which firms you apply to.

Timing

Many firms and chambers look to fill their training places two years in advance. For law students, this means applying during the summer vacation between the second and third year of your law degree. Non-law students should apply before starting the GDL.

While budding solicitors should apply directly to firms for training contracts, the recruitment process for the Bar is different. Certain applications must be made through the centralised online pupillage application system, the Pupillage Gateway (www. pupillagegateway.com). See "Training as a barrister" for further details.

Some smaller organisations accept applications just one year in advance. If you have left your application late or were unsuccessful in your first round of applications, use the "Jobs" section of www.LawCareers.Net to source up-to-date information and availability.

Many recruiters mention the importance of applying well before the official closing date: first, so you don't have to rush to get the application done; second, because the most popular firms may well fill their quota of trainees before the deadline. Mirrick Koh, former head of graduate recruitment and development at CMS, says: "Know your deadlines and find out whether the firm you are applying to recruits on a rolling basis, as this could influence when you submit your application." The message here is clear – don't let it go down to the wire.

Presentation

An application may be the first contact that you have with prospective employers. Make a good impression by convincing them that you have the necessary skills, experience, qualifications and enthusiasm for the job in question.

Make sure that you know how the firm or chambers wants you to apply – the vast majority use online application forms, although some may still prefer CV and covering letter. Where possible, obtain the name of the person to whom your application should be addressed. Don't just send in a CV when the firm or chambers clearly wants you to tackle its application form.

We can't stress enough that the best applications are tailored to each individual firm or chambers. Tell a firm or set why you are choosing to apply to it rather than any of its competitors. Most recruiters complain about applications that are littered with misspellings and puffery about the nature of the organisation. A head of chambers in the Southeast agreed: "We had an application from someone allegedly impressed by 'the ethos of our set and the fact that it had kept it touch with its roots'. Our advice? Don't write guff like that on your applications. Flattery will get you nowhere – it's just padding and it doesn't impress."

Puneet Tahim, senior recruitment coordinator at Latham & Watkins, adds: "Candidates should avoid using broad statements such as, 'I am a good team player, with excellent communication skills who is extremely ambitious and driven'. All these are valued skills and attributes, but you need evidence to back up your claims. You would be better placed to talk about a particular activity you are involved in and explain all of the skills you have developed as a result. Keep it simple and avoid unnecessary jargon. When you consider the volume of applications a firm receives, it's important to focus on the key information you want to convey. Don't use 10 words when five will suffice."

Competition is stiff and some firms and chambers receive thousands of applications for just a few places – never more so than in the current climate. Don't give recruiters the easy option to eliminate you from their lists – so no spelling mistakes, grammatical errors or casual language. And get someone who can spell to check the final version (errors through familiarity and repetition creep in otherwise). Alix Balfe-Skinner, HR manager at Taylor Vinters, says: "Attention to detail is everything – small things such as making sure you use capitals in the correct places are crucial. It makes an application seem more professional and as though more time and care has been taken."

Here are a few more top tips from recruiters:
- "Spelling and grammar are absolutely vital. Ask someone else to read through your form for you to check it makes sense. Copy and paste the text into Word and apply spellcheck. If you haven't got anyone to check it for you, review it. Leave it for a couple of hours then review again with fresh eyes before submitting" – Danielle White, graduate recruitment and development manager at Mayer Brown International.
- "Bear in mind that graduate recruiters will know little or nothing about you before receiving your application form. By the end of each form, candidates should have explained why they want to be a solicitor, why they are applying to that particular firm and why they feel the firm should hire them" – Puneet Tahim, Latham & Watkins.
- "You must check your spelling – otherwise it just looks sloppy. Where there is a word count, make sure that you are succinct. It's all about attention to detail and presentation, which is of course what we're looking for in our future lawyers – we wouldn't send out something with mistakes in it to a client" – Caroline Walsh, former head of legal trainee recruitment and development, Clyde & Co LLP.

• "Think carefully about what is distinctive about a particular set of chambers or area of practice and explain why that interests you. You should also identify what is distinctive about you and why you should be picked above the other candidates" – Matthew Parker, barrister, 3 Verulam Buildings.
• "Be interesting, but not contrived. Interviewers have to read dozens of these forms. The more you can engage them, the better – but don't try to do so artificially. And be positive; being negative about anything on your application form can create a bad impression" – barrister at leading London set.

Application forms

Many students struggle with the open-ended or competency questions on application forms. These questions vary, but tend to focus on teamwork, problem solving, communication and judgement (eg, "Outside of your studies, describe a situation where you have worked with a group of people to achieve a goal"). As a rule, the best answers are as significant and unique to you as possible, easy to discuss at interview and relevant to the job. Tackle the question by breaking it down into the situation or context, the task or problem faced and the outcome or result.

Make sure that you read instructions very carefully. Don't be like this candidate for a regional firm: "We ask people to list their strengths and weaknesses. One student obviously did not read the question properly and listed her strengths as being 'honest, competent and hardworking' – so far, so good – but unfortunately went on to list her weaknesses as 'dishonest, incompetent and lazy'. Needless to say, she was not invited for an interview."

And keep an eye on word limits, as one barrister advises: "Brevity is key; don't waste words on things that are irrelevant, so abstract as to lack sense or by trying to be funny. Save your humour for interviews." Naomi Winston of Ten Old Square agrees: "Don't write reams and reams, just because you can – remember that someone has to read your application (and maybe a couple of hundred others, too)."

Don't underestimate the amount of time it takes to complete an application form (hours rather than minutes). Plan to do them well in advance and don't leave it to the last minute on deadline day to submit. Lucie Rees, graduate manager at Watson Farley & Williams LLP, suggests "saving the form as you go along – there's nothing worse than spending hours doing something only for a technical hitch to mean you have to do it all again". Always read through the entire form, including the small print, which may contain important instructions; and practise on a photocopy of the form first. It may be time consuming, but it is crucial to approach each application individually, back up your work regularly and avoid the temptation to copy and paste. Michelle Ruddle, recruitment marketing manager at Hogan Lovells, says: "Tailor your answers; don't just copy and paste content from another application form, as you may end up referring to the wrong firm name in error, which shows lack of attention to detail. You should also have someone else check your application form before you click 'submit' to pick out any grammatical or spelling mistakes."

And while some recruiters say never copy and paste under any circumstances, others accept that you probably will, so take some advice on how to do it successfully, such as from this London barrister: "Be careful when copying and pasting. It saves time, but you won't endear yourself to a set if you are obviously describing how much you want to join their main rival." Similarly, Laura Newton of Brick Court Chambers says: "If you must copy and paste, do so with care! Make sure that the 'variable' parts get updated and that the text fits in with the rest of the form."

Covering letters

Unless the employer's instructions state otherwise, you should send a short covering letter with the application form (or CV). A covering letter gives you the opportunity to highlight your unique selling points, provide extra information in support of your application and convey your motivation for the job. The golden rule of covering letters is to keep them brief – no longer than one A4 page. The first paragraph should mention the position that you are applying for, the year of entry and, if it was advertised, where you saw the vacancy. The second paragraph should say why you want to work for the firm or set and what you can offer it. The third paragraph should close on a positive note, saying you look forward to hearing from the recruiter at his or her convenience, with your mobile number and any dates on which you are unavailable for interview.

Never write a standard covering letter to accompany all of your applications. 'Dear Sir or Madam' will not do. Be sure to tailor each letter to the firm/chambers to which you are applying. Clarity, neatness and courtesy are all equally important.

CVs
If one of your target firms or sets requires a CV rather than its own form, use this to your advantage. Unlike application forms, a CV gives you the chance to create your own personal record of achievements in a format that you control. The content of your CV should comprise the following.
- Personal details - include your name, address, telephone number and email address. Nationality and date of birth are optional.
- Education and qualifications - set out your most recent achievements in detail. Recruiters are more interested in how you performed in your year-end exams than how

good you were at GCSE metalwork.
- Work experience/employment history - use reverse chronological order. Show the dates of work experience, including the name of the employer and the town/city it is based in. Mention any work experience, including any voluntary and seemingly less relevant jobs – for example, bar work can be sold as demonstrating your ability to perform a customer/client-facing role under pressure.
- Other skills and interests - non-academic skills include leadership, teamwork, flexibility, judgement, commercial awareness, imagination, adventurousness and diligence. They are often best illustrated and reflected through cultural, social, sporting, travel and independent activities and hobbies. But remember: the facts must ultimately support your application to become a lawyer. In particular, non-law graduates should highlight any legal work experience that they have in order to prove their commitment to law.
- Referees - it is standard practice to include two referees: one academic and one relating to work experience or general character. Check with your intended referees in advance that it's okay to mention them and offer to send them a copy of your application.

Further reading:
There is plenty more useful application advice on LawCareers.Net:
- Application master class – www.lawcareers. net/Information/Features/03072018-Here-is-our-training-contract-application-master-class
- Guide to formal application writing - www.lawcareers.net/Information/ Features/28062016-CVs-cover-letters-and-applications-LCNs-guide-to-formal-writing

Reality check: A key point when applying: tell the truth. Seems obvious, but sometimes it's worth reiterating, as one barrister we spoke to emphasised: "Don't lie and don't write about things that you don't know anything about. If you are caught out, it is incredibly embarrassing and the end of your chance of a pupillage." You have been warned.

Ten top tips for online apps

You should approach an online form exactly as you would a paper form – take your time, carefully prepare your responses and pay attention to detail. Here are our top 10 tips for online apps:

- Do read through the whole application form before you start, keeping a close eye on all instructions.

- Do plan where all your main boasts will be made. It would be a shame to work a slightly tangential skill or experience into one answer when you turn out to be questioned directly on the issue on the next page.

- Don't complete the form with your caps lock on, except where specified – it looks as if you're SHOUTING.

- Do take care with the layout of your application. Consider writing the longer sections using Word and then copying the text over, checking that the formatting (eg, bullet points) have transferred properly.

- Don't succumb to 'copy and paste' fatigue. This opens the door wide to calling the firm by the wrong name – recruiters' most-hated mistake.

- Do use the spell check, although not the US version, which will let annoying Americanisms through.

- Don't be tempted to use email or text talk (eg, 'It wld be wkd to work 4 u'). Write in full sentences and do not abbreviate words.

- Do make sure that there is some way of keeping a record of your application. Whereas previously you would have photocopied it, make sure you either save it, print it or copy it into a separate document.

- Do read through your completed application at least three times before you submit it. Boasting of your 'excellen eye for deetail' will not get you the training contract/pupillage.

- Do use a sensible email address that you will be able to access throughout the recruitment period. If you graduate in June, your university email address will be shut down, but firms will want to contact you throughout the summer.

Interview technique

When you are invited to an interview, the first thing you should do is pat yourself on the back. The process to get to this stage is highly competitive, so you have already shown that you are a good candidate for a training contract. Nerves will probably soon follow, too, and you are bound to wonder what you will be asked and what the process will be like.

Read on for advice on how to maximise your chances of success.

Preparation
It's your application that has aroused the firm's/chambers' interest, so reread it. Try to imagine some of the things which your interviewers might focus on (eg, what you have gained from your experiences in terms of skills and personal development). Caroline Lindner, global communications lead at Norton Rose Fulbright, advises: "Interviewers will want to test how the candidate can respond to unseen materials or topics, so expect to be taken out of your comfort zone and be willing to debate and discuss topical commercial issues which you may not know a lot about. After all, we are looking for agile minds!"

Read the firm's/chambers' recruitment literature and browse its website. Read the trade press, such as *The Lawyer*, *Legal Week* and *Law Society Gazette*, as well as the law sections of *The Times* and *The Guardian*, so that you are aware of current legal issues. If you can't face trawling through the broadsheets, go to www.LawCareers.Net for its News section.

Alix Balfe-Skinner, HR manager at Taylor Vinters is keen to emphasise the importance of research and preparation: "It is vital that students understand and know as much as possible about the firm they are applying to and the challenges and opportunities currently faced by the firm. This is often a key questioning area in training contract

and other interviews. You don't need to know everything, but you need to be able to give your opinion coherently and concisely. Reading the legal press is also essential, as candidates are likely to be asked about current affairs and the wider legal market."

On the day itself, arrive with time to spare. Being late is likely to be viewed as a sign of arrogance or rudeness, not confidence. Make sure you have a mobile phone and the number of the firm in case you are unavoidably detained, so you can let them know what's happening. Don't follow the example of the applicant from Leeds who turned up two hours late for an interview with a firm in London armed with several Harrods shopping bags, or the candidate who failed to show up for an interview without explanation, then rang the chambers a week later demanding to know why she hadn't heard from them.

Having done your preparatory homework and got yourself safely to the correct location, let's take a look at the sort of thing you can expect when you get there.

Assessment days
Firms and sets are increasingly using a variety of ways to assess your suitability to be a lawyer. Selection procedures can range from a series of interviews to a day of group exercises and tests, devised to ascertain whether you have the skills and qualities which they are looking for. In some ways, assessment days are a bit like a mini-vacation scheme – they are a chance for the firm to put you through your paces in a variety of different ways rather than just talking to you at an interview.

A typical assessment day (if there is such a thing) might include group exercises, ability tests, presentations and in-tray exercises. In a brutal twist, there may even be a cull at lunchtime where poorer performers are sent home, while the remainder might have a formal panel interview in the afternoon. One recruiter mentions an incident that occurred during the chambers' assessment day: "We do an X-Factor style goodbye halfway through the day, inviting only a few to stay for lunch and second interview. We were joined at lunch one year by someone we had rejected, but who could not understand the word 'goodbye'." The lesson here is to learn when to take a hint!

> ❝ Don't ask a question that, had you done any research on the firm, you would have found out the answer ❞

Remember that although they might sound intimidating, the exercises generally aren't set to trick you, but rather are intended to reveal what sort of person you are and the sort of lawyer you might become. One firm likes to test applicants' initiative by asking in a written assessment whether you know its address and phone number (the answers are on the pen you are given to write the answer!). Be your best self on the day and don't let nerves get the better of you. Lucie Rees, graduate manager at Watson Farley & Williams, offers some reassurance: "Assessment centres are designed to put candidates at their ease and give them the best chance to showcase the skills we are looking for. More times than not, successful candidates tell us they actually enjoyed the day, which is great to hear. There is a mix of group and individual work, all of which fits into a client scenario that runs throughout the day. Try to relax and be yourself – you're more likely to perform well and find the firm that is right for you."

Each firm/chambers will have its own way of going about things and, with a bit of luck, will

brief you properly in advance. If it doesn't, there's no harm in asking, but don't be too pushy as surprises might be a deliberate part of the day.

Psychometric tests

Psychometric tests are supposedly the Holy Grail, bringing science into the recruitment equation. With employers seeking not only ability, but also candidates with an appropriate temperament and character profile, psychometric tests are designed to work this out. While they are somewhat imperfect and should always be used in conjunction with other methods, it is fair to say that they represent a useful tool for recruiters. One graduate recruitment manager told us that psychometric tests can provide "a strong indication of a participant's potential".

The key to psychometric tests is that there is no 'right' answer. Often, similar questions are asked in a number of ways. The aim is to discourage candidates from trying to guess what answer is expected and instead give a genuine picture of themselves. As such, it is hard to offer advice on how to approach them, beyond being honest. Some firms will even give an identical test immediately after the first, to ensure that people are being honest – as our recruiter says: "Nobody can remember how they responded previously if they were trying to suppress their true nature!"

Interviews
During

An interview is a two-way process, designed for both you and the interviewer to decide whether you meet each other's needs. A recruiter at a City firm told us: "An interview day at our firm starts with candidates arriving an hour before their interview slots. They are given a written question and asked to orally present the advice they would give in that scenario for five minutes at the start of the interview. The remainder of the interview is spent discussing the application form and the candidate in general, as well as the firm." During the interview, you should do the following:

- Listen carefully to all questions and think for a moment before answering.
- Speak in a clear voice and be positive and alert throughout.
- Remember your manners. One City firm recruiter mentions an interviewee who asked "whether there were any David Brent characters in the office – it might have been funny if the candidate hadn't been performing so badly".
- Be aware of your body language. Look the interviewer in the eye when speaking to him or her, but without staring psychotically.
- In a panel interview, make eye contact with everyone, not just one person throughout. And do try to get people's names right – one interviewer recalls "making such an impression on the candidate that she called me David; my name is Robert!"
- Try to be relaxed and enthusiastic, without being too laid-back. One partner at a City firm recalls the candidate who swore during the interview, but had no recollection of doing so: "It just goes to demonstrate that people are often oblivious to how they come across."
- Be yourself, urges Danielle White, graduate recruitment and development manager at Mayer Brown International LLP: "It's always nice to see someone who is passionate and motivated, and who is able to show his/her personality as well as capability during the interview."

We mention eye contact for a reason. Talking to graduate recruiters, it's an issue for many candidates. Whether you want to or not, you must make eye contact with the interviewer(s). Simply put, avoiding eye contact makes you look shifty, whereas making it projects confidence and self-assurance. One recruitment manager says: "Try to sit still – being nervous often causes fidgeting which you may not be aware of. This can be off-putting to interviewers, so be self-aware." Another London recruiter, giving an example of how not to do an interview, recalled in horror "the candidate who spent 40 minutes staring at a speck on the wall because she just could not make eye contact with us". Equally bad was the interviewee who "listed effective communication as one of his main strengths, but did not once make eye contact, rather disproving his claim".

> **❝ Try to sit still – being nervous often causes fidgeting which you may not be aware of ❞**

Although there is no way to find out the interview questions in advance, you can make an educated guess about some of them (the box on p43, which lists some of the most commonly asked questions, is a good place to start). Prepare your answers accordingly and think about one or two clever questions that you can ask your interviewers. Remember also that there is not necessarily always going to be a 'correct' answer - some of the questions will be asked in order to gauge how well you express yourself. Puneet Tahim, senior recruitment coordinator at Latham & Watkins, says: "Candidates should try to pre-empt what an interviewer might ask them and prepare for these questions. In doing this they will be able to engage in a meaningful discussion/debate which demonstrates their communication and influencing skills."

You're likely to get asked at least one question designed to assess your business understanding, advises Danielle: "Commercial awareness is very important and will almost certainly be tested at some point during the process. It is of fundamental importance that candidates understand what is happening in the business world and how this will potentially impact on the legal industry."

We know it's hard, but do try to speak intelligently while thinking on your feet during the interview. Examples of how not to do it include naming Lauren Goodger when asked whom in the world you most admire; declaring that you don't know who David Gauke is or whether Nigel Farage is leftwing or rightwing; and mentioning the importance of presenting a professional appearance while sporting zebra-striped hair, a skirt with the hem hanging off, a creased jacket and scuffed shoes.

On the question of attire, matching neon green tights and nail varnish do not go down well with the rather staid legal profession. One regional recruiter gives this sartorial example: "One candidate arrived dressed more appropriately for nightclubbing than an interview. She wore a very orange, very short skirt and a low-cut pink top with a low-slung belt around her hips. When she stood up to leave her belt fell to the floor, leaving her face as pink as her top!"

Ask questions to which you genuinely want to know the answers – but not those for which you could have found out the answer beforehand. One northwest graduate recruitment adviser comments: "Don't ask a question that, had you done any research on the firm, you would have found out the answer. There are no brownie points for asking the obvious."

We asked recruiters what sorts of questions would impress them. Most said anything that reflects an interest in and understanding of the commercial world, clients and their business needs, or something that demonstrates specific knowledge of the

firm without merely parroting the graduate recruitment literature or the firm's/chambers' website. Amy Kisser, barrister at QEB and a member of the pupillage committee, says: "Candidates always seem to think that they need to ask an 'impressive question' of their interviewers – we think this is nonsense. We want them to use this part of the interview as an opportunity to ask us any questions they may still have – having looked at our website already – rather than for us to use it as an opportunity to assess them. We are clear that interviews are very much a two-way street; our candidates are assessing us as much as we are them!" It is also important to remain unfazed and appear confident. Some recruiters mentioned being both impressed and flummoxed by questions about why they like their job and what would make them leave!

> ££ Reading the legal press is also essential, as candidates are likely to be asked about current affairs and the wider legal market ££

After

Try to end things on a positive note, shaking hands with your interviewer(s) and thanking them for their time. If you feel comfortable doing so, ask for some feedback. Ways not to end an interview? One candidate concluded by saying: "I like to try lots of things, but rarely succeed at any of them." We suspect that didn't leave a very positive impression. Another barged back into the room, interrupting another interview, to ask whether the interviewers had his bus ticket.

As soon as you come out of the interview, it's a good idea to find somewhere quiet to sit and write down all the questions you can remember being asked. Then write down what you gave as an answer. Later, work through the questions again, this time writing out what you would have said, given time to think and no interview nerves. By taking time to reflect on the interview, you'll be making the most of the experience (whether good or bad) and preparing yourself for the next one.

Offers

You will hear back from most recruiters quickly. If you receive an offer, most firms will give you four weeks in which to respond. If you are certain that you want to accept, respond in writing as soon as possible. If you are unable to give a decision at the time of receiving an offer, let them know and give a date by which you should have a final answer. Once you have accepted an offer, inform all other firms/chambers that have invited you for interview or that have made you an alternative offer. If no deadline is given, don't feel pressured to give an answer if you think that other offers may still be forthcoming.

Further advice appears throughout LCNH. In particular, be sure to read the profiles of individual solicitors and barristers in the practice area sections, many of whom offer their take on the application and interview process.

Further reading

There is plenty more useful interview advice on LawCareers.Net, including:
* Training contract interviews made easy - www.lawcareers.net/Information/LCNSays/ Training-contract-interviews-made-easy
* A dedicated guide to pupillage interviews www.lawcareers.net/Information/ Features/03012017-Acing-that-pupillage-interview

Reality check: Remember that you won't be successful in your interview endeavours without preparing thoroughly, dressing smartly, arriving punctually and making eye contact.

Ten top interview questions

Naturally, what you will be asked in interviews can vary from firm to firm and set to set. However, here are 10 commonly asked questions to give you an idea of what recruiters are keen to know:

* Why are you applying to this firm/chambers?
* What are your long-term objectives in terms of career development?
* What do you really want in life?
* Are you satisfied with your academic achievements to date?
* What sorts of qualities do you feel you can bring to a job or career?
* What do you see as your personal strengths?
* What do you see as your faults or weaknesses?
* What is the worst mistake you have ever made and what did you learn from it?
* Have there been any commercial stories in the news over the last week that have interested you?
* Is there any aspect of the law or criminal justice system you would like to change?

Scotland and Northern Ireland

As we already have a firm handle on how things work in England and Wales, let us now look at how lawyers are trained in other parts of the United Kingdom. Here follows a brief explanation of what happens in Scotland and Northern Ireland.

Scotland

Over the last few years, legal education and training in Scotland have undergone a major review. The "standard" route to qualification that most Scottish solicitors take is to do a four-year undergraduate degree in Scots law, followed by a mandatory one-year course called the Diploma in Professional Legal Practice and finally a two-year "traineeship" at a solicitors' firm. Non-law graduates must complete a two-year accelerated LLB in Scots law, after which the route is the same as the above. There is also a third option for those who do not want to – or are unable to – attend university. Instead of university, candidates can complete a three-year pre-professional education and training (PEAT) training contract (yes, they like the word "training" so much they have used it twice). The compulsory Diploma in Professional Legal Practice follows this and the process ends with a further two-year traineeship. For the most up-to-date information, visit www.lawscot.org.uk.

Undergraduate study

It is possible to study for an LLB in Scots Law/Foundation Programme at 10 universities in Scotland. The ordinary degree takes three years, while the honours degree takes four. There are also accelerated degree options, which can be taken if you have a non-law first degree. Students on the Scottish law degree at either the University of Dundee or the University of Strathclyde can take enough English law modules to earn a dual-qualified law degree, enabling them to progress to qualification in England and Wales or Scotland.

If you do not wish to do an LLB, it is possible to do a three-year, pre-diploma training contract with a qualified Scottish solicitor, at the end of which you sit the Law Society of Scotland's professional exams. During the three years you must receive training in various prescribed areas.

Vocational study

All those who intend to practise as a solicitor or advocate (the equivalent of a barrister) must complete the Diploma in Legal Practice, a 26-week full-time course offered at six universities, namely Aberdeen, Dundee, Glasgow, Strathclyde, Edinburgh and Robert Gordon. The course imparts knowledge and skills necessary for working life, with an emphasis on practical application and much of the teaching carried out by practising lawyers.

Training

Solicitors

To qualify as a solicitor, individuals must complete a two-year traineeship. Trainees are usually paid by the training firm at least the minimum amount set by the Law Society of Scotland (from June 2018 £19,000 in the first year, £22,000 for the second year). During the training contract, trainees must complete a minimum of 60 hours of trainee continuing professional development, which is structured learning over and above the trainee's office work. It is possible to be admitted as a solicitor after one year of training (especially useful if the trainee is to appear in court on behalf of clients); but normally, at the end of the two years – and provided that all conditions have been met – the trainee is admitted as a fully qualified solicitor.

Advocates

The body that administers the Scottish Bar is the Faculty of Advocates. Having completed the diploma, a trainee advocate (or 'intrant') must undertake a 21-month period of paid training in a solicitors' office (as for a trainee solicitor above, although slightly shorter), followed by a nine-month period 'devilling' as an unpaid pupil to an advocate. The intrant must then pass an exam set by the Faculty of Advocates covering written and oral advocacy. At this stage, he or she is admitted as an advocate.

Prospective students should note that a law degree from an English university will not form part of the qualification process in Scotland. Nor will a Scottish law degree be recognised by the Law Society of England and Wales as part of its qualification process. If you train in, say, Scotland, you will have to retrain to practise in England and Wales or Northern Ireland, and the same applies for movement in the opposite direction – unless you hold the special dual-qualified degree on offer from the universities of either Dundee or Strathclyde.

For more details visit www.lawscot.org.uk and www.advocates.org.uk.

Northern Ireland
Undergraduate study
Law degrees are offered at Queen's University Belfast (QUB) and the University of Ulster in Northern Ireland. However, law degrees from a number of other universities in England, Wales and Ireland are also accepted as qualifying law degrees for the purposes of passing on to the next stage: apprenticeship.

Non-law graduates must complete a two-year master's in legal science at QUB before they can progress to their apprenticeship.

Vocational study/training
Solicitors
The vocational study and practical training aspects that are found separately in England, Wales and Scotland are combined in Northern Ireland. Trainee solicitors must undertake a two-year apprenticeship under a supervising solicitor (called a 'master').

The practical component comes first, with a four-month period of office-based training. This is followed by one year studying for the Certificate of Professional Studies at the Institute of Professional Legal Studies at QUB or the Graduate School of Professional Legal Education at the University of Ulster. This is then followed by a further eight months of office-based work.

There is a reciprocal arrangement whereby English and Welsh-qualified solicitors may transfer to Northern Ireland without taking further qualifications or examinations. They need only complete an application form, supply any proofs asked for and pay a fee. However, Scottish solicitors are required to take further examinations and complete a period of apprenticeship before they can be admitted in Northern Ireland.

Barristers
Trainee barristers must undertake the Bar Postgraduate Diploma in Professional Legal Studies at the Institute of Professional Legal Studies at QUB. They are then called to the Bar; but before they can practise, they must enter into one year of pupillage with a practising barrister of not less than seven years' standing.

For more details visit www.lawsoc-ni.org and www.barofni.com.

Alternative careers

Nobody ever said that having a law degree condemns you to life as a lawyer – far from it, in fact. There are many alternatives to becoming a solicitor or barrister, and routes to qualification other than the standard training contract or pupillage. Employers will value the skills you have learned through your legal training, such as the ability to research, collect and analyse large amounts of information, and to create a logical argument and reasoned conclusion from a set of facts. The ability to communicate clearly with the public and the profession alike is another sought-after skill. Discretion and a first-class memory are all highly valued in the general careers market.

Read on to see whether any of these alternative careers or routes to law tickle your fancy.

Alternative professions

Accountancy and taxation

Many accountancy firms recruit law students to specialise in tax work because, arguably, there are few differences between the job of a tax accountant and that of a tax lawyer. In addition, three of the 'big four' accountancy firms – PricewaterhouseCoopers, KPMG and Ernst & Young – have secured alternative business structure licences, allowing them to launch and run their own law firms.

Accountancy exams are tough, but the potential rewards – both professional and financial – are excellent. A move into accountancy also offers the opportunity to branch out into other careers (with positions in industry, management and consultancy). For further details of careers in accountancy, contact the Institute of Chartered Accountants in England and Wales or the Chartered Institute of Taxation (see "Useful addresses").

Finance

Banks are keen to recruit law graduates, as are building societies, insurance companies, stockbrokers and related professions. Those who thrive in a competitive, high-pressure environment may find a financial services or City career attractive. Most of the leading financial institutions offer summer work placement programmes, which are a good starting point for you to explore this further.

Civil service

There are opportunities throughout the civil service. Law graduates may wish to pursue a career in the Home Office, the Ministry of Justice, the diplomatic service or the Foreign Office. Her Majesty's Revenue & Customs employs tax inspectors and those with an ability to understand the intricacies of tax law are especially suited to such jobs. The UK Border Agency also welcomes applications from candidates with a legal background. It is worth investigating the Civil Service Fast Stream, an accelerated training scheme for graduates (www.faststream.gov.uk).

Media

Writing about the law can be a creative way in which to use your legal knowledge. Specialist publishers occasionally advertise for law graduates or qualified lawyers to train as legal editors. There is a wide variety of potential employers, ranging from international publishing houses with large legal departments to small companies that produce legal news and features, reference works and directories. In addition, a number of international law firms have publishing departments that provide newsletters and briefings for clients.

Newspapers and television and radio stations all employ legal correspondents. Here, an understanding of how the law works is invaluable.

Police

Those with a keen interest in law and order may wish to consider joining the police force; opportunities abound for graduates to achieve accelerated promotion. For further details, look at recruit.college.police.uk/pages/home.aspx.

European Commission

The European Commission often advertises for law graduates to work in its directorates. To get a taste of what that might be like, the commission offers five-month periods of in-service training (known as 'traineeships') for people who have recently obtained a university degree/diploma. The programme has been running for over 50 years and tens of thousands of people have benefited – in fact, many of them have gone on to become European civil servants and even European commissioners. Although traineeships are only open to EU nationals and the United Kingdom has voted to leave the European Union, Britain will still be a full member until March 2019, throughout the long and complicated process of leaving. This means that these opportunities should still be open to UK graduates. For more information, contact the European Commission's London office (see "Useful addresses").

Court reporting

Court reporters record verbatim court hearings for official transcripts of court proceedings. Increasingly, reporters use a computer-aided transcription system rather than traditional shorthand. Court reporters need not be legally qualified to enter the profession, although it is an advantage. Details of training and careers are available through the British Institute of Verbatim Reporters (see "Useful addresses").

Conveyancing

Licensed conveyancers deal with property transactions worth nearly £10 billion each year. Conveyancing is the process of legally transferring title or ownership of property from one person to another. A licensed conveyancer is a specialist lawyer qualified in all aspects of property law in England and Wales. They are also commissioners for oaths and more and more of them do probate, which is the process for enacting someone's will after their death. They work in a wide range of organisations, including specialist firms, landowning estates and local authorities, and are regulated by the Council for Licensed Conveyancers (CLC) (see "Useful addresses").

The Scottish Qualifications Authority has developed a range of new diplomas in partnership with the CLC, which replace the previous CLC qualifications. It is possible to study to become a licensed conveyancer while working, by either distance learning or part-time study. Most students spread the course over three to four years, although it is possible to complete it in two. To find out more, call the CLC on 020 3859 0904 or email traineelawyer@clc-uk.org.

Alternative qualification opportunities
In-house lawyers

Approximately 28,000 lawyers work in-house in commercial and industrial organisations in the United Kingdom. The main characteristic of the in-house role is that lawyers deal exclusively with their employer's legal business. This close involvement enables the lawyers to develop detailed knowledge of all aspects of their employer's business and provide advice that is in tune with the employer's commercial needs.

Although commercial organisations are usually the main employers of in-house lawyers, an increasing number of non-profit making bodies (eg, charities and trade unions) are hiring legal advisers to work in-house. One interesting aspect of working as a lawyer within a non-profit-making organisation is that many of its legal concerns relate to its own particular interests, in addition to the general laws that affect other companies.

However small, most in-house legal departments are expected to provide cost-effective, commercially attractive and legally correct solutions to problems. Common to most legal departments is a requirement to draft and maintain up-to-date standard contract documents. In-house lawyers may also be involved in planning business strategies with commercial colleagues and negotiating the terms of deals with customers or other lawyers. Other responsibilities could include advising on the supply of goods and services, leases, mortgages, mergers and acquisitions, and cooperation agreements for research, production, distribution or marketing, as well as litigation stemming from disputes arising from any of these activities.

Ensuring the company's compliance with UK and EU law is an important part of the in-house lawyer's remit. Specialist knowledge of the law relating to the employer's business may be necessary (eg, financial services, pharmaceuticals or telecommunications). Besides a thorough and analytical approach to business and the relevant law, it is also important for in-house lawyers to have excellent communication skills, a flexible and confident attitude, the ability to work as part of a team and sound commercial awareness.

For more information contact the Commerce & Industry Group (www.cigroup.org.uk) or the Bar Association for Commerce, Finance and Industry (www.bacfi.org).

Government lawyers

The work carried out by government lawyers covers virtually every aspect of the law you can think of. The diversity of the work reflects the variety of activities within government, these range across issues of national and international significance and across public and private law (covering advisory and legislative work, litigation, commercial, employment and a wealth of specialist areas).

Jenny Underhill at the Government Legal Secretariat says: "Lawyers and legal trainees within government will advise and represent their client, the government of the day, on a huge range of domestic and European

matters. Government lawyers advise not only on what the law is, but also on what it should be. This type of work is quite simply unique. Approximately 50 trainee solicitors and pupil barristers positions are advertised each year. What many of our trainees find attractive is that they are given a high level of responsibility at an early stage and have the option to work in a variety of fields of law throughout their career."

For those who are successful in obtaining a training contract or pupillage, government departments will pay LPC or BPTC fees in full, provided you have not yet started either course. Where the course has already begun, they will pay the fees for the remainder of the course. Those intending to study the LPC or BPTC on a full-time basis can also expect to receive a bursary of between £5,400 and £7,600 for the vocational year.

Crown Prosecution Service

The Crown Prosecution Service (CPS) is the largest legal employer in England and Wales, with around 2,800 lawyers who conduct criminal prosecutions on behalf of the Crown.

Crown prosecutors weigh up evidence and public interest factors in all cases and decide those which should be heard by the courts. They also advise the police on matters relating to criminal cases. CPS caseworkers assist prosecutors in case management as well as attending court, dealing with post-court administration, assessing professional fees and liaising with witnesses and other organisations within the criminal justice system.

Martin McKay-Smith, training principal and director of pupil training at the CPS, says: "The CPS offers a varied, challenging and interesting career for those focusing on criminal litigation. The role of the modern prosecutor provides a true public service, encompassing charging decisions, advocacy and victim and witness care. Our mission is to deliver justice transparently, through the independent and effective prosecution of crime, fostering a culture of excellence in the way we analyse, advocate and progress our cases, reflecting always on what we do to learn and improve."

Applicants for the role of lawyer within the CPS must be solicitors admitted in England and Wales with a full current practising certificate or barristers called to the English Bar who have completed pupillage. In addition, the CPS recruits annually through a Legal Trainee Scheme, with around 40 positions available for trainee solicitors and pupil barristers. Those interested in applying are advised to visit the CPS website (www. cps.gov.uk/careers).

Law centres

For over 40 years, law centres have provided an invaluable service to those in need of legal help and advice, often in deprived inner-city areas. With around 44 centres nationwide, the non-profit-making service is free for clients and centres are funded through local authorities. The nature of the work is dictated by local needs; workers are likely to need to know something about the law relating to immigration, employment, crime and landlord and tenant. Jobs are advertised in the local and national press, and in specialist publications such as the Legal Action Group's magazine or the *Law Gazette*.

Although not financially rewarding, law centre work is one of the most satisfying ways in which a lawyer can use his or her legal expertise. For more information, contact the Law Centres Federation (see "Useful addresses").

Citizens Advice

Citizens Advice is a professional national agency offering free, confidential, impartial and independent advice. In operation since 1939, Citizens Advice provides a service similar to law centres at around 2,700 community locations throughout England and Wales. Information and advice are dispensed in person, and by telephone and email, to millions of people every year – 2.6 million in 2016-17 alone.

Advisers can help to fill out forms, write letters, negotiate on behalf of clients and represent them at courts or tribunals in matters ranging from debt and benefits to housing, employment and immigration. Most centres offer legal advice and some employ their own lawyers. Contact Citizens Advice for further information (see "Useful addresses").

Court work

Over 95% of all criminal cases are dealt with by magistrates. Her Majesty's Courts and Tribunals Service employs many qualified solicitors and barristers as justices' clerks. Clerks advise lay magistrates on law and procedure, and are key figures in the daily running of the courts and the administration of justice. They also play a vital role in the management and administration of the service, organising the arrangement of court time, payment of fines and other related matters.

Stipendiary magistrates are largely chosen from practising solicitors and barristers, although it is possible for a lawyer to progress through the magistrates' courts to the circuit bench and beyond. Clerks who are interested in administration can work towards becoming a justices' chief executive, with responsibilities for increasingly large groupings of magistrates' courts. Further information is available from the Magistrates Association (see "Useful addresses").

Her Majesty's Courts and Tribunals Service also provides administrative support to the higher courts and tribunals. More information can be found at www.gov.uk/government/organisations/hm-courts-and-tribunals-service.

Alternative routes into law
Paralegals

There are a number of other opportunities to work in a solicitors' firm other than as a trainee. As well as administrative, business support and specialist non-legal fee-earner roles, many graduates get work as paralegals. The standing of paralegals is rising, especially as many firms are favouring paralegals over trainees or even some junior solicitors. This is particularly true in alternative business structure (ABS) law firms, which are permitted to have paralegal partners. Paralegals with paralegal practising certificates under the Professional Paralegal Register (PPR) have the added credibility of a voluntary regulator behind them, making them ideal as freelancers. Paralegals with sufficient experience can now also apply for junior judicial office.

While it is now possible to complete a paralegal apprenticeship, it is not in fact essential to have any legal qualifications whatsoever to work as a paralegal – according to the website of the Institute of Paralegals (IoP – www.theiop.org), of the approximately 60,000 paralegals working in solicitors' firms, most do not have any legal qualifications and only a minority are graduates.

Rita Leat, chief executive of the IoP, says: "There has never been a better time to become a professional paralegal, as they are now recognised as the fourth arm of the legal profession. Paralegals make up the highest proportion of legal service providers in the United Kingdom, many of whom are self-employed or paralegal businesses. Many law graduates seeking careers as barristers or solicitors may find that working as a paralegal will enable them to develop their knowledge and experience if they wish to resume their progress towards qualifying as a solicitor or barrister at a later date."

Rita's advice is especially apt as in July 2014 the Solicitors Regulation Authority (SRA) announced changes to the training regulations that allow LPC graduates to qualify as solicitors without doing a training contract – provided that they can show to the SRA's satisfaction that they have achieved equivalent training elsewhere. In April 2015 Robert Houchill of Bates Wells Braithwaite became the first paralegal to qualify in this way.

Most paralegals specialise in one type of law – commonly personal injury, family, criminal, conveyancing, debt recovery, probate or commercial law – so most vacancies are in these practice areas (there is more variety if you work for an in-house legal department). Unless you have previous practice experience, you will be applying for entry-level positions, even as a law graduate. As entry-level positions tend not to be advertised, you should apply direct to the firms you would like to work for.

Competition is fierce and preference tends to be given to those who have some experience or practical legal training. Optional training valued by employers is available from a variety of providers. The IoP's new training arm, IoP Law School, to be launched in the autumn 2018 will provide specialist paralegal training programmes and qualifications that are mapped to the paralegal competency standards.

CILEx legal executives

CILEx was established in 1963 with the aim of recognising the skills offered by lawyers' clerks in England and Wales. CILEx now represents around 20,000 individuals who are employed in various legal institutions in the United Kingdom, including private practice law firms, local government, and commerce and industry.

Chartered legal executives are qualified lawyers who have at least three years' experience of working under the supervision of a solicitor and who have passed the CILEx exams. Their daily work is similar to that of solicitors, but they have a narrower training than that of a qualified solicitor. They often specialise in one or two areas of the law.

Depending on his or her area of specialisation, a chartered legal executive may brief barristers, advise a party to a matrimonial dispute, draft a will or draw up documentation for the formation of a company. Chartered legal executives are recognised by the Ministry of Justice as qualified lawyers and are eligible for judicial appointments and partnerships in law firms, and can also be advocates.

There are certain suggested minimum qualification requirements, but an introductory qualification course is provided for those who do not have the necessary grades or legal background. Most aspiring chartered legal executives combine study for their CILEx exams (through evening classes, day release or distance learning) with the practical experience of working in a firm, building up a client base and becoming a fee earner.

A representative from CILEx told us: "CILEx gives individuals the opportunity to study for a career in law without incurring huge debts and at the same time gain worthwhile on-the-job experience. Any gap between the day-to-day work of a solicitor and a chartered legal executive lawyer is ever closing. CILEx is even currently applying for greater independent practice rights. There has never been a better time to be a chartered legal executive lawyer."

Most employers will pay for CILEx tuition and examination fees and, of course, the trainee is earning a living as he or she progresses. For further information contact CILEx (see "Useful addresses"). For more detail, see the CILEx chapter on page 147.

Legal apprentices

A legal apprentice is an individual who joins a law firm straight from school, rather than going to university, to work in a role similar to that of a paralegal. Apprentices also receive on-the-job training that takes them towards a formal qualification – for example, as a chartered legal executive, paralegal or solicitor.

Over the past few years, a number of firms have launched their own internal apprenticeship schemes (including DWF, Kennedys, Clyde & Co and Browne Jacobson). There are currently four separate levels of legal apprenticeship – Intermediate, Paralegal, Chartered Legal Executive and Solicitor. Both the Paralegal and the Solicitor Apprenticeships require three A levels graded C or above.

This area of the legal market is relatively new and constantly changing, so if you are seriously considering doing an apprenticeship, you will find much more information about the work involved and the different possible career paths in *The Law Apprenticeships Guide 2019*. Pick one up from your careers adviser or read the guide online at www.lawcareers.net.

Chartered secretaries

Chartered secretaries work as company secretaries and in other senior positions in companies, charities, local government, educational institutions and trade bodies. They are qualified in company law, accounting, corporate governance, administration, company secretarial practice and management. They are trained to deal with regulation, legislation and best practice, and to ensure effective operations. See the website of the Institute of Chartered Secretaries and Administrators at www.icsa.org.uk.

Where did it all go wrong?

As you may have already discovered, finding a training contract or pupillage involves careful planning and application. It's a case of ensuring that what you have to offer is presented as efficiently and attractively as possible, while avoiding the kind of faux pas that will haunt you for years after the event. Inevitably, you will make mistakes, but rest assured: whatever has gone wrong for you has been trumped many times over. Here we look at some of the pitfalls encountered in the past, based on a survey of actual recruiters. We urge you not to reprise them!

First impressions…

…or falling at the first hurdle. While it's important for your application to stand out from the pack, bear in mind that grabbing the interviewer's attention should only be for the right reasons. You don't want your well-crafted application to end up being forwarded around the firm for giggles.

One firm was dismayed to be confronted with an inspirational quote from *The Lion King* at the head of an application. Meanwhile, one recruiter at a commercial firm describes with horror two cringe-worthy instances of applicants trying a bit too hard to stand out: "A candidate once set out her application in the format of a play, with Act One, Scene One featuring a lost law student looking for a training contract and Act Three, Scene Three 'still to be written'. Another applicant began her covering letter with a line about how she flailed her arms around when excited. She then elaborated to say that friends had commented that our firm was the only one that was making her flail! There are better ways to demonstrate enthusiasm and commitment to a firm. My advice? Don't go with quirky!"

One well-known commercial and chancery London set was bemused by the applicant who, when asked about his motivation to apply for pupillage, wrote "I have always wanted to work for a leading tax chambers." Nice sentiment, "except tax was not one of our core areas of law; obviously, this was a copy and paste job that had gone horribly wrong", recalls the chambers' marketing and business development manager.

On a more mundane level, recruiters are adept at spotting mass applications, even if the candidate has managed to match up firm, recruitment contact and the type of work the firm does (apparently quite an achievement for many; one hapless applicant included the names of three other firms – yes, three – in her application to a fourth). Published example letters should likewise be treated as a guide and shouldn't be copied out verbatim. You really aren't the only one who's found that website, you know.

Equally, sometimes a strikingly original example or an answer that is just a bit too candid can be just as damning, as one recruiter recalls: "One hot Friday afternoon, I reviewed two applications which had been sent in from the same address, although in two different names with different details and experiences. The first applicant, answering the question about their greatest achievement, wrote something so blue, it is unrepeatable. The second applicant, answering the question about extracurricular activities, said that they spent their time 'going down the pub and drinking lots of beer'. It gave me a laugh, but perhaps their time could have been better spent."

And make sure that you use decent examples when trying to demonstrate that you have the necessary skills. One recruiter recalls a candidate who really scraped the barrel: "The applicant described how his parents went on holiday and left him in charge of the house and his younger siblings. The story ended with him changing a lightbulb, which he said he had not expected to have to do. The applicant claimed that 'the fact that I did this successfully shows that I react to challenges well', but I'm afraid we're looking for slightly bigger challenges than that!"

Face to face
So you've made it to interview. Well done, but don't be complacent. You can rewrite an application, but once you've got it very wrong in front of an interviewer, there's not a lot you can do, so stay focused. There are three main ways that an interview can go awry on the interviewee's part: nervousness, rudeness and inappropriateness.

Lawyers are generally a sociable breed whose work involves a high degree of interaction with both colleagues and clients. This means that recruiters are looking for a modicum of social ability, confidence and grace. Nervousness at interview is understandable and all but the most callous of interviewers will allow for this.

Before you go to the interview, think about your appearance. As with your application, it's best not to stand out for the wrong reasons: don't wear anything too outlandish and do check everything's done up properly! On your arrival, remember to be respectful. One junior tenant on a set's interview panel went to the door to meet the applicant, who later described the tenant as "just a receptionist".

Once in the interview room, remember all that experience you've had of sitting on – not falling off – chairs and drinking glasses of water rather than pouring them down your front. Similarly, it's best to wipe clean your specs if they've misted up (unlike one candidate who conducted his whole interview through a fog). And remember, the firm wants to interview you; if you bring your mother along, it is unlikely that you, or she, will get a training contract.

Think about what you say, too: a candidate who claimed to have a lifelong love of shipping and the sea (in an application to a shipping firm) eventually revealed that this 'love' amounted to a one-week family cruise 15 years previously; while the candidate who admitted to informing herself of current affairs via the tabloids (apparently she found broadsheets boring) was rather ill-advised. It also pays to pay attention at all times – a recruiter at a large, full-service national firm shares this example of how switching off can lead to embarrassment: "Following a series of talks given by our lawyers at an open day, an attendee casually asked one of the speakers (a senior associate) if she thought she might apply for a training contract with the firm following the experience of the open day. Clearly, this individual had been sleeping through the talks!" Further, don't massively confuse things by answering "Why do you want to be a lawyer?" with "I don't want to be a lawyer"!

One recruiter from a US firm recalls this tricky encounter with an interviewee who was asked for an example of using their initiative: "The candidate talked about working in insurance, cold calling an elderly lady and essentially ripping her off by selling her all of the insurance under the sun! The initiative part related to making more money for the business without being asked to!" Don't forget that ethics play a big part in a successful lawyer's career.

There are lots of old interview chestnuts that you can expect to be asked, so have an answer ready. These include (with less than ideal answers): what is your greatest achievement? ("Stopping biting my nails.") What are your hobbies? ("Playing with my girlfriend.") Why do you want to become a lawyer? ("I used to be a doctor, but I'm tired of having to use my judgement.") Why are you applying to this firm? ("My zodiac sign is Libra, the symbol for justice.") Having something positive to say about the town or city you are in is helpful – definitely don't be like the candidate who, when asked why he wished to move to Norwich, replied: "This is Norwich?" And possibly not best to tell the partners interviewing you how very hungover you are.

Outright rudeness will make you the stuff of legend at a firm or chambers, but won't get you a job. One City firm tells how an interview was interrupted by the candidate's mobile phone ringing (bad). The candidate answered her phone (very bad) and then asked for some privacy while she conducted her conversation (very, very, very bad). Another candidate, when asked why he had applied only to City firms, bar the northern firm interviewing him, replied: "You must have slipped through the net!"

Remember that you're not in your living room. One top national firm describes how a candidate was making a presentation in front of a panel of recruiters, but "decided to demonstrate a particularly flamboyant cricket move and split his trousers". And the interviewer certainly isn't your "mate": especially not when you try to stretch a personal contact by saying: "I'm a great friend of your wife, you know."

Accidental disaster

It happens. You've covered every angle, done your research, arrived hours early and while you're waiting, you manage to spill coffee on your shirt. Don't panic. Tell somebody what has happened. Don't be like the woman who walked into her interview in an inappropriate party dress for this reason, but only told the firm after the interview, or the man who arrived covered in blood from a stress-induced nosebleed and likewise gave no explanation. Pouring a cup of scalding tea into the lap of the interviewer can also be a tricky situation, as a candidate in Yorkshire

discovered. As long as you apologise for any mistakes, you should be OK.

Hopefully this chapter puts things in perspective. If you do have a rush of blood to the head and pull off something similar to the above, don't despair – just move on to the next application. And remember, mishaps don't only happen to candidates. A recruiter in Bath conducted an interview using the wrong candidate's name throughout and then fell down the stairs while showing her out.

Work experience

Work experience

Here at *The LawCareersNet Handbook*, we like to tell it to you straight. The bottom line is that without relevant work experience, you are not going to get a training contract/pupillage.

You see, dazzling academics and personality are not enough to satisfy recruiters in the legal profession. They also want hard evidence that you are committed to a career in law. This is for two reasons. First, they want to know that law isn't so much a passing fancy for you as a serious ambition. Second, they want your decision to be an informed one, based on your experience to date.

An ideal start to your career is to get a place on a formalised work placement scheme/mini-pupillage. You know the drill: they are run by firms and chambers, and no expense is spared during your two weeks (most even pay you to be there!). In an ideal world, everyone who wanted a place on one of these would get one. They're the perfect foot in the door of a firm/chambers: you get to make crucial contacts and put across the real you, rather than the tongue-tied version that recruiters tend to meet at interview. However, there just aren't enough places to go round. Fear not, though, as we will show you how to create your very own work placement.

How do I get involved?
Formal schemes
During formal work placements and mini-pupillages, firms and chambers will make every effort to ensure that you get a wide range of experience and a real taste of life as one of their own. The schemes normally offer a chance to get involved with real legal work, meet trainees, associates and partners, and enjoy an array of social events. All this and you get paid as well – usually between £200 and £300 a week, but sometimes more. On these sorts of scheme

you're effectively becoming a trainee for two weeks, dipping your toe in the water, seeing if you like the firm and vice versa. The same goes for a good mini-pupillage, which will give you the chance to attend court and conferences with members of chambers, see barristers at their day-to-day work and get a flavour of how the particular set operates. During assessed mini-pupillages, you may be asked to prepare a piece of written work in order to develop a feel for the practical application of law. Generally, you should see the two to three weeks as a time to get a sense of the work, the people and the culture, while being sure to make the best possible impression. Katie Makey, recruitment officer at Shearman & Sterling, says: "Being a trainee is not all glamour, so when we see candidates who have done comprehensive stints in comparable law firms, we hope that they have seen the true picture of trainee life – if they are still keen on applying to us, then we are reassured that they have carefully considered the career and are committed."

With any luck, your positive impression will lead to the offer of a training contract or pupillage. Fiona Medlock, former graduate recruitment manager at Mills & Reeve, says: "Many firms use their placements as part of their training contract recruitment process. It is an opportunity for you to see first-hand if a firm is the type of place you can envisage yourself starting your career, while the firm has the opportunity to assess whether you have the potential they are looking for." But can we suggest that you don't follow the lead of one work placement student at an international firm who "constantly posted his experiences with us on the satirical RollOnFriday website. Sadly, his efforts to remain nameless failed!" Equally, we think it may not be sensible to resort to violence, as one placement student did on a night out with a Newcastle firm: "The candidate picked a fight with one of our trainees on a social night during a work placement. We didn't take his application any further and he didn't ask for any feedback!"

Work placement: case study

Adam Blin, formerly of Linklaters and now at Lazard, remembers his work placement at Linklaters well: "The tasks you get involved in as a vacation scheme student are very similar to what you would undertake as a trainee. You'll get involved in a wide range of work, with the support of a principal and a trainee buddy, which really helps you to understand the role of a trainee within the firm. You are given the opportunity to learn a lot about Linklaters, our culture and the work we do through various seminars and workshops throughout the vacation scheme. The best advice I can give to students is to always ask questions when visiting a firm; everybody is really friendly and wants you to make the most of your time here. It's a two-way process, which people can sometimes forget."

The experience has also stood Adam in good stead when bringing through subsequent generations of vac schemers: "I was a trainee buddy during this year's summer vacation scheme and was really impressed by the quality of the work the students were able to produce. I managed to get involved in some of the scheme's social events, which provided an informal environment for students to network with lawyers from across the firm while also showcasing some of the fun opportunities that sometimes come our way."

Another former vac schemer, now an associate at a City firm, gave this advice: "Get stuck in to the work; I was certainly made to feel that I could ask any questions. Also, get to know the people, from your fellow schemers to the graduate recruitment team to the associates and partners. Go to as many of the social events as you can.

You are trying to work out whether that firm is right for you, so make the most of your time there. The placement is a two-way process, for them to impress you as well as you to impress them. I found it a very beneficial experience." He also points out that it takes you one step closer to a training contract, as most firms will guarantee you an interview if you attend their work placement scheme.

Mini-pupillage: case study

One barrister-to-be says of his mini-pupillage experiences: "Mini-pupillages were an invaluable part of the pupillage application process. By doing them, I was able to get a proper feel for the work that a chambers did and the set's atmosphere. Mini-pupillages (though they are often unassessed) also give chambers the opportunity to have a look at you and see whether you could be a good candidate for pupillage. I would strongly advise anyone applying for pupillage to do several mini-pupillages – particularly at the sets they might end up applying to. My favourite mini-pupillage was at the set where I ultimately ended up doing pupillage and getting tenancy."

Alternative experience

Those of you who aren't lucky enough to get a place on one of the formalised programmes must be resourceful. It's not the end of the world if you don't get a place, but you will have to take the initiative and create opportunities for yourself.

Lucie Rees, graduate manager at Watson Farley & Williams, says: "All experience is relevant and shapes you into the person you are. Firms are looking for well-rounded candidates and experience in a variety of areas will help with this. All the work experience you have will build your knowledge and transferable skills – it's how you then choose to make it work for you on your application form that counts."

Work experience

Puneet Tahim, senior graduate recruitment and development coordinator at Latham & Watkins, agrees: "Non-legal work experience can be incredibly valuable to students in terms of developing their wider skill sets. Where they can sometimes let themselves down is not really thinking about using it in their application forms to sell themselves. Rather, they need to take the time to explain what they were doing, the skills they developed and how these will be useful to them in a career in law."

Andy Creer, barrister at Hardwicke Chambers, adds: "We recognise that people have different opportunities according to their socioeconomic backgrounds. It is therefore more important to demonstrate what you have got out of your work experience, than what you have done *per se.*"

Alternative work experience in the business world can also help you to build your commercial awareness, as Matthew Parker, barrister at 3 Verulam Buildings, points out: "Non-legal work experience is very useful if it involves skills that are important at the Bar, such as public speaking, collecting and presenting information or dealing with clients. For the commercial Bar, it is often very helpful to have had some experience in a business environment, which will help develop commercial awareness and enable you to engage with clients' concerns on their level."

Citizens Advice
One option is to volunteer at your local Citizens Advice Bureau (CAB). Maxine Cole, a senior crown prosecutor at the Crown Prosecution Service, volunteered for about a year at the Barking and Dagenham CAB following her master's degree. She comments: "I provided advice on housing law, landlord and tenant issues, claims for disrepair and welfare law. When it came to applying for training contracts, I was able to talk about some of my experiences at CAB – for example, when asked to discuss how I dealt with a difficult situation, I referred to an incident at the CAB involving a client with Alzheimer's. I would certainly recommend CAB work because the training is excellent: you are trained in all the areas that they expect you to advise on and in how to use their files to find information. It teaches you how to apply the law in reality and hones your interview and advice skills."

Even a two or three-week stint at the CAB could work to your advantage. Like Maxine, you will be able to include the experience on your CV and then talk about it at interview.

Court work
Court work is another option. Fatim Kurji, a barrister at Birmingham superset No5 Chambers, explains what marshalling involves: "The point of marshalling is to spend some time with a judge to see the litigation process from a judicial perspective. I spent my time reading the skeleton arguments and papers before the court and then watching the trial unfold. The process is immensely useful: you quickly learn which advocacy styles are effective and which to avoid. When it came to applying for pupillages, my marshalling experience in particular helped me to answer those standard interview questions, such as 'What makes a good barrister?' I would recommend it as a good introduction into seeing how trials are run and putting into perspective the roles of the advocates and the ultimate aim – persuading the judge."

Free Representation Unit
Other options include volunteering for the Free Representation Unit (FRU), a charity that provides free legal representation to those who cannot afford it. FRU trains you to represent its clients at tribunals. Lots of barristers/solicitors look favourably on this

practical experience, which is invaluable when applying for pupillage and training contracts. We spoke to a pupil at Blackstone Chambers, who said: "I volunteered at FRU for almost two years while on the GDL and BPTC. Outside of studying, I think it was the most useful thing I did. FRU gives you the opportunity to get stuck into practical elements of law in a way that not many other pro bono organisations do. You have to meet and advise clients, run a piece of litigation on your own and ultimately may have to argue a case before the Employment or Social Security Tribunal. In short, you get real experience of what being a barrister is like."

The first step in volunteering is to attend an induction day for the area in which you are interested. They are usually held eight times a year, with four of the days focused on training in employment law and the other four in social security. You can attend either employment, social security or both, depending on your level of experience. To undertake employment training, you must be at least a master's, GDL, LPC or BPTC student. To undertake social security training, you must be at least a final-year LLB or GDL student.

To read an interview with a former FRU volunteer and the charity's chief, see our "Free Representation Unit" chapter in this section. Find out more about FRU at www. thefru.org.uk or by ringing 020 7611 9555.

Pro bono work
Many universities and postgraduate study providers operate pro bono clinics, which are a great chance to get involved in providing legal advice at the front line. John Watkins, director of employability at The University of Law, talks about the University's schemes and their benefit to both students and the wider community: "Pro bono at the University consists of three broad programmes: legal advice clinics, where students answer legal enquiries from the general public under supervision; external opportunities, where students gain experience of working for not-for-profit organisations; and public legal education, raising legal awareness in communities through schemes such as the Streetlaw initiative. All our students are encouraged to participate, and with a wide range of over 3,300 opportunities and placements available each year, students can get involved whatever their field of interest. Students appreciate the many benefits that flow from developing their knowledge and skills in a challenging but secure real-life setting. The additional benefits to the wider community reinforce the positive nature of the work."

Sarah Stockley, member of the trainee recruitment team and former senior associate at Vinson & Elkins, says of pro bono: "Pro bono is an excellent way for students to practise giving legal advice and also giving something back to the community. A lot of firms offer pro bono services, so it is a good skill to learn early on."

Martin Barnes, chief executive of LawWorks, adds: "I would encourage every law student to get involved in pro bono activities. There is a range of potential opportunities available, including helping people with real-life issues as well as developing legal and practical skills."

For more on LawWorks and what it does, see the "LawWorks" chapter in this section. For more on getting involved with pro bono in general, see www.lawworks.org.uk and www.studentprobono.net.

European Union
Although no one knows what the outcome of the Brexit negotiations will mean, currently graduates might like to consider doing a traineeship (formerly known as a 'stage') at the EU institutions. The European Parliament,

the Council, the European Commission, the European Court of Justice, the Social and Economic Committee, the Committee of the Regions and the European Ombudsman all organise traineeships, each lasting between three and five months. Traineeships may be paid or unpaid. For further details visit http:// ec.europa.eu/stages/index_en.htm.

What else can I do?
Staying closer to home, you could send a speculative letter to local high-street law firms asking to shadow a partner (or a trainee) for a few days or offer to answer the phones at a nearby legal advice centre. Court ushering at your nearest magistrates' court and outdoor clerking are suggested for those unable to get on a formal mini-pupillage.

We asked graduate recruiters how non-law graduates in particular can get a foot on the ladder if they cannot get onto a formal work placement. All said that non-law graduates should at least make the effort to research the profession, speak to solicitors/ trainees about their experiences and visit firms or attend open days. In addition, they suggest using personal contacts to obtain work experience, either in law or in a related field (eg, banking or accountancy). Diana Spoudeas, graduate recruitment and development manager at Jones Day, says: "Work of all types – including cleaning and waiting – shows grit and determination, as well as a willingness to roll up your sleeves and get on with the job. We recruit candidates with wide interests and if you have experienced other careers, you can speak from the heart at interview about the reasons you have excluded those careers and feel propelled towards law."

One recruiter talked about the non-law student candidate who was studying business management, but joined his university law society and enjoyed the benefits it gave him.

Best suggestion of all: write speculatively to firms for experience in some sort of support capacity (eg, legal secretarial work or paralegalling). Commercial experience, perhaps in-house, is also regarded as valuable. A recruiter at one international firm says: "Previous non-legal work experience can help students understand businesses or individuals that they are working with and the challenges they face."

A graduate recruitment assistant at another international firm suggests: "Try to get other business experience in order to develop yourself in all areas. It's worth trying to make contact with the firm you're interested in (eg, attend a law fair or phone up the graduate recruitment team), so that your name is remembered positively. In relation to extracurricular activities, we like to see anything that demonstrates commitment and an ability to take something to a high level. Activities that show responsibility, leadership or team cooperation are also valued."

Students with disabilities would do well to contact the Lawyers with Disabilities Division. This division of the Law Society aims to achieve equality of opportunity for people with disabilities, whether they be qualified solicitors, trainee solicitors, law students, clients or members of the public. One of the things that the division does is contact firms to encourage them to offer work placements to disabled students. For more details visit www.lawsociety.org.uk/ support-services/practice-management/ diversity-inclusion/lawyers-with- disabilities-division.

When should I do it?
It's never too early to start. In terms of formal schemes, law students should try to secure a placement in the summer before their final year at university at the latest; non-law students should apply during the summer following their third year. In fact, more firms

than ever are running schemes aimed at first years, so you need to be on the ball right from the beginning of your university career.

Most formal schemes last between two and three weeks. Take a look at the "Insider reports" chapter for a selection of application deadlines for formal work placement schemes. Otherwise, check individual firms' websites.

With regard to informal DIY experience, just get writing!

How do I get the most out of it?

Without a shadow of a doubt, most firms use their formal and informal work experience schemes as part of the recruitment process. A solicitor at national firm Freeths says: "You can only learn so much from an application form and interview. However, a week or two spent with lawyers and support staff is the best way for both firm and student to make an informed decision about each other. Because they are so useful, I suggest you treat your applications for summer schemes as seriously as – if not more seriously than – your training contract applications."

This is your opportunity to show off your skills and charms to their very best advantage. So while there, make sure that you really do all you can to be your best possible self. That means:
• asking questions;
• showing enthusiasm and initiative;
• taking advantage of all opportunities that are offered;
• behaving professionally; and
• acting appropriately (so no getting drunk or being rude!).

Equally, if you are at a firm or chambers, you should be assessing whether it is the sort of place in which you can imagine working. If you are at one of the other voluntary schemes (eg, Citizens Advice or a pro bono clinic), make sure you are taking mental notes about how you respond to the type of work to which you are being exposed. What sparks your interest? What makes you switch off? What would you like to learn more about? Don't forget, it's a two-way process.

What about afterwards?

Send a brief letter thanking the recruiter for your placement/mini-pupillage/DIY work experience. Add a personal touch along the lines of how you think the experience has helped you at the outset of your career and what you most enjoyed.

It may be worth jotting down some thoughts and impressions of the experience to focus your mind. This will allow you at interview to talk about how it helped in terms of your future plans and overall knowledge of the legal profession.

Reality check: A large number of firms recruit trainees directly from work placements, so it is worth getting onto a scheme if possible. In addition, you should be asking family members, friends, teachers and even friends of friends if they know anyone working in the legal profession who might be able to help you get some work experience. Introductions are important!

LawWorks

There is a long history of lawyers doing pro bono work, going back to medieval times and beyond; for many people, pro bono was the only means to seek redress or justice. Restrictions in the scope of legal aid and the impact of local authority spending cuts on law centres and advice agencies have contributed to a contemporary access to justice crisis, with those who cannot access legal aid and who cannot afford to pay potentially being denied advice or representation.

Pro bono is not, and should not become, an alternative to a properly funded system of legal aid – it simply cannot fill the vacuum and need caused by policy change and cuts – but its importance and value have never been greater.

Any lawyer has the ability (with the right temperament and commitment) to do pro bono that makes a difference, whether you become a lawyer in private practice or an in-house lawyer working for a company or a charity, or in local or central government. You may have legal expertise or knowledge which can help an individual or a charity to resolve a legal problem. What you definitely will have is valuable training, skills and aptitudes that are readily translatable to real-life situations and problems. And you can make a valuable pro bono contribution as student, trainee or pupil – early experience of pro bono can instil a passion and commitment that lasts a career and beyond.

Pro bono for students

LawWorks launched its Students and Law Schools Project (funded by the Law Society) in 2007. Since then, pro bono has strengthened and grown, and is increasingly seen as a key part of legal education. The benefits of pro bono as a student, trainee or pupil can include developing legal skills, such as interviewing clients and drafting letters; gaining practical research skills, based on real legal problems for real clients; exploring practice in new areas of law; developing contacts and links to legal professionals, firms, charities and others; and making a contribution to your local community.

There are different ways to get involved in pro bono as a student:
- Legal education for the public – your law school may have links with local community groups or schools interested in knowing more about areas of law or the legal system. You could research relevant topics and prepare for or contribute to presentations and workshops.
- Student placement – your law school may not be able to support pro bono opportunities internally, but may arrange for you to volunteer with a local advice agency or community group.
- Legal advice clinic – your law school may run or be part of a legal advice clinic (including being part of the LawWorks Clinics Network, as below). With supervision (often provided by lawyers from the local community), pro bono activity may include drafting letters, researching legal problems and providing face-to-face advice.
- Tribunal representation – the Free Representation Unit (FRU) provides a good opportunity for students to acquire advocacy experience. FRU volunteers help with case preparation and representation in tribunal cases (see p65 for more on FRU).
- Internships with charities – legal and pro bono organisations such as LawWorks, the Bar Pro Bono Unit, the Access to Justice Foundation and the London Legal Support Trust are often looking for interns to support the work of their organisations. There may be opportunities with other charities and organisations.

The Bar Pro Bono Unit acts as a clearing house, matching barristers prepared to undertake pro bono work with those who need their help. Applications are reviewed by one of a number of senior barristers and the unit then makes a decision as to whether to try to find a volunteer barrister to assist.

LawWorks encourages and supports the development of law school clinics and also organises the annual Student Pro Bono Awards, run in partnership with the attorney aeneral with a ceremony held at the House of Commons. By recognising and celebrating student pro bono, the awards help encourage an interest and passion that will last and grow.

Pro bono for qualified lawyers
Opportunities for pro bono volunteering continue during training and pupillage. Increasingly, aspiring lawyers see opportunities for pro bono as informing their career decisions. For many, pro bono is an essential part of being a lawyer. It can help to build skills and confidence, develop teams and team spirit, and offers the chance to test oneself as a lawyer, perhaps in a new environment or a different area of law.

LawWorks is the operating name of the Solicitors Pro Bono Group. Established in 1997, it is a charity providing support for local independent pro bono advice clinics and supporting the pro bono work of our members – largely law firms and in-house teams – and others. LawWorks' programmes include the following:
• The LawWorks Clinic Network – LawWorks supports a network of over 230 independent clinics, providing free advice to individuals, predominantly in areas of social welfare law (eg, social security benefits, housing, family and employment). Advice is delivered face to face, over the phone and via Skype.

• The Not-for-Profit Programme – LawWorks connects smaller charities and community groups with the skills and expertise of pro bono lawyers, strengthening their capacity and avoiding or resolving problems.
• Secondary specialisation – in response to growing need for legal advice and representation, LawWorks supports more in-depth pro bono casework and representation, including training and supervising lawyers to develop expertise in areas of social welfare law. This includes a project for solicitors taking on first-tier social security tribunal cases, and working with the charity Together for Short Lives to provide legal advice for families and carers of children with life-limiting conditions.

LawWorks is also developing a 'policy voice' for pro bono, drawing on the experience of clinics, our members and the wider profession, to address barriers to pro bono and, more broadly, to better enable access to justice for all.

Working together to achieve more
In recent years, the support and co-ordination of pro bono in England and Wales has strengthened.

Supported by LawWorks, the Law Society of England and Wales has produced a Pro Bono Manual (to support solicitors to develop or extend pro bono practice) and a Pro Bono Charter, encouraging the profession to make a public commitment to pro bono.

The National Pro Bono Centre was established in Chancery Lane, London, to house and support national pro bono organisations and others working to maximise access to justice. The centre represents the creation of a single, physical hub for the coordination and development of national pro bono services (www.nationalprobonocentre.org.uk).

Conclusion

Pro bono has an important and significant contribution to make in enabling access to justice. The important debates about legal aid provision and policy reform will continue. Whatever direction your future career may take, you can personally make a difference through pro bono. It truly is part of being a lawyer.

Martin Barnes is the chief executive of LawWorks. For more information about LawWorks, visit www.lawworks.org.uk or follow on Twitter @Law-Works.

The Free Representation Unit

The Free Representation Unit (FRU) is a charity that provides individuals with representation that they could not afford otherwise and gives junior lawyers a valuable opportunity to get practical advocacy experience.

FRU represents clients in employment tribunals, social security tribunals and a small number of criminal injuries compensation cases. FRU has a handful of staff to oversee the cases and provide advice and support to the representatives, run the office and raise funds; but the volunteers take responsibility for case preparation and advocacy in the tribunals. Cases are passed on by over 200 referring agencies or by self-referral for some employment cases.

David Abbott has been the charity's chief executive since June 2017. He says: "FRU owes its success to a simple model, matching unrepresented clients facing tribunals with junior lawyers seeking the opportunity to handle cases. In bringing together these two parties, we promote access to justice and help junior lawyers gain experience that will be valuable in their future careers. Without our service, some clients might not attend their hearing or would be left with the daunting prospect of representing themselves. We don't operate a merits test when accepting referrals, but our volunteers still have a high success rate."

FRU's office is in Holborn, close to the heart of the legal profession and several law schools. Volunteers use the office to prepare their cases, carry out research, make use of its facilities, seek advice from the legal officers, hold conferences with clients and discuss cases and tactics with fellow volunteers.

With over 300 volunteers working on cases in any given year, FRU has a rigorous training process. Would-be volunteers must attend a day-long technical training course in one of FRU's practice areas and then complete a test. "Only about two-thirds of the volunteers pass this test at the first attempt," explains David. "People who pass then have to observe a tribunal case and attend an office induction, at which point they are ready to take on their first case. Volunteers can take on as few or as many cases as they wish, although many enjoy building on the skills gained in their first case and the buzz created by knowing that they did a great job for their client."

Allison Crabtree started volunteering with FRU when she was studying for the GDL at The University of Law in Moorgate, continuing through her LPC year. "I attended a training day and was attracted by the chance to do a real case," recalls Allison. "I took the test, which was challenging but very much like one of the practical scenario-based problems I was set on the GDL. FRU has been flexible in a way that many volunteering opportunities aren't; you have to meet with your new client quickly, stay in touch with them as things progress and be available for the tribunal date, and you often need to put in many hours of preparation, but there are no specific days or weeks to be in an office. That has made it possible for me to combine it with studying full time."

Allison explains why FRU is useful for both would-be barristers and solicitors: "Most of the other FRU volunteers I've met hope to become barristers and are drawn to FRU because of the advocacy experience, but I think it's just as helpful for aspiring solicitors. Volunteers interview clients and witnesses, draft documents and prepare bundles. And of course many solicitors do a lot of advocacy; in employment cases, the employer's representative in tribunal is quite often a solicitor."

FRU's legal officers maintain close contact with the volunteers, particularly during the ratification process for the first case. "The legal officers oversee cases, provide support to the volunteers throughout and are always available to talk things through," comments David. "It is a big step to take your first case to tribunal and we are very keen to ensure that representatives do not feel that they have been thrown in at the deep end. We encourage volunteers to share their experiences and try to promote a collaborative learning experience. We always remember that we are providing a service to clients who need to be confident that their FRU representative will do the best possible job on their behalf."

Allison confirms the important role that the FRU legal staff play: "They are a major reason I wanted to volunteer, as they are passionate about the work and an absolute goldmine of information. But the staff are there to help you get things right; they will not hold your hand through the work. No one will be in your client conference or at tribunal with you. It is your case and your responsibility. You need to develop a sense of when to ask for help and I think that's a useful skill to take to a training contract or pupillage."

David explains why volunteering for FRU is such a good experience for people who want a career at the Bar: "The essence of being a barrister is advocacy, which is something you can only learn through practical experience. Although you practise cross-examination and making submissions on the BPTC, it does not compare to the experience FRU offers by giving you the opportunity to appear as a representative in a tribunal. When you are in front of the judge, you know that it's down to you and this makes it particularly rewarding, whatever the outcome. In addition, FRU provides essential experience in client care and in taking on a case that may have been prepared by the client themselves or another agency." David also emphasises the relevance of FRU to aspiring solicitors: "A 'magic circle' firm, Linklaters LLP, has placed

a trainee at FRU for six months of each year for several years now. Linklaters does so because it recognises the value of FRU work to solicitors, whatever field of law they eventually plan to specialise in."

Allison adds: "FRU work helps you to develop a real feeling for the strengths and weaknesses of a case, and then see it play out with all the unpredictable things that spring up along the way. Clients and cases are very diverse – for example, you might have a seriously mentally ill client in a social security case, who would struggle to attend their tribunal without your help, and then an employment client with a professional background who is legally knowledgeable and well prepared. Sometimes the work is about helping a client present the facts in the clearest way and sometimes there are points of law or complicated evidential issues – I have cross-examined a HR director over the calendar settings on his IT network!"

FRU helps volunteers to develop the ability to put someone at ease and listen to them, while keeping the legal issues in mind and getting the necessary information, explains Allison: "Clients may be very angry about how they've been treated at work or embarrassed to be applying for benefits and discussing personal medical issues with strangers. There can be a lot at stake financially too."

Finally, it feels great to be praised for your work by a member of the judiciary, reflects Allison: "One of the most rewarding aspects has been the respect and appreciation I've received from many judges. Judges know about FRU and some have even been volunteers themselves. They appreciate that we help tribunals run more smoothly and fairly."

For more information about FRU and how to become a volunteer, visit www.thefru.org.uk.

Vacation scheme insider reports

Chris Watkins studied law at the University of Leicester. He attended a 10-day scheme in December 2015 and is now a second-seat trainee at Allen & Overy.

What did you do while on the vacation scheme?
I sat in the banking department throughout the scheme, with my trainer who was a several-years' qualified associate. My time was split between presentations on the types of work the firm does and life as a trainee, as well as desk time doing work given to me by various members of the department. We also had several assessments, one of which was a client pitch which involved us working in groups and culminating in a presentation to a panel of partners and business development executives. The social aspect was great, with drinks and dinners, but just the right amount – I've been on other schemes where you're wined and dined the entire time! That can be fun, but you don't get a true sense of the firm and whether it's somewhere you'd want to join.

What did you feel that you gained from the placement?
A real idea of what it would be like to be part of team and firm; we were truly integrated into things. For example, as I joined banking, they invited me to be part of the department's football team. I also loved having the chance to speak to trainees face to face, in an environment where they were able to be honest about their experiences.

Which were the most enjoyable – and most challenging – aspects of the scheme?
The graduate recruitment team did a great job of buddying people up with trainees; they looked after us all week. As a vacation scheme student, I felt that the work we did was valued, and my trainer took the time to go through it with me and give feedback.

The client pitch was a challenge – although we had done plenty of preparation and felt ready, it was a real grilling! The partners were very specific about what they wanted to know and we had to answer on the spot. Having to think on your feet and trying to answer questions from people with years of combined experience was challenging, but it was good to have had the experience. It has made me ensure that I am prepared for anything!

Did the scheme end with a training contract interview or some other kind of further recruitment process?
There was no formal interview, as the process we'd already gone through to get on the scheme was the same as for a training contract. Rather, we were assessed throughout the week, including on our work, client pitch, written assessment and drafting exercise. Then we had to indicate on the last day whether we'd be interested in being considered for a training contract. They let us know whether we'd been successful within a couple of weeks.

Is there one key thing that you took away from the experience that you would pass on as advice to others?
The most important thing is to integrate as much as you can. For example, playing with the football team got me off on the right foot with other members of the department, who were enthused by how keen I was! Another example was Christmas jumper day; we weren't entirely sure if we should join in, as we had been dressed quite formally, but we were absolutely encouraged to take part. It all helps to demonstrate that you are adaptable and able to fit in.

No of scheme places
50

Location of schemes
London

Length of schemes
Varies

Remuneration (per week)
Competitive

Dates of schemes
December 2018
July 2019

Closing date for applications
Winter:
31 October 2018
Summer:
31 December 2018

Application procedure
Online application form
www.aograduate.com

For full contact information and details of Training Contract, see the firm's full entry in the main directory on p287

Remember to cite *The LawCareers.Net Handbook* on your application form if you apply to this law firm.

WORK EXPERIENCE **69**

MOVE YOUR MIND

Aim beyond pure legal knowledge. Beyond commercial advice. Be known for something more: a clarity of thought and an instinct for problem solving that can influence governments and leading businesses the world over. Join us and we'll help you enrich and expand your worldview, grow your skills and influence new ways of thinking. In other words, we'll help you move minds.

Begin now at www.ashurst.com/en/careers

 AshurstGraduates AshurstGraduates **in** Ashurst

ashurst

Gareth Mair completed a vacation scheme with Ashurst in December 2017. He studied law at the University of Warwick.

What did you do while on the vacation scheme?

I was with the corporate transactions team, where I sat in on several client calls with the managing partner, Simon Beddow, and also conducted research tasks. Vacation schemers were set a project to work on over the week, which culminated in a group presentation in front of a panel of partners on the last day. We also attended sessions organised by the graduate recruitment team – one was a trainee-led discussion of secondment opportunities, while on another occasion we participated in speed networking with partners in different departments. On the social side, there was an after-work event with the other vacation schemers and those of us in the corporate team were also invited to the department's Christmas party.

What did you feel that you gained from the placement?

I gained a valuable insight into how commercial lawyers work, including how they interact with clients. I was able to get a good sense of what life as a trainee at the firm would be like thanks to the sessions put on by the graduate recruitment team, as well as of the firm's overall direction and strategy through meeting with partners, who were happy to give me their time and advice when I reached out.

Which were the most enjoyable - and most challenging - aspects of the scheme?

Talking to people at the firm was probably the most enjoyable aspect – everyone was genuinely approachable and generous with their time, from trainees to the managing partner. I was made to feel comfortable from the first day and was able to make the most of the experience through learning about specific deals and the experiences of different people at Ashurst. The experience was challenging because it was my first vacation scheme, so everything was new and I was constantly learning. The presentation was also quite daunting beforehand, as I knew I would be speaking in front of three partners and a member of the graduate recruitment team.

Did the scheme end with a training contract interview or some other kind of further recruitment process?

We were assessed on our project work and then had to submit a new training contract application after the scheme ended, based on the form we had completed to apply for a place on the scheme, but adding experiences from our week with the firm. About a month after the vacation scheme itself, I was invited to an interview with two partners.

Is there one key thing that you took away from the experience that you would pass on as advice to others?

The most valuable part of the scheme for me was the opportunity to reach out to people at the firm and benefit from one-to-one discussions with them over a coffee. Before you start the scheme, look up people you want to speak to on LinkedIn, particularly those in practice areas that you will not be exposed to during the scheme itself. You can find out a lot more by talking to people than just relying on researching online. More generally, be enthusiastic, smile and make the most of the opportunity that you have been given – it will be over in a flash!

No of scheme places
70-80

Location of schemes
London

Length of schemes
Spring: 1 weeks
Summer: 3 weeks

Remuneration (per week)
£400

Dates of schemes
Winter:
December 2018
Spring:
April 2019
Summer:
June 2019
July 2019

Closing date for applications
Winter:
5 November 2018
Spring and Summer:
6 January 2019

Application procedure
Online application accessed via the firm's website at www.ashurst.com/en/careers

For full contact information and details of Training Contract, see the firm's full entry in the main directory on p292

Remember to cite *The LawCareers.Net Handbook* on your application form if you apply to this law firm.

WORK EXPERIENCE **71**

OPPORTUNITY

If you're one of the handful of graduates who join Bristows LLP as trainee solicitors each year, you'll be exposed to a world of opportunity right from the start...

...opportunity to get involved with top tier work for clients in the most innovative industries.

...opportunity to work side-by-side with some of the most respected lawyers in their fields.

...opportunity to build your career in an environment where you'll be stretched but also get plenty of support and encouragement.

If we sound like the firm for you and you want to find out more, please visit training.bristows.com.

BRISTOWS

Portia Guidotti studied pharmacology at the University of Bristol. She attended a two-day workshop at Bristows in December 2017 and will be starting her training contract at the firm in September 2020.

Insider report

Bristows LLP

What did you do while on the vacation scheme?
Initially, I wasn't entirely sure what to expect from the workshop. By the end however, I felt I gained amazing insight into the firm and the type of work it does. There were 12 workshop students and we had several presentations over the two days from different areas of the firm. The first was an icebreaker, and then representatives from the different departments came and spoke to us. Obviously Bristows is well known for its IP expertise, but we also heard about its corporate, competition and real estate work. We were also given two really interesting case studies, the first on patent litigation and the other on a corporate case, giving us exposure to both the firm's core business and beyond. We also took part in some speed networking with lots of different members of the firm – not just lawyers – which was a lot of fun.

What did you feel that you gained from the placement?
As for any prospective trainee, it can be hard to identify which firms you want to work for, because all the information that is online looks the same! It can be hard to distinguish between marketing and reality. So having first-hand experience really helped – I met a lot of different people, got a feel for the work, and whether I could imagine working here. It really helped to solidify my decision. Bristows is unique in the UK in that there's not a firm of similar size of its standing that does this type of work, so I got to know a lot of people that I might not have at a bigger firm. We also learnt a lot about the commercial side of IP law and the firm's strategy for the future.

Which were the most enjoyable – and most challenging – aspects of the scheme?
I really enjoyed the speed networking, but in terms of work, the IP case study was fascinating. We were given an actual physical product that was the subject of the litigation, and we had to figure out how it worked and how it matched up to the patent. You had a sense that you were actually doing the work of a patent litigator, with the product right in front of you.

At the beginning, it was a challenge to know how much to say during the presentations, but we were quickly encouraged to treat it informally and ask questions regularly, so pretty soon we all felt much more comfortable.

Did the scheme end with a training contract interview or some other kind of further recruitment process?
At the end of two days, we had a session with May Worvill from the grad rec team, who gave us advice on the interview and the process generally, and then we had to write a letter updating our application and reflecting on what we'd learnt. Once that was done, you were invited back for the first, and hopefully second, round of interviews.

Is there one key thing that you took away from the experience that you would pass on as advice to others?
Although applying for training contracts is a very competitive and stressful process, remember to be respectful to your competitors when you meet them; it will affect how you come across to the people who may hire you. Focus on being your true self and respect everyone you encounter.

No of scheme places
36

Location of schemes
London

Length of schemes
Winter: workshop
(two days)
Spring: workshop
(two days)
Summer: workshop
(two days)

Dates of schemes
Winter
December 2018
Spring
April 2019
Summer
June 2019

Closing date for applications
Winter:
18 November 2018
Spring and Summer:
31 January 2019

Application procedure
Online application form

For full contact information and details of Training Contract, see the firm's full entry in the main directory on p310.

Insider report

Bryan Cave Leighton Paisner

Krish Raichura completed a vacation scheme with Bryan Cave Leighton Paisner (BCLP) in July 2018. He completed his undergraduate and master's degrees in English literature at Queen Mary University of London.

What did you do while on the vacation scheme?
I was with the structured debt team during the first week and one of the firm's real estate teams for the second. With the structured debt team, I researched how new regulations would affect a client's business within the European Economic Area, while in real estate I was doing things such as drafting letters for agreements of tenancy surrender. There were some great networking opportunities, including an informal partner lunch and socials with my fellow vacation schemers and our trainee buddies, which gave me a real insight into the firm's culture and the people who work at BCLP. We also attended talks given by partners and trainees. The former explored the firm's different specialisms and explained how the various teams work, while the latter gave us an insight into what the training contract would be like, including the opportunities on offer to go on client and international secondments.

What did you feel that you gained from the placement?
There is only so much you can glean from attending law fairs and open days, and reading recruitment literature. The experience imbued me with a much richer understanding of what a career in commercial law entails. Doing work that would ultimately end up in front of clients and seeing how the firm worked from the inside proved invaluable. I also gained an insight into the law firm as a business and the decisions it must make as a commercial entity, which is often overlooked – as students we often focus on the client side of commercial awareness.

Which were the most enjoyable - and most challenging - aspects of the scheme?
Something that I found really summed up BCLP was that people would happily take time out of their busy schedules to talk to me about their careers and life at the firm, and explain concepts that were not necessarily relevant to the work that I was doing, but which improved my general understanding of commercial law. It showed that the firm is committed to its learning culture and investing in its people. The most challenging aspect for me as a non-law graduate was the complex legal terminology involved in some contracts that we worked on, but my trainee buddy was always there to point me in the right direction.

Did the scheme end with a training contract interview or some other kind of further recruitment process?
I had a one-hour interview with two partners during the second week, in which we discussed my career motivations as well as my competencies and commercial awareness.

Is there one key thing that you took away from the experience that you would pass on as advice to others?
Treat it as a learning experience. Obviously you are being assessed, but if approach the scheme with the mindset that you want to absorb as much as possible, you will get much more out of the various networking opportunities and have a more productive and rewarding experience overall.

No of scheme places
London approx 80
Hong Kong approx 18

Location of schemes
London
Hong Kong

Length of schemes
London
1 or 2 weeks
Hong Kong
2 or 4 weeks

Remuneration (per week)
London £400
Hong Kong undisclosed

Dates of schemes
December 2018
April 2019 (London only)
June 2019
July 2019

Closing date for applications
Winter:
October 2018
Spring:
February 2019
Summer:
January 2019

Application procedure
Online application

For full contact information and details of Training Contract, see the firm's full entry in the main directory on p311

Remember to cite *The LawCareers.Net Handbook* on your application form if you apply to this law firm.

74 THE LAWCAREERS.NET HANDBOOK

Olivia Ved has just completed her law degree at UCL. She took part in Clifford Chance's first-year springboard scheme (now known as 'Clifford Chance SPARK') in Spring 2016 and will start at the firm in August 2019.

What did you do while on the scheme?

The springboard scheme was a great introduction to the firm. Initially there was a welcome talk from the managing partner and a personal impact session delivered by a comedian. That was a great icebreaker as we learnt how to improve our public speaking, project our voices, and to think about the types of emotions we convey.

Throughout the week we had presentations from various departments which consisted of a partner or senior associate explaining what the department did within the firm as a whole, and on a day-to-day basis. They used high-profile deals to demonstrate the scale of the firm's work and to give us real-life examples. Every morning we had a networking breakfast with a different department which allowed us to speak to trainees, associates and partners, and ask them further questions about their work. Listening to their personal experiences helped to shape a bigger picture of their practice areas.

We also visited Clifford Chance's Paris office one day (although the firm now takes students to the Amsterdam office), which gave us the chance to find out more about the firm's international strategy. At the end of the week we were given a litigation and corporate case study. That meant we could use the information we had learnt about the firm, plus our common sense and practical skills, to work out deals and settlements of a piece of litigation, and to avoid the pitfalls of an M&A deal.

What did you feel that you gained from the placement?

The scheme gave me a much clearer insight into the firm, as well as a better understanding of its culture and how that's reflected in the firm's business structure and long-term strategy. Also, it gave me an appreciation for the trainee workload!

Which were the most enjoyable – and most challenging – aspects of the scheme?

I found the case study really enjoyable because I could use and apply all the information I had learnt so far during the scheme. We also had a session with David Adams, who oversees capital markets and finance training at the firm, where he explained very simply and practically what a derivative is. It was valuable to walk away from the scheme with knowledge about the basics of financial instruments that are used every day.

Did the scheme end with a training contract interview or some other kind of further recruitment process?

At the end of the scheme I submitted answers to four reflective questions that focused on my understanding of the firm, and the insider information I had acquired. From that I was invited to a training contract interview.

Is there one key thing that you took away from the experience that you would pass on as advice to others?

I would definitely recommend first years to apply – and to take your time researching the firm and speaking to representatives before submitting your application. You should do your homework before the scheme starts as well. The Clifford Chance website has so much accessible information that provides the answers to basic questions, as well as a platform for more complex topics you might need to address in your training contract interview.

No of scheme places
35

Location of schemes
London

Length of schemes
1 week

Remuneration (per week)
£350

Dates of schemes
June 2019
July 2019

Closing date for applications
16 December 2018

Application procedure
Via our website careers.
cliffordchance.com/london

For full contact information and details of Training Contract, see the firm's full entry in the main directory on p321

Remember to cite The LawCareers.Net Handbook on your application form if you apply to this law firm.

Melissa Montford studied law at Coventry University and is currently working as a paralegal. She did a two-week spring scheme at Dechert in 2018 and will join the firm as a trainee in September 2019.

What did you do while on the vacation scheme?
I spent my first week in the employment department and the second in financial services. The work was varied and exciting. While in employment for example, I worked on live client matters, some of which included drafting clauses for a company employee handbook, compiling a summary advice note and conducting legal research. With the help of my supervisor and reading relevant materials, I was able to understand technical concepts and assist a client on a Brexit-related project. We attended presentations from the various practice groups, which was helpful to get a sense of the firm's strategy and how the departments work with one another. To commemorate Women's History Month, Dechert hosted an inspiring discussion with one of Britain's greatest Paralympians, Tanni Grey-Thompson. The various social events were great as we were able to find out more about Dechert in an informal setting; my personal favourite was our night at Swingers Crazy Golf!

What did you feel that you gained from the placement?
The scheme presented an invaluable opportunity to immerse yourself into the firm. It was exceptionally well curated, designed to challenge us as well as give us scope to showcase our potential. I also gained an accurate depiction of the culture of the firm and what it would be like to train at Dechert.

Which were the most enjoyable – and most challenging – aspects of the scheme?
I was fortunate enough to attend a client meeting with an employment partner; he briefed me in advance and gave me materials to read, so that I would be able to understand the intricacies of the case. It was fascinating to watch the partner lead the meeting; I felt very trusted and enjoyed the face-to-face client interaction.

We were given a group presentation task, which we delivered in small groups to a panel at the end of the week. This was the most challenging part of the scheme as we had to get to know each other, learn each other's different working styles and agree a plan of action simultaneously. It also tested our time management skills as we had to balance our preparation alongside our day-to-day workloads.

Did the scheme end with a training contract interview or some other kind of further recruitment process?
At the start of the scheme, the graduate recruitment team outlined the ways in which we would be assessed during the two weeks, including supervisor feedback, individual performance during the group presentation, teamwork skills, as well as the overall quality of our work. We were also told that all Dechert employees have the opportunity to provide feedback on the vacation scheme students. I was offered a training contract on the final day of the scheme and I was truly overwhelmed – it was my dream job at my dream firm, so I was absolutely ecstatic!

Is there one key thing that you took away from the experience that you would pass on as advice to others?
Be the best version of yourself that you can be; the firm buys into you as an individual and they value personality. Also, use your time to get to know the people who work there and build relationships. Be inquisitive, proactive and get stuck in. You gain knowledge and useful skills that, irrespective of the outcome, will only contribute to your future success.

No of scheme places
20

Location of schemes
London

Length of schemes
2 weeks

Dates of schemes
April 2019
June 2019

Closing date for applications
Spring:
31 December 2018
Summer:
31 January 2019

Application procedure
Online application, video interview, assessment day, face-to-face interview, written exercise and an office tour with a current trainee. Please note, an application for a place on one of Dechert's vacation schemes in 2019 is also an application for a training contract commencing in September 2021

For full contact information and details of Training Contract, see the firm's full entry in the main directory on p334

Remember to cite *The LawCareers.Net Handbook* on your application form if you apply to this law firm.

WORK EXPERIENCE 77

Abisola Yussuf completed a vacation scheme at Hogan Lovells in Winter 2017. She studied international development at King's College London.

What did you do while on the vacation scheme?

The scheme was split into two seats. In my first week, I sat in the financial institutions retail banking team and my second was in international arbitration, which is one of the firm's key practice areas. In both seats I gained a practical, commercial insight into the type of work completed by commercial lawyers on a weekly basis. In my first seat, I worked closely with my supervisor and a few trainees to draft summary reports on recent EU legislations affecting Fintech companies, payment service providers as well as traditional lending institutions. I found that it was important to move beyond the analysis of black letter law and regulations, and assess the different ways in which regulations will affect the firm's clients and how as a lawyer, I could help clients navigate the risks associated with the changing regulatory landscape. The arbitration seat was equally challenging. Speaking as a non-law student, I initially believed that a legal background would have been beneficial for this practice area, as I analysed previous court proceedings to interpret an ambiguous line of legislation. However, I soon found after presenting my findings to a partner that the onus was on my personal interpretation and analysis.

What did you feel that you gained from the placement?

I found that my interest in commercial law was solidified by taking on different tasks that brought me out of my comfort zone. This helped me to gain a first-hand understanding of what is expected of trainees at the firm.

Which were the most enjoyable – and most challenging – aspects of the scheme?

I particularly enjoyed the commercial awareness and financial case study workshops, in which vacation scheme students and trainees discussed how to help prospective clients navigate the potential risks that arise during an M&A transaction. We also had a workshop which was led by Christopher Stoakes, author of Know the City and a former banking lawyer at Hogan Lovells. I had already read the book, so being able to watch him share his insights was a real highlight.

Another challenging yet enjoyable aspect of the scheme was the group presentation, which was judged by a panel of partners and members of the graduate recruitment team. To encourage cross-selling of practice areas at the firm, we had to pitch a new practice area to one of the firm's existing clients.

Did the scheme end with a training contract interview or some other kind of further recruitment process?

On the final Thursday of the scheme, we each had an interview with two partners. Before this interview, the graduate recruitment team were available throughout the week to share feedback and advice from the previous recruitment interview to help you prepare – I would certainly urge future vacation schemers to take this opportunity.

Is there one key thing that you took away from the experience that you would pass on as advice to others?

Once you have secured a place on a scheme, make sure to further research the firm, as well as the practice areas in which you will be sitting, so that you can hit the ground running when you start the scheme.

No of scheme places
55

Location of schemes
London

Length of schemes
2-3 weeks

Remuneration (per week)
£450

Dates of schemes
Winter:
December 2018
Summer:
June 2019
July 2019
August 2019

Closing date for applications
Winter:
31 October 2018
Summer:
6 January 2019

Application procedure
Visit our website at www.hoganlovells.com/graduates to find out more information and complete an application form online

For full contact information and details of Training Contract, see the firm's full entry in the main directory on p375

Insider report

Howes Percival LLP

Oluwatobi Taiwo graduated with a degree in business management in Canada before moving to the UK and studying law at the University of Leicester. She completed a vacation scheme with Howes Percival in July 2017.

What did you do while on the vacation scheme?
A lot was packed into the week-long scheme. During the first four days, I rotated across each of Howes Percival's core practice areas. I sat with the company-commercial team – Co-Co, followed by the intellectual property team on the second day; the commercial property team on the third and the employment team on the fourth. My interest in these areas was one of the main reasons I applied to Howes Percival. In each seat, I was set realistic tasks that a typical trainee solicitor would do during their training contract. For example, in the company-commercial seat, I had to draft a legal memorandum that provided solutions to a series of contractual and commercial law issues. At the end of each day, I reviewed my tasks with my supervising trainees, Charlotte and Victoria, and received helpful feedback and insight into the practicality of my answers. I was also pleasantly surprised to learn that all of my tasks were based on real cases that the firm had handled in the past. This made the experience more meaningful and exciting. On the last day, I had the chance to revisit one of the areas from earlier in the week, and I happily chose to spend the morning with the co-co team. In the afternoon, I competed in a fun negotiation competition with the other vacation schemers. There were also a lot of opportunities in between work to socialise with other trainees, associates and even partners.

What did you feel that you gained from the placement?
The scheme gave me further insight into the firm, its values, work and culture. The people are friendly, hardworking, and dedicated to providing excellent legal advice to their clients. This experience also reaffirmed my initial impression and knowledge of the firm and motivated me to apply for the training contract.

Which were the most enjoyable - and most challenging - aspects of the scheme?
This might make me sound like a nerd, but the most enjoyable aspects of the scheme was learning more about different areas of law and seeing their practical applications in various situations. However, the most challenging aspect of the scheme was trying to understand property law during the commercial property seat when I had not yet studied land law.

Did the scheme end with a training contract interview or some other kind of further recruitment process?
Believe it or not, I didn't complete the training contract section of my vac scheme application because I was unsure about which year I would be eligible to start. Fortunately, on the first day one of the firm's employment solicitors, Hannah, sat with me and explained that I could join the 2019 intake and invited me to be considered. Shortly after the scheme, I was invited to attend an assessment centre at the Leicester office, and later offered a training contract.

Is there one key thing that you took away from the experience that you would pass on as advice to others?
Take full advantage of your time on the scheme – don't be afraid to ask questions and talk with other trainees and lawyers at the firm.

No of scheme places
24

Location of schemes
Leicester, Northampton, Norwich

Length of schemes
1 week

Dates of schemes
June 2019
July 2019

Closing date for applications
31 March 2019

Application procedure
Online application form

For full contact information and details of Training Contract, see the firm's full entry in the main directory on p377

Ayshea Baker completed a vacation scheme at Jones Day in Winter 2017. She studied English literature and French at the University of Birmingham.

Insider report
Jones Day

What did you do while on the vacation scheme (eg, type of work, networking, presentations or social events)?
We got straight into doing interesting work on the first day of the scheme, when we were given free reign to knock on doors and seek out tasks across the firm's different teams, encompassing a range of practice areas. Over the course of the scheme I worked for the employment, corporate, global disputes and intellectual property teams, and the variety of opportunities was really beneficial to me as someone with a non-law background. All the work was on live matters for the firm's clients.

There were lots of social events throughout the two weeks – I think there was something to do almost every evening after work, including ice skating at Somerset House as the scheme took place close to Christmas. As soon as we arrived there was a welcome drinks reception where we had a chance to meet lawyers in the firm as well as the other vacation schemers, and there was also a tapas evening and a visit to an art gallery. I was able to do some pro bono work for a legal advice clinic during the scheme, and there were opportunities to attend partner-led talks on the firm's different practice areas. There was also a business discussion exercise involving a one-to-one discussion with a partner or senior associate, as well as a group negotiation task.

What did you feel that you gained from the placement (eg, insight into the firm, useful contacts or an appreciation of a trainee's workload)?
Jones Day's vacation scheme was unlike any other that I have experienced because I didn't feel like a work experience person and was treated as a valued team member. People seemed genuinely interested in my opinion, while the work I did was really beneficial because I was able to see that law in practice is not black and white, and that there is always room for interpretation.

Which were the most enjoyable – and most challenging – aspects of the scheme?
Going from door to door to seek work was a great experience – it was good to take the initiative and I probably took just as much away from my conversations with partners while doing this as I did from doing the work itself. The whole scheme was challenging as no two days were the same – I had different work and new experiences every day. During the second I week I found that I had a higher workload because by that point I was trusted enough to be given more to do, so there was the challenge of juggling different priorities.

Did the scheme end with a training contract interview or some other kind of further recruitment process?
Yes, everyone had a training contract interview in the second week, which was with two partners that we hadn't necessarily worked with previously.

Is there one key thing that you took away from the experience that you would pass on as advice to others?
Make the most of every opportunity that comes your way. The firm doesn't expect the finished article but wants to see that you are willing to learn and that you are open-minded. The more you put into the Jones Day scheme, the more you will get out of it.

No of scheme places
70

Location of schemes
London

Length of schemes
2 weeks

Remuneration (per week)
£500

Dates of schemes
Winter:
December 2018
Spring:
March 2019
April 2019
Summer:
July 2019

Closing date for applications
Applications open on 1 September 2018. We recruit on a rolling basis and cannot guarantee availability, so apply early. Final deadlines:
Winter:
26 October 2018
Spring:
14 December 2018
Summer:
10 January 2019
We recruit nearly all trainees from our placement candidates.

Application procedure
Online at www.jonesdaylondon.com

For full contact information and details of Training Contracts, see the firm's full entry in the main directory on p382

LawCareers.Net™

Delivering your future in law

Our newsletter, LCN Weekly, is packed with news, profiles, opinion and advice about becoming a lawyer.

Sign up to *LawCareers.Net*™

Daniel Kellard completed a vacation scheme at Kennedys in January 2018. He studied politics and international relations at the University of Bath.

What did you do while on the vacation scheme?
Before the scheme we were asked to put forward two preferred practice areas that we would like to spend time in during the week. I was fortunate to be given my first preference and sat with the healthcare department. I dealt primarily with litigation work on the defendant side, which mostly involved clinical negligence claims. I was assigned a trainee buddy in the same team, which helped me to settle in. Over the course of the scheme I attended a hearing at the Royal Courts of Justice, a tribunal hearing and a trial at Clerkenwell and Shoreditch County Court, which concerned an employer's liability claim. I also did a number of research tasks, including one on the law surrounding eviction notices for NHS patients and another for a partner on the Jackson reforms. In addition, there were talks on the firm's different practice areas throughout the week, which gave me the opportunity to learn more about the firm's business beyond the department I was placed in.

What did you feel that you gained from the placement?
The experience improved my understanding of the procedural aspects of law. You learn the substantive side of the law when studying, but not the practicalities of lodging a claim, time-pressured working or talking with clients when waiting for a court hearing to start.

Which were the most enjoyable - and most challenging - aspects of the scheme?
I really enjoyed the variety of work and situations that I had the opportunity to experience. This included working alongside people at different levels within the firm, from trainees, to senior associates, to partners. If I had to pick one event that stood out, it would have to be the mid-week pizza making social, which was very fun! Getting to grips with the practical elements of being a lawyer was challenging because it was all new, but as I mentioned, it was hugely beneficial.

Did the scheme end with a training contract interview or some other kind of further recruitment process?
There wasn't an interview or assessment centre. Instead we met the HR team for a debriefing session at the end of the week and found out whether we were being offered a training contract a couple of weeks later.

Is there one key thing that you took away from the experience that you would pass on as advice to others?
Be proactive and take advantage of the different opportunities that will come your way, while making sure that you are still able to meet your deadlines and are not overloaded. I would also say that it is wise to carry a notepad and pen everywhere you go, as you will be given lots of important information and it's best to write down key points immediately so that you don't forget anything.

No of scheme places
12

Location of schemes
London

Length of schemes
1 week

Remuneration (per week)
£370

Dates of schemes
January 2019

Closing date for applications
30 September 2018

Application procedure
Online application form, video interview, critical thinking test and assessment day

For full contact information and details of Training Contract, see the firm's full entry in the main directory on p386

Remember to cite *The LawCareers.Net Handbook* on your application form if you apply to this law firm.

WORK EXPERIENCE **83**

WHAT IF YOU WANT TO STAND OUT FROM THE CROWD?

At Kirkland & Ellis we keep our trainee intake small giving you the chance to shine.

We hire just 10 trainees each year and provide them with high quality work from day one. You will be treated as a lawyer from the start and be given every opportunity for success.

Graduate careers in law
UKGRADUATE.KIRKLAND.COM

KIRKLAND & ELLIS INTERNATIONAL LLP
The Gherkin, 30 St Mary Axe, London

Georgia Cooper-Dervan completed a vacation scheme at Kirkland & Ellis in Summer 2017. She studied law at the London School of Economics.

What did you do while on the vacation scheme?
The vacation scheme candidates were divided between the corporate and debt finance teams, and I spent both weeks with the corporate team. There was a big pharmaceutical deal in progress during the first week so the team were busy, and I gained a good insight into how such transactions work by reading all the key documents, learning the client's business objectives behind the transaction and trying my hand at drafting. We were also encouraged to seek work from elsewhere, so I was able to meet people from across the corporate department and participate in other transactions.

Beyond the work itself, there was a mixture of formal and informal events to attend, both inside and outside the office. These involved the wider firm and were not put on especially for vacation schemers, which was great because it enabled us to gain a clearer insight into life at the firm. For example, one talk was organised by the Women's Leadership Initiative at the firm and was given by the rower and Olympian Dame Katherine Grainger. There was also a mock transaction in which we were divided into two teams of legal advisers for two parties negotiating a sponsorship agreement, with the clients played by a partner and a senior associate.

What did you feel that you gained from the placement?
The experience gave me an accurate picture of Kirkland & Ellis as a whole, as the firm is smaller than others that do comparable work and I was able to meet and work alongside lawyers from many different practice areas. The people I met were diverse and there was no sense of rigid hierarchy, with everyone able to talk to each other regardless of their level of seniority. This was very different to the cultures at some firms where I have had work experience, where people were referred to by how many years of post-qualifying experience they had. Being encouraged to seek work from different practice areas was good for my confidence, whereas on other schemes I was simply given work to do by a supervisor.

Which were the most enjoyable - and most challenging - aspects of the scheme?
I really enjoyed the mock transaction – it enabled me to see what working on a deal from start to finish involves, which is something that I probably would not have experienced otherwise in just two weeks. The most challenging part of the scheme was a debt finance exercise that we were given at short notice, which tested our ability to think on our feet and use common sense, as we were not allowed to do any research for it.

Did the scheme end with a training contract interview or some other kind of further recruitment process?
Yes, there were two back-to-back partner interviews of 30 minutes each over the last two days of the scheme, focusing on my experience on the scheme and what I had learnt.

Is there one key thing that you took away from the experience that you would pass on as advice to others?
When you're going into an interview, try to feel confident and positive because you have already done so well to get there.

No of scheme places
30

Location of schemes
London

Length of schemes
2 weeks

Remuneration (per week)
£500

Dates of schemes
Spring and Summer 2019

Closing date for applications
6 January 2019

Application procedure
Apply online at
ukgraduate.kirkland.com

For full contact information and details of Training Contract, see the firm's full entry in the main directory on p389

Remember to cite *The LawCareers.Net Handbook* on your application form if you apply to this law firm.

LawCareers.Net™

Are you a non-law student who is keen on becoming a lawyer?

LawCareers.Net's non-law zone tells you everything you need to know about the conversion course (GDL), transferable skills, and valuable work experience opportunities.

Sign up to LawCareers.Net™

Matthew Carpenter has recently completed his law degree at the University of Leeds. He took part in Linklaters' spring vacation scheme in April 2018 and will start at the firm in March 2020.

What did you do while on the scheme?

My vacation scheme was two weeks long and I sat in the dispute resolution team for both weeks. In addition to the work given to me by my principal, I was also given a due diligence project to complete. This was a good experience because it tested my time-management and communication skills.

During the scheme, there were also frequent networking opportunities with partners and associates, including a networking breakfast with different practice groups and a number of presentations about the firm. I also had the chance to meet several trainees when they joined us at social events which included a trip to the theatre.

What did you feel that you gained from the placement?

I gained an insight into the firm. Everyone was very friendly and approachable despite working in such a high-pressure environment – that speaks volumes about Linklaters' culture. The practice area presentations by partners and associates helped develop my commercial awareness and understanding of Linklaters as an international law firm.

Which were the most enjoyable – and most challenging – aspects of the scheme?

I worked with my principal on live cases, some of which are still ongoing. To be given hands-on experience at such a big firm during the scheme was a bit of a shock! But I thoroughly enjoyed being involved in real work.

I also enjoyed taking part in the client pitch exercise. During the pitch, we worked in small groups and acted as representatives of Linklaters. We conducted thorough research into the company we were pitching to, which gave a real insight into the varied businesses that Linklaters represent and the realities of working with clients. At the end of the exercise, we presented our ideas to three Linklaters partners who were acting as senior members of companies' boards. The presentations were not assessed, but were particularly challenging due to the technical nature of the questions we were asked.

Did the scheme end with a training contract interview or some other kind of further recruitment process?

At the end of the scheme, I interviewed for a training contract. During the interview with a partner and managing associate we discussed my vacation scheme project in more detail as well as what I had learnt during the scheme. The final interview is about testing your knowledge and seeing what you've taken in over the two weeks.

Is there one key thing that you took away from the experience that you would pass on as advice to others?

When applying, you must have a firm grasp of what the firm does and think about what they are trying to do in the future. In my application I wrote about the emerging use of law tech and AI in the legal industry, and displayed my research into Linklaters' 'Nakhoda' technology.

During the scheme, be prepared to ask questions – this shows your enthusiasm for the firm's work. It's ok to not understand everything you read because it is very complex, but my principal appreciated my enthusiasm and happily took the time to explain things.

No of scheme places
100

Location of schemes
London

Length of schemes
Winter: 2 weeks
Spring: 2 weeks
Summer: 4 weeks

Remuneration (per week)
£400

Dates of schemes
Winter, Spring, and Summer (penultimate-year and final-year undergraduates, graduates and postgraduates)

Closing date for applications
Winter:
25 October 2018
Spring:
8 January 2019
Summer:
8 January 2019

Application procedure
Online application form, critical thinking test, case study and two interviews

For full contact information and details of Training Contract, see the firm's full entry in the main directory on p394

Remember to cite *The LawCareers.Net Handbook* on your application form if you apply to this law firm.

WORK EXPERIENCE **87**

MACFARLANES

EXCEPTIONAL LAWYERS. WITHOUT EXCEPTION.

Chanel Yusuf studied law at the University of Exeter. She attended a two-week scheme at Macfarlanes in Summer 2017 and will be starting as a trainee at the firm in September 2020.

What did you do while on the vacation scheme?
I sat in two different departments, private client and financial services, both of which I had an interest in prior to starting. I was immediately immersed in a variety of tasks, which were given to me by the supervising trainees. This included helping to prepare wills, conducting research on the tax implications of an international trust, and taking part in the departmental education seminars. Throughout the duration of the vacation scheme we had a 'mock' transaction, which we negotiated in our teams on the last day and which was followed by a completion team social.

We also enjoyed a broad range of networking and social events, including playing darts at Flight Club and the London Legal Walk. I particularly enjoyed meeting with a newly qualified solicitor from my university alumni; it was a good opportunity to talk through the Macfarlanes training programme, LPC and qualification process.

What did you feel you gained from the placement?
It was a great opportunity to learn about the firm, its culture and the breadth of work available to you as a future trainee. It was also the best opportunity to confirm that Macfarlanes was right for me, through asking questions, meeting a broad range of lawyers and shadowing the work performed by current employees. There were partner-led departmental talks throughout the week, focusing on the firm's core practice areas which were comprehensible for both law and non-law students. I found it interesting listening to various partners from different departments, talking about what they and their trainees do.

Which were the most enjoyable – and most challenging – aspects of the scheme?
The most enjoyable aspect was negotiating the mock transaction; it involved quite an eccentric fictional character, and was a great way to form bonds with the other vac schemers. It was great to prepare all of the terms and see all of our hard work come to fruition at the deal completion event.

The most challenging aspect was conducting the research for the solicitor I was sharing an office with; the initial volume of books was alarming! However, once I was fully immersed and familiar with the terminology I found it really interesting and fulfilling to independently provide a valued answer.

Did the scheme end with a training contract interview or some other kind of further recruitment process?
Participants were invited to complete assessments during the vacation scheme. The recruitment process consisted of a written exercise, competency interview and case study interview. After the hard work was complete, we celebrated with a farewell dinner.

Is there one key thing that you took away from the experience that you would pass on as advice to others?
Just be yourself; although it may feel as though you are under constant assessment, you will come across much better if you act naturally. I believe it is always obvious if you're trying too hard. Always ask relevant questions and think about what you want to know. The vacation scheme is a great opportunity to learn about the firm, as well as for them to see you. It's very much a two-way process.

No of scheme places
55

Location of schemes
London

Length of schemes
2 weeks

Remuneration (per week)
£330

Dates of schemes
Easter:
April 2019
Summer
June 2019
July 2019

Closing date for applications
31 January 2019

Application procedure
Online application via our website www.macfarlanes.com/join-us followed by an assessment day

For full contact information and details of Training Contract, see the firm's full entry in the main directory on p396

Remember to cite *The LawCareers.Net Handbook* on your application form if you apply to this law firm.

WORK EXPERIENCE   89

Let's talk
rays

Practise across inspiring industries and sectors, including cutting-edge solar energy production.

From energy companies and investment banks, to media moguls and sports stars, our trainees help advise some of the most influential corporations and individuals in the world. Their stories are challenging and diverse. By working with them, yours can be too.

Get the full story at **www.mayerbrownfutures.com**

MAYER · BROWN

Law worth talking about

Open days | Vacation schemes | Training contracts

Anthony Cunningham has just completed his law degree at the University of Kent. He took part in Mayer Brown's vacation scheme earlier this summer and will start at the firm in September 2020.

What did you do while on the scheme?
The vacation scheme took place over two weeks. In the first week I was in the banking and finance department and this included lots of hands-on tasks such as creating transactional documents and drafting letters for a big mining project finance deal. I sat with the litigation team for the second seat, with a focus on insurance. This involved conducting legal research and proofreading skeleton arguments. It was great to experience both the commercial and litigation side of law during the vacation scheme. There were various skill sessions throughout the placement and my favourite was about the law as a business. As a student we're always told to focus on the commercial side of law firms, so it was interesting to hear from somebody in the firm's business development department. In terms of social events, it was a good experience to meet with the current trainees outside of the office during the weekly evening activities, and to see that they are all good friends. It shows how welcoming the firm is. We also visited the firm's Paris office in the second week.

What did you feel that you gained from the placement?
It was invaluable to experience the type of work that trainees do, from drafting and researching, to bundling. The amount of work made me realise just how important organisation is – you are given so many tasks, so it's necessary to prioritise and manage your time effectively. Everybody tells you that it's a lot of work, but you don't realise until you're actually doing it!

Which were the most enjoyable – and most challenging – aspects of the scheme?
The most challenging task I completed was during my second week where I researched how a certain article was used in international arbitration proceedings. I went through over 100 cases and summarised my findings into a one-page document to present to a senior associate. It was difficult because there was so much material to read through and some of it wasn't in English, but it was certainly a great insight into the kinds of work I will be doing in the future.

The most enjoyable part was the progression throughout the work, as by the end of the week I was able to complete much more complicated and difficult tasks. This was especially true of my time in the banking and finance team as I learned the technical terms and abbreviations.

Did the scheme end with a training contract interview or some other kind of further recruitment process?
There was a short interview with two partners at the end of the second week, but it was much more of an informal chat. The process stood the firm apart from others as it was less about whether I was good enough, and more about how I enjoyed my time at the firm and the work I had completed.

Is there one key thing that you took away from the experience that you would pass on as advice to others?
My advice would be to remember that although you will be interacting with successful and inspirational lawyers during the scheme, you shouldn't forget that they are human beings too. I spent the first week being too nervous to knock on a partner's door but soon realised that the more you talk to them, the better insight you will get into the firm and the more varied and interesting work you will receive.

No of scheme places
30

Location of schemes
London

Length of schemes
2 weeks

Remuneration (per week)
£275

Dates of schemes
Spring 2019
Summer 2019

Closing date for applications
31 January 2019

Application procedure
Online

For full contact information and details of Training Contract, see the firm's full entry in the main directory on p400

Insider report

Mills & Reeve LLP

Johannes Arens studied history and politics at the Ludwig Maximilians University of Munich. He attended the firm's 2017 summer placement scheme and will start his training contract in September 2019.

What did you do while on the vacation scheme?
The scheme comprises mini seats in four different departments; I sat in employment, real estate, projects, and regulatory, public and commercial disputes. As such, my tasks varied greatly throughout. For example, I attended and took notes at an employment tribunal, drafted a lease report, undertook research on rights of way, took notes during a client conference call, and much more. It was all actual work for clients that went out once it had been checked by my supervisors. I also attended a staff briefing by the managing partners, which helped me to understand how the firm operates as a business. Socially, there was something happening almost every evening, including hockey, punting, a quiz and dinner with the current trainees.

What did you feel that you gained from the placement?
I gained a practical understanding of legal work and experienced first-hand what a pleasant, friendly and supportive culture the firm has – something which is not always a given! Working with the trainees, I had the chance to understand their tasks, and how they manage and prioritise their workload day to day. It was also the first time that I had worked in an open-plan office, which I really enjoyed. It's so much easier to chat to people that way.

Which were the most enjoyable – and most challenging – aspects of the scheme?
The most enjoyable was being exposed to a broad variety of tasks and matters, and getting to know many different people and departments. The flipside of that is it can be a challenge to adjust to a new team every couple of days. However, the format does give you more opportunity to make an impression and learn about the firm. Of course my biggest challenge – and triumph! – was setting a new grape-eating record at a charity event; 51 grapes in 60 seconds!

Did the scheme end with a training contract interview or some other kind of further recruitment process?
We knew from the outset that there would be no interview at the end of the scheme; rather, it all depended on the impression we made throughout. The teams you work with give feedback to HR on your performance, so it's just an informal chat on the last day with the graduate recruitment manager. Successful applicants receive their training contract offer a couple of weeks later – so that was a very special day! I appreciated this approach, as you have two weeks to work with different individuals on different matters, which allows them to make a more solid and objective decision based on whether you and the firm are a good fit.

Is there one key thing that you took away from the experience that you would pass on as advice to others?
The main thing is showing that you are enthusiastic about the law and that specific firm. Don't be lukewarm or shy; instead be proactive, get involved, ask questions, take on work and show that you're interested in both the detail and the bigger picture. That enthusiasm will make sure that you stand out as someone with the potential to be a great trainee.

No of scheme places
36

Location of schemes
Birmingham, Cambridge, Manchester, Norwich

Length of schemes
2 weeks

Remuneration (per week)
£306.25

Dates of schemes
June 2019
July 2019

Closing date for applications
31 January 2019

Application procedure
Firm's online application form

For full contact information and details of Training Contract, see the firm's full entry in the main directory on p406

Sampaguita Tarrant studied law at the University of Bristol. She took part in Morrison & Foerster's vacation scheme in Summer 2016 and started her training contract at the firm in 2017.

What did you do while on the scheme?
I spent the first week in the corporate department and the second in litigation. I listened to the recording of an AGM and drafted a set of board minutes for a pro bono client, helped to map out a group structure of a multinational conglomerate, attended meetings and assisted with general proofreading and research. We were also given a research task to work on over the two weeks.

Throughout the scheme there were talks by partners from different practice areas. We also had a presentation from the managing partner of Europe about the firm's wider strategy and five-year plan. On the first day we went for lunch with trainees and junior associates and asked the questions we had already submitted – that took the pressure off thinking of questions on the spot!

We attended numerous social events, from drinks with our supervisors to cooking classes, bowling, and even a Harry Potter escape room. We were also invited to the summer party, and as a group organised the firm's cheese and wine night.

What did you feel that you gained from the placement?
Morrison & Foerster is good at getting vac schemers involved, so you get a sense of the culture and people of all levels. You learn things about the firm that you simply can't get from preliminary research. Colleagues thanked me for my work and copied me into external emails, so I could see the part that I'd played. Because Morrison & Foerster's London office is smaller than, say, magic circles firms, they are very flexible in catering to your interests. My supervisor helped me to set up meetings with people in other departments I had an interest in.

Which were the most enjoyable – and most challenging – aspects of the scheme?
There was a lot crammed in, so it was challenging to keep on top of everything. But that also plays into what was most enjoyable as I really got stuck in. Everybody at the firm was friendly and made an effort to get to know me, and I felt well-acquainted with most people by the end.

Did the scheme end with a training contract interview or some other kind of further recruitment process?
There was an exit interview with the head of legal recruitment. We discussed how I found the scheme, what I most enjoyed and the work I had got involved with. But this was not a formal assessment as the firm uses your performance on the scheme to assess your relationship building skills and your ability to succeed as a trainee.

Is there one key thing that you took away from the experience that you would pass on as advice to others?
Be as enthusiastic as possible. The firm likes to see that you are genuinely interested and willing to get involved and interact with people. This is the best way for you and the firm to find out if you are a good fit. And show initiative in your work: people don't mind if you get things wrong, but they will respond well if you show sensible reasoning and are diligent and thoughtful.

No of scheme places
15

Location of schemes
London

Length of schemes
2 weeks

Remuneration (per week)
£350

Dates of schemes
June 2019
July 2019

Closing date for applications
6 January 2019

Application procedure
Online application

For full contact information and details of Training Contract, see the firm's full entry in the main directory on p410

Remember to cite *The LawCareers.Net Handbook* on your application form if you apply to this law firm.

WORK EXPERIENCE **93**

Insider report

Osborne Clarke LLP

George Oakes has just finished his law degree at the University of Manchester. He attended a two-week scheme at Osborne Clarke in Summer 2017 and will start his training contract at the firm in September 2019.

What did you do while on the vacation scheme?
My scheme was in the Bristol office and I sat in two departments – commercial litigation and corporate – both of which I had expressed interest in prior to the scheme. The types of work were very different, with litigation involving research using various new sources such as Practical Law, while in corporate I was drafting ancillary documents for various deals. We also visited the London office, where we had a talk from the UK managing partner and met all the other vac schemers, and enjoyed several networking lunches and social events. There were also numerous presentations, including one on career progression, which was unique to any other vac scheme I had experienced.

What did you feel that you gained from the placement?
Vac schemes are so important from a cultural perspective. Culture is something you can only learn so much about by reading up on the firm; you don't get a tangible understanding until you go into the firm, be yourself in that environment and see how comfortable you feel. It has to be right for you as well as the firm. Personally, I just threw myself into it and felt comfortable from the first day. Everyone I met had a genuine interest in me and overall I felt that I thrived at OC.

Also, having access to the firm's intranet was amazing – it gives you so much information that's not in the public domain. When I was preparing for my final interview, I was able to answer the 'Why OC?' question much more intelligently, relating it back to me and the firm. Make sure you use the intranet while you can!

Which were the most enjoyable – and most challenging – aspects of the scheme?
My favourite part was knowing that I was doing real work for real clients; none of it was hypothetical. I also received lots of useful feedback from both trainees and partners, so I learnt a huge amount in just two weeks. More challenging was the stamina required – the 9-5 is hard enough when you're a student, but feeling that you need to constantly be on top form means that you have a heightened sense of self-awareness throughout. However, it's an excellent insight into the busy life of a trainee – I just made sure I got lots of sleep at the weekend!

Did the scheme end with a training contract interview or some other kind of further recruitment process?
We had an interview with two partners on the final day, where we discussed my experience on the scheme and how I would approach life as a trainee. There were also group and written exercises over the two weeks, so I took comfort that I was assessed in the round.

Is there one key thing that you took away from the experience that you would pass on as advice to others?
Approach everything with enthusiasm, as it's a two-way process. If you are lucky enough to have a choice of offers, you want to be informed and know that you're making the right decision. Demonstrate your enthusiasm by asking for feedback and about the wider context of the work you're doing. Overall, throw yourself into it – that's how you'll get the most from your scheme.

No of scheme places
35

Location of schemes
Bristol, London and Reading

Length of schemes
2 weeks

Remuneration (per week)
£275

Dates of schemes
June 2019
July 2019

Closing date for applications
15 January 2019

Application procedure
Please visit our website www.joinoc.com and complete our online application form.

For full contact information and details of Training Contract, see the firm's full entry in the main directory on p417

Terry Prempeh completed a vacation scheme at Reed Smith in Summer 2017. He studied theology and philosophy at Durham University.

What did you do while on the vacation scheme?
I spent the first week in the energy and natural resources team and then moved to the funds team, in the financial industry group for my second. In energy, I sat with a senior associate and eased into things well. This was helped by the fact that my supervisor let others in the group know that I was keen and available to help, which resulted in a steady flow of work from lots of different people. Matters ranged from legal research, which was new to me, as I had not studied law as an undergraduate; to creating a timeline of a transaction for an associate advising one of the firm's banking clients. The work was geared toward showing that I could solve problems and approach issues logically, rather than demonstrating legal knowledge. The social side of the scheme set Reed Smith apart – there were networking lunches, after-work socials and presentations on different departments for trainees choosing their seats, which we were invited to observe. We were also invited to attend the firm's summer party, which allowed us to network with employees across the business.

What did you feel that you gained from the placement?
There were two parts of the scheme that really stood out and made me decide that Reed Smith was the place for me. The first was a cultural intelligence presentation given by Peter Alfandary, who emphasised the global nature of the training contract. It was about improving our understanding of cultural differences that you would encounter when working in different offices around the world. That was a big thing for me because it's my ambition to work with people from different countries and backgrounds. The second was a workshop, where a public speaking expert coached us on our presentation skills – this was invaluable training for the skills required to work in the commercial world, that I had not seen on other schemes.

Which were the most enjoyable - and most challenging - aspects of the scheme?
A particularly enjoyable aspect of the scheme was a mock employment tribunal in which we were advocates, it was hugely beneficial. The onus of the scheme is not on feeling comfortable, but on challenging you. I was in the privileged position of having a few training contract offers when I started the scheme, so I was really looking to get as much of an insight as I could into what life at the firm would be like. The firm certainly wanted to see what I was capable of and I was consistently challenged with the work I was given.

Did the scheme end with a training contract interview or some other kind of further recruitment process?
There is an assessment day on the penultimate day of the scheme consisting of a case study, a group exercise and an interview.

Is there one key thing that you took away from the experience that you would pass on as advice to others?
If you are enthusiastic and show a genuine interest, you will find so many people are willing to help you and give you their time. There is a real sense of camaraderie at the firm.

No of scheme places
20

Location of schemes
London

Length of schemes
2 weeks

Remuneration (per week)
£330

Dates of schemes
June 2019
July 2019

Closing date for applications
31 January 2019

Application procedure
Online application form via our website
www.reedsmith.com/ukgraduates

For full contact information and details of Training Contract, see the firm's full entry in the main directory on p428

Remember to cite *The LawCareers.Net Handbook* on your application form if you apply to this law firm.

WORK EXPERIENCE **95**

Ela Broderick-Bassar has just finished the LPC at the University of Law. She completed RPC's vacation scheme in July 2017 and will start at the firm in September 2019.

What did you do while on the vacation scheme?

At RPC vac schemers split their time between two departments and I was fortunate to get my top choices for both; commercial, technology & outsourcing and general, liability & medical. Our tasks included conducting research, putting together client bundles and taking notes in client meetings, as well as producing a business presentation, which we gave to partners and senior associates. There were also a number of social activities organised to help us to get to know the other vac schemers and the RPC team; we had a cocktail-making class one evening, as well as a dinner with the current trainees who were very approachable and answered any questions we had. I was lucky enough to attend court in both of my seats. It was a unique experience and definitely not part of your average placement, as a lot of my friends kept telling me!

What did you feel that you gained from the placement?

I am currently a paralegal for an in-house legal team, so I'm used to working with law firms as a client. It was an entirely different experience to be on the other side of the instructions and I learnt a lot about client care.

Although I was fortunate enough to attend court in both departments, I also gained a huge amount of experience from the other tasks given to me . It highlighted how varied and interesting the firm's work is, as well as the culture of everyone throwing themselves into it – especially when it's time-sensitive.

Which were the most enjoyable – and most challenging – aspects of the scheme?

I was asked by a partner to research a new client's issues in preparation for the initial client meeting. My research proved useful in the dispute and helped the partner find a solution. It was rewarding to have my work appreciated by both the partner and the client, and to feel part of the RPC team.

The most challenging part was keeping the balance between my work and the social opportunities – the vacation scheme is well organised by HR, and they were really understanding when I had to prioritise other commitments like attending court over social events. It was clear that RPC encourages a healthy work and social life balance.

Did the scheme end with a training contract interview or some other kind of further recruitment process?

On the last morning I was interviewed by the director of people and talent development and a partner from the corporate team. They had a set amount of questions to ask within the hour, which meant that I had to get straight to the point! I was offered a training contract the following week.

Is there one key thing that you took away from the experience that you would pass on as advice to others?

If you are in your second or final year, or have even graduated, and haven't got a vacation scheme or training contract – don't give up. My applications were much better after getting my paralegal work experience, so there is nothing wrong with taking a year or two to get legal work experience elsewhere. General office work experience is also very useful. Although it may seem trivial, the team really appreciated that I knew how to use the printers and scanners!

No of scheme places
24

Location of schemes
London

Length of schemes
2 weeks

Remuneration (per week)
£300

Dates of schemes
Summer:
June 2019
July 2019

Closing date for applications
19 January 2019

Application procedure
Recruitment for our summer schemes usually takes place in either January or February. Shortlisted candidates will be invited to one of our assessment days during which they will meet our existing trainees, associates, legal directors and partners

For full contact information and details of Training Contract, see the firm's full entry in the main directory on p432

Remember to cite *The LawCareers.Net Handbook* on your application form if you apply to this law firm.

WORK EXPERIENCE **97**

APPLICATIONS ARE NOW OPEN!

Develop your career at a firm with a consistent, open and collaborative approach to business where the past few years have seen transformative growth and development.

INSIGHT EVENING

30th November 2018

Come and meet Shoosmiths' partners, solicitors and current trainees. Learn about the company culture, build your network and ask questions.

PLACEMENT SCHEME

28th February 2019

Come for a week in June and experience what working in our firm is all about. This is a perfect opportunity to gain quality work experience, see how we live our values and find out if we are right for you!

TRAINING CONTRACT

30th June 2019

In our opinion the best way to learn is in practice, that's why you'll be given responsibility and your own case files to manage. The tasks that you will undertake are engaging, interesting and often with familiar topics, brands and products with which you can easily identify.

Office locations
Belfast
Birmingham
Edinburgh
Leeds
London
Manchester
Milton Keynes
Northampton
Nottingham
Southampton
Thames Valley

SHOOSMITHS

www.shoosmiths.co.uk/graduates

 joinus@shoosmiths.co.uk
 @shoosmithsgraduates
 @shoosmithsgrads
 @shoosmithsgrads

Abi Wood completed a vacation scheme at Shoosmiths in Summer 2017. She studied law at the University of Liverpool.

What did you do while on the vacation scheme?
I spent the full week in the corporate team, where I experienced a good mix of real responsibility and shadowing. This included company searches, checking non-disclosure agreements and sitting in on conference calls. Vacation schemers were also set work by the graduate recruitment team – halfway through the week there was a mini-assignment and the scheme ended with each of us giving a 15-minute presentation to an audience of partners and members of HR. On a few different days we went out for lunch with trainees, while I was also able to attend a firm-wide party to celebrate moving into the firm's new offices. In addition, I attended the firm's end-of-year brief given by the chairman, Peter Duff, which gave me a great insight into the firm's business strategy and its plans for the year ahead – this was also very helpful in my interview!

What did you feel that you gained from the placement?
By the end of the week, I felt that I had gained an insight into Shoosmiths' values, from how clients are treated to the office culture. I had spent a week seeing what it would really be like to be a trainee at the firm. The scheme also helped me to improve key skills, for example, I was required to prioritise my tasks and maintain good communication with the lawyers assigning me tasks to give them realistic information about when the work would be completed.

Which were the most enjoyable - and most challenging - aspects of the scheme?
Meeting people from across the firm, including many who had trained at Shoosmiths and others who had joined from other firms, was fantastic. The quality of work that a firm offers is very important, but so too is the culture if you're planning to start a career there. The most challenging aspect was definitely the presentation at the end of the week. The experience was a good one, though, because I received valuable feedback and was able to have a great conversation about the firm based on that.

Did the scheme end with a training contract interview or some other kind of further recruitment process?
There was an informal chat about how I had found the week and I was then invited to the assessment centre later in the summer. The interview was part of the assessment centre and, like the end of the vacation scheme, also included a mini-presentation.

Is there one key thing that you took away from the experience that you would pass on as advice to others?
My advice would be to be confident – or at least not appear nervous. One piece of feedback I received was that I didn't appear as confident throughout the week as I did in my presentation. Nerves are bound to be present on a vacation scheme, but try not to show them and just make sure that you immerse yourself into everything and speak to as many people as you can.

No of scheme places
60

Location of schemes
Birmingham, Edinburgh, Leeds, Manchester, Milton Keynes, Northampton, Nottingham, Reading, Solent

Length of schemes
1 week

Remuneration (per week)
£310

Dates of schemes
June 2019

Closing date for applications
28 February 2019

Application procedure
Apply online at www.shoosmiths.co.uk

For full contact information and details of Training Contract, see the firm's full entry in the main directory on p438

Remember to cite *The LawCareers.Net Handbook* on your application form if you apply to this law firm.

WORK EXPERIENCE 99

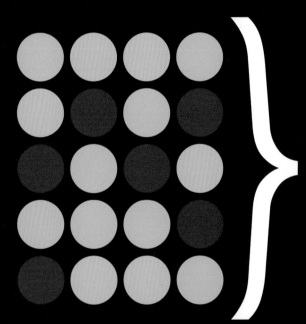

Yuki Yue is studying law at the University of Exeter. She attended Stephenson Harwood's one-week winter scheme in December 2017 and will start at the firm as a trainee in September 2019.

Stephenson Harwood LLP

What did you do while on the vacation scheme?
Despite the scheme only being one-week long, it was action packed! I had expressed a preference to work in the marine and international trade group. This was a unique experience as it's not an area of law that is normally covered in your legal studies at university. In terms of work, I completed a research task on a point of law regarding shipment terms and two case summaries. These tasks gave me a clear idea of what trainees are expected to complete. We were also given the opportunity to attend networking lunches with trainees, associates and partners, and ask them lots of questions about the firm. We also met with the chief executive, Sharon White, where she explained to us the trajectory of the firm and some future developments, all of which helped us with our understanding of the firm. In terms of social events, we were invited to firm events, including the Christmas concert, which really made us feel a part of things.

What did you feel that you gained from the placement?
The best thing was gaining an insight into the firm and the work it does. Representatives from each of the practice groups gave presentations, including in-depth analysis of their types of cases/deals. In addition, it was great to find out more about the strong support network at the firm. There were only eight of us on the scheme, which meant that the HR team could really focus on us and our wellbeing. We were each assigned a trainee buddy, who gave us a tour on the first day and offered guidance throughout the week.

Which were the most enjoyable – and most challenging – aspects of the scheme?
I most enjoyed the interactive practice group presentations, which were very engaging, and interacting socially with other members of the firm. For example, the trainees really took an interest in helping us to get the most out of the scheme, organising lots of events, including cocktail-making, lunches and court visits.

My biggest challenge was trying to fit everything into just one week; there was a lot of information to digest. Despite that, I'm glad our schedules were tightly packed, because it was very fruitful and we managed to get a well-rounded view of the firm.

Did the scheme end with a training contract interview or some other kind of further recruitment process?
In the one-week scheme, the assessment day was held in the middle, and included an interview, presentation and other components.

Is there one key thing that you took away from the experience that you would pass on as advice to others?
Embark on a placement with a curious mind, wanting to know as much as you can about the firm. I found at Stephenson Harwood that everyone was very willing to answer questions – you could talk to anyone – and it felt very open and supportive in that way. They really wanted us to understand the firm.

No of scheme places
40

Location of schemes
London

Length of schemes
Winter: 1 week
Spring and Summer: 2 weeks

Remuneration (per week)
£360

Dates of schemes
Winter:
December 2018
Spring:
April 2019
Summer:
June 2019
July 2019

Closing date for applications
Winter:
11 November 2018
Spring and Summer:
31 January 2019

Application procedure
Apply online at
www.shlegal.com/graduate

For full contact information and details of Training Contract, see the firm's full entry in the main directory on p444

Remember to cite *The LawCareers.Net Handbook* on your application form if you apply to this law firm.

WORK EXPERIENCE **101**

SULLIVAN & CROMWELL LLP

AN EXCEPTIONAL OPPORTUNITY

Sullivan & Cromwell provides the highest quality legal advice and representation to clients around the world.

The results we achieve have set us apart for more than 130 years and serve as a model for the modern practice of law.

If you are considering a career as a solicitor, interested in working with the world's leading companies on their most challenging matters, and feel that you have the qualities we are looking for, we encourage you to apply for a place on the 2019 summer vacation scheme or for a training contract in our London office, to commence September 2021.

Please send a copy of your CV (including a full classification and percentage breakdown of all academic results) and a covering letter to: traineesolicitors@sullcrom.com. We will be accepting applications for the 2019 summer vacation scheme from **1st November 2018** through **11th January 2019**, and applications for our 2021 trainee intake from **1st May 2019** through **12th July 2019**.

www.sullcrom.com

LONDON · PARIS · FRANKFURT · BRUSSELS

NEW YORK · WASHINGTON, D.C. · LOS ANGELES · PALO ALTO

TOKYO · HONG KONG · BEIJING · MELBOURNE · SYDNEY

Hannah Cockle is studying law at the University of Oxford. She attended Sullivan & Cromwell's Summer 2017 scheme and will start her training contract with the firm in September 2019.

What did you do while on the vacation scheme?
The work itself was very varied, with many different trainees and associates asking for our help. Commonly, it was research tasks, although I spent a large proportion of my time with one associate, going through the due diligence process for one transaction. This gave me the chance to read through contracts and contribute to an overview document. All our tasks went towards actual work, so we weren't filling our time with fabricated exercises. We also sat in on team meetings and trainee educational seminars, which gave us a sense of what we'd be doing when we start our training contract. We were taken out for lunch and coffee by the trainees, which was an informal chance to chat, and we had had a lovely dinner following our trip to the London Eye, and a really interesting tour around the Lloyd's Building and the Royal Courts of Justice!

What did you feel that you gained from the placement?
As much insight into life as a trainee as is possible within a fortnight. I spoke to most trainees about what they're working on and their experiences of the firm so far. I also feel that I was exposed to real work, as opposed to just studying it in an academic context, so am more prepared for what to expect as a trainee.

Which were the most enjoyable – and most challenging – aspects of the scheme?
The most challenging was completing work for various people simultaneously, which was a good test of my ability to manage my time. At university, you are left mostly to motivate yourself, whereas in a firm you are part of a large team which is relying on you to finish on time in order for everyone to meet their deadlines.

Most enjoyable was having the chance to see what a cohesive office it is. Everyone eats lunch together, and you find yourself sitting next to a mix of trainees, associates and partners. High standard of work aside, I was really looking for an environment that I would enjoy being in, so it was great to see that Sullivan & Cromwell offered that.

Did the scheme end with a training contract interview or some other kind of further recruitment process?
I had a brief meeting with Ben Perry, the grad rec partner; I'd chatted to him before, so it wasn't daunting at all. He mostly wanted to know if I'd enjoyed the scheme and was looking for honest feedback. The grad rec team were infinitely helpful throughout and I had an informal chat with them at the end as well. I also handed in a log of the work I'd done and the people that I'd worked with.

Is there one key thing that you took away from the experience that you would pass on as advice to others?
Everyone is so eager to help, even when they're busy, so you should use the people around you as a resource. It's all a learning curve and you're not expected to know everything, so ask questions and show enthusiasm. You are assigned a trainee buddy, who is only a few years ahead of you; asking for help is not nearly as intimidating as you might think!

No of scheme places
6-8

Location of schemes
London

Length of schemes
2 weeks

Remuneration (per week)
£500

Dates of schemes
July 2019

Closing date for applications
11 January 2019

Application procedure
By CV (including a full classification and percentage breakdown of all academic results) and a covering letter to traineesolicitors@ sullcrom.com

For full contact information and details of Training Contract, see the firm's full entry in the main directory on p447

Insider report

Vinson & Elkins RLLP

Maitilda Dolin completed a vacation scheme at Vinson & Elkins in June 2017. She studied law at the University of Sheffield.

What did you do while on the vacation scheme?
My placement was non-rotational, meaning that I spent the whole week with the same department, which in my case was the energy and projects team, but I received work from the whole office. This mirrored the firm's non-rotational training contract structure, which enables trainees to be involved in matters from the start, right through to their conclusion. I was one of two vacation schemers at the firm that week. I was supervised by an associate, who provided me with work and was there to answer questions, and was also assigned a trainee buddy. Many of my tasks were research-based, but I also had the opportunity to draft some deeds, which was really interesting, particularly because it was not something that I had done before at law school – it was an exciting challenge to be thrown in at the deep end. The non-rotational format of training means that trainees at Vinson & Elkins can work on matters in a range of different practice areas from start to finish, and this is also the case for vacation schemers. It meant that I gained some experience of different areas of law, as well as a realistic insight into what life as a trainee is like. The scheme was centred around the firm's work and that was the main difference I found compared to other placements I have attended. However, that's not to say that there were no social events – I went out to lunch with my fellow vacation schemer and our supervisors on the first day, and attended networking drinks to finish off the scheme.

What did you feel that you gained from the placement?
The experience gave me a valuable insight into working at an international, commercial law firm. I'm very interested in the oil and gas industry (having spent time working with an oil major previously), so it was particularly great to be able to spend time with the energy and projects team. Also the fact that the group was so small – just me and one other vacation schemer – meant that I was able to ask lots of questions and really get involved in the work.

Which were the most enjoyable - and most challenging - aspects of the scheme?
The fact that I was made to feel like a valued member of the team really stood out. It helped instil the confidence I needed to knock on doors and find work. The non-rotational structure of the scheme was nonetheless challenging, though, because it meant that I received tasks on tight deadlines from different departments and therefore had to balance my workload and priorities to get everything done.

Did the scheme end with a training contract interview or some other kind of further recruitment process?
I had an exit interview on the Thursday which focused on a task that my fellow vacation schemer and I were set separately at the beginning of the week. The task was a problem question that I then researched throughout the week – the focus wasn't particularly on law, ensuring a level playing field for law and non-law students. I was offered a training contract following the exit interview.

Is there one key thing that you took away from the experience that you would pass on as advice to others?
Be confident and be yourself! I would encourage anyone doing a vacation scheme to try to make as many connections as possible at the start of the week, and to ask lots of questions. Even if you don't end up being offered a training contract at the end of the scheme, the contacts you establish and insights you gain could be highly valuable in the future.

No of scheme places
Approximately 25

Location of schemes
London

Length of schemes
1 week

Remuneration (per week)
£250

Dates of schemes
Summer 2019

Closing date for applications
31 January 2019

Application procedure
Online application form

For full contact information and details of Training Contract, see the firm's full entry in the main directory on p456

Becky Delaney studies Law with European Legal Studies at Newcastle University. She completed Walker Morris' vacation scheme in April 2018 and will start at the firm in 2020.

What did you do while on the vacation scheme?

During the week's scheme I was placed in the commercial department. Although the department wasn't my initial choice, I enjoyed experiencing something unfamiliar. I'd recommend going for a department that's outside your comfort zone as it was interesting to be doing something I knew little about!

The work was varied all week; it started off with tasks like proofreading and moved onto drafting contract terms and carrying out red flag reports. Some of the tasks were quite challenging, but the trainee buddy I was paired with and my supervisor (a senior associate) were always on hand to offer guidance. There was also plenty of opportunity to explore other departments through networking, and question and answer sessions. For instance, I am interested in competition law and the director was more than happy to give me an insight into that department over coffee.

There were two assessments throughout the week, which were both engaging, fun tasks – an individual written exercise and a group negotiation. Social events included a lunch with trainees and associates on the first day, and a mid-week social attended by partners. I was also invited to attend a social client event within the commercial department. This was a great insight into how Walker Morris interacts with their clients.

What did you feel that you gained from the placement?

For me, it was a two-way process. From reading the website to speaking to people at the firm and experiencing the culture first hand, the scheme was a confirmation that Walker Morris was right for me. I also really enjoyed that I was given current client work, so I now feel more prepared for what to expect as a trainee and their fast-paced workload.

Which were the most enjoyable – and most challenging – aspects of the scheme?

I enjoyed the entire week, but I really liked the close interaction with the trainees. It was useful to gain a realistic insight from people who are only a few steps ahead of you. Additionally, I enjoyed the responsibility of assisting with current client work. On the flipside, it was challenging at first to adjust from an academic to a client-focused mindset – but we were given ample support from our supervisors.

Did the scheme end with a training contract interview or some other kind of further recruitment process?

On the last day there was an informal chat with a partner and HR about how I had found the week and the work I had done. I was offered a training contract shortly afterwards.

Is there one key thing that you took away from the experience that you would pass on as advice to others?

The firm is looking for individuality, so the more things you get involved with, the more chances they have to see if your personality fits with them. I also advise researching the department you'll be in; once I knew I was in commercial, I did some research into the head of department, so that when I first went to introduce myself I had talking points and genuine questions which made it less daunting. Overall, enjoy the week because it goes so fast!

No of scheme places
48

Location of schemes
Leeds

Length of schemes
1 week

Remuneration (per week)
£175

Dates of schemes
April 2019
June 2019

Closing date for applications
31 December 2018

Application procedure
Online application form

For full contact information and details of Training Contract, see the firm's full entry in the main directory on p458

WATSON FARLEY & WILLIAMS

SEEKING EXCELLENCE

Ella Harold completed a vacation scheme at Watson Farley & Williams in July 2017. She studied modern languages – French and German at the University of Oxford.

Insider report

Watson Farley & Williams LLP

What did you do while on the vacation scheme?

I was in the litigation department for the entirety of the two weeks, which enabled me to get to know the members of the team and be more involved with the team's work. The team had been working on a big case for weeks and I was lucky to start my placement when the case was being heard in court, so on several occasions I was able to accompany the trainees to watch it unfold, as well as assist with the preparation of documents. Outside of this, I was assigned various research tasks by my supervisor, an associate, as well as by partners in the department. My fellow vac schemers and I were also introduced to the firm's different departments in a series of lunchtime workshops. There was another workshop – this time led by trainees – about the opportunity to go on international secondment which is a guaranteed part of the training contract. In addition, we were tasked with a group research project which we had to coordinate in between everything else we were doing, which culminated in giving a presentation at the end of the two weeks. The scheme also included social activities, including a fun cocktail making class, an evening meal out and a farewell lunch on the last day.

What did you feel that you gained from the placement?

I gained a valuable insight into the culture of the firm. Spending the whole placement with the same team meant that I was able to get to know the people I was sitting with and learn what litigation lawyers do. The opportunity to attend court also helped me to appreciate the reality of the matters I was working on and the wider importance that they have. It was great to be able to bond with the other vac schemers, which was helped by the fact that we were part of a small group – the firm runs several schemes rather than having everyone attend one big placement. This also enabled each of us to fully integrate into the firm.

Which were the most enjoyable - and most challenging - aspects of the scheme?

I really enjoyed getting to know the trainees, who were all on hand to answer questions. I was paired with a trainee buddy who showed me around, which I really appreciated. Being able to interact with current trainees enabled me to gain a realistic sense of what life as a trainee at the firm would be like. The most challenging aspect was juggling the various priorities and making sure that I had time to finish everything.

Did the scheme end with a training contract interview or some other kind of further recruitment process?

During the last week of the scheme I was interviewed by a partner and a member of the graduate recruitment team. Although the interview was formal, I felt comfortable and relatively at ease by that point, as I had gotten to know quite a few people over the two weeks, including the recruiters. I quite enjoyed it, which is not something I would say about any other interview I have had!

Is there one key thing that you took away from the experience that you would pass on as advice to others?

Talk to people and get involved as much as you can – say yes to tasks and ask people if they have any work that you could do. Getting to know people and immersing myself in the work really helped me to work out whether the firm would be a good fit for me, as well as the recruiters and partners tasked with deciding whether I would be a good fit for them.

No of scheme places
Up to 30

Location of schemes
London

Length of schemes
2 weeks

Remuneration (per week)
£325

Dates of schemes
April 2019
June 2019
July 2019

Closing date for applications
14 January 2019

Application procedure
Online application

For full contact information and details of Training Contract, see the firm's full entry in the main directory on p461

Remember to cite *The LawCareers.Net Handbook* on your application form if you apply to this law firm.

WORK EXPERIENCE **107**

Georgie Moule studied French and Spanish at the University of Newcastle. She attended the Summer 2017 scheme at Withers and will start her training contract at the firm in September 2019.

What did you do while on the vacation scheme?

I sat in the family department in my first week and corporate in my second. It was great to have exposure to two such different practice areas – especially as I'd never considered corporate work before. My supervisors got me involved with various matters, including due diligence tasks, reviewing documents from the other side of a transaction, and attending an Employment Tribunal hearing, following which we had to present our findings to an employment partner. I even had the chance to help to draft a divorce petition. We also took part in a role play, acting as lawyers on either side of a dispute over a will. Throughout the two weeks, it felt that we were doing trainee-level work, in a safe environment! Socially, we had drinks and dinner with trainees and partners on our first and last nights, and went to the trainee summer party that featured a cocktail-making class!

What did you feel that you gained from the placement?

I gained excellent insight into the firm, its work and the type of people that work there. I had been on a couple of other schemes at other firms, and Withers really struck me as having a very friendly environment.

Which were the most enjoyable – and most challenging – aspects of the scheme?

I enjoyed the entire experience, but the trip to the tribunal was great – I probably wouldn't have otherwise had the chance to do that and it was a great way to put the work into context. It was a challenge to adapt to two very different seats, getting out of the family and into the corporate mindset, but in hindsight I'm so pleased I had the chance to do so. Juggling responsibilities, especially with the role-play element thrown in, and managing expectations was another challenge, but a good introduction to working life.

Did the scheme end with a training contract interview or some other kind of further recruitment process?

I had an informal chat with HR on the last day of the scheme, and was then invited back to the assessment centre a few weeks later. That featured an interview and presentation to two partners, a group exercise and document analysis. It really helped to have done the scheme, in terms of greater knowledge of the firm and its work, and even just knowing my way around the office and seeing some familiar faces.

Is there one key thing that you took away from the experience that you would pass on as advice to others?

Say yes to as many things as you can (within reason!) and talk to as many different people as you can. It's the best way to get a true sense of the firm. And ask lots of questions!

No of scheme places
18

Location of schemes
London

Length of schemes
2 weeks

Remuneration (per week)
£350

Dates of schemes
Easter
April 2019
Summer
June 2019
July 2019

Closing date for applications
31 January 2019

Application procedure
Online application form

For full contact information and details of Training Contract, see the firm's full entry in the main directory on p469

Remember to cite *The LawCareers.Net Handbook* on your application form if you apply to this law firm.

WORK EXPERIENCE **109**

Firms that offer work placement schemes

Firms in **bold** have provided detailed information in the directory section
Firms in purple have provided an Insider Report

Abode Solicitors
ACA Law Ltd
Acuity Legal Limited
Addleshaw Goddard
Adlams LLP
Akin Gump Strauss Hauer & Feld
Allan Janes
Allen & Overy LLP
Allington Hughes Law
Amicus Solicitors LLP
Ams Solicitors Limited
Anglo-Thai Legal (ATL)
Anthony Collins Solicitors
Anthony Jacobs & Co
AP Law Solicitors Ltd
Arlingtons Sharmas Solicitors
Arnold & Porter Kaye Scholer (UK) LLP
asb law LLP
Aschfords Law
Ashfords
Ashton Bell
Ashtons Legal
Ashurst LLP
Aston Bond
Atkins Hope
Austin Kemp Solicitors Limited
Avadis & Co Solicitors
Avery Emerson
B P Collins LLP
Baines Wilson LLP
Baker McKenzie
Barlow Robbins LLP
Baron Grey
Bastian Lloyd Morris LLP
Bates Wells Braithwaite
Bevan Brittan LLP
Beviss & Beckingsale
Bhatt Murphy
Bhogal Partners Solicitors
BHW Solicitors
Bilton Hammond
Bircham Dyson Bell LLP
Bird & Bird
Birkett Long LLP
Birketts LLP
Blacks Solicitors LLP
Blake Morgan LLP
Blandy & Blandy LLP
BLM
Boodle Hatfield LLP
Bosley & Co
Boyes Turner
BPE Solicitors LLP
Brachers LLP
Bridge McFarland
Bridger & Co Solicitors

Bristows LLP
Bross Bennett
Browne Jacobson LLP
Bryan Cave
Bryan Cave Leighton Paisner
BS Singh & Co LLP
BTMK Solicitors Ltd
Burges Salmon LLP
Burnetts
Burton & Co LLP
Cains Advocates Limited
Caldicotts
Campbell-Taylor Solicitors
Camps
Canter Levin & Berg
Capital Law
Cartmell Shepherd
Caytons Law
CFG Law (part of the client first group)
Charles Russell Speechlys
Chatham Chambers Solicitors
Churchers Bolitho Way
Clarion Solicitors
Cleary Gottlieb Steen & Hamilton LLP
Clifford Chance
Clyde & Co LLP
CMS
Coffin Mew LLP
Cohen Davis Solicitors
Coles Miller
Collyer Bristow LLP
The Commercial Law Practice
Conrad King & Solomon Solicitors
Cooley (UK) LLP
Covington & Burling LLP
Cripps LLP
Cunningtons
Curtis Law Solicitors LLP
Curzon Green Solicitors
DAC Beachcroft LLP
Darlingtons
David Gray Solicitors LLP
David Phillips & Partners
Davis Polk & Wardwell London LLP
Dawson Cornwell
Daybells LLP
De Marco Solicitors
Dean Manson LLP - Solicitors
Debevoise & Plimpton LLP
Dechert LLP
Dentons
Dexter Montague LLP
Df Legal LLP
DH Law Solicitors Ltd
DLA Piper UK LLP
DMH Stallard LLP

Donald Race & Newton
Druces LLP
Duncan Lewis Solicitors Ltd
DW Law
DWF LLP
Eb Legal
Edmondson Hall
Edwin Coe LLP
Elliott Bridgman Limited
Ellis Jones Solicitors LLP
Emery Johnson Astills
EMW Law LLP
The Endeavour Partnership LLP
Eversheds Sutherland (International) LLP
Express Solicitors
Faegre Baker Daniels LLP
Faradays Solicitors
Farrer & Co LLP
Fellowes Solicitors LLP
Field Seymour Parkes
Fieldfisher
Foot Anstey LLP
Forbes Solicitors
Forsters LLP
Fountain Solicitors Limited
Fox Williams LLP
Franklins Solicitors LLP
Freeman Johnson
Freshfields Bruckhaus Deringer LLP
Furley Page LLP
Gamlins Law
Garden House Solicitors
Gateley Plc
GHP Legal
Gibson, Dunn & Crutcher UK LLP
Girlings
Glaisyers Solicitors LLP
Goodwin Procter (UK) LLP
Goody Burrett LLP
Gowling WLG (UK) LLP
Greenberg Traurig LLP
Greenhouse Stirton & Co
Greenwoods GRM LLP
Gregory Abrams Davidson LLP
Guile Nicholas Solicitors
Harding Evans LLP
Harris & Harris Legal Services LLP
Harris Waters & Co
Harrison Clark Rickerbys Solicitors
Hatten Wyatt Solicitors & Advocates
Hay & Kilner Law Firm
Heald Solicitors LLP
Henry's Solicitors Limited
Herbert Smith Freehills LLP
Hewitsons LLP
HFW

Hibberts LLP
Higgs & Sons
Hill & Abbott
Hill Dickinson LLP
HKH Kenwright & Cox
Hogan Lovells
Horwich Farrelly
Howarth Goodman
Howes Percival LLP
Hugh James
Humphreys & Co
Humphries Kirk LLP
Hunters
Huttons
Inghams
Irwin Mitchell
Jeremy Roberts & Co
John Hodge Solicitors
Johns & Saggar LLP
The Johnson Partnership
Jones Day
Joseph Hill & Co
Joves Solicitors
K&L Gates LLP
Katten Muchin Rosenman UK LLP
KC Law Chambers Solicitors
Keebles LLP
The Keith Jones Partnership
Kennedys
Kesar & Co Solicitors
Kingsley Napley LLP
Kirkland & Ellis International LLP
Kiteleys
Kotecha & Co
Kuit Steinart Levy
Kundert Solicitors LLP
LA Steel
Langleys Solicitors LLP
Latham & Watkins
Latimer Lee
Laytons Solicitors LLP
Leathes Prior
Lee Bolton Monier-Williams
Leigh Day
Lester Aldridge LLP
Lewis Silkin
Linklaters LLP
Lodders Solicitors LLP
London Solicitors
M Olubi Solicitors
Macfarlanes LLP
Major & Co
Makka Solicitors Ltd
Makwana Solicitors
Malcolm C Foy & Co Ltd
Malik & Malik

Firms that offer work placement schemes

Firms in **bold** have provided detailed information in the directory section
Firms in purple have provided an Insider Report

Malik Legal Solicitors Ltd
Marriott Harrison LLP
Martin Cray and Co
Matrix Solicitors
Maurice Turnor Gardner LLP
Mayer Brown International LLP
McMillan Williams Solicitors
Meikles
Memery Crystal LLP
Michelmores LLP
Middleton Solicitors
Middleweeks
Milbank Tweed Hadley & McCloy
Milburns Solicitors Limited
Millan Solicitors
Miller Evans & Co
Mills & Co. Solicitors Limited
Mills & Reeve LLP
Mincoffs Solicitors LLP
Minster Law Solicitors
Mishcon de Reya LLP
MLP Law LLP
Mohammed & Co
Moosa-Duke Solicitors
Morgan, Lewis & Bockius UK LLP
Morrison & Foerster (UK) LLP
Moss & Co
Muckle LLP
Murrell Associates Limited
Myerson Solicitors LLP
Nash & Co Solicitors LLP
Noble Solicitors
Nockolds
North Yorkshire County Council
Norton Rose Fulbright
Obaseki
O'Melveny
Osborne Clarke LLP
Osbornes Solicitors LLP
Osmond & Osmond
Ozoran Turkan
Palmers
Paragon Law Limited
Paris Smith LLP
Parker Bullen LLP
Paul Hastings
Peters & Peters
Philcox Gray Ltd
Pinsent Masons LLP
Pope & Co
Premier Solicitors LLP
Prettys
Punch Robson
PwC
Quality Solicitors J A Hughes
Quality Solicitors John Barkers

QualitySolicitors Mirza
Rai Solicitors
Ratcliffe & Bibby Solicitors
Rawal & Co
Reed Smith
Rest Harrow & Co Solicitors
Reynolds Colman Bradley LLP
Riaz Solicitors
Rippon Patel & French LLP
Rix & Kay Solicitors LLP
Roberts Jackson Solicitors
Rollits
Ropes & Gray International LLP
Royds Withy King
Roythornes Solicitors
RPC
Russell-Cooke Solicitors
Samuel Phillips Law Firm
Savas & Savage Solicitors Limited
Schofield Sweeney LLP
Sentinel Solicitors
The Sethi Partnership Solicitors
Sharpe Pritchard LLP
Shearman & Sterling (London) LLP
Sheikh & Co
Shoosmiths
Sidley Austin LLP
Sills & Betteridge LLP
Silverdale Solicitors
Simkins LLP
Simmons & Simmons LLP
Sintons LLP
SJP Law
Skadden, Arps, Slate, Meagher & Flom (UK) LLP
Slaughter and May
Smith Llewelyn Partnership
SO Legal Limited
Sonn Macmillan Walker
Spelthorne Borough Council
Spence & Horne
Squire Patton Boggs (UK) LLP
Sri Kanth & Co
Stephens Scown
Stephenson Harwood LLP
Stephensons
Stevens & Bolton LLP
Stone King
Stowe Family Law LLP
STS Solicitors
Stuart Miller Solicitors
Sullivan & Cromwell LLP
Surrey Law Centre
Sweetman Burke & Sinker
Talbot & Co
Tassells
Taylor & Emmet LLP

Taylor Vinters LLP
Taylor Walton LLP
Taylor Wessing
Teacher Stern LLP
Tees
Thaliwal & Co Solicitors
Thomson Snell & Passmore LLP
Thorne Segar Ltd
Tim Johnson / Law
TLT LLP
TMJ Legal Services Ltd
Toussaints
Tozers LLP
Travers Smith LLP
Trowers & Hamlins LLP
TV Edwards Solicitors
Vinson & Elkins RLLP
Vodafone Group Services
VWV (Veale Wasbrough Vizards)
Vyman Solicitors Ltd
Wainwright & Cummins
Wake Smith Solicitors
Walker Morris LLP
Walter Wilson Richmond
Walters & Plaskitt
Ward Hadaway
Watkins Solicitors
Watson Burton LLP
Watson Farley & Williams LLP
Watson Legal
Watson Watson Solicitors
Wedlake Bell LLP
Weightmans LLP
Weil, Gotshal & Manges (London) LLP
White & Case LLP
White & Co
Wilkin Chapman LLP
Wilsons Solicitors
Wilsons Solicitors LLP
Winckworth Sherwood LLP
Winston & Strawn London LLP
Withers LLP
WLL Solicitors
Womble Bond Dickinson
Woodfines LLP
Wright Hassall LLP
Zyda Law

Chambers that offer mini-pupillages

Chambers in **bold** have provided detailed information in the directory section

Albion Chambers
Amethyst Chambers
Angel Chambers
Apex Chambers
Arden Chambers
Atkin Chambers
Atlantic Chambers
Bank House Chambers
2 Bedford Row
7 Bedford Row
36 Bedford Row
42 Bedford Row
29 Bedford Row Chambers
Blackstone Chambers
4 Breams Buildings
One Brick Court
4 Brick Court
Brick Court Chambers
Broadway House Chambers
Carmelite Chambers
1 Chancery Lane
Charter Chambers
Chartlands Chambers
Citadel Chambers
Cloisters
College Chambers
Coram Chambers
Cornerstone Barristers
12CP Barristers
Criminal Defence Solicitors
Crown Office Chambers
One Crown Office Row
Crown Office Row Chambers
Deans Court Chambers
Dere Street Chambers
Devereux
Doughty Street Chambers
2 Dr Johnson's Buildings
Three Dr Johnson's Buildings
East Anglian Chambers
Enterprise Chambers
Erskine Chambers
39 Essex Chambers
One Essex Court
5 Essex Court
Essex Court Chambers
23 Essex Street
Exchange Chambers
Falcon Chambers
Farrar's Building
Farringdon Chambers
Fenners Chambers
Field Court Chambers
187 Fleet Street
Foundry Chambers
Fountain Court Chambers

Francis Taylor Building
1 Garden Court
Garden Court Chambers
Goldsmith Chambers
9 Gough Square
Gough Square Chambers
4-5 Gray's Inn Square
1 Gray's Inn Square
Gray's Inn Tax Chambers
GT Stewart Solicitors
Guildford Chambers
Guildhall Chambers
Hailsham Chambers
2 Harcourt Buildings
Harcourt Chambers
Hardwicke
1 Hare Court
3 Hare Court
7 Harrington Street Chambers
Henderson Chambers
1 High Pavement
Hogarth Chambers
Invictus Chambers
Iscoed Chambers
One ITL
KBG Chambers
KBW
11KBW
6KBW College Hill
KCH Garden Square Barristers
Keating Chambers
Kenworthy's Chambers
1 King's Bench Walk
2 King's Bench Walk
2 King's Bench Walk
4 King's Bench Walk
5 King's Bench Walk
7 King's Bench Walk
9 King's Bench Walk
12 King's Bench Walk
Kings Chambers
Lamb Building
Landmark Chambers
Lincoln House Chambers
Linenhall Chambers
Maidstone Chambers
Maitland Chambers
1 MCB
Monckton Chambers
New Court Chambers
New Park Court Chambers
3 New Square
4 New Square
8 New Square
New Square Chambers
No5 Chambers

Northampton Chambers
Ten Old Square
15 Old Square
Old Square Chambers
Old Square Chambers (Bristol)
Oriel Chambers
Outer Temple Chambers
Five Paper
4 Paper Buildings
5 Paper Buildings
9 Park Place
30 Park Place
Park Square Barristers
Parklane Plowden Chambers
3PB
4 Pump Court
5 Pump Court
6 Pump Court
Pump Court Chambers
1 Pump Court Chambers
Pump Court Tax Chambers
QEB Hollis Whiteman
Quadrant Chambers
Queen Elizabeth Building
Queen Square Chambers
Radcliffe Chambers
5RB
Red Lion Chambers
Selborne Chambers
Serjeants' Inn Chambers
Serle Court
South Square
11 South Square
5 St Andrew's Hill
St Ives Chambers
9 St John Street Chambers
18 St John Street Chambers
St John's Buildings
St John's Chambers
St Mary's Chambers
St Paul's Chambers
St Philips Chambers
Staple Inn Chambers
Three Stone
4 Stone Buildings
5 Stone Buildings
9 Stone Buildings
Stone Chambers
Stour Chambers
Sussex Chambers
Tanfield Chambers
Fourteen
Temple Garden Chambers
3 Temple Gardens
2TG
Thomas More Chambers

Trinity Chambers
Trinity Chambers
Unity Street Chambers
3 Verulam Buildings
Westgate Chambers
Wilberforce Chambers
15 Winckley Square
XXIV Old Buildings

*Law**Careers.Net**™*

Delivering your future in law

Our newsletter, LCN Weekly, is packed with news, profiles, opinion and advice about becoming a lawyer.

Sign up to *Law**Careers.Net**™*

Postgraduate training

Postgraduate training

Broadly speaking, the Solicitors Regulation Authority (SRA) and the Bar Standards Board (BSB) are responsible for laying down the training requirements for qualification as a solicitor or barrister in England and Wales. The past few years have seen a lot of change in the postgraduate training world, for both would-be solicitors and barristers, especially since the publication in 2013 of the cross-profession Legal Education and Training Review (LETR). The final report offered 26 key recommendations related to the effectiveness of legal teaching and training methods, including a number of ways in which quality, accessibility and flexibility must be enhanced. Since then, both the SRA and BSB have released plans and consulted on how to implement the recommendations, and some important changes have been made in the last two years.

Changes ahead

As of 2015-16, firms are now allowed to recruit solicitors from the second year of university onwards (previously training contracts were only supposed to be offered in the final year). Most firms are sticking broadly to the traditional 31 July application deadline, but others are recruiting earlier in the year and directly from their vacation schemes. Another change has been to abolish the term 'training contract' in favour of the less specific 'period of recognised training' (although confusingly, most firms and providers still refer to 'training contract'!).

In practical terms, this means that law firms and aspiring solicitors have been given much greater flexibility in how they gain the necessary skills and experience to qualify. For example, it is now possible to apply to the SRA to be granted qualification if you have completed a law degree or the Graduate Diploma in Law (GDL), the Legal Practice Course (LPC), and gained all the necessary skills and experience (as set out by the SRA) while working as a paralegal. Meanwhile, it is no longer necessary to gain a mixture of contentious and non-contentious experience in order to qualify and changes have also been made to continuing professional development training, which you undertake when you start practising.

Another major development is the proposed introduction by the SRA of a Solicitors Qualifying Examination (SQE), which all prospective solicitors – whether coming through the university, equivalent means (see explanation under "GDL" below) or apprenticeship routes – would have to take in order to qualify. The proposal met with widely published opposition, particularly from universities and academics, but the SRA has confirmed that the SQE will go ahead – the exam is expected to be introduced in 2020 "at the earliest".

The Bar, too, is looking at the future training of barristers and has decided to introduce a limited number of new routes to train as a barrister, which could be in place by 2019. A central tenet is that training as a barrister needs to become more flexible and accessible to a more diverse range of candidates. As of August 2018, what those new routes will be exactly has not yet been revealed. Another big timetable change occurred in January 2017 when the Pupillage Gateway opened for applications in January rather than April. This change was made to stop the application season clashing with exams and to allow students to know whether they have secured a pupillage before committing to the expensive Bar Professional Training Course (BPTC). Find detailed information about the SQE and the planned changes at the Bar on LawCareers.Net.

So things are very fluid at the moment; but as they stand, the below describes the postgraduate training landscape.

Two-stage training

For both solicitors and barristers, training comprises two stages: academic and vocational. The academic stage can be completed in one of three ways:
- a law degree;
- the GDL for non-law graduates; or
- the CILEx exams for those wishing to qualify as chartered legal executives, which enable people who are already in legal employment to qualify while they are working (see "Alternative careers").

The vocational stage involves completion of the LPC or BPTC, plus a two-year training contract or one-year pupillage.

GDL

The GDL is a conversion course that non-law graduates can take to enable them to apply for an LPC or BPTC place. It is normally a one-year, full-time course designed to enable non-law graduates to fulfil the academic stage of legal training. The course can also be taken over two years, either part time or by distance learning.

If you intend to study full time, you should apply through the Central Applications Board (www.lawcabs.ac.uk) from September onwards in your final year at university. There is no closing date for applications; rather, applications are dealt with as they are submitted and institutions are notified weekly of new submissions. Applications for part-time courses must be made directly to the provider.

To be eligible for the GDL, students must hold a degree from a UK university or recognised overseas university. As a non-graduate, it may still be possible to commence the GDL based on the SRA's "equivalent means" test, which assesses whether the individual holds other "academic or vocational qualifications that the SRA considers equivalent to a degree". Subject

to various criteria, the following people may be eligible for exemption: mature students; chartered legal executives; assistant justices' clerks; and those with professional qualifications equivalent to a degree (eg, obtained through the Institute of Chartered Accountants). If you think you might fall within one of these categories, you should contact the SRA (www.sra.org.uk/contactus or 0370 606 2555) or consult its "Equivalent means information pack" page.

Course content

The GDL is an intensive, demanding programme focusing on the seven foundations of legal knowledge, which are:
- contract;
- tort;
- criminal;
- equity and trusts;
- European Union;
- property/land; and
- public.

Be aware that this stage of training is widely regarded as extremely difficult. Specific course content is set internally by individual institutions. However, for full-time students, the final examination will normally comprise a three-hour paper in each of the seven core areas. All papers will usually need to be passed on the same occasion. Although you have up to three years to complete the GDL, you will not be allowed to attempt any paper more than three times. Part-time and distance-learning GDL students must attend a recognised course which lasts two years and must complete the course in not more than four years.

As an alternative to the GDL, a two-year, senior-status law degree can be studied. After this degree, students go straight on to the appropriate vocational stage of legal training (ie, LPC or BPTC). A number of UK universities offer senior-status degrees. To check whether your preferred university offers a senior status degree, contact the SRA, as above.

Finally, it is worth taking into account the fact that many institutions teaching both the GDL and LPC will automatically offer you a place on the latter if you successfully complete the former.

LPC

All institutions that offer the full-time LPC are managed by the Central Applications Board. You should contact them for an application form or apply online at www.lawcabs.ac.uk.

The LPC is the vocational stage of training to be a solicitor. It aims to provide students/ trainees with sufficient knowledge and skills to ensure that they are well equipped to undertake the work of a solicitor. It is a one-year, full-time (or two-year, part-time) course designed to bridge the academic degree and training contract. Although the length of time it takes to complete remains the same, it is possible to split the course into core and elective stages, enabling you to start your training contract sooner (ie, after having completed the core stage only).

The LPC focuses on practical skills and the instilling of professional conduct and ethical standards. Teaching methods are no longer just academic: the emphasis is on workshops, continuous assessment, independent research and group discussions. The course also permits some specialisation through a range of optional subjects.

In Stage One, the core subjects cover litigation, property, business, professional conduct and regulation, taxation, wills and the administration of estates. This stage also teaches students specific skills such as advocacy, drafting and writing, interviewing and advising, problem solving and legal research. This stage is completed at law school.

It is now possible to complete Stage Two during your training contract or while working at a law firm in another role (eg, as a paralegal or legal secretary), should you wish to do so. This stage consists of electives from a range of subjects in private and corporate client work, including commercial law and practice, employment, intellectual property, consumer, housing, family and immigration.

BPTC

Anyone wanting to become a barrister must pass the BPTC, which effectively bridges the gap between the study of law and work as a pupil. Students seeking a place on the BPTC must go through the centralised online application process at www.barsas.com.

The full-time BPTC is a one-year course; the part-time course takes two years. All students must be admitted to an Inn of Court before registration on the BPTC. The BSB also requires that applicants must:
- hold at least a 2.2 degree (in either law or non-law plus the GDL);
- gain a score of at least 7.5 in all subjects of the British Council's IELTS test, if English is not their first language; and
- pass the Bar Course Aptitude Test (BCAT), which tests critical thinking and reasoning, and is designed to assess chances of success at the Bar. Applicants must pay £150 to sit the test.

The main areas of knowledge taught on the BPTC are civil litigation and remedies, criminal litigation and sentencing, evidence and professional ethics. It also teaches skills related to advocacy, conferencing, drafting and resolution of disputes out of court. Students are then allowed to choose two optional subjects from areas that include family, intellectual property, immigration, personal injury and employment law. Assessment varies from institution to institution. However, the BSB sets three standard exams in civil litigation, criminal litigation and professional ethics.

If a BPTC graduate seeks to pursue a career as a solicitor, he or she may be granted exemption from attendance and assessment in several areas of the LPC, including litigation, advocacy, drafting, practical legal research and two vocational electives. Students must have completed the BPTC no earlier than five years before enrolling on the LPC.

LLM
A master's degree in law is a popular option as the profession grows more competitive and students seek to add an extra edge to their CV. The LLM is a sure-fire way of developing your expertise in a niche area of the law, but be aware that it is unlikely to make the difference that lands you a training contract or pupillage. This is especially so if you see doing an LLM as the way around a lower-than-expected first degree result in order to get a training contract/pupillage. Few law firms/chambers will take account of an LLM if your first degree result falls below their entry requirement and you have no genuine mitigating circumstances.

In marketing your LLM to potential employers, you will be able to point out that you have not only gained a thorough knowledge of a particular area of law or legal practice, but also improved your communication and research skills. But do bear in mind that while most firms don't mind where you have studied the GDL, this isn't the case with LLMs. LLM programmes are as much governed by snobbery as undergraduate law degrees and there is no point pretending otherwise. Thus, our advice for LLMs is to use the same principles for selecting a course as you would at undergraduate level.

What to look for in a postgraduate provider
You have a wide range of choice when it comes to the postgraduate law courses. There are over 30 institutions – some with more than one site – offering the LPC alone. Whether you are about to do the GDL, LPC or BPTC, a number of factors should guide which law schools you apply to. Those of you with the easiest choice have already secured a training contract or pupillage and your future firm/chambers will have specified the provider that you should attend. It is also possible that your prospective firm/chambers is paying your fees, in which case you don't have to pay too much heed to financial considerations.

The rest (and the majority) of you should pay close attention to each of the factors listed below.

Course fees
This boils down to how much money you can afford to hand over for the privilege of attending the course. Fees for a one-year course can be as much as £19,070 (for the BPTC in London in 2018-19). However, do not make the mistake of thinking that the more expensive the course is, the better it will be. That's not always the case.

Both BPP and The University of Law make financial offers to LPC and BPTC students who have failed to secure either a training contact or pupillage having completed the course. First, BPP's 'career guarantee' says that if within six months of graduating no training contract or pupillage is forthcoming, a student will be given the chance to study another of BPP's courses for free (from an approved list). Next, The University of Law's 'employment promise' provides that if a student fails to secure a job within nine months of graduating, he or she will get all of the course fees back, made up of 50% cashback and 50% credit towards any further courses. A note of caution: both these offers are heavily caveated, so it is worth reading the small print before basing your decision to apply to either on this reason alone.

Course structure/type

It is essential to do an LPC or BPTC that reflects the type of law you wish to practise. The LPC at its core remains the same course for everyone, but institutions offer versions with different emphases. For example, BPP Law School offers a business-focused LPC, developed in conjunction with leading firms that include Clifford Chance, Freshfields Bruckhaus Deringer, Allen & Overy and Herbert Smith Freehills. The University of Law's standard LPC is now the LLM LPC, offering students the chance to gain both a master's and the LPC during the one-year course. It also offers firm-specific LPCs to future trainees at firms that include magic circle stalwart Linklaters. Ask potential providers what they have to offer and how this differs from what is available elsewhere.

Teaching quality

Some courses have better teachers and teaching methods than others. The SRA continually monitors course quality and rates LPC courses, focusing on six different areas:
• teaching, learning and the curriculum;
• assessment;
• students and their support;
• learning resources;
• leadership and management; and
• quality assurance and enhancement.

Contact the SRA to find out more (www.sra.org.uk/contactus or 0370 606 2555).

Facilities

Not all courses and institutions offer the same level of facilities, resources, support and class sizes. Some institutions include books and materials, while at others these are additional costs. Don't be afraid to ask questions about what you get for your money.

Housing/living costs

London is an expensive city in which to live, while the rest of the country is (mostly) cheaper. This should be factored in when you consider how much you will be paying for the course. Ask the questions and do your research.

Location

If you study somewhere near home, you can live there and save on costs. If you are keen to move elsewhere, first work out whether you are likely to be happy there – a preliminary visit is a good idea. The BPTC and LPC are usually completed in a year, which is a manageable amount of time wherever you are, but be sure to consider the factors that are important to you.

Reputation

This is possibly the most nebulous of considerations. There are plenty of people whose opinion you can elicit (potential employers, tutors, careers advisers, friends, relations, colleagues and fellow students). With all that advice, you should garner a fair amount of insight into the best place of study for you. Just remember to pay more heed to those who actually know what they are talking about!

Further reading on LawCareers.Net:
• GDL – www.lawcareers.net/Solicitors/GDL
• LPC – www.lawcareers.net/Solicitors/LPC
• BPTC – www.lawcareers.net/Barristers/BPTC

Financing the vocational courses

Training to be a lawyer is not cheap. The reality is that if you have to pay for all your university tuition fees and vocational courses, you could incur debts of many tens of thousands of pounds. And it's not just course fees that have to be taken into account – there are also the other expenses of books, accommodation, food, transport and at least one good suit!

So with that in mind, how do you go about financing the vocational stage of your study? Thankfully, there are a variety of options. For those who secure a training contract or pupillage before they begin their vocational training (which is recommended), sponsoring firms or chambers may pay fees and/or a maintenance grant. For those who are self-funding this stage, careful financial planning is essential. In 2018-19 Graduate Diploma in Law (GDL) course fees were as much as £11,250. Fees for the Legal Practice Course (LPC) and the Bar Professional Training Course (BPTC) were even higher, with the LPC costing as much as £16,200 and the BPTC up to £19,070. Clearly, these fees represent the upper limits of what you can expect to pay, but the courses are always a significant financial undertaking - especially given the rising cost of living throughout the country.

Sponsorship
An increasing number of firms and chambers offer financial assistance to their future trainees and pupils, from full payment of fees and maintenance for up to two years of postgraduate study to the provision of an interest-free loan towards LPC/BPTC course fees. One thing to remember is that the terms of sponsorship may tie you to the firm for a period of time after your training contract. Details of individual policies can be found in the directory section of this book.

Local authority grants
Such grants are available, but funds are extremely limited. In addition, grants are discretionary for the GDL and LPC, which means that they are difficult to get. As a result, you should contact your local authority as soon as possible to find out the situation and apply immediately. Local authorities will supply a booklet describing the details of their award policies. Most authorities require you to complete an application form with details of your education history and financial circumstances.

Law Society
The Law Society lists a variety of trusts and scholarships designed to support the development of individuals who can demonstrate exceptional academic ability and potential as a solicitor. For application details, visit the Junior Lawyers Division website and go to its "Funding your studies" page.

The Law Society also runs a Diversity Access Scheme, which provides support to talented people who will have to overcome a specific obstacle in order to qualify. Such obstacles might include social, educational, personal or financial factors. The scheme provides scholarships to cover LPC course fees and successful applicants will automatically qualify for support through the Law Society's mentoring scheme.

Inns of Court
In recent years the four Inns have dished out millions of pounds in awards. They all seem to use the umbrella term 'award' to describe scholarships, bursaries and grants. Inner Temple even calls them 'exhibitions'. Curiously, most wannabe barristers know little about the awards available and although the Inns' websites provide some information, there's a complex web of requirements and application procedures, meaning that working out exactly what is available can be a challenge.

Eamonn O'Reilly, formerly the scholarships and students manager at Inner Temple, said:

Financing the vocational courses

"All the four Inns are different and it's difficult to get your head around all the different awards. We all have a scholarships fund and we all give money out, mostly on merit, using different kinds of means testing to fine tune that. The scholarships committees think: 'Does this person have a good chance of succeeding at the Bar?' That's the bottom line."

The Inns' websites have application forms for you to complete and send to the relevant person. The forms ask for character details, legal experience, income/funds and references. You can only apply for scholarships at one Inn. If the scholarships committee likes your application, it will invite you to an interview.

Here is a breakdown of what's on offer.

Lincoln's Inn
Lincoln's Inn offers 32 scholarships ranging from £3,000 to £8,000 for those studying the GDL and 110 scholarships and bursaries for those on the BPTC. The total value of the Inn's awards in 2018-19 is just over £1.57 million. Lincoln's Inn has many other awards and bursaries available, from its £60,000 fund for up to 50 awards of up to £1,500 for pupillage to the £3,500 Peter Duffy Human Rights Award for young barristers to spend three months at the European Court of Human Rights in Strasbourg. There are also scholarships of £3,500 to the other European courts in The Hague and Luxembourg. Students are recommended to apply for awards in their third year at university or the year prior to starting the GDL or BPTC. The majority of the scholarships are now applied for via the Inn's online portal, scholarships. lincolnsinn.org.uk, but any questions about the process should be sent to the scholarships coordinator (scholarships@ lincolnsinn.org.uk).

Inner Temple
Probably the Inn with the most accessible information, Inner Temple handed out £1,786,306 in awards in 2018. The number of awards is not fixed, but the Inn usually offers 80 to 100 scholarships per year for those on the BPTC. These vary in value, with a maximum award of £22,000. For those on the GDL a number of scholarships are available, of values up to £10,000. A small number of pupillage awards are available, as well as small disability and internship awards. The Inn has a scholarships and students manager, Sellisha Lockyer (slockyer@ innertemple.org.uk), and its website (www. innertemple.org.uk) has all the info you need and you can apply online.

Middle Temple
In 2018 Middle Temple was due to make awards worth around £1.3 million, with £1.1 million of that going to BPTC students and most of the rest to GDL students. While the awarding of scholarships is based purely on merit, the sizes of the awards are based on the applicant's financial means. The Inn also has a pupillage hardship fund for pupils who experience severe, unforeseen financial difficulties and a pupillage support grant for pupils on low awards in publicly funded areas of law. The website (www. middletemple.org.uk) tells you a lot about the scholarship scheme and has a downloadable application form with clear instructions. Scholarships are part of the education department within the Inn's Treasury and Christa Richmond is the director of education services. Contact the education services manager, Sally Yorke (s.yorke@ middletemple.org.uk), with questions.

Gray's Inn
Although Gray's Inn is the smallest of the four Inns, in 2016 (the most recent statistic available at time of writing) it awarded in excess of £890,000 in scholarships, awards and prizes. In 2017 the Inn awarded £90,000 in CPE/GDL scholarships, and £838,5000 to scholars undertaking the BPTC. Residential, pupillage and internship awards are also

available, as are prizes for mooting, debating and. Detailed information on all of Gray's Inn's scholarships can be found at www.graysinn.org.uk/education/scholarships. All enquiries should be sent to scholarships@graysinn.org.uk or to Sam Wingrove via the online form at www.graysinn.org.uk/education/contact-the-department.

College access funds

College access funds are available to postgraduate students at universities and publicly funded colleges, mainly to provide additional assistance to meet living costs. The funds are available at the discretion of your college and are intended for those who are experiencing particular difficulties in meeting their living costs. Students should contact the student support department of their institution for further details.

Loans

Some high-street banks offer specialised loans for those wishing to study for professional qualifications. However, there does seem to be an increasing unwillingness to lend to students, with most of the major banks withdrawing their loan schemes over the past few years. The University of Law offers loans to its master's, LPC and BPTC students, via the Student Loans Company, for up to £10,609. BPP offers a similar postgraduate loan, but only to its master's students, as well as its scheme Future Finance Loans.

Professional and Career Development Loans are deferred repayment loans that are available to help pay for vocational courses, including fees and any related expenses, not exceeding a total of £10,000. One month after finishing the course, you must begin to repay the loan to the Cooperative Bank – the only bank that offers the loan – over an agreed period and at an agreed rate. Applicants must show that they intend to use the resulting qualification for the purposes of finding employment in the United Kingdom or European Union. Worth noting is that career development loans cannot be used to fund a course that leads to another course rather than employment, so they are not available to help fund the GDL.

More importantly, these loans will no longer be available from 25 January 2019, so apply now if you intend to do so. More information and an application form may be obtained from the Cooperative Bank, the National Careers Service helpline on 0800 100 900 or the www.gov.uk website (search for "career development loan").

Charities and grant-making trusts

Some grant-making trusts and charities may offer financial assistance to those seeking to qualify as a lawyer. The application criteria for these awards vary enormously, but they are often so specific that eligibility is limited to just a few and only small amounts of money are available. The best place to find a full list of such organisations is in publications such as *The Guide to Educational Grants*, *The Directory of Grant-Making Trusts*, *The Grants Register*, *A Guide to Grants for Individuals in Need* and *Charities Digest*. However, each is expensive to purchase, so try the reference section of your local library.

Reality check: The road to becoming a trainee or pupil is a huge financial investment, with no guarantee of a training contract or pupillage at the end of it. Make sure you've got what it takes before committing thousands of pounds to the process.

Course directory

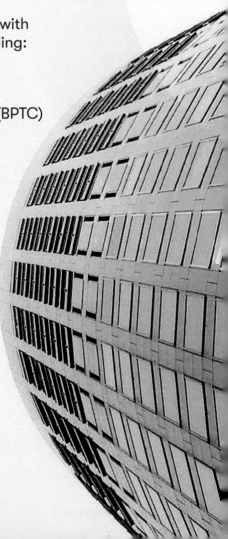

BPP University Law School

68-70 Red Lion Street, London WC1R 4NY
Tel: 0333 1223 604
Email: admissions@bpp.com
Web: www.bpp.com/courses/law
f bpplawschool 🐦 bpplawschool

With over 25 years' experience in delivering professional legal qualifications, we have proudly earned our place as one of the leading law schools in the UK.

We build and shape legal careers. We focus on your employability, developing your skills as a lawyer and giving you the edge to secure a training contract or pupillage.

Our courses are taught in small groups and delivered by highly skilled tutors, who use realistic case studies to thoroughly prepare you for your career in law. That is why over 60 leading law firms trust us to exclusively train their future solicitors.*

Don't let finances stand in the way of your legal training. Our LLM courses incorporate the essential legal training you need to become a solicitor or barrister, and are eligible for a government postgraduate loan up to £10,609.

Secure your legal future with our Career Guarantee. Gain a training contract or pupillage within six months of completing our LPC or BPTC, or study another course to enhance your CV at no extra cost.**

Graduate Diploma in Law (GDL)/LLM (Law Conversion) (full time, part time and distance learning) If you are a non-law graduate, the GDL or LLM (Law Conversion) is your path to a career in law, designed to prepare you for the next stage of legal training to become a solicitor or barrister. Tailor your studies to your career ambitions with our additional GDL Extra lecture series and Skills in Practice workshops.

Legal Practice Course (LPC)/LLM Legal Practice (Solicitors) (full time and part time) Our LPC or LLM Legal Practice (Solicitors) will give you the best possible start to your career as a solicitor. Designed in close collaboration with law firms and delivered by experienced lawyers, you will be taught through simulated client portfolios and learn how to develop client relationships, as well as technical legal practice. Tailor your training to your ambitions and explore different practice areas with our wide range of electives. Enhance your employability with additional study options, including our cutting-edge legal technology innovation and design module. LPC students have the option to top up to a full Masters' degree at no extra cost.

Bar Professional Training Course / LLM Legal Practice (Barristers) (full time and part time) Our BPTC/LLM Legal Practice (Barristers) will provide you with the best possible preparation to secure pupillage and start your career as a barrister. Learn from experienced practitioners with links to chambers who can help develop your legal career. Create your own competitive niche with our wide selection of optional modules – more than any other provider. BPTC students can also top up to a full Masters' degree at no extra cost

*As of September 2018. **T&Cs apply.

Apply to

Visit www.bpp.com/
courses/law

Funding
Scholarships and funding options are available:
www.bpp.com/students/
funding-your-studies

Location
Birmingham, Bristol, Cambridge, Leeds, London (Holborn and Waterloo), Manchester

BPP
UNIVERSITY
LAW SCHOOL

Remember to cite *The LawCareers.Net Handbook* if you apply to this law school.

POSTGRADUATE TRAINING 【129】

Bristol Law School

University of the West of England, Coldharbour Lane, Frenchay, Bristol BS16 1QY
Tel: 0117 328 3333
Email: admissions@uwe.ac.uk
Web: www.uwe.ac.uk/professionallawcourses
f uwebristol **🐦** uwebristol

College overview UWE Bristol Law School is widely recognised as one of the leading providers of professional legal education in the UK. We have a reputation for excellence and for delivering courses of the very highest quality. UWE Bristol Law School offers the full range of professional law programmes. Our courses are taught by the tutors who design and write them; experienced solicitors or barristers teaching within their own subject areas. From our dedicated law facilities to our events and pro bono activities, we have everything you need to enhance your career prospects and have a very strong track record of assisting students that have not secured training contracts or pupillage.

Our benefits: regional law fair and meet the employers fair; networking and careers events (including our distinguished executive address series); dedicated professional law teaching and common rooms; mock courtrooms (used by legal practitioners and students); comprehensive online resources, including recorded lectures; extensive law library; pro bono unit, with a range of award-winning activities. Both the LPC and BPTC are offered as Masters programmes, allowing eligible students to apply for a postgraduate loan to fund their studies. There are different options to complete the Masters programme, and these focus on continuing your professional development, as a reflective practitioner with responsibility for your own development and learning.

Graduate Diploma in Law Our GDL enables you as a non-law graduate to progress with confidence to the LPC/BPTC, and is supported by a dedicated team of tutors who understand the demands of the GDL route. Teaching is not shared with undergraduates. The curriculum is divided into two teaching blocks with assessments after each block, which greatly assists our students in managing workload. Tuition will develop you for the demands of the legal profession, equipping you with the necessary legal skills to thoroughly apply the law to a set of facts and the ability to solve legal problems.
Places offered: 100 split between full time and part time.

LLM Advanced Legal Practice Whether you are intending to practise in a commercial or high street firm, the practical, wide-ranging Legal Practice Course leading to a Masters qualification will provide the broad and rigorous foundation you need to be 'practice ready'. Workshop teaching happens in small, interactive groups with an emphasis on intensive, personal tuition. Here, you will learn by doing within a supportive, friendly environment, developing the skills and knowledge to excel in your role as a solicitor. You will benefit from flexible modes of study and a choice of timetabling options. There are strong links to local and regional practice, including a placement scheme run in conjunction with Bristol Law Society.
Places offered: 100 (full time) 100 (part time).

LLM Bar Professional Training Studies With its reputation for teaching excellence, high levels of student satisfaction and outstanding pastoral care, our BPTC leading to Masters qualification is highly commended by the Bar Standards Board (BSB) and will equip you with key skills to excel in practice. There are exceptional links with the local Bar including participation in mock pupillage interviews, chambers sponsored advocacy and mooting competitions annually and an additional Western Circuit sponsored advocacy prize. As part of the programme you have the opportunity to become an accredited civil commercial mediator.
Places offered: 120 (full time) 48 (part time).

CPE/GDL	100
LPC	300
BPTC	168

Apply to

GDL Central Applications Board (full time), direct to UWE Bristol (part time)
LPC Central Applications Board (full time), direct to UWE Bristol (part time)
BPTC Bar Professional Training Online

Contact names

GDL
Delyth James
delyth.james@uwe.ac.uk

LPC
Jane Waddell
jane.waddell@uwe.ac.uk

BPTC
Delyth James
delyth.james@uwe.ac.uk

PSC/CPD
Philip Millington
philip.millington@uwe.ac.uk

DREAM
BIG

The University of Law

Braboeuf Manor, Portsmouth Road, Guildford GU3 1HA
Tel: 01483 216 500
Email: admissions@law.ac.uk
Web: www.law.ac.uk/postgraduate
f universityoflaw **𝕏** universityoflaw

University overview The University of Law is the UK's longest-established specialist provider of legal education and training in the UK. Our expert Employability Service gives students access to work experience, pro bono opportunities and legal vacancies as soon as they accept their place. The result is excellent employability statistics: 97% of our full-time 2016/17 and accelerated 2016/17 LPC students graduating in summer 2017 secured employment, a training contract, or further study within nine months of successfully completing their course. In 2017, we were awarded a gold ranking in the government-led Teaching Excellence Framework (TEF) for delivering consistently outstanding teaching, learning and outcomes for our undergraduate students, making us one of the highest quality providers of higher education in the UK.

Graduate Diploma in Law (full time/part time/online) Our unique modular GDL spreads the workload for a better paced approach. Unlike linear GDL courses, our modular course structure is spread over two semesters, so you can 'bank' some exams in the first semester, therefore reducing any excessive end of course assessment burden. With a range of study options to suit you, including online (i-GDL), you can now study full-time over 12 months or part-time over 21 months.

MA Law (full time)) Our MA Law course is designed for non-law graduates to gain a legal qualification at Master's level. An internationally recognised qualification, it is ideal if you're considering a career path in or outside of the legal sector. We now offer part-time and online (i-MA Law) options over 12 months or 21 months. MA Law students may also be eligible for a postgraduate loan.

Legal Practice Course (full time/part time/online) Our career-focused LPC will prepare you for life as a solicitor. Improve your career prospects by learning the essential professional skills that legal employers are looking for. At no extra cost, you can gain an MSc in Law, Business and Management or an LLM in Professional Legal Practice. LPC Master's degree students may also be eligible for a postgraduate student loan. We offer a range of study options to suit you, including online (i-LLM LPC), full-time over 11 months or part-time over 22 months. With a clear focus on your employability, we can offer you our LPC Employment Promise. Get a job in nine months or receive 50% of your fees as cashback plus 50% of your fees as credit towards any further courses.

Bar Professional Training Course (full time/part time) Our BPTC is designed to help you secure pupillage and prepare you for life as a barrister. You'll get to study in small groups, with plenty of opportunities to test your advocacy skills. With our BPTC LLM you can gain additional practical experience representing real clients in courts and tribunals. Master's degree students may also be eligible for postgraduate funding.

LLM Legal Practice Programmes (full time/online) English Law plays an important role in various areas of business. We offer a range of Master of Laws (LLM) programmes enabling you to specialise in a particular area of the law. LLM students may also be eligible for postgraduate funding.

MSc Programmes Build on your ICA Professional Diploma expertise and develop your compliance or wealth management knowledge with our career enhancing Master's programmes.

Events We run events of all types, including open days, law fairs and insight days, as well as lawyers den, barrister insight days and our annual national law fair. Check them out at law.ac.uk/events/postgraduate.

Contact

Admissions
01483 216 000
admissions@law.ac.uk

Apply to

GDL, MA Law and LPC full time
Central Applications Board
www.lawcabs.ac.uk

GDL, MA Law and LPC part time and online
Apply directly to
The University of Law
www.law.ac.uk/postgraduate

BPTC full and part time
Bar Student Application Service
www.barsas.com

LLMs and MSc Programmes
Apply directly to
The University of Law
www.law.ac.uk/postgraduate

Locations
Birmingham, Bristol, Chester, Exeter, Guildford, Leeds, Liverpool, London (Bloomsbury and Moorgate), Manchester, Reading

The
University of
Law

LawCareers.Net™

Delivering your future in law

Our newsletter, LCN Weekly, is packed with news, profiles, opinion and advice about becoming a lawyer.

Sign up to *LawCareers.Net*™

Liverpool John Moores University

Redmonds Building, Brownlow Hill, Liverpool L3 5UG
Tel: 0151 231 5175
Email: apsadmissions@ljmu.ac.uk
Web: www.ljmu.ac.uk
🐦 ljmulaw

College overview Liverpool John Moores University (LJMU) is a contemporary university in one of the most famous cities in the world. We aim to give people the opportunity to maximise their potential in an environment that is stimulating, challenging and exciting, but also caring and supportive.

The School of Law offers a broad portfolio of academic, vocational and professional programmes in both full-time and part-time modes. The School provides undergraduate, postgraduate and professional programmes in law, legal practice and criminal justice. It also offers opportunities to study for an MPhil or PhD by research. School staff are engaged in a wide range of law and criminal justice research, and the School hosts the Centre for Criminal Justice.

The School of Law has invested significantly in staff development, with an emphasis on enhancing the status and quality of teaching and learning, and also in providing excellent information technology facilities.

The School is part of the Faculty of Arts, Professional and Social Studies, based in the £38 million Redmonds Building close to the heart of Liverpool City Centre. Liverpool is a vibrant city and the cultural capital of the North of England.

Legal Practice Course (full, part time and combined LLM LPC courses offered) The LPC at LJMU has been designed to meet the requirements and needs of the legal profession of the 21st century. The LPC aims to produce a highly skilled, commercially aware and effective trainee solicitor, who is prepared for the rigours and demands of a training contract. Students will join a team of professional lawyers who are highly committed, enthusiastic and skilled teachers.

LPC students are able to volunteer for the School of Law's pro bono Legal Advice Centre. The service, which is open to residents around Merseyside, gives students real-life client and case management experience working across a variety of legal areas, from family to employment and commercial law.

LLM Qualifying Law The LLM Qualifying Law offers students a broad range of learning options selected from across the School of Law's diverse module portfolio. The LLM Qualifying Law degree replaces the GDL and offering candidates a fully validated (SRA/BSB) masters qualification. The degree can be studied in both full-time and part-time patterns and offers excellent preparation for a professional legal career.

Other postgraduate courses (one-year full time or two-year part time)
LLM in Legal Practice (top-up masters allows you to convert your existing LPC or BVC/BPTC Postgraduate Diploma to an LLM)
LLM in International Business, Corporate and Finance Law
LLM Global Crime, Justice and Security
MA Criminal Justice

LJMU also offers a range of postgraduate and professional programmes in business, arts, humanities and media. For further details visit our website www.ljmu.ac.uk/courses or telephone 0151 231 5175.

LPC   144

Apply to

Full time Central Applications Board

Part time Apply direct

Admissions contact LPC and LLM LPC
Fiona Fargher
f.l.fargher@ljmu.ac.uk
0151 231 3930

Admissions contact LLM
Sarah Stirk
s.k.stirk@ljmu.ac.uk
0151 231 3986

Admissions contact LLM Qualifying Law
Anita Ellis
a.ellis@ljmu.ac.uk
0151 231 3936

Admissions contact LLM in Legal Practice
Laura Samaroo
l.a.samaroo@ljmu.ac.uk
0151 231 3832

Admissions contact LLM International Business, Corporate and Finance Law
Blanca Mamutse
b.c.mamutse@ljmu.ac.uk
0151 231 4735

Admissions contact LLM Global Crime, Justice and Security
Dr Gary Wilson
g.wilson@ljmu.ac.uk
0151 231 3397

Admissions contact MA Criminal Justice
Dr Noel Cross
n.cross@ljmu.ac.uk
0151 231 3902

#TakeOnTomorrow

AT A LAW SCHOOL THAT REALLY MAKES AN IMPACT

Since 2005, Northumbria's Student Law Office has represented more than **3,000 clients** and secured them **over £1.5 million** in compensation.

Considering a GDL, LPC, BPTC or LLM?

Register your details with Northumbria for your chance to win a Surface Pro†.

northumbria.ac.uk/lawsurfacepro

† Prize draw will be made on 28 June 2019. For full terms and conditions please see website.

Northumbria Law School

City Campus East, Newcastle upon Tyne NE1 8ST
Tel: 0191 227 4494
Email: law@northumbria.ac.uk
Web: www.northumbria.ac.uk/law
f northumbrialaw **𝕏** northumbrialaw

University overview Northumbria Law School is one of the largest law schools in the UK, with a national and international reputation for excellence in legal education. We have won numerous awards for the outstanding work of our student law office – the largest university law clinic in the UK. We focus on law in practice and are committed to ensuring that students develop the knowledge and skills needed to become successful legal professionals. We have a suite of long-standing and well-regarded professional programmes, to which we have recently added Masters options for both routes of the profession.

Graduate Diploma in Law GDL (full time or distance learning) Our GDL is taught using a practical, student-focused approach providing a solid grounding in the major areas of law. It covers the foundations of legal knowledge, which are taught by means of lectures, other large group sessions and seminars. Students are provided with comprehensive study materials, webcasts and step-by-step workbooks to support their studies. Successful GDL students who continue to study at Northumbria are guaranteed a place on the Legal Practice Course (LPC).

Legal Practice Postgraduate Diploma LPC (full or part time) Our LPC provides vocational training across a range of subjects and practical skills, enabling students to learn how to apply their legal knowledge in a practical context. The well-established, highly successful programme offers a strong staff/student ratio, a guaranteed legal placement or professional mentor and a wide range of electives tailored to both general and commercial practice.

LLM Legal Practice (full or part time) This programme will enhance the students' legal knowledge and allow them to develop the skills and values necessary to become an effective and successful legal professional. This Masters degree offers students the opportunity to gain an internationally recognised LLM qualification in addition to the LPC, and will prepare students for a training contract and life as a solicitor. It will also enable eligible students to apply for postgraduate funding.

Bar Professional Training Course BPTC (full or part time) Our BPTC is student-centred with skills taught in small group and practical sessions. Students develop a range of essential skills, which include advocacy, drafting, opinion writing, conference skills and resolution of disputes out of court. Evidence, criminal and civil litigation are taught as discrete subjects, as well as being integrated within the five main skill areas. The majority of teaching staff are practising legal professionals, including senior prosecutors and a retired judge.

LLM Bar Practice (full or part time) This programme allows students to enhance their BPTC qualification by enabling them to gain a Masters (LLM) award as part of the BPTC course. The LLM can be obtained by completion of a project, which provides students with the opportunity to explore in great depth areas of law in which they may wish to practice. This programme will also enable eligible students to apply for postgraduate funding.

LLM Advanced Legal Practice (distance learning) Designed for qualified lawyers (solicitors and barristers, or their international equivalent) who want to develop their knowledge in a specialist area of law. Students develop their skills in legal research and its written presentation, through an in depth study of an agreed legal topic under individual tutor supervision.

We offer a range of other specialist LLM programmes taught by leading academics and experienced lawyers.

LPC	150 (full time)
	50 (part time)
GDL	100 (full time)
	50 (distance)
BPTC	100 (full time)
	48 (part time)

Contact

Admissions
0191 406 0901
bc.applicantservices
@northumbria.ac.uk

Apply to

GDL & LPC (full time)
www.lawcabs.ac.uk

BPTC & LLM Bar Practice (full and part time)
www.barsas.com

GDL (distance learning), LPC (part time) and LLM
Direct to Northumbria
www.northumbria.ac.uk/law

Northumbria University
NEWCASTLE

Nottingham Law School

Burton Street, Nottingham NG1 4BU
Tel: 0115 848 4460
Email: nls.enquiries@ntu.ac.uk
Web: www.ntu.ac.uk/nls
f ntulawschool **𝕐** lawnls

School overview One of the largest and most diverse law schools in the UK, Nottingham Law School has been delivering excellence in legal education for over 50 years. We seek to ensure that all of our clients, from students to experienced practitioners, receive the best practical legal education and training. You will be taught by a unique mix of qualified lawyers with a proven track record in practice and legal education. As an acknowledgement of our commitment to legal education, we were voted Legal Education Provider of the Year at the 2016 *Solicitors Journal Awards*.

Nottingham Law School has an excellent record of graduate employability. Our focus on practical skills and our dedicated careers and recruitment service ensures that you get the best possible start to your career. We have an award-winning pro bono scheme and our commitment to practical legal education is epitomised by the purpose-built Nottingham Law School legal advice centre. This centre provides a multitude of opportunities for students as well as access to justice for a variety of clients.

Graduate Diploma in Law (full time or distance learning) This conversion course is designed for any non-law graduate who intends to become a solicitor or barrister in the UK. The intensive course effectively covers the seven core subjects of an undergraduate law degree in one go. It is the stepping stone to the LPC or the BPTC and to a legal career thereafter.

Legal Practice Course (full time or part time) At Nottingham Law School we strive to provide you with the practical knowledge and insight that employers regard as essential. This is why we have enhanced our LPC so that the successful completion of all its elements will result in the award of a Masters degree. As well as providing you with an internationally recognised qualification, our LLM Legal Practice Course will provide enhanced insight into the legal profession. On the LLM part of the course you will have the opportunity to complete a project or dissertation, focusing on aspects of legal practice that interest you. You will also benefit from a series of lectures delivered by experts within the legal profession, a bridge to practice module and commercial awareness training.

Bar Professional Training Course (full time) Nottingham Law School designed its BPTC to develop a range of core practical skills, and to equip students to succeed in the fast-changing environment of practice at the Bar. We have enhanced our BPTC so that the successful completion of all its elements will result in the award of a Masters degree: LLM Bar Professional Training Course. Particular emphasis is placed on the skill of advocacy and Nottingham Law School is home to the UK's first centre for advocacy. The BPTC is taught entirely by qualified practitioners, and utilises the same integrated and interactive teaching methods as all of the school's other professional courses. Essentially, students learn by doing. Students are encouraged to realise, through practice and feedback, their full potential.

Other postgraduate courses We offer LLMs in a number of subject areas including international trade and commercial law; oil, gas and mining law; human rights law; intellectual property law; health law and ethics; corporate and insolvency law and sports law. We also provide research degrees, a professional doctorate in legal practice and intellectual property courses for practitioners.

Apply to

GDL (full time)
www.lawcabs.ac.uk

GDL distance learning
www.ntu.ac.uk/apply

LPC (full time)
www.lawcabs.ac.uk

LPC (part time)
www.ntu.ac.uk/apply

BPTC
www.barsas.com

Other postgraduate law courses
www.ntu.ac.uk/apply

Location
Nottingham

NOTTINGHAM LAW SCHOOL
NOTTINGHAM TRENT UNIVERSITY 🡇

Course providers

Institutions that offer the GDL
Birmingham City University
Bournemouth University
BPP Law School
Bristol, University of the West of England
Cardiff University
The City Law School
De Montfort University
University of East Anglia
University of Central Lancashire
The University of Law
Leeds Beckett University
London Metropolitan University
London South Bank University
Manchester Metropolitan University
Northumbria University
Nottingham Law School
Oxford Brookes University
University of Plymouth
Roehampton University
University of Sheffield
Staffordshire University and Worcester College of Technology at Worcester
University of Sussex
Swansea University
University of Westminster

Institutions that offer the LPC
Anglia Ruskin University
Birmingham City University
Bournemouth University
BPP Law School
Bristol, University of the West of England
Cardiff Law School
The City Law School
De Montfort University
University of Central Lancashire
The University of Law
Leeds Beckett University
Liverpool John Moores University
London Metropolitan University
Manchester Metropolitan University
Northumbria University
Nottingham Law School
University of Plymouth
University of Sheffield
University of South Wales
Staffordshire University
University of Sunderland
Swansea University
University of West London
University of Westminster
University of Wolverhampton

Institutions that offer the BPTC
BPP Law School
Bristol, University of the West of England
Cardiff Law School
The City Law School
The University of Law
Manchester Metropolitan University
University of Northumbria
Nottingham Law School

Solicitors

LEADERS ARE ~~BORN~~ MADE

We place a huge emphasis on providing the right support and training so you can truly fulfil your potential.

That's why, at Gowling WLG, you'll get the training and support you need to become a dynamic, well-rounded lawyer, and you'll work alongside inspirational colleagues who are at the top of their field. Best of all, you'll begin your career at the only law firm to appear in the Great Place to Work UK 2018 rankings.

Join us – to find out more and apply today go to
gowlingwlgcareers.co.uk

GRADUATE OPPORTUNITIES
An international law firm that's ambitious for your success

The Law Society and the Junior Lawyers Division

The Law Society

The Law Society is the independent professional body for solicitors in England and Wales. We are run by and for our members. Our role is to be the voice of solicitors, to drive excellence in the profession and to safeguard the rule of law.

On behalf of the profession, we influence the legislative and regulatory environment in the public interest. At home we promote the profession and the vital role legal services play in our economy. Around the word we promote England and Wales as a global legal centre, open new markets and defend human rights.

Our commitment is to put members at the heart of everything we do. Whether you are working in a high-street practice, a commercial, regional or City firm, an alternative business structure (ABS) or in-house for a private, public or charitable organisation, the Law Society exists for you.

We are committed to ensuring that you can make the most of opportunities and can respond to the challenges of a changing legal sector. Our aim is to deliver value for money for the public interest funding contribution that you make as part of your practising fee and when you choose to pay for additional products and services.

Supporting students and solicitors

We provide a range of services for students, trainees and newly qualified solicitors, including information and training. Our weekly *Law Society Gazette* includes news, commentary and features on different areas of law. Our website is a comprehensive and regularly updated source of information for the entire profession.

Every year we run over 400 national and regional conferences, workshops and seminars, including careers workshops for undergraduates and LPC students. Once qualified, members can subscribe to a range of networks. Benefits include exclusive access to training events, conferences and seminars, dedicated web areas and web-based forums, newsletters and alerts, practice toolkits and quarterly magazines.

As the sole national representative body for all solicitors in England and Wales, we are the voice of the profession, making sure that its members' views are heard by regulators, government and other decision makers. We campaign for better law, lobby and work with parliamentary members, and challenge the government where necessary.

Promoting equality and diversity

Our Diversity Access Scheme helps talented, committed people to overcome social, economic or personal barriers to becoming a solicitor. It funds LPC places at a number of teaching institutions and offers mentoring support and work placements.

Junior Lawyers Division

With approximately 70,000 members, the Junior Lawyers Division (JLD) is one of the largest communities within the Law Society. It represents, supports and provides services to junior lawyers at the start of their careers to help them develop, progress and diversify within the legal profession. Membership of the JLD, which is free and automatic, includes LPC students, LPC graduates such as those working as paralegals, trainee solicitors and solicitors up to five years' qualified.

A local presence

Local JLD groups exist across the country. They run events ranging from lectures to monthly meetings and social events and offer an opportunity to socialise with junior lawyers who work and live in the area. They can often be a lifeline for trainees who may be alone in their firms, as well as giving junior lawyers the chance to connect and build their professional networks.

Campaigning on key issues
The JLD ensures that members' views are heard and campaigns to bring about real change to further members' interests. JLD campaigns and lobbying activities over the years have covered issues such as the trainee minimum salary, work experience, cuts to legal aid, student funding and successfully lobbying the Solicitors Regulation Authority to amend their proposals for a centralised assessment.

Events
The JLD offers opportunities to attend national events and engage with support services. The main events include the following:
- Forums – one-day careers events, held around the country, focusing on issues that affect the membership, from how to get a training contract to practical skills and advice for junior lawyers in the work environment.
- Conference – an annual event, featuring interesting speakers and lively debate with the focus on taking control of your career.
- International weekend – once a year the JLD, the Young Barristers' Committee, the European Young Bar Association and the London Young Lawyers Group organise a two-day training conference that is attended by lawyers from around the world.
- Essay competition – a 2,000-word essay competition that gives the JLD's student, paralegal and trainee members the chance to compete for prize money, as well as honing their drafting skills on a subject of professional relevance.
- International networking – opportunities to meet and network with junior lawyers from other legal jurisdictions through membership of international organisations.

Advice and information
The JLD aims to be a source of information on everything you need to know about becoming a solicitor and the issues facing junior lawyers. Its website includes information about legal career paths, national and regional events, ongoing policy projects, webinars, initiatives involving junior lawyers and articles of interest to the junior profession. Its social media pages – on Twitter, Facebook and LinkedIn – provide updates on JLD activity and upcoming events.

Getting involved
The JLD is always looking for active participation; its committee has positions available each year, including a specific LPC student seat.

This information is provided by the Law Society. Learn more about the Law Society at www.lawsociety.org.uk. Learn more about the JLD and sign up for the JLD e-newsletter at www.lawsociety.org.uk/juniorlawyers, or contact them via email at juniorlawyers@ lawsociety.org.uk.

The Solicitors Regulation Authority

The Solicitors Regulation Authority (SRA) is the regulator of solicitors and law firms in England and Wales, protecting consumers and supporting the rule of law and the administration of justice. It does this by overseeing all education and training requirements necessary to practise as a solicitor, licensing individuals and firms to practise, setting the standards of the profession and regulating and enforcing compliance against these standards. Further information is available at www.sra.org.uk.

In order to practise, all would-be solicitors need to be admitted to the roll. Under current regulations, to be eligible to apply for admission you must have satisfactorily completed:
- the academic stage of training (ie, a qualifying law degree (QLD), the Graduate Diploma in Law (GDL) or the Common Professional Examination (CPE));
- the vocational stage of training which comprises:
  - the Legal Practice Course (LPC);
  - a period of recognised training (formerly referred to as 'training contract'); and
  - the Professional Skills Course (PSC).

Any part of the academic or vocational stages may be met by equivalent means (see www.sra.org.uk/students/resources/equivalent-means-information-pack.page).

This is known as the domestic route to qualification. Alternative routes may be available to those who have CILEx qualifications, or who have already qualified in another jurisdiction.

You must also satisfy the SRA that you are of the right character and suitability to be a solicitor. As part of this, you must undertake screening, which includes a standard disclosure from the Disclosure and Barring Service (DBS).

Regulatory reform
The SRA is transforming the way it regulates for the benefit of consumers and in the public interest.

The SRA will be changing its qualification requirements (see "Changes ahead" below). However, the following information sets out the current requirements for admission as a solicitor.

LPC
If you are planning on becoming a solicitor through the domestic route outlined above, you need to complete the LPC. Before enrolling on the LPC, you need to satisfy the provider that you have met the academic requirements for admission.

Period of recognised training
The period of recognised training is a period of supervised training with an SRA-registered training establishment (eg, a firm of solicitors, local authority or legal department within a commercial organisation). It usually lasts for two years, but can be completed over a longer period if working or studying part time.

The following criteria must be met during your period of recognised training:
- You will gain experience in at least three areas of English or Welsh law and develop your skills in contentious and non-contentious areas of practice. The SRA's Practice Skills Standards set out the extent and level of the experience that you will need to gain.
- You will need to keep a record of the work you have done and the skills you have gained.
- You will have informal performance reviews with your training principal or supervisor.
- You will have at least three formal appraisals over the period, at which you can discuss your development and progress.

You may also demonstrate that you have met the requirements of the period of recognised training through equivalent means (see SRA website, as above).

Admission to the roll
Approximately 10 weeks before the end of your training, the SRA will contact you to

complete a declaration agreeing to screening checks. This includes financial and identity checks plus a Standard Disclosure from the DBS. The fee for this is £42.

Eight weeks before the end of your training, you will be sent an application for admission. There are two admission dates each month and applications must be received at least 28 days before the date on which you wish to be admitted (see www.sra.org.uk/trainees/admission/admission.page).

Once admitted, solicitors are under a professional duty to make sure they can offer a proper standard of service to their clients. They must therefore make sure they stay up to date and are competent to practise in their particular field of work.

Changes ahead

In April 2017 the SRA announced that it would introduce a new national licensing exam for intending solicitors – the Solicitors Qualifying Examination (SQE). The target date for the introduction of the SQE is September 2020.

Once the SQE is introduced, the SRA will no longer require aspiring solicitors to take the QLD, GDL or LPC. Instead, candidates will be free to do the training they need to prepare themselves for the SQE.

The SQE will consist of two stages. Stage one will primarily test functioning legal knowledge; stage two will test practical legal skills. The SRA will not specify when the tests need to be taken, but it is likely many candidates will take SQE stage one at or shortly after they complete their law degree. The SRA anticipates that candidates will need to complete a substantial period of legal work experience in order to be able to pass stage two (the skills test).

There will continue to be a requirement for two years' work experience before admission. However, the SRA will recognise a wider range of legal work experience, not just formal training contracts, but also working as a paralegal or in a student law clinic, provided that the experience gives a candidate the opportunity to develop the competencies required for practice as a solicitor. These are set out in the Competence Statement for Solicitors, which the SRA published in 2015.

The SRA consulted on transitional arrangements in Autumn 2017. Anyone who has started a QLD or GDL before the SQE is introduced will have the choice about whether to qualify under the existing route to qualification, or to qualify under the SQE.

More information about the SQE can be found on the SRA's website at www.sra.org.uk/t4t.

Further information

This is a broad outline of what you need to do to start your career as a trainee solicitor. If you need more details, please visit www.sra.org.uk/students and www.sra.org.uk/trainees, where comprehensive student and trainee sections include the training regulations in full, a list of training firms and organisations, institutions that provide academic and vocational courses, and more. If you need to talk to someone, call the SRA's contact centre on 0370 606 2555 or email contactcentre@sra.org.uk.

The SRA works closely with the Junior Lawyers Division (JLD) throughout the year in hosting events for students and young lawyers, such as webinars, to help address some of the issues they face. For example, it has held sessions with JLD members to discuss the SQE. For more on the JLD, see www.lawsociety.org.uk/juniorlawyers or page 143.

This information is supplied by the SRA.

The Chartered Institute of Legal Executives

The Chartered Institute of Legal Executives (CILEx) is the professional association representing around 20,000 qualified chartered legal executive lawyers, paralegals and other legal practitioners. Changes in legislation mean that chartered legal executive lawyers are increasingly on a level playing field with solicitors or barristers, as they can now become judges, coroners, advocates and partners in law firms.

CILEx is recognised as one of the three professional bodies of the legal profession, alongside the Bar Council (see page 472) and the Law Society (see page 143). The role of a chartered legal executive lawyer is now so similar to that of a solicitor that the average client is unlikely to be able to distinguish between them. In fact, many chartered legal executives supervise solicitors. The difference is that a chartered legal executive is a qualified lawyer who is trained to specialise as an expert in one or two particular areas of the law, whereas solicitors have a broader, more general legal training.

There are alternative academic routes to becoming a chartered legal executive lawyer. If you don't have a law degree, you will need to take the traditional CILEx route, which is comprised of the level 3 CILEx qualification (set at A-level standard) and the level 6 CILEx qualification (studied to the same standard as an honours degree). This full CILEx route costs on average around £9,500, depending on where and how you choose to study. This will typically take four years to complete part time and can be completed alongside full-time working. Timescales can be flexible and study can be tailored according to your personal and professional needs.

If you already have a qualifying law degree, irrespective of when this was achieved, CILEx offers a cost-effective alternative to the LPC or BPTC through its graduate fast-track diploma, which usually takes around a year to complete part time and costs approximately £3,250.

Regardless of whether you follow the traditional CILEx route or the graduate fast-track diploma pathway, you will need to complete a three-year period of qualifying employment and submit a portfolio of evidence called work-based learning. Work completed as a paralegal, while studying, may be used towards part of this requirement; a minimum of one year of your qualifying employment needs to fall after you've completed your CILEx academic qualification. The last two years of your qualifying employment must be continuous.

If you already hold an LPC or BPTC, you will be exempt from all CILEx qualifications and can immediately apply to become a graduate member of CILEx and use the designatory letters 'GCILEx'. You will still need to complete the qualifying employment requirement. On successful completion of the academic stage and the qualifying employment stage of training, you will become a fellow of the chartered institute and have the right to call yourself a chartered legal executive lawyer.

CILEx has a network of over 80 accredited study centres in England and Wales that are approved to deliver CILEx courses and quality assured to CILEx standards. CILEx examinations take place twice a year, in January and June, and may be taken at separate examination sittings to suit your plans and study needs. Distance learning is offered through specialist study centres, including at CILEx Law School.

Training to be a solicitor

A career as a chartered legal executive lawyer is a worthwhile, rewarding and fulfilling career in its own right, but CILEx does recognise that there are those who have more traditional ambitions. CILEx qualifications can be used to count towards qualifying as a solicitor.

As a fellow of the Institute, you may be exempt from the Solicitors Regulation Authority (SRA) training contract. It is important that you contact the SRA to get full details, as this exemption is wholly at its discretion.

Salaries

Salaries will vary according to your location and legal specialism. Starting salaries are usually up to £20,000 per year while qualifying. Many trainee CILEx members report that they are on higher salaries than the trainee solicitors they work alongside. After completion of your CILEx qualifications, you can expect to earn on average up to £26,500.

Once fully qualified (having completed three years of qualifying work experience), you can expect to earn on average up to £45,500; if you work in a big city or become a partner in a firm, you can earn much more (salaries of over £100,000 have been stated).

CILEx qualifications are highly valued by employers and, as such, recent surveys have found that around 67% of CILEx students have their membership fees paid for by their employers.

What chartered legal executive lawyers do

Professional responsibilities increase with experience. Fully qualified and experienced chartered legal executives are able to undertake many of the legal activities that solicitors do and often supervise solicitors and other legal staff. They will have their own clients and represent them in court. Although chartered legal executives can be involved in many areas of law, the most common areas of specialism are:

- conveyancing – the legal side of buying and selling property;
- family – advising on divorce and matters

affecting children;
- crime – defending and prosecuting people accused of crimes;
- company and business law – advising on legislation that affects clients' businesses such as tax, contract and employment law;
- litigation – advising clients who are in dispute with someone else;
- probate – dealing with wills, trusts and inheritance tax; and
- personal injury – handling accident claims.

All CILEx members are independently regulated and must adhere to a code of conduct. They are required to continue training throughout their careers in order to keep abreast of the latest developments in the law.

The move to allow CILEx fellows to apply for judicial positions has seen the appointment of the first chartered legal executive judges. Additionally, there is a growing number of chartered legal executives acquiring their own advocacy rights in higher courts. Many are partners in legal practices.

Where chartered legal executives work

Chartered legal executives are found in over 60% of *The Lawyer's* list of top 200 UK law firms, but it is not just legal firms that employ them. Such lawyers fill key legal roles in a wide variety of government bodies, local authorities, charities and business organisations, including Caterpillar, HSBC, Admiral Insurance, Disney Corporation, UK Border Agency, Ministry of Defence, Crown Prosecution Service, NHS, county councils, RSPCA and The Peabody Trust.

Partnership is the aspiration of most solicitors in private practice and that ambition is also shared by chartered legal executives. The legal market has seen many changes since the Legal Services Act 2007, which formally recognised chartered legal executives as fully fledged lawyers and enabled them to become partners in law firms.

The future

The quality of chartered legal executives as specialist lawyers is increasingly being recognised. Since early 2015 CILEx has been able to grant its members additional rights to conduct litigation in civil, criminal and family matters, and provide probate and conveyancing services, as well as immigration advice, independently of solicitors.

Combined, these will essentially give chartered legal executives all the rights they need to practise on their own without being in partnership with a solicitor or under supervision.

If you are looking for an affordable and flexible career in law, CILEx is worth serious consideration.

Sharon Bruty is head of communications at CILEx. For all the latest information, visit www.cilex.org.uk. For details on becoming a chartered legal executive, visit www.cilexcareers.org.uk.

Becoming a solicitor

Solicitors provide legal advice and representation. They work directly with their clients and are usually the first point of contact for anyone seeking legal advice. In general practice, solicitors may be called on to advise on issues ranging from crime, personal injury, contracts and wills to buying houses and taking over a business.

One important thing to note: in 2017 the Solicitors Regulation Authority (SRA) confirmed that it would be introducing in 2020 its Solicitors Qualifying Examination (SQE), which all prospective solicitors will have to pass in order to qualify. The SQE will bring about fundamental changes to the way that would-be solicitors are educated and trained, but for now, the information below remains current. To learn more about what the SQE will mean, read the SRA chapter on p145 or go to www.sra.org.uk/home/hot-topics/Solicitors-Qualifying-Examination.

Training contract/period of recognised training

The traditional training contract – or 'period of recognised training', as it is now termed by the SRA – is a two-year employment contract with a law firm or other approved organisation, akin to an apprenticeship. The two years provide an opportunity for trainees to put into practice all the knowledge and skills they have acquired so far, with the firm assessing the trainee's suitability for retention upon completion of the training period. Trainees may also study elective LPC modules if they choose to begin the training contract upon completion of the initial core LPC modules.

Trainee solicitors are required to meet the SRA's competence statement (released in 2015 and forming the basis of the proposed SQE) and most training contracts are based on the following format.

Structure

The training contract format varies between firms. Most (although not all) firms operate a 'seat' system, in which trainees spend six months in four different departments. This gives trainees exposure to different practice areas. As far as possible, firms will try to accommodate the individual wishes of trainees in terms of seats, although they have to consider the overall needs of the firm as. In some firms, trainees may also have the opportunity to spend a seat in an overseas office or on secondment to a client.

Training contracts may be less structured in smaller and high-street firms than those with the larger commercial firms – an approach that might appeal to those who fear a 'conveyor-belt' training mentality in the City firms. As many small firms cannot offer detailed training over a wide spread of specialisations, trainees are sometimes permitted to undertake consortium training, fulfilling different training seats in different firms.

Content

What trainees learn during the training contract will depend on the type of firm and its solicitors. Clearly, the practice areas you learn about as a solicitor working at a commercial firm in the City are going to differ from those learnt by your peers at regional high-street firms. The smaller firms that mainly concentrate on a single area of work will obviously provide the most limited experience, but conversely can offer the most responsibility.

Assessment and support

Trainee solicitors are assessed continuously throughout their training contract, a fact from which you should take comfort – it means that problems are likely to be nipped in the bud, not left to snowball.

Almost without exception, firms have a three and six-monthly appraisal for each training contract seat. In this way trainees get good feedback about their performance both during and after a seat, and get to have their say about anything they're not 100% happy with. Nobody will expect you to know everything from day one of your training contract; indeed, some firms dedicate the first few weeks to induction lectures and presentations to get you up to speed with the firm, its clients and its different practice areas. Most of your work will involve drafting, writing and researching, with everything being checked by a qualified solicitor and your supervision overseen by a partner (many trainees share an office with their supervisor during their seats).

Other training opportunities exist with the Crown Prosecution Service and within the government, and with some companies outside private practice in commerce and industry (see "Alternative careers").

LPC electives

Trainees who have completed only Stage One (the core modules) of the LPC will also need to complete Stage Two (the elective modules) during their training contract. Some postgraduate course providers now offer different ways of doing this, from flexible tutor time (weekends and evening classes) to online tutorials.

Equivalent means

The changes in 2014 to the SRA regulations allowed for qualification via "equivalent means", which in practice means that in some circumstances it may be possible to qualify as a solicitor without having done a training contract. Instead, the individual is required to prove that he or she has the necessary skills and training to become a solicitor by evidencing

his or her achievements while working in other, non-solicitor legal roles – most obviously as a paralegal. Again, this is in its infancy and is the exception rather than the rule, but that may change when the SQE is introduced.

Professional Skills Course

You cannot qualify as a solicitor without passing the Professional Skills Course (PSC). This is a modular course which aims to ensure that you have reached the appropriate level of skills and knowledge during the LPC and the training contract. Firms must pay for their trainees to attend the PSC. The three core modules are:
- financial and business skills;
- advocacy and communication skills; and
- client care and professional standards.

There is a written exam for the financial and business skills module, but no formal assessment of the others. You will also need to complete 24 hours' worth of elective modules. If it is taken full time, the PSC will last up to 12 days. However, each module can be taken individually. Many of the larger firms run the PSC in house as part of their ongoing training programmes.

Non-graduates

Non-graduates can qualify as a solicitor by way of the Chartered Institute of Legal Executives (CILEx), which involves completing several years' qualifying employment (usually in a law firm), passing specific CILEx exams to qualify first as a member, then as a fellow, and then applying to the SRA to be considered as exempt from various of its qualification requirements. For more on CILEx, see "Alternative careers" and the CILEx chapter on page 147.

Reality check: Remember that although most firms currently use the four-seat training contract model described here, this could change over the coming years – a few also run training on a non-rotational basis. A smaller number of firms also choose to operate a six-seat training system, exposing trainees to a wider variety of practice areas.

Career timetable: solicitors

Before we launch into this chapter, you need to be alert to the fact that in April 2017 the Solicitors Regulation Authority (SRA) confirmed that it would be going ahead with its new 'super exam', which all prospective solicitors will have to pass in order to qualify. The Solicitors Qualifying Examination (SQE) is to be introduced in 2020, although the SRA has warned this could be delayed; for now, all students and trainee solicitors will still be able to qualify by the current route, while those who commence training just before or at the point at which the SQE is introduced will also be able to continue via the traditional route. All those who begin legal education and training once the SQE has been introduced will have to train under the new system and pass the SQE.

This means that as things stand, the information below is correct, but fundamental change is not far away. For more on the SQE and what it requires, read the SRA chapter on p145 and keep alert to things by going to the SRA's website, www.sra.org.uk/home/hot-topics/Solicitors-Qualifying-Examination.

First-year law and second-year non-law students

What does it mean to be a solicitor? Am I cut out for the work? Why do I want to be a solicitor rather than a barrister? Do I want to practise in London or the regions? In which practice area? These are the questions to be asking around this time. Answers can be gleaned by delving into the law section of your university careers centre, attending your university's law fair (usually held in October/November) and undergoing a healthy dose of self-analysis.

You should try to arrange some summer work experience to begin checking out the different types of firm. In addition to informal work experience, some of the bigger firms now run formal work placement schemes specifically aimed at first-year law students,

so keep an eye out for these. Above all, work at achieving and maintaining good grades – when it comes to applying for work placement schemes and training contracts, firms will definitely want to know your first and second-year grades.

Second-year law and final-year non-law students

Autumn term, winter holidays and spring term

Decide whether you genuinely believe that law is a career which will suit your character and skills through further research into the profession. Go to the careers advice service and discuss the profession generally with a careers adviser. Attend law firm presentations on campus and at firms' offices, and research and apply for work placement schemes for your summer vacation – 31 January is a significant deadline. It's a good idea to do a few schemes in order to get a feel for the range and types of practice available to you. Note that some firms also offer winter and spring holiday work schemes.

Worth noting is that as of July 2015, the Voluntary Code of Practice for the Recruitment of Trainee Solicitors (which most firms adhere to) was amended to "reflect modern practices". The most significant change is that firms may now (i) set their deadlines for training contract applications at any point, although not before candidates' penultimate year of undergraduate study, and (ii) make training contract offers at any point during candidates' penultimate year of undergraduate study. In essence, this means that the traditional deadline of 31 July may change, as more firms recruit and offer earlier. However, for now a very large number of firms still place their application deadlines on 31 July.

As mentioned above, virtually all university law career fairs take place in October/

November. They represent your best chance to meet firms face to face. It is sensible to have done some preliminary research so that you can ask intelligent questions. Many firms also organise on-campus presentations during these two terms.

Look into the funding possibilities for your postgraduate legal training (eg, local education authority grants) and check closing dates for applications.

Non-law degree students will need to apply for a place on the conversion course, known as the Graduate Diploma in Law (GDL). If you intend to study full time, you should apply through the Central Applications Board (www.lawcabs.ac.uk) from September onwards in your final year at university. There is no longer a closing date for applications; rather, applications are dealt with as they are submitted and institutions are notified weekly of new submissions. Applications for part-time courses must be made directly to the provider.

Spring holidays
Apply for further work placements for the summer vacation. Thoroughly research the applications procedure for training contracts, especially those at firms you are interested in. By now, you should be beginning to shortlist the firms to which you want to apply.

Summer holidays
Most major law firms have training contract application deadlines during this period, although note the point above in relation to the revised code of conduct; the major deadline of 31 July could change as more firms set their own deadlines and choose to recruit earlier. Gain some further work experience, either on a formal work placement scheme or through other means. You may also be interviewed for training contracts during this period.

Final-year law and GDL students
Autumn term
You must also apply for a place on the Legal Practice Course (LPC) through the Central Applications Board from September onwards in your final year at university. As described above, the application system has changed so that there is no longer a closing date for applications; rather, applications are dealt with as they are submitted and institutions are notified weekly of new submissions. Applications for part-time courses must be made directly to the provider.

Spring term
The SRA runs character and suitability checks on students wishing to train as solicitors, and requires people to disclose any information related to this. If you do have such issues (eg, a police caution), you need to disclose these at the earliest opportunity – and at least six months before you would anticipate starting a training contract. Undergoing a character and suitability check before starting the LPC costs £100.

Summer term
If you have not succeeded in obtaining a training contract, keep applying! You might want to consider delaying starting the LPC if you are yet to find a training contract, given the competitiveness of the job market; time spent gaining experience and focusing on applications should give you a better chance of success.

LPC
If you have yet to find a training contract, keep making further applications throughout your LPC year until you get one. Attend as many law fairs as possible and check for adverts in the *Law Society Gazette* and on www.LawCareers.Net.

The SRA requires providers to split the LPC in half, separating the compulsory Stage One subjects from the elective Stage Two subjects, which can then be completed during the training contract. However, the one-year option remains the most popular way of doing the course.

Training contract/period of recognised training

The traditional training contract – or 'period of recognised training', as it is now termed by the SRA – is a two-year employment contract with a law firm or other approved organisation, akin to an apprenticeship. In July 2014 the SRA implemented a number of changes to its training regulations, including a move to a more outcomes-focused approach which allows firms greater freedom to design the structures of their own training contracts. However, trainee solicitors are still required to meet the SRA's competence statement (released in March 2015 and forming the basis of the proposed SQE) and most training contracts are still based on the following format.

Year one

Ensure that your training contract has been registered with the SRA (your firm will usually do this for you). Most firms operate a series of departmental rotations (usually four seats in separate departments, each lasting six months). On-the-job training is provided throughout and is supplemented by courses and lectures during the two-year training period. If you've so far only completed Stage One of your LPC, you'll need to complete Stage Two during your training contract.

Year two

Around the middle of your second year, most firms will run through their post-training job offer process and you will know whether you are going to be offered a position at the end of your training – hopefully in your preferred department. Approximately 12 weeks before your training contract is due to end, the SRA will send you the necessary forms so that you can apply to be formally admitted to the roll of solicitors. Provided that all necessary training conditions have been satisfied, you will be admitted to the roll. Congratulations – you are a solicitor!

Types of law firm

There are many different kinds of law firm, and where you train has a significant influence on your career, as the style, size and clientele of each will vary. Consider the following broad categories to establish which type of law firm might best match your career goals and working style.

International firms

These are mainly located in the City of London. For the UK-born 'Anglo' firms, London is the hub of their international operations, which can range from just a couple of strategically located offices to a sprawling global network – Clifford Chance, for example, has 33 in 25 countries. Among these Anglo firms are some of the world's legal giants, reflecting the fact that English law governs complex, big-ticket transactions across the globe, and is the law of choice for high-value disputes. The appeal of English law is not the only asset for UK firms: they also reap dividends from the ubiquity of the English language, the City's status as a key financial centre and the convenience of European time zones for coordinating cross-border deals.

A firm's footprint determines the availability of overseas secondments for trainees, and in the current economic climate these opportunities are more important than ever. Wherever you are based, expect to work mostly on multi-jurisdictional matters for either UK or foreign-based corporate clients. As well as providing a comprehensive commercial offering, each will have its own strong suits; for example, Allen & Overy is dominant in all things finance-related, while Clyde & Co excels in disputes. It's important to understand the key practice areas and client sectors of the firms you apply to.

People sometimes refer to the 'magic circle' and 'silver circle'. These expressions have historical resonance, but no real significance. The magic circle comprises Allen & Overy, Clifford Chance, Freshfields Bruckhaus Deringer, Linklaters and Slaughter and May. The so-called silver circle firms are not quite as big as their magic circle peers, although one or two are equally profitable.

US firms in London used to be viewed as a separate category, having offered English law advice only since the mid-1990s. However, there are now around 75 US-born firms in the United Kingdom and around a dozen more hybrid Anglo-US firms. Approximately 40 run training schemes, some with 30-plus trainees and others just a handful. Yet small in London need not equate to small globally: Arnold & Porter Kaye Scholer LLP, for example, employs some 1,000 lawyers across 14 global offices, but takes on just two UK trainees each year.

Staff work long hours in return for top dollar. If you join a big London office, you'll have resources, amenities and peers aplenty, and probably a relatively bureaucratic working environment. While potential seat options will be abundant, competition for the most popular ones will be stiff and you will have to spend much of your time in core departments.

For a profile of a solicitor at an international firm, see Farmida Bi of Norton Rose Fulbright in the "Islamic finance" chapter, p194.

UK-focused City firms

Exclusively UK-based firms typically offer a broad commercial training, emphasising one or two specialist areas; some will also have a private client practice, reflecting longstanding relationships with wealthy individuals and trusts. Bristows, for example, is a market leader in IP law; meanwhile, Boodle Hatfield LLP has a real estate focus, resulting from its connection to vast landowner The Grosvenor Estate. Most domestic firms cultivate relationships with overseas lawyers and this attracts some multi-jurisdictional work. If you think you would be happiest working in a smaller, less frenetic environment, then there are plenty of firms to choose from. Starting salaries are typically in the high £20,000s to low £30,000s.

For a profile of a solicitor at a UK City firm, see Nadine Bleach of Bristows in the "Intellectual property" chapter, p192.

National/regional firms

Beyond London, the most active cities are Manchester, Birmingham, Leeds, Bristol, Liverpool, Cardiff, Newcastle and Nottingham. National firms have offices in several cities (and perhaps also Scotland), whereas a 'regional' firm might limit itself to say, the north or the southwest, perhaps with an additional office in London. A regional firm could have just one office or several. Clients are mostly UK public and private companies, local and public authorities, and possibly also international businesses with UK interests. As a rule of thumb, smaller firms are also likely to prioritise private client work.

Expect to spend your training contract in a single region, potentially visiting different offices. Salaries vary by location, with Birmingham, Manchester and Bristol faring relatively well (low £20,000s to low £30,000s) compared to, say, Wales or Kent (from around £16,500 to mid £20,000s). Regional trainees typically work more manageable hours than their City counterparts; however, there is a strong emphasis on gaining practical experience and client exposure. Available seat options will depend on the firm's business model, so do your research. For a profile of a solicitor at a national/regional firm, see Grace Malone of Burges Salmon in the "Employment" chapter, p178.

General practice, legal aid and advice centres

Law on the high street is undergoing a revolution as a result of the Legal Services Act 2007. Some predict that thousands of tiny partnerships and sole practitioners will give way to large franchises (eg, QualitySolicitors) and alternative business structures. Your clients will be ordinary people with a house to buy, a spouse to divorce, an ex-employer to sue, a will to write or an injury to be compensated for. Some will be entrepreneurs in need of a steer through an exceptional phase of their business plan.

It's been a torrid decade for lawyers assisting publicly funded clients and opportunities for new trainees are fewer than ever. Legal aid has become unprofitable – so much so that many practitioners in the field must bolster their income from privately paying clients, while the government has plans to cut legal aid even further. Even within law centres and other advice bureaux, priorities and clients must be selected carefully. This kind of work is only for those truly committed to universal access to justice. You will encounter abusive neighbours, rogue landlords, recidivist teens, individuals struggling to cope with disability or debt, and endless need in your local community.

For an example of a solicitor at a general practice firm, see Adam Cooper of Blake Morgan LLP in the "Family" chapter, p184. And for an example of a solicitor working in the legal aid sector, see Susie Labinjoh of Hodge Jones & Allen in the "Human Rights" chapter, p186.

Reality check: In 2014 the minimum trainee salary was abolished and firms are now entitled to pay trainees the national minimum wage. While many – particularly in the commercial sector – will continue to pay their trainees well above that, it is likely that some increasingly squeezed high street and criminal firms will make use of the rule change.

Solicitor practice areas

Banking

Banking and finance is a global industry involving a wide variety of financial products, ranging from simple bank loans to companies to highly structured financing arrangements across multiple jurisdictions. The rise of internationalisation and the development of increasingly sophisticated financing structures mean that modern banking law and practice is becoming ever more complex. In the post-financial crisis era, banking and finance lawyers find themselves at the forefront of the evolution and recovery of the industry.

As part of Sarah Greenwood's four-year law degree, she spent a placement year as a paralegal in the real estate team at Mills & Reeve, at the end of which she applied for – and gained – a training contract. She rejoined the firm after completing her LPC in 2010.

Now a senior associate, Sarah looks back at the choice between life as a solicitor versus a career at the Bar: "I'd enjoyed mooting at university and had done some mini-pupillages, so it wasn't out of the question. However, having had the chance to be a paralegal for a year, I realised that the life of a solicitor was for me. I like the structure and routine of working as a solicitor in a law firm and understand a barrister's career has a bit less of that. I also enjoy working as part of a team, with the high levels of client exposure and different types of work that you get as a commercial solicitor."

Real work

The banking team at Mills & Reeve enjoys an excellent reputation for its expertise in real estate finance (Sarah's specialism), corporate finance and asset-based lending, among others. "We employ a different model to most other firms, so that in real estate finance, for example, we carry out both the due diligence and the financing in team, offering a very joined-up approach to clients," she explains. "Clients appreciate being able to speak to just one person on all aspects of a deal. It

also means that our work is extremely varied – I might be conducting due diligence on a high-value investment asset one day, going on a site visit the next, and negotiating and drafting finance documents the next."

She goes on to extol the virtues of this approach: "I enjoy helping clients, be they lenders or borrowers, to find a solution to commercial problems and to get the deal done. If we understand both the property and the finance, it makes it far easier for us to join the dots between the two and enables us to give commercial and practical advice that moves things along. Firms have to be able set themselves apart and offer something new to clients, including acting as trusted business advisers and finding innovative ways to do things." Sarah is one of the firm's 'innovation champions', helping to drive and explore innovative ways of working and encouraging innovation throughout the firm, which she says is "a great addition to the legal work that I do".

Currently working on a cross-jurisdiction corporate acquisition of a property-owning company, Sarah explains some of the mechanics behind such a deal: "We are acting for the borrower, who is also the buyer. There are a lot of moving parts; obviously, you're always dealing with deadlines in this job, but in this instance they are very specific and set in stone. I have to keep on top of these and make sure that all the relevant third parties are lined up to deliver on time to ensure we can secure funding and ultimately achieve completion of the acquisition for the client."

She recalls a similar deal for one for the firm's key clients a couple of years ago: "It was a complicated corporate acquisition involving a number of different jurisdictions. As a result of a very tight timetable, everything had to be completed by midnight on a particular date just before Christmas. There was a massive flurry of activity with more lawyers involved than I could count, but we completed at

For more firms that work in this practice area, please use the "Training contract regional indexes" starting on p211.

Name: **Sarah Greenwood**
Firm: **Mills & Reeve LLP**
Location: **Cambridge**
University: **Nottingham Trent University**
Undergraduate degree: **Law**

11:57pm, so all the hard work was worth it and everyone was extremely happy."

The chance to meet and interact with a wide variety of clients and colleagues as part of her daily working life is one of the most pleasing aspects of the job. "We're a large firm, with 1,000 people based across six offices, and we often work cross-office, especially if it is a large property portfolio-based transaction," she describes. "For example, we recently worked on a deal that involved over 100 different properties, so we involved a large cross-office team to deliver the transaction for the client."

As is usual in the legal profession, the fact that the job is far from nine-to-five means that sometimes commitments outside work suffer as a result: "But I work with great people and for great clients, and am passionate about the work itself, so although the hours can sometimes be long, it would only be a hardship if I wasn't enjoying it!"

Banking on Legal Tech
Sarah's view is that one of the biggest developments to hit the profession is artificial intelligence (AI) – with junior lawyers being the most deeply affected by its arrival. "The programmes that I've seen replace some work historically undertaken by junior lawyers, doing it much more quickly," she reflects. "Although there is a way to go, especially with accuracy issues, it's moving in the right direction and will really help to speed up transactions for clients. For example, if you have a portfolio acquisition financing and you want to establish if the seller has been using the same form of lease consistently across the portfolio AI can run those sorts of queries quickly, saving hundreds of person-hours. It also frees lawyers up to do more interesting work that actually requires human intervention."

However, there is a flipside to this tech innovation: "Junior lawyers will lose the opportunity to perform certain tasks where often you spot things and learn by asking questions as you go along. It's all about how to fill that knowledge gap and how to help lawyers coming up through the ranks adapt. We just have to find a new way to give those learning opportunities to juniors as AI takes hold."

Skills to get ahead
Perhaps no surprise, Sarah's view is that as for any transactional lawyer, being organised is key: "Developing your project management skills is essential – there are often so many individual elements and it's your job to ensure that everything lines up and is in hand. If this is the type of work you're keen on, then those skills are essential. You also need an eye for detail and an ability to be commercial – finding solutions that work for all parties and that get the deal done are essential."

On that point, being commercially minded and putting yourself in the shoes of your client is also a key skill: "Clients are looking for lawyers who can explain not only the legal position, but also the commercial risks and benefits. They're not interested in the academic elements of the law. Commerciality is about looking at the wider picture and realising why a client wants to do a deal; if something is particularly important to them, they might be prepared to take a view on what you identify as a key legal issue."

More generally, when thinking about where you might want your career to go, Sarah suggests being alert to what you enjoy doing and where your interests lie – "you are far better working in something that you are passionate about" – and taking some ownership of its direction: "Don't expect others to do it for you; if you want to get involved with things, ask. It's your career and it will be what you make it."

Capital markets

'Capital markets' is the term used for financial markets where debt or equity securities are traded. Capital markets lawyers work primarily with transactions involving the issue of debt or equity securities either to the public or to a group of investors. Capital markets practice is closely connected to derivatives and financial regulation. Capital markets lawyers conduct due diligence review on the issuer of the securities, draft the prospectus and other disclosure documents describing the issuer and its securities to the potential investors, negotiate agreements between the issuer and its advisers and navigate the transaction through regulatory hurdles. London's pivotal position in the global debt and equity markets makes this a significant element of the City's legal activity.

Choosing a career is a long-term commitment, so it is important to think about whether you will continue to enjoy doing something years down the line – a consideration that was key in Macfarlanes partner Harry Coghill's decision to become a solicitor. "I considered becoming a barrister when I was starting out, but I wanted to be part of a team and to be doing transactions," he explains.

Following a modern languages degree at Oxford and a law conversion, Harry trained as a solicitor at Slaughter and May, before making the move to Macfarlanes in 2011. As corporate lawyers, he and his team have "a broad practice which includes a mix of both private and public M&A, private equity and equity capital markets. I personally focus on the private M&A and public company sides," he elaborates.

City finance
Equity capital markets work, Harry explains, is about "advising clients on the different methods of raising equity finance and the regulatory framework around those methods. That involves drafting documents, but also management of the process. Equity capital markets deals can be large and complex because there are often a lot of advisers involved, so some types of transaction are six months in the making. On the regulatory side, we liaise with the UK Listing Authority, the regulator that reviews the transaction documents that we draft."

Mastering both the granular detail and the wide scope of these transactions takes time, so while trainees learn the ropes, at partner level the role is more centred around management. "A transaction will likely involve trainees verifying and drafting ancillary documents and associates being responsible for drafting the prospectus," Harry explains. "Being at partner level means I now spend more time giving advice and managing the team."

> ❝ Building client relationships is part of the fun of the job and the clients with whom I have the best relationships are those who end up calling me about all sorts of different things – not just corporate law, but about their wider businesses ❞

The scale of finance in this practice area naturally means that transactions often involve household names. "The biggest highlight of my career so far is probably the landmark Verizon-Vodafone transaction in 2014," he recalls. "It involved issuing $60 billion of shares and listing them on the London Stock Exchange – I don't think I'll be doing that very often!"

For more firms that work in this practice area, please use the "Training contract regional indexes" starting on p211.

Name: **Harry Coghill**
Firm: **Macfarlanes LLP**
Location: **London**
University: **University of Oxford**
Degree: **Modern languages – German and Italian**

However, the real satisfaction of the job for Harry is on a more personal scale. "I enjoy being an adviser to our clients and that my judgment is valued," he confides. "Building client relationships is part of the fun of the job and the clients with whom I have the best relationships are those who end up calling me about all sorts of different things – not just corporate law, but about their wider businesses."

And what about the job does he like least? "Not being in control of my own destiny. As a corporate lawyer your life can turn on a sixpence – that gets better as you become more senior because you can manage teams and clients more, but certainly when you start out you have to be prepared to be very flexible with your plans."

Hot topics: Brexit, corporate governance and AI
Harry is – understandably – reluctant to speculate about what form Brexit will take and how it will affect lawyers in this area, but notes an interesting trend: "In 2018 a lot of the firms listing are financial services firms, accounting for just over half of the total proceeds raised on the London stock market, which is a positive indicator for the future of London as a financial centre."

An issue that aspiring trainees should certainly read up on, however, is "the interesting debate going on regarding the standards of corporate governance on the London stock market, particularly the recent changes to the rules to accommodate sovereign wealth funds owning large chunks of listed companies, which arguably have one eye on attracting Saudi Aramco to listing on the London stock market when it comes to market."

Looking at the wider solicitors' profession, Harry identifies artificial intelligence (AI) as a key issue that will affect lawyers over the next few years and beyond. "At trainee level, it will

be important to ensure that trainees are still able to do some of the work – such as due diligence – which has traditionally been one of the ways of learning the job, but which AI might be able to do more efficiently in the future," he observes.

The value of experience
Legal work experience is crucial for candidates aiming to join a City firm to work on these kinds of large-scale corporate transaction. To that end, Harry recommends applying for vacation schemes: "Vacation schemes are a great way to gain experience and it is important to gain as much as you can. The experience will improve your CV, but vacation schemes are also a major part of the training contract recruitment process at many firms in the City."

Finally, Harry shares some valuable advice that he was given as an associate: "Someone once told me that to be a good solicitor you need to be the 'three As' – able, available and affable. That means being bright and knowing the law, being flexible and able to put the client first – we are in a competitive world where clients expect to be able to get hold of you and for you to enthusiastically embrace their issues – and being able to get on with the client on a personal level and build a relationship with them." If you can do all that, this could well be the career for you.

Commercial

Commercial lawyers focus on trade and work on a wide range of commercial agreements dealing with the supply, manufacture and distribution of goods and services, agency agreements and franchising deals, as well as identifying and establishing the best routes to market. Recently, there has been increased focus on ecommerce, online sales and software agreements. The work involves advising clients on the best trade arrangements, drafting, negotiating and signing off contracts, assisting with the day-to-day running of commercial business and advising on new products. Commercial law is often a key component in other projects and touches many areas of law, making it a highly varied legal arena.

At school Charlotte Wright discovered her love for advocacy and debating, so much so that she began to picture a career as a barrister. However, she tells us that "as a commercial lawyer, you are a draftsman", so it was Charlotte's love for English which has proved to be her greatest career ally.

Charlotte studied law at Durham University and graduated in 2010. Once out of university she worked for four months at a family law firm in Wakefield, but it was not right for her. It was during her time as a paralegal in the commercial team's head office at Asda House in Leeds that Charlotte had her first taste of commercial law and found the fit that suited her best. During that time, Charlotte was involved in a lot of exciting work; implementing training, dealing with competition and information requests and assisting with contract management for big suppliers.

Variety is the spice of life

Her Walker Morris training contract enabled Charlotte to experience numerous areas of law. She touched on property development, corporate, employment, banking and litigation. The fast-paced world of litigation was exhilarating, but Charlotte explains that while the "adrenaline rush" was fun, the lifestyle "wasn't for me". A secondment back to Asda and a further secondment to Hargreaves brought the "variety and range" of an in-house workload, making the decision of where to qualify much easier: "Even though I hadn't sat in the commercial department at Walker Morris at that time, I knew from my experience during my secondments that it was what I wanted to do."

It is the variety that Charlotte loves the most. The "big deals come three or four times a year – the time you put in, the build-up; that's a huge accomplishment". In between the big deals there is the "bread and butter" work, the day-to-day trading advice, contracts and terms of sale and building relationships: "It's nice sometimes to get a piece of work and to sit down and lock yourself away, or work from home and get your head down and get quite creative to make the document the best you can make it."

You work for your clients

Charlotte's days involve advising on, drafting and negotiating a wide spectrum of commercial agreements. She interacts with her clients through conference calls and meetings, as well as occasional visits to other cities. International clients are not always available to meet face to face, but video-calling and screen sharing are just a click away.

Charlotte explains that Walker Morris is supportive of business development and encourages building client relationships: "You don't always think about it, but law is all people based, you work for your clients, so building those relationships is important".

She likes organising activities and explains that there is ample opportunity for social events. "Historically, it was quite male dominated", all "golf days" and brandy, but things are much more open now: "If you have a good idea, you have the freedom to roll with

For more firms that work in this practice area, please use the "Training contract regional indexes" starting on p211.

Name: **Charlotte Wright**
Firm: **Walker Morris LLP**
Location: **Leeds**
University: **University of Durham**
Undergraduate degree: **Law**

it – if you are happy to get involved with the planning then there is nothing to stop you from doing that."

Milestones

Charlotte is eager to share a career highlight where she was acting for a client launching a new product with a major bank. She was running it herself, with support where required, and working through the night liaising with City partners, drafting documents and handling client calls at 1:00am: "Completing this deal was a milestone in my career. Having the responsibility for getting a deal completed is scary at the time, but you know you have to do it and you will get it finished. It gives you a real sense of satisfaction. The recognition that you get from the team, the sense of accomplishment in yourself – it's a proud moment!"

When it comes to what Charlotte enjoys least, she struggles for an answer – she enjoys her job and turns the negatives into positive advice: "When you get bogged down, you might be in the middle of a three-week period when it's been really busy, and you are getting in at 7:00am and not leaving until 10:00pm and it can just seem a bit relentless. I compare it to when you are doing exams, and when you are in the middle of those exams you just can't see a way out, but you just have to keep going. In those periods it can be hard, but you have to learn your own coping mechanisms. So even if I know I'm going to be working to 11:00pm, I'll try and get out to the gym around the corner to get some time back for myself."

Automated future?

Charlotte has many friends in commercial law and they often discuss their legal future. Technology and contract automisation are the big changes that Charlotte sees affecting commercial law: "If clients continue to instruct firms to come in and automise documents and fast-draft paperwork themselves, then this could really start to change how lawyers

work. There will always be a need for lawyers, as there will always be a need for complex legal knowledge, delicate negotiations and fine tuning of drafted documents. It will be very interesting over the next five to 10 years to see how this will shape contract drafting."

Explore your options

Charlotte advises budding lawyers not to "feel trapped" by the traditional route of A levels and law degrees when there are numerous opportunities to train on the job or try a non-law degree: "At my school in particular, there weren't many people that went to university or stayed for sixth form, so I was in a minority of students applying to university and career advice wasn't great at the time. Looking back, I really enjoyed English and writing, which is really useful and helps me in my day-to-day job – now, if I'd have had better career advice at the time, I may have chosen an English degree and done a GDL conversion. I don't think I had realised that there were different routes to the qualification."

Charlotte is keen to promote on-the-job experience: "If you get the opportunity, do a secondment. And if you don't get the opportunity to do a secondment, or if people are graduating without a training contract to go straight into, get experience within a commercial environment. It means that when you do qualify in commercial law, you understand the business drivers that the clients are facing and what is important to them. So, working in a law firm, sometimes it can feel that you are in a bit of a vacuum if you don't appreciate and understand your clients' needs – they are asking you to do the work and you are just doing it. But you can add a lot more value if you appreciate where they are coming from, then you can suggest other things that they might not have thought about."

Commercial property

Commercial property (or real estate) lawyers act for a variety of domestic and international clients – including investors and developers, governments, landowners and public sector bodies – on a wide range of transactions, involving everything from offices to greenfield and retail developments, infrastructure projects and the management of shopping malls. The work itself focuses on the sale, purchase and lease of land; development; investment; and leasehold management. This touches on a range of other legal disciplines, including planning, environmental, construction, litigation and tax law. Property may also be a key component of other projects, including mergers and acquisitions, property finance and commercial projects. It crosses most sectors: investment, banking, insolvency, education, hotels, health, transport, agriculture, charities and private wealth.

Working out how best to convert the experience he had gained in the financial services sector saw Tom Newborough consider life as a lawyer, as he explains: "A couple of years after I graduated, I was working in a senior customer services role in a financial company. I enjoyed it, but wondered how I could use the skills I had developed in a more challenging setting, so I decided to take the plunge in to law." Still focused on skills, being a solicitor made the most sense: "Going to the Bar was never something that I really considered because I thought that my skills leant themselves more to the solicitor route. I also had the – possibly wrong – impression that becoming a barrister was less accessible for someone with no prior legal background."

Tom describes his year doing the GDL as predictably tough. "I was working part time at the same time as studying full time, and the pressure really kicked in in the last couple of months, with exams and my dissertation due in," he recalls, "but it was the same for everyone. And it's a good test of what to expect as a lawyer – you need to be able to manage your time well."

A training contract at Shoosmiths beckoned, where Tom was happy to be thrown in at the deep end: "I was given responsibility where I asked for it and showed that I was capable. It was a very focused training contract, where I realised quite early on that transactional work was my preferred option." After a stint first in property litigation, followed by corporate, he spent his two final seats in commercial property, where he went on to qualify.

Retail heaven
The wide-ranging nature of this practice area – due in part to the many different types of client that the firm serves – is one of the things that Tom particularly values about his career: "The work you do is often dependent on the type of client. For example, we currently deal with lots of retail clients, including a number of household names in relation to tenancy leases. We also act for institutional landlords and investors. One example is a client who owns a large shopping centre which requires a lot of asset management work, including new leases, lease variations or granting licences. You very rarely get the same sort of work, and retail leasehold work has built my experience up quickly and keeps me on my toes!"

Tom identifies a few of the key developments from the past couple of years in commercial property: "In city centres, the rise of trendy retail and leisure spaces continues, such as gastro pubs, craft ale bars and pop-up shops and restaurants. Distribution warehouses are also a big thing, with ever more demand for online shopping. In Nottingham there is increased investment in infrastructure, particularly around transport hubs, that is linked to the general rejuvenation of the city centre."

A career highlight centred on being part of the team selling a large property portfolio on behalf of an investment client. "It coincided with my starting as a third-seat trainee and finished near the end of my fourth seat," explains Tom. "Being involved with all the

For more firms that work in this practice area, please use the "Training contract regional indexes" starting on p211.

Name: **Tom Newborough**
Firm: **Shoosmiths**
Location: **Nottingham**
University: **University of Leeds**
Undergraduate degree: **Psychology**

elements and seeing the first large-scale project all the way through was great, especially seeing it all come together." But it's not just the headline, big-deal work that makes it mark: "I got as much satisfaction from the first time I negotiated a lease over the phone with a solicitor or explained some complicated legal issues to a client in a conference call. Although these matters are smaller scale for the firm, they're big for a trainee or NQ as they can be daunting to contemplate at the outset."

This feeds into the point that you continue to grow as a professional, even beyond the point of qualification: "This is a challenging role and you're always learning; every day there is something new, you feel your expertise growing and that is very rewarding."

One of the downsides to such a challenging – and rewarding – job is the obvious demands it can make on life beyond the office, as Tom explains: "Especially in real estate, you never feel that you're completely in control of your workload. There is always something more you could be doing, so it can be a challenge to decide when to go home! It comes down to prioritising the urgent work, but also finding time to fit in everything else that's required of you. That can be difficult and stressful, and you need to become comfortable with not being able to tick everything off your to-do list each day!"

The full implications of Brexit remain a mystery (to us all!), but it is the one thing that Tom and his colleagues are keeping the closest eye on, especially in terms of their investor clients: "It's mostly about what decision making is going on during the negotiation process – for example, are clients holding back until they know what the outcome of the UK deal? Will they move their head offices elsewhere? From a property perspective, it's about those clients potentially being less active in the market."

Commercial experience

So what do clients need from their lawyers right now? Tom thinks there are several key skills: "Commerciality is really important; clients want to get stuff done and it's your job as their lawyer to assess the risks and work out how to do things in the best possible way. Also important are soft skills such as time management and an ability to deal with pressure. Both your verbal and written communication skills need to be strong; the worst thing you can do is give an ambiguous response. You have to be very clear, even down to the way you structure your emails and present information; you could reel off all the legal issues to a client, but they only really care what the outcome is. Anything superfluous should be left out."

In terms of getting ahead of the pack at training contract application time, work experience is non-negotiable. Tom explains: "It can be hard when applying for a training contract, having come straight from university, to provide practical examples to go with your application. Don't get hung up on it having to be legal experience; any work experience, even in shops or restaurants, is great if you're learning about the commercial aspect of the job." If you can get legal experience, all the better: "I did a placement at a criminal firm with a solicitor specialising in mental health; it wasn't my preferred type of law, but having got something on my CV, it set the ball rolling. Also, don't panic if you're not hired straightaway – I was 25 when I received my training contract offer, so keep trying."

Remain open to what working in a law firm is going to be like: "My preconception was perhaps that law firms were fairly stuffy and people were likely to be unapproachable; the reality is of course completely different. I felt relaxed here from the very beginning. You are learning quickly and you don't need to have all the answers straightaway. It is better to say that you don't know and go and check. Ask questions as often as you need to, as everyone wants you to learn and progress."

Competition

Typically, competition and regulatory work includes merger control under the Enterprise Act 2002 and the EU Merger Regulation, regulatory and court proceedings under the Competition Act 1998 and EU legislation, issues arising from sector-specific regulation, state aid, public sector and utility procurement issues. There has been significant reform of both UK and EU competition law and practice in recent years, and further proposals are being considered. An interesting recent development in the area is the reform of the cartel offence giving rise to criminal liability for individuals. Private competition law actions are also a particular area to watch, with both the UK and EU authorities keen to encourage such suits.

When choosing her legal career path, Danica Barley was mainly attracted to the teamwork and client contact involved in being a solicitor. She is now an associate at Ashurst and previously trained at the firm. "I really enjoyed my training contract – it's a great way of getting to experience different areas of law and working out which is best suited to you," she explains. "I think the six-month rotational aspect of it is really valuable." While her current work involves more substantial drafting and direct client contact than it did as a trainee, she was brought in on cases from an early stage: "The team here is great at making sure that trainees are involved on a day-to-day basis, so I got a good flavour of the work that was involved in different types of matters."

Having studied economics at university, Danica chose a practice area which overlaps with her degree subject. While she has certainly found this beneficial, she is keen to emphasise that such a background is not a prerequisite to a career in competition law. However, an enthusiasm for keeping on top of legal developments and understanding business sectors is key. "I'm sure all practice areas would say this, but I think a genuine interest in the specialism is crucial," she explains. "It can be quite a technical area in terms of research and analysing case law. It involves in-depth analysis of markets and businesses, gaining a detailed understanding of specific products and services, and how it all works in an economic context – so it helps to find that interesting if you want to go into this area."

Tumultuous times

Danica describes what are currently interesting times for competition law, citing technological advances and the uncertain political climate as particular catalysts for change. "The Competition and Markets Authority – CMA – and other regulators are considering a number of different issues, including digital technological advances and innovation, which are posing interesting issues from a competition law perspective," she observes. "And of course, depending on the economic situation going forward, Brexit may result in more merger control filings if companies are required to notify both the European Commission and the CMA – and it may also lead to parallel abuse of dominance and cartel investigations by the European and UK authorities."

Day to day, her work mainly involves advising on matters such as merger control: "I often work with clients in relation to a potential merger, including assessing whether the transaction would require notification under the different merger control regimes around the world, assessing whether substantive issues are likely to arise, and assisting clients throughout the filing process," she continues. "We are also involved in competition law investigations, where the regulator is investigating potential anti-competitive agreements and abuse of dominance, as well as advising on general competition law compliance – helping

For more firms that work in this practice area, please use the "Training contract regional indexes" starting on p211.

Name: **Danica Barley**
Firm: **Ashurst LLP**
Location: **London**
University: **London School of Economics**
Undergraduate degree: **Economics**

businesses to ensure that they're meeting their competition law obligations."

Danica feels fortunate to have been involved in a wide range of work so far at Ashurst and identifies this variety as one of the most enjoyable aspects of the job. She has also had the opportunity to go on secondment: "I spent six months with Lloyds Banking Group, which I really enjoyed – it was great to work with the in-house team there. I've also worked with lots of different clients and on a range of matters during my time at Ashurst, including the merger between Arla Foods and part of Yeo Valley Dairies, which was recently cleared by the CMA at phase one; the recent AVEVA/Schneider Electric transaction which involved a number of filings; and being involved in advising a leading bank in relation to the CMA's retail banking market investigation."

whether law is for them at the outset of their studies, she would encourage them not to rule it out. "I think often people don't consider it as a possible career for them, whereas actually, you can study something else first and then decide to qualify as a solicitor." Far from being an obstacle, a non-law degree can prove a real asset to prospective lawyers – as Danica knows from experience. "It can be really beneficial to have studied another subject – for example, economics, languages or maths – which can provide valuable and transferable skills."

66 It can be quite a technical area in terms of research and analysing case law 99

Finding the right fit

To others considering a career in law, she stresses the value of work experience in discovering what practice area – and firm – is right for you. "I think vacation schemes are very useful – they're a really good way of working out whether law is for you, because it can be tricky to know exactly what's involved on a day-to-day basis until you've experienced it," she advises. "These schemes not only give you a flavour of the different departments, but also help you to decide if a firm's culture is suitable for you."

When asked what one thing aspiring solicitors should know, Danica emphasises that "you don't have to have studied law at university!" Even if someone is unsure

Construction

Contentious construction work involves the resolution of disputes by way of litigation, mediation, adjudication or arbitration. Non-contentious work involves drafting and negotiating contracts and advising on projects, insurance, health and safety, environmental matters and insolvency. Clients range from industry associations, insurers, contractors, architects, engineers, public authorities and government bodies to major companies and partnerships.

While it is self-evident that the majority of solicitors follow the most common route to professional qualification – undergraduate degree, law school (GDL and/or LPC) and training contract – it should always be remembered that other paths do exist, and that law is a career that remains accessible to those who commit to practising it at various different stages of their professional lives.

Paul Hargreaves is one of those who took "a more alternative route", although his career with his current law firm Walker Morris began long before his formal legal education. "I started working for Walker Morris in 1999, in what was then WM Claims, our personal injury unit," he explains. "I had no formal legal qualifications; a lot of personal injury firms will have a select number of qualified lawyers, the rest will be case handlers/fee earners, and I started as a case handler. In 2001 I left Walker Morris because I wanted to travel; I visited a variety of different countries and ended up in Australia working for Aon Insurance. When I returned to the United Kingdom, I came back to Walker Morris and decided that law was the career for me. I did a law degree part time at Leeds Metropolitan University (as it was called then). It was two evenings a week for a four-year period. While studying, I was working full time."

Hard work pays

All the hard work and effort paid off; Paul did the LPC in 2008 and was offered a training contract with Walker Morris which began in 2009. Two years later Paul qualified as a solicitor, was shortlisted for "Associate Solicitor of the Year" at the British Legal Awards 2015 and is now a partner at the firm. He admits that he did consider training at a few other firms, but Walker Morris won out. "It was an easy choice, really," he says. "I knew the people, I knew and liked the firm, and I liked what it stands for. I knew my training contract would provide me with close personal supervision and also a high level of responsibility to get involved in cases and run my own files. Although I did research other firms and thought about going down to London, at heart I knew that what I was looking for was here."

At the start of his training contract, Paul thought that his previous experiences would mean he would specialise and qualify into a litigation role, but during his six-seat rotation he briefly dabbled with the idea of regulatory law, before settling in the firm's construction and engineering department.

Big ticket to ride

"It was the big-ticket litigation that did it," he recalls. "What I find in construction is that it's a great area in which to be a litigator as there are still a large number of disputes, which is great for us. Walker Morris is quite unique in its approach at getting junior lawyers more involved at an earlier stage than other firms; since qualification I have been involved in a number of significant cases, including representing 96 claimants in a claim involving issues arising out of the Defective Premises Act 1972 and which included a four-week trial before Mr Justice Edwards-Stuart in the Technology and Construction Court."

Not all trainees will be lucky enough to get involved in such high-rolling cases, of

For more firms that work in this practice area, please use the "Training contract regional indexes" starting on p211.

Name: **Paul Hargreaves**
Firm: **Walker Morris LLP**
Location: **Leeds**
University: **Leeds Beckett University**
Undergraduate degree: **Law**

course, but Paul assures us that there is very real work to keep them busy: "We make sure that the trainees are part of the team from the word go. You are given work to do and you're certainly not spending your days photocopying – we see that as a waste of talent. We want them to be trained up as quickly as possible, working as quickly as possible and fee-earning as quickly as possible. One of the things I know from speaking to peers at other firms is that we are known for giving trainees a large amount of responsibility. This means that trainees can hit the ground running in the departments into which they qualify."

❝ What I find in construction is that it's a great area in which to be a litigator as there are still a large number of disputes ❞

The construction and engineering team as a whole does a mix of contentious and non-contentious work, such as drafting building contracts, bond guarantees and warranties. This insulates it to a degree from the infamous changes of fortune that characterise the construction industry, which are traditionally closely linked to the political and economic climate.

"No one really knows how Brexit will affect things," muses Paul. "I think it is going to be quite challenging for all sectors, including construction. There certainly needs to be a lot more building within the United Kingdom – certainly more houses, as there is a massive shortage – but to be able to do that we need money. That said, in construction, when it's boom time we are dealing with a lot of development work and we are doing a lot of non-contentious work. As soon as you get a recession, people are more inclined to revisit issues and that is when you get

involved in litigation. So you get both ends, and at the moment we have a good mix here at Walker Morris."

Fledgling lawyers keen to get involved in the non-contentious side of the practice should show an interest in construction work in general, believes Paul, so they should be looking at the building press and architectural journals to find out what is happening in the sector.

As for those interested in the contentious side of construction – which, as Paul confirms, is an excellent place for litigation-hungry lawyers – they need to be able to process large volumes of technical data. "In law generally there is a significant amount of information that you have to be able to digest and assimilate," he explains. "But certainly in construction work, and defect work in particular, you can be faced with 300-page reports about a subject in which you have limited knowledge and you have to be able to pick that up relatively quickly and be able to put it to your client in a succinct manner that they will understand. That is a skill in itself."

Paul finishes with a word of warning for those who are not sure they are cut out for the legal profession: "If you don't really like this job, don't do it! That applies to all areas of the law. It's not a soft option. It is hard work and long hours sometimes. But it can be incredibly intellectually satisfying and worthwhile – or at least I think so; but then I am very interested in the law."

Corporate finance

Corporate finance lawyers advise companies on all aspects of the buying and selling of whole businesses or business assets. This requires guidance on how to comply with company law procedures, the raising of funds and, in the case of cross-border transactions, compliance with foreign laws. It is possible to work primarily on mergers and acquisitions (M&A) with public or privately owned companies. Alternatively, a corporate lawyer may focus on the private equity, venture capital or hedge fund sectors, or spend his or her whole career as a generalist assisting SMEs and small-scale entrepreneurs.

First-hand experience is the best way to decide whether a career path is really for you, and work placements at both solicitors' firms and barristers' chambers informed Michael Mountain's choice to become a solicitor. "I was attracted to a career as a solicitor by the team-focused nature of the role, as opposed to the more individualistic nature of working as a barrister," he explains. "I also liked the idea of being involved in deals from start to finish, which involves a closer working relationship with the client – in contrast, barristers usually receive their instructions from solicitors. Barristers get involved at quite a late stage and while they are then involved at the 'business end', I find that contributing from a deal's inception all the way through to completion provides a certain satisfaction that is hard to match. Solicitors often have a broader mandate than barristers, which is something that I believed I would enjoy."

After graduating from his law degree and completing the Legal Practice Course, Michael trained at magic circle firm Slaughter and May. "It is an excellent place to train and my experiences there instilled the highest standards into my work," he recalls. "My training set up a really good foundation for my career and I think that would be the case whether I stayed in law or decided to do something else. I qualified into the corporate department at Slaughters – I gained exposure to a wide variety of work and enjoyed the dynamics of deals in this practice area."

> ❝ It is unpredictable from day to day, but I like the build-up to completing a transaction, which necessarily involves different stages and different levels of intensity ❞

Michael later joined international law firm White & Case. "I specialise in M&A, including advice on joint ventures, minority investments and also do a range of general advisory corporate work. Of late, this has particularly involved working for investment funds."

Investment funds

A key aspect of Michael's role, inevitably, is documenting the transactions that his team shepherds to close. "There is often both an equity and a debt component in the deals that we help to execute on behalf of investment fund clients, as their investments take the form of ownership in entities, as well as debts which have been lent to those entities," he explains. "Part of the strategy for many investment funds is to invest in the asset in a variety of different ways. Any deal will involve negotiating with the other stakeholders invested in the asset and carrying out due diligence. As a lawyer on the transaction, you will often be documenting two principal aspects, being the purchase agreement for the acquisition itself and then the shareholders'/investment agreement, which concerns the ongoing relationship between the shareholders/stakeholders invested in the asset."

Michael has been heavily involved in the expansion of this area of White & Case's

For more firms that work in this practice area, please use the "Training contract regional indexes" starting on p211.

Name: **Michael Mountain**
Firm: **White & Case LLP**
Location: **London**
University: **University of Oxford**
Undergraduate degree: **Law**

corporate practice in London. "Perhaps the highlight of my career so far is being part of forming a new unit within the corporate team, which focuses on investment fund clients and works in tandem with the restructuring and private debt teams," he explains. "It has been challenging, but satisfying and enjoyable to help this part of the firm's practice grow and thrive over the last 18 months."

Ebb and flow

The workload in this transactional area is not necessarily steady or predictable – it inevitably involves a lot of peaks and troughs. "It isn't for everyone – it depends on how you like your working days to ebb and flow," says Michael. "It is unpredictable from day to day, but I like the build-up to completing a transaction, which necessarily involves different stages and different levels of intensity. The moments that bring the most happiness and satisfaction are when you get recognition from clients with whom you have been working for a number of weeks or months on a deal – appreciation from people you have come to really respect is a great reward for hard work, and it feels good to be seen as a valued adviser."

A familiar bugbear of working in commercial law is time recording. "It's certainly not a highlight – trying to accurately account for every minute of your day is quite challenging," observes Michael. "It is also quite particular to the legal profession, as the work of many other professional advisory firms is accounted for in a different way."

Commercial lawyers are currently weighing up the consequences of Brexit and how it might transform the landscape. "It has already had an impact on M&A and will continue to do so," explains Michael. "That isn't to say that M&A activity is just going to stop, or indeed that other areas in which corporate lawyers play a part are not going to continue to thrive, but certainly clients are assessing the impact of Brexit and will be taking that into account

in their investment strategies and transaction planning. I would also say more generally that, in terms of the business we are in, London is a very legal competitive market, so it is becoming increasingly important for firms and lawyers to stand out from their competitors anyway. Finding innovative ways to develop your business is a constant challenge."

Quick off the mark

To succeed in corporate finance and M&A, you need several key skills, not least the ability to remain calm under pressure. "As I mentioned, the way that deals can ebb and flow means that there is usually a crescendo to the transaction which is very busy and intense, so you need to be able to remain focused under those conditions," explains Michael. "You also need to be able to quickly identify the key issues in any situation. You may have more time to deal with them, but finding the crux in a matter in short order is expected, which is a real skill. Flexibility and the ability to multitask are also important, as you need to be able to manage multiple transactions at once, which could be of a completely different nature."

Michael also has the following general tips for those keen to embark on a career in law: "It is a great idea to meet and talk to lawyers at law fairs, open days and the other opportunities available. The day-to-day job can be very different depending on which type of firm you join, so it's useful to do your research and speak to a broad range of people at different kinds of firm. One thing I would also recommend is not to be afraid to take time out to travel or work in a different environment before you start your legal career. These experiences can be beneficial when you're writing applications and attending interviews, and I don't think that you would miss out by coming to the profession a year or two later. However, it can be difficult to drop your responsibilities and take that kind of time out further down the line. You certainly don't have to rush in."

Corporate tax

Virtually all commercial transactions have tax implications. Corporate tax is thus an important practice area for any major law firm. Working in corporate tax involves advising on the most tax-efficient means of acquiring, selling or restructuring assets, negotiating and documenting the transaction, and ensuring the smooth completion of the deal. On the contentious side, corporate tax lawyers advise on all aspects of tax litigation and investigations, including negotiating with tax authorities.

Lizzie James' expertise as a lawyer channels the same skills she honed sifting through sources and fine details during her history degree at University College London. Painstaking analysis and problem solving are just as important as advocacy and making arguments, and her aptitude in the former helped to decide her path into the solicitors' profession. She explains: "I've always enjoyed working behind the scenes more than public speaking and the whole performative aspect of law."

After converting to law, Lizzie trained at Burges Salmon, where she is now an associate. Her training contract was "a really positive experience – there was a wider variety of work than at other firms due to Burges Salmon's six-seat programme." And the breadth of experience provided by the firm's six-seat system was what first introduced her to her eventual specialism, corporate tax law. "It was not something that I had any knowledge of before I became a solicitor," she explains. "But it felt like a good match because I have an eye for detail and have always been interested in the technical side of how things work. As well as history, I enjoyed studying economics and maths at A level, and if I hadn't become a lawyer I may well have been an accountant – it's fair to say that I enjoy problem solving! That said, a career in corporate tax does not actually involve any number crunching – it is all about technical detail and analysis."

Thinking on your feet
Her work covers all aspects of UK tax law – corporate, VAT, property, stamp – and a wide range of tax issues. "My time is split evenly between transactional work – corporate tax support roles for large M&A deals – and advising individual clients," she elaborates. "On the transactional side, I support the corporate department with M&A transactions, which involves negotiating tax warranties and covenants with solicitors for the other side. This is really interesting because it involves negotiation skills, complex drafting and thinking on your feet, as no two deals are ever the same."

Meanwhile, the advisory work "spans from answering technical queries that require interpreting legislation and reporting your conclusions, to much larger projects where I am advising clients on their tax structuring and putting together detailed technical documents."

> ❝ It is fast-paced, and the law is always changing and being interpreted differently – often just when you become familiar with something ❞

Variety is the spice of life
Tax is a challenging area to work in, as Lizzie explains: "It is fast-paced, and the law is always changing and being interpreted differently – often just when you become familiar with something. There are two sides to this – on one hand you can feel that you're never quite on top of the law, but it also ensures that the work is constantly interesting and varied. One of the most enjoyable aspects of my role is that no two

For more firms that work in this practice area, please use the "Training contract regional indexes" starting on p211.

Name: **Lizzie James**
Firm: **Burges Salmon LLP**
Location: **Bristol**
University: **University College London**
Degree: **History**

days are the same. I could be working on my own on a small technical tax issue one moment and a large, multi-team project the next. On the other side, one frustration is the negative perception that people sometimes have about the tax profession, as the reality is completely different."

Brexit

Lizzie highlights two key issues that readers interested in commercial law, or tax more specifically, should look out for: "Brexit is certainly one issue that tax lawyers are watching closely, along with much of the rest of the profession, as it could have a significant effect on European legislation generally. There is also increased scrutiny from HMRC on the profession itself to ensure that it is above board, which is driven by political pressure. Tax is an issue that gets more attention in the media than used to be the case."

She also offers the following advice for those considering a career in this area: "A successful tax solicitor need an eye for detail and to be analytical, but also able to get to the heart of complex issues quickly. It is also important to be flexible about the specialisms you explore within your practice area. Go into it without preconceptions and don't rule anything out or maintain a fixed idea of what you want to specialise in, as the reality of actually practising an area of law is so different studying it at university. I had never considered corporate tax as a student but it fits me perfectly! Having an open mind is so important."

Crime

Criminal solicitors advise and appear in court on behalf of both accused persons and the prosecution, handling the full spectrum of offences, from minor motoring misdemeanours to more serious crimes, including murder. They deal with all aspects of the criminal justice system, from the initial police interview to trial before the court.

Despite being a history graduate, Matthew Hardcastle had always had an eye on a legal career – and in fact feels that his non-law background has enhanced his day-to-day lawyering: "I always had an interest in law but I enjoyed my time as a history student, particularly the research aspect of it. I found it an attractive prospect to spend my professional life in a job that would allow me to continue to use those skills; a career in law has allowed me to continue with a mix of research and practical application. I find that a history background has helped me to take a rounded approach to cases."

The courtroom side of a barrister's career initially appealed, but further research revealed that he was better suited to life as a solicitor: "Advocacy was something I was interested in, but after speaking to several people about which route to take, there was a consistent theme of the difficulties faced by junior members of the criminal Bar. I thought that the solicitor route offered more stability and, in some ways, a more traditional route to advocacy with a greater exposure to the magistrates' courts at an early stage."

Matthew joined TV Edwards, a large high-street practice specialising in criminal defence, first as a paralegal and then as a trainee. "I absolutely loved it – Anthony Edwards, who was head of the firm, teaches other lawyers about criminal law, so the training I received was first rate," Matthew recalls. "It was very hands-on experience, which you would expect in a publicly funded firm. I couldn't have asked for anything more."

After three years post-qualification at TV Edwards, Matthew moved to Kingsley Napley. He describes his current practice: "My work is split between white collar cases and more traditional criminal cases. There is a very supportive atmosphere at Kingsley Napley with the partners working very much as a team with their associates; this allows a good balance on every type of case."

❝ You can have a fantastic knowledge of the law, but if you can't connect with your client then it will be very difficult to practise effectively ❞

Part of what appeals to Matthew about his career is the variety afforded by a mix in type and size of work: "As a profession we get pushed more and more into specialising at a very early stage of our careers, but for me, I think the combination of large financial crime and general crime is a nice balance. Large matters can take on a life of their own and develop slowly, so they require a different approach. Having said that, underneath it all, it's the same law and rules of evidence."

Human beings on trial

Reflecting back on some of the most significant professional moments of his career, Matthew recalls a long-running case, acting for an individual "who was essentially in the wrong place at the wrong time". He expands: "He had been very good at his job, without realising that his job involved working for a firm that was practising illegally. He had everything to lose and when the jury acquitted him, the relief for him and his family was palpable."

The human element is one of the most satisfying aspects of the job, but also the one that requires a lot of skilled handling. "I

For more firms that work in this practice area, please use the "Training contract regional indexes" starting on p211.

Name: **Matthew Hardcastle**
Firm: **Kingsley Napley LLP**
Location: **London**
University: **University of Hull**
Undergraduate degree: **History**

meet people from varied backgrounds, who find themselves in need of advice for many different reasons," explains Matthew. "But, if you are going to do the best job for your client then you have to understand their individual needs as well as the specifics of the case."

He expands on the need for finely honed people skills: "You can have a fantastic knowledge of the law, but if you can't connect with your client then it will be very difficult to practise effectively. You are often meeting them at the most stressful point in their life and you have to build a sufficient relationship so that they are able to trust your judgement – that includes when you give tough advice." It also includes your perception of what the 'best' strategy would be: "You must always be alive to your client's desired outcome as any disconnect can lead to a pyrrhic victory."

Criminally underfunded

For Matthew, the consistent underfunding of the criminal justice system is one of the most troubling aspects of the job: "There is an extreme lack of funding at the moment and that causes systemic issues. Many good lawyers – be that for the prosecution or for the defence – are unable to progress a case in the way that they would want to because they have too much work and too little time. There is no certainty or stability in the system and a delay at any point can have a knock-on effect during the life of a case. That can be difficult to manage and I suspect it will only get worse."

Some have suggested that the increasing digitalisation of criminal legal proceedings may help alleviate some of the problems of underfunding: "At some point, a decision will have to be made about how publicly funded work, and criminal justice as a whole, will be funded. Will there be a new approach or will there be sufficient savings derived from digitalisation to carry on in the same way?"

Getting work experience to learn more about the profession you hope to join is important, explains Matthew, but it needn't be on a formal vacation scheme: "I got my training contract at TV Edwards, following work experience and a period paralegalling there. However, I had also walked around the area where I lived, clutching a copy of my CV, and knocking on the doors of local firms, hoping to get some experience. I managed to secure one day a week at a firm, which was invaluable in terms of what I learnt. People think that way of getting experience has gone out of fashion and it's not for everybody – you have to have the spare time to do it for one thing – but especially in criminal law, you can learn so much from high-street experience."

On that point, Matthew is keen to emphasise that career progression from trainee upwards is possible in the publicly funded side of the profession. "It's a shame that some don't consider the high street an entry point anymore because there is real expertise in the high street firms – some of the most remarkable lawyers I know are on the high street. And it is also possible to progress from the high street to the City, if that's what you choose. Equally, I have seen first hand how consistently impressive the new qualified solicitors are at Kingsley Napley; their ability on qualification is a clear result of high-quality training they receive. Overall, the single most important factor is to ensure that you receive excellent training – it is what frames your career."

Dispute resolution

Commercial litigation involves the resolution of disputes in the corporate and commercial sphere, including those arising out of joint venture projects, civil fraud, commercial and banking transactions, corporate governance, financial services regulation and professional negligence. The Jackson Reforms, which came into force in April 2013, have significantly changed the court process, including the way litigation is managed, especially in relation to directions and costs.

Susan Garrett's introduction to the legal world could not have been more dramatic; whilst at school she was hit by a car driven by one of her teachers, who then failed to offer an adequate apology. As a result, Susan encouraged her parents to instruct a solicitor and to take him to court. Despite the case being somewhat boring and pretty uneventful, it sparked Susan's interest in law and inspired her to embark on a career as a lawyer.

From this young age Susan began to explore where her legal interests lay and went on to study law at Durham University. She took up a number of vacation placements to better understand the difference between the work of a barrister and a solicitor. She decided that a career as a solicitor was most appealing for two reasons: "Firstly, I liked the team spirit and that you get involved in bigger teams and being a barrister seemed to be a bit more of a lonely profession. Secondly, in a law firm as a solicitor you are closer to the clients, especially commercial clients. I like to really get under the skin of clients in a commercial context and as a barrister you are one step further removed."

Susan completed her training contract at what was Herbert Smith (now Herbert Smith Freehills) and describes it fondly as "a fantastic two years. I was one of many trainees and made some great friends, I was part of a great cohort of trainees and I was lucky enough to do 12 months of litigation; six months of shipping litigation and six months of commercial litigation. I had the opportunity to do some great work and had a great time working in the City."

The opportunity to get stuck into big litigation cases during her training contract meant that Susan knew that this was the field that she wanted to work in. She is now a commercial litigation partner at Addleshaw Goddard and her work mainly involves running large commercial conflicts and disputes of an incredibly varied nature, including "shareholder disputes, warranty claims, judicial reviews and a lot of tax litigation and pension litigation in particular."

Variety is key

The variety of matters that Susan takes on means that her workload is spread across multiple cases simultaneously: "I have quite a few big disputes that take years to resolve, they may be going to trial in the next year or in 2019 and some of which may be on trial for a month or more. I also have many matters that are not based in the courts, there are many disputes that clients need to sort out before the commencement of proceedings, through mediation or commercial negotiation, so I have a real mixture of cases and can be involved in up to 30 or more at any one time."

Susan has always been keen to work on a diverse selection of matters, but as a partner she now bears ultimate responsibility for the outcome of the cases she takes on: "The main difference of being a partner to when I was a junior solicitor is that, essentially, the buck stops with me and I have overall strategic responsibility for the cases while leading my team. Whereas, when you are newly qualified or a trainee, you are part of a team and you usually work on one small specific element of a case or help on a

For more firms that work in this practice area, please use the "Training contract regional indexes" starting on p211.

Name: **Susan Garrett**
Chambers: **Addleshaw Goddard**
Location: **Manchester**
University: **University of Durham**
Degree: **Law**

selection of different aspects, but you don't have the overall responsibility of running a large case."

However, the pressure of being ultimately responsible is offset by the high that comes with working through a difficult case and securing a great result for a client: "I'm an adrenaline junky and as a litigator you move from one high to the next, it's always great winning trials, obtaining worldwide freezing injunctions and getting a really good settlement for a client. Often the client is in a very difficult position and they are trying to resolve something that is really critical for the survival of their business, and what I enjoy is devising a strategy to help get clients through the process with their business intact."

❛❛ You've got to have an eye for detail and be analytical, and you've got to think strategically and enjoy problem solving ❜❜

On the flip side of this, the mundanity of one aspect of the role can be frustrating: "Recording time in six-minute units is a less enjoyable aspect of my job, I am lucky enough for most of my work to be enjoyable, but time recording is a bit tedious."

Competition is on the rise
Looking to the future, Susan anticipates that increasing competition will precipitate change in the market: "Price pressures, the cost of regulation and the fact that it is a very competitive market means that I would expect to see some consolidation in the market, but perhaps not as much as in other areas. A number of law firms have failed but we are fortunate that Addleshaw is financially strong and we have fantastic clients, but weaker firms will start to fall by the wayside and we will see more consolidation."

In the dispute resolution sector, funding is a key talking point: "Addleshaw Goddard is at the forefront of how litigation is funded and the market for third-party funders has become very competitive, so we are going to see more and more big group litigation funded by third-party professional funders." For those looking to pursue a career in dispute resolution, an aptitude for analysis is an absolutely crucial part of being a successful litigator: "You've got to have an eye for detail and be analytical, and you've got to think strategically and enjoy problem solving, as these are the kinds of things you will do on a daily basis". Equally, collaboration is key, as Susan advises: "If you want to work in a law firm you have to enjoy working as a team, whether you are in private practice or in-house, it is hard work but it is incredibly interesting and rewarding."

Broadening your horizons is also important – getting as much experience as possible as early as you can will make things much easier in the long run: "Try and get internships at a variety of different firms doing different work and build up your experience early on," offers Susan. "Get a wide variety of experience in different kinds of disputes and work areas. Then you can decide whether you want to specialise in something and identify what really interests you. Doing disputes in diverse areas helps you to develop the necessary skills to analyse any problem so that you can work with the client to create a resolution."

Susan stresses that utilising the opportunity to gain experience was absolutely invaluable in determining what field she most enjoyed working in and that this enjoyment has been key in helping her build a successful and rewarding career: "Ultimately, if you do what you enjoy you will have a great career and won't grow weary of it, and you will end up being really successful as you are doing what you enjoy."

Employment

Employment lawyers work across all areas of employment law, including, for example, handling discrimination, staff restructuring and whistleblowing issues. There has been increased focus on employment law in recent years, due to a combination of new legislation, government policies and employees' increased awareness of their rights. Trainees assist with a wide variety of work, such as the employment aspects of corporate or commercial transactions, preparations for tribunal claims, attending hearings and meetings, and helping to draft documents such as employment contracts or policies.

Grace Malone was attracted to the study of law by the flexibility that it affords later down the line: "I always preferred words to science or maths, and thought that law seemed like a sensible undergraduate degree to do. I wasn't certain I wanted to be a lawyer when I applied for university, but felt that because of its academic nature, a law degree could take you in all sorts of directions." Going to the Bar was never on the radar: "I was swept up into the training contract application process by my second year and really liked the idea of working in a big firm, with lots of colleagues in a supportive environment."

Having secured a training contract at Burges Salmon in her second year, Grace relished the chance to learn more about what daily lawyering really means, in a variety of different departments. "It is quite a big annual intake of trainees, around 20 to 25, and I liked the fact that you were surrounded by people at the same stage as you, forming friendships from the very beginning," Grace reflects. "Also, our six-seat system means that you get to try a large number of different areas within the two years. You are given enough responsibility, without it being overwhelming; there is a real focus on ensuring trainees get lots from the training experience and work out where their skills lie,

rather than more senior lawyers expecting you to be perfect. The firm wants you to get a sense of what lies ahead after qualification."

Grace's second seat was in employment, where she first formed an opinion on what the practice area could offer and whether it might suit her career aspirations: "I enjoyed all my seats and there were aspects of them all that I would have enjoyed if I had qualified there. I was drawn to employment, however, because it is a 'people-based' area. The style of advising is different to other areas – the issues are often very pressing, sensitive or reputational, and there are lots of daily conversations and meetings with clients. I really like the story and human element of it; it is all very tangible and relatable, which I think makes it easier to get your teeth into as a junior lawyer."

Employment work at the firm is a varied mix of contentious and non-contentious work, which keeps things interesting for practitioners. "We do advisory work, such as guiding clients through a restructure or reorganisation, or assisting with tricky grievance or disciplinary scenarios" describes Grace. "We also support our commercial, pensions or corporate teams with transactions that they're working on – for example, the employment elements of an outsourcing deal. On the contentious side, we help to manage clients' tribunal claims, mostly acting for the employer. A claim might be related to whistleblowing or disability or sex discrimination, for example."

Second to none
Both as a trainee and since qualification, Grace has benefited from the professional opportunities that come with going on client secondments: "Last year I was seconded to a business to help with a specific project, a large-scale redundancy. It was really interesting to be based within a projects team because you realise the amount of work that goes on behind the scenes – I had

For more firms that work in this practice area, please use the "Training contract regional indexes" starting on p211.

Name: **Grace Malone**
Firm: **Burges Salmon LLP**
Location: **Bristol**
University: **University of Exeter**
Undergraduate degree: **Law**

good visibility of what it means to implement the advice we give, and an appreciation for the complexities of decision making and administering such a project. Now, when I give advice, I can picture that all going on in the background. What different clients do with our advice, how it is implemented, some of the different business drivers – if you can get a handle on how different businesses operate, then you can advise your clients much better."

Developing the ability to offer timely and strategic advice can be hard for junior lawyers: "One of the most difficult things as a junior lawyer is that there are a lot of grey areas in employment. Often you are giving your view on the best strategic option to get your client to where they want to go and that can be hard before you have a sufficient breadth of experience. It doesn't take long to see similar scenarios and have an idea of what to do though, and there are always more senior lawyers around to ask what their view is."

Employment law is also a very fast-moving area compared to some others, because it is heavily case-law driven, so Grace urges the need to keep updated and on top of trends – many of which appear in the national press: "Because the issues are relatable and interesting, employment law gets a lot of coverage in the press. 'Hot topics' recently have been the calculation of holiday pay, gender pay reporting and a focus on the status of gig economy workers. There are always consultations and case law to keep on top of – you can't rest on your laurels!"

Have you got skills?
Grace reiterates the need to hone your people skills in this very human and emotional field of law: "You have to be personable and able to relate to people; the issues involved are often more sensitive than in other areas of law. You also need

empathy; it's very important to understand what drives individuals. For example, in a tribunal claim if you can understand what is driving both of the parties, there may be a way to resolve things quickly and commercially rather than going through the entire hearing process."

Commerciality is also essential: "Each client has different drivers and appetites for risk – for example, some clients may be unionised, or reputation may be very important to them, and maintaining good employee relations and avoiding criticism will be their primary motivator. Compare that to other businesses where cost may be the ultimate driver. You have to be able to step into your client's shoes and understand what is important to them." This ties in with the need to grasp that being brilliant at law is only one aspect of being a good lawyer: It is important to listen to what your client wants to achieve and connect that to your advice. It's not just an understanding of the legislation; you have to appreciate what that advice will be used for. This helps build strong relationships with your clients."

Grace's top tips centre on the need to find a firm that is a good match with your aspirations. She explains: "In terms of what you can do to make yourself more marketable, you need to show you have taken time to identify which firms might suit you and why, as opposed to just applying to any firm. You want to end up at a firm that suits you, culture and values wise.

And a reassuring final note: "The job is not as difficult or as different to life as a student as you might expect – you're working with people who are there to support you and help you develop, and they recognise that it takes time for you to be confident about what you're doing. You don't need to be a fully formed lawyer on day one – it's a much gentler introduction to the career than that."

Energy and natural resources

The energy and natural resources sector is an important part of the legal landscape and is currently making more headlines than ever before. It covers, among other things, oil and gas projects, pipelines, refineries, liquefied natural gas, nuclear, renewables, and water and wastewater. Emerging energy initiatives such as biofuels and carbon capture and trading also feature. The key legal issues centre on the development and financing of projects, M&A, disputes and trading, and may be either domestic or international in scope.

William Jones, a senior associate in RPC's energy insurance practice, always wanted to be a spy. However, rather than embarking on a career in espionage following university, William focused on his other major passion. "I'd always been interested in the law. I chose the solicitor route rather than the Bar because I enjoy working in teams, dealing directly with commercial clients, and taking account of your clients' commercial drivers. I also like taking a more holistic view of a commercial disagreement rather than looking at it in strictly legal terms."

Following his legal studies, William undertook a training contract at RPC. "I was looking for a firm that had a broad range of practice areas" he remarks, "because as a law student it's quite difficult to really know what you want to end up doing until you've done it. I wanted to go somewhere that offered me four very different seats and at the end feel confident that I was doing something that interested me and that I wanted a career in."

At the end of his training contract, William chose to specialise in the energy insurance field: "I was very much drawn in by the international nature of the work and the fact that, having a politics background, it had a political angle, and it was often contentious."

Each day is different

Coverage advice and litigation are the two main planks of William's job. As he explains, the coverage side entails "advising insurance companies in respect of large energy and industrial claims, for example, if their insured has encountered a peril such as a hurricane, defective machinery or terror attack, and seeks to recover under their insurance policy. You're advising insurers in those circumstances as to whether the insurance policy will respond to the claim. Occasionally, insurers and insureds have very different interpretations of a peril or a policy term and you end up in court."

> **❝ I like having to become very knowledgeable about very niche issues very quickly ❞**

William enjoys the litigation side of his job because "it's multi-faceted, often involves ultra-high value claims of $100 million or more, the claims tend to be based overseas and subject to different law and jurisdiction, and you tend to have to take account of all sorts of geopolitical issues in the context of advising your clients. When people read the word 'insurance', they tend to switch off, however, in this context it's actually very interesting."

A recent case saw William working at the cutting edge of artificial intelligence (AI) and the law through the use of predictive coding. "In essence, it's a computer programme that can be trained to understand relevance," he explains. "You train the software to understand what documents are likely to be relevant within a large volume of material. It saves a huge amount of money as you only have to review a fraction of the documents, which is great news for clients and for paralegals! It's one way I think

For more firms that work in this practice area, please use the "Training contract regional indexes" starting on p211.

Name: **William Jones**
Firm: **RPC**
Location: **London**
University: **University of Bristol**
Degree: **Politics**

that technology and AI is advancing the legal profession. In our particular case, we worked with data scientists in California and developed a methodology that would enable two disputing parties to work together to train the software so that it would recognise both parties' understanding of relevance."

Above all, William enjoys the variety of his job and the fact that each day is different. "I like having to become very knowledgeable about very niche issues very quickly," he says. "You come in one morning knowing nothing about something to do with a particular pipeline, for example, and by the next day you need to have ingested enough information to have a considered argument with another lawyer about that pipeline in circumstances where you know that they too have only been reading about it for two days."

Key variables

The price of oil is a key variable in the energy insurance world. "Where the price is high, companies in the oil business have more profit and it effects the way in which they deal with risk and with their insurance companies," he explains. "That dynamic changes with the oil price and it will be interesting to see how it shifts now that oil prices are on the up."

Cyber risk is another hot topic. "Generally, I think people are unaware of its potential significance," William says, "but there's every possibility that where control systems aboard a vessel are compromised, or an oil refinery cooling system is hacked, it could result in very significant damage. Insurance companies are coming to terms with how to write these risks, whether they agree to cover them and on what terms, and whether they need a separate policy for this type of peril. Insurance is about risk; it's about determining how likely something is to happen and how severe the problem would be if it happened. In the context of cyber risks, it's very difficult for insurers

and insureds to get a proper grip of that at present, so the next five years will be interesting in this regard."

Be open minded

Understanding your clients' business and commercial pressures are considerations that trainees hoping to work in commercial law, including the energy insurance field, should keep in mind. "When you're studying law, you really see the law as an end in itself," he observes. "However, the law for your clients is an expensive tool that they use when necessary to achieve their ends. It's not an end in itself. Understanding that early is quite important. You work in a service sector and you are a cost. You need to justify your existence."

Working well with other people is another fundamental aspect of the job. "You are always working with someone, be it your clients or other lawyers based overseas, technical experts, professors from obscure universities with very niche interests as well as your team," William explains. "There's a lot of time spent working alongside other people and if that's not something you enjoy this might not be an area of law that would interest you."

William also recommends being open minded at the start of your career. "Try to do four varied seats and keep an eye on the day-to-day job and the work-life balance of the senior members of the team, and ask yourself whether you want their job. That's the key question. Your experience as a trainee is not your experience as an associate, senior associate or partner. You need to consider whether you like the work that you're going to be doing and the pressure that it brings."

Environment

Issues such as climate change and the need for alternative energy sources make environmental laws more important than ever. Environmental regulations seek to limit pollution and to minimise the impact of human activity on the natural world. This sweeping objective means that environmental lawyers are involved in a wide range of matters, from health and safety, risk management, contaminated land, waste, renewable energy and environmental finance; to commercial and property transactions, nuclear law and litigation. Clients can include individuals, community groups, companies of all sizes, local authorities and governments.

Ben Standing's career choices have always been driven by his passions, rather than the potential pay packet. His interest in law was first ignited during his undergraduate years at the University of Birmingham. "I studied labour economics as part of my degree and one of the modules was employment law. I really enjoyed it and decided to study the Graduate Diploma in Law – my interest just kept growing from there," he explains.

After jumping through the qualification hoops with ease, Ben secured a training contract at Browne Jacobson. "It's always quite hectic, being a trainee," he recalls. "You get pulled in all sorts of directions and get on with some teams more than others, but I really enjoyed the experience. It's all about finding your niche and the people you can work with."

That niche turned out to be environmental law, which involves issues that are close to Ben's heart. In fact, Browne Jacobson's prestigious environmental and public planning practice was a key reason that Ben chose to apply to train at the firm. He has not been disappointed – since joining, he has risen through the ranks to represent bodies such as Natural England and has even played a role in the creation of a new Welsh environmental protection body, Natural Resources Wales (NRW). He describes the diversity of the practice area: "A lot of environmental law focuses on property. My team primarily represents public sector clients – such as local councils and environmental bodies – but we also work alongside our colleagues in the property team, whose clients are often in the private sector. We look at environmental issues which come up in relation to land – how they affect planning permission, and sale and purchase agreements when land is sold. We also advise local authorities and private bodies in relation to the contaminated land regime. Another aspect of our work is reviewing environmental reports to look at potential issues that could arise regarding liability and identify relevant clauses which could therefore be required. I personally help to advise public bodies, such as Natural England, on environmental impact assessments and matters concerning sites of special scientific interest. My work on environmental impact assessment in relation to agriculture for the Welsh government sees me travelling all over Wales to present cases in front of planning inspectors."

Ins and outs of judicial review

Public and administrative law is another important element of the practice. Judicial review is central to this area and, as a representative of several public bodies, Ben spends a lot of his time defending clients against judicial review challenges. "Our job is to make sure that the decisions which public bodies enter into are lawfully made and cannot be reversed or quashed," he explains. "The first stage is the permission stage, where someone submits a claim and the defending party then has 21 days to respond by submitting summary grounds of resistance. A decision is then made by the court on whether to grant permission for the claimant to progress the matter; he or she is only allowed to do so if there is an arguable case which

For more firms that work in this practice area, please use the "Training contract regional indexes" starting on p211.

Name: **Ben Standing**
Firm: **Browne Jacobson LLP**
Location: **Nottingham**
University: **University of Birmingham**
Undergraduate degree: **International commerce**

justifies full investigation of the substantive merits. If permission is granted, we move on to the substantive stage. In our practice, often matters don't go to a substantive hearing because we are successful at the permission stage. However, if necessary we will robustly defend our client's decision in court."

When it comes to judicial review, a lot depends on the cards you are dealt initially. "The point at which we become involved has an impact," admits Ben. "If you're instructed when a decision is being made, you look to ensure that all the correct procedures have been followed and that the regulations are being complied with. A common reason for challenge is that the body has not adequately explained in writing its reasons for doing something. Coming up with a reasoned, logical decision and explaining why you have made it is the best way to defend against judicial review. However, if you're instructed after a decision has already been made, you just have to make the best of the situation and try to collect evidence to explain why the body has made its decision. In the worst-case scenario, you have to advise your client that it has made a mistake."

Green at heart

Flying the flag for causes that he cares about is an understandable source of job satisfaction. "I like the feeling of being on the right side, to be honest," says Ben. "I care about green issues and working for these bodies to protect the environment by making people comply with their environmental responsibilities makes me feel that I might be doing some good." Nowhere was this more evident than in Browne Jacobson's role in the formation of NRW: "The firm's property team handled the property aspect of the deal, while our job was to transfer responsibilities from the Countryside Council for Wales, the Environment Agency and the Forestry Commissioners to the new body, which involved amending the relevant

legislation by drafting an order which transferred those powers. I had only just qualified, so the experience stands out as a highlight – it was really rewarding to see what we had written become law."

Looking ahead, Ben is concerned at the amount of holes that remain to be filled in the environmental regime, as well as the possibility of existing protections being eroded. "We're primarily involved in making sure that people comply with the legislation that is there, but there should be more legislation being put in place to protect the environment," he says. "Meanwhile, the decision to leave the European Union is hugely significant, because most of our environmental law – on water, waste, birds and habitats, to name a few – stems from EU directives. I am concerned that some people are looking to unpick the legislative framework concerning the environment and this could have significant negative impacts, especially in relation to biodiversity."

Ben goes on to advise that succeeding in this area of law requires serious dedication. "There aren't many of us environmental lawyers out there, are there?" he muses. "You need to be passionate about what you're doing because, whether you're acting for public bodies or claimants, you won't want to be in this for the money – neither of these types of client have much to spend on legal fees. That said, it's a hard area to get into – there aren't that many firms practising environmental law and I was fortunate enough to join one of them, complete a seat with the team during my training and fill a vacancy when the opportunity arose. When choosing your firm, it would be wise to apply to those which practise a broad range of environmental law, not just the property side, which a lot of firms do. This area of law would be quite difficult to cross into at a later date, I think – you need to get some experience early on."

Family

Family and divorce is very much a people-focused area of law. Family and divorce lawyers deal with diverse legal issues including marriage, civil partnerships and unmarried couples, cohabitation, separation, divorce, financial claims and the now common pre and post-nuptial/civil partnership agreements. Work on matters relating to children also form a big part of a family lawyer's daily caseload. Family and divorce lawyers are often litigators, but also negotiate out-of-court settlements. Family law cases often grab the media headlines, particularly when they involve people with high wealth or high-profile personalities. While the role of a family lawyer calls for an astute legal mind, strong communication and pastoral skills are also needed to support clients through often difficult times.

Adam Cooper always knew that he wanted to work with individuals and, despite preferring history at school, he always had a legal career at the back of his mind. "I wanted to have the chance to establish a relationship with the client," he explains, and family law offered the ideal opportunity. During his training contract with Blake Morgan, Adam decided against any particularly corporate or finance-heavy seats in order to focus on private client sectors. Motivated by the fact that "every client you see is different and every case varies", he found that the family law team offered a nurturing environment for trainees: "You hear about firms where trainees are treated like work horses, but I felt I was given tasks to help me develop." Being based outside London also helped. "There's a different focus in regional offices," he observes. "They're important in their communities." However, that is not to say that trainee life is easier outside the capital. "The work was challenging," Adam recalls. "But I was well supported. The focus was on helping me to develop professionally."

Modern family

The department continued to offer a natural progression for Adam after he qualified. When it comes to the day-to-day tasks of a family law solicitor, "the starting point is divorce, but that is very much a starting point". With a case load spanning marital finances on separation to child contact disputes and issues arising from the relocation of a parent, there is always something new to learn. "I'm still learning from colleagues every day," he admits; with such a broad range of disputes, "cases and clients can go various ways".

What's more, the profession is changing. With the evolving face of the modern family, Adam acknowledges that "there's an increase in work for cohabiting couples". Considering that such individuals do not enjoy the same rights as married couples, his team often has to apply different aspects of the law.

> **“ Attention to detail and a good understanding of the law go hand in hand with the softer skills of being client-focused. You need to understand what the client's going through, but also to look at it objectively ””**

One particular Supreme Court case is being closely watched by family law practitioners around the United Kingdom. At present, "there are five facts to petition for divorce", Adam explains, "and couples are often forced to find claims of unreasonable behaviour". But *Owens v Owens* has raised serious questions around what constitutes 'unreasonable'. "There's a growing campaign for a no-fault divorce," he enthuses. Those working in family law

For more firms that work in this practice area, please use the "Training contract regional indexes" starting on p211.

Name: **Adam Cooper**
Firm: **Blake Morgan LLP**
Location: **Southampton**
University: **University of Leeds**
Degree: **History and politics**

anticipate that the Supreme Court's decision in this case, which held that a wife must remain married to her husband, could lead to big changes in the sector.

Firms mean business

Despite these noble aims, Adam remains cautious. "You might have the best intentions to help people, but you still have to meet targets and bring in billable hours," he warns. There is a significant difference between studying the law and its developments academically and working in a legal environment. "You know this in principle, but it's about making that work in practice."

Joining Blake Morgan as a paralegal before starting his training contract helped Adam to make that transition. Having already invested in the firm's culture, he was able to hit the ground running as a trainee. Understanding the demands of the workplace needs more than just in-house experience, though. "Having experience of how other businesses or sectors run really helps," Adam stresses. "Working in other businesses helps you to understand companies and their motivations." And if there is one thing that budding solicitors should bear in mind, it is that law firms are businesses. With a background teaching English to adults abroad and working at a small company, for Adam, wider work experience has been essential. "Firms are looking for the 'right fit'. They want good academics, but not necessarily the top grades." Finding your place in a firm takes the right personality, then. "Firms want to employ a well-rounded person, someone who will contribute to the office", he elaborates. The key question is: "How do they interact and how committed are they?"

Balancing empathy and professionalism

Succeeding in family law is as much about approachability as it is about competence. "Attention to detail and a

good understanding of the law go hand in hand with the softer skills of being client-focused," explains Adam. "You need to understand what the client's going through, but also to look at it objectively." Although compassion is vital in a family law solicitor, "you also need to be able to give bad news". Ultimately, it comes down to "finding a balance between being a professional and remaining empathetic".

Children law work is especially tough, but the rewards of undertaking it are all the greater. Reflecting on his achievements so far, Adam reveals that he recently acted to secure the return of a young child, who had been removed from the client's care against a court order. "It was a delicate situation," he says, "but it's rewarding when you're helping someone personally". In family law, every case is personal – if the opportunity is there to help bring a child home, it may be more than just a career highlight to know that you can make a positive difference to peoples' lives. "Every client I see, I'm helping someone through a really difficult, stressful period and trying to resolve their situation, collaboratively where possible, fighting their corner where not, but always furthering their best interests."

Human rights

Human rights law has long been a popular choice for students and practitioners, with universities increasingly offering human rights modules as part of their law degrees, and ever more firms and chambers boasting specialisms in the field. It covers a wide range of legal matters, but broadly refers to the fundamental rights and freedoms set out in the Human Rights Act 1998, which made the European Convention on Human Rights (ECHR) directly enforceable in the UK courts.

For civil liberties specialist Susie Labinjoh, a career in law presented a way to make a positive difference: "When I finished my philosophy degree, I was looking everywhere for jobs – there aren't many for philosophers, as you can imagine – and I saw job advert for a mixed administrative and HR role at Hodge Jones & Allen. I joined the firm and saw what the solicitors were doing – how they could change clients' lives – and thought 'I really want to do that'."

Determined to become a solicitor, Susie continued working while studying the GDL in the evenings part time, before going full time for the LPC. She then secured a training contract at the firm: "My previous role did not mean that there was an easy way in, though. I still had to complete the usual application process."

Miscarriages of justice
Civil liberties work encompasses many different areas of law. Broadly, Susie's practice centres on miscarriages of justice and wrongdoing by the state. "I work on civil claims against the police and public authorities, for example, inquests involving deaths in prison or police custody, or in other forms of state detention, such as mental health detention," she explains. "My work also includes judicial reviews and compensation claims for miscarriages

of justice – something I used to do much more of before the government changed the compensation scheme. A recent development has been an increase in Data Protection Act claims, where the police have released information that they shouldn't have about somebody."

❝ I work on civil claims against the police and public authorities, for example, inquests involving deaths in prison or police custody, or in other forms of state detention, such as mental health detention ❞

The current political climate presents serious challenges to solicitors working in civil liberties, particularly in securing funding from the Legal Aid Agency for otherwise meritorious cases. "We are in an age of austerity where cuts in legal aid funding have made resources far scarcer," Susie observes. "The lack of any increase to rates in many years also works as a real-terms cut."

The result of the cuts driven through by the austerity agenda of the last three successive governments has been that "the number of people eligible for legal aid has been drastically reduced," she explains. "This is to the point where even a student's maintenance loan will be considered 'income' that makes their case ineligible for funding, which seems bizarre given that student loans have to be repaid. Access to justice is a massive challenge for most people, because unless you are rich and have the resources to pay, or your income is so low that you are eligible for legal aid funding, you will be among the majority of people in the middle who cannot afford to

For more firms that work in this practice area, please use the "Training contract regional indexes" starting on p211.

Name: **Susie Labinjoh**
Firm: **Hodge Jones & Allen LLP**
Location: **London**
University: **University of Hull**
Degree: **Philosophy**

address wrongs when they happen to you. Securing public funding for cases is also incredibly tedious and bureaucratic, and while legal aid is not always the only means of funding available, it is vital for many of the cases on which I work."

In a democratic society, there is no substitute for a properly funded legal aid system. Nonetheless, Susie and her colleagues have been doing their bit to find creative ways to fund cases: "Cases have been crowdfunded in a few examples, and crowdfunding is a new area that is likely to expand in the future. Meanwhile, we have to keep fighting to secure the provision that there is."

A vocation, not just a career
That provision is vital because it is often the only way of setting right issues that would otherwise result in injustice for people of modest means. And it is the chance to prevent – or at least overturn – injustice that drives Susie in her work, even when her efforts don't succeed, as a major case from earlier in her career illustrates: "I took a case to the House of Lords in the days before the Supreme Court was established in 2009. The claim sought compensation for a miscarriage of justice, where people found to have been wrongly imprisoned after their convictions were overturned had applied for compensation, only to find that the government now intended to deduct thousands of pounds for 'board and lodging' from their awards – they were effectively being charged for their food and accommodation costs whilst they had been in prison. The case wasn't ultimately successful, and the House of Lords upheld the principle, but it raised the issue on a national level."

As a solicitor, she relishes the opportunity to see cases through from start to finish – a privilege not often shared by her barrister colleagues. "I enjoy the challenge and the fact that if you succeed, you are righting a wrong," she continues. "And remember that you can be a solicitor and do advocacy – you don't necessarily have to go to the Bar. Most of the solicitors in our criminal department have higher rights of audience."

Remember the spider
To succeed in this highly challenging area, she advises that "you have to be resilient, tenacious, extremely organised, empathetic, a good communicator, and to have a great eye for detail. You also need to be creative and flexible in the way that you approach problems."

With that taken into account, there is no better way to find out if this is the career path for you than to try it. "Do some vacation schemes and mini-pupillages," she urges. "Volunteer at law centres or branches of Citizens Advice. You will gain a sense of whether you want to be a solicitor or barrister, and whether you want to work with people or with businesses."

And for those who share her sense of justice and determination to succeed in this area, Susie finally counsels patience: "Remember the story of Robert the Bruce and the spider – he watched one try – and fail – to spin a web between two points on his ceiling before it succeeded on the third attempt. You might apply for work experience or a training contract and not get it, but don't be dissuaded – keep going. Rejections are good training for navigating the challenges and obstacles you will come up against on the job."

Immigration

Immigration lawyers deal with all legal matters relating to immigration and nationality. The work ranges from asylum and human rights claims through applications by family members and students to how businesses can secure immigration status for their employees. There is a significant and increasing EU law element, and many cases raise important human rights issues. The law is rapidly developing in terms of both statute law and jurisprudence, and procedural timeframes are tight. There is a good deal of overlap with employment, tax, social welfare, mental health, prison law, criminal law and civil actions.

Rizwana Quazi, now a business immigration lawyer, never dreamed of being a solicitor: "I didn't choose to be a solicitor initially. I always said that if I were to go into the legal profession, I would want to be a barrister, so I did my law degree and Bar Professional Training Course thinking that was the route I was going to pursue."

From asylum seekers to business immigration

Following her degree, Rizwana began looking for experience: "I started looking for a pupillage, but during that time I needed experience, so I began doing advocacy at a solicitors' firm. I do business immigration now, but when I started it was just about getting experience. We were asked to go to the immigration tribunal and represent asylum seekers. It was a good way to get the experience that I needed because it was all advocacy. If you were lucky enough to be a case worker – which I was – you got to do everything end-to-end. Because I was taking cases from the start all the way through to the finish, I felt I was getting the best of both worlds."

Rizwana eventually became a senior case worker and was offered an opportunity to take part in the Qualified Lawyers Transfer Scheme in order to switch to become a solicitor – something which was ultimately a hard decision: "I didn't want to let the barrister route go, even though I was quite senior, because I had invested a lot. I eventually moved firms and continued with immigration, but I started to steer away from asylum and human rights. I decided to go into business immigration because the points-based system launched in 2008 and I wanted to focus on a different aspect of immigration."

Over time, Rizwana has fully immersed herself into the sector: "Now I strictly do business immigration and 90% of what I do is corporate. It's a very different process and incredibly fast-paced. There is a lot of strategy involved and our focus is on helping businesses add to their workforce, whether this is highly skilled workers or transfers." Ultimately, according to Rizwana, "it's all about finding solutions for your clients – we have to work with clients to come up with the best solutions for them."

Implications of shifting immigration policies

There are undoubtedly significant changes happening to the United Kingdom's immigration policies, but the results of these changes are thus far unclear: "Brexit is challenging the industry as a whole because we don't know what its impact will be, but it will certainly be wide ranging. Brexit is working in our favour for now because there are an awful lot of clients that don't know what's happening or how to manage their workforce. Global businesses don't know whether they'll stay in the United Kingdom or relocate."

Not only that, says Rizwana, but "a lot of employers haven't needed to worry about their European workforce – there were no issues and now all of a sudden there is a lot of uncertainty about whether they can keep this workforce, how to look after them and how best to plan for employees' futures."

For more firms that work in this practice area, please use the "Training contract regional indexes" starting on p211.

Name: **Rizwana Quazi**
Firm: **Kingsley Napley LLP**
Location: **London**
University: **London Metropolitan University (formerly the University of North London)**
Degree: **Law**

In light of all of the uncertainty, there has been a focus on providing clients with the most up-to-date information: "We spend a lot of time explaining the facts, but these keep changing, so we consistently hold workshops to keep everyone in the know. Once Brexit happens, the dynamics will change, as will our role. The question will become whether companies have a need to relocate workers to the United Kingdom."

ɟɟ There is a lot of strategy involved and our focus is on helping businesses add to their workforce, whether this is highly skilled workers or transfers ͻͻ

Rizwana's personal experience highlights how quickly everything is changing: "It's quite frustrating because you don't know. You can only plan hypothetical situations. Companies may decide to leave even though they don't need to, whereas other clients are willing to wait and see – you have to manage everyone's expectations. It will certainly have an impact on us directly, but our duty and role in the current climate is to give clients the necessary knowledge."

Wellbeing in the workplace
Rizwana serves on the wellbeing committee at Kingsley Napley and believes that a healthy work-life balance is essential: "There is a big emphasis at Kingsley Napley on wellbeing and mental health. Our industry is stressful and the hours are long. When I started, I didn't know that my career would have such an impact on my mental wellbeing.

"Especially in business immigration, it doesn't matter how much you prepare or how many hours you work, you're always faced with situations that you haven't planned for.

Some people live off this stress, so it can work – but I think it's important to realise that it doesn't work for everyone. I believe that there is far more awareness of this in our industry and certainly at my firm. At Kingsley Napley, we are big on work-life balance."

Expert advice
Rizwana concludes with some advice for aspiring solicitors: "Be proactive and have foresight. You must also be able to manage and work with your clients. Often, you'll have clients that are set in their ways. As their solicitor, you should be able to communicate what the implications are if they don't want to make changes. You also have to manage expectations and be frank, firm and – most importantly – fair."

Another hugely important aspect is business development: "Because we do a lot of seminars, webinars and marketing, there is a big focus on business development at whatever level you're at. Whether you're a paralegal, trainee or partner, business development is so much more important now. Yes, you have to know the law and keep up to date, but law students will benefit from being able to make friends and network. It's important to be well-rounded."

Above all, Rizwana says "you need to believe in the same values as your firm. If you have things that are very important to you, try to get your experience with a firm that values those things too. I've worked for various businesses and firms and I love where I am now because of their values and integrity. Your wellbeing is so important."

Her parting advice is to "develop your career in a place you feel comfortable, a place where you're not afraid to say what you believe or voice your opinion. It's so important to feel accepted for who you are and know that you're a valid person. I believe that you can't develop unless you get the freedom to be who you are."

Insurance

Insurance (and reinsurance – the insurance of insurers) is an integral part of commercial activity throughout the world. The insurance practices of top-end firms advise on a range of areas, including coverage disputes, investment management, documentation, mergers and acquisitions of insurers, and the transfer of books and business between insurers. Regulatory law governs matters such as the establishment and regulation of insurance companies throughout the world. Clients include insurers, reinsurers and UK insurance institutions, as well as major insured companies and their captive insurers.

Stephanie Castell's journey into the legal profession began at the University of Kent, where she gained her law degree; and continued at The University (then College) of Law for the Legal Practice Course stage. She joined BLM, well known for its status as a leader in the field of insurance law, as a trainee in the Southampton office in 2010, where her experiences during the training contract proved to be ideal preparation for her future practice: "I spent one of my seats on secondment at the Association of British Insurers (ABI), which was a very interesting and beneficial experience, seeing bills being written and presented through Parliament and particularly as many of the firm's customers work with the ABI on current topical issues."

Now a partner at the firm, Stephanie is part of the catastrophic injury team, where she acts on behalf of insurers defending high-value claims brought against them or their insured's involving serious injuries. "My caseload involves defending claims for traumatic brain and spinal injuries as well as amputation cases, with most claims valued above £1 million," she explains.

In addition to the kinds of claim already described, Stephanie has worked on a number of complex cerebral palsy cases where there is dispute as to whether injuries may have been caused by, for example, a road traffic accident, or an unexplained and unregistered insult to the foetus *en ventre sa mere* (in the womb).

Complex investigations

Such serious issues require sensitivity and the opinions of medical experts – and sometimes those in other fields, as well – to establish the facts and arrive at an appropriate level of damages. "Some cases can take years to run from start to finish given the complexity of the medical problems and investigations needed," she explains. "Part of my role is to investigate liability and determine fault, which may involve analysing an accident scenario, conducting interviews and considering expert reconstruction evidence. The next stage is to consider quantum, which is the value of the injuries as set out by the courts and the compensation that should be paid to put the claimant back in the position they would have been in pre-accident. These valuations are based on medical evidence, so in the case of a traumatic brain injury with ongoing effects, we would usually instruct a neurologist who will not only comment on the severity of the injury, but also any risk of post-traumatic epilepsy and any effect on life expectancy. There is often an array of evidence to get through and experts to consult." Clearly, solicitors who work on cases involving catastrophic injury can foster very different relationships with the solicitors on the opposing side than might be the case with solicitors in other practice areas, as the severity of the injuries involved in such cases requires, more often than not, a collaborative approach to securing the right level of damages.

One of the most appealing aspects of the role is the regular opportunity to consult

For more firms that work in this practice area, please use the "Training contract regional indexes" starting on p211.

Name: **Stephanie Castell**
Firm: **BLM**
Location: **Southampton**
University: **University of Kent**
Undergraduate degree: **Law**

with experts who are frequently leaders in their fields. "The same applies on the purely legal side," she adds. "I instruct top QCs and work with excellent solicitors. The variety of professionals that I work with is another attraction of the role." But an interesting, high-value caseload is not without its pressures: "The workload is not for the faint hearted, dealing with complex medical terminology and conditions, while balancing court-imposed time limits to factor in with many other cases as part of one's caseload; it can be demanding."

❝ The workload is not for the faint hearted, dealing with complex medical terminology and conditions, while balancing court-imposed time limits ❞

As for highlights in Stephanie's career so far, becoming a partner would be a tough one to surmount: "I have helped to build a strong catastrophic injury team in the Southampton office and have responsibility not only to conduct my own caseload, but also to train and develop the more inexperienced members of the team."

Unknown territory
Stephanie comments on the recent change to the discount rate causing concern in the insurance industry, which has sparked wide debate as to how such a rate should be set in the future: "We are still very much in unknown territory. Such uncertainties, and the status of the industry, mean that there is an onus on solicitors' firms to continue adapting to meet the challenges of an environment that is as competitive as ever where you are judged not only on your ability to carry out the work, but what 'extras' you can bring to the table."

Finally, Stephanie has the following advice for those aspiring to join the solicitors' profession themselves. "A strong academic record and the ability to manage complex information to arrive at good solutions is essential, but there is much more to being a solicitor than legal expertise – you need a much wider skill set. Excellent interpersonal and communication skills are also essential in addition to prioritising your workload and the ability to adapt and understand evidence in an array of often unfamiliar fields of expertise."

Intellectual property

IP work can be divided into two main areas: so-called 'hard' and 'soft' intellectual property. 'Hard' intellectual property generally relates to registered IP rights such as patents, while 'soft' intellectual property includes registered trademarks and registered designs, copyright, unregistered design rights, database rights, trade secrets, confidential information and passing off. IP lawyers advise on issues ranging from commercial exploitation to infringement disputes, and agreements that deal either exclusively with IP or with IP rights in the wider context of larger commercial transactions. Many lawyers specialise in either contentious or non-contentious IP work.

As is the case for many IP lawyers, Nadine Bleach took her undergraduate background in the sciences and converted it into a career in law: "I wanted to use my physics degree, but not necessarily in a purely scientific field. IP law, which requires the application of technical understanding to a legal framework, seemed like a sound option. Although it was intellectual property that drew me in, looking at many different areas of law made me realise that even without the direct use of science, there are a lot of transferable skills, including problem-solving and analysis, and the ability to structure and work through issues in a logical way."

Patently clear
Nadine trained at Bristows, enjoying among other things the fact that she was able to undertake six seats, which offered the chance to try a variety of departments and make an informed choice at the point of qualification. That led her to join their market-leading IP department in 2014. "At Bristows there is a split between transactional and litigious intellectual property; I'm in the litigation department, specialising in patents," she explains. "I work on disputes in all kinds of scientific area, but I am drawn more to the technological areas – such as telecoms, engineering and mechanics.

It is a mix of advising clients who can be at various stages of the dispute process, and running litigation at court."

Nadine was a part of one of the most high-profile patent cases of recent years, *Unwired Planet v Huawei, Samsung & others*, acting for Samsung: "It was my first telecoms case at Bristows and I was involved from the very beginning and throughout the life cycle of the case. Piecing it all together, working on the high-level strategy as well as getting to grips with the technical detail and then attending court and watching it all unfold – it was very interesting and exciting."

Day to day, what you will find yourself doing depends largely on the type of matter you are involved in and, if it is a court case, the stage the trial has reached, as Nadine explains: "At the beginning of a trial, you're getting into the subject matter, working with the client to understand what the case is all about, including any products, features of the market and the issues in dispute. You need to understand things from the client's perspective, including their commercial goals. The focus then turns to strategy, including finding and working with experts in the particular field. Cases often feel fast-moving and before you know it you are in the nitty gritty of trial preparation, working with barristers on the strategy for presenting the case to the court."

One of the most interesting things about the job is the opportunity to work with and meet a huge variety of people: "Clients, barristers, experts; they all have a role to play in preparing patent cases for court. Much of it is often understanding complicated technical information; despite having a scientific background, we will work with experts who know these areas in incredible detail. I love working with people who are the best in their fields; you learn about some very interesting things, which you wouldn't otherwise have access to. You also become something of a

For more firms that work in this practice area, please use the "Training contract regional indexes" starting on p211.

Name: **Nadine Bleach**
Firm: **Bristows LLP**
Location: **London**
University: **Imperial College London**
Undergraduate degree: **Physics**

mini-expert in each area as you go from case to case. For example, I might move from telecoms to medical devices to product packaging!"

The unpredictability of hours and workload is one of the few disadvantages to this exciting career: "Especially coming up to deadlines, you don't always know in advance how busy you're going to be. Things come up when you least expect them to and that can be tough. But I like that we are often working in teams – working things through together. As a junior lawyer, that's a great way to learn."

Nadine explains the significance of the much-anticipated launch of the Unified Patent Court (UPC): "For example, rather than having to launch a patent action in each country of infringement, under the UPC it will be possible to bring a single action, provided the countries in which infringement is alleged are part of the UPC. A similar principle applies for invalidating patents. It will be quite different to the current UK system, including different rules of procedure and involving judges from all over Europe. While Brexit certainly muddied the waters, the plan is still for the UPC to open in 2018-19 and for the United Kingdom to be part of the system. What is less certain is the United Kingdom's longer term participation."

There is also a concern among some patent lawyers that the United Kingdom may lose some work as a result of the UPC because all European lawyers will be competing for the same work. However, there remains confidence in the ability to win work and there is also the prospect of work flowing in from across the Atlantic: "There has been a change in the United States in the rules as to where patent infringement proceedings can be brought. This restricts a patentee's ability to bring cases in the most patentee-friendly jurisdictions in the United States, such as the Eastern District of Texas. This may drive more work in the direction of the future UPC, where the patentee will have more options as to where it can bring its claims. In

fact the UPC could well cause a global shift in litigation from the United States to Europe."

Skills and challenges

Nadine reflects on some of the most important skills associated with a successful career in IP law. "Teamwork is a huge part; the more experienced I get, the more I realise its importance, in terms of working more efficiently and making me a better lawyer," she says. "You need an eye for detail – that's very important. The entire strategy in a case can change on the smallest of details. It's also essential to be logical and not jump to conclusions and do things in a methodical way. You also need to be able to look at what the client wants and needs, their commercial goals, as well as the technical case, as it all feeds into a cohesive whole. This is both challenging and enjoyable – I feel fulfilled when I've manged to put together what can be a very complicated puzzle. I enjoy this mental challenge."

A challenge ahead of would-be lawyers is finding the firm that is the best fit for them. Nadine has a few suggestions on how to go about doing that: "Do your research to work out what firms do and specialise in. All firms are different, they are different sizes, working in different ways with different types of client; so you need to identify what is best for you. Try to understand about a firm before you apply, so that you can make a targeted application." The best way of doing that is to get out there and talk to people: "Go to open days and law fairs; they're really helpful to get insight into a range of firms. I realised that I wanted to work here at Bristows when I did the vacation scheme – I really liked the people and the work I was exposed to. Understanding a firm's culture and type of work is best done through speaking to people first hand, especially trainees but also more senior lawyers, who can offer insight into life at the firm once qualified. If you like what you hear, then it's a good indicator that the firm will suit you too."

Islamic finance

The term 'Islamic finance' refers to a system of banking that is consistent with *Sharia* law. In particular, interest is prohibited, as is investing in businesses considered unlawful, such as those which trade in pork or alcohol. Although Islamic finance was initially important predominantly to commercial firms with interests in the oil-rich countries of the Middle East, it is now a practice area in every major international firm. Banks, financial institutions, sovereigns and corporates worldwide still take a great interest in traditional Islamic finance markets such as Malaysia, the United Arab Emirates and Saudi Arabia, but there are also significant Islamic financial centres in London, Hong Kong and Singapore. This, combined with the growth of Islamic finance throughout Asia and Africa, is leading to an increased need for lawyers who understand Islamic finance.

Farmida Bi was initially drawn to the law by the prospect of "going out there and righting wrongs and helping people" – a lofty ideal, and not uncommon when the notion of becoming a lawyer is dreamed up in childhood. It took a law degree and a few stints of work experience to discover that in fact, she wanted to be an entirely different type of lawyer: "I did a vacation scheme at Clifford Chance in my second year. I loved the international nature of the work, and the informality when compared to the chambers at which I'd done mini-pupillages." Another reason for turning down the Bar was financial: "At that time, you generally had to fund your way through Bar school and pupillage, whereas the big law firms paid for law school, a maintenance grant and your training. For me, the financial imperatives were decisive."

Farmida studied her finals (now the LPC) at The College of Law (now The University of Law) in Guildford and went on to do her articles (now the training contract) at Clifford Chance. She recalls the time fondly: "We had about 80 people in our intake, so there were lots of us in the same position. It was a well-organised programme and you got a real sense of the different options available to you. I also spent six months in Singapore, which I loved."

> ££ The workload is not for the faint hearted, dealing with complex medical terminology and conditions, while balancing court-imposed time limits JJ

Leader in the field

Leaving Clifford Chance when she was four years' qualified, and after a brief spell in-house at JP Morgan, Farmida moved to US firm Cleary Gottlieb and qualified at the New York Bar. That was, she enthuses, "a wonderful experience; I had a much broader range of work than before, with a huge amount of responsibility – it was exhilarating". She then became a partner at Denton Wilde Sapte (now Dentons), which is where, as part of the capital markets team, she first encountered Islamic finance; in 2008 she joined Norton Rose (now Norton Rose Fulbright) as a partner, where she is European head of Islamic finance. She is the only woman ranked for Islamic finance in *Chambers UK* and has also added to her trophy cabinet by scooping 'Best in Banking and Finance' at the European Women in Business Law Awards in 2011 and 2013.

Farmida's practice is primarily focused on capital markets and she explains where Islamic finance fits into that: "Islamic finance can be used for all sorts of deals – be that financing an aeroplane, constructing a building or going out into the markets and raising money – while fulfilling the requirements of *Sharia* law, which includes a prohibition on the charging of interest."

For more firms that work in this practice area, please use the "Training contract regional indexes" starting on p211.

(194) THE LAWCAREERS.NET HANDBOOK

Name: **Farmida Bi**
Firm: **Norton Rose Fulbright**
Location: **London**
University: **University of Cambridge**
Undergraduate degree: **Law**

Change is afoot

She describes the changing nature of Islamic finance: "For us as a firm, and for me personally, Islamic finance has become quite specialised. Three or four years ago, if you were an Islamic finance lawyer, you could work on a fund one day, a property acquisition the next and a *sukuk* (a *Sharia*-compliant bond issue) on the third. Nowadays, it is more common to specialise in a particular area – such as capital markets – and you have to work on that in both a conventional and an Islamic way. Some clients can switch from one option to the other – they might start out with a conventional deal and then find an investor that wants it to be *sharia* compliant, so it changes, and vice versa." Farmida's advice to those interested in Islamic finance is to think instead about becoming a lawyer who can work in both a conventional and an Islamic speciality: "The skills you will be offering are those of a lawyer. Our job is to structure a transaction which satisfies the client's commercial needs and meets the requirements of the *Sharia*, as evidenced by a fatwa provided by an Islamic scholar. We have to understand that we are not the scholars and we have been employed for our legal skills rather than our religious beliefs."

As a partner, Farmida's day is a mix of client work and general firm-related matters: "On any given day, I could be meeting clients, reviewing the work of associates in the team, structuring a new deal and marketing the firm, as well as dealing with internal administrative issues. There is also some travel – particularly to the Middle East, although not exclusively: "We also have a lot of clients in Europe who are interested in Islamic finance and potentially looking to do deals which are sharia compliant."

Ground-breaking work

A professional highlight for Farmida was working on the first UK corporate *sukuk* for IIT: "It was a small deal, but the fact that it was the first of its kind made it interesting.

By contrast, a few years ago I worked on one of the biggest deals in the market – the $3.5 billion Dubai Ports acquisition. That really changed the market. Most of the deals I work on have an average lifespan of around three months, so you work on something, it comes to market and you move on to the next one. That's satisfying."

For those keen to find out more, Farmida recommends starting with the press, such as the *Financial Times* and the *Economist*, to "get a general idea of what's happening in the world and with Islamic finance in particular, as it gets significant coverage". A number of textbooks are also available. And a familiarity with Islam itself will help: "If you speak Arabic or have an understanding of the principles of Islam, it makes a big difference. Having said that, there are plenty of successful people in the industry who are not Arabic speakers or Muslims; but an interest in the religion and the culture definitely helps."

Finally, Farmida stresses the importance of experience – and not just of the legal variety: "Getting a training contract now seems more difficult, so it's important to be an interesting and engaged person. Legal work experience gives you an advantage, but so can other experience. I interviewed a solicitor recently who'd taken a couple of years off to manage a jazz band. The skills she had picked up, such as managing a business, researching the market and meeting client needs, were all relevant for a successful lawyer. She had also done something she was interested in. I think that people can be narrowly CV-focused these days; general life experience and doing things you're interested in will also help you to be a more attractive candidate as you try to build a career."

Personal injury

Personal injury (PI) law falls under the law of tort. It involves civil law cases brought to obtain compensation for injuries sustained, to restore the injured person to the position he or she would have been in had the injury not happened. The subject matter varies considerably and can range from controversial, high-profile disasters to road traffic accidents to health and safety cases. A related specialised practice area of PI law is clinical negligence, which involves injuries suffered during medical procedures.

Although he can't pinpoint exactly why, law was always where Matt Bacon imagined himself ending up: "I studied it at A level and at university; I just never wanted to do anything else. I've always been interested in litigation – I like putting together arguments to see how they play out. I also have some family members in law, so having spoken to them and others, it sounded even more like something I would enjoy."

Matt secured his training contract at what was then Henmans (although the firm announced its merger with Freeths just a few days later). He benefited from having spent time paralegalling elsewhere, which meant that he was able to knock six months off his training contract as 'time to count', and went on to qualify into the defendant personal injury team. "I only do defendant work, and we mainly receive our instructions from insurers or corporate clients that have large self-insured elements of their business", Matt explains. "I specialise in employers' liability, covering any accident that occurs at work, public liability and product liability. I'm also involved with defending health and safety prosecutions – so those companies that are prosecuted by the Health and Safety Executive as a result of a one-off accident or breaches in relation to health and safety in general."

As a trainee, Matt enjoyed great exposure to work of this nature and he still works closely with his former supervisor: "Now I have my own caseload, which I run from start to finish, and which involves thinking of my own tactics. It allows me to be more independent with the way I deal with cases. On top of that, I help my supervisor with his cases. Things do ramp up in terms of responsibility when you qualify, but you can always run tactics past your supervisor and there is continued support."

Tactical advantage

Matt recalls as a highlight his first experience of a case discontinuance – "we presented evidence in defence and the claimant discontinued the claim" – but generally speaking, it is the process of working through a PI matter that provides the everyday satisfaction: "I enjoy when you get a case in and you're deciding on tactics and formulating the best arguments." He makes the point that sometimes, the best way forward is not to defend a claim, especially if there is little chance of success and it may be better for the client simply to take it on the chin: "Most clients just want you to be open and honest with your advice; if there isn't a case to defend, they don't want to waste money on defending it. Economics plays a big part in what we do and you have to be commercially minded, putting pragmatic business interests first."

Not unique to PI lawyers, but certainly something with particular resonance to them, the profession is keeping a close eye on changes relating to costs, particularly those of the claimant. "There was a change in legislation a few years ago – and there are others in the pipeline – to make most personal injury claims up to £25,000 subject to fixed costs, so as the lawyer, you would receive a fixed amount as opposed to an hourly fee," Matt explains. There is also the small claims track for low-value claims,

For more firms that work in this practice area, please use the "Training contract regional indexes" starting on p211.

Name: **Matt Bacon**
Firm: **Freeths LLP**
Location: **Oxford**
University: **University of Reading**
Undergraduate degree: **Law**

where you can't usually recover the costs of instructing a lawyer. The government is looking at increasing the claim limit for that from £1,000."

More generally, lawyers must keep up with clients' evolving needs and expectations – particularly as these relate to the use of technology – in order to maintain a successful practice: "Especially in light of the changeable economy, clients expect you to be doing the work on the most cost-efficient basis, using all the tech that is available. Every firm has to keep abreast of that now."

> ❝ **Being commercial is something to remember; you have to understand your clients' businesses, establish what they're looking for and tailor your advice to their particular needs** ❞

Keep cool

Something else that clients want from their legal adviser is the ability to stay both cool under pressure and commercially attuned, as Matt notes: "Given the often very tight timescales, and as you normally have several cases going on at once, you have to remain calm and deal with them all as efficiently as you can. Being commercial is something to remember; you have to understand your clients' businesses, establish what they're looking for and tailor your advice to their particular needs. When you're dealing with insurers, who are very knowledgeable about the law because they handle it every day, your advice has to be pitched at someone who is an experienced user of the legal profession. Conversely, if it's an individual who is not familiar with the law or the system, you have to adjust your advice to that."

In order to stand out from the hordes of other would-be lawyers, Matt suggests talking to those already in the profession as a way to learn more and to establish whether it's right for you: "It's very important to get yourself out there, so do some work experience and try to meet as many people as possible. Law fairs are another important way of gaining exposure to firm reps, so that when you come to apply, you're not doing so from a completely blank background. Firms have so many people applying, it's important you have something that separates you from the pack."

While you shouldn't be put off by the levels of competition, you also have to be realistic about your chances: "One thing that didn't really strike me until I was through the process is how competitive it is and how many people are going for each vacancy; I didn't get my training contract until after law school and it was a real eye-opener to see how many of us there didn't have training contracts. I wouldn't change the way I did it, but it is very competitive and you have to put yourself out there."

Private client

A private client solicitor looks after the affairs of individual clients and trustees, planning and managing all aspects of their personal wealth, including wills and probate, onshore and offshore trusts, and tax matters. Private client lawyers also handle a wide range of charity work, advising on specific legal issues as well as on commercial and property matters that affect charitable organisations and the establishment of charities. Private client work is booming and, increasingly, multi-jurisdictional issues are becoming more important for private client lawyers as a result of acting for clients who are based outside the United Kingdom or who own assets in various countries throughout the world.

"It could have been quite a dry degree with all that jurisprudence!" quips Laura Paterson on her decision not to study law at undergraduate level. Opting to read history at the University of Edinburgh instead, Laura discovered that she wanted to be a solicitor through a more hands-on approach: "I had the opportunity to have a few weeks of work experience, both at solicitors' firms and with two sets of barristers' chambers. I really enjoyed the discipline of the law but much preferred the analytical to the adversarial side of it."

"The work experience that I had done had been predominantly at private client firms," she continues, describing what first attracted her to this area of law as she studied for her GDL and LPC at BPP University in London. After completing a vacation scheme at Forsters, Laura was offered a training contract and qualified into the firm's private client practice in 2015. Since then, she hasn't looked back, and conducts most of her work "for UK resident domiciled clients, advising on tax and succession issues".

Collaborative approach

Laura explains why being a barrister never really appealed to her: "I enjoy public speaking, but it was a lot to do with the work experience. I found the work that barristers do and their core process very interesting, but I thought I might prefer being part of a team to the solitary nature of barristers' work. I enjoy the more collaborative approach to problem solving and I thought that becoming a solicitor would suit my personal attributes better."

In fact, this collaborative approach is one of the things that Laura enjoys most about her work as a private client solicitor. "Tax legislation changes so often because it is inherently political, which makes our job more interesting. "Even at the more junior end, you can participate in debates because it's sometimes the case that the people who are more junior are more familiar with the rules, because they might have learnt them recently or have advised on them with a different partner."

Political risk

Such a focus on legislation means that the private client sphere can be particularly academic: "If you're one of those people at law school who really enjoys doing research then it might be the practice area for you."

The political nature of tax, though, comes with its own challenges. Laura highlights "the risk of changes to legislation which make the UK a less attractive place for international individuals to live, work and invest in" as one issue facing the profession at present. With widespread changes to legislation affecting the taxation of non-domiciled individuals having been implemented in April 2017 and earlier this year, Laura adds that "it's a very interesting time in terms of public policy and generally the way that new legislation is affecting our clients".

For more firms that work in this practice area, please use the "Training contract regional indexes" starting on p211.

Name: **Laura Paterson**
Firm: **Forsters LLP**
Location: **London**
University: **University of Edinburgh**
Undergraduate degree: **History**

Client focus

Day-to-day, Laura explains, there is "lots of drafting – wills, letters of wishes, lasting powers of attorney, trust instruments and other subsidiary documents – and preparing detailed tax advice". However, private client law is intrinsically client-focused, meaning that there is also an abundance of client facetime. "Unlike with other practice areas where you don't get to meet with clients very often, I usually have one or two client meetings each day. If you're drafting someone's will, for example, you need to have a clear understanding of how their personal wealth is structured and how they relate to the rest of their family, which can often only be gleaned from face-to-face meetings."

> ## 66 Unlike with other practice areas where you don't get to meet with clients very often, I usually have one or two client meetings each day 99

This mix of the technical and the personal demands a varied skill set, Laura suggests, highlighting three particularly important attributes for private client solicitors: "The first is to have an analytical mind, as lots of the work is interpreting black letter law." Second, it is useful to have a good memory "because of the longstanding relationships with clients – you might be in a meeting and someone will say 'oh we did this planning the other day' and 'the other day' might have been seven or eight years ago!"

Finally, it is absolutely crucial to have excellent interpersonal skills. "Much like family law, you may be advising clients at tricky personal times; there's no escaping that much of the work that we do revolves around death," Laura warns. "You need to have high levels of emotional intelligence."

Human element

However, this only makes the job even more rewarding. "The real highlights for me are the personal thank yous from clients, which often mean much more than highly technical achievements," Laura reflects. "You know that you've done a good job when clients seek your opinion on matters which are entirely non-legal. Building up a role as a trusted adviser is always the aim."

She continues: "A lot of the work involves drafting entirely bespoke documents, because no two families are ever the same. Ultimately, we give personal advice – the reward feels much greater, because you've done a good job for the client personally, rather than the entity for which they work. I like the human element of it."

Go in with your eyes open

Laura's main advice for those contemplating a career as a solicitor is to do as much research as possible. "Speak to people who work in the industry, as many as you can, because then you're really going into it with your eyes open," she suggests. "One thing I wish I'd known is how all law firms are very different, so think about the type of firm you might want to work for – not just in terms of culture but in terms of clients and practice area. I was lucky in that I knew that I wanted to qualify as a private client lawyer so applied to firms with that offering, but if you don't have an idea of which specialism you want to go into, do your research. Not all firms offer the same practice areas so do your homework!"

Restructuring and insolvency

Restructuring and insolvency lawyers are called in when a company, individual or other organisation is in financial difficulties and is facing possible liquidation, administration or bankruptcy. In such situations, restructuring and insolvency lawyers work to advise the organisation's management and other stakeholders on what to do next, which could be filing for administration or a distressed merger. A restructuring and insolvency lawyer's work is also to advise organisations that have not yet become insolvent on how to avoid such a situation and formulate contingency plans. In addition, restructuring and insolvency lawyers will also advise an organisation's creditors where their borrower is facing financial problems.

When studying and training to be a lawyer in her native Australia, Hanh Nguyen may not have imagined that she would be a partner, specialising in restructuring and insolvency, in a respected City firm a decade later. However, she had always been open to wherever her legal career might take her: "I always wanted to keep my options open, which is why I did a double degree. However, towards the end of the degree when I was looking for part-time work, I was drawn to legal secretary roles and having secured one, realised that the practical element of law really resonated with me."

After qualification in 2004, Hanh spent seven years at a boutique general practice firm in Sydney, before sitting the Qualified Lawyers Transfer Test and coming to the United Kingdom. She spent time at both Teacher Stern LLP and Salans LLP, where she first explored corporate and personal insolvency work, coinciding as it did with the global recession. She then joined Speechly Bircham LLP (which merged with Charles Russell LLP in 2014 to form Charles Russell Speechlys LLP), for what was supposed to be a six-month contract: "Seven years on, I'm still here – and now a partner!"

Cradle to grave

Hanh explains the way in which the firm occupies a unique place in terms of restructuring and insolvency work, aiming to be a one-stop-shop for clients. "We do both contentious and non-contentious work, so consider our role to be from cradle to grave," she explains. "Stage one is where a company or individual is in financial difficulties and our client – for example, the company's board of directors, shareholders or bank – gets us involved to see if we can restructure or rescue the company, to avoid it going into an insolvency process. In that case, you're looking at ways to avoid the company being wound up or placed into another insolvency process, such as via restructuring its debt or minimising its liabilities. In those cases we work closely with our corporate finance and banking colleagues to see what can be done."

Stage two is when the company moves officially into the relevant insolvency process, and Hanh and her colleagues find themselves usually acting for the office holder that has been appointed as the agent of the company, namely, an insolvency practitioner – for example, Deloitte, KPMG, Duff & Phelps or Grant Thornton: "Our role then is to advise on whatever needs doing, such as selling the business or making employees redundant – whatever needs to be done in order to realise assets for the company's creditors."

The third and final stage can involve pursuing delinquent directors or others who may carry fault for the failure of the company: "The situation may involve fraudulent or questionable conduct by directors, such as stripping the company of assets before it was wound up. We then issue court proceedings to recover assets that rightfully belong to the company. Again, the main objective is to achieve a result for the creditors."

For more firms that work in this practice area, please use the "Training contract regional indexes" starting on p211.

Name: **Hanh Nguyen**
Firm: **Charles Russell Speechlys LLP**
Location: **London**
University: **University of Sydney**
Undergraduate degree: **Commerce and law**

Variety is the spice

This full-service offering means work is never dull and the chance to work internally with many of the firm's different teams is a key feature of her practice: "No two days are the same. I work with our corporate finance, employment, banking and private client colleagues, which keeps thing interesting. I'm not an expert in any of these areas, I have to be aware of them and liaise with colleagues accordingly. Compared to other firms that might just do contentious or non-contentious work, we have always thought it was useful to have both skill sets, even though my preference is probably for the advisory and transaction work."

There is also satisfaction to be derived from the variety of clients that Hanh deals with on a daily basis: "It ranges from fellow professionals in accountancy firms to personnel at all manner of different companies. It's good not to get too entrenched with one type of client."

Hanh reflects on some of the challenges that come with being made partner: "It requires a different skill set, namely learning to manage people, supervise and delegate. It's assumed that you're technically sound and competent by this point in your career, but there are new people skills that you can only really learn on the job. Business development and marketing is also part of it – and again, not something that you're taught at uni! Developing long-term relationships with clients is a real skill. Still, I welcome the challenge – BD is encouraged by the firm from a very junior stage, especially developing networks among your peer group, both within and outside of the firm."

There is also real satisfaction from working on matters that non-lawyers can understand. "I like it when I'm involved with something that's in the press or quite high profile, such as the Borders or East Retail insolvencies.

They may not be billion-pound-deals, but it's nice to have some spark of recognition from people, in terms of them understanding what I do. I worked on a case that involved a power plate manufacturer, which friends I talked to found relatable! I also find that friends use me as a sounding board if they want advice about investing; I can offer a different perspective that has been gained by working in restructuring and insolvency, even though sometimes it is all a bit doom and gloom!"

As you might expect, the spectre of Brexit looms large on the horizon, as Hanh describes: "There is a lot of uncertainty ahead. All law firms and accountants can do briefings about what might happen, but who really knows? There might be a decline in investment, fewer exports and imports, but it's all speculation. The key issues facing our area of law and the profession generally will be founded in the outcome of the Brexit negotiations and where that takes us."

Sage advice

Hanh's top tips to would-be lawyers include the need to "research firms well; don't just apply to the top five firms just for the sake of it or because everyone else is." She cites client interaction or being part of a team as two potential motivators and, more broadly, a need to think about what you really want out of your career: "It's a long-term commitment and you have to be certain it's right for you. What are your strengths and are they something that you can apply to a particular practice area or way of working? One example – if the idea of advocacy makes you want to jump out of bed, then life as a barrister could be for you. If it fills you with dread, then it's probably not! Working culture and environment are also important. Listen to what others have to say about the firms you're interested in – it's not just the quality of work, but also the quality of colleagues; a good environment and sound career progression may become more important than massive deals."

Shipping

Shipping law tends to fall into two areas: contentious and non-contentious. On the contentious side, 'dry' shipping involves contractual issues such as bill of lading and charterparty disputes, whereas 'wet' shipping tends to involve issues of international law, tort and jurisdiction (eg, collisions). Non-contentious work includes ship finance (eg, lending and security) and the drafting of commercial agreements (eg, charters and shipbuilding contracts). Whereas the shipping industry is by its nature international, London remains the pre-eminent venue for dispute resolution and marine insurance, and English law is the legal system of choice.

Matt had visions of joining the army, but the dream was not to be. The army's loss, however, was law's gain: "Although I had originally planned to join the army, law seemed like a good solid degree, and it felt to me that you could do a lot with it. I had also had the chance to do some work experience at a firm in the shipping department; at 18 years old, it felt pretty exciting to be dealing with claims from Japan, the US and all over the world!"

Going on to train at Walton & Morse, which is now part of Kennedys, Matt had another taste of life as a shipping lawyer: "It was a small and very traditional London market firm, and while there, I'd often been on the opposite side to HFW lawyers. When I had the chance to shift to HFW on qualification, I jumped at the chance. That's an opportunity as an NQ that you don't turn down."

Navigating the high seas of law
Now a senior associate at the firm, Matt works within the disputes section of the shipping department – there are also finance and corporate sections. His clients are predominantly shipowners, transport operators, ports and terminal operators, and insurers, and he tends to be defending them in relation to a variety of logistics and supply-chain related disputes and projects, which "could be worth £50,000 or £50 million".

He is also involved in more general commercial disputes: "For example, there may have been a falling out with customers over the provision of a particular service or the contractual renegotiation of pricing levels. Another common example is where a UK retailer has gone bust, owing many different companies money, and a shipowner wants to exercise its right of lien over the goods, but the administrators are screaming for the goods to be returned. That type of claim tends to come in cycles, often following on from retail premises rent reviews."

> **Generally speaking, lawyers who work in shipping are passionate about it – I'd even say borderline nerdy; I know a lot of people with Lego ships!**

There was a run of high street collapses in 2012, including Jane Norman, Focus DIY, Peacocks, JJB Sports and La Senza. "They came thick and fast, so we had a lot of work on – the La Senza claim went to court on expedited proceedings, and from start to finish it took just two weeks," he recalls. "We were working round the clock on witness statements, culminating in a good win for our client, changing the law and even making it into *The Sun!*"

Matt describes a couple of the court proceedings he's currently involved with: "We have a number of cases for shipowners whose vessels were hijacked by pirates in 2011 and who are trying to recover part of the ransom-associated costs from the owners of the cargo that was being transported. We are invoking a mechanism called a general average claim, which is essentially about sharing the cost involved with getting goods

For more firms that work in this practice area, please use the "Training contract regional indexes" starting on p211.

Name: **Matthew Wilmshurst**
Firm: **HFW**
Location: **London**
University: **De Montfort University**
Undergraduate degree: **Law**

to their destination. I'm also involved in a claim that centres on damage to parts of large oil pipes that occurred in transit, and a series of cases relating to high-value designer clothing, which was being transported by road, where interesting arguments are being raised including whether some of the drivers were gassed while sleeping and whether others may have been involved in the theft."

Matt also sees some collision work, much of which involves intense crisis management: "We've had situations where a big vessel comes into a container terminal and fails to stop, knocking down cranes and worse! I have been involved in cases where vessels collide and sink, where they ground themselves on an island or a beach(!) and where they have suffered an explosion. These types of case require working non-stop for a few weeks, dealing with the fallout." As you'd expect, it is very international work: "The main region I deal with is the far east, which has a lot of container lines and is where most of the goods we consume here in the UK come from, but other colleagues focus on different geographies."

Matt notes that one of the best bits of the job is the excellent people he works with: "Generally speaking, lawyers who work in shipping are passionate about it – I'd even say borderline nerdy; I know a lot of people with Lego ships! So we all enjoy what we do, which creates a great atmosphere in the team."

Riding the tech wave
In terms of how shipping law and its practice might change, Matt cites Blockchain and technology generally as the developments that are likely to have the greatest impact. He says: "Every week there's a seminar on Blockchain and tech, including autonomous vehicles or going paperless. It has the potential to change everything. Cyber issues are also becoming more and more common. Last summer one of the world's biggest

container lines was crippled by a cyberattack, so it's very real. Companies are looking at their crisis management plans, whether they have the correct insurance in place, and changing their contracts to cater for these events so as to avoid or minimise liability."

Technology also has the ability to enhance – and disrupt – daily lawyering: "In terms of how we practise, tech is creeping in, with many more firms using automatic contract review programmes and so on. I'm slightly sceptical, as a lot of what we bring to the table is strategy and not pure law, but the tech certainly has the potential to make our lives easier on some fronts. For example, the client that dumps eight folders of documents on us: tech can sort that out more efficiently than we can!"

There is also a trend among shipping lawyers for many to have had a career in another, related industry: "We're seeing more people come to us who have had a previous career, often in insurance, or with a shipowner or operator, and as a result they understand the work that we do and what clients need. It's taken as given that everyone is good at law – that's a small part of what we do really – but it's all about how we can help clients."

Matt offers a few tips on how to stand out from among the hordes of others seeking training contracts: "Everyone has straight As and has done their volunteering, so when it comes to standing out on paper, I'm impressed by the slightly off-the-wall answers to the questions about what the future might hold for the profession or the firm. It's preferable to reading the same thing over and over again, often simply regurgitating what is on our website. Then, once you're at the assessment centre, it's always a good start if someone comes in smiling and is personable. You also then need to be able to do well in the exercises, follow instructions and try not to show off!"

Sports

Sports law involves the legal issues at play in the worlds of both amateur and professional sport. Although perhaps now a distinct area of law, it draws in particular on employment, contract, competition, commercial and intellectual property, public and tort law.

Tim knew from a very early stage that he was keen on the law and at one point thought that the Bar might be calling his name: "At the beginning, I was more interested in the barrister route. However, I didn't particularly enjoy studying law at university, but really enjoyed the LPC. My sense was that if you liked the case law and academic aspect of the undergraduate degree, then the Bar could be more for you; whereas the LPC is much more akin to the day-to-day life of a solicitor." In fact, the one thing that he wished he'd known about being a lawyer was "that you don't have to do a law degree! That's something that I might have explored more fully – other than that, I have no regrets about my career."

Tim went on to train at a smaller firm in Norwich, Steeles, staying on for another four years PQE. "Being at a smaller firm has definite advantages," he recalls, "in that you get more direct exposure to clients and more responsibility for matters that you might not get in a bigger firm. It provided a very good foundation." He then moved to Collyer Bristow, leaving there in 2014 to join Squire Patton Boggs.

Game of two halves
Now a director in the firm's litigation practice group, Tim has built on his expertise in sports law. He explains the two distinct sides that are a feature of the work: "First, there is general legal work that is required for our sports clients, be they individuals, clubs or organisations, such as contractual drafting or disputes, employment matters or property work. Many firms do that kind of work.

Second, and the much more specialised element, relates to regulatory and disciplinary sports matters. That sort of work is only dealt with by a handful of UK firms, including ours." He goes on to offer some examples of both types: "At the moment, we're dealing with a couple of matters in relation to the sale of a football club, which falls into the High Court litigation category but which are essentially contractual disputes for a sports client. Conversely, on the regulatory side, I may deal with a challenge by a football club against a red card given unfairly to a player, a specific disciplinary matter dealt with under the FA's Regulation, or a lengthy investigation into allegations of corruption involving officials within a sport."

From the beginning of his career, Tim has worked in the reputation management sphere, including for one of the most headline-grabbing media cases in recent years. "When I was at Steeles, we had done a lot of work for Formula One which led to us acting for then FIA President Max Mosley in relation to his privacy claim against the *News of the World*," explains Tim. "That was a real career highlight – but again, it was more privacy related than anything specific to sport; it's just that he was a high-profile sports figure. In fact, he's probably remembered more for the privacy claims than any of the amazing work he's done then or since to do with road safety!"

Romance v reality
Tim reflects on the true nature of sports law, keen to dispel the myth that it's all impossibly glamorous: "Working with clubs or governing bodies throws up myriad issues, which are normally pretty interesting – although at the end of the day, they're commercial bodies. So for every sexy legal issue to do with the transfer of a famous player, there is also a dispute with the caterer that has to be resolved or, for a governing body, how it deals with its responsibilities

For more firms that work in this practice area, please use the "Training contract regional indexes" starting on p211.

Name: **Tim Lowles**
Firm: **Squire Patton Boggs (UK) LLP**
Location: **London**
University: **University of East Anglia**
Undergraduate degree: **Law**

to the various stakeholders within its sport. Certainly, the media will be keener to cover the former, which is probably how this field gets its reputation!"

But that variety – from high-profile players to everyday legal matters – is one of the many things that keeps Tim interested: "I have always really enjoyed the work and the variety plays a big part in that – you never really know what issue you'll be dealing with next. Sometimes, it can be the larger cases that go on for a long time; the excitement comes in the initial stages, when you're having heated discussions with the other side, but you must remain focused solely on what the client's objectives are. I was always going to be in contentious law though, as I think that's what the law is all about – arguing the point."

> ❝ **If you're applying to a firm that does any sort of sports work, you have to put your hand up and let it be known that you're interested – don't just wait for it to land on your desk** ❞

Tim identifies the growth of the number of practitioners working in this area, commonly in house. This in turn "means that there has been a change in focus in what the genuine leaders in the industry are working on. While we still undertake commercial, employment/HR or transfer matters, most in-house teams will not have the time or specialist expertise to handle the contentious work, be that in the courts or arbitral tribunals, such as the Court of Arbitration for Sport (CAS), or the investigatory work associated with some of the issues facing sports."

Work on your form

There are ways in which you can learn more about sports law, if you think it might be the field for you. Tim suggests: "If it is something of interest, then you need to make sure that you are aware of some of the common legal issues and read up on some of the specific jurisprudence that exists in the CAS. If you're applying to a firm that does any sort of sports work, you have to put your hand up and let it be known that you're interested – don't just wait for it to land on your desk." He offers the example of writing blogs or articles, or volunteering in the sports sector as a way to stand out in the crowded undergraduate market.

He also thinks that future trainees should consider whether their prospective firms are offering a sufficiently decent work-life balance: "Firms recognise the need to offer more flexible and agile working, and while not every firm is doing so, many are. It's about finding the right balance between what clients need with what the firm should offer its employees."

He also urges students to discover which firms are leaders in this field if they've got their heart set on life as a sports lawyer: "Many firms say that they do sports law, but there aren't really more than a handful of firms that genuinely do a large amount of the more specialist work. One good indicator is whether the firm offers a seat in it – it's worth asking that question. Equally though, don't put all your eggs in one basket – this is a very small area. Sometimes when we interview would-be trainees, and they say they want to be a sports lawyer, it can serve to put off an interviewer. Rather, keep an open mind and make sure your firm knows that you have an open mind – you might do a seat in tax and love it! There are lots of variables in what makes an interesting career, and the people you work with are a massive part of it."

Technology, media and telecommunications

Technology, media and telecommunications (TMT) is one of the fastest-developing sectors of the legal market. The constant evolution of technology pushes legal boundaries and begs for the provision of innovative legal advice. In advising their clients, TMT lawyers are required not only to apply black letter law, but also to take into account market developments, regulatory considerations and commercial and technical issues. Outsourcing continues to be a particularly hot topic.

Leo Spicer-Phelps settled on the idea of becoming a solicitor after completing his politics degree at the University of Nottingham. This understanding of the machinations of politics has instilled in him an underlying interest in scrutinising the regulation of the ever-changing and evolving world of technology law in which he now practices. While he did not really consider taking the Bar, Leo was immediately drawn to the business-focused world of being a solicitor: "I wanted to work in a broadly commercial space, working directly with companies in a more engaged fashion rather than on an *ad hoc* basis and being a solicitor seemed like the best way to do that."

Early responsibility
During his training contract, Leo appreciated the opportunity to get stuck into all aspects of practising as a solicitor and believes that the on-the-job training and the level of responsibility afforded to him, helped him to hone his craft and develop the skills required as a junior and mid-level associate: "I really valued the training experience and think it played in to how I learn best. As a trainee at Cooley, if you demonstrate that you are capable of doing something, you are happy and engaged with that work and you are curious to learn more, there is a huge will to ensure that you get to take on greater responsibilities."

Passionate about all things tech-related, things began to fall into place when Leo secured a secondment at an internet powerhouse in his second seat during his training contract. "I absolutely always wanted to work in technology and I love learning about technology," and in a market that is constantly shifting and developing, this desire for knowledge has proven to be invaluable, particularly as Cooley is well-established in Silicon Valley and the venture market, serving clients "who are trying to do new things in new ways, or old things in new ways".

> ££ There must be some point where a self-driving car has to make a decision between injuring the driver of the car or injuring a third party on the street. Is there a regulatory framework that coders would follow in creating the code which makes that decision? ££

Building client relationships
Leo obviously made a great impression during his secondment and that client still calls on him directly for a selection of commercial contract work. It is this aspect of the job that Leo enjoys most; building a relationship with a client who then seeks out his input and uses him as a sounding board for new ideas and ventures. As a tech law specialist Leo also relishes collaborating with companies and watching as they grow from a nascent brand tapping into a niche in the technology market, to an established and successful name. The fact that the world of technology is continuously shifting and evolving means that the expertise of technology lawyers is in constant demand; whether that be for a US company looking to

For more firms that work in this practice area, please use the "Training contract regional indexes" starting on p211.

Name: **Leo Spicer-Phelps**
Firm: **Cooley LLP**
Location: **London**
University: **University of Nottingham**
Degree: **Politics**

launch a new product in the United Kingdom or for a global household tech brand that is looking to acquire a key player in a disruptive technology.

However, this perpetually changing market means that tech solicitors must be readily available and as Leo advises, this can be difficult to get a handle on: "There is a need to ensure you integrate your work and life in a sustainable way. In a world where we are expected respond to clients immediately, this needs to be factored in to how you do your job. However, this becomes more manageable if you can effectively find a way to blend the two and strike a balance."

Looking at the state of the profession generally, Leo has concerns that solicitors are falling behind when it comes to accurately reflecting the community at large and this is something that needs to be addressed: "There is a real need to ensure that we meet the moral and business imperative to be representative of our clients, as well as the wider society and nation in which we live. Across the legal profession, our clients are, generally speaking, way ahead of us and we should take equivalent steps to ensure diversity and inclusiveness occurs across the legal world."

The question of AI
Looking specifically at the tech sector, Leo's passion is palpable when he ponders the conundrum of how governments must work out how to regulate evolving and future technology: "The regulatory framework for the world of tech is not moving fast enough, take artificial intelligence (AI) for example, how will they regulate it? There must be some point where a self-driving car has to make a decision between injuring the driver of the car or injuring a third party on the street. Is there a regulatory framework that coders would follow in creating the code which makes that decision? They are really

behind the regulatory curve when it comes to the development of AI."

For budding lawyers, Leo suggests that one characteristic is key and that is enthusiasm: "You really have to be genuinely enthusiastic about what you do. Try and work out what sectors you are most interested in and what you enjoy most at law school or university – whether that be mooting or negotiation workshops – and then try and find something which incorporates those elements. Then you can target in on firms that publicly manifest an interest in that sector or area. Firms want to see applicants with enthusiasm in a given field, two lawyers working together will have an infinitely better relationship if they are both interested and passionate about the work they are doing."

Aside from enthusiasm, Leo is keen to stress the fact that the route to becoming a successful solicitor is varied and that it is an incredibly diverse career: "My job and profession is too varied for an easy one-size-fits-all piece of advice. Not all solicitors are the same and you can really carve out a niche and make your own path. When firms look for entrepreneurial individuals, what they really want is someone who can take the initiative, identify what they enjoy and carve out their own path within and without the firm."

Training contract directory

How to use the training contract regional indexes and directory

Solicitors' regional indexes

These tables are designed to allow you to shortlist firms by particular criteria. Further information about each firm is contained within the training contract directory.

The tables detail:
- the number of annual vacancies at the firm (unless a particular year has been specified);
- the number of partners (which generally includes equity and salaried partners) and total staff;
- whether work placement schemes are available; and
- up to five general practice and 19 specialisation work areas.

Firms that claim to have an office in a particular region are listed from A to Z in the appropriate regional table.

For the purposes of the indexes we have used the 10 standard economic planning regions of Great Britain (not including Scotland), and London is dealt with separately. There is also a table for the Channel Islands and the Isle of Man, and an international table.

Please note, the following abbreviations have been used for the specialisation work areas:
- 'Banking' refers to Banking and finance;
- 'Property' refers to Commercial property; and
- 'Comp/comm' refers to Company/ commercial.

It should be noted that the information has been provided by the firms themselves and has generally not been verified by us. We do not, therefore, claim that the information is fully accurate and comprehensive, only that it can be used as a starting point for shortlisting appropriate firms. Furthermore, although we have attempted to contact every firm that is authorised to provide training contracts, not all firms that take trainees have supplied their details.

Training contract directory

The directory contains contact information and a brief practice description for all firms that are authorised to offer training contracts by the SRA and have supplied us with their details. It is therefore an essential reference guide to firms that offer work placement schemes, training contracts and funding.

The basic entry includes the firm's application address (not necessarily its main office), telephone number, email address, the applications contact and a brief description of the firm, together with the number of vacancies per year (unless a particular year is specified), the number of current trainees, partners and total staff, and whether the firm offers work placement schemes. Firms with a more detailed directory entry appear in bold in the regional indexes.

Every effort has been made to collate accurate information from all firms that are authorised to provide training contracts and we are confident that the directory is the most comprehensive of its kind. However, as LCNH is published in October and firms may change their information at any point, we recommend that you double check key information on firms' own websites. Deadlines can also be checked on www.LawCareers.Net.

These resources should be used in conjunction with the section on law firm practice areas, which features in-depth interviews with numerous solicitors who are keen to pass on their advice about making it in the legal profession.

Training contract regional indexes

Channel Islands

	Vacancies	Partners	Total staff	Work placement	Corporate/commercial	General commercial	Niche	General practice	High street/legal aid
Collas Crill	3(19)	33	183		•			•	

East Anglia

	Vacancies	Partners	Total staff	Work placement	Corporate/commercial	General commercial	Niche	General practice	High street/legal aid
Accutrainee	Varies			•	•	•	•		
Adlams LLP	0	4	23	✔				•	•
Ashtons Legal	4(20)	30	300	✔	•	•	•	•	
Barker Gotelee	0	8	54					•	
Birkett Long LLP	2(20)	26	170	✔	•	•		•	
Birketts LLP	7	59	504	✔	•				
Buckles Solicitors LLP	2	14	100		•	•		•	
Chamberlins	0	5	32					•	•
Chelmsford Borough Council	0		16				•		
Cozens-Hardy LLP	1(19)	13	70				•	•	
Crown Prosecution Service	1(19)	2315	6051				•		
Cunningtons	Varies	9	60	✔				•	•
Edmondson Hall	0	3	20	✔	•	•			
Ellisons	1(20)	17	160					•	
England & Co	0	6	25					•	•
Eversheds Sutherland (International) LLP	50	395	3235	✔	•	•			
Fisher Jones Greenwood Solicitors	0	21	141		•	•	•	•	•
Fosters	0	13	130					•	•
Goody Burrett LLP	1(20)	4	30	✔	•			•	•
Gotelee	0	19	122		•				
Greenwoods GRM LLP	3	10	140	✔	•	•			
Gross & Co	0	5	28		•	•	•	•	
Hayes + Storr	2	11	90		•	•		•	
Her Majesty's Courts & Tribunals Service	0		1200					•	
Hewitsons LLP	15	45	254	✔	•	•	•	•	
Hilliers HRW	0	2	32		•	•		•	
Holmes & Hills	0	9	105		•	•		•	
Hood Vores & Allwood	0	5	25					•	
Howes Percival LLP	8	43	208	✔	•	•			
Hunt and Coombs Solicitors	2	8	85				•	•	•
Irwin Mitchell	45	260	2500	✔	•	•		•	
Jeremy Roberts & Co	1	1	8	✔					

Banking	Comp/comm	Competition	Construction	Corporate tax	Crime	Dispute resolution	Employment	Environment	Family	Human rights	Insurance	IP	Personal injury	Private client	Property	Shipping	Sport	TMT
•	•			•		•	•				•	•	•		•	•		•
•	•	•	•	•		•	•	•	•		•		•	•	•		•	•
	•					•						•	•	•				
	•		•	•		•	•	•	•			•	•	•			•	•
•	•					•	•	•	•			•		•			•	
•	•	•	•	•		•	•	•	•			•	•	•			•	
•	•	•	•	•	•	•	•	•	•			•	•	•	•	•		•
	•					•	•	•	•			•	•	•				
	•				•													
	•					•	•	•	•			•	•	•				
	•					•	•	•	•		•	•	•	•	•			
	•					•	•	•	•			•	•	•				
•	•	•	•	•	•	•	•	•		•	•	•		•	•			•
•	•				•	•	•	•	•	•	•	•	•	•				•
•	•					•	•	•	•			•	•	•				
	•	•	•	•		•	•	•				•	•	•				
•	•	•	•	•		•	•		•		•	•	•	•		•	•	•
	•						•		•			•	•					
	•					•	•	•	•			•	•	•				
•	•	•	•	•		•	•		•		•	•	•	•			•	•
	•		•	•		•	•		•			•	•	•				
•	•			•		•	•	•	•			•	•	•			•	
•	•					•	•	•				•	•	•		•		•
•	•	•	•	•		•	•	•	•	•		•	•	•	•			•
	•		•		•	•	•	•	•	•		•	•	•				•
				•		•	•	•	•		•	•	•	•				•

	Vacancies	Partners	Total staff	Work placement	Corporate/ commercial	General commercial	Niche	General practice	High street/ legal aid
Kennedys	20(20)	393	1900	✔	•	•			
Lawtons Solicitors	2(19)	2	25						•
Leathes Prior	1-4	13	100	✔	•	•	•	•	
Metcalfe Copeman & Pettefar	1(19)	15	120		•	•	•	•	
Mills & Reeve LLP	20	122	994	✔	•	•			
Morgan Jones & Pett	0	3	23					•	
Nockolds	4(20)	13	140	✔	•	•		•	
Norton Peskett	0	6	118					•	•
Palmers	1	8	100	✔	•	•		•	
Park Woodfine Heald Mellows LLP	0	7	60			•		•	•
Paul Robinson Solicitors LLP	1	9	85		•			•	•
Penningtons Manches LLP	14-16	113	700		•	•		•	
Plexus Law	0	117	1800				•		
Prettys	3-4	6	75	✔	•	•	•	•	
Ronaldsons	1	1	10				•		•
Roythornes Solicitors	6(20)	26	194	✔	•	•	•	•	
The Sethi Partnership Solicitors	1	3	25	✔	•	•		•	
Shoosmiths	22	190	1630	✔	•	•	•	•	
Steeles Law Solicitors Ltd	0	4	50		•	•	•	•	
Stone King	4	42	200	✔	•	•	•	•	
Taylor Vinters LLP	6	29	170	✔	•	•	•	•	
Tees	3	24	250	✔					
Terrells LLP	1	2	18						•
Thompson Smith and Puxon	Poss	11	75		•	•	•	•	
Thomson Webb & Corfield	1(19)	9	39		•			•	
Tollers Solicitors	4	18	140		•	•		•	
Ward Gethin Archer	1(20)	16	149		•	•		•	
Watson Legal	1(19)	1	2	✔				•	
Wilkinson & Butler	0	4	20					•	•
Woodfines LLP	3(20)	22	140	✔	•	•		•	

Banking	Comp/comm	Competition	Construction	Corporate tax	Crime	Dispute resolution	Employment	Environment	Family	Human rights	Insurance	IP	Personal injury	Private client	Property	Shipping	Sport	TMT
•	•		•		•	•	•	•				•	•	•	•	•	•	
					•													
•	•		•		•	•	•	•	•	•		•	•	•			•	
	•		•			•	•	•	•				•	•	•			
•	•	•	•		•	•	•	•	•		•	•	•	•			•	•
								•					•					
	•					•		•				•	•	•	•			
	•				•	•	•	•					•	•	•			
	•		•	•	•	•	•	•					•	•	•			•
	•	•	•		•	•	•	•					•	•	•			
•	•		•	•		•	•	•				•	•	•	•		•	•
	•	•	•	•		•	•	•	•		•	•	•	•	•	•	•	•
	•		•	•		•	•	•	•	•			•	•	•			
	•		•			•		•			•		•	•	•			
•	•	•	•	•		•	•	•				•	•	•	•	•	•	•
•	•		•	•		•	•	•			•		•	•	•		•	•
	•		•			•	•	•					•	•	•			•
•	•	•	•	•		•	•	•					•	•	•			•
	•			•		•	•	•					•	•	•			
						•		•				•						
	•		•			•	•	•					•	•	•			
	•			•		•	•	•					•	•	•			
•	•	•	•			•	•	•					•	•	•			
	•			•		•	•	•	•				•	•	•			
						•	•		•					•	•			
					•													
•	•	•		•	•	•	•	•				•	•	•				•

East Midlands

	Vacancies	Partners	Total staff	Work placement	Corporate/commercial	General commercial	Niche	General practice	High street/legal aid
Accutrainee	Varies				•	•	•	•	
Actons	2	16	70		•	•		•	
Banner Jones	0	10	90					•	•
Beetenson & Gibbon Solicitors	0	5	30					•	•
Bhatia Best	0	11	128					•	•
BHW Solicitors	2-4[20]	9	62	✔				•	
Bilton Hammond	0	6	35	✔				•	•
Bird & Co Solicitors LLP	0	4	50					•	
BLM	23	196	1595	✔		•			
Bray & Bray	1	12	95					•	
Bridge McFarland	2[19]	25	176	✔	•	•		•	
Browne Jacobson LLP	20	142	981	✔	•	•	•		
Bryan and Armstrong	0	4	21					•	•
Buckles Solicitors LLP	2	14	100		•	•		•	
Burton & Burton Solicitors Ltd	0-1	4	20					•	
Burton & Co LLP	0	5	40	✔	•	•		•	•
Cartwright King	0	24	211					•	•
Cocks Lloyd	0	5	50		•			•	•
Crown Prosecution Service	1[19]	2315	6051				•		
Emery Johnson Astills	2	5	45	✔			•	•	•
Eversheds Sutherland (International) LLP	50	395	3235	✔	•	•			
Fishers	0	5	38		•	•	•	•	
Franklins Solicitors LLP	0	14	100	✔	•	•		•	
Fraser Brown	0	15	107		•	•		•	
Freeths LLP	20	147	750		•	•		•	
Gateley Plc	16	143	883	✔	•	•			
Geldards LLP	6[20]	57	352		•	•	•		
Greenwoods GRM LLP	3	10	140	✔	•	•			
Her Majesty's Courts & Tribunals Service	0		1200					•	
Hewitsons LLP	15	45	254	✔	•	•	•	•	
Howes Percival LLP	8	43	208	✔	•	•			
HSR Law	0	7	42		•	•		•	•
Jeremy Roberts & Co	1	1	8	✔				•	
JH Powell & Co	0	6	20		•	•		•	
Johar & Co	1	2	25					•	•
The Johnson Partnership	1-2	13	110	✔				•	
Langleys Solicitors LLP	5	34	335	✔	•	•		•	•
M & S Solicitors Limited	0	3	10		•		•		
Matrix Solicitors	0	1	7	✔	•		•		
Moosa-Duke Solicitors	1[19]	2	11	✔			•		
Nelsons	0	48	193		•	•		•	•

Banking	Comp/comm	Competition	Construction	Corporate tax	Crime	Dispute resolution	Employment	Environment	Family	Human rights	Insurance	IP	Personal injury	Private client	Property	Shipping	Sport	TMT
•	•	•	•	•		•	•	•	•		•	•	•	•	•	•	•	•
	•					•	•		•			•	•	•	•			
		•			•	•	•		•				•	•	•			
									•				•	•	•			
					•			•	•				•	•	•			
	•					•	•		•		•		•	•	•			•
	•				•	•	•		•				•	•	•			
		•			•	•	•	•	•		•		•	•	•	•		•
	•		•		•	•	•		•			•	•	•	•		•	•
	•		•	•	•	•	•		•			•	•	•	•		•	•
•	•	•	•	•	•	•	•	•	•			•	•	•	•		•	•
	•		•		•	•	•		•			•	•	•	•		•	•
	•				•	•	•	•	•	•			•	•	•			
	•				•	•	•	•	•				•	•	•			
					•	•	•	•	•				•	•	•			
					•				•				•	•				
•	•	•	•	•	•	•	•	•	•		•		•	•	•	•	•	•
	•			•		•	•	•				•		•	•			
	•					•	•	•				•		•	•			
•	•		•	•		•	•	•				•	•	•	•			•
•	•	•	•	•	•	•	•	•	•	•	•	•	•	•	•	•	•	•
•	•	•	•	•		•	•	•			•		•	•	•	•	•	•
•	•		•	•		•	•	•				•	•	•	•		•	•
•	•	•	•	•		•	•	•			•		•	•	•		•	•
•	•	•	•	•		•	•	•					•	•	•			
•	•	•	•	•		•	•	•			•		•	•	•		•	•
	•				•	•	•	•				•	•	•	•			
					•	•	•	•				•		•	•			
	•		•		•	•	•	•		•		•	•	•	•			•
				•														
•	•		•	•	•	•	•		•		•		•	•	•		•	
	•					•	•							•	•	•		
	•						•		•				•	•	•			
•	•	•	•	•	•	•	•	•	•	•	•	•	•	•	•		•	•

	Vacancies	Partners	Total staff	Work placement	Corporate/ commercial	General commercial	Niche	General practice	High street/ legal aid
Oldham Marsh Page Flavell	Poss	3	30					•	•
Paragon Law Limited	1	5	30	✔	•		•		•
Park Woodfine Heald Mellows LLP	0	7	60			•		•	•
Phillips	0	2	9						•
QualitySolicitors Davisons	0	7	150					•	
Robinsons	0	7	61		•	•		•	
Roythornes Solicitors	6[20]	26	194	✔	•	•	•	•	
Shacklocks LLP	2-4[19]	4	43					•	
Shakespeare Martineau LLP	8	131	717		•				
Shoosmiths	22	190	1630	✔	•	•	•	•	
Sills & Betteridge LLP	2[20]	43	265	✔	•	•		•	•
Slater & Gordon (UK) LLP	53	86	3500		•			•	
Smith Partnership	4	28	250		•	•	•	•	•
Spearing Waite LLP	2-4[20]	22	98		•	•		•	
Stowe Family Law LLP	Varies	30	100	✔			•		
Talbot & Co	1	1	20	✔	•	•	•	•	
Tallents Solicitors	0	5	51					•	•
Taylor Rose TTKW	1-2	13	250		•	•	•	•	
Thaliwal & Co Solicitors	0	1	11	✔			•		
Thompsons Solicitors	0	50	888				•		
Tinn Criddle & Co	0	4	10					•	
Tollers Solicitors	4	18	140		•	•		•	
Vincent Sykes	0	1	6			•		•	
Vincent Sykes & Higham LLP	0	5	26					•	
Weightmans LLP	Up to 18	188	1277	✔	•	•	•		
Wilkin Chapman LLP	5[20]	45	378	✔	•	•		•	
Wilson Browne Solicitors	0	16	118		•			•	
Woodfines LLP	3[20]	22	140	✔	•	•		•	

Banking	Comp/comm	Competition	Construction	Corporate tax	Crime	Dispute resolution	Employment	Environment	Family	Human rights	Insurance	IP	Personal injury	Private client	Property	Shipping	Sport	TMT
					•		•		•				•		•			
														•				
	•	•	•			•	•		•				•	•	•			
			•			•	•		•				•	•	•			
	•					•	•		•				•	•	•			•
	•		•	•		•	•	•	•				•	•	•			
	•					•	•		•				•	•	•			
•	•	•	•	•		•	•	•	•		•	•	•	•	•			•
•	•	•	•	•	•	•	•	•	•		•	•	•	•	•	•	•	•
•	•		•			•	•	•	•			•	•	•	•		•	•
	•		•	•	•	•	•		•	•	•	•	•	•	•		•	•
•	•	•	•		•	•	•		•			•	•	•	•		•	•
									•				•					
	•					•	•		•			•	•	•	•			
		•			•	•	•		•			•	•	•				
•	•					•							•		•			
					•		•						•					
	•												•					
•	•	•	•			•			•			•	•	•	•			
	•						•		•			•	•	•	•			
	•						•		•			•		•	•			
•	•	•	•	•	•	•	•	•	•		•	•	•	•	•	•	•	•
•	•	•	•	•	•	•	•	•	•			•	•	•	•	•		
	•						•	•		•			•	•	•			
	•	•	•		•	•	•	•	•			•	•	•	•			•

International

	Vacancies	Partners	Total staff	Work placement	Corporate/ commercial	General commercial	Niche	General practice	High street/ legal aid
Addleshaw Goddard	46	239	1500	✔	•				
Allen & Overy LLP	No fixed quota	554	5400	✔	•				
Anglo-Thai Legal (ATL)	Varies	1	5	✔			•	•	
Arnold & Porter Kaye Scholer (UK) LLP	2	23	117	✔	•	•	•		
Ashurst LLP	40-45	395	1978	✔	•				
Beale & Company Solicitors LLP	5-6[20]	23	130		•	•	•		
Bird & Bird	18	298	3000	✔	•				
Brown Rudnick LLP	4	35	130		•				
Bryan Cave Leighton Paisner	35	200	1600	✔	•	•			
Cains Advocates Limited	2	5	52	✔	•	•	•		
Charles Russell Speechlys	24	150	1020	✔	•	•		•	
Cleary Gottlieb Steen & Hamilton LLP	15-20	193	2500	✔	•				
Clifford Chance	Up to 90	570	6115	✔	•	•			
Clyde & Co LLP	45-50	415	3800	✔	•	•			
CMS	120	1000	7500	✔	•	•			
Collyer Bristow LLP	4-5	30	140	✔	•	•		•	
Curtis Mallet-Prevost Colt & Mosle LLP	2[19]	7	14	✔	•				
DAC Beachcroft LLP	13[20]	240	2300	✔	•	•		•	
Davis Polk & Wardwell London LLP	Approx 4	8	90	✔	•				
Debevoise & Plimpton LLP	8	21	213	✔	•			•	
Dechert LLP	10	312	2295	✔	•				
Dentons	50	2892	10455	✔	•	•	•		
DLA Piper UK LLP	Up to 70	1300	8500	✔	•				
Dorsey	2	14	45		•				
DWF LLP	40	316	2800	✔	•	•			
Eversheds Sutherland (International) LLP	50	395	3235	✔	•	•			
Faegre Baker Daniels LLP	2	8	46	✔	•	•			
Fieldfisher	18	223	986	✔	•	•			
Freshfields Bruckhaus Deringer LLP	80	381	4925	✔	•				
Gide Loyrette Nouel LLP	4	6	46				•		
Greenberg Traurig LLP	4+[19]	25	105	✔	•				
Herbert Smith Freehills LLP	60[20]	468	4932	✔	•				
HFW	15	167	1016	✔	•	•	•		
Hill Dickinson LLP	10	175	840	✔	•	•	•		
Jones Day	20	60	350	✔	•				
K&L Gates LLP	TBD	53	232	✔	•	•			
Katten Muchin Rosenman UK LLP	2-3	18	66	✔				•	
Kennedys	20[20]	393	1900	✔	•	•			
Kirkland & Ellis International LLP	10	900	3978	✔	•				
Latham & Watkins	24	77	600	✔	•				
Lewis Silkin	Up to 6	58	350	✔	•	•			

Banking	Comp/comm	Competition	Construction	Corporate tax	Crime	Dispute resolution	Employment	Environment	Family	Human rights	Insurance	IP	Personal injury	Private client	Property	Shipping	Sport	TMT
•	•	•	•	•		•	•	•			•	•		•	•		•	•
•	•	•	•	•		•	•	•			•	•		•				•
		•		•	•	•	•	•	•	•		•	•	•	•			
•	•	•		•	•	•	•					•	•					•
•	•	•	•		•	•	•				•	•		•	•			•
	•		•			•	•	•	•		•	•		•				
•	•	•	•	•		•	•	•			•	•			•		•	•
	•			•	•	•	•				•	•						
•	•	•	•	•		•	•	•			•	•		•	•	•	•	•
•	•	•	•			•	•				•	•		•	•	•	•	•
•	•	•	•	•		•	•	•	•		•	•	•	•	•	•		•
•	•	•	•	•		•	•	•			•	•			•			•
•	•	•	•	•		•	•	•			•	•	•	•		•	•	•
•	•	•	•	•		•	•	•			•	•			•			•
•	•	•	•			•	•	•	•		•	•		•	•			•
•						•						•						
•	•	•	•	•		•	•	•			•	•	•	•				•
•						•					•				•			•
•	•	•	•	•		•	•				•			•				•
•	•	•	•	•		•	•	•			•	•		•	•	•		•
•	•	•	•			•	•	•			•	•			•			•
•	•	•	•	•		•	•	•			•	•	•	•	•			•
•	•	•	•	•	•	•	•	•			•	•			•			•
•	•	•				•	•				•	•		•	•			•
•	•	•	•	•		•	•	•	•		•	•	•	•	•		•	•
•	•	•	•			•	•	•			•	•			•			
•			•			•	•	•			•			•	•			
•	•	•	•	•		•	•	•			•	•	•	•		•	•	•
•	•	•	•			•	•	•	•		•	•	•	•	•		•	•
•	•	•	•	•	•	•	•	•			•				•		•	•
•	•	•	•			•	•				•	•	•	•	•			•
	•	•				•	•				•				•			
•	•		•			•	•	•			•				•		•	
•	•	•		•		•	•				•				•		•	•

	Vacancies	Partners	Total staff	Work placement	Corporate/commercial	General commercial	Niche	General practice	High street/legal aid
Linklaters LLP	100	490	5270	✔	•				
Magrath Sheldrick LLP	2[19]	8	65		•	•	•		
Malik Legal Solicitors Ltd	4	3	14	✔		•			
Mayer Brown International LLP	15	75	460	✔	•	•			
McDermott Will & Emery UK LLP	2	566	2167		•	•			
McGuireWoods London LLP	1	13	50					•	
Milbank Tweed Hadley & McCloy	5	28	195	✔	•				
Morgan, Lewis & Bockius UK LLP	8	34	160	✔	•	•			
Norton Rose Fulbright	Up to 45	1200	4000	✔	•	•			
Obaseki	1[20]	3	11	✔		•		•	
O'Melveny	Up to 3	7	50	✔	•				
Orrick, Herrington & Sutcliffe (UK) LLP	6-8	33	168		•				
Osborne Clarke LLP	20	258	1632	✔	•	•	•		
Paragon Law Limited	1	5	30	✔	•			•	•
Paul Hastings	6-8	28	150	✔	•				
Pinsent Masons LLP	68	430	3000	✔	•		•		
Reed Smith	25	649	2939	✔	•				
RPC	12[20]	79	800	✔	•		•		
Shearman & Sterling (London) LLP	Approx 15	35	300	✔	•				
Sidley Austin LLP	12	43	270	✔	•				
Simmons & Simmons LLP	25	280	1600	✔	•	•			
Skadden, Arps, Slate, Meagher & Flom (UK) LLP	Approx 10	31	250	✔	•				
Slaughter and May	80-85	112	1200	✔	•	•			
Squire Patton Boggs (UK) LLP	25	494	3000	✔	•	•			
Stephenson Harwood LLP	20	170	1000	✔	•				
Sullivan & Cromwell LLP	4-6	19	140	✔	•				
Systech Solicitors Limited	0		25				•		
Taylor Vinters LLP	6	29	170	✔	•	•	•	•	
Taylor Wessing	Up to 35	400	1800	✔	•	•			
Thomas Cooper LLP	Up to 3	32	103		•		•		
TLT LLP	Up to 15	110	1020	✔	•	•	•	•	
Travers Smith LLP	25	83	660	✔	•	•			
Trowers & Hamlins LLP	23	157	894	✔		•			
Vinson & Elkins RLLP	5	16	100	✔	•				
Watson Farley & Williams LLP	18	157	850	✔	•	•			
Weil, Gotshal & Manges (London) LLP	15	33	297	✔	•				
White & Case LLP	50	101	828	✔	•				
Withers LLP	11	167	1000	✔	•		•	•	•
Womble Bond Dickinson	Up to 25	123	1200	✔	•	•			

Banking	Comp/comm	Competition	Construction	Corporate tax	Crime	Dispute resolution	Employment	Environment	Family	Human rights	Insurance	IP	Personal injury	Private client	Property	Shipping	Sport	TMT
•	•	•	•	•		•	•	•			•	•			•			•
						•	•											
	•				•	•			•	•			•	•				
•	•	•		•		•	•	•			•	•			•			•
	•			•		•	•							•				
•	•	•		•		•	•	•				•			•		•	•
•	•	•		•		•					•	•			•			•
•	•	•	•	•		•	•	•			•	•			•	•		•
					•				•						•			
•	•			•		•	•								•			•
•	•	•		•		•	•	•							•			•
•	•	•	•	•		•	•	•			•	•		•	•			•
						•								•				
•	•	•		•		•	•	•			•	•			•			•
•	•	•	•	•		•	•	•			•	•			•	•	•	
•	•	•	•	•		•	•	•			•	•	•		•			•
•	•	•	•	•		•	•				•	•			•			•
•	•	•		•		•	•	•			•	•			•			•
•	•	•		•		•	•	•			•	•			•			•
•	•	•		•		•					•				•			•
•	•	•	•	•		•	•	•			•	•			•		•	•
•	•	•	•	•		•	•	•			•	•	•		•		•	•
•	•	•	•	•		•	•	•			•	•			•	•		•
•	•	•				•												•
			•			•												
•	•	•	•	•		•	•		•			•			•	•		•
•	•	•	•	•		•	•	•			•	•		•	•	•	•	•
•	•	•	•	•		•	•				•	•	•	•	•	•	•	•
•	•		•	•		•	•	•	•			•			•	•		•
•	•	•		•		•	•				•	•			•	•		•
•	•		•	•		•	•						•	•				•
•	•	•	•	•		•	•				•			•	•			•
•	•	•		•		•	•				•	•		•	•			•
•	•	•	•	•		•	•	•			•	•		•	•	•	•	•
•	•	•	•	•		•	•	•				•		•	•	•		•

London

	Vacancies	Partners	Total staff	Work placement	Corporate/ commercial	General commercial	Niche	General practice	High street/ legal aid
Abrahams Dresden LLP	2(19)	3	29		•	•			
ACA Law Ltd	Varies	1	24	✔					•
Accutrainee	Varies				•	•	•	•	
Addleshaw Goddard	46	239	1500	✔	•				
Ahmed & Co	0	2	15						•
Akin Gump Strauss Hauer & Feld	4	39	190	✔	•				
Akin Palmer LLP	0	4	10				•		
Allen & Overy LLP	No fixed quota	554	5400	✔	•				
Alpha Lexis Law Firm	0	2	8					•	
Anthony Gold Solicitors	4(19)	32	160			•		•	•
Anthony Louca Solicitors	1	3	7				•		•
AP Law Solicitors Ltd	0	2	50	✔	•		•	•	•
AP Solicitors	2	2	6				•		
Arbis Sutherland LLP	1-2	5	18				•		
Archon Solicitors Limited	0	5	19				•		
Arlingtons Sharmas Solicitors	Poss	2	14	✔	•	•		•	
Arnold & Porter Kaye Scholer (UK) LLP	2	23	117	✔	•	•	•		
Aschfords Law	1	3	5	✔				•	
Ashfords	9	74	540	✔	•	•			
Ashurst LLP	40-45	395	1978	✔	•				
Aston Clark Solicitors	0	3	12					•	•
Atkins Hope	0	4	35	✔				•	•
Avadis & Co Solicitors	1	1	5	✔				•	•
Avery Emerson	2	1	6	✔				•	
Baker McKenzie	30	90	900	✔	•				
Bargate Murray	0	3	11		•		•		
Baron Grey	0	1	9	✔		•		•	
Batchelors		14	55			•			
Bates Wells Braithwaite	6	38	270	✔	•	•	•		
Beale & Company Solicitors LLP	5-6(20)	23	130		•	•	•		
Bevan Brittan LLP	10	60	435	✔	•	•			
Bhatt Murphy	0	2	33	✔				•	
Bhogal Partners Solicitors	1	3	19	✔	•	•			•
Bindmans LLP		14	114					•	•
Bircham Dyson Bell LLP	5	49	280	✔	•	•		•	
Bird & Bird	18	298	3000	✔	•				
Birnberg Peirce	1(20)	3	42						•
Bishop & Sewell LLP	0	9	54		•	•		•	
Blake Morgan LLP	18	114	800	✔	•	•	•	•	
Blandy & Blandy LLP	2-3(20)	20	104	✔	•	•		•	
Blaser Mills Law	4	22	125		•	•		•	•

Banking	Comp/comm	Competition	Construction	Corporate tax	Crime	Dispute resolution	Employment	Environment	Family	Human rights	Insurance	IP	Personal injury	Private client	Property	Shipping	Sport	TMT
	•					•	•		•					•	•			
									•	•								
•	•	•	•	•		•	•	•	•		•	•	•	•	•	•	•	•
•	•	•	•	•		•	•	•			•	•		•	•		•	•
			•															•
•	•	•	•	•		•								•	•			
	•					•			•					•	•			
•	•	•	•	•		•	•	•			•	•		•	•			•
	•					•			•					•	•			
									•				•	•	•			
									•					•	•			
	•					•	•		•					•	•			
•	•	•				•					•						•	
•	•		•			•	•						•	•	•	•	•	
•	•	•		•		•	•						•	•	•			•
									•									
•	•	•	•	•		•					•			•	•	•	•	•
•	•	•		•		•	•						•	•	•	•	•	•
						•												
									•				•	•	•			
									•				•	•	•			
	•					•			•					•	•			
•	•	•	•	•		•	•				•			•	•			•
•	•					•	•				•			•	•	•		
	•					•							•	•	•			
	•		•			•	•				•			•	•			
•	•	•		•		•	•	•			•			•	•		•	•
	•		•			•	•	•					•	•				•
	•		•			•	•				•			•	•			•
									•									
	•					•	•		•					•	•			
			•			•	•	•	•			•	•					
•	•	•	•	•		•	•	•			•			•			•	•
•	•	•	•	•		•	•				•				•		•	•
						•			•					•	•			
	•		•			•			•		•			•	•	•		
	•					•	•		•					•	•			•
	•	•		•		•	•	•	•			•		•	•	•	•	•

	Vacancies	Partners	Total staff	Work placement	Corporate/ commercial	General commercial	Niche	General practice	High street/ legal aid
BLM	23	196	1595	✔		•			
Bolt Burdon	3	14	65			•		•	
Bonnett Son & Turner LLP	0	3	30					•	
Boodle Hatfield LLP	4	33	150	✔	•	•	•		
Bristows LLP	10	40	275	✔	•				
Bross Bennett	0	5	20	✔			•		
Brown Rudnick LLP	4	35	130		•				
Browne Jacobson LLP	20	142	981	✔	•	•	•		
Bryan Cave	0	15	80	✔	•				
Bryan Cave Leighton Paisner	35	200	1600	✔	•	•			
Burges Salmon LLP	20	87	750	✔	•	•		•	
BWF Solicitors	2	2	5					•	
Campbell Chambers	0	2	10				•		•
Campbell-Taylor Solicitors	0	1	10	✔			•		
Cannings Connolly Solicitors	1	7	25		•				
Capsticks Solicitors LLP	8[20]	51	403		•	•	•		
Carpenter & Co	0-1	3	25					•	•
Carter Lemon Camerons LLP	1[19]	11	38				•		
Cartwright King	0	24	211					•	•
Caytons Law	1	6	28	✔			•		
Charles Russell Speechlys	24	150	1020	✔	•	•		•	
Chhokar & Co	1	3	11					•	
Clarke Willmott LLP	TBC	112	642		•	•		•	
Clarkslegal LLP	2	13	70			•			
Clarkson Wright & Jakes Ltd	0	15	71		•	•		•	
Cleary Gottlieb Steen & Hamilton LLP	15-20	193	2500	✔	•				
Clifford Chance	Up to 90	570	6115	✔	•	•			
Clifford Harris & Co	0	2	8		•	•			
Clintons	2	21	75			•	•		
Clyde & Co LLP	45-50	415	3800	✔	•	•			
CMS	120	1000	7500	✔	•	•			
Cohen Davis Solicitors	3[19]	1	4	✔			•		
Collyer Bristow LLP	4-5	30	140	✔	•	•		•	
Community Law Clinic Solicitors	0	1	24					•	•
Cooley (UK) LLP	4	28	180	✔	•	•			
Covington & Burling LLP	8	30		✔	•	•	•	•	
Cripps LLP	7	51	360	✔	•	•		•	
Crown Prosecution Service	1[19]	2315	6051				•		
Cunningtons	Varies	9	60	✔				•	•
Curtis Mallet-Prevost Colt & Mosle LLP	2[19]	7	14		•				
Curwens LLP	2[19]	15	90					•	

Banking	Comp/comm	Competition	Construction	Corporate tax	Crime	Dispute resolution	Employment	Environment	Family	Human rights	Insurance	IP	Personal injury	Private client	Property	Shipping	Sport	TMT
				•		•	•	•	•		•		•			•		•
	•					•	•		•					•	•			
							•						•	•	•			
	•		•	•		•		•						•	•			
	•	•		•		•	•							•				•
								•										
•	•			•	•	•						•						
•	•	•	•	•		•	•	•	•		•	•	•		•		•	•
•	•	•	•			•	•							•	•			
•	•	•	•	•		•		•			•	•	•	•	•		•	•
•	•	•	•	•		•	•	•	•		•	•	•	•	•	•	•	•
					•			•										
	•		•			•								•				
	•		•			•		•			•		•	•	•			
							•		•	•			•	•	•			
•	•		•			•	•	•	•		•	•	•	•	•		•	•
					•		•	•	•									
											•			•				
•	•	•	•	•		•	•	•	•		•	•	•	•	•		•	•
	•						•		•			•		•	•			
•	•	•	•	•		•	•	•	•		•	•	•	•	•		•	•
•	•	•	•	•		•	•	•			•	•	•	•	•		•	•
•	•	•	•			•	•	•			•		•	•	•		•	•
•	•	•	•			•	•	•			•		•	•	•		•	•
•	•	•	•	•		•	•	•			•		•	•	•	•		
•	•					•	•	•			•		•	•			•	•
	•	•	•	•		•	•	•					•	•	•		•	•
•	•	•	•	•		•	•	•			•		•	•	•		•	•
	•					•	•	•			•			•				•
						•		•			•			•				
•	•	•	•			•		•			•		•	•				•
						•	•				•			•				
•	•	•		•		•	•				•		•		•		•	•
	•		•	•		•			•		•	•	•	•				•
			•				•		•									
	•					•	•		•				•	•	•			
	•	•				•		•			•		•	•				

	Vacancies	Partners	Total staff	Work placement	Corporate/ commercial	General commercial	Niche	General practice	High street/ legal aid
Curzon Green Solicitors	2(19)	3	22	✔				•	
DAC Beachcroft LLP	13(20)	240	2300	✔	•	•		•	
Darlingtons	1	6	42	✔	•			•	
David Phillips & Partners	0	15	75	✔			•	•	•
Davies and Partners	1(19)	12	170		•	•		•	
Davis & Co	0	1	2				•		
Davis Polk & Wardwell London LLP	Approx 4	8	90	✔	•				
Dawson Cornwell	1(20)	10	54	✔			•		
Daybells LLP	1(20)	3	10	✔				•	
Dean Manson LLP - Solicitors	4	2	10	✔				•	
Debevoise & Plimpton LLP	8	21	213	✔	•			•	
Debidins	0	2	4					•	
Dechert LLP	10	312	2295	✔	•				
Dentons	50	2892	10455	✔	•	•	•		
Devonshires Solicitors	6(20)	35	240		•		•		
DH Law Solicitors Ltd	0	1	10	✔					•
DLA Piper UK LLP	Up to 70	1300	8500	✔	•				
DMH Stallard LLP	0	59	259	✔	•	•		•	
Dorsey	2	14	45		•				
Dowse & Co	0	3	14						•
Druces LLP	2	21	86	✔	•	•			
Duncan Lewis Solicitors Ltd	100	33	421	✔	•				•
DWF LLP	40	316	2800	✔	•	•			
EC3 Legal LLP	0	6	24		•				
Edwards Duthie	0	12	85		•	•		•	•
Edwin Coe LLP	4	39	172	✔	•	•	•	•	
Elborne Mitchell LLP	2	8	21		•		•		
EMW Law LLP	5	34	172	✔	•				
Everatt's LLP	1	2	6		•	•		•	
Eversheds Sutherland (International) LLP	50	395	3235	✔	•	•			
Everys	0	10	100		•	•		•	•
Ewings & Co	0	3	30					•	•
Faegre Baker Daniels LLP	2	8	46	✔	•	•			
Faradays Solicitors	Varies	4	20	✔				•	•
Farrer & Co LLP	10	80	450	✔	•	•	•	•	
Fellowes Solicitors LLP	1	4	14	✔				•	•
Fentons	0	24	210					•	•
Fieldfisher	18	223	986	✔	•	•			
Fisher Jones Greenwood Solicitors	0	21	141		•	•	•	•	•
Fisher Meredith	2(20)	11	41					•	
Fladgate LLP	6	74	261		•	•			

Banking	Comp/comm	Competition	Construction	Corporate tax	Crime	Dispute resolution	Employment	Environment	Family	Human rights	Insurance	IP	Personal injury	Private client	Property	Shipping	Sport	TMT
	•		•			•	•		•				•		•		•	•
•	•	•	•	•		•	•	•			•	•	•		•		•	•
	•		•			•	•					•		•	•			
					•			•					•	•				
	•		•			•	•	•	•			•		•	•			•
						•					•			•		•		
•	•		•			•								•				
	•					•			•					•				
	•					•						•						
									•									
•	•					•					•			•				•
						•	•		•				•	•				
•	•	•	•	•		•	•	•			•	•		•		•	•	•
•	•					•						•		•				
						•	•		•	•			•	•				
•	•		•		•		•		•		•	•	•	•	•		•	•
•	•					•	•		•	•		•	•	•	•			•
	•		•			•					•			•				
•			•			•	•		•	•		•		•	•			•
	•	•	•	•	•	•					•	•		•	•			•
•	•	•				•	•				•			•	•			
	•					•	•							•		•		
					•	•	•		•			•		•	•			
•	•	•	•	•	•	•	•	•			•			•			•	•
•	•		•			•	•		•			•		•	•			
•	•					•	•		•					•		•		
	•		•	•		•	•		•			•		•	•			•
					•	•	•		•					•	•			
•	•					•			•			•		•	•		•	
	•				•	•	•		•				•	•			•	•
					•	•	•		•					•	•			
•	•	•	•	•		•	•		•		•	•	•	•	•		•	•
	•				•	•	•		•	•	•		•	•	•			
	•					•	•		•	•								•
•	•	•	•	•		•	•		•			•	•	•	•		•	•

London continued

	Vacancies	Partners	Total staff	Work placement	Corporate/ commercial	General commercial	Niche	General practice	High street/ legal aid
Fletcher Dervish	0	1	20					•	•
Forsters LLP	7-9	53	400	✔			•		
Fox Williams LLP	3[20]	34	118	✔	•	•	•	•	
Frank Brazell & Partners	0	3	28						•
Freeths LLP	20	147	750		•	•		•	
Freshfields Bruckhaus Deringer LLP	80	381	4925	✔	•				
Fried, Frank, Harris, Shriver & Jacobson (London) LLP	2	15	100		•				
Galbraith Branley	1	1	15						•
Gateley Plc	16	143	883	✔	•	•			
Geldards LLP	6[20]	57	352		•	•	•		
Gibson, Dunn & Crutcher UK LLP	7-8	404	2694	✔	•				
Gide Loyrette Nouel LLP	4	6	46				•		
Gill & Co	1	2	14					•	•
Glovers Solicitors LLP	2	11	38				•		
Goodman Derrick LLP	3	35	112		•	•	•	•	
Goodman Ray	0	5	20					•	•
Goodwin Procter (UK) LLP	6	23	140	✔	•				
Gordon Dadds LLP	6	39	236		•	•		•	
Government Legal Profession	50		2000						
Gowling WLG (UK) LLP	25	593	3171	✔	•				
Greenberg Traurig LLP	4+[19]	25	105	✔	•				
Greenhouse Stirton & Co	0	2	3	✔					•
Greenwoods GRM LLP	3	10	140	✔	•	•			
Gregory Abrams Davidson LLP	0	9	78	✔				•	
GRM Law	0	11	40					•	
Guile Nicholas Solicitors	0	5	30	✔				•	•
Hanne & Co Solicitors	3[20]	12	60					•	
Harbottle & Lewis LLP	6	42	186		•	•			
Harper & Odell	TBC	2	5				•		
Harris Waters & Co	1	2	11	✔	•	•		•	•
Hempsons	3	46	300				•		
Her Majesty's Courts & Tribunals Service	0		1200					•	
Herbert Smith Freehills LLP	60[20]	468	4932	✔	•				
Hewitsons LLP	15	45	254	✔	•	•	•	•	
Hextalls Ltd	0	8	30				•		
HFW	15	167	1016	✔	•	•	•		
Hill Dickinson LLP	10	175	840	✔	•	•	•		
Hilliers HRW	0	2	32		•	•		•	
Hine Solicitors	10	8	180					•	•
HKH Kenwright & Cox	0	2	19	✔	•			•	•

Banking	Comp/comm	Competition	Construction	Corporate tax	Crime	Dispute resolution	Employment	Environment	Family	Human rights	Insurance	IP	Personal injury	Private client	Property	Shipping	Sport	TMT
					•	•			•				•	•	•			
•	•		•	•		•	•		•					•	•			
•	•	•		•	•	•	•	•			•	•		•			•	•
					•				•					•				
•	•	•	•	•		•	•	•	•	•	•	•		•	•		•	•
•	•	•	•	•		•	•	•	•		•	•		•				•
•			•			•			•			•		•				
					•				•					•				
•	•	•	•	•		•	•	•	•			•		•	•	•	•	•
•	•		•	•		•	•	•			•	•	•	•	•		•	•
•	•	•		•		•	•				•	•		•				•
•			•			•			•					•				
				•				•						•	•			
•	•	•	•	•		•	•		•		•	•		•			•	•
	•		•						•					•				
•	•	•	•	•		•	•	•	•	•	•	•	•	•	•		•	•
•	•	•	•			•	•	•	•		•	•	•	•	•		•	•
•	•	•	•	•		•	•				•	•	•	•	•		•	•
						•	•		•					•	•			
•	•	•	•	•		•	•	•			•	•	•	•	•		•	•
	•					•	•		•			•	•	•	•		•	•
	•					•	•		•				•	•	•		•	•
						•	•		•					•	•			
•			•		•	•	•		•				•	•			•	•
	•					•	•		•			•	•	•				
						•			•					•	•			
•						•	•		•				•	•	•			
•		•			•	•			•					•	•			
•	•	•	•	•		•	•	•			•	•		•	•			•
•	•	•	•	•		•	•	•			•	•		•	•		•	•
•			•			•	•	•			•	•	•				•	
•			•	•		•	•						•	•	•	•	•	
•	•	•	•	•		•	•				•		•	•	•		•	•
	•		•	•			•				•		•	•				
					•		•							•	•			
					•	•		•				•		•	•			•

	Vacancies	Partners	Total staff	Work placement	Corporate/ commercial	General commercial	Niche	General practice	High street/ legal aid
Hodders	0	5	65		•	•		•	•
Hodge Jones & Allen LLP	6-10[20]	46	216				•		•
Hogan Lovells	50	800	5000	✔	•				
Horwich Farrelly	15	35	730	✔		•			
Howard Kennedy	10[20]	53	350					•	
Howell Jones LLP	0	14	75					•	
Hugh James	10	64	680	✔	•	•	•	•	
Humphries Kirk LLP	1[19]	20	180	✔				•	
Hunters	1-2	28	71	✔				•	
Ikie Solicitors LLP	0	2	5						
Irwin Mitchell	45	260	2500	✔	•	•		•	
Jay Vadher & Co	1	3	8			•		•	•
Jeffrey Green Russell Limited	2	21	76		•				
Joelson JD LLP	4[19]	14	80		•	•	•		
John Chapman and Co	0	4	22					•	•
Johns & Saggar LLP	0	2	13	✔	•			•	
Jones Day	20	60	350	✔	•				
Joseph Hill & Co	5[19]	2	12	✔				•	•
Joves Solicitors	0		3	✔				•	
K&L Gates LLP	TBD	53	232	✔	•	•			
Kaim Todner Solicitors Ltd	0	8	70					•	•
Katten Muchin Rosenman UK LLP	2-3	18	66	✔					
KC Law Chambers Solicitors	2[19]	2	5	✔				•	
Kennard Wells Solicitors	1	5	35					•	•
Kennedys	20[20]	393	1900	✔	•	•			
Kingsley Napley LLP	6[20]	53	378	✔					
Kirkland & Ellis International LLP	10	900	3978	✔	•				
Kotecha & Co	0	2	5	✔		•			
Laderman and Co	Poss	2	13		•	•		•	
Latham & Watkins	24	77	600	✔	•				
Laytons Solicitors LLP	6	29	118	✔	•	•			
Lee Bolton Monier-Williams	2	8	45	✔		•	•	•	
Leigh Day	8-10[20]	44	420	✔			•		•
Lester Aldridge LLP	8	46	324	✔	•	•	•	•	
Lewis Silkin	Up to 6	58	350	✔	•	•			
Linklaters LLP	100	490	5270	✔	•				
London Solicitors	3	2	14	✔				•	
Luqmani Thompson & Partners	0	5	9				•		•
Lyons Davidson	4-6	36	1200		•	•		•	
M Olubi Solicitors	4	1	7	✔				•	
Macfarlanes LLP	30	85	723	✔	•				

Banking	Comp/comm	Competition	Construction	Corporate tax	Crime	Dispute resolution	Employment	Environment	Family	Human rights	Insurance	IP	Personal injury	Private client	Property	Shipping	Sport	TMT
	•					•	•		•					•	•			
					•	•	•	•	•	•			•	•				
•	•	•	•	•			•	•	•		•	•			•	•		•
						•							•					
•	•		•	•			•		•	•		•		•	•		•	•
	•						•		•				•		•			
•	•		•			•	•	•	•		•	•		•	•		•	•
	•		•			•	•		•			•		•	•			
	•					•	•		•					•	•			
					•		•		•			•			•			
•	•	•	•	•	•	•	•	•	•	•	•	•		•	•			•
	•						•		•			•		•	•			
•	•		•	•		•	•		•			•		•	•		•	•
	•	•		•			•		•			•						•
									•				•					
	•						•		•						•			
•	•	•	•	•		•	•	•			•	•		•	•			•
					•									•				
							•											
									•	•								
•		•	•				•	•	•		•	•			•			•
				•				•						•				
•			•	•		•	•				•	•	•					
					•		•	•	•			•		•	•			
					•		•	•	•			•		•	•			
•	•		•			•	•	•			•	•	•	•	•	•	•	
•	•		•	•		•	•		•		•			•	•		•	•
•	•	•									•				•			
							•						•		•			
	•						•		•					•				
•	•	•			•		•	•			•			•			•	•
•	•	•	•	•	•		•	•			•	•		•			•	•
	•		•			•	•				•			•			•	•
							•	•		•			•					
•	•	•	•	•	•	•	•	•	•		•	•	•	•	•	•		•
	•		•		•	•	•				•			•			•	•
•	•	•	•	•		•	•				•	•		•				•
						•	•		•	•				•	•			
										•								
	•						•	•	•		•		•	•	•			
					•						•	•		•	•			
•	•	•	•	•		•	•	•			•	•			•		•	•

	Vacancies	Partners	Total staff	Work placement	Corporate/commercial	General commercial	Niche	General practice	High street/legal aid
MacRae & Co LLP	0	3	7					•	
Magrath Sheldrick LLP	2(19)	8	65		•	•	•		
Makka Solicitors Ltd	1	3	8	✔				•	•
Makwana Solicitors	1	1	2	✔				•	
Malik & Malik	1	2	15	✔				•	
Maples Teesdale LLP	3(20)	18	68			•			
Marriott Harrison LLP	2-3(20)	19	58	✔	•	•	•		
Martin Murray & Associates	0	9	70					•	•
Martin Shepherd Solicitors LLP	0	6	34					•	
Maurice Turnor Gardner LLP	1-2(20)	10	38	✔			•		
Mayer Brown International LLP	15	75	460	✔	•	•			
McDermott Will & Emery UK LLP	2	566	2167		•	•			
McGuireWoods London LLP	1	13	50		•	•			
McMillan Williams Solicitors	Varies	60	400	✔	•	•	•	•	•
Memery Crystal LLP	4	33	140	✔	•	•	•		
Michelmores LLP	9	66	440	✔	•	•	•		
Milbank Tweed Hadley & McCloy	5	28	195	✔	•				
Miller Evans & Co	1	2	10	✔				•	
Mills & Reeve LLP	20	122	994	✔	•	•			
Mills Chody LLP	1-2	4	15					•	
Mishcon de Reya LLP	12-15	124	910	✔	•	•			
Monro Wright & Wasbrough LLP	2(20)	9	35				•		
Moore Blatch LLP	3(20)	42	270					•	
Morgan, Lewis & Bockius UK LLP	8	34	160	✔	•	•			
Morrison & Foerster (UK) LLP	6	19	90	✔	•				
Moss & Co	1(19)	2	10	✔					•
Mundays LLP	2	25	94		•	•	•	•	
Nandy & Co	0							•	
Nockolds	4(20)	13	140	✔	•	•			
Norton Rose Fulbright	Up to 45	1200	4000	✔	•	•			
Obaseki	1(20)	3	11	✔		•			
O'Melveny	Up to 3	7	50	✔	•				
Orrick, Herrington & Sutcliffe (UK) LLP	6-8	33	168			•			
Osborne Clarke LLP	20	258	1632	✔	•	•	•		
Osbornes Solicitors LLP	4	18	110	✔				•	•
Osmond & Osmond	1(19)	2	8	✔		•		•	
Oury Clark Solicitors	1	7	21		•	•	•		
Ozoran Turkan	2	2	10	✔			•	•	
Paragon Law Limited	1	5	30	✔	•		•		•
Paul Hastings	6-8	28	150	✔	•				
Payne Hicks Beach	2	26	146					•	

Banking	Comp/comm	Competition	Construction	Corporate tax	Crime	Dispute resolution	Employment	Environment	Family	Human rights	Insurance	IP	Personal injury	Private client	Property	Shipping	Sport	TMT
•	•	•	•			•	•						•		•			•
						•	•								•			
						•			•						•			
			•			•			•				•					
						•			•						•			
•	•		•			•									•			
•	•					•	•		•				•		•		•	•
			•			•									•			
	•					•			•					•	•			
														•	•			
•	•	•	•	•		•	•	•			•	•			•			•
	•			•		•	•							•				
•	•	•				•	•	•							•			
	•	•	•	•	•				•	•		•	•	•				•
•	•	•	•	•		•	•				•	•			•		•	•
•	•	•	•	•		•	•	•	•	•	•	•			•			•
	•	•	•	•		•	•							•	•		•	•
	•					•			•			•		•	•		•	•
•	•					•	•	•			•	•		•	•		•	•
	•					•			•					•	•			•
	•					•			•					•	•			
•	•	•				•	•								•			•
•						•						•						•
				•						•								
•	•	•	•	•		•	•							•				•
									•	•								
	•					•	•		•					•	•			
•	•	•	•	•		•	•	•			•	•		•	•	•		•
									•			•			•			
•						•	•					•			•			
•	•	•		•		•									•			•
•	•	•	•	•		•	•	•				•		•	•			•
						•	•		•				•	•	•			
	•					•	•		•					•	•			
	•					•						•			•			
		•			•									•				
														•				
•	•			•		•	•								•			•
	•		•			•	•		•					•	•		•	•

	Vacancies	Partners	Total staff	Work placement	Corporate/ commercial	General commercial	Niche	General practice	High street/ legal aid
Peacock & Co	1	8	30					•	
Pemberton Greenish LLP	0	14	89		•	•	•		
Penningtons Manches LLP	14-16	113	700		•	•		•	
Peter Brown & Co Solicitors LLP	1	6	20		•	•		•	
Peters & Peters	2	10	75	✔			•		
Philcox Gray Ltd	0	4	23	✔					•
Pinsent Masons LLP	68	430	3000	✔	•	•			
Pitmans LLP	8	36	210		•	•	•	•	
Plexus Law	0	117	1800				•		
Portner	1	4	29		•	•	•		
Pothecary Witham Weld	1(19)	4	28				•		
Powell & Co	0	2	14				•		•
Powell Spencer & Partners	0	2	44						•
PwC	25	35	320	✔	•				
QualitySolicitors Mirza	2	4	18	✔				•	•
RadcliffesLeBrasseur	4	40	170		•	•	•	•	
Rai Solicitors	0	3	✔				•		
Raj Law Solicitors	0	2	8				•		•
Ratna & Co	Poss	2	7					•	•
Rawal & Co	1	1	7	✔				•	•
Reed Smith	25	649	2939	✔	•				
Rest Harrow & Co Solicitors	0	2	3	✔				•	
Reynolds Colman Bradley LLP	2	4	26	✔			•		
Rippon Patel & French LLP	1	2	6	✔			•	•	
Ronald Fletcher Baker LLP	3	9	40			•		•	
Rooks Rider	0	7	37		•	•	•	•	
Ropes & Gray International LLP	7	25	204	✔	•	•			
Rosling King LLP	4(20)	14	85			•			
Royds Withy King	12	67	484	✔	•	•		•	•
RPC	12(20)	79	800	✔	•	•			
Russell-Cooke Solicitors	9-10	62	343	✔	•	•		•	•
Russells	0	10	45			•	•		
SB Solicitors	0	2	4						•
Schillings International	0	9	62		•	•	•		
Seddons	2	32	116		•	•			
Sentinel Solicitors	2(19)	3	6	✔				•	•
The Sethi Partnership Solicitors	1	3	25	✔	•	•			
Shakespeare Martineau LLP	8	131	717		•				
Sharpe Pritchard LLP	3 or 4	24	77	✔			•	•	
Shearman & Sterling (London) LLP	Approx 15	35	300	✔	•				
Sheikh & Co	2	3	35	✔				•	•

Banking	Comp/comm	Competition	Construction	Corporate tax	Crime	Dispute resolution	Employment	Environment	Family	Human rights	Insurance	IP	Personal injury	Private client	Property	Shipping	Sport	TMT
	•			•			•				•			•	•			
•	•		•	•		•	•					•	•	•	•		•	•
	•														•			
		•			•	•												
							•											
•	•	•	•	•		•	•	•	•		•	•			•	•	•	•
•	•			•		•		•			•	•	•	•				•
			•			•				•		•						
		•				•	•							•	•			
	•					•								•	•			
							•					•						
					•			•				•						
•	•		•			•	•				•	•		•				
					•		•						•	•	•			
•			•			•	•	•			•			•	•		•	•
					•			•						•	•			
							•	•							•			
•	•	•	•	•			•	•	•		•	•			•	•		•
						•	•								•			•
		•				•					•			•				•
	•				•		•					•	•	•				
•	•	•	•			•	•		•		•		•	•	•			•
•			•					•					•		•			
•	•		•	•		•	•	•			•	•	•	•			•	•
•	•	•	•	•		•	•	•			•	•	•	•			•	•
•	•	•	•	•	•	•	•	•			•	•	•	•			•	•
						•	•				•			•				•
						•	•				•		•	•				•
	•				•	•	•				•	•	•	•				•
								•	•									
	•			•		•	•		•				•	•	•			•
•	•	•	•	•	•	•	•	•			•	•	•	•				•
	•		•			•	•	•				•		•				•
•	•	•	•	•	•	•	•	•						•				•
					•	•		•						•				

	Vacancies	Partners	Total staff	Work placement	Corporate/ commercial	General commercial	Niche	General practice	High street/ legal aid
Sherrards Solicitors LLP	1	15	90		•	•	•		
Shoosmiths	22	190	1630	✔	•	•	•	•	
Shranks	0	2	9			•	•		
Sidley Austin LLP	12	43	270	✔	•				
Simkins LLP	2	20	45	✔	•	•	•		
Simmons & Simmons LLP	25	280	1600	✔	•	•			
Skadden, Arps, Slate, Meagher & Flom (UK) LLP	Approx 10	31	250	✔	•				
Slater & Gordon (UK) LLP	53	86	3500			•		•	
Slater Gordon Solutions Legal Ltd	1	5	1150				•		
Slaughter and May	80-85	112	1200	✔	•	•			
Sonn Macmillan Walker	2[20]	3	25	✔					•
Sookias & Sookias	0	4	20			•			
Spence & Horne	0	1	4	✔				•	•
Squire Patton Boggs (UK) LLP	25	494	3000	✔	•	•			
Sri Kanth & Co	2	2	11	✔				•	
Steeles Law Solicitors Ltd	0	4	50		•	•	•	•	
Stephenson Harwood LLP	20	170	1000	✔	•				
Stone King	4	42	200	✔	•	•	•	•	
Stone Rowe Brewer	1-2	5	50		•	•	•		
Stowe Family Law LLP	Varies	30	100	✔			•		
STS Solicitors	2	1	5	✔		•		•	
Stuart Miller Solicitors	1	2	32	✔					•
Sullivan & Cromwell LLP	4-6	19	140	✔	•				
Sweetman Burke & Sinker	Poss	3	16	✔				•	•
Systech Solicitors Limited	0		25				•		
Taylor Rose TTKW	1-2	13	250		•	•	•	•	
Taylor Vinters LLP	6	29	170	✔	•	•	•		
Taylor Wessing	Up to 35	400	1800	✔	•	•			
Teacher Stern LLP	3	30	121	✔	•	•			
Thomas Cooper LLP	Up to 3	32	103		•		•		
Thompsons Solicitors	0	50	888				•		
Thrings	7[20]	58	224		•	•	•	•	
Tim Johnson / Law	1	1	8	✔			•		
Tinklin Springall	2[19]	7	50				•		
TLT LLP	Up to 15	110	1020	✔	•	•	•	•	
Travers Smith LLP	25	83	660	✔	•	•			
Trowers & Hamlins LLP	23	157	894	✔		•			
TV Edwards Solicitors	0	13	120	✔				•	•
TWM Solicitors LLP	0	32	220		•	•		•	
Vinson & Elkins RLLP	5	16	100	✔	•				
VWV (Veale Wasbrough Vizards)	8-10	72	411	✔	•	•	•	•	

Banking	Comp/comm	Competition	Construction	Corporate tax	Crime	Dispute resolution	Employment	Environment	Family	Human rights	Insurance	IP	Personal injury	Private client	Property	Shipping	Sport	TMT
•	•					•	•				•		•	•	•			•
•	•	•	•			•	•	•	•		•	•	•	•	•	•	•	•
	•					•	•						•	•	•			
•	•	•		•		•	•				•	•		•				•
•	•	•		•		•	•	•			•	•		•				•
•	•	•				•	•				•			•				
		•		•		•	•		•			•	•	•	•			•
												•						
•	•	•	•	•		•	•	•			•	•		•		•	•
					•													
	•						•							•				
							•							•	•			
•	•	•	•	•		•	•	•			•	•		•	•	•	•	•
•	•	•	•	•		•	•	•	•		•	•	•	•	•		•	•
	•		•	•		•	•		•			•		•	•			•
				•									•	•				
					•			•						•	•			
•	•	•		•		•									•			
				•		•		•						•				
•	•		•			•								•	•			
•	•	•	•	•		•	•		•		•	•		•	•		•	•
•	•	•	•	•		•	•	•			•	•	•	•	•	•	•	•
•	•	•		•		•	•					•		•		•	•
					•							•						
•	•	•	•	•		•	•	•			•	•		•	•	•	•
	•					•								•	•			
•	•	•	•	•		•	•	•			•		•	•	•		•
•	•	•		•		•	•	•			•	•				•	•
•	•			•		•							•	•		•	•
						•	•	•	•	•			•	•			
	•			•		•	•		•					•	•		
•	•		•	•		•	•										•
•	•	•	•	•		•	•		•		•			•	•		•

	Vacancies	Partners	Total staff	Work placement	Corporate/commercial	General commercial	Niche	General practice	High street/legal aid
Vyman Solicitors Ltd	2	4	24	✔	•				•
W H Matthews & Co	0	12	49					•	
Wainwright & Cummins	0	4	35	✔					•
Wallace LLP	2(19)	17	60		•	•			
Walter Wilson Richmond	0	1	7	✔				•	•
Watson Burton LLP	3(20)	14	110	✔	•				
Watson Farley & Williams LLP	18	157	850	✔	•	•			
Wedlake Bell LLP	8	60	250	✔	•	•			
Weightmans LLP	Up to 18	188	1277	✔	•	•	•		
Weil, Gotshal & Manges (London) LLP	15	33	297	✔	•				
Wellers Law Group LLP	1(20)	3	85		•	•		•	
White & Black Limited	2	10	20		•				
White & Case LLP	50	101	828	✔	•				
Whitehead Monckton	Varies(20)	11	118					•	
Wilson Solicitors LLP	5	12	70						•
Wilsons Solicitors LLP	4	30	164	✔	•	•		•	•
Winckworth Sherwood LLP	8	62	344	✔				•	
Winston & Strawn London LLP	2	14	58	✔	•	•			
Withers LLP	11	167	1000	✔	•	•	•	•	•
WLL Solicitors	2	1	7	✔				•	
Womble Bond Dickinson	Up to 25	123	1200	✔	•	•			

North

	Vacancies	Partners	Total staff	Work placement	Corporate/commercial	General commercial	Niche	General practice	High street/legal aid
Accutrainee	Varies				•	•		•	•
Anglo-Thai Legal (ATL)	Varies	1	5	✔				•	•
Ben Hoare Bell LLP	3	9	75					•	•
Bevan Brittan LLP	10	60	435	✔	•	•			
BHP Law	0	10	125		•			•	
BLM	23	196	1595	✔		•			
Cartmell Shepherd	2	7	90	✔				•	
Cartwright King	0	24	211					•	•
Clyde & Co LLP	45-50	415	3800	✔	•	•			
Crown Prosecution Service	1(19)	2315	6051				•		
Darlington Borough Council	0		19					•	
David Gray Solicitors LLP	0	9	67					•	•

Banking	Comp/comm	Competition	Construction	Corporate tax	Crime	Dispute resolution	Employment	Environment	Family	Human rights	Insurance	IP	Personal injury	Private client	Property	Shipping	Sport	TMT
•					•	•									•			
	•		•		•	•	•		•				•	•	•			
					•		•		•									
	•					•							•	•	•		•	•
						•	•	•	•					•				
•	•		•	•		•	•	•				•			•			•
•	•	•	•	•		•	•				•				•	•		
•	•	•	•	•		•	•				•			•	•			•
•	•	•	•	•	•	•	•	•	•		•	•	•	•	•	•	•	•
•	•	•		•		•	•				•			•	•			
	•					•	•	•	•			•		•	•			
	•					•						•		•	•		•	
•	•	•	•	•		•						•		•	•			
	•					•						•		•	•			
					•				•	•								
•	•	•		•		•	•	•	•			•		•	•			•
•	•		•	•		•	•	•	•			•		•	•			
•	•	•		•		•	•	•				•		•	•	•	•	•
						•												
•	•	•		•		•	•					•	•	•	•	•		•

Banking	Comp/comm	Competition	Construction	Corporate tax	Crime	Dispute resolution	Employment	Environment	Family	Human rights	Insurance	IP	Personal injury	Private client	Property	Shipping	Sport	TMT
•	•	•	•		•		•	•	•		•	•	•	•	•	•	•	•
	•		•			•	•		•	•		•	•	•	•			
			•						•	•				•				
	•	•	•			•	•	•					•	•				•
•	•			•		•	•		•			•	•	•	•			•
			•			•	•	•	•		•		•		•	•		•
	•				•	•	•	•	•					•	•			
					•		•	•	•					•				
•	•	•	•		•		•	•	•		•	•		•	•	•		
					•													
					•	•			•					•	•			

	Vacancies	Partners	Total staff	Work placement	Corporate/commercial	General commercial	Niche	General practice	High street/legal aid
Davies Johnson	0		26				•		
DMA Law	0	5	34					•	
DWF LLP	40	316	2800	✔	•	•			
The Endeavour Partnership LLP	3	10	55	✔	•	•			
Eversheds Sutherland (International) LLP	50	395	3235	✔	•	•			
Freeman Johnson	1	8	45	✔				•	•
Hay & Kilner Law Firm	3	24	82	✔	•	•		•	
Hempsons	3	46	300				•		
Her Majesty's Courts & Tribunals Service	0		1200					•	
Hethertons LLP Solicitors	0	3	31					•	•
Hewitts	0	13	103					•	•
Horwich Farrelly	15	35	730	✔			•		
Irwin Mitchell	45	260	2500	✔	•	•		•	
Jacksons Law Firm	2	11	70		•	•		•	
K J Commons & Co	Poss	2	55					•	•
Latimer Hinks	Poss	9	51					•	
Meikles	1[20]	9	52	✔				•	•
Mills & Co. Solicitors Limited	1	13	31	✔			•		
Mincoffs Solicitors LLP	1[20]	10	70	✔	•				
Mortons	0	6	35					•	
Muckle LLP	4	30	137	✔	•				
Plexus Law	0	117	1800				•		
Punch Robson	1-2[19]	7	53	✔	•	•	•	•	•
QualitySolicitors Lawson & Thompson	0	6	30					•	•
Reed Smith	25	649	2939	✔	•				
Samuel Phillips Law Firm	1	4	44	✔		•	•	•	
Short Richardson & Forth LLP	1	8	23					•	
Sintons LLP	3	26	200	✔	•	•			
Slater & Gordon (UK) LLP	53	86	3500			•			
Stone King	4	42	200	✔	•	•	•	•	
Stowe Family Law LLP	Varies	30	100	✔			•		
Thompsons Solicitors	0	50	888				•		
Tilly Bailey & Irvine LLP	TBC[20]	13	146		•	•		•	•
TLT LLP	Up to 15	110	1020	✔	•	•	•	•	
TMJ Legal Services Ltd	Poss	3	35	✔				•	•
Ward Hadaway	10-15	85	450	✔	•	•			
Watson Burton LLP	3[20]	14	110	✔	•				
Weightmans LLP	Up to 18	188	1277	✔	•	•		•	
Womble Bond Dickinson	Up to 25	123	1200	✔	•	•			

Banking	Comp/comm	Competition	Construction	Corporate tax	Crime	Dispute resolution	Employment	Environment	Family	Human rights	Insurance	IP	Personal injury	Private client	Property	Shipping	Sport	TMT
						•					•		•			•		
					•				•					•				
•	•	•	•	•		•	•	•			•	•	•	•	•	•		•
	•		•			•	•				•				•			•
•	•		•	•		•	•	•			•		•	•	•			•
	•			•		•	•	•					•	•	•			
•	•		•			•	•	•	•				•	•	•			•
	•			•		•							•					
						•	•		•				•					
	•		•			•	•		•				•	•	•			
						•			•				•					
•	•	•	•	•	•	•	•	•	•	•	•	•	•	•	•			•
	•	•	•			•	•	•	•	•			•	•	•			•
	•		•			•	•	•	•	•			•	•	•			•
						•			•				•					
•	•					•			•				•		•	•		
						•			•				•					
•	•		•			•	•		•			•	•	•	•		•	•
	•		•			•	•		•		•		•		•			
	•					•	•		•				•	•	•			
						•	•		•				•	•	•			
•	•	•	•	•		•	•		•		•	•	•	•	•	•		•
	•					•	•		•				•	•	•			
	•					•	•		•			•	•	•	•			
•	•		•			•	•	•	•				•	•	•		•	•
	•		•	•		•	•		•				•	•	•			•
						•	•		•		•		•	•	•			
			•		•		•						•					
	•		•			•	•		•			•	•	•				
•	•	•	•	•	•	•	•	•	•			•	•	•	•	•		•
						•	•		•				•					
•	•	•	•	•		•	•	•	•		•	•	•	•	•		•	•
•	•		•	•		•	•	•			•		•	•				•
•	•	•	•	•	•	•	•	•	•		•	•	•	•	•	•	•	•
•	•	•	•	•	•	•	•		•		•	•	•	•	•	•	•	•

Northwest

	Vacancies	Partners	Total staff	Work placement	Corporate/commercial	General commercial	Niche	General practice	High street/legal aid
Aaron and Partners	0	24	124		•	•	•		
Accutrainee	Varies				•	•	•	•	
Addleshaw Goddard	46	239	1500	✔	•				
Alfred Newton Solicitors	0	4	25					•	•
Allington Hughes Law	2(19)	14	82	✔				•	•
ALP LAW LLP	Poss	4	90				•		
Amicus Solicitors LLP	1	2	7	✔				•	
Ams Solicitors Limited	2	2	16	✔	•			•	
Antony Hodari & Co	0	6	110					•	
Arnold Greenwood Solicitors Ltd	0	4	16					•	
Baines Wilson LLP	2(19)	9	30	✔	•	•			
Barnetts	0	6	135				•		
Bermans	2(19)	12	70		•	•	•		
Birchall Blackburn Law	0	21	240		•			•	•
Blackhurst Swainson Goodier LLP t/a BSG Solicitors	1	5	27		•	•	•	•	•
BLM	23	196	1595	✔		•			
Bott & Company Solicitors LTD	0	3	102					•	
Bowcock Cuerden LLP	1	3	28		•	•			
Brabners LLP	6	60	375		•	•			
Brian Koffman & Co	0	1	2				•		
Brighouse Wolff	1	10	80					•	
Browne Jacobson LLP	20	142	981	✔	•	•	•		
Bryan Cave Leighton Paisner	35	200	1600	✔	•	•			
Burnetts	2	7	143	✔				•	
Butcher & Barlow LLP	2(20)	24	139					•	
Camps	0	5	170	✔			•		
Canter Levin & Berg	1-2	10	91	✔				•	•
Cartmell Shepherd	2	7	90	✔				•	
Cartwright King	0	24	211					•	•
CFG Law (part of the client first group)	4	1	75	✔				•	
Chenery Maher	0	2	11				•		
Clyde & Co LLP	45-50	415	3800	✔	•	•			
CMS	120	1000	7500	✔	•	•			
Colemans-ctts t/a Simpson Millar	0	12	200		•			•	
Crown Prosecution Service	1(19)	2315	6051				•		
Cumbria Law Centre	0		13				•		•
Curtis Law Solicitors LLP	8	4	115	✔				•	
DAC Beachcroft LLP	13(20)	240	2300	✔	•	•		•	
David Phillips & Partners	0	15	75	✔			•	•	•
Davis Blank Furniss LLP	2	10	60		•	•		•	

Banking	Comp/comm	Competition	Construction	Corporate tax	Crime	Dispute resolution	Employment	Environment	Family	Human rights	Insurance	IP	Personal injury	Private client	Property	Shipping	Sport	TMT
•	•	•	•			•	•	•	•			•		•	•		•	•
•	•	•	•	•			•	•	•	•	•	•	•	•	•	•	•	•
•	•	•	•	•		•	•	•	•		•	•	•	•	•		•	•
			•					•	•				•	•	•			
	•				•	•	•		•				•	•	•			
													•					
									•				•	•	•			
													•					
						•	•		•					•	•			
•	•		•			•	•					•			•			
	•					•							•	•	•			
•		•				•	•					•		•	•		•	•
	•				•		•		•	•			•	•	•			
	•					•	•	•	•		•	•	•	•	•	•		
			•				•	•	•	•	•			•		•		•
	•						•	•	•					•	•			
•	•	•	•	•		•	•	•			•	•	•	•	•		•	•
				•														
						•		•						•	•			
•	•	•	•	•		•	•	•			•	•	•	•	•		•	•
•	•	•	•	•		•	•	•			•	•	•	•	•	•	•	•
•	•		•			•	•	•			•	•		•	•			•
	•		•			•	•		•				•	•				
					•		•		•				•	•				
	•				•		•	•	•				•	•	•			
					•		•	•	•				•					
													•					
							•								•			
•	•	•	•	•		•	•	•			•	•	•		•	•		
•	•	•	•	•			•	•			•	•		•	•		•	•
	•					•	•						•		•			
					•													
										•								
	•								•				•	•				
•	•	•	•			•	•	•			•	•	•		•			•
					•				•				•	•				
•	•	•	•				•		•			•	•		•		•	•

	Vacancies	Partners	Total staff	Work placement	Corporate/ commercial	General commercial	Niche	General practice	High street/ legal aid
Dean Solicitors	0	2	9					•	
Denby & Co	1	5	26		•			•	•
Derek B Forrest Solicitors	0	2	8					•	
DLA Piper UK LLP	Up to 70	1300	8500	✔	•				
Donald Race & Newton	0	6	47	✔				•	•
Duncan Gibbins Solicitors	2	2	34				•		
DWF LLP	40	316	2800	✔	•	•			
Eb Legal	1	1	5	✔			•		
Eversheds Sutherland (International) LLP	50	395	3235	✔	•	•			
Express Solicitors	5[19]	22	230	✔			•		
Farleys Solicitors LLP	2[19]	12	170		•	•		•	•
Fentons	0	24	210					•	•
Fieldfisher	18	223	986	✔	•	•			
Fieldings Porter	3-4	11	76		•	•		•	•
Forbes Solicitors	4	44	320	✔	•	•	•	•	
Forresters Solicitors Limited	0	2	15						•
Freeths LLP	20	147	750		•	•			
Gateley Plc	16	143	883	✔	•	•			
GHP Legal	0	10	87	✔				•	•
Glaisyers Solicitors LLP	0	11	85	✔	•	•		•	
GLP Solicitors	0-1	4	9					•	•
Government Legal Profession	50		2000						
Gregory Abrams Davidson LLP	0	9	78	✔				•	
Hall Smith Whittingham	0	5	40					•	
HCB Solicitors	1	8	52		•	•		•	•
Hempsons	3	46	300				•		
Henry's Solicitors Limited	1		25	✔				•	
Her Majesty's Courts & Tribunals Service	0		1200					•	
Hibberts LLP	1[19]	9	96	✔		•		•	•
Hill Dickinson LLP	10	175	840	✔	•	•	•		
Hillyer McKeown LLP	1	12	80		•	•	•	•	
Horwich Farrelly	15	35	730	✔			•		
Howarth Goodman	Poss	2	11	✔	•	•			
Howes Percival LLP	8	43	208	✔	•	•			
Inghams	Poss	7	43	✔		•		•	•
Irwin Mitchell	45	260	2500	✔	•	•		•	
The Jackson Lees Group	0		280					•	
James Murray Solicitors	0	4	68					•	•
JMW Solicitors	Approx 10	35	380		•	•	•	•	
JWK Solicitors	0	5	34					•	•
The Keith Jones Partnership	0	3	15	✔		•	•		

Banking	Comp/comm	Competition	Construction	Corporate tax	Crime	Dispute resolution	Employment	Environment	Family	Human rights	Insurance	IP	Personal injury	Private client	Property	Shipping	Sport	TMT
													•					
	•				•		•	•	•				•	•	•			
	•				•		•		•				•	•				
•	•	•	•	•			•	•	•						•	•	•	•
					•		•		•									
													•	•				
•	•	•	•	•			•	•	•		•	•	•	•	•	•	•	•
					•								•					
•	•	•	•	•	•		•	•	•		•	•			•		•	•
													•					
	•				•		•	•	•				•	•		•		
													•					
•	•	•	•	•			•	•	•		•	•	•	•	•		•	•
•	•		•		•		•		•		•	•	•	•	•			
•	•	•	•	•	•		•	•	•	•	•	•	•	•	•			•
					•				•				•	•				
•	•	•	•	•			•	•	•	•	•	•	•	•	•	•	•	•
•	•	•	•	•			•	•	•			•	•	•	•	•	•	•
•	•				•		•					•	•	•	•			
•	•	•	•				•	•	•	•		•	•	•	•	•	•	•
									•					•	•			
	•						•	•	•				•	•	•			
	•				•		•		•				•	•	•			
	•	•			•		•						•	•				
					•		•		•				•					
	•						•	•	•					•	•			
•	•	•	•	•			•	•	•			•	•	•	•		•	•
	•						•	•	•			•	•	•	•	•		•
							•						•					
	•	•							•				•		•			
•	•	•	•	•			•	•	•				•	•	•		•	•
	•						•						•	•	•			
•	•	•	•		•		•	•	•	•	•	•		•	•			•
	•	•			•		•		•	•			•	•				
					•				•									
	•				•		•					•	•	•	•		•	•
					•													

	Vacancies	Partners	Total staff	Work placement	Corporate/ commercial	General commercial	Niche	General practice	High street/ legal aid
Kennedys	20(20)	393	1900	✔	•	•			
Kirwans	0	5	80			•		•	•
Kuit Steinart Levy	6	35	185	✔	•	•	•	•	
Land Law LLP	0	6	46			•			
Latimer Lee	0			✔		•			
Laytons Solicitors LLP	6	29	118	✔	•	•			
Leigh Day	8-10(20)	44	420	✔			•		•
Malik Legal Solicitors Ltd	4	3	14	✔			•		
McHale & Company	1	5	40		•	•		•	•
Middleton Solicitors	1(19)	3	25	✔		•		•	
Middleweeks	0	2	19	✔			•		
Milburns Solicitors Limited	1(19)	8	50	✔		•		•	•
Mills & Reeve LLP	20	122	994	✔	•	•			
Milne Moser	0	6	27						
MLP Law LLP	3(20)	6	22	✔	•	•	•	•	
Mohammed & Co	0	1	13	✔				•	•
Myerson Solicitors LLP	3	20	93	✔	•	•	•		
Napthens	2-4(20)	27	229					•	
Nexus Solicitors	0	9	45		•	•			
Oglethorpe Sturton & Gillibrand	1-2	8	46			•		•	
O'Neill Patient Solicitors LLP	0	10	240					•	
Pearson Hinchliffe LLP	2(19)	8	49		•	•		•	•
Pinsent Masons LLP	68	430	3000	✔	•	•			
Plexus Law	0	117	1800				•		
QualitySolicitors Turnerlaw	0	3	25					•	
Ralli Ltd	0	5	45		•	•	•		
Ratcliffe & Bibby Solicitors	0	5	45	✔				•	•
Robert Lizar	Poss	6	22					•	
Robert Meaton and Co Solicitors	1	2	13			•		•	
Roberts Jackson Solicitors	6	9	220	✔			•		
The Roland Partnership	0	2	20				•		•
Russell & Russell	0	26	200					•	•
SAS Daniels LLP	4	20	150	✔	•	•		•	
Savas & Savage Solicitors Limited	4(19)	3	25	✔				•	
Shoosmiths	22	190	1630	✔	•	•	•	•	
Silverdale Solicitors	0	4	25	✔	•	•		•	
Slater & Gordon (UK) LLP	53	86	3500		•	•		•	
Slater Gordon Solutions Legal Ltd	1	5	1150				•		
Southerns	0	6	63					•	•
Squire Patton Boggs (UK) LLP	25	494	3000	✔	•	•			
Stephensons	5	26	325	✔	•			•	•

Banking	Comp/comm	Competition	Construction	Corporate tax	Crime	Dispute resolution	Employment	Environment	Family	Human rights	Insurance	IP	Personal injury	Private client	Property	Shipping	Sport	TMT
•	•		•			•	•	•			•	•	•	•	•		•	
					•	•	•	•					•	•	•			
•	•	•	•	•		•	•			•		•		•		•		•
	•	•		•	•	•	•		•			•	•	•	•			
							•	•		•		•						
	•		•			•	•			•			•	•	•		•	
•	•					•	•		•		•		•	•				
					•								•	•				•
•	•	•	•	•		•	•	•	•		•	•	•	•			•	•
	•						•	•				•	•	•				•
	•					•	•						•	•	•			
•	•	•		•		•	•	•	•			•	•	•				•
	•		•	•		•	•	•	•		•	•	•	•				
	•					•	•					•	•	•		•	•	
	•					•	•	•				•	•	•				
•							•						•	•				
	•		•			•	•		•				•	•				
•	•	•	•		•	•	•	•			•	•			•	•	•	
		•				•					•		•					
					•		•		•				•	•				
	•		•		•	•	•					•	•	•	•		•	•
	•					•	•		•				•	•	•			
					•		•	•	•				•					
	•					•	•						•	•	•			
					•								•	•	•			
	•		•			•	•		•		•		•	•	•			
•	•	•	•	•		•	•	•	•		•	•	•	•	•	•	•	•
	•				•	•	•		•				•	•				
		•			•							•	•	•	•			•
	•					•	•	•		•			•	•	•			
•	•	•	•	•		•	•	•	•		•	•		•	•	•	•	•

	Vacancies	Partners	Total staff	Work placement	Corporate/commercial	General commercial	Niche	General practice	High street/legal aid
Storrar Cowdry	0	7	24					•	
Stowe Family Law LLP	Varies	30	100	✔		•			
Systech Solicitors Limited	0		25			•			
Temple Heelis LLP	0	6	30					•	
Thompsons Solicitors	0	50	888				•		
TLT LLP	Up to 15	110	1020	✔	•	•	•	•	
Trowers & Hamlins LLP	23	157	894	✔		•			
Ward Hadaway	10-15	85	450	✔	•	•			
Weightmans LLP	Up to 18	188	1277	✔	•			•	
WH Darbyshire & Son	0	5	13			•		•	•
Winckworth Sherwood LLP	8	62	344	✔			•		
Wrigley Claydon	1	5	26					•	•

Scotland

	Vacancies	Partners	Total staff	Work placement	Corporate/commercial	General commercial	Niche	General practice	High street/legal aid
Addleshaw Goddard	46	239	1500	✔	•				
BLM	23	196	1595	✔		•			
Clyde & Co LLP	45-50	415	3800	✔	•	•			
CMS	120	1000	7500	✔	•	•			
Corries Solicitors Ltd	0	2	47					•	
Dentons	50	2892	10455	✔	•	•	•		
DLA Piper UK LLP	Up to 70	1300	8500	✔	•				
DWF LLP	40	316	2800	✔	•	•			
Eversheds Sutherland (International) LLP	50	395	3235	✔	•	•			
Irwin Mitchell	45	260	2500	✔	•	•		•	
Pinsent Masons LLP	68	430	3000	✔	•	•			
Shoosmiths	22	190	1630	✔	•	•	•	•	
Slater & Gordon (UK) LLP	53	86	3500			•		•	
TLT LLP	Up to 15	110	1020	✔	•	•	•	•	
Weightmans LLP	Up to 18	188	1277	✔	•	•	•		
Womble Bond Dickinson	Up to 25	123	1200	✔	•	•			

Banking	Comp/comm	Competition	Construction	Corporate tax	Crime	Dispute resolution	Employment	Environment	Family	Human rights	Insurance	IP	Personal injury	Private client	Property	Shipping	Sport	TMT
	•						•		•				•	•	•			
							•							•				
			•			•												
	•					•	•		•				•	•	•			
					•								•					
•	•	•	•	•		•	•	•	•		•		•	•	•	•		•
•	•	•	•	•		•	•	•	•		•	•	•	•	•		•	•
•	•	•	•	•	•	•	•	•	•		•	•	•	•	•	•	•	•
					•				•				•	•	•			
•	•					•	•		•		•			•	•			•
	•					•	•		•				•	•	•			•

Banking	Comp/comm	Competition	Construction	Corporate tax	Crime	Dispute resolution	Employment	Environment	Family	Human rights	Insurance	IP	Personal injury	Private client	Property	Shipping	Sport	TMT
•	•	•	•	•		•	•	•			•	•		•	•		•	•
	•					•	•	•	•		•		•			•		•
•	•	•	•	•		•	•	•			•	•	•		•	•		•
•	•	•	•	•		•	•	•			•	•		•			•	•
											•		•	•				
•	•	•	•	•		•	•	•			•	•		•	•	•		•
•	•	•	•	•		•	•	•			•	•	•	•	•	•	•	•
•	•	•	•	•		•	•	•			•	•		•	•	•	•	•
•	•	•	•	•	•	•	•	•			•	•	•	•	•			•
•	•	•	•	•	•	•	•	•	•	•	•	•	•	•	•		•	•
•	•	•	•	•		•	•	•			•	•	•	•	•	•	•	•
			•		•			•			•		•	•	•			•
•	•	•	•	•		•	•	•			•		•	•	•			•
•	•	•	•	•		•	•	•			•	•	•	•	•	•	•	•
•	•	•	•	•		•	•	•			•	•		•	•	•		•

Southeast

	Vacancies	Partners	Total staff	Work placement	Corporate/commercial	General commercial	Niche	General practice	High street/legal aid
Accutrainee	Varies				•	•	•	•	
Alan Simpson & Co	0-1	1	12					•	
Allan Janes	1	5	20	✔	•				
Antony Clapp Solicitors	0	2	13				•		
asb law LLP	2(19)	17	134	✔	•	•		•	
Aston Bond	1	3	20	✔	•	•			
Atkins Hope	0	4	35	✔				•	•
B P Collins LLP	3-4(20)	14	110	✔	•	•		•	
Barlow Robbins LLP	4	18	178	✔	•			•	
Basingstoke & Deane Borough Council	1-2	1	20				•		
Bastian Lloyd Morris LLP	0	3	14	✔					•
Batchelors	0	14	55			•			
Berry & Lamberts Solicitors	1(19)	12	80					•	•
BG Group Plc	1		100				•		
Bhogal Partners Solicitors	1	3	19	✔	•	•		•	
Bircham Dyson Bell LLP	5	49	280	✔	•	•		•	
Birkett Long LLP	2(20)	26	170	✔	•	•		•	
Blake Morgan LLP	18	114	800	✔	•	•	•	•	
Blandy & Blandy LLP	2-3(20)	20	104	✔	•	•		•	
Blaser Mills Law	4	22	125		•	•	•	•	•
BLM	23	196	1595	✔		•			
Boodle Hatfield LLP	4	33	150	✔	•	•	•		
Bosley & Co	1	3	13	✔				•	•
Boyes Turner	3	23	160	✔	•	•	•	•	
Brachers LLP	3(20)	26	196	✔	•	•		•	
Bramsdon & Childs	1	5	34			•		•	•
Breeze & Wyles Solicitors Ltd	4(19)	9	180			•			
Brignalls Balderston Warren	0	13	57					•	
Brooks & Partners	0	1	24		•	•		•	
BTMK Solicitors Ltd	0	10	110	✔	•	•	•	•	•
Buss Murton Law LLP	2(20)	9	70					•	
Carpenter & Co	0-1	3	25					•	•
Carter Bells LLP	0	7	25					•	
Charles Russell Speechlys	24	150	1020	✔	•	•		•	
Chatham Chambers Solicitors	1	2	6	✔		•	•	•	
Churchers Bolitho Way	0	7	22	✔	•	•		•	•
Clarke Kiernan	1(19)	2	27						•
Clarke Willmott LLP	TBC	112	642		•	•		•	
Clarkslegal LLP	2	13	70			•			
Clarkson Wright & Jakes Ltd	0	15	71		•	•		•	
Clyde & Co LLP	45-50	415	3800	✔	•	•			

Banking	Comp/comm	Competition	Construction	Corporate tax	Crime	Dispute resolution	Employment	Environment	Family	Human rights	Insurance	IP	Personal injury	Private client	Property	Shipping	Sport	TMT
•	•	•	•	•		•	•	•	•		•	•	•	•	•	•	•	•
	•						•		•				•		•			
	•		•			•	•	•				•	•	•	•		•	
								•										
•	•	•	•	•		•	•	•	•		•	•	•	•	•		•	•
	•		•			•	•	•				•		•				•
								•	•		•		•	•	•			
•	•	•	•	•		•	•	•	•		•		•	•	•		•	•
	•					•		•	•			•		•	•			•
			•	•		•	•	•	•			•		•			•	•
	•		•			•	•	•				•		•	•			
	•		•				•	•				•		•	•			
	•		•					•								•		
•	•	•	•	•		•	•	•	•		•	•	•	•	•			•
•	•	•	•	•		•	•	•	•	•	•	•	•	•	•		•	•
•	•	•	•	•		•	•	•	•		•	•	•	•	•		•	•
	•						•	•				•		•	•			
	•					•	•	•	•		•	•	•	•	•		•	•
	•		•			•	•	•				•		•	•			
•	•	•	•			•	•	•	•			•	•	•	•			•
•	•		•	•		•	•	•	•		•	•	•	•	•			
			•			•	•	•				•		•	•			
	•		•	•		•	•	•				•		•	•			
	•		•	•		•	•	•				•		•	•			
	•		•	•		•	•	•		•	•	•	•	•			•	•
	•	•	•			•	•	•		•		•		•	•		•	•
							•	•						•	•	•		•
	•					•	•	•				•		•	•			
•	•	•	•	•		•	•	•	•		•	•	•	•	•		•	•
	•					•	•	•				•		•	•			
	•		•	•		•	•	•				•		•			•	•
	•		•			•	•							•	•			
•	•	•	•	•		•	•	•	•		•	•	•	•	•		•	•
•	•	•	•	•		•	•	•	•		•	•	•	•	•			•
•	•	•	•	•		•	•		•		•	•	•	•	•	•		•

	Vacancies	Partners	Total staff	Work placement	Corporate/ commercial	General commercial	Niche	General practice	High street/ legal aid
Coffin Mew LLP	8	20	220	✔	•	•	•	•	
Colemans-ctts t/a Simpson Millar	0	12	200		•			•	
Collins Solicitors	0	5	24				•		•
Cowans Solicitors LLP	0	2	25					•	•
Cripps LLP	7	51	360	✔	•	•		•	
Crown Prosecution Service	1[19]	2315	6051				•		
Cunningtons	Varies	9	60	✔				•	•
Curwens LLP	2[19]	15	90					•	
Curzon Green Solicitors	2[19]	3	22	✔				•	
DAC Beachcroft LLP	13[20]	240	2300	✔	•	•			
Dakers Marriott Solicitors	0	3	12			•			
Darlingtons	1	6	42	✔	•				
David Phillips & Partners	0	15	75	✔			•	•	
Dawson Hart	0	7	42					•	
Dean Wilson LLP	2[20]	13	76		•	•			
Debenhams Ottaway LLP	0	11	120					•	
Dentons	50	2892	10455	✔	•	•	•		
Dexter Montague LLP	1[20]	4	24	✔				•	•
DMH Stallard LLP	0	59	259	✔	•	•			
Drysdales Solicitors LLP	1	3	20					•	
DW Law	0	2	8	✔					•
East Hampshire District Council	0		7						
Edwards Duthie	0	12	85		•	•		•	•
EMD Law LLP	0	3	13						
EMW Law LLP	5	34	172	✔	•				
Eric Robinson Solicitors	2	9	140					•	
Essex Legal Services	0		120						
Fearon & Co	0	1	6				•		
Field Seymour Parkes	3	19	114	✔	•	•		•	
Fitz Solicitors	0	1	5		•	•		•	
Frances Lindsay & Co	0	1	5				•		
Franklins Solicitors LLP	0	14	100	✔	•	•		•	
Furley Page LLP	2	18	150	✔	•			•	
Gaby Hardwicke	2[20]	17	150		•	•		•	
Garden House Solicitors	1	1	10	✔				•	
Gateley Plc	16	143	883	✔	•	•			
GC Solicitors	0	2	17					•	•
Gepp & Sons Solicitors LLP	2[19]	17	91					•	
Gill Turner Tucker	0	4	27		•	•		•	
Girlings	2[20]	14	100	✔	•	•		•	
Glanvilles	0	13	100		•	•		•	•

Banking	Comp/comm	Competition	Construction	Corporate tax	Crime	Dispute resolution	Employment	Environment	Family	Human rights	Insurance	IP	Personal injury	Private client	Property	Shipping	Sport	TMT
•	•	•	•			•	•		•			•	•	•	•		•	•
	•					•	•						•		•			
								•	•				•	•				
					•				•									
•	•		•		•		•		•			•			•			•
	•				•		•		•				•	•	•			
	•	•				•	•		•			•		•				
	•		•			•	•		•				•	•	•			
•	•	•	•	•	•	•	•	•			•	•	•	•	•		•	•
	•					•	•		•				•	•				
	•		•			•	•		•					•	•			
					•	•		•					•	•				
	•					•	•		•					•	•			
•	•					•	•		•				•	•	•			
•	•	•	•	•		•	•	•			•	•			•	•	•	•
•	•		•			•	•		•		•	•	•		•			•
				•		•		•						•				
				•		•		•					•	•				
				•		•	•		•				•					
•	•		•			•	•		•			•		•	•			•
	•				•	•	•		•		•	•	•	•	•			
							•	•	•		•		•					
	•							•					•	•	•			
•	•	•	•	•		•	•		•				•		•		•	•
	•				•	•	•		•					•				
									•									
	•					•	•		•			•	•	•	•			•
	•				•	•	•		•			•	•	•				•
	•					•	•		•			•	•	•				
•	•	•	•	•	•	•	•		•			•	•		•	•	•	•
				•		•		•				•		•	•			
	•					•	•		•					•	•			•
	•					•	•		•				•	•	•			
	•								•					•	•			•

	Vacancies	Partners	Total staff	Work placement	Corporate/ commercial	General commercial	Niche	General practice	High street/ legal aid
Goodhand & Forsyth	0	2	31					•	•
Government Legal Profession	50		2000						
Graeme Quar & Co	0	1	9		•				
Hart Reade	2	6	60			•		•	
Hatten Wyatt Solicitors & Advocates	4[20]	9	80	✔	•	•		•	•
Heald Solicitors LLP	1[20]	4	30	✔	•	•		•	
Helix Law	2[20]	4	14				•		
Her Majesty's Courts & Tribunals Service	0		1200					•	
Herrington Carmichael LLP	3-4[20]	13	95		•	•		•	
Hill & Abbott	0		40	✔				•	
Hine Solicitors	10	8	180					•	•
HKH Kenwright & Cox	0	2	19	✔	•			•	•
Hodders	0	5	65		•	•		•	•
Holden & Co. LLP	1	4	23					•	•
Horsham District Council	1		15						
Horwood & James LLP	0	5	28					•	
Howell Jones LLP	0	14	75					•	
HRJ Foreman Laws	0	5	35				•		
Irwin Mitchell	45	260	2500	✔	•	•			
John Chapman and Co	0	4	22					•	•
Judge & Priestley LLP	1	11	130					•	
Kaim Todner Solicitors Ltd	0	8	70					•	•
Kennard Wells Solicitors	1	5	35					•	•
Kennedys	20[20]	393	1900	✔	•	•			
Kesar & Co Solicitors	2[20]	1	29	✔				•	
Kingsley Smith Solicitors LLP	0	4	20		•	•			
Lamport Bassitt	0	11	80		•	•	•		
Larcomes LLP	1	6	40			•		•	•
Lawtons Solicitors	2[19]	2	25						•
Laytons Solicitors LLP	6	29	118	✔	•	•			
Lennons Solicitors Ltd	1[19]	4	42					•	
Leonard Cannings Solicitors LLP	2	3	20						•
Lester Aldridge LLP	8	46	324	✔	•	•	•	•	
Lewis Silkin	Up to 6	58	350	✔	•	•			
Lightfoots LLP	0	10	107		•	•	•	•	
Machins Solicitors LLP	4[20]	12	100		•	•	•	•	•
Mackarness & Lunt	0	3	18					•	
Major & Co	0	1	8	✔				•	
Martin Cray and Co	1	2	22	✔				•	
Martin Murray & Associates	0	9	70					•	•
Martin Searle Solicitors	0	2	15				•		

Banking	Comp/comm	Competition	Construction	Corporate tax	Crime	Dispute resolution	Employment	Environment	Family	Human rights	Insurance	IP	Personal injury	Private client	Property	Shipping	Sport	TMT
					•		•		•				•	•				
•	•	•		•			•	•		•			•	•	•	•	•	•
	•					•	•	•						•				
	•					•	•	•	•					•				
	•	•			•	•	•	•	•				•	•				
•	•	•	•			•	•	•	•				•	•	•		•	•
	•					•			•									
	•			•	•		•		•					•	•			
	•						•	•						•	•	•		
						•	•		•				•	•	•			•
	•				•		•		•									
•						•	•		•					•	•			
					•				•				•	•				
						•	•		•					•	•			
	•					•	•		•					•	•			
	•	•				•	•	•	•				•	•	•		•	•
•	•	•	•	•	•	•	•	•	•	•	•	•	•	•	•	•	•	•
									•									
	•					•			•					•	•			
					•				•						•			
•	•					•	•	•	•		•	•	•	•	•	•	•	
					•				•				•					
	•	•	•			•	•	•	•		•			•	•		•	•
	•					•	•		•				•	•	•			
	•				•		•		•					•	•			
•	•	•	•	•		•	•	•	•				•	•	•			•
	•					•	•	•	•				•	•	•			
					•			•	•									
•	•	•	•	•	•	•	•	•			•		•	•	•	•		•
	•		•	•		•	•						•		•		•	•
•	•		•			•	•		•				•	•	•			
									•					•	•			
	•					•	•		•				•	•	•			
			•		•	•	•		•				•	•	•			
					•				•									

	Vacancies	Partners	Total staff	Work placement	Corporate/ commercial	General commercial	Niche	General practice	High street/ legal aid
Mayo Wynne Baxter LLP	1(19)	31	214					•	
McMillan Williams Solicitors	Varies	60	400	✔	•	•	•	•	•
Moore Blatch LLP	3(20)	42	270					•	
Morrisons Solicitors LLP	2-4(20)	13	140					•	
Mowll & Mowll	0	5	24		•	•			
Mullis & Peake	Poss(19)	7	56					•	
Mundays LLP	2	25	94		•	•	•		
Noble Solicitors	0	3	40	✔					•
Osborne Clarke LLP	20	258	1632	✔	•	•	•		
Owen White	2	6	40		•	•	•		
Owen White and Catlin	3	11	130			•		•	•
Palmers	1	8	100	✔	•	•		•	
Paris Smith LLP	5	37	200	✔	•	•		•	
Parker Bullen LLP	2(20)	7	60	✔	•	•		•	
Paul Robinson Solicitors LLP	1	9	85		•			•	•
Peacock & Co	1	8	30					•	
Penningtons Manches LLP	14-16	113	700		•	•		•	
Pitmans LLP	8	36	210		•	•	•	•	
Pope & Co	0	2	12	✔				•	•
Premier Solicitors LLP	20	8	100	✔				•	
Prettys	3-4	6	75	✔	•	•	•	•	
QualitySolicitors Howlett Clarke LLP	2(20)	3	45	✔				•	
QualitySolicitors Large & Gibson	0	2	20		•	•			
QualitySolicitors Truemans	0	3	18					•	•
Raj Law Solicitors	0	2	8					•	•
Rawlison Butler LLP	0	14	74		•	•	•		
Reena Ghai Solicitors	0-1	1	6						•
Rix & Kay Solicitors LLP	1(19)	22	125	✔	•				
Robson & Co	0	2	8					•	
Royds Withy King	12	67	484	✔	•	•		•	•
SA Law	2(19)	15	90		•	•			
The Sethi Partnership Solicitors	1	3	25	✔	•	•		•	
Sherrards Solicitors LLP	1	15	90		•	•	•		
Shoosmiths	22	190	1630	✔	•	•	•	•	
SO Legal Limited	5(20)	2	22	✔	•	•			
Spelthorne Borough Council	0		12	✔					
Stephen Rimmer LLP	1(19)	11	92			•		•	•
Stevens & Bolton LLP	5	42	229	✔	•	•		•	
Stone King	4	42	200	✔	•	•	•	•	
Stowe Family Law LLP	Varies	30	100	✔			•		
Surrey Law Centre	0		9	✔					•

Banking	Comp/comm	Competition	Construction	Corporate tax	Crime	Dispute resolution	Employment	Environment	Family	Human rights	Insurance	IP	Personal injury	Private client	Property	Shipping	Sport	TMT
	•					•	•		•			•	•	•	•			•
	•	•	•	•	•	•	•		•	•		•	•	•	•			•
	•			•		•	•	•	•			•	•	•	•			
•	•			•		•	•		•			•	•	•	•			
	•					•	•		•			•		•	•			
•	•	•	•	•		•	•		•			•		•	•			•
					•													
•	•	•	•	•	•	•	•	•				•		•	•			•
	•	•	•			•	•		•			•		•	•			•
				•		•		•	•			•		•				
	•		•			•	•		•			•	•	•	•			
•	•	•	•	•		•	•	•	•			•	•	•	•		•	
•	•	•	•		•	•	•	•	•			•	•	•	•	•		
	•			•		•	•		•			•	•	•				
•	•		•	•		•	•		•			•	•	•	•		•	•
•	•		•			•	•		•		•	•	•	•				
						•	•		•			•		•				
	•					•	•		•			•	•	•	•			
	•	•	•	•		•	•	•	•		•	•	•	•	•	•	•	•
	•					•	•		•			•	•	•				
	•		•	•		•	•		•			•	•	•	•			
	•					•	•		•			•	•	•				
				•									•					
	•	•	•			•			•			•	•	•	•		•	•
				•				•										
	•		•			•	•		•		•	•	•	•		•		
								•					•					
•	•	•	•	•		•	•		•			•	•	•	•		•	•
•	•					•	•		•			•		•		•	•	•
	•		•			•	•		•			•	•	•	•			
•	•					•	•		•			•		•	•			
•	•	•	•	•		•	•	•	•		•	•	•	•	•	•	•	
	•		•			•	•		•			•		•	•		•	
	•					•		•						•				
	•		•		•	•	•	•			•	•		•	•			•
•	•	•	•	•		•	•		•		•	•		•	•			•
	•		•	•		•	•		•			•		•	•			•
								•						•				
							•		•									

	Vacancies	Partners	Total staff	Work placement	Corporate/ commercial	General commercial	Niche	General practice	High street/ legal aid
Talbot Walker LLP	1	3	14					•	
Tassells	1	7	21	✔		•		•	
Taylor Walton LLP	4	28	160	✔	•	•		•	
Tees	3	24	250	✔				•	
Thackray Williams LLP	3[20]	18	140		•	•		•	•
Thompson Smith and Puxon	Poss	11	75		•	•	•	•	
Thompsons Solicitors	0	50	888				•		
Thomson Snell & Passmore LLP	6	41	235	✔	•	•		•	
Thomson Webb & Corfield	1[19]	9	39		•			•	
Tinklin Springall	2[19]	7	50					•	
Trethowans LLP	3-4	40	235		•	•		•	
TWM Solicitors LLP	0	32	220		•	•		•	
Vodafone Group Services	0		110	✔	•	•			
VWV (Veale Wasbrough Vizards)	8-10	72	411	✔	•	•	•	•	
W H Matthews & Co	0	12	49					•	
Wannop & Fox	0	6	52					•	•
Warner Goodman LLP	2-4	17	160		•	•		•	•
Warners Solicitors	2[20]	22	111					•	
Weightmans LLP	Up to 18	188	1277	✔	•	•	•		
Wellers Law Group LLP	1[20]	3	85		•	•		•	
White & Black Limited	2	10	20		•				
White & Co	1[19]	2	12	✔			•		•
Whitehead Monckton	Varies[20]	11	118					•	
Wilson & Bird	1	1	6					•	
Wilsons Solicitors	2	1	5	✔				•	•
Winckworth Sherwood LLP	8	62	344	✔			•		
Womble Bond Dickinson	Up to 25	123	1200	✔	•	•			
Woodfines LLP	3[20]	22	140	✔	•	•		•	
Wortley Byers LLP	0	11	60		•	•		•	

Southwest

	Vacancies	Partners	Total staff	Work placement	Corporate/commercial	General commercial	Niche	General practice	High street/legal aid
Accutrainee	Varies				•	•	•	•	
AMD Solicitors Limited	1	2	30		•			•	•
Ashfords	9	74	540	✔	•	•		•	
Awdry Bailey & Douglas	0	7	95		•	•		•	
Barcan+Kirby	0	17	170		•	•		•	
Battens Solicitors Limited	0	6	170					•	•
Beale & Company Solicitors LLP	5-6(20)	23	130		•	•	•		
Bennetts Solicitors & Attorneys	0	4	15		•	•	•	•	
Bevan Brittan LLP	10	60	435	✔	•	•			
Beviss & Beckingsale	1(19)	7	50	✔				•	
Blanchards Bailey LLP	0	6	66					•	
BLM	23	196	1595	✔		•			
BPE Solicitors LLP	4	21	130	✔	•	•			
Browne Jacobson LLP	20	142	981	✔	•	•	•		
BS Singh & Co LLP	2	2	4	✔			•	•	
Burges Salmon LLP	20	87	750	✔	•	•		•	
Burroughs Day	1	10	100		•	•		•	
Capsticks Solicitors LLP	8(20)	51	403		•	•	•		
Charles Russell Speechlys	24	150	1020	✔	•	•			
Charlesworth Nicholl & Co	0	2	20						•
Clarke & Son Solicitors LLP	0	7	37		•	•		•	
Clarke Willmott LLP	TBC	112	642		•	•		•	
CMS	120	1000	7500	✔	•	•			
Coles Miller	3	12	110	✔	•	•		•	•
The Commercial Law Practice	0	4	11	✔	•	•			
Crosse & Crosse	0	8	56		•	•			
Crown Prosecution Service	1(19)	2315	6051				•		
DAC Beachcroft LLP	13(20)	240	2300	✔	•	•		•	
Davies and Partners	1(19)	12	170		•	•		•	
Davies Johnson	0		26				•		
Devon & Cornwall Constabulary	0	1	12				•		
DWF LLP	40	316	2800	✔	•	•			
Ellis Jones Solicitors LLP	2	12	130	✔	•	•		•	
Everys	0	10	100		•	•		•	•
Farnfields	0	4	65					•	•
Foot Anstey LLP	12(20)	49	500	✔	•	•		•	
Ford Simey LLP	0	11	64					•	
GA Solicitors	2(19)	18	77		•	•		•	
Gilbert Stephens LLP	1	12	126		•	•		•	•
Gordon Dadds LLP	6	39	236		•	•		•	
Government Legal Profession	50		2000						

Banking	Comp/comm	Competition	Construction	Corporate tax	Crime	Dispute resolution	Employment	Environment	Family	Human rights	Insurance	IP	Personal injury	Private client	Property	Shipping	Sport	TMT
•	•	•	•	•		•	•	•	•		•	•	•	•	•	•	•	•
								•						•	•			
•	•	•	•	•	•	•	•	•		•		•	•	•	•	•	•	•
	•		•			•	•		•				•	•	•			
	•					•	•		•					•				
	•		•			•	•	•			•				•			•
•	•	•		•		•	•					•		•			•	•
	•	•	•			•	•	•			•		•		•			•
	•					•		•		•			•	•	•			
	•						•		•				•	•	•			
		•				•	•	•	•		•		•			•		•
	•		•	•		•	•				•			•				•
•	•	•	•	•		•	•	•	•		•	•	•	•	•		•	•
					•				•					•	•			
•	•	•	•	•		•	•	•	•		•	•	•	•	•		•	•
	•		•			•	•		•			•		•				•
	•	•	•			•	•	•			•		•	•				•
•	•	•	•	•		•	•	•	•		•	•	•	•	•		•	•
	•						•		•				•	•	•			
•	•	•	•	•		•	•	•	•		•	•	•	•	•		•	•
	•		•			•	•	•	•			•	•	•				
	•					•		•	•				•	•	•			
	•		•			•	•	•				•	•	•				
					•													
•	•	•	•	•		•	•	•			•	•	•	•	•			•
	•		•			•	•	•	•			•	•	•				
						•				•			•		•		•	
					•		•											
•	•	•	•	•		•	•				•	•	•	•				•
•	•	•			•	•	•				•	•	•	•				
	•					•	•		•	•			•	•	•			
	•					•	•		•				•	•	•			
•	•	•	•			•	•	•			•	•	•	•				•
						•		•					•	•	•			
	•					•	•		•			•	•	•				
	•					•	•					•	•	•				
•	•	•	•	•		•	•		•		•	•	•	•			•	•
•	•	•		•			•	•		•		•	•	•	•	•	•	•

	Vacancies	Partners	Total staff	Work placement	Corporate/ commercial	General commercial	Niche	General practice	High street/ legal aid
Harris & Harris Legal Services LLP	1(19)	7	50	✔				•	•
Harrison Clark Rickerbys Solicitors	Approx 10	70	460	✔	•	•			
Her Majesty's Courts & Tribunals Service	0		1200					•	
Hine Solicitors	10	8	180					•	•
Hooper & Wollen	0	11	84					•	•
Hotchkiss Warburton	0	2	6					•	•
Howard & Over	0	2	32					•	•
Hughes Paddison	2	11	60					•	
Humphreys & Co	1-2	4	30	✔	•	•	•	•	
Humphries Kirk LLP	1(19)	20	180	✔				•	
Irwin Mitchell	45	260	2500	✔	•	•		•	
Jacobs & Reeves	0	6	45		•	•		•	•
John Hodge Solicitors	0	4	65	✔				•	
Kennedys	20(20)	393	1900	✔	•	•			
Kiteleys	0	4	50	✔				•	
Kitsons LLP	Poss(19)	16	100		•	•		•	
Laceys Solicitors LLP	2	13	110					•	
Langley Wellington LLP Solicitors	0	8	70					•	•
Lester Aldridge LLP	8	46	324	✔	•	•	•	•	
Lyons Davidson	4-6	36	1200		•	•		•	
Makka Solicitors Ltd	1	3	8	✔				•	•
McMillan Williams Solicitors	Varies	60	400	✔	•	•	•	•	
Metcalfes Solicitors	0	6	55		•	•	•	•	
Michelmores LLP	9	66	440	✔	•	•		•	
Middleton & Upsall LLP t/a Middletons	0	4	30					•	
Murrell Associates Limited	0	3	16	✔	•				
Mustoe Shorter	0	7	50					•	•
Nash & Co Solicitors LLP	0	12	72	✔	•	•		•	•
Osborne Clarke LLP	20	258	1632	✔	•	•	•		
Over Taylor Biggs	1	5	20					•	
Pardoes Solicitors LLP	1(20)	7	76					•	•
Paris Smith LLP	5	37	200	✔	•	•		•	
Parker Bullen LLP	2(20)	7	60	✔	•	•		•	
Plexus Law	0	117	1800		•		•		
Porter Dodson	Poss	22	120		•	•		•	•
Rawlins Davy Plc	0	8	45		•	•		•	
Reynolds Colman Bradley LLP	2	4	26	✔			•		
RJR Solicitors	0	5	45						•
Royds Withy King	12	67	484	✔	•	•		•	•
RPC	12(20)	79	800	✔	•	•			
Samuels Solicitors LLP	0	3	16					•	

Banking	Comp/comm	Competition	Construction	Corporate tax	Crime	Dispute resolution	Employment	Environment	Family	Human rights	Insurance	IP	Personal injury	Private client	Property	Shipping	Sport	TMT
	•					•	•	•						•	•			
•	•	•	•	•	•	•	•	•	•	•	•	•	•	•	•	•	•	•
			•				•	•					•	•				
	•					•	•	•	•			•	•	•	•	•	•	
															•			
			•					•					•	•				
•	•	•				•	•	•			•	•	•	•	•		•	•
•	•	•	•	•	•	•	•	•	•	•	•	•	•	•	•			•
						•	•	•					•	•	•			
•						•	•	•				•	•		•			
						•	•	•					•	•				
•			•			•	•	•				•	•	•	•			•
•	•		•			•	•	•				•		•	•			
						•		•					•	•	•			
•	•	•	•	•	•	•	•	•	•		•	•	•	•	•	•		•
	•		•			•	•	•			•			•	•			
							•		•				•	•	•			
	•	•	•	•	•		•			•		•		•				
•	•		•	•		•	•	•				•	•	•	•			
•	•	•	•			•	•	•				•		•	•			•
						•	•						•	•	•			
	•							•				•	•	•	•	•		
					•		•	•					•	•				
•	•		•	•		•	•	•				•	•	•	•		•	•
•	•	•	•		•	•	•	•				•	•	•	•	•	•	•
			•			•	•				•		•	•				
	•		•			•	•	•				•	•	•	•			
	•					•	•					•		•	•			
			•			•					•							•
	•				•		•						•					
•	•	•	•	•		•	•					•	•	•	•		•	•
•	•	•	•	•		•	•				•		•	•	•		•	•
						•							•	•	•			

	Vacancies	Partners	Total staff	Work placement	Corporate/commercial	General commercial	Niche	General practice	High street/legal aid
Scott Rowe Solicitors	1[19]	3	26			•		•	
Sewell Mullings Logie LLP	1[20]	7	42				•	•	
Shoosmiths	22	190	1630	✔	•	•	•	•	
Simmons & Simmons LLP	25	280	1600	✔	•	•			
Steele Raymond LLP	2-3	14	80		•	•		•	
Stephens Scown	8	55	300	✔	•			•	
Stone King	4	42	200	✔	•	•	•	•	
Stowe Family Law LLP	Varies	30	100	✔			•		
Thompsons Solicitors	0	50	888				•		
Thorne Segar Ltd	1	2	27	✔				•	
Thrings	7[20]	58	224		•	•	•	•	
TLT LLP	Up to 15	110	1020	✔	•	•	•	•	
Tozers LLP	Poss	20	120	✔	•	•		•	•
Trethowans LLP	3-4	40	235		•	•		•	
Trowers & Hamlins LLP	23	157	894	✔		•			
VWV (Veale Wasbrough Vizards)	8-10	72	411	✔	•	•	•	•	
Waller & Hart Solicitors Limited	1	2	14			•	•	•	
Wansbroughs	2-3[19]	16	90					•	
Watkins Solicitors	0	3	32	✔				•	•
Willans LLP	0	14	70		•	•			
Wilsons Solicitors LLP	4	30	164	✔	•	•	•	•	
Womble Bond Dickinson	Up to 25	123	1200	✔	•	•			

Wales

	Vacancies	Partners	Total staff	Work placement	Corporate/commercial	General commercial	Niche	General practice	High street/legal aid
Accutrainee	Varies				•	•	•	•	
Acuity Legal Limited	2-3[19]	16	62	✔	•				
Allington Hughes Law	2[19]	14	82	✔				•	•
Anthony Jacobs & Co	2[19]	1	5	✔				•	
Bennetts Solicitors & Attorneys	0	4	15		•	•	•	•	
Blake Morgan LLP	18	114	800	✔	•	•	•	•	
Bridger & Co Solicitors	1	3	8	✔				•	
Cameron Jones Hussell & Howe	0	5	28					•	
Capital Law	4[20]	20	140	✔	•	•			
Carmarthenshire County Council	0	6	16		•				
City and County of Swansea	0		46						

Banking	Comp/comm	Competition	Construction	Corporate tax	Crime	Dispute resolution	Employment	Environment	Family	Human rights	Insurance	IP	Personal injury	Private client	Property	Shipping	Sport	TMT
	•					•	•		•				•	•	•			
	•					•	•		•					•	•			
•	•	•	•	•		•	•	•	•		•	•	•	•	•	•	•	•
•	•	•		•		•	•	•			•	•			•			•
•	•	•		•	•	•	•	•			•	•		•	•			•
	•		•	•		•	•	•	•		•	•		•	•			•
								•					•					
				•			•						•					
							•							•				
•	•	•	•	•		•	•	•	•		•	•	•	•	•	•	•	•
•	•	•	•	•		•	•	•	•			•		•	•	•		•
	•					•	•	•				•		•	•	•	•	
•	•					•	•		•			•	•	•	•			
•			•	•		•	•	•	•			•		•	•			
•	•	•	•	•		•	•	•	•			•	•	•	•			•
	•					•	•	•				•		•	•			
	•		•			•	•	•	•			•		•	•		•	
•	•	•	•			•	•		•			•		•	•			•
	•			•		•	•		•			•		•	•			
•	•	•	•	•		•	•		•		•	•		•	•			•

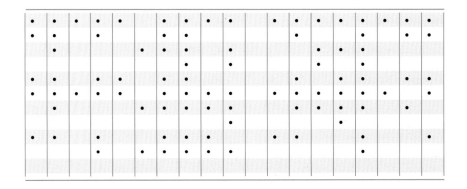

	Vacancies	Partners	Total staff	Work placement	Corporate/ commercial	General commercial	Niche	General practice	High street/ legal aid
Crown Prosecution Service	1(19)	2315	6051				•		
Cyril Jones & Co	0	5	20					•	•
DAC Beachcroft LLP	13(20)	240	2300	✔	•	•		•	
Darwin Gray LLP	0	7	22		•	•			
David & Snape	0	4	26			•		•	•
Dolmans Solicitors	0	9	39		•	•	•		
Douglas-Jones Mercer	1	6	50		•	•		•	
Eversheds Sutherland (International) LLP	50	395	3235	✔	•	•			
Fountain Solicitors Limited	1(19)	1	40	✔				•	•
Gabb & Co	0	6	36					•	
Gamlins Law	2(19)	11	70	✔	•	•		•	•
Geldards LLP	6(20)	57	352		•	•	•		
GHP Legal	0	10	87	✔				•	•
Gordon Dadds LLP	6	39	236		•	•		•	
Government Legal Profession	50		2000						
Hains & Lewis	0	4	30					•	•
Harding Evans LLP	1	10	120	✔				•	
Her Majesty's Courts & Tribunals Service	0		1200						
Hugh James	10	64	680	✔	•	•	•	•	
Huttons	0	3	25	✔				•	•
JNP Legal	1(19)	4	48					•	•
JW Hughes & Co	0	6	34					•	•
Kirwans	0	5	80			•		•	•
Lanyon Bowdler Solicitors LLP	3(20)	26	225		•			•	
Leo Abse & Cohen	0	13	140		•	•		•	•
Lewis Silkin	Up to 6	58	350	✔	•	•			
Lyons Davidson	4-6	36	1200		•	•		•	
Patchell Davies	0	2	7					•	
PJE Solicitors	0	2	10					•	
Quality Solicitors J A Hughes	1	6	30	✔				•	•
RadcliffesLeBrasseur	4	40	170		•	•	•	•	
Slater & Gordon (UK) LLP	53	86	3500			•		•	
Smith Llewelyn Partnership	1	4	40	✔				•	•
The Speakeasy	0		14					•	
Thompsons Solicitors	0	50	888					•	
Wendy Hopkins Family Law Practice	1	4	27					•	

Banking	Comp/comm	Competition	Construction	Corporate tax	Crime	Dispute resolution	Employment	Environment	Family	Human rights	Insurance	IP	Personal injury	Private client	Property	Shipping	Sport	TMT
					•													
•	•	•	•	•			•	•	•		•	•	•	•	•			•
	•						•	•				•		•	•		•	•
	•			•			•	•	•			•		•	•			
	•		•				•	•	•		•	•	•	•	•		•	•
•	•	•				•	•	•	•		•	•	•	•	•			•
•	•	•	•	•	•	•	•	•	•		•	•	•	•	•		•	•
							•		•	•			•					
	•						•							•	•			
	•				•	•	•	•	•		•	•		•	•		•	•
•	•		•	•			•	•				•	•	•	•	•		•
	•		•		•	•		•				•		•	•		•	•
•	•	•	•	•			•				•	•		•			•	•
•	•	•		•			•	•		•		•	•	•	•	•	•	•
	•				•		•	•					•	•			•	
•			•				•	•	•		•	•		•	•		•	•
	•					•	•	•			•			•	•			
•	•	•	•		•	•	•	•	•		•	•	•	•	•		•	•
	•				•	•	•	•				•		•	•			
					•	•	•	•				•		•	•			
					•	•	•	•				•		•	•			
	•		•			•	•	•	•			•		•	•			•
	•					•	•	•			•		•	•	•			
	•		•			•	•	•			•		•	•	•		•	•
	•					•	•	•			•			•	•			
•	•	•		•	•	•	•	•	•			•	•	•	•		•	•
			•			•	•	•			•		•	•	•		•	•
						•	•		•	•			•	•	•		•	
					•		•					•						
						•						•						

	Vacancies	Partners	Total staff	Work placement	Corporate/ commercial	General commercial	Niche	General practice	High street/ legal aid
Accutrainee	Varies				•	•	•	•	
Alsters Kelley	0	4	90			•		•	•
Anthony Collins Solicitors	8	29	298	✔	•	•	•	•	•
Atter Mackenzie & Co	2[19]	5	26			•	•	•	•
Bell Lax Solicitors	2	3	25					•	
Bevan Brittan LLP	10	60	435	✔	•	•			
BLM	23	196	1595	✔	•	•			
Browne Jacobson LLP	20	142	981	✔	•	•	•		
Caldicotts	0	4	19	✔					•
Capsticks Solicitors LLP	8[20]	51	403		•	•	•		
Cartwright King	0	24	211					•	•
CBTC Rawstorne	0	1	7		•			•	•
Clarke Willmott LLP	TBC	112	642		•	•		•	•
Cocks Lloyd	0	5	50		•			•	•
Cotterhill Hitchman LLP	0	3	15			•			
Coventry City Council	0		52						
Cowlishaw & Mountford	0	1	10					•	
Crown Prosecution Service	1[19]	2315	6051				•		
Cunningtons	Varies	9	60	✔				•	•
DAC Beachcroft LLP	13[20]	240	2300	✔	•	•			
David Phillips & Partners	0	15	75	✔			•	•	•
Davies and Partners	1[19]	12	170		•	•		•	
De Marco Solicitors	0	1	12	✔	•	•		•	
Df Legal LLP	2	3	24	✔				•	
DLA Piper UK LLP	Up to 70	1300	8500	✔	•				
DWF LLP	40	316	2800	✔	•	•			
Elliott Bridgman Limited	2	1	21	✔		•	•	•	•
Enoch Evans LLP	Poss[19]	13	75		•	•		•	•
Eversheds Sutherland (International) LLP	50	395	3235	✔	•	•			
FBC Manby Bowdler LLP	0	29	182					•	
Ferdinand Kelly	0	1	5			•	•		
Fieldfisher	18	223	986	✔	•	•			
Fountain Solicitors Limited	1[19]	1	40	✔				•	•
Freeths LLP	20	147	750		•	•		•	
Gateley Plc	16	143	883	✔	•	•			
George Green LLP	2	15	81		•	•			
GHP Legal	0	10	87	✔				•	•
Gough-Thomas & Scott	1	4	18					•	
Government Legal Profession	50		2000						
Gowling WLG (UK) LLP	25	593	3171	✔	•				
Harrison Clark Rickerbys Solicitors	Approx 10	70	460	✔	•	•		•	

Banking	Comp/comm	Competition	Construction	Corporate tax	Crime	Dispute resolution	Employment	Environment	Family	Human rights	Insurance	IP	Personal injury	Private client	Property	Shipping	Sport	TMT
•	•	•	•	•	•	•	•	•	•	•		•	•	•	•	•	•	•
	•				•	•	•	•		•			•	•	•			
		•		•		•	•		•		•		•	•	•			
				•			•		•	•	•		•	•				
•	•		•			•	•		•		•		•	•				
	•	•	•			•	•	•					•	•		•		•
		•		•		•	•	•	•		•		•	•		•		•
•	•	•	•	•	•	•	•	•			•		•	•		•	•	•
					•		•	•		•				•				
	•	•	•			•	•	•			•		•	•				
		•			•		•		•					•				
•		•		•	•	•	•		•		•		•	•			•	•
	•				•	•	•		•				•	•	•			
	•			•		•	•	•	•					•				
				•		•				•								
	•				•		•		•				•	•				•
•	•	•	•	•		•	•		•		•		•	•	•			•
	•			•		•		•			•		•	•				
	•		•			•		•				•	•	•				
	•					•	•		•			•	•	•				
•	•	•	•	•		•	•		•		•	•	•	•		•	•	•
•	•	•	•	•		•	•		•		•	•	•	•	•	•		•
							•		•				•					
•	•	•	•	•	•	•	•		•		•	•	•	•			•	•
•	•	•	•	•		•	•		•		•		•	•		•	•	•
	•					•	•	•	•			•	•	•	•			•
	•					•	•		•			•	•					
•	•	•	•	•		•	•		•		•		•	•		•	•	
•	•					•	•	•	•	•	•		•	•	•			•
•	•	•				•	•	•					•	•				•
•	•			•		•	•	•	•				•	•	•		•	
•	•						•	•	•				•	•				•
	•			•			•	•		•			•	•				
						•	•		•				•					
•	•	•		•		•	•	•		•			•	•	•		•	•
•	•	•	•	•		•	•	•	•		•	•	•	•	•	•		•

	Vacancies	Partners	Total staff	Work placement	Corporate/commercial	General commercial	Niche	General practice	High street/legal aid
Hatchers Solicitors	0	13	90		•	•	•	•	•
Her Majesty's Courts & Tribunals Service	0		1200					•	
Herefordshire District Council	0		31						
Hibberts LLP	1(19)	9	96	✔	•			•	•
Higgs & Sons	6	35	227	✔	•	•	•	•	
Hine Solicitors	10	8	180					•	•
Hogan Lovells	50	800	5000	✔	•				
Irwin Mitchell	45	260	2500	✔	•	•		•	
Kangs Solicitors	1-2(20)	1	10				•		
Kennedys	20(20)	393	1900	✔	•	•			
Kundert Solicitors LLP	0	4	30	✔				•	•
Lanyon Bowdler Solicitors LLP	3(20)	26	225		•			•	
Lodders Solicitors LLP	3	28	130	✔	•			•	
Lyons Davidson	4-6	36	1200		•	•		•	
Mander Hadley Solicitors	0	9	45		•	•		•	•
Martin-Kaye LLP	Poss	6	60		•	•	•	•	•
mfg Solicitors LLP	2-4(20)	30	140		•	•	•	•	•
Mian & Co	0	2	9						•
Mills & Reeve LLP	20	122	994	✔	•	•			
Newcastle under Lyme Borough Council	0		2						
Painters	0	9	50			•		•	•
Pickerings Solicitors	1	4	57		•	•	•	•	•
Pinsent Masons LLP	68	430	3000	✔	•	•			
Plexus Law	0	117	1800				•		
QualitySolicitors Davisons	0	7	150					•	
Rees Page	0	8	46					•	•
RN Williams & Co	1(19)	3	19					•	•
Scaiff LLP	0	3	21						
Shakespeare Martineau LLP	8	131	717		•				
Shoosmiths	22	190	1630	✔	•	•	•	•	
Slater & Gordon (UK) LLP	53	86	3500			•		•	
Squire Patton Boggs (UK) LLP	25	494	3000	✔	•	•			
Stone King	4	42	200	✔	•	•	•	•	
Stowe Family Law LLP	Varies	30	100	✔			•		
Terry Jones Solicitors	Poss	4	120					•	
Thaliwal & Co Solicitors	0	1	11	✔				•	
Thompsons Solicitors	0	50	888				•		
Tinsdills	TBC(19)	11	97					•	
Toussaints	0	1	1	✔				•	•
Trowers & Hamlins LLP	23	157	894	✔		•			
VWV (Veale Wasbrough Vizards)	8-10	72	411	✔	•	•	•	•	

Banking	Comp/comm	Competition	Construction	Corporate tax	Crime	Dispute resolution	Employment	Environment	Family	Human rights	Insurance	IP	Personal injury	Private client	Property	Shipping	Sport	TMT
	•		•		•	•	•	•	•			•	•	•	•			
	•	•					•	•	•		•			•				•
	•					•		•						•	•			
•	•	•	•	•	•		•	•	•			•		•	•			•
						•		•			•			•	•			
•	•	•	•	•		•	•	•	•			•		•	•	•	•	•
•	•	•	•	•			•	•	•	•	•	•	•	•	•			•
					•			•										
•	•		•			•		•	•			•		•	•	•	•	•
	•					•		•	•					•	•			
	•					•		•	•			•		•				•
	•				•			•						•	•			
	•					•		•	•		•			•	•			
	•					•		•	•					•	•			
	•			•		•	•		•			•		•	•			
					•													
•	•	•	•	•		•	•	•	•		•	•		•	•		•	•
	•					•	•		•					•	•			
	•					•		•	•			•		•	•		•	
•	•	•	•	•		•	•	•			•	•		•	•	•	•	•
			•			•		•			•		•					
						•	•		•			•	•	•	•			
	•					•		•	•			•	•	•	•			
					•		•		•			•	•	•				
	•					•		•	•			•		•	•			
•	•	•	•	•		•	•	•	•		•	•	•	•	•			•
•	•	•	•	•		•	•	•	•		•	•	•	•	•	•	•	•
			•		•	•		•				•	•	•	•			
•	•	•	•	•		•	•	•	•		•	•	•	•	•	•	•	•
	•		•	•		•	•		•			•		•	•			
						•	•		•					•	•			
	•					•	•	•	•					•	•			
					•								•					
			•			•		•						•	•			
					•				•									
•	•	•	•	•		•	•	•	•			•	•	•	•			
•	•	•	•	•		•	•	•	•				•	•	•			•

	Vacancies	Partners	Total staff	Work placement	Corporate/ commercial	General commercial	Niche	General practice	High street/ legal aid
Wall James Chappell	1	7	35					•	
Wallace Robinson & Morgan	0	6	41		•	•		•	
Walters & Plaskitt	Poss	4	60	✔				•	•
Watson Watson Solicitors	2	2	20	✔	•	•	•		
Weightmans LLP	Up to 18	188	1277	✔	•	•	•		
WH Law Ltd	0	3	10					•	
The Wilkes Partnership	4	21	160		•	•			
Wright Hassall LLP	4	35	280	✔	•	•	•	•	
Zyda Law	1	1	5	✔		•	•		

Yorkshire

	Vacancies	Partners	Total staff	Work placement	Corporate/ commercial	General commercial	Niche	General practice	High street/ legal aid
Abode Solicitors	1[20]	4	46	✔				•	
Addleshaw Goddard	46	239	1500	✔	•				
Addlestone Keane Solicitors	0	3	14		•	•	•		
Ashton Bell	0	1	6	✔	•	•	•	•	
Atherton Godfrey LLP	2[20]	8	120					•	
Austin Kemp Solicitors Limited	2[19]	1	10	✔			•		
Bassra Solicitors (incorporating John Kelly & Co)	0	2	8						
Blacks Solicitors LLP	3	16	170	✔	•	•			
Bridge McFarland	2[19]	25	176	✔	•	•		•	•
Bridge Sanderson Munro	0	4	20					•	
Bury & Walkers LLP	0	6	68		•	•		•	•
Capsticks Solicitors LLP	8[20]	51	403		•	•	•		
Cartwright King	0	24	211					•	•
Clarion Solicitors	6[20]	24	175	✔	•	•		•	
CMS	120	1000	7500	✔	•	•			
Conrad King & Solomon Solicitors	2	1	6	✔				•	
Corries Solicitors Ltd	0	2	47					•	
Crockett & Co	0	2	8				•		•
Crown Prosecution Service	1[19]	2315	6051				•		
DAC Beachcroft LLP	13[20]	240	2300	✔	•	•		•	
Devonshires Solicitors	6[20]	35	240		•		•		
DLA Piper UK LLP	Up to 70	1300	8500	✔	•				
Eaton Smith LLP	0	7	80		•	•		•	•

Banking	Comp/comm	Competition	Construction	Corporate tax	Crime	Dispute resolution	Employment	Environment	Family	Human rights	Insurance	IP	Personal injury	Private client	Property	Shipping	Sport	TMT
	•					•	•		•					•	•			
	•					•	•		•				•	•	•			
			•				•	•					•	•				
	•	•													•			
•	•		•	•	•	•	•	•	•		•	•	•	•	•	•	•	•
							•	•					•	•				
	•		•		•	•	•		•			•	•	•	•			
•	•	•	•	•		•	•	•	•		•	•	•	•	•		•	•
								•						•				

Banking	Comp/comm	Competition	Construction	Corporate tax	Crime	Dispute resolution	Employment	Environment	Family	Human rights	Insurance	IP	Personal injury	Private client	Property	Shipping	Sport	TMT
															•			
•	•	•	•	•		•	•	•			•	•		•	•		•	•
	•					•						•	•	•	•			•
	•					•	•		•	•		•	•	•				
								•										
•						•			•									
	•					•	•		•			•	•	•	•		•	
	•		•	•		•	•		•			•	•	•	•	•	•	
•			•	•	•	•	•	•	•	•		•	•	•	•		•	•
	•	•	•			•		•	•		•	•		•				
				•		•	•	•					•					
•	•	•	•			•	•	•			•	•		•			•	•
•	•	•	•	•		•	•	•			•	•		•			•	•
	•					•		•					•					
								•	•				•	•				
								•										
			•															
•	•	•	•	•		•	•	•			•	•	•		•			•
•	•		•			•	•					•	•	•	•			
•	•	•	•	•		•	•	•			•			•	•	•	•	•
	•		•	•		•	•		•			•	•	•	•		•	•

	Vacancies	Partners	Total staff	Work placement	Corporate/commercial	General commercial	Niche	General practice	High street/legal aid
Emsleys Solicitors Limited	1[20]	6	120					•	
Eversheds Sutherland (International) LLP	50	395	3235	✔	•	•			
Finn Gledhill	0	6	50					•	
Forbes Solicitors	4	44	320	✔	•	•	•	•	•
Freeths LLP	20	147	750		•	•		•	
Gateley Plc	16	143	883	✔	•	•			
Gordons LLP	4	26	200		•				
Gosschalks	3	28	124		•	•	•	•	
Government Legal Profession	50		2000						
Graham & Rosen	0	6	45					•	
Grays	0	5	26				•		
Harrowells	4	20	135					•	
Hawkswell Kilvington Ltd	1	3	15				•		
Hempsons	3	46	300				•		
Heptonstalls	1-2	6	100					•	•
Her Majesty's Courts & Tribunals Service	0		1200					•	
Hethertons LLP Solicitors	0	3	31					•	•
Hill Dickinson LLP	10	175	840	✔	•	•	•		
HSR Law	0	7	42		•	•		•	•
Irwin Mitchell	45	260	2500	✔	•	•		•	
Jacksons Law Firm	2	11	70		•	•		•	
The Johnson Partnership	1-2	13	110	✔					•
Jordans	1[20]	4	65					•	•
Keebles LLP	4	36	280	✔	•	•	•	•	
Kennedys	20[20]	393	1900	✔	•	•			
Kingsley Brookes	0	2	5				•		•
LA Steel	0		8	✔			•		
Langleys Solicitors LLP	5	34	335	✔	•	•		•	•
LCF Law	2[19]	21	134		•	•			
Lester Morrill	0	4	38				•		•
Lyons Davidson	4-6	36	1200		•	•		•	
Makin Dixon Solicitors	0	2	70						•
Malcolm C Foy & Co Ltd	1	8	57	✔				•	•
Millan Solicitors	0	1	2	✔				•	
Mills & Reeve LLP	20	122	994	✔	•	•			
Minster Law Solicitors	0		500	✔			•	•	
Morrish Solicitors LLP	0	15	90					•	•
Musa Patels	0	2	16					•	•
North Yorkshire County Council	0		43	✔					
Parker Rhodes Hickmotts	0	3	49					•	•
Pattersons Solicitors	0	1	7						•

Banking	Comp/comm	Competition	Construction	Corporate tax	Crime	Dispute resolution	Employment	Environment	Family	Human rights	Insurance	IP	Personal injury	Private client	Property	Shipping	Sport	TMT
									•				•	•	•			
•	•	•	•	•	•	•	•	•			•	•			•	•		•
	•				•	•	•	•	•				•	•	•			
	•	•	•	•	•	•	•	•	•	•	•	•	•		•		•	•
•	•	•	•	•		•	•	•	•		•		•	•	•	•	•	•
•	•	•	•	•		•	•	•				•	•	•	•	•	•	•
•	•	•		•		•	•		•			•	•	•	•			•
•	•		•			•	•	•		•		•	•	•	•	•	•	•
	•					•	•		•				•	•	•			
						•	•					•	•	•				
	•					•	•		•			•	•	•				
			•			•												
	•		•			•		•				•		•				
													•					
						•	•		•				•	•	•			
•	•	•	•	•	•	•	•	•	•			•	•	•	•	•	•	•
	•				•	•	•		•				•	•	•			
•	•	•		•		•	•	•	•	•		•	•	•	•			•
	•	•				•	•	•	•	•		•	•	•	•			•
					•													
•	•		•		•		•		•			•	•	•	•		•	•
•	•		•			•	•	•			•	•	•	•	•	•	•	
					•							•						
•	•		•	•		•	•		•		•	•		•	•			•
	•					•	•		•		•	•	•	•			•	•
						•				•		•	•	•	•			
	•							•				•						
						•			•			•	•	•	•			
								•				•						
•	•	•	•	•		•	•	•	•		•	•		•	•		•	•
						•						•	•	•				
					•	•		•					•	•	•			
			•												•			
	•	•					•	•	•		•				•			
	•						•		•					•	•	•		
					•													

	Vacancies	Partners	Total staff	Work placement	Corporate/commercial	General commercial	Niche	General practice	High street/legal aid
Pinsent Masons LLP	68	430	3000	✔	•	•			
Quality Solicitors John Barkers	Poss	2	6	✔	•	•	•	•	
QualitySolicitors Bradbury Roberts & Raby	1(19)	4	49					•	•
RadcliffesLeBrasseur	4	40	170		•	•	•	•	
Read Dunn Connell	0	4	23			•		•	
Riaz Solicitors	0			✔				•	•
Rollits	2-3	21	118	✔	•	•			
Schofield Sweeney LLP	3(20)	31	161	✔	•	•			
Sergeant & Collins	0	2	15					•	•
Shoosmiths	22	190	1630	✔	•	•	•	•	
Shulmans LLP	3	23	214		•				
SJP Law	2	5	50	✔	•	•			
Slater & Gordon (UK) LLP	53	86	3500		•		•		
Slater Gordon Solutions Legal Ltd	1	5	1150				•		
Squire Patton Boggs (UK) LLP	25	494	3000	✔	•	•			
Stone King	4	42	200	✔	•	•	•	•	
Stowe Family Law LLP	Varies	30	100	✔			•		
Switalskis Solicitors LLP	0	12	250		•				•
Systech Solicitors Limited	0		25				•		
Taylor & Emmet LLP	2	21	210	✔	•	•		•	•
Thompsons Solicitors	0	50	888				•		
Thorpe & Co	0	8	55					•	•
W Brook & Co	1(19)	2	20						•
Wake Smith Solicitors	1	19	98	✔	•	•		•	
Walker Morris LLP	15	46	450	✔	•	•			
Ward Hadaway	10-15	85	450	✔	•	•			
Watson Burton LLP	3(20)	14	110	✔	•				
Weightmans LLP	Up to 18	188	1277	✔	•	•	•		
Wilkin Chapman LLP	5(20)	45	378	✔	•	•		•	
Wilkinson Woodward Limited	1-2	8	92					•	•
Wrigley Claydon	1	5	26					•	•
Wrigleys Solicitors LLP	2	27	200				•		
Yorklaw Ltd t/as Burn & Company	0	5	20					•	

Banking	Comp/comm	Competition	Construction	Corporate tax	Crime	Dispute resolution	Employment	Environment	Family	Human rights	Insurance	IP	Personal injury	Private client	Property	Shipping	Sport	TMT
•	•	•	•	•		•	•	•			•	•		•	•	•	•	•
•	•	•				•	•		•			•	•	•	•			
	•					•	•		•			•		•	•			
•	•	•		•	•	•	•	•	•			•	•	•	•		•	•
	•					•		•	•			•						
				•									•					
•	•		•			•	•	•	•			•	•	•	•			•
•	•		•	•		•	•	•	•			•	•	•	•			•
							•		•			•		•	•			•
•	•	•	•	•		•	•	•	•		•	•	•	•	•	•	•	•
•			•	•		•	•	•	•		•	•	•	•	•	•	•	•
	•						•	•				•	•	•	•			•
							•						•					
												•						
•	•	•	•	•		•	•		•		•	•	•	•	•	•	•	•
	•		•	•		•	•		•		•		•	•				•
							•		•					•				
				•			•		•	•			•					
	•					•												
				•			•					•						
				•			•					•	•					
				•			•											
•		•	•				•		•		•	•	•	•				•
•	•	•	•	•		•	•	•	•		•	•	•	•			•	•
•	•	•	•			•	•	•	•		•	•	•	•			•	•
•	•		•	•		•	•	•	•		•	•	•	•				•
•	•	•	•	•	•	•	•	•	•		•	•	•	•			•	•
•	•	•	•			•	•	•	•		•	•	•	•	•		•	•
	•			•	•	•	•		•				•	•	•			
	•						•	•					•	•	•			•
	•							•				•		•	•			
	•						•							•	•			

Training contract directory

AARON AND PARTNERS
Grosvenor Court, Foregate Street, Chester CH1 1HG
Tel: 01244 405555
Email: careers@aaronandpartners.com
Apply to: Ms Catherine Hughes

Working principally for business clients providing general commercial services (property, litigation and company/commercial) plus specialist areas - planning, minerals, environmental, transport, construction and insolvency.

V	0
T	4
P	24
TS	124
WP	no

ABODE SOLICITORS
The Studio, Greengate, Harrogate HG3 1GY
Tel: 01423 535600
Email: info@actionconveyancing.co.uk
Apply to: Mr R Ali

Specialist property firm dealing with residential and commercial property. Welcomes applications from all graduates.

V	1[20]
T	1
P	4
TS	46
WP	yes

ABRAHAMS DRESDEN LLP
111 Charterhouse Street, London EC1M 6AW
Tel: 020 7251 3663
Email: careers@ad-solicitors.co.uk
Apply to: Miss Alexandra Protopapas

Small progressive commercial firm committed to providing a superior service and excellent client care.

V	2[19]
T	4
P	3
TS	29
WP	no

ACA LAW LTD
168-172 Kentish Town Road, London NW5 2AG
Tel: 020 7485 6677
Email: lawyers@acalaw.co.uk
Apply to: Ms Lisa Cutting

Young, expanding firm involved primarily in publicly funded work, committed to providing high quality advice and representation. The firm is a member of the specialist fraud panel.

V	Varies
T	6
P	1
TS	24
WP	yes

ACTONS
20 Regent Street, Nottingham NG1 5BQ
Tel: 0115 910 0200
Email: caroline.pearson@actons.co.uk
Apply to: Mrs Caroline Pearson

Full range of services to businesses and private clients. Particularly strong reputation in insolvency, personal injury, commercial and property work.

V	2
T	5
P	16
TS	70
WP	no

ACUITY LEGAL LIMITED
3 Assembly Square, Britannia Quay, Cardiff Bay, Cardiff CF10 4PL
Tel: 029 2048 2288
Email: rsellek@acuitylegal.co.uk
Apply to: Mrs Rachelle Sellek

Commercial firm specialising in corporate finance, commercial property, commercial advice, commercial litigation, construction, employment, commercial projects and public sector.

V	2-3[19]
T	4
P	16
TS	62
WP	yes

ADDLESTONE KEANE SOLICITORS
Regent House, 5 Queen Street, Leeds LS1 2TW
Tel: 0113 244 6700
Email: brianaddlestone@aklaw.co.uk
Apply to: Mr Brian Addlestone

Niche commercial practice advising PLCs, substantial private clients and companies across a broad range including litigation, employment, commercial property and debt recovery.

V	0
T	-
P	3
TS	14
WP	no

ADLAMS LLP
37b Market Square, St Neots, Cambridgeshire PE19 2AR
Tel: 01480 474061
Email: info@adlams.co.uk
Apply to: Ms Connie Johnstone

Long-established small high street practice specialising in conveyancing, family, probate and some commercial work. Good IT skills an advantage for candidates.

V	0
T	1
P	4
TS	23
WP	yes

V = Vacancies / **T** = Trainees / **P** = Partners / **TS** = Total Staff / **WP** = Work Placement

Accutrainee

200 Aldersgate Street, London EC1A 4HD
Tel: 020 7040 0973
Email: info@accutrainee.com
Web: www.accutrainee.com
f accutrainee **🐦** accutrainee

The firm Accutrainee was created to help graduates reach qualification. We recruit trainee solicitors and send them on secondments lasting between 6 to 24 months to a range of both private practice and in-house clients. Our clients include FTSE 100 organisations, global investment banks and both UK and international law firms ranging from large City firms to small niche practices. We offer a unique route to qualification as each training contract is designed around the trainee. You may be seconded to just one organisation for the duration of your training contract or you could gain experience within several businesses, enabling you to broaden your commercial understanding. Trainees are placed where there is a genuine business need, which means you will quickly become an integral part of the team, carrying out high-quality work.

Types of work Accutrainee training contracts offer high quality work at an impressive range of client organisations. The type of work you will be involved in will be dependent on the secondments you complete. The majority of secondments are within corporate and commercial practice areas although some of our most popular secondments are in media, trade finance, privacy, fraud, commercial litigation and financial services.

Who should apply Accutrainee is looking for candidates who can demonstrate a high standard of academic achievement at A level (or equivalent) and degree level. If you have a 2.2 degree or lower A level grades, we still welcome your application, but you must be able to demonstrate academic excellence. The qualities we look for include strong interpersonal skills, resilience, a drive to succeed, the ability to show initiative and a common sense approach to problems-solving. You will need to demonstrate excellent verbal and written communication skills, commercial awareness, organisational skills, an ability to manage responsibility and a strong desire to add value and make your mark. You will be given opportunities to demonstrate these qualities in your application and throughout our selection process.

Training programme As we were the first to pioneer this unique approach to training contracts, we are naturally passionate about what we do: attracting and developing talented individuals, offering outstanding secondments and supporting and enabling trainees to thrive, develop and reach qualification. We pride ourselves on our collaborative culture, which prioritises training and support and encourages networking. As an Accutrainee, you will receive considerable mentoring, supervision and guidance, which includes training sessions, workshops and meeting regularly with highly-experienced solicitors, with whom you can discuss your development, gain feedback and review your training preferences as you progress. We want you to fulfil your potential, which is why we expect nothing but your full commitment to each firm or in-house legal department you are seconded to. Secondments give you the opportunity to demonstrate your capabilities and work towards a newly qualified role at the end of your training. Many of our trainees have approached qualification with more than one offer of employment.

When and how to apply We welcome applications throughout the year. There are no deadlines as we are always looking to fill specific business needs for our clients. Candidates must complete an online application form on our website.

Work placements We do not have any vacation schemes or work placement programmes, but we do offer paralegal roles, please apply via our website for a paralegal position.

Vacancies	Varies
Trainees	Varies

Training contract deadline
See website for details

Apply
Online at
www.accutrainee.com

Minimum qualifications
All applications considered

Offices
London

Addleshaw Goddard

Milton Gate, 60 Chiswell St, London EC1Y 4AG
Tel: 020 7606 8855
Email: grad@addleshawgoddard.com
Web: graduates.addleshawgoddard.com
🐦 aggrads

The firm Addleshaw Goddard is a premium international law firm with an exceptional breadth of services. Our reputation for outstanding quality and service is built upon long term relationship investment and a deep understanding of client markets combined with high calibre expertise, straight talking advice and a collaborative team culture. By delivering what clients want wherever they need it, from high value strategic advice, to the everyday, we pride ourselves on a service which is high quality, focused, relevant and consistently excellent. The firm is an FT Innovative Lawyers Award winner and is pioneering new ways of delivering legal services, through its intelligent delivery approach, which brings added efficiencies and value for clients. As a firm, AG continues to look at the changes to the profession and what this means for the lawyers of tomorrow, developing innovation initiatives to training and development.

Types of work The firm's client portfolio is testament to its strength and range of expertise, and includes financial institutions, public sector bodies, successful businesses and private individuals. It is a leading advisor to FTSE 100 companies, and a market leader across its business divisions – corporate and commercial, finance and projects, litigation and real estate – as well as in specialist fields such as private capital, and across its chosen sectors: digital, energy and utilities, financial services, health, industrials, real estate, retail and consumer, transport.

Who should apply We are looking for candidates who can demonstrate commercial awareness, teamwork, motivation and drive. Applications from law and non-law graduates are welcomed, as are applications from those who may be considering a change of direction.

Training programme As a trainee, you'll work on everything from multi-million pound banking deals and cross-border mergers and acquisitions to the most high profile fraud cases, complex technology contracts, employment disputes and transformational construction assignments. During each six-month seat, there will be regular two-way performance reviews with the supervising partner or solicitor. Trainees may have the opportunity to spend a seat in one of the firm's other offices and there are a number of secondments to clients available. Seated with a qualified solicitor or partner and working as part of a team enables trainees to develop the professional skills necessary to deal with the demanding and challenging work the firm carries out for its clients. Practical training is complemented by high-quality training courses provided by both the in-house team and external training providers. A trainee buddy programme is in place with the trainee predecessor for the first seat.

When and how to apply Apply online at graduates.addleshawgoddard.com by 31 July 2019 to begin 2021.

Work placements We offer a week long Easter scheme in Edinburgh and London, and two-week summer schemes in Edinburgh/Glasgow, Leeds, London and Manchester. During the scheme you will experience life as a trainee at AG. Students are allocated a department to sit in and swap into a different department in the second week (if undertaking the summer scheme). During your time in the department you will be supervised by an experienced solicitor who will welcome you to the department and allocate you work. You will also be paired up with a trainee buddy throughout the duration of the scheme who will be on hand to help.

Vacancies	46
Trainees	99
Partners	239
Total staff	1,500+
Work placement	yes

Training contract deadline
31 July 2019

Apply
Online at graduates.
addleshawgoddard.com

Starting salary
London – £39,500
Leeds and
Manchester – £27,000
Scotland – £21,500

Minimum qualifications
2.1 degree and ABB at
A level

Sponsorship
GDL/LPC

Offices
Aberdeen, Edinburgh,
Glasgow, Leeds, London,
Manchester, Dubai,
Hong Kong, Muscat, Doha,
Singapore, Tokyo*
*Alliance office

ADDLESHAW GODDARD

Akin Gump Strauss Hauer & Feld

Eighth Floor, Ten Bishops Square, London E1 6EG
Tel: 020 7012 9600
Email: graduaterecruitment@akingump.com
Web: www.akingump.com/uk-students
🐦 akin_gump

The firm Akin Gump's London office is the main hub of the firm's international offices and its strategy is to grow practices that complement core strengths of the firm. It is an integrated office practising at the top of its markets. The firm has 20 offices worldwide and clients range from corporations and financial institutions to foreign governments and individuals.

Types of work Market leading practices including; financial restructuring, corporate transactions (including mergers and acquisitions, joint ventures and private equity), banking and finance, energy and project finance, debt and equity capital markets, securities, financial services regulatory, litigation and international arbitration, investment funds (hedge, private equity, real estate and infrastructure), international trade and EU competition and tax.

Who should apply We hire the best and brightest. We look for exceptional and consistent academic achievement combined with evidence of a driven outlook through extracurricular achievements.

To thrive in our fast-paced commercial environment our future trainees need to be on track for a 2.1 degree at minimum. You should demonstrate intellectual curiosity, be solution-driven and keen for early responsibility. Diverse professional and personal backgrounds broaden perspectives throughout the firm. Our complementary strengths make for a truly dynamic atmosphere.

Training programme Our London office is an exciting and inspiring environment to train as a lawyer as evidenced by the office winning 'Best Trainer – US Firm in the City' at the LawCareers.Net Training and Recruitment Awards in 2016 and 2018. We offer up to four trainee places per year. By focusing on a smaller intake we maintain flexibility and seek to grow through our junior lawyer retention. Trainees have the choice of sitting within the financial restructuring, corporate and M&A, energy, finance, financial regulatory, funds and investment management, litigation and arbitration, competition or tax practice areas. Seats can be tailored to three or six-month durations across the two-year training programme to provide a breadth of experience. Some of our trainees have enjoyed the experience of a seat in an international office.

When and how to apply Online application via the firm's website at www.akingump.com/en/careers/uk-students. The deadline for 2021 training contracts is 14 July 2019.

Work placements Our two-week summer vacation scheme is held in July each year. We introduce participants to our practices and support their exposure to the work the firm does through integration into two practices and tailored development sessions. The application deadline for our 2019 programme is 31 January 2019.

Sponsorship GDL and LPC course fees. Maintenance grants of £8,000 per academic year.

Vacancies	4
Trainees	9
Partners	40
Total staff	190
Work placement	yes

Training contract deadline
14 July 2019

Apply
Online

Sponsorship
GDL/LPC

Offices
Abu Dhabi, Beijing, Dallas, Dubai, Fort Worth, Frankfurt, Geneva, Hong Kong, Houston, Irvine, Longview, London, Los Angeles, Moscow, New York, Philadelphia, San Antonio, San Francisco, Singapore, Washington DC

Akin Gump
STRAUSS HAUER & FELD

AHMED & CO
67a Camden High Street, London NW1 7JL
Tel: 020 7383 2243
Email: mail@ahmedco.com
Apply to: Ms Nosheen Saleem

Specialist services provided in crime, housing, immigration/nationality and welfare benefits law for individuals who are disadvantaged in some way to enable them to seek justice.

V	0
T	4
P	2
TS	15
WP	no

AKIN PALMER LLP
3 Angel Gate, 326 City Road, London EC1V 2PT
Tel: 020 7833 8828
Email: law@akinpalmer.com
Apply to: Mr Dele Ogun

A full service four-partner commercial law firm established since 1997 with a fast-growing reputation.

V	0
T	1
P	4
TS	10
WP	no

ALAN SIMPSON & CO
Mill Court, 19 London Hill, Rayleigh SS6 7HW
Tel: 01268 745406
Email: ajs@alansimpson.com
Apply to: Mr AJ Simpson

General high street practice serving private and commercial clients.

V	0-1
T	1
P	1
TS	12
WP	no

ALFRED NEWTON SOLICITORS
49-51 Wellington Road South, Stockport, Cheshire SK1 3RX
Tel: 0161 480 6551
Email: mail@alfrednewton.com
Apply to: Mr A Penman

We have three offices based in Stockport providing a wide range of legal services including family, property, wills, probate, mental health, employment, PI and housing.

V	0
T	2
P	4
TS	25
WP	no

ALLAN JANES
21-23 Easton Street, High Wycombe HP11 1NT
Tel: 01494 521301
Email: enquiries@allanjanes.com
Apply to: Mr CJG Hitchen

Niche commercial practice focusing on the South Bucks geographical area with a private client department servicing high-net worth clients.

V	1
T	1
P	5
TS	20
WP	yes

ALLINGTON HUGHES LAW
10 Grosvenor Road, Wrexham LL11 1SD
Tel: 01978 291000
Email: trainingcontract@allingtonhughes.co.uk
Apply to: Mr Ian Barnes

V	2[19]
T	2
P	14
TS	82
WP	yes

ALP LAW LLP
Sherrington House, 66 Chorley Street, Bolton BL1 4AL
Tel: 01204 454333
Email: mail@alplaw.co.uk
Apply to: Mr TB Walters

A unique and leading firm specialising exclusively in accident cases on a nationwide basis, and dedicated to the pursuit of professionalism and results.

V	Poss
T	2
P	4
TS	90
WP	no

ALPHA LEXIS LAW FIRM
Boundary House, Barnet Lane, Hertfordshire WD6 3JP
Tel: 0845 194 7340
Email: info@alphalexislaw.co.uk
Apply to: Mr Mahesh Kakkar

We are a forward-thinking, efficient practice specialising in contentious and non-contentious company commercial law, property law and private client work.

V	0
T	0
P	2
TS	8
WP	no

V = Vacancies / **T** = Trainees / **P** = Partners / **TS** = Total Staff / **WP** = Work Placement

Allen & Overy LLP

One Bishops Square, London E1 6AD
Tel: 020 3088 3399
Email: graduate.recruitment@allenovery.com
Web: www.aograduate.com
f allenoverygrads 🐦 allenoverygrads

The firm Allen & Overy is an international legal practice with approximately 5,400 people in 44 major centres worldwide. Our client list includes many of the world's leading businesses, financial institutions and governments. Naturally, we are committed to providing the highest quality advice, which is driven by innovation. By developing tailored solutions to a wide range of business issues, our partners are recognised as leaders in their areas of expertise and we have earned an enviable reputation and outstanding success in high-profile deals.

Types of work We are renowned for the high quality of our banking, corporate and international capital markets advice, but also have major strengths in areas such as dispute resolution, employment and benefits, real estate and tax.

Who should apply We expect to see a strong, consistent academic performance with at least a 2.1 and 135 UCAS (AAB) (or equivalent) predicted or achieved. At Allen & Overy we are looking for driven, collaborative and creative individuals to become lawyers of the future. Here, you will be working in a team where you will manage your own time and workload, so we look for candidates who can act on initiative, build strong relationships and prioritise effectively.

Training programme The Allen & Overy training contract is characterised by flexibility and choice. The seat structure ensures that you get hands on learning by sitting with an experienced associate or partner each time, allowing you to see as many parts of the firm as possible. Given the strength of the firm's international finance practice, trainees are required to spend a minimum of 12 months in at least two of the three core departments of banking, corporate and international capital markets. The firm offers its trainees the option of completing a litigation course. This means that trainees do not need to spend time in the firm's litigation and dispute resolution department to gain their contentious experience if they are sure their interests lie elsewhere. There are also opportunities for trainees to undertake an international or client secondment during their final year of training.

Please follow us on facebook www.facebook.com/allenoverygrads and twitter www.twitter.com/allenoverygrads. Plus also add us on snapchat: allenoverygrads.

When and how to apply Both law and non-law students can apply from October 2018. Please visit our website for full details about closing dates.

Work placements We recruit around 50 vacation students across the year from all degree disciplines. We have opportunities for students in their penultimate year and onwards, including graduates, on our vacation schemes. We also offer A&O first as a work experience programme and support network designed exclusively for around 30 undergraduate first-year students in the UK, as well as for those in their second year of a four-year course. Full details about eligibility requirements and application deadlines are available on our website at aograduate.com.

Sponsorship We pay your GDL and LPC course fees and contribute to your maintenance costs. We pay a £10,000 maintenance grant for the Allen & Overy LPC (with LLM Qualification) and also a £9,000 maintenance grant for the GDL in London.

Partners	554*
Total staff	5,400*
	*denotes approximate worldwide figures

Work placement yes
(see Insider Report on p69)

Apply
Online at
www.aograduate.com

Starting salary
£45,000

Minimum qualifications
2.1 degree and 135 UCAS
(AAB) (or equivalent)

Sponsorship
GDL/LPC

Offices
Abu Dhabi, Amsterdam, Antwerp, Bangkok, Barcelona, Beijing, Belfast, Bratislava, Brussels, Bucharest (associated office), Casablanca, Doha, Dubai, Düsseldorf, Frankfurt, Hamburg, Hanoi, Ho Chi Minh City, Hong Kong, Istanbul, Jakarta (associated office), Johannesburg, London, Luxembourg, Madrid, Milan, Moscow, Munich, New York, Paris, Perth, Prague, Riyadh (cooperation office), Rome, São Paulo, Seoul, Shanghai, Singapore, Sydney, Tokyo, Warsaw, Washington DC, Yangon

ALLEN & OVERY

Proud diversity and inclusion partner of

2S aspiringsolicitors

ALSTERS KELLEY
Hamilton House, 20-22 Hamilton Terrace,
Leamington Spa CV32 4LY
Tel: 01926 356000
Email: alison.field@alsterskelley.com
Apply to: Mrs Julie Richardson

Four-partner, three-office practice in Coventry and Warwickshire undertaking private client and commercial work.

V	0
T	2
P	4
TS	90
WP	no

AMD SOLICITORS LIMITED
100 Henleaze Road, Henleaze, Bristol BS9 4JZ
Tel: 0117 962 1205
Email: admin@amdsolicitors.com
Apply to: Mrs MK Davies

High street firm undertaking residential conveyancing, commercial and company work, probate, trusts, family (both private and legal aid) and education.

V	1
T	0
P	2
TS	30
WP	no

AMICUS SOLICITORS LLP
761 Wilmslow Road, Didsbury, Manchester M20 6RN
Tel: 0161 434 4448
Email: enquiries@amicussolicitors.co.uk.
Apply to: Mr Aneil Naeem

We offer a wide range of services to both international and domestic clients. We have a wealth of experience in a wide range of disciplines.

V	1
T	2
P	2
TS	7
WP	yes

AMS SOLICITORS LIMITED
Wentworth, 1B Fairways Office Park, Preston PR2 9LF
Tel: 01772 653 333
Apply to: Mr A Suleman

We are an upcoming and rapidly expanding firm specialising in litigation, personal injury and commercial property.

V	2
T	1
P	2
TS	16
WP	yes

ANGLO-THAI LEGAL (ATL)
24 Houghton Street, Warrington WA2 7DD
Tel: 01925 414308
Email: john.lewis@anglothailegal.com
Apply to: Mr John Lewis

Anglo-Thai Legal (ATL) is an international law company regulated to provide legal services in England [SRA no. 559208] and Thailand [Thai Lawyers Council no. 7082/2552].

V	Varies
T	1
P	1
TS	5
WP	yes

ANTHONY COLLINS SOLICITORS
134 Edmund Street, Birmingham B3 2ES
Tel: 0121 200 3242
Email: trainingcontract@anthonycollins.com
Apply to: Online

Fast-growing niche commercial and private client practice with a national client base boasting the largest social housing, charities and community regeneration operations outside London.

V	8
T	9
P	29
TS	298
WP	yes

ANTHONY GOLD SOLICITORS
The Counting House, 53 Tooley Street, London Bridge SE1 2QN
Tel: 020 7940 4000
Email: clare.kelly@anthonygold.co.uk
Apply to: Ms Clare Kelly

General practice with excellent reputation for family work, plaintiff personal injury/medical negligence, CoP and housing. Offices in London Bridge, Streatham and Elephant & Castle.

V	4[19]
T	9
P	32
TS	160
WP	no

ANTHONY JACOBS & CO
91 Albany Road, Cardiff CF24 3LP
Tel: 029 2048 3509
Email: anthonyjacobs@btconnect.com
Apply to: Mr Anthony Jacobs

General practice with emphasis on property law and family law. No criminal law or legal aid.

V	2[19]
T	2
P	1
TS	5
WP	yes

V = Vacancies / T = Trainees / P = Partners / TS = Total Staff / WP = Work Placement

ANTHONY LOUCA SOLICITORS
24 Lisson Grove, Marylebone, London NW1 6TT
Apply to: Mr F Argyrou

Anthony Louca Solicitors is seeking a trainee solicitor with a good class degree for an early start. No transfers accepted.

V	1
T	0
P	3
TS	7
WP	no

ANTONY CLAPP SOLICITORS
Holly Bank Chambers, Oasts Business Village, Maidstone ME18 5NN
Tel: 01622 815 940
Email: antony.clapp@antonyclappsolicitors.co.uk
Apply to: Mr AEJ Clapp

We are a specialist firm dealing exclusively in family law. We have a distinguished reputation built up over many years.

V	0
T	1
P	2
TS	13
WP	no

ANTONY HODARI & CO
34 High Street, Manchester M4 1AH
Tel: 0161 832 4781
Email: careers@antonyhodari.co.uk
Apply to: Mr T Pope

Establsihed in 1984, specialists in RTA personal injury claims.

V	0
T	6
P	6
TS	110
WP	no

AP LAW SOLICITORS LTD
257 Balham High Road, London SW17 7BD
Tel: 020 8672 2488
Email: ap@aplaw.co.uk
Apply to: The Business Manager

High quality of work in specialist areas. Fast expanding, highly motivated young firm. Strong team spirit and excellent opportunities.

V	0
T	5
P	2
TS	50
WP	yes

AP SOLICITORS
Second Floor, 19 Gerrard Street, London W1D 6JG
Tel: 020 7287 7880
Email: info@apsolicitors.com
Apply to: Ms Vivienne Poon

A modern and expanding law firm practising in the heart of London.

V	2
T	-
P	2
TS	6
WP	no

ARBIS SUTHERLAND LLP
Marble Quay, St Katharine's Dock, London E1W 1UH
Tel: 020 7553 8000
Email: azm@arbis-sutherland.com
Apply to: Mr Andrew Murray

Leading shipping and commodity trading boutique with London and Geneva offices, in combination with major US firm Sutherland Asbill & Brennan since March 2014.

V	1-2
T	1
P	3
TS	18
WP	no

ARCHON SOLICITORS LIMITED
Martin House, 5 Martin Lane, London EC4R ODP
Tel: 020 7397 9650
Email: reception@archonsolicitors.com
Apply to: Ms Corinne Aldridge

Niche employment law practice offering advice in relation to all aspects of employment law to both employers and senior employees.

V	0
T	1
P	5
TS	19
WP	no

ARLINGTONS SHARMAS SOLICITORS
6 Arlington Street, St James's, London SW1A 1RE
Tel: 020 7299 8999
Email: law@arlingtons.co.uk
Apply to: Mrs Awal

A well-established firm with a strong client base covering commercial work, litigation, property (commercial and residential), employment, trusts, probate and private client work.

V	Poss
T	1
P	2
TS	14
WP	yes

V = Vacancies / **T** = Trainees / **P** = Partners / **TS** = Total Staff / **WP** = Work Placement

Arnold & Porter Kaye Scholer (UK) LLP

Tower 42, 25 Old Broad Street, London EC2N 1HQ
Tel: 020 7786 6100
Email: london.graduate.recruitment@arnoldporter.com
Web: www.arnoldporter.com

The firm Arnold & Porter is a US-headquartered firm with a deserved reputation for its quality of service and expertise in handling the most complex legal and business problems, which require innovative and practical solutions.

Types of work Our London lawyers advise on a full range of regulatory, transactional and litigation matters, with a particular focus on intellectual property transactions, pharmaceuticals and medical device regulation and litigation, telecommunications, media and technology, employment, competition and trade regulation, international arbitration, UK enforcement and dispute resolution, corporate and finance, product liability and commercial litigation. Providing our clients with an excellent service is our number one priority, and our lawyers need to be commercially minded, approachable and able to work with our clients as part of a team on complex and often high-profile legal issues.

Who should apply We are looking for talented law and non-law graduates from all backgrounds and cultures who share our commitment to excellence, and who want to be part of the continued growth of our London office and become our next generation of partners and lawyers. Candidates applying to Arnold & Porter need to demonstrate a consistently high academic background. We expect candidates to have at least a 2.1 degree, AAB at A level or equivalent, and look for well-rounded individuals who can demonstrate their participation in a range of extra-curricular activities and achievements.

Training programme Trainees will have the opportunity to spend six months working within four of our practice groups: life sciences and healthcare regulatory, intellectual property, corporate, competition, international arbitration and white collar crime. Arnold & Porter encourages individuals to work across specialisms, so trainees may find that while working in one practice group, they undertake work in a variety of different areas, and for a variety of partners and fee-earners throughout the firm. Trainees will be expected to work on several matters at once and to assume responsibility at an early stage. We emphasise teamwork and trainees will be exposed to working for a variety of partners and fee earners throughout the office and the firm. Trainees may have an opportunity to work in our Brussels office and, where the occasion permits, to work on projects in one of our US offices. There are also opportunities for client secondments. Trainees are invited to attend the annual new associates retreat in our Washington DC office. We also encourage trainees to take part in our pro bono programme and devote 15% of their time to it, reflecting the firm's strong commitment to pro bono, helping young lawyers to develop their client management skills from an early stage.

When and how to apply For our 2019 summer vacation scheme, by 3 March 2019. For training contracts commencing in September 2021, by 4 August 2019. Apply online at the London trainees page of our website.

Work placements We take around 10 summer vacation students each year. Students will spend two weeks working on a variety of projects and workshops with partners and associates throughout the London office. In addition to this, social events are organised for our summer vacation students to encourage them to meet the partners and associates in our London office.

Sponsorship Arnold & Porter will pay your fees for the LPC and GDL. In addition we will pay a maintenance grant for each course.

Vacancies	2
Trainees	4
Partners	23
Total staff	117

Work placement yes

Training contract deadline
4 August 2019

Apply to
Graduate Recruitment

Starting salary
£46,000

Minimum qualifications
2.1 degree

Sponsorship
GDL/LPC

Offices
London, Washington DC, Brussels, Chicago, Frankfurt, New York, Los Angeles, Denver, Houston, San Francisco, Shanghai, Silicon Valley, West Palm Beach

Arnold & Porter

Remember to cite *The LawCareers.Net Handbook* on your application form if you apply to this firm.

290   THE LAWCAREERS.NET HANDBOOK

ARNOLD GREENWOOD SOLICITORS LTD
Exchange Chambers, 8 & 10 Highgate, Kendal,
Cumbria LA9 4SX
Tel: 01539 720049
Email: brichardson@arnoldgreenwood.co.uk
Apply to: Miss B Richardson

V	0
T	1
P	4
TS	16
WP	no

ASB LAW LLP
Origin Two, 106 High Street, Crawley, West Sussex
RH10 1BF
Tel: 01293 603600
Email: hr.team@asb-law.com
Apply to: Ms Kelly-Anne Goodall

Award-winning practice servicing businesses, public sector bodies and private clients with recognised expertise in a number of sectors including aviation and travel.

V	2^{19}
T	4
P	17
TS	134
WP	yes

ASCHFORDS LAW
79 College Road, Harrow, Middlesex HA1 1BD
Tel: 020 3586 4050
Email: info@aschfordslaw.com
Apply to: Ms Shalini V Bhargava

Aschfords Law Solicitors is a UK based immigration specialist firm. We are authorised to train trainee solicitors. We also provide the opportunity to enthusiasts looking for work experience (unpaid) and paralegals.

V	1
T	1
P	3
TS	5
WP	yes

ASHFORDS
Ashford House, Grenadier Road, Exeter EX1 3LH
Tel: 01392 333 634
Email: traineerecruitment@ashfords.co.uk
Apply to: Ms Jordan Harris

Ashfords is a national provider of legal, professional and regulatory services to businesses and individuals throughout the UK and abroad.

V	9
T	20
P	74
TS	540
WP	yes

ASHTON BELL
19 Hanover Square, Leeds LS3 1AP
Tel: 0113 2438688
Apply to: Ms Maxine Brown

Predominantly private client practice. Most high street work undertaken except crime. Significant personal injury and divorce work.

V	0
T	0
P	1
TS	6
WP	yes

ASHTONS LEGAL
The Long Barn, Fornham Business Court, Fornham
St Martin, Bury St Edmunds, Suffolk IP31 1SL
Tel: 01284 732120
Email: graduaterecruitment@ashtonslegal.co.uk
Apply to: Miss Claire Hughes

A leading East Anglian medium-sized law firm. This award winning practice stands out through its reputation for excellence and its friendly, approachable ethos.

V	4^{20}
T	6
P	30
TS	300
WP	yes

ASTON BOND
135-137 High Street, Slough SL1 1DN
Tel: 01753 486 777
Email: info@astonbond.co.uk
Apply to: Mr Stephen Puri

We are a young energetic and entrepreneurial law firm specialising in general commercial and corporate matters involving property and have a strong reputation for excellence.

V	1
T	1
P	3
TS	20
WP	yes

ASTON CLARK SOLICITORS
225-227 High Street, Acton, London W3 9BY
Tel: 020 8752 1122
Email: solicitors@astonclark.co.uk
Apply to: Personnel Department

Busy high street practice offers a professional, efficient, friendly, cost-effective service from pleasant West London offices.

V	0
T	1
P	3
TS	12
WP	no

V = Vacancies / **T** = Trainees / **P** = Partners / **TS** = Total Staff / **WP** = Work Placement

Ashurst LLP

Broadwalk House, 5 Appold Street, London EC2A 2AG
Tel: 020 7638 1111
Email: gradrec@ashurst.com
Web: www.ashurst.com/en/careers
f ashursttrainees

The firm With 26 offices in 16 countries and a number of referral relationships we offer the reach and insight of a global network, combined with the knowledge and understanding of local markets. Our 395 partners and further 1,200 lawyers work across 10 different time zones, responding to our clients wherever and whenever they need us.

Types of work Ashurst advance; banking and finance; capital markets; competition and antitrust; corporate and M&A; digital economy; dispute resolution; employment; financial regulation; insurance and reinsurance; intellectual property; investigations; investment funds; projects; real estate; restructuring, insolvency and special situations; tax.

Who should apply We expect a lot of ourselves – and so, as you would expect, you will need to be comfortable with challenges and pressure. You should also be able to express yourself confidently on paper and out loud, whether that's among your team or in a client's boardroom.

You'll need to become a shrewd negotiator, have an ability to read both balance sheets and behaviours, and become a commercial strategist with a deep understanding of specific industries.

Training programme We will plan closely with you four seats of six months each, that will broaden your world view and hone your talents. At least one seat will be in a finance practice and another within a transactional department. You will also have the opportunity to apply for an overseas or client secondment.

When and how to apply Complete an online application form addressed to Nick Wong, early careers partner. We will be accepting training contract applications to start in September 2021/March 2022 from 1 September 2018 to 6 January 2019 and then again from 1 May 2019 to 31 July 2019.

Work placements We run a one-week winter vacation scheme and one three-week vacation scheme during the summer.

Our winter scheme is designed for final-year students or graduates from any degree discipline. Applications open on 1 September 2018 and close on 4 November 2018.

Our summer vacation scheme has been designed for penultimate-year law students. Applications open on 1 September 2018 and close on 6 January 2019.

We also host a first-year programme in the spring for law students. Apply online between 1 September 2018 and 6 January 2019.

Sponsorship For the Graduate Diploma in Law (GDL) and Legal Practice Course (LPC), we offer scholarships that cover your course fees and provide £8,000 per year towards the cost of maintenance (£7,000 if you choose to study the GDL outside of London).

Vacancies	40-45
Trainees	90
Partners	395
Total staff	1,978

Work placement yes
(see Insider Report on p71)

Training contract deadline
6 January 2019

Apply
Online

Starting salary
£44,000

Minimum qualifications
2.1 degree

Sponsorship
GDL/LPC

Offices
Abu Dhabi, Beijing, Brisbane, Brussels, Luxembourg, Canberra, Dubai, Frankfurt, Glasgow (support office), Hong Kong, Jakarta (associated office), Jeddah (associated office), London, Madrid, Melbourne, Milan, Munich, New York, Paris, Perth, Port Moresby, Shanghai, Singapore, Sydney, Tokyo, Washington DC.

ATHERTON GODFREY LLP

8 Hall Gate, Doncaster, South Yorkshire DN1 3LU
Tel: 01302 320 621
Email: d.parker@athertongodfrey.co.uk
Apply to: Ms Diane Parker

A high street firm doing claimant personal injury work, clinical negligence, family, company and commercial, domestic conveyancing, wills and probate and general litigation.

V	2[20]
T	2
P	8
TS	120
WP	no

ATKINS HOPE

74-78 North End, Croydon, Surrey CR9 1SD
Tel: 020 8680 5018
Email: cc@atkinshope.co.uk
Apply to: Ms Greta Carpenter

Chambers listed and Jordans Awards shortlisted firm with four partners and three offices, undertaking all aspects of family law, mediation, PI and non-contentious work.

V	0
T	1
P	4
TS	35
WP	yes

ATTER MACKENZIE & CO

Bridge Court, 64 Bridge Street, Evesham WR11 4RY
Tel: 01386 425300
Email: ah@attermackenzie.co.uk
Apply to: Mr Amer Hussain

Legal aid franchised high street general practice. Litigation orientated.

V	2[19]
T	3
P	5
TS	26
WP	no

AUSTIN KEMP SOLICITORS LIMITED

7 Northumberland Street, Huddersfield HD1 1RL
Tel: 0845 862 5001
Email: mail@austinkemp.co.uk
Apply to: Vivienne Rudd

Niche firm of specialist divorce lawyers with a particular focus on high-net worth complex finance divorce cases.

V	2[19]
T	1
P	1
TS	10
WP	yes

AVADIS & CO SOLICITORS

7 - 9 Ferdinand Street, London NW1 8ES
Tel: 020 7267 8864
Email: lavadis@aol.com
Apply to: Mr L Avadis

We are offering an opportunity for some hands-on unpaid work experience for law students.

V	1
T	-
P	1
TS	5
WP	yes

AVERY EMERSON

Gloucester House, 335 Green lane, Ilford, Essex IG3 9TH
Tel: 020 8215 0884
Email: reception@ae-law.co.uk
Apply to: The Recruitment Officer

Proactive and innovative law firm which undertakes a wide variety of work: employment; immigration; conveyancing; family; wills and probate; landlord and tenant; litigation; and business.

V	2
T	1
P	1
TS	6
WP	yes

AWDRY BAILEY & DOUGLAS

33 St Johns Street, Devizes SN10 1BW
Tel: 01380 722311
Email: david.turley@awdrys.co.uk
Apply to: Mr Andrew Douglas

General high street practice.

V	0
T	5
P	7
TS	95
WP	no

BAINES WILSON LLP

2 Merchants Drive, Carlisle CA3 0JW
Tel: 01228 552600
Email: j.holborn@baineswilson.co.uk
Apply to: Joanne Holborn

We are one of the North of England's leading specialist commercial law firms. Our lawyers work from Carlisle and Lancaster, serving clients throughout the UK.

V	2[19]
T	2
P	9
TS	30
WP	yes

V = Vacancies / **T** = Trainees / **P** = Partners / **TS** = Total Staff / **WP** = Work Placement

Baker McKenzie LLP

100 New Bridge Street, London EC4V 6JA
Tel: 020 7919 1000
Email: londongraduates@bakermckenzie.com
Web: www.bakermckenzie.com/londongraduates
f bakermckenziegraduates ✖ bakermckenzie

The firm Baker McKenzie is a leading global law firm based in over 75 locations in nearly 50 countries. With a presence in nearly all of the world's leading financial and commercial centres, our strategy is to provide the best combination of local legal and commercial knowledge, international expertise and resources. Our trainee solicitors are a vital part of that strategy, exposed to the international scope of the firm from the moment they start. There is also the possibility of an overseas secondment, with recent secondees spending time in San Francisco, Singapore, Washington DC and Hong Kong.

Types of work London is home to the firm's largest office where Baker McKenzie has been well established since its opening in 1961. With more than 400 legal professionals, we have a substantial presence in the legal and business community.

We deliver high-quality local solutions across a broad range of practices and offer global advice in conjunction with our international offices. Our client base consists primarily of venture capital funds, investment banks, technology powerhouses and household name brands. And as a firm with a very strong international client base, we have considerable expertise in acting on, and coordinating, complex cross-border transactions and disputes.

Who should apply The firm strives to enable trainee solicitors to be the best they can be. We are looking for trainees who are stimulated by intellectual challenge, and respect and enjoy the diversity of cultural, social and academic backgrounds found in the firm. Effective communication skills, together with the ability to be creative and practical problem solvers, and a team player are qualities which will help applicants stand out from the crowd.

Training programme The two-year training contract comprises four six-month seats which include a corporate and/or banking seat and a contentious seat, usually within our highly regarded dispute resolution department, together with the possibility of a secondment abroad or with a client. During each seat you will have formal and informal reviews to discuss your progress and regular meetings to explore subsequent seat preferences. Your training contract commences with a highly interactive and practical induction programme which focuses on key skills including practical problem solving, presenting and the application of information technology. The firm's training programmes include important components on management and other business skills, as well as seminars and workshops on key legal topics for each practice area. There is a trainee solicitor liaison committee which acts as a forum for any new ideas which may occur during the training contract.

When and how to apply The firm is aiming to recruit 30 individuals looking to commence their training contracts in either March 2021 or September 2021. Applicants can apply through our online application form, which can be found on our website along with our deadlines.

Work placements The firm offers a two-week spring vacation scheme, two three-week summer vacation schemes and a first-year insight scheme. During the schemes you will gain experience within one or more of our practice areas, network with partners, trainees and associates and gain exposure to live projects and transactions.

Sponsorship The firm will cover the payment of the GDL and LPC and a maintenance grant of £8,000 for the LPC and £6,000 for the CPE/GDL.

Vacancies	30
Trainees	65
Partners	90
Total staff	900
Work placement	yes

Apply to
Graduate Recruitment Team

Starting salary
£45,000

Minimum qualifications
340 UCAS points,
2.1 degree or equivilent

Sponsorship
GDL/LPC

Offices
Over 75 offices in nearly 50 countries

Baker McKenzie.

Proud diversity and inclusion partner of

 aspiringsolicitors

BANNER JONES 24 Glumangate, Chesterfield S40 1UA **Tel:** 01246 560 560 **Email:** info@bannerjones.co.uk **Apply to:** Mr Robert Banner	General firm with six offices throughout North Derbyshire and Sheffield. The firm incorporated in 2008 and has 10 directors and a staff of approaching 90.	V T P TS WP	0 0 10 90 no
BARCAN+KIRBY 111/117 Regent Street, Kingswood, Bristol BS15 8LJ **Tel:** 0117 3252929 **Email:** b.humanresources@barcankirby.co.uk **Apply to:** Mrs Claire Pennell	Six office Bristol based practice.	V T P TS WP	0 4 17 170 no
BARGATE MURRAY 44 Worship Street, London EC2A 2EA **Tel:** 020 7375 1393 **Email:** info@bargatemurray.com **Apply to:** Mr Quentin Bargate	We are an expanding City of London law firm with niche expertise in superyachts, shipping, litigation, ADR, commercial and corporate.	V T P TS WP	0 0 3 11 no
BARKER GOTELEE 41 Barrack Square, Martlesham Heath, Ipswich IP5 7RF **Tel:** 01473 611211 **Email:** bg@barkergotelee.co.uk **Apply to:** Mr Toby Pound	A regional commercial and private client firm with a national reputation in agricultural, property and private client work. We offer broad and practical training.	V T P TS WP	0 2 8 54 no
BARLOW ROBBINS LLP The Oriel, Sydenham Road, Guildford, Surrey GU1 3SR **Tel:** 01483 562 901 **Email:** trainees@barlowrobbins.com **Apply to:** Mrs Jo Vernon	Established Surrey based law firm servicing individuals, families, businesses, schools and charities with offices in Guildford and Woking. A member of Law South.	V T P TS WP	4 8 18 178 yes
BARNETTS Southport Buiness Park, Wight Moss Way, Kew, Southport PR8 4HQ **Tel:** 0844 800 5600 **Email:** andrea.parry@barnetts.co.uk **Apply to:** Mrs Andrea Parry	Niche property and personal injury practice. Applicants must have completed both LLB (or equivalent) and LPC and work as an assistant for 12 months.	V T P TS WP	0 12 6 135 no
BARON GREY Langtry House, 441 Richmond Road, Middlesex TW1 2EF **Tel:** 020 8891 4311 **Email:** info@barongrey.co.uk **Apply to:** Mr Vincent Hambleton-Grey	Multi-discipline practice with general commercial and family clientele, specialising in litigation, conveyancing and probate.	V T P TS WP	0 1 1 9 yes
BASINGSTOKE & DEANE BOROUGH COUNCIL Civic Offices, London Road, Basingstoke, Hampshire RG21 4AH **Tel:** 01256 845402 **Email:** chris.guy@basingstoke.gov.uk **Apply to:** Mrs Nicki Beck	Leading e-enabled local government practice. High-value development, regeneration and commercial property projects. Trainees have own caseloads with opportunities for advocacy. Applications continually sought.	V T P TS WP	1-2 4 1 20 no

V = Vacancies / **T** = Trainees / **P** = Partners / **TS** = Total Staff / **WP** = Work Placement

Bates Wells Braithwaite

10 Queen Street Place, London EC4R 1BE
Tel: 020 7551 7777
Email: training@bwbllp.com
Web: www.bwbllp.com/training-contracts
f bateswellsbraithwaite ⅶ bwbllp

The firm Bates Wells Braithwaite is a professional services firm, combining a UK 100 legal practice with consultancy services in impact measurement, outcomes-based planning and strategy, and financial services regulatory compliance. The firm works with a wide range of clients, large and small, across a variety of sectors – from established businesses, charities and social enterprises and public bodies to innovative start-ups and high-profile individuals. We stand out as a law firm – combining practical, commercial legal expertise with the deep understanding of the third sector that comes from working with more charities and social enterprises than any other UK firm. We are not only recognised as the leading charity law firm in the UK; we are also ranked in the major UK legal directories for our excellence across many of our specialist practice areas. We are proud to be the first UK law firm to achieve B corporation certification.

Types of work Advertising and marketing, brand and reputation management, charity, competition law, compliance, corporate and commercial, dispute resolution and litigation, electoral and political activities, employment, fraud prevention and cure, IT and outsourcing, immigration, insolvency, intellectual property and Information law, legacies, trusts and probate, disputes, media disputes, patents, public and regulatory law, real estate, real estate disputes, safeguarding, trademarks, consultancies, advisory and impact.

Who should apply BWB has a unique profile. We want to attract the best possible potential commercial lawyers who understand the work we undertake, the clients we work for and who are committed to our principles. We are not looking for the person who for whatever reason has failed to get the big-firm training contract they really want. We expect an applicant to have a sound academic background plus an ability to communicate clearly and effectively. Most importantly we want an applicant who is positively looking to join a firm with our work mix and approach. We are also looking for candidates with interests outside work which we would expect to be maintained if not developed.

Training programme During the two years of the training contract our trainees undertake two six-month seats in the first year and three four-month seats in the second year. All trainees do seats in charity and social enterprise and dispute resolution or public and regulatory. Other seats available are immigration, corporate and commercial, employment and real estate. Our flightpaths are allocated following consultation to ensure that consideration is given to their preferred career path as well as to our needs, but we aim to give each trainee a balanced experience in several areas of practice.

When and how to apply Apply online via our website.

Work placements We will be offering 12 two-week placements during Easter and Summer 2019 as part of our recruitment process for training contracts commencing in August 2021.

Sponsorship We will provide full financial support for both the LPC and GDL course. Fees will only be paid for courses that commence after the offer of a training contract has been made. We also pay interest on loans taken out during either or both of these courses from the signing of the training contract to the contract end date.

Vacancies	6
Trainees	12
Partners	38
Total staff	270

Training contract deadline
1 June 2019

Apply
Online

Minimum qualifications
2.1 degree

Sponsorship
GDL/LPC

Offices
London

Firm	Description	V	T	P	TS	WP
BASSRA SOLICITORS (INCORPORATING JOHN KELLY & CO) 89/93 Manningham Lane, Bradford, West Yorkshire BD1 3DN **Tel:** 01274 307060 **Apply to:** Mr John Kelly	Small North West Yorkshire firm specialising in crime. Legal aid franchise.	0	2	2	8	no
BASTIAN LLOYD MORRIS LLP Sovereign Court, Witan Gate East, Milton Keynes MK9 2HP **Tel:** 01908 546 580 **Email:** jab@blmsolicitors.co.uk **Apply to:** Mr Syvil Lloyd Morris	Bastian Lloyd Morris Solicitor Advocates specialise in all aspects of criminal law, including police stations, family law, including care proceeding and injunctive relief.	0	1	3	14	yes
BATCHELORS Charles House, 35 Widmore Road, Bromley, Kent BR1 1RW **Tel:** 020 8768 7000 **Email:** batchelors@batchelors.co.uk **Apply to:** Ms Sarah Brannigan	Medium-sized practice providing services for commercial and private clients including housing management, real estate, wills, trust and probate. No vacancies at present.	0	0	14	55	no
BATTENS SOLICITORS LIMITED Mansion House, Princes Street, Yeovil BA20 1EP **Tel:** 01935846043 **Email:** cath.knapman@battens.co.uk **Apply to:** Mrs Cath Knapman	Battens is a progressive firm with offices in Somerset, Dorset and Bath. Long established it has strong presence in most practice areas except criminal.	0	3	6	170	no
BEALE & COMPANY SOLICITORS LLP Capital House, 85 King William Street, London EC4N 7BL **Tel:** 020 7469 0400 **Email:** traineeapplications@beale-law.com **Apply to:** Mrs Donna Clarke	A commercial law firm with specialist experience in construction, engineering and infrastructure, insurance, and technology sectors.	5-6[20]	10	23	130	no
BEETENSON & GIBBON SOLICITORS 12-18 Frances Street, Scunthorpe, North Lincolnshire DN15 6NS **Tel:** 01724 847888 **Email:** ruth.gilliatt@bgsolicitors.com **Apply to:** Miss J Moorhouse	Friendly high street practice specialising in personal injury, family and property.	0	1	5	30	no
BELL LAX SOLICITORS New Bank House, 21 Maney Corner, Sutton Coldfield B72 1QL **Tel:** 0121 355 0011 **Email:** liam.owen@belllax.com **Apply to:** Mr Liam Owen	Specialist litigation practice - 65% commercial litigation, 35% personal injury and relationship disputes. Trainees given considerable responsibility, but benefit from close supervision on all matters.	2	2	3	25	no
BEN HOARE BELL LLP 19 John Street, Sunderland SR1 1JQ **Tel:** 0191 565 3112 **Email:** rachelfloyd@benhoarebell.co.uk **Apply to:** Miss Rachel Floyd	Clinical negligence, crime, housing, family, mental health, personal injury. Strong links to universities and other key agencies.	3	6	9	75	no

V = Vacancies / **T** = Trainees / **P** = Partners / **TS** = Total Staff / **WP** = Work Placement

BENNETTS SOLICITORS & ATTORNEYS Barley Wood Stables, Long Lane, Wrington, Bristol BS40 5QB **Tel:** 01934 862786 **Email:** info@bennettlaw.co.uk **Apply to:** Mr Craig Smith	Training at Bennetts is practical, gives broad but specialist commercial and private client experience, develops problem solving, client care and high professional standards.

V	0
T	1
P	4
TS	15
WP	no

BERMANS Exchange Station, Tithebarn Street, Liverpool L2 2QP **Tel:** 0151 224 0500 **Email:** alex.chapman@bermans.co.uk **Apply to:** Mr Alex Chapman	No nonsense business lawyers. Niches in asset based lending, invoice finance and asset finance/leasing.

V	2[19]
T	4
P	12
TS	70
WP	no

BERRY & LAMBERTS SOLICITORS 11 Church Road, Tunbridge Wells TN1 1JA **Tel:** 01892 526344 **Email:** schapman@the-solicitors.co.uk **Apply to:** Miss Sue Chapman	A general practice carrying out contentious and non-contentious work for individuals and businesses. A member of LawNet. Applications only accepted in January and February.

V	1[19]
T	3
P	12
TS	80
WP	no

BEVAN BRITTAN LLP Kings Orchard, 1 Queen Street, Bristol BS2 0HQ **Tel:** 0370 194 3050 **Email:** hr.training@bevanbrittan.com **Apply to:** HR Department	Bevan Brittan provides legal and advisory services to 300 businesses and is a market-leader advising health and social care, housing and local and central government.

V	10
T	18
P	60
TS	435
WP	yes

BEVISS & BECKINGSALE Law Chambers, Silver Street, Axminster, Devon EX13 5AH **Tel:** 01297 630700 **Email:** enquiries@bevissandbeckingsale.co.uk **Apply to:** Ms Anna Leavy	Award-winning law firm across East Devon and Somerset specialising in private client, agricultural matters, residential and commercial property work, litigation and family law.

V	1[19]
T	1
P	7
TS	50
WP	yes

BG GROUP PLC 100 Thames Valley Park Drive, Reading RG6 1PT **Tel:** 0118 935 3222 **Email:** info@bg-group.com **Apply to:** Mr Howard Landes	BG is a global business and a leader in exploration, production and delivery of natural gas. Our lawyers are integral to our success.

V	1
T	2
P	-
TS	100
WP	no

BHATIA BEST 12 Carrington Street, Nottingham NG1 7FF **Tel:** 0115 950 3231 **Email:** info@bhatiabest.co.uk **Apply to:** Ms Jayne Sheehan	A city centre legal aid franchise practice with a dynamic, progressive approach. Specialising in crime, matrimonial, public law, community care, civil litigation, PI, commercial debt.

V	0
T	4
P	11
TS	128
WP	no

BHATT MURPHY 10 Tyssen Street, London E8 2FE **Tel:** 020 7729 1115 **Email:** mail@bhattmurphy.co.uk **Apply to:** Ms Diane Fisher	Bhatt Murphy is a human rights practice specialising in the protection of civil liberties, dealing particularly with actions against the police, public and prison law.

V	0
T	5
P	2
TS	33
WP	yes

V = Vacancies / **T** = Trainees / **P** = Partners / **TS** = Total Staff / **WP** = Work Placement

BHOGAL PARTNERS SOLICITORS
33 Bath Road, Hounslow, London TW3 3BW
Tel: 020 8572 9867
Email: info@bhogalpartners.co.uk
Apply to: Mr Kritpal Bhogal

Established for over 20 years, we are a dynamic and forward-thinking legal firm providing services in various areas of law and notarial services.

V	1
T	3
P	3
TS	19
WP	yes

BHP LAW
Westgate House, Faverdale, Darlington DL3 0PZ
Tel: 01325 466 794
Email: lisac@bhplaw.co.uk
Apply to: Mrs Lisa Cairns

V	0
T	4
P	10
TS	125
WP	no

BHW SOLICITORS
1 Smith Way, Grove Park, Enderby, Leicester LE19 1SX
Tel: 0116 289 7000
Email: nick.bridle@bhwsolicitors.com
Apply to: Nick Bridle

A progressive eight-partner firm providing a high quality legal service to business clients ranging from national PLCs to local entrepreneurs.

V	2-4^{20}
T	4
P	9
TS	62
WP	yes

BILTON HAMMOND
The Corner House, Union Street, Mansfield, Nottinghamshire NG18 1RP
Tel: 01623 675 800
Email: markbilton@biltonhammond.co.uk
Apply to: Mr Mark Bilton

Progressive firm specialising in family, crime and property. Only applicants living within 10 miles of Chesterfield or Mansfield will be considered for the vacation scheme.

V	0
T	2
P	6
TS	35
WP	yes

BINDMANS LLP
275 Gray's Inn Road, London WC1X 8QB
Tel: 020 7833 4433
Email: info@bindmans.com
Apply to: Ms Lynn Knowles

A highly successful law firm offering a wide range of services with a reputation for excellence, we are often at the cutting edge of legal developments.

V	0
T	9
P	14
TS	114
WP	no

BIRCHALL BLACKBURN LAW
36-48 Avenham Street, Preston PR1 3BN
Tel: 01772 561663
Email: cjharris@birchallblackburn.co.uk
Apply to: Mrs Christine Harris

Well-established and progressive firm with seven offices, offering services to business and private clients. Also cover insolvency and are specialists in family law, particularly childcare.

V	0
T	2
P	21
TS	240
WP	no

BIRCHAM DYSON BELL LLP
50 Broadway, London SW1H 0BL
Tel: 020 7227 7000
Email: graduate@bdb-law.co.uk
Apply to: Graduate Recruitment Team

Broad based, friendly firm with strong private client, charities and parliamentary public law and planning practices. Trainees given good training with responsibility under supervision of partners.

V	5
T	10
P	49
TS	280
WP	yes

BIRD & BIRD
12 New Fetter Lane, London EC4A 1JP
Tel: 020 7415 6000
Email: london.graduates@twobirds.com
Apply to: Graduate Recruitment & Trainee Development Team

Bird & Bird is an international law firm serving clients in 118 countries from 28 offices across Europe, the Middle East and the Asia-Pacific region.

V	18
T	36
P	298
TS	3000
WP	yes

V = Vacancies / **T** = Trainees / **P** = Partners / **TS** = Total Staff / **WP** = Work Placement

Blake Morgan LLP

New Kings Court, Tollgate Chandler's Ford, Eastleigh Hampshire SO53 3LG
Tel: 0238 090 8090
Email: graduateinfo@blakemorgan.co.uk
Web: www.blakemorgan.co.uk
f blakemorganllp 𝕏 bm_careers

The firm At Blake Morgan we have always excelled in finding the best possible solutions for our clients. With exceptional talent and leading lawyers working across southern England and Wales, Blake Morgan has a highly skilled workforce, giving our clients access to a wide range and depth of skills and experience. We act for large corporates, entrepreneurs and owner-managed businesses, public sector, charity organisations and private individuals.

Types of work Banking and finance, commercial contracts, commercial recoveries, construction and engineering, corporate transactions, dispute resolution, driver defence, employment, family, financial services, franchising, insurance, intellectual property, licensing, pensions and benefits, planning, professional regulatory, property litigation, public procurement, real estate, regulatory risk and compliance, residential property, restructuring and insolvency, rural and agriculture, interventions, technology and outsourcing, trademarks and registrations, wills, probate, tax and trusts.

Who should apply When recruiting our trainee solicitors we are looking for ability, enthusiasm, commitment and contribution. We recruit high-calibre people with proven analytical ability, strong interpersonal skills, good commercial awareness and an excellent academic record. We look for individuals with a record of significant personal achievement, who are willing and flexible, and who care about their communities as much as we do. To be successful at the application screening stage, we need to see evidence of the skills and attributes needed to be a successful lawyer within your application, including those such as attention to detail, research and individuality.

Training programme Training is carefully structured and designed to provide variety, responsibility and intellectual challenge. Working closely alongside partners and associates, the aim is to give you experience of a wide range of clients and practice areas through a series of six-month placements. We also offer client secondment opportunities. Your seat supervisor will involve you directly in work so you learn from personal experience as well as observation and instruction. The more competence you demonstrate, the more responsibility we will give you. We offer a comprehensive development programme alongside the compulsory Professional Skills Course. You will have a review meeting every three months with your supervisor and the trainee regional partner to monitor your progress.

When and how to apply All applications must be made via our online application form at www.blakemorgan.co.uk. We regret that we cannot accept applications made by any other means.

Work placements We offer a one-week vacation scheme to those applying for a training contract. We structure the week to allow you to spend quality time within a legal team learning about the work they do and their clients. It is also important to us that you have a chance to really understand our culture and what being a trainee at Blake Morgan is like so you also complete client research and charity-related projects. The final day is an assessment day where candidates will have a first-round interview with an associate and take part in group and individual exercises. Insights days are a great way to learn more about us and to confirm that we're the right firm for you. After a warm welcome from the trainee regional partner, you'll hear more about Blake Morgan, attend a recruitment workshop and enjoy a networking lunch before shadowing a current trainee for the afternoon.

Vacancies	18
Trainees	37
Partners	114
Total staff	800

Work placement yes

Training contract deadline
31 May 2019

Apply
Online

Sponsorship
LPC

Offices
Cardiff, London,
Southampton, Portsmouth,
Oxford, Reading

Proud diversity and inclusion
partner of

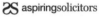

Blaser Mills Law

40 Oxford Road, High Wycombe HP11 2EE
Tel: 020 3814 2020
Email: enquiries@blasermills.co.uk
Web: www.blasermills.co.uk
🐦 blasermillslaw

The firm Blaser Mills Law is a leading law firm based in the South East with over 60 lawyers. We are a full-service firm, offering a comprehensive range of legal services to businesses and private individuals. Our highly regarded firm has a strong business services offering, including corporate and commercial, employment, commercial property and dispute resolution. We also have experienced private client and family lawyers, as well as specialist lawyers in personal injury, child care, residential property and criminal defence. We offer a fresh approach to law, with a focus on not only building relationships with clients, but also building employee relationships. The success of our business, and the high-quality service we provide for our clients comes from nurturing the skills and promoting the talent and diversity of our staff.

Types of work Corporate and commercial, commercial property, employment, dispute resolution, residential property and development, wills, trusts and probate, personal and serious injury, family and divorce (including child care), criminal defence.

Who should apply We are proud of the diversity of our teams of lawyers, in terms of experience, background and approach. We look for diversity in our trainees too. As well as a strong academic background, excellent communication skills and analytical ability, we look for talented individuals who have a strong team ethic, ambition and who embrace responsibility. Trainees are right at the heart of the firm and nothing demonstrates this more clearly than the fact that the majority of our partners trained with us. Progression to partnership is strictly on merit and excellence is continuously rewarded.

Training programme From the moment that our future trainees receive their official offer, they become a valued member of the team. The firm organises a number of events throughout the two year gap to give them an opportunity to get to know the firm before they officially start their training contract. Training starts in September with a full induction day. Trainees will have varied (four six-month) seats in both non-contentious and contentious practice areas, giving them the opportunity to gain experience across a broad range of legal disciplines in a variety of locations. From day one, trainees are given plenty of responsibility and hands-on experience, with the ongoing support from experienced training supervisors. In addition, we operate a mentor scheme that gives trainees confidential access to recently qualified lawyers who can offer first-hand experience and advice. Part of the mentor scheme includes getting the trainees together three times a year for social events. Throughout the training contract, trainees will develop their technical skills, department knowledge and client care. Business development is a further skill that we look to develop in our trainees, so when it comes to qualifying, they are confident to approach prospective clients and build their own client list. Trainees will have access to multiple business development opportunities, whether that be through article writing, presenting at seminars or attending networking events.

When and how to apply For training contracts to commence September 2021, applications open on 1 March 2019 and close on 28 June 2019. Please complete the online application form accessible on our website. We no longer accept applications by CV and covering letter.

Vacancies	4
Trainees	8
Partners	22
Total staff	130

Training contract deadline
28 June 2019

Apply
Online

Offices
High Wycombe, Amersham, Rickmansworth, Silverstone, London

BLM

Kings House, 42 Kings Street West, Manchester M3 2NU
Tel: 0161 236 2002
Email: graduaterecruitment@blmlaw.com
Web: www.blmlaw.com/graduatecareers
🐦 blm_grads

The firm BLM is an insurance risk and commercial law firm with both a domestic and international focus. We now work with an increasing number of customers, across more lines of business, in more locations throughout the UK and Ireland as well as across the world, than ever before. We have established a deep-rooted presence in the general insurance sector, the London market and amongst brokers. We also have a significant presence among corporate businesses many of whom are multi-national, the public sector and the health and care industry.

Types of work Insurance risk and commercial law, including (but not limited to): catastrophic injury, casualty, clinical negligence, fraud, housing, motor, occupational disease, commercial litigation and commercial property.

Who should apply We look for a blend of high academic ability and people who fit with our dynamic, ideas led and ambitious culture.

You should be confident and resilient in your approach and demonstrate exemplary interpersonal written and verbal communication skills; you should look forward to assuming real responsibility in a supportive environment from an early stage.

Training programme Our two-year trainee solicitor programme has been designed to maximise your potential. You'll complete four six-month seats, giving you exposure to a variety of teams across the business. You'll also gain the experience and develop the skills required of a qualified solicitor within insurance law.

You may also have the opportunity to spend time on secondment with one of our customers or with the Association of British Insurers. Throughout your programme you will work with our partners and associates on a variety of cases from low to complex, high-value claims, from initial investigation through to trial. You will have all of the support that you need from your assigned supervisor and our in-house talent development team.

Partners encourage early responsibility and expect trainees to manage workloads autonomously and as part of a team. We will provide a supportive and friendly working environment and you can expect clear opportunities for career progression and a broad scope of challenging and interesting work.

When and how to apply Please apply directly through our website www.blmlaw.com/join-us/graduates.

Work placements BLM's vacation scheme gives you the opportunity to spend two weeks in one of our offices. You'll be paired up with one of our current trainees and will have the opportunity to really get to grips with what we do 'day-to-day'. You'll work with our partners and associates too, contributing to live cases and be given real responsibility.

Sponsorship BLM will fund the LPC for future trainees who have not already completed this.

Vacancies	23
Trainees	50
Partners	196
Total staff	1,595
Work placement	yes

Apply
Online

Starting salary
London – £31,000
Regional offices – £22,000

Minimum qualifications
2.1 degree

Sponsorship
LPC

Offices
Edinburgh, Glasgow, Liverpool, Manchester, Birmingham, London, Southampton

 BLM

BIRD & CO SOLICITORS LLP
15 Castlegate, Grantham, Lincolnshire NG31 6SE
Tel: 01476 591711
Email: enquiries@birdandco.co.uk
Apply to: Mrs E Conron

Four-partner firm with offices in Grantham, Newark and Lincoln. Young and progressive high street practice. Core areas are criminal, family, civil litigation, PI, conveyancing, wills and probate.

V	0
T	2
P	4
TS	50
WP	no

BIRKETT LONG LLP
1 Amphora Place, Sheepen Road, Colchester CO3 3WG
Tel: 01206 217300
Email: liz.omahony@birkettlong.co.uk
Apply to: Miss Liz O'Mahony

Pre-eminent Essex firm - general services; specialisms in commercial, environmental, agricultural, education, employment, computer law, family and private client. Other offices in Chelmsford and Basildon.

V	2[20]
T	4
P	26
TS	170
WP	yes

BIRKETTS LLP
Providence House, 141-145 Princes Street, Ipswich IP1 1QJ
Tel: 01473 232300
Email: graduate-recruitment@birketts.co.uk
Apply to: Mrs Suzannah Rogers

Award-winning, top 100 law firm based in the East of England, providing a full range of legal services: corporate and commercial, property and private client.

V	7
T	20
P	59
TS	504
WP	yes

BIRNBERG PEIRCE
14 Inverness Street, London NW1 7HJ
Tel: 020 7911 0166
Email: sibleyc@birnbergpeirce.co.uk
Apply to: Mrs Claire Sibley

Leading criminal defence, immigration and civil liberties firm.

V	1[20]
T	1
P	3
TS	42
WP	no

BISHOP & SEWELL LLP
59-60 Russell Square, London WC1B 4HP
Tel: 020 7631 4141
Email: mail@bishopandsewell.co.uk
Apply to: Mr Michael Gillman

Bishop & Sewell is a firm offering a comprehensive range of legal services to both private and commercial clients. We are not currently inviting applications for training contracts.

V	0
T	2
P	9
TS	54
WP	no

BLACKHURST SWAINSON GOODIER LLP T/A BSG SOLICITORS
10 Chapel Street, Preston PR1 8AY
Tel: 01772 253841
Email: info@bsglaw.co.uk
Apply to: Miss Andrea Brown

General practice. Holder of legal aid franchise. Applications for training contracts and vacation placements accepted at any time.

V	1
T	3
P	5
TS	27
WP	no

BLACKS SOLICITORS LLP
Citypoint, 29 King Street, Leeds LS1 2HL
Tel: 0113 207 0000
Email: tmoyes@lawblacks.com
Apply to: Mr Tom Moyes

General commercial practice with increasing emphasis on company commercial and commercial property areas of work but also servicing private clients.

V	3
T	6
P	16
TS	170
WP	yes

BLANCHARDS BAILEY LLP
Bunbury House, Stour Park, Blandford St Mary, Dorset DT11 9LQ
Tel: 01258 459361
Email: pat.mapstone@blanchardsbailey.co.uk
Apply to: Ms Pat Mapstone

Blanchards Bailey is a six-partner firm with approximately 66 staff across three offices dealing with a wide range of legal work.

V	0
T	1
P	6
TS	66
WP	no

V = Vacancies / **T** = Trainees / **P** = Partners / **TS** = Total Staff / **WP** = Work Placement

Boyes Turner

Abbots House, Abbey Street, Reading RG1 3BD
Tel: 0118 952 7191
Email: graduates@boyesturner.com
Web: www.boyesturner.com
🐦 boyesturner

The firm Boyes Turner is continuing to flourish in the Thames Valley legal market. The strategy for 2019 and onwards is to continue the growth and development of the firm, its employees and its work.

The firm demands a high standard of quality work from its partners, associates, assistants and trainee solicitors, together with those employees providing support services. However, the firm also recognises its employees' desire to enjoy their time outside of work which results in highly motivated employees.

The firm's values fall into the following categories: accessibility, quality client contact, commercial awareness, approachability, openness, honesty, enthusiasm and respect. Boyes Turner prides itself on being a modern, forward thinking, friendly team.

Types of work We are one of the UK's leading full-service law firms. Our lawyers regularly work with many of the world's largest multinationals as well as successful UK and European businesses. Our highly ranked commercial and specialist claims groups are regularly rated amongst the best in the UK.

Who should apply If you are an enthusiastic, practical and pragmatic individual who takes pride in your work and are prepared to go the extra mile to provide high quality services to clients, colleagues and the firm as a whole, then apply to Boyes Turner for a 2021 training contract.

Training programme The training principal, Andrew Chalkley, and the human resources manager, Helen Barnett, oversee the training of all trainee solicitors. Each trainee has a tutor who is one of the firm's partners. The tutors meet the trainees on a regular basis throughout the training contract to review the trainees' progress on two levels: (a) how the trainees are developing as lawyers and (b) how the trainees are developing as individuals.

Training seats are currently organised into six-month seats in four practice areas, offering our trainees experience in both commercial and private client areas of law. For each area, a supervisor from the relevant practice group will oversee day-to-day training and work. Boyes Turner seeks to give as much client contact to trainees as possible.

When and how to apply If you are interested in applying for a training contract with Boyes Turner commencing in 2021, please do so via our online application at www.boyesturner.com. The deadline for receipt of 2021 applications is June 2019. The application form will be published on our website from January 2019.

Work placements Boyes Turner's vacation placement scheme provides a unique opportunity to gain an insight into what it is like to work for our law firm. We offer eight students one-week placements (four placements in the spring and four placements in the summer). We use the vacation placement scheme to identify potential recruits for our training contracts. The placement also allows you to find out if you would like to train with us.

Sponsorship Candidates who accept a training contract with Boyes Turner prior to beginning their LPC will receive part sponsorship of LPC tuition fees.

Vacancies	3
Trainees	6
Partners	23
Total staff	160

Work placement yes

Training contract deadline
June 2019

Apply
Online at
www.boyesturner.com

Minimum qualifications
2.1 degree

Sponsorship
LPC terms apply, see website

Offices
Reading

B P Collins LLP

Collins House, 32-38 Station Road, Gerrards Cross SL9 8EL
Tel: 01753 889995
Email: jacqui.symons@bpcollins.co.uk
Web: www.bpcollins.co.uk
🐦 bpcollinslaw

The firm Established in 1966 and with over 60 lawyers, B P Collins LLP is an award-winning law firm based in Gerrards Cross, Buckinghamshire. Heralded a 'regional heavyweight' and top ranked by independent legal directories, its teams of legal experts provide advice and support to both businesses and private individuals across a range of corporate, employment, real estate, dispute resolution, family law and wills, trusts and probate matters.

Celebrating 50 years in 2016, the firm has built its reputation helping successful people with significant assets achieve peace of mind. Its lawyers are dedicated to delivering the best legal advice, through solving problems, managing risk and adding value. Lexcel accredited, B P Collins' commitment to and enduring relationships with clients, whether a private individual or thriving business, ensure delivery of an outstanding service.

Most lawyers have worked in London, but have opted to work in more congenial surroundings where they can enjoy a higher quality lifestyle. Gerrards Cross is a very pleasant town surrounded by beautiful countryside, but within 20 minutes commuting distance of London Marylebone. It is an affluent area and we are conveniently located to serve the extremely active business communities of West London, Heathrow, Uxbridge, Slough and High Wycombe.

Types of work Corporate and commercial, commercial and residential property, employment law, family law, litigation and dispute resolution and private client.

Who should apply Bright, hard-working, lateral thinkers who are good communicators with plenty of initiative will thrive in the B P Collins environment. You should be adaptable and self starting in approach and possess a degree of robustness to cope with the changing demands which you will face during the contract.

Training programme The firm aims to have six to eight trainee solicitors at different stages of their training contracts at all times. Trainees complete five months in four different practice groups of their choice. The final four months is spent in the practice group in which the trainee intends to specialise. The firm has a training partner with overall responsibility for all trainees and each practice group has its own trainee supervisor who is responsible for day-to-day supervision. Trainees are given early responsibility which includes plenty of client contact and professional work. There are regular meetings between the supervisor and the trainee to monitor progress and a review meeting with the training partner midway through and at the end of each practice group seat. Trainees are encouraged to participate in social and marketing events. The firm has a very high trainee retention rate.

When and how to apply CV with a handwritten letter from 1 March through to 31 May 2019 (email applications will not be considered).

Work placements See website for details.

Sponsorship The firm makes a contribution towards LPC fees.

Vacancies	3-4
Trainees	7
Partners	14
Total staff	110
Work placement	yes

Training contract deadline
31 May 2019

Apply to
Jacqui Symons,
HR Manager

Starting salary
£26,400

Minimum qualifications
2.1 degree, As and Bs at A level

Sponsorship
LPC

Offices
Gerrards Cross, Bucks

BPE Solicitors LLP

St James House, St James Square, Cheltenham GL50 3PR
Tel: 0124 222 4433
Email: amanda.coleman@bpe.co.uk
Web: www.bpe.co.uk
f bpecommunity 🐦 bpe_solicitors

The firm BPE Solicitors is an entrepreneurial firm working with like-minded businesses and individuals, supporting them at home and at work. Many clients have been retained for decades and the firm has supported young businesses in their growth to become multi-million pound, multi-national operations.

With more than 130 staff including 60 lawyers, BPE continues to grow through its collaborative approach, providing clients with a team of specialists. Its lawyers have extensive sector experience and great networks of contacts. As comfortable working directly with owner-managers and directors of growing firms, as with in-house counsel, government agencies, or private clients seeking help with family issues, BPE provides versatility, expertise and a personal approach.

Headquartered in Cheltenham, Gloucestershire and with an office in London and a presence in Bristol and Oxford, BPE clients are located throughout the UK.

Operating for close to 35 years, for the past eight the firm has been led by senior partner John Workman.

Types of work Property, corporate, construction and engineering, commercial, employment, litigation, science and technology, family, private client, contentious probate and residential.

Who should apply BPE is different. We want you to share our ambition. We are looking for bright, passionate and driven individuals who are able to think on their feet, learn from each other, and enjoy being part of a dynamic, entrepreneurial team. You will need a minimum 2.1 degree with strong A levels and relevant work experience.

Training programme Each trainee will spend six months in four seats across the firm. We offer corporate and commercial seats along with a private client seat option, covering both contentious and non-contentious disciplines, giving you the chance to find out which area of law suits you best.

Our teams provide an exciting and stimulating training environment with a very hands on approach. You will find yourself getting involved in client matters, networking events, conference calls, ADR, target client research, and much more. We guarantee your training will be wide ranging, intensive and well balanced.

But it's not all work and no play – we make the most of any opportunity to get together and have fun! From our mix of sports teams and Friday nights out to firm-wide summer and Christmas parties and team away days, there's always plenty of opportunities to get to know your colleagues outside of work.

When and how to apply Contact HR Manager Amanda Coleman at amanda.coleman@bpe.co.uk for more information.

Work placements Placements are available throughout the summer depending on the availability of both the student and BPE.

Sponsorship We do not offer any form of sponsorship.

Vacancies	4
Trainees	10
Partners	24
Total staff	130

Training contract deadline
31 May 2019

Apply
Online

Starting salary
£24,500

Minimum qualifications
2.1 degree

Offices
Cheltenham, Stonehouse

BLANDY & BLANDY LLP
One Friar Street, Reading RG1 1DA
Tel: 0118 951 6800
Email: hr@blandy.co.uk
Apply to: Mrs Anne Laflin

The firm offers a full range of commercial and private client services (except criminal work). Clients include public and private companies, landed estates and individuals.

V	2-3[20]
T	5
P	20
TS	104
WP	yes

BOLT BURDON
Providence House, Providence Place, London N1 0NT
Tel: 020 7288 4700
Email: people@boltburdon.co.uk
Apply to: Ms Lucy Croucher

A modern professional firm providing swift practical advice and the highest levels of service to business and personal clients, and in negligence cases.

V	3
T	3
P	14
TS	65
WP	no

BONNETT SON & TURNER LLP
33 Bath Road, Hounslow TW3 3BW
Tel: 020 8570 5286
Apply to: Mrs N Bowman

Established practice with two offices specialising in company, commercial property, litigation, employment, residential conveyancing, and wills and probate.

V	0
T	1
P	3
TS	30
WP	no

BOODLE HATFIELD LLP
240 Blackfriars Road, London SE1 8NW
Tel: 020 7629 7411
Email: traineesolicitors@boodlehatfield.com
Apply to: Miss Jenny Andrews

Boodle Hatfield is a highly successful law firm which advises wealthy individuals, families, property owners and businesses in the United Kingdom and internationally.

V	4
T	8
P	33
TS	150
WP	yes

BOSLEY & CO
5 Marlborough Place, Brighton BN1 1UB
Tel: 01273 608 181
Email: sb@bosley.co.uk
Apply to: Mr Stanley Bernard

V	1
T	-
P	3
TS	13
WP	yes

BOTT & COMPANY SOLICITORS LTD
St Ann's House, Parsonage Green, Wilmslow, Cheshire SK9 1HG
Tel: 01625 415 800
Email: info@bottonline.co.uk
Apply to: Ms Claire Walsh

V	0
T	0
P	3
TS	102
WP	no

BOWCOCK CUERDEN LLP
South Cheshire House, Manor Road, Nantwich, Cheshire CW5 5LX
Tel: 01270 611106
Email: jpc@bowcockcuerden.co.uk
Apply to: Mr JP Cuerden

Three-partner LLP niche commercial firm with specialist private client department; longstanding Lexcel accreditation; progressive; quality oriented. NFU legal panel firm covering Cheshire and Derbyshire.

V	1
T	0
P	3
TS	28
WP	no

BRACHERS LLP
Somerfield House, 59 London Road, Maidstone MEI6 8JH
Tel: 01622 690691
Email: humanresources@brachers.co.uk
Apply to: Mrs Jacqueline Shepherd

Providing extensive legal services to corporate and private clients throughout London and the South East.

V	3[20]
T	3
P	26
TS	196
WP	yes

V = Vacancies / **T** = Trainees / **P** =.Partners / **TS** = Total Staff / **WP** = Work Placement

Brabners LLP

1 Horton House, Exchange Flags, Liverpool L2 3YL
Tel: 0151 600 3000
Email: trainees@brabners.com
Web: www.brabners.com
🐦 brabnersllp

The firm A leading North West commercial legal practice, Brabners LLP has offices in Liverpool, Manchester and Preston. The firm has over 361 staff including 57 partners across its three offices, with nationally recognised experts in its key practice areas of corporate, commercial, property, employment and pensions, litigation, sports, social housing, charity, family and private client.

Types of work The firm provides a wide range of specialist legal services and its client base includes PLCs, public sector bodies, banks, other commercial, corporate and professional businesses and high-net-worth individuals

Brabners' legal teams are made up of sector specialists. This ensures clients are given legal advice in the context of the commercial environment their businesses operate in. The firm has specialists in a number of core sectors including real estate, business services, healthcare, media, technology, retail, sport and charity.

Who should apply Graduates and those undertaking the GDL or LPC, who can demonstrate intelligence, intuition, humour, approachability and commitment.

Training programme Brabners is one of the few law firms that holds Investor in People status and has a comprehensive training and development programme, which is one of the highest ranked in the student law firm guide *The Lex 100*. Brabners places in the top 20 law firms for work-life balance and stress levels, and was named the friendliest in the UK in 2017.

Trainees are given a high degree of responsibility and are an integral part of the culture of the firm. Each trainee will have partner-level supervision and personal development appraisals are conducted at three six-monthly intervals to ensure that progress is as fast and seamless as possible.

The training programme is overseen by the firm's director of training, Dr Tony Harvey. Tony is a solicitor, holds a master's degree and doctorate in ethics and law and is also the firm's head of risk and compliance and oversees the firm's ethical guidance.

He said: "Our trainee programme is a fundamental part of the firm's long-term plan for sustainable growth. We're a business built on finding and nurturing talent."

It is not all hard work and the firm has an excellent social programme, including an extensive schedule of charity events. Brabners holds an annual charity challenge where employees head to the Lake District to take part in a number of physical activities, including kayaking, cycling and fell walking to raise money for good causes.

The firm also hosts several networking and sector insight events throughout the year. A great example of this is the high-profile state of play conference on sporting governance, which included a keynote speech from Olympic medallist Beth Tweddle.

When and how to apply Apply online by 30 June 2019 for training contracts commencing September 2021.

Vacancies	6
Trainees	12
Partners	57
Total staff	361

Training contract deadline
30 June 2019

Apply
Online

Starting salary
Not less than £24,000

Minimum qualifications
2.1 degree or postgraduate degree

Offices
Liverpool, Manchester, Preston

Brabners

BRAMSDON & CHILDS 141 Elm Grove, Southsea, Portsmouth PO5 1HR **Tel:** 023 92821251 **Apply to:** Mr Andrew White	Well-established firm with offices in Southsea, Portsmouth and Fareham with a general practice.	V 1 T 1 P 5 TS 34 WP no
BRAY & BRAY Spa Place, 36-42 Humberstone Road, Leicester LE5 0AE **Tel:** 0116 254 8871 **Email:** info@braybray.co.uk **Apply to:** Mr ID Lewis	Well-established firm with strong private client and SME commercial client base. Wide variety of work including legal aid.	V 1 T 1 P 12 TS 95 WP no
BREEZE & WYLES SOLICITORS LTD Second Floor, Stag House, Old London Road, Hertford SG13 7LA **Tel:** 01992 558411 **Email:** recruitment@breezeandwyles.co.uk **Apply to:** Ms Janani Ganay	Established for 100 years, progressive and forward thinking. Covers domestic conveyancing/commercial conveyancing and litigation, company commercial, matrimonial, probate and private client.	V 4[19] T 8 P 9 TS 180 WP no
BRIAN KOFFMAN & CO New Maxdov House, 130 Bury New Road, Prestwich, Manchester M25 0AA **Tel:** 0161 832 3852 **Email:** briankoffman@motoringoffencesolicitors.co.uk **Apply to:** Mr B Koffman	Privately funded road traffic and crime.	V 0 T - P 1 TS 2 WP no
BRIDGE MCFARLAND Sibthorp House, 351-355 High Street, Lincoln LN5 7BN **Tel:** 01522 518888 **Email:** recruitment@bmcf.co.uk **Apply to:** Mrs Tracey Inkpin	Offices in Grimsby, Lincoln, Hull, Louth and Market Rasen. Particular expertise in medical negligence, personal injury, commercial, civil and construction litigation, family, and property.	V 2[19] T 3 P 25 TS 176 WP yes
BRIDGE SANDERSON MUNRO 55 Hallgate, Doncaster DN1 3PD **Tel:** 01302 321621 **Email:** info@bsmlaw.co.uk **Apply to:** Mr PD Davies	Long-established franchised general practice with four partners in three offices.	V 0 T 0 P 4 TS 20 WP no
BRIDGER & CO SOLICITORS Old Bank Chambers, 35 High Street, Builth Wells, Powys LD2 3DL **Tel:** 01982 559292 **Email:** philip@bridgerandco.co.uk **Apply to:** Mr Philip Bridger	Bridger & Co is a fast growing practice, based at Llandovery, Llandrindod Wells and Builth Wells with plans to open further branches. We specialise predominantly in high street work as well as agriculture and planning.	V 1 T 2 P 3 TS 8 WP yes
BRIGHOUSE WOLFF Whelmar House, Southway, Skelmersdale WN8 6NX **Tel:** 01695 722577 **Email:** mgh@brighouse-wolff.co.uk **Apply to:** Mr MG Hagerty	Large general practice specialising in conveyancing probate litigation, crime, mental health and family law. Legal aid franchise and estate agency.	V 1 T 1 P 10 TS 80 WP no

V = Vacancies / **T** = Trainees / **P** = Partners / **TS** = Total Staff / **WP** = Work Placement

Bristows LLP

100 Victoria Embankment, London EC4Y 0DH
Tel: 020 7400 8000
Email: trainee.recruitment@bristows.com
Web: training.bristows.com
🐦 bristowsgrad

The firm Bristows is a medium-sized firm that handles the types of work you might normally associate with only the very largest firms. Established 180 years ago, we have built up a client list that includes leading businesses from a variety of cutting-edge industries. Working with so many ambitious organisations, we are often advising on issues that shape entire industries and on which a company's future might depend.

Our strength in the intellectual property field means we have a great many clients from the life sciences, technology and consumer products sectors, as these are areas where organisations often need to protect their ideas, inventions and brands. Our clients range from fast-growing start-ups and medium-sized enterprises, to global corporations, financial institutions and high-profile charities. It's a real mix of organisations and, whatever your specialism, as a lawyer at Bristows you could find yourself working with any of them.

Types of work Bristows has one of the foremost intellectual property practices in the world. Our lawyers are recognised as leading authorities in a wide variety of legal disciplines and as a firm we offer a true breadth of expertise. Our core practice areas are: IP, IT and data protection, corporate, commercial technology and copyright disputes, real estate, regulatory, EU and competition, employment, tax and charities.

Who should apply Each year we ask around 10 graduates to join our team and are extremely selective because we are looking for trainees with true partner potential. We place great importance on having a diverse and inclusive environment and recruit trainees from all degree disciplines (including those with a science and engineering background) from a wide range of universities.

Training programme As part of a small, select and high-calibre intake, our trainees work alongside our partners dealing directly with clients right from the start. There's plenty of responsibility, but this is matched by an extremely supportive and friendly culture so trainees are never far from encouragement and advice when they need it. During the two years' training we offer a mixture of three-month and six-month seats which may include a three-month secondment to the UK in-house legal department of one of our leading multi-national clients. We also guarantee a seat in IP – this is rare even among firms with a strong IP practice!

When and how to apply To apply for a training contract position commencing in August 2021, please complete our online application form which can be found on the firm's trainee recruitment webpage. The deadline for training contract applications is 31 July 2019.

Work placements We run a number of two-day workshops and open days which offer the chance to find out more about Bristows and are a great opportunity to assess whether law as a career, and Bristows as a firm, are for you. While in the office you will take part in a range of activities to enable you to get a real sense of the firm and find out first-hand what life is like as a lawyer at Bristows. Please visit our website for the dates of our winter, spring and summer workshops, our open days and application deadlines.

Sponsorship Payment of full fees and a maintenance grant of £8,000 for both the LPC and GDL (where applicable).

Vacancies	10
Trainees	20
Partners	41
Total staff	275

Work placement yes
(see Insider Report on p73)

Training contract deadline
31 July 2019

Apply
Online

Starting salary
£38,000

Minimum qualifications
2.1 degree preferred

Sponsorship
GDL/LPC

Offices
London

BRISTOWS

Proud diversity and inclusion partner of

 **2S** aspiringsolicitors

Bryan Cave Leighton Paisner LLP

Adelaide House, London Bridge EC4R 9HA
Tel: 020 3400 1000
Email: abby.sanders@blplaw.com
Web: www.blplaw.com/trainee
🐦 bclplaw

The firm Formed by the merger of Bryan Cave and Berwin Leighton Paisner, global law firm Bryan Cave Leighton Paisner LLP is purposely structured in a way few other law firms are, as a fully integrated international team that provides clients with clear, connected legal advice, wherever and whenever they need it.

Types of work The firm is structured in four large departments: real estate, corporate, finance, and litigation and corporate risk (LCR). There are various seats available in each department, in addition there is an opportunity for trainees to second internationally and to clients. Trainees work on challenging projects from the outset and are given a high level of responsibility. Completing tasks such as drafting submissions, completing due diligence reports or working with internationally renowned clients such as, AIG, Balfour Beatty, Tesco and The Football Association.

Who should apply We welcome applications from various, diverse backgrounds; whether you are a non-law student, graduate, career changer or qualified lawyer, we would love to hear from you. We look for enthusiastic, commercial individuals who possess a resilient, can-do attitude. Our culture is important to the firm and we look for individuals who will thrive in our meritocratic, innovative environment, whilst understanding the importance of respect and collaboration.

Training programme Hong Kong and London trainees rotate through four, six-month seats in different parts of the business. Trainees in Manchester are allocated work on a pooled basis. All trainees will gain contentious, non-contentious experience during their two year training contract.

When and how to apply All candidates must apply online to be considered, jobs are offered on a rolling bases, so applying early is advantageous. The application process is outlined here:

Online application form and verbal reasoning test – Your application form and verbal reasoning test are reviewed in combination. The application includes your personal details, academics, work experience and a mix of research based and situational questions. After your application has been reviewed and if you meet our benchmark, you'll then be progressed to the next stage of our application process, the assessment centre.

Assessment centre – The assessment centre includes a drafting, role play and negotiation exercise. If applying to a vacation scheme and you are successful at this stage you will be offered a position, your application will be progressed to vacation scheme, if applying directly for a training contract please refer to partner interview.

Vacation scheme – Throughout the vacation scheme you'll be assigned various tasks by your trainee and partner buddy, including at least one piece of written work to assess your drafting skills. The scheme will also include department workshops, partner lunch, social events and partner interview. We collect feedback from your buddies and interviewers, if feedback is positive you'll be offered a training contract – Congratulations!

Partner interview – The partner interview is scheduled for one hour, be expected to interview with two senior representatives of the firm. If successful at partner interview you'll be offered a training contract – Congratulations!

Sponsorship GDL and LPC course fees plus maintenance grant.

Vacancies	35
Trainees	78
Partners	200
Total staff	1,600

Work placement   yes
(see Insider Report on p74)

Training contract deadline
31 May 2019

Apply
Online

Minimum qualifications
2.1 degree

Sponsorship
GDL/LPC

Offices
32 offices across Europe, the United States and Asia

BRYAN
CAVE
LEIGHTON
PAISNER

BRIGNALLS BALDERSTON WARREN Forum Chambers, The Forum, Stevenage, Hertfordshire SG1 1EL **Tel:** 01438 359311 **Apply to:** Mr B C Lendrum	General high street practice dealing with conveyancing, probate, wills and trusts, family, crime, corporate and commercial matters, employment and general civil litigation.	V 0 T 2 P 13 TS 57 WP no
BROOKS & PARTNERS Lyons House, 2 Station Road, Camberley, Surrey GU16 7JA **Tel:** 01276 681217 **Email:** law@brooks-partners.co.uk **Apply to:** Mrs V Lennard	A progressive law firm based in Surrey handling a wide range of private client and business work. Our strength is the quality of our people.	V 0 T 1 P 1 TS 24 WP no
BROSS BENNETT Stable House, 64A Highgate High Street, London N6 5HX **Tel:** 020 8340 0444 **Email:** gen1@brossbennett.co.uk **Apply to:** Mrs Sharon Bennett	The firm specialises in family law and is one of the largest niche practices outside of central London.	V 0 T 1 P 5 TS 20 WP yes
BROWN RUDNICK LLP 8 Clifford Street, London W1S 2LQ **Tel:** 020 7851 6000 **Email:** employmentopportunities@brownrudnick.com **Apply to:** Ms Valerie Jones	An AmLaw 200 firm with offices in the United States and Europe. The firm represents clients in high stakes litigation and business transactions.	V 4 T 6 P 35 TS 130 WP no
BROWNE JACOBSON LLP Mowbray House, Castle Meadow Road, Nottingham NG2 1BJ **Tel:** 0808 1789064 **Email:** traineeapplications@brownejacobson.com **Apply to:** Trainee Recruitment	A full service national law firm with expertise across both private and public sector specialisms. Offering excellent opportunities for quality people.	V 20 T 36 P 142 TS 981 WP yes
BRYAN AND ARMSTRONG The New Meeting House, Station Street, Mansfield NG18 1EF **Tel:** 01623 624505 **Email:** enquiries@bryanandarmstrong.co.uk **Apply to:** Mr N Croston	Legal aid, matrimonial, personal injury and litigation, commercial and residential property, small business advice. One office in Mansfield. Lexcel and CQC accredited.	V 0 T 1 P 4 TS 21 WP no
BRYAN CAVE 88 Wood Street, London EC2V 7AJ **Tel:** 020 3207 1100 **Email:** clinton.baker@bryancave.com **Apply to:** Mr Clinton Baker	Extensive banking, corporate/commercial practice with offices worldwide. Bryan Cave is one of the leading firms in the US and offers clients a comprehensive service.	V 0 T 4 P 15 TS 80 WP yes
BS SINGH & CO LLP 182 Stapleton Road, Easton, Bristol BS5 0NZ **Tel:** 0117 935 4500 **Email:** info@bssinghsolicitors.co.uk **Apply to:** Mr Bhupinder Singh	Bristol-based high street niche practice. Specialising in immigration, family, children matters, conveyancing (residential, commercial), wills and probate, litigation, employment, crime and general.	V 2 T - P 2 TS 4 WP yes

V = Vacancies / **T** = Trainees / **P** = Partners / **TS** = Total Staff / **WP** = Work Placement

Burges Salmon

1 Glass Wharf, Bristol BS2 OZX
Tel: 0117 939 6938
Email: anna.dixon@burges-salmon.com
Web: www.burges-salmon.com
🐦 burgessalmonts

Law Careers.Net
AWARDS
2018
BEST WORK PLACEMENT SCHEME
REGIONAL FIRM

The firm Burges Salmon is the independent UK law firm which delivers the best mix of advice, service and value. We pride ourselves on delivering an excellent standard of legal and business advice to our clients, which has led to many of our practice areas and sectors winning awards and recognition as best in class. Our national and international client base ranges from private individuals to government departments and FTSE 100 companies including The Crown Estate, Nationwide, Lloyds Banking Group, John Lewis, The Nuclear Decommissioning Authority, FirstGroup and the Crown Commercial Service. We believe it is our people that make the firm great. Our values of ambition, collaboration, commitment, fairness, quality and respect shape our distinctive culture and are evident across the firm. All our people are based in our HQ in Bristol. This means we all know and work with each other. In fact, team playing is core to our approach to delivering a great client experience. We are accredited by Investors in People Gold and offer our people a generous benefits package, career development and progression, and a strong corporate responsibility programme.

Types of work The quality of the firm's expertise is widely recognised across its main departments including banking and finance, commercial, corporate, dispute resolution, employment, private client, projects and real estate.

Who should apply There is no 'standard' Burges Salmon trainee. The one thing all our people have in common is their ambition and drive to deliver top quality work for colleagues and clients. We therefore welcome applications from the widest pool of candidates. As an undergraduate you can apply from your penultimate year. We also welcome applications from graduates and those considering a change in career. Successful candidates will have achieved or expect to achieve a 2.1 at degree level in any discipline and have achievements which demonstrate the exceptional personal skills necessary to become a lawyer at Burges Salmon.

Training programme Our six-seat training contract is designed to provide you with the greatest breadth of experience possible as a trainee. While traditional training contracts normally include four six-month seats, ours includes six four-month placements. This ensures you gain the maximum exposure to our varied practice areas and experience a wide range of contentious and non-contentious work from across our main departments.

When and how to apply Our online application form can be found within the careers section of our website.

Work placements We run winter (one-week), spring and summer (two-week) schemes across the year. During the vacation scheme you will have the opportunity to visit two departments of your choice. The emphasis is on 'real work' and, under the guidance of your supervisor, you will have the chance to attend court visits or client meetings as well as skills sessions run by trainees and solicitors. In addition to this, there are many social and sports events throughout the placement that offer a real insight into life as a trainee solicitor. Allowance: £250 per week.

Sponsorship The firm pays GDL and LPC fees. Maintenance grants of £7,000 are paid to LPC students and £14,000 to students studying for both the GDL and LPC (£7,000 pa).

Vacancies	20
Trainees	56
Partners	87
Total staff	750
Work placement	yes

Training contract deadline
31 July 2019

Apply
Online

Starting salary
£35,000

Minimum qualifications
2.1 degree, any discipline

Sponsorship
GDL/LPC

Offices
Bristol, London

Remember to cite *The LawCareers.Net Handbook* on your application form if you apply to this firm.

TRAINING CONTRACT DIRECTORY **313**

BTMK SOLICITORS LTD 19 Clifftown Road, Southend-On-Sea, Essex SS1 1AB **Tel:** 03300 585 222 **Email:** info@btmk.co.uk **Apply to:** Mrs Judith Kundi	One of the largest commerical and personal law firms in Essex with expertise covering all aspects of company and business law and personal legal services.	V T P TS WP	0 5 10 110 yes
BUCKLES SOLICITORS LLP Grant House, 101 Bourges Boulevard, Peterborough PE1 1NG **Tel:** 01733 888722 **Email:** hr@buckles-law.co.uk **Apply to:** Mrs Christine Walker	Buckles Solicitors LLP are a regional firm dedicated to the provision of quality legal services to individual and commercial clients. We are a progressive and developing firm.	V T P TS WP	2 2 14 100 no
BURNETTS Victoria House, Wavell Drive, Rosehill, Carlisle CA1 2ST **Tel:** 01228 552222 **Email:** kas@burnetts.co.uk **Apply to:** Mrs Kate Sowerby	We are one of the largest law firms in Northern England providing grounded and expert legal advice nationally to individuals, businesses and the public sector.	V T P TS WP	2 2 7 143 yes
BURROUGHS DAY 14 Charlotte Street, Bristol BS1 5PT **Tel:** 0117 929 0333 **Email:** recruitment@bd4law.com **Apply to:** Ms Michelle Groom	Burroughs Day Solicitors is a leading South West law firm offering advice to start-ups, owner-managed businesses and individuals.	V T P TS WP	1 1 10 100 no
BURTON & BURTON SOLICITORS LTD Fox House, 17 Dale Street, Nottingham, Nottinghamshire NG2 4LE **Tel:** 01159 859 059 **Email:** enquiries@burtonandburton.co.uk **Apply to:** Mr Mohammed Mahruf	High street firm which also deals with wide range of work specialising in immigration, family, personal injury and property.	V T P TS WP	0-1 2 4 20 no
BURTON & CO LLP Stonebow, Lincoln LN2 1DA **Tel:** 01522 523215 **Email:** inmail@burtonlaw.co.uk **Apply to:** Mrs Judith Brennan	A very well established, well known firm located in the centre of Lincoln, undertaking all types of work for a small city and country clientele.	V T P TS WP	0 1 5 40 yes
BURY & WALKERS LLP Britannic House, Regent Street, Barnsley S70 2EQ **Tel:** 01226 733533 **Email:** info@burywalkers.con **Apply to:** Mr John Clark		V T P TS WP	0 1 6 68 no
BUSS MURTON LAW LLP Wellington Gate, 7-9 Church Road, Tunbridge Wells, Kent TN1 1HT **Tel:** 01892 510222 **Email:** psimpson@bussmurton.co.uk **Apply to:** Ms Patricia Simpson	Medium-sized regional law firm covering most aspects of the law in both commercial and private client areas. Modern open-plan working environment in town centre.	V T P TS WP	2^{20} 3 9 70 no

V = Vacancies / **T** = Trainees / **P** = Partners / **TS** = Total Staff / **WP** = Work Placement

BUTCHER & BARLOW LLP 2 Bank Street, Bury BL9 0DL **Tel:** 0161 764 4062 **Email:** cb@butcher-barlow.co.uk **Apply to:** Mr Charles Barlow	We prefer candidates who can develop their careers in any of our offices in Greater Manchester and Cheshire.	V 2²⁰ T 4 P 24 TS 139 WP no
BWF SOLICITORS 529 Kingsland Road, Dalston, London E8 4AR **Tel:** 020 7241 7180 **Email:** admin@bwfsolicitors.com **Apply to:** Mr B Owusu	Small highly professional solicitors, specialising in family, immigration, civil litigation, conveyancing, personal injury, and wills and probate.	V 2 T 0 P 2 TS 5 WP no
CAINS ADVOCATES LIMITED Fort Anne, Douglas, Isle of Man IM1 5PD **Tel:** 01624 638300 **Email:** tristan.head@cains.com **Apply to:** Mr Tristan Head	Cains advises many of the world's largest financial and commercial institutions in areas including project finance, corporate law, financial services, commercial litigation and commercial property.	V 2 T 2 P 5 TS 52 WP yes
CALDICOTTS 21 Burgess Street, Leominster, Herefordshire HR6 8DE **Tel:** 01568 614168 **Email:** lawyers@caldicotts.com **Apply to:** Mr Bruce Gray		V 0 T 3 P 4 TS 19 WP yes
CAMERON JONES HUSSELL & HOWE 1/3 Grove Place, Port Talbot, West Glamorgan SA13 1HX **Tel:** 01639 885261 **Email:** jghussell@cjhh.com **Apply to:** Mr JG Hussell	Sound base in conveyancing and probate. Experienced in civil litigation. Franchise for matrimonial and family work including child care.	V 0 T 1 P 5 TS 28 WP no
CAMPBELL CHAMBERS 25 Hatton Garden, London EC1N 8BQ **Tel:** 020 7691 8777 **Apply to:** Ms A Campbell	The firm is progressive and forward-thinking, valuing the diversity of its client base. We aim to recruit a workforce that reflects this. No vacancies at present.	V 0 T 4 P 2 TS 10 WP no
CAMPBELL-TAYLOR SOLICITORS 3 Bradbury Street, London N16 8JN **Tel:** 020 7923 9583 **Email:** admin@rhctlegal.co.uk **Apply to:** Mr Rod Campbell-Taylor		V 0 T 1 P 1 TS 10 WP yes
CAMPS 1 Europa House, Conway Street, Birkenhead CH41 4FT **Tel:** 0151 201 8080 **Email:** cdb@camplaw.co.uk **Apply to:** Mr Colin Billing	Specialist plaintiff litigation using dedicated software.	V 0 T 0 P 5 TS 170 WP yes

V = Vacancies / **T** = Trainees / **P** = Partners / **TS** = Total Staff / **WP** = Work Placement

Capsticks Solicitors LLP

1 St George's Road, Wimbledon, London SW19 4DR
Tel: 020 8780 4900
Email: career@capsticks.com
Web: www.capsticks.com
🐦 capsticksllp

The firm Capsticks is a leading provider of legal services to the health, social care and housing sectors, as well as in the field of professional discipline. The firm has a turnover of c£38m and 400 staff – including more than 250 fee earners – across its four offices in London, Birmingham, Leeds and Winchester and acts for a wide range of long standing clients in both the public and private sector including all forms of NHS organisations, governmental and regulatory bodies, registered providers, insurers, defence organisations, independent healthcare providers, charities and GP practices. Further details about the firm and the type of work carried out can be found on our website at www.capsticks.com.

Types of work Clinical negligence, advisory, inquests, employment, housing development, housing management, real estate, commercial, litigation and regulatory.

Who should apply Capsticks is committed to recruiting the best people to maintain its market leading position. We recruit eight trainee solicitors each year and welcome applications from candidates who are either on course for or have achieved at least a 2.1 (or equivalent) in their undergraduate degree. The firm also expects candidates to be able to demonstrate they are committed to a career in health, housing and social care as well as being highly driven, but well rounded, team players, with good problem solving and communication skills. Capsticks is committed to providing equal opportunities for all and to encouraging diversity through recruitment. Applications are welcome from all sections of the community and decisions to progress will be made with reference to entirely objective criteria only.

Training programme Capsticks' broad range of practice areas and clients enables it to provide its trainees with an opportunity to experience a wide variety of legal work. Trainees rotate every six months undertaking seats in the firm's practice areas, which include clinical law, housing, employment, real estate, commercial, litigation and regulatory. Trainees are therefore able to acquire an in-depth knowledge of both the law and the health, social care and housing sectors, in addition to developing the skills that any good lawyer needs. Where possible, we qualify our trainees after 18 months if they have prior paralegal experience that can form part of their period of recognised training. This is a real attraction for our trainees.

When and how to apply The firm welcomes applications for training contracts commencing in September 2020 and September 2021. The closing date for applications is 5:30 pm on Monday 3 June 2019. Further details are available on our website www.capsticks.com/careers/trainee-solicitors.

Work placements Capsticks recruits to its trainee solicitor positions through an application process and assessment centre. We do not offer work placements as part of our recruitment process.

Sponsorship For those who have not already completed their GDL (if applicable) and LPC, Capsticks will pay the course/qualification provider directly. Funding for this training is structured in the following way: 50% of the total course registration and examination fees will be paid by the firm; and the remaining 50% of course registration and exam fees will be paid by the firm as an interest-free career loan up to a total value of £10,000 repayable in monthly instalments from the trainee's salary upon commencement of employment. Please note that Capsticks will not reimburse any costs previously incurred for such courses.

Vacancies	8
Trainees	14
Partners	51
Total staff	403

Apply
Online

Minimum qualifications
2.1 degree

Sponsorship
GDL/LPC

Offices
London, Leeds, Birmingham, Winchester

CANNINGS CONNOLLY SOLICITORS 16 St Martin's-le-Grand, London EC1A 4EE **Tel:** 020 7003 8124 **Email:** sjones@cclaw.co.uk **Apply to:** Mr Simon Jones	Two six-months seats in real estate and a further six months in each of dispute resolution and corporate/commercial.	V 1 T 2 P 7 TS 25 WP no
CANTER LEVIN & BERG The Temple, 1 Temple Square, 24 Dale Street, Liverpool L2 5RL **Tel:** 0151 239 1000 **Email:** martinmalone@canter-law.co.uk **Apply to:** Ms Hayley Roberts	Offices in Liverpool and Kirkby.	V 1-2 T 1 P 10 TS 91 WP yes
CAPITAL LAW Capital Building, Tyndall Street, Cardiff CF10 4AZ **Tel:** 0333 2400 489 **Email:** recruitment@capitallaw.co.uk **Apply to:** Miss Lauren Peach	Specialising in commercial litigation, employment, non-contentious corporate/commercial matters, insolvency and commercial property.	V 4[19] T 6 P 18 TS 85 WP yes
CARMARTHENSHIRE COUNTY COUNCIL County Hall, Carmarthen, Carmarthenshire SA31 1JP **Tel:** 01267 224012 **Email:** direct@carmarthenshire.gov.uk **Apply to:** Mr Lyn Thomas	Local government legal service.	V 0 T 2 P 6 TS 16 WP no
CARPENTER & CO 46 Woodcote Road, Wallington, Surrey SM6 0NW **Tel:** 020 8669 5145 **Apply to:** Mr Paul Verlander	A general well-established high street practice including family, conveyancing, probate and civil litigation.	V 0-1 T 0 P 3 TS 25 WP no
CARTER BELLS LLP Kings' Stone House, 12 High Street, Kingston-upon-Thames KT1 1HD **Tel:** 020 8939 4000 **Email:** mail@carterbells.co.uk **Apply to:** Mr Frank Horder	This well-established high street practice covers all areas of law apart from crime and can provide a good grounding for enthusiastic trainees.	V 0 T 0 P 7 TS 25 WP no
CARTER LEMON CAMERONS LLP 10 Aldersgate Street, London EC1A 4HJ **Tel:** 020 7406 1000 **Email:** janetdayman@cartercamerons.com **Apply to:** Mrs Janet Dayman		V 1[19] T 4 P 11 TS 38 WP no
CARTMELL SHEPHERD Viaduct House, Carlisle CA3 8EZ **Tel:** 01228 516666 **Email:** scott.garson@cartmells.co.uk **Apply to:** Mr Scott Garson	Cartmell Shepherd is a large, broadly-based general practice with five offices throughout Cumbria and Northumbria.	V 2 T 5 P 7 TS 90 WP yes

V = Vacancies / **T** = Trainees / **P** = Partners / **TS** = Total Staff / **WP** = Work Placement

CARTWRIGHT KING
Lock House, Wilford Road, Nottingham NG2 1AG
Tel: 0115 9587 444
Email: personnel@cartwrightking.co.uk
Apply to: Mrs Ellen Nightingale

We are a national firm specialising in practice areas including family and care, mental health, court of protection, motoring, fraud, immigration and crime.

V	0
T	2
P	24
TS	211
WP	no

CAYTONS LAW
85 Gracechurch Street, London EC3V 0AA
Tel: 020 7398 7600
Email: baker@caytonslaw.com
Apply to: Mrs Emma Baker

Caytons Law is a leading insurance litigation practice based in the City of London. The majority of our cases involve representing professionals and their insurers.

V	1
T	3
P	6
TS	28
WP	yes

CBTC RAWSTORNE
27a Windsor Street, Stratford-Upon-Avon CV37 6NL
Tel: 01789 267 646
Email: enquiries@cbtcrawstorne.co.uk
Apply to: Mrs Melanie Mellichap

Main areas of practice are criminal, mental health, family, childcare, civil litigation, residential conveyancing, company and commercial, wills, trust and probate law.

V	0
T	0
P	1
TS	7
WP	no

CFG LAW (PART OF THE CLIENT FIRST GROUP)
Oakwater House, 4 Oakwater Avenue, Cheadle Royal Business Park, Cheshire SK8 3SR
Tel: 0161 437 9999
Email: recruitment@cfglaw.co.uk
Apply to: Ms Allyson McCahill

Specialist personal injury practice with a commitment to providing an interesting and challenging case load, excellent training and full support.

V	4
T	6
P	1
TS	75
WP	yes

CHAMBERLINS
4, 5 & 6 Crown Road, Great Yarmouth, Norfolk NR30 2JP
Tel: 01493 857621
Email: info@chamberlins.demon.co.uk
Apply to: Mr JB Thackray

General practice with four branches. The firm has been established for over 100 years. The first firm in Great Yarmouth to be recommended for a legal aid franchise.

V	0
T	0
P	5
TS	32
WP	no

CHARLESWORTH NICHOLL & CO
31 High Street, Crediton, Devon EX17 3AJ
Tel: 01363 774706
Email: sp@charlesworthnicholl.co.uk
Apply to: Miss CS Nicholl

A high street practice specialising in residential, agricultural and commercial property work, wills and probate, and family work. We have Lexcel and Investors in People.

V	0
T	1
P	2
TS	20
WP	no

CHATHAM CHAMBERS SOLICITORS
136 Chatham Street, Reading, Berkshire RG1 7HT
Tel: 0118 958 5855
Email: contact@chathamchambers.co.uk
Apply to: Mr I Nawaz-Chechi

We are a dynamic high street practice specialising in immigration, property and private client work. Based in Reading.

V	1
T	1
P	2
TS	6
WP	yes

CHELMSFORD BOROUGH COUNCIL
Legal Services, Civic Centre, Duke Street, Chelmsford CM1 1JE
Tel: 01245 606606
Email: susan.deval@chelmsfordbc.gov.uk
Apply to: Mrs Susan De Val

An in-house service providing a comprehensive range of legal services to the council and other public bodies including advice, litigation, advocacy and mediation services.

V	0
T	0
P	0
TS	16
WP	no

V = Vacancies / **T** = Trainees / **P** = Partners / **TS** = Total Staff / **WP** = Work Placement

Charles Russell Speechlys LLP

5 Fleet Place, London EC4M 7RD
Tel: 020 7203 5353
Web: www.charlesrussellspeechlys.com
🐦 crs_trainees

The firm At Charles Russell Speechlys we have an unusually broad range of skills and experience across the full spectrum of business and personal needs. This gives us a wider perspective, clear insight and a strongly commercial long-term view. We use this approach to secure the growth of our clients as they move confidently into the future.

It has made us a leader in the world of dynamic growth and family businesses, and among the world's leading creators and owners of private wealth and their families. Major corporates and institutions find our more considered and personal approach a refreshing alternative to conventional business law firms.

Types of work As a trainee you will have the opportunity to experience seats in the following areas: banking and finance, commercial, commercial dispute resolution, construction, engineering and projects, contentious trusts and estates, corporate, corporate tax, corporate restructuring and insolvency, employment, pensions and immigration, family, financial services, IP litigation, private property, property litigation, real estate and tax, trusts and succession. These practice areas are focused on the following sector areas: charities/not for profit, construction and infrastructure, energy and natural resources, financial services, healthcare, private wealth, real estate, retail and leisure, sport and TMT.

Who should apply We require candidates to achieve a minimum of a 2.1 in their degree and be able to demonstrate other key attributes outside of academia, such as teamwork, leadership, communication skills and initiative. People come to us from a range of backgrounds and degree disciplines, with a range of views that combine to give us our distinctive perspective on the law.

Training programme The two-year training contract at Charles Russell Speechlys is divided into four seats, giving trainees the opportunity to experience a range of different practice areas before qualification where they engage in high level work with both private clients and commercial clients. Throughout the training contract, there are regular meetings and reviews between the trainees and their supervisors to ensure they are continuing to receive a broad range of quality work and that they are developing the required skills and knowledge as they progress through their seats. There are also a number of CSR and pro-bono initiatives that the trainees are encouraged to get involved with.

When and how to apply Online applications to be submitted via our website www.charlesrussellspeechlys.com.

Work placements Our summer placement scheme takes place in each of our UK offices: London, Cheltenham and Guildford, and offers a detailed introduction to the legal world. Each week is spent in a different practice area where you will carry our real fee earning work that could include attending client meetings and going to court. You will have support from trainees and solicitors in each of the teams and have the opportunity to meet a number of different people, either at our organised social events or as part of your day to day interactions.

Sponsorship We undertake to pay impending GDL and/or LPC course fees together with a maintenance grant.

Vacancies	24
Trainees	48
Partners	150
Total staff	1,020
Work placement	yes

Training contract deadline
30 June 2019

Apply
Online via www.
charlesrussellspeechlys.
com

Starting salary
London – £40,000
Guildford – £33,000
Cheltenham – £29,500

Sponsorship
GDL/LPC

Offices
London, Cheltenham, Guildford, Doha, Dubai, Geneva, Hong Kong, Luxembourg, Manama, Paris, Zurich

Proud diversity and inclusion partner of

Remember to cite *The LawCareers.Net Handbook* on your application form if you apply to this firm.

TRAINING CONTRACT DIRECTORY **319**

		V	0
CHENERY MAHER	Small semi-niche firm committed	T	0
21 Church Street, Clithero, Lancs BB7 2DF	to provision of quality professional	P	2
Tel: 01200 422264	services in conveyancing, wills and	TS	11
Email: mail@chenerymaher.co.uk	probate, and family specialisation.	WP	no
Apply to: Mrs N Bradbury			

		V	1
CHHOKAR & CO	Established quality driven West	T	1
29a The Broadway, Southall, Middlesex UB1 1JY	London practice committed to	P	3
Tel: 020 8574 2488	delivering a superior service in	TS	11
Email: law@chhokar.com	property (residential and commercial),	WP	no
Apply to: Mr SS Chhokar	family, wills and probate, immigration and litigation.		

		V	0
CHURCHERS BOLITHO WAY	General practice with specialism	T	2
13-18 Kings Terrace, Portsmouth PO5 3AL	in commercial work (particularly	P	7
Tel: 023 92820747	software licensing). Applications by	TS	22
Apply to: Mr DJ Grinstead	post.	WP	yes

		V	0
CITY AND COUNTY OF SWANSEA	Large, busy local government legal	T	0
Civic Centre, Oystermouth Road, Swansea SA1 3SN	department dealing with litigation, commercial property, planning,	P	0
Tel: 01792 636000	contracts, employment, housing,	TS	46
Email: vivienne.rees@swansea.gov.uk	social services, childcare and	WP	no
Apply to: Legal Services Department	education matters.		

		V	6[20]
CLARION SOLICITORS	Clarion has a reputation regionally,	T	12
Elizabeth House, 13-19 Queen Street, Leeds LS1 2TW	nationally and internationally and it has become renowned for being	P	24
Tel: 0113 246 0622	forward-thinking and commercially	TS	175
Email: hrteam@clarionsolicitors.com	savvy. Clarion offers three key service	WP	yes
Apply to: Mrs Helen Saunders	areas: business services, private client services and recovery and insolvency.		

		V	0
CLARKE & SON SOLICITORS LLP	Established 1862, our goal is to be	T	1
Manor House, 8 Winchester Road, Basingstoke RG21 8UG	the best law firm in Basingstoke. An experienced and dynamic team, our	P	7
Tel: 01256 320555	primary focus is our clients.	TS	37
Email: mail@clarkeandson.co.uk		WP	no
Apply to: Mrs Nia Wharry			

		V	1[19]
CLARKE KIERNAN	Two offices. High street practice	T	1
2-4 Bradford Street, Tonbridge TN1 1DU	offering specialist deparments in	P	2
Tel: 01732 360 999	family and criminal work, growing	TS	27
Email: cmc@clarkekiernan.com	litigation, housing and prison law	WP	no
Apply to: Ms Catherine McCarthy	departments, principally legal aid work.		

		V	TBC
CLARKE WILLMOTT LLP	We are a national law firm with seven	T	15
138 Edmund Street, Birmingham B3 2ES	offices around the UK providing a wide	P	112
Tel: 0345 209 1729	range of legal services to corporate	TS	642
Email: heather.cooper@clarkewillmott.com	clients, organisations and individuals.	WP	no
Apply to: Mrs Heather Cooper			

V = Vacancies / **T** = Trainees / **P** = Partners / **TS** = Total Staff / **WP** = Work Placement

Clifford Chance

10 Upper Bank Street, Canary Wharf, London E14 5JJ
Tel: 020 7006 4005
Email: graduate.recruitment@cliffordchance.com
Web: careers.cliffordchance.com/london
f cliffordchancegrads ✔ ccgradsuk

The firm We are one of the world's pre-eminent law firms, with significant depth and range of resources across five continents. As a single, fully integrated, global partnership, we pride ourselves on our approachable, collegial and team-based way of working. We always strive to exceed the expectations of our clients, which include corporates from all the commercial and industrial sectors, governments, regulators, trade bodies and not-for-profit organisations. We provide them with the highest-quality advice and legal insight, which combines the firm's global standards with in-depth local expertise.

Types of work Our clients look for expert advice and solutions for a host of different commercial issues, which we divide into six key practice areas: corporate; finance; capital markets; real estate; litigation and dispute resolution; and risk management; and tax, pensions and employment.

Who should apply We are looking for individuals with a strong and consistent academic record along with a keen interest in commercial affairs and the law. This is a client-orientated vocation so excellent commnication skills are key. Teamwork, resilience, planning and organisation, problem solving and attention to detail are all vital attributes we are looking for in our applicants.

Training programme Over the course of the 24-month training contract you'll rotate through four of our core areas: finance, corporate, capital markets and one other of your choice. In each seat, you'll have in-depth, sector-specific training, which will bring you up-to-date with the latest trends, ideas and innovations in that area. You'll also have the support of our graduate development team, as well as a dedicated supervisor.

The support doesn't end there either. You'll also have access to not just a legal support manager and a career development partner, but also the award-winning Clifford Chance academy. This acclaimed centre works to develop innovative learning tools and offers exceptional training courses, led by internal and external experts. The academy also holds regular talks with clients, to give you an idea of the wider industry.

We offer client secondments and international seats as part of the training contract subject to business need.

When and how to apply Apply via our website careers.cliffordchance.com/london for training contracts in 2021. All of our applications open on 1 August 2018 – 16 December 2018.

Work placements We are running two first-year schemes and one summer vacation scheme. We will also be hosting open days throughout the year so please visit our website to find out more and how to apply.

Sponsorship Please refer to website for details.

Vacancies	Up to 90
Trainees	200
Partners	570
Total staff	6,115

Work placement yes
(see Insider Report on p75)

Training contract deadline
16 December 2018

Apply
Online

Starting salary
1st year – £46,600
2nd year – £52,500
(September 2018)

Sponsorship
Please refer to website

Offices
Abu Dhabi, Amsterdam, Bangkok, Barcelona, Beijing, Brussels, Bucharest, Casablanca, Dubai, Düsseldorf, Frankfurt, Hong Kong, Istanbul, Jakarta, London, Luxembourg, Madrid, Milan, Moscow, Munich, New York, Paris, Perth, Prague, Rome, São Paulo, Seoul, Shanghai, Singapore, Sydney, Tokyo, Warsaw, Washington DC

C L I F F O R D
C H A N C E

CLARKSLEGAL LLP
One Forbury Square, The Forbury, Reading RG1 3EB
Tel: 0118 958 5321
Email: contact@clarkslegal.com
Apply to: Ms Denise Taylor

Based in Reading and London, a leading commercial practice offering a comprehensive service to a wide range of business clients.

V	2
T	4
P	13
TS	70
WP	no

CLARKSON WRIGHT & JAKES LTD
Valiant House, 12 Knoll Rise, Orpington BR6 0PG
Tel: 01689 887887
Email: hr@cwj.co.uk
Apply to: Ms Jill Lawton

CWJ sees itself as providing capital quality to its clients (corporate, commercial and private client) without the rat race for its staff.

V	0
T	1
P	15
TS	71
WP	no

CLEARY GOTTLIEB STEEN & HAMILTON LLP
City Place House, 2 London Wall Place, London EC2Y 5AU
Tel: 020 7847 6861
Email: lonlegalrecruit@cgsh.com
Apply to: Graduate Recruitment

Cleary Gottlieb is a leading international law firm with 16 closely integrated offices located in major financial and political centres around the world.

V	15-20
T	27
P	193
TS	2500
WP	yes

CLIFFORD HARRIS & CO
58 Queen Anne Street, London W1G 8HW
Tel: 020 7486 0031
Email: sv@cliffordharris.co.uk
Apply to: Mr Sunil Varma

Small West End commercial practice dealing with general litigation, insolvency, conveyancing, and company/commercial work for established corporate and private clients.

V	0
T	1
P	2
TS	8
WP	no

CLINTONS
55 Drury Lane, London WC2B 5RZ
Tel: 020 7379 6080
Email: pnewton@clintons.co.uk
Apply to: Mr Paul Newton

One of the foremost law practices in entertainment, sport and media, with an extensive general practice covering contentious and non-contentious commercial work, family and property.

V	2
T	4
P	21
TS	75
WP	no

CLYDE & CO LLP
The St Botolph Building, 138 Houndsditch, London EC3A 7AR
Tel: 020 7876 5555
Email: graduaterecruitment@clydeco.com
Apply to: Ms Victoria de Jonge

Clyde & Co is a sector-focused global law firm. We advise on a full range of contentious, non-contentious and transactional matters.

V	45-50
T	72
P	415
TS	3800
WP	yes

COCKS LLOYD
Riversley House, Coton Road, Nuneaton, Warwickshire CV11 5TX
Tel: 024 7664 1642
Email: sol@cockslloyd.co.uk
Apply to: Mrs Sharon Wilkinson

Largest firm in Nuneaton/North Warwickshire; all general practice areas covered including some significant commercial work more normally associated with larger 'city' practices.

V	0
T	1
P	5
TS	50
WP	no

COFFIN MEW LLP
1000 Lakeside, North Harbour, Portsmouth PO6 3EN
Tel: 023 9238 8021
Email: careers@coffinmew.co.uk
Apply to: Mrs Jody Nash

A full service firm providing services for individuals and business across the Solent region and beyond, with a strong focus on delivering client service excellence.

V	8
T	15
P	20
TS	220
WP	yes

V = Vacancies / **T** = Trainees / **P** = Partners / **TS** = Total Staff / **WP** = Work Placement

CMS

Cannon Place, 78 Cannon Street, London EC4N 6AF
Tel: 020 7367 3000
Email: grad.rec@cms-cmno.com
Web: www.cms.law
f cmsuk_graduates **𝕐** cmsuk_graduates

The firm With 74 offices in over 42 countries, CMS is a global elite law firm. In 2017, CMS UK, Nabarro LLP and Olswang LLP combined in what was the largest ever merger in the UK legal industry. The new combined firm, CMS, is now the sixth largest in the UK by revenue and the sixth largest globally by headcount.

Types of work Across its six core sectors of energy, financial services, infrastructure and project finance, life sciences and healthcare, real estate and technology, media and communications, CMS has some of the brightest and most creative legal minds. Its lawyers are immersed in the clients' worlds, are genuine experts in their fields and knowledgeable about the issues that lie ahead.

Who should apply Eligibility for our graduate opportunities will vary depending on your year of study; therefore, please visit our website for further details. Our minimum criteria requires candidates to have an ABB at A level (or equivalent) and be on track to achieve/have achieved a 2.1 at degree level (or equivalent). We will take into account mitigating circumstances.

Training programme Prior to starting a training contract, trainees complete a comprehensive induction programme. During the training contract, trainees undertake four six-month seats across various practice areas. There may be the opportunity to be seconded to one of the firm's clients or to a UK or international office. To secure a training contract, candidates will need to successfully complete the CMS academy.

When and how to apply Applications are likely to open in October 2018 and close in early January 2019. Please follow us on social media for further details.

Work placements Our first steps programme offers an introduction to commercial law and working in a global elite law firm. The programme comprises an introduction to CMS, skills sessions and an opportunity to shadow our fee earners. A case study and social events will both enhance your technical skills, interpersonal skills and networking skills. Attending our first steps programme will put you in a strong position to apply for any of our other graduate opportunities. Each student is paid £350 to attend the programme for one week.

The CMS academy is CMS's next generation vacation scheme starting with innovative leadership development training in London. This comprises panel discussions with clients, case studies, work simulation exercises and client visits amongst other things! It is an intense but fully rewarding week where you will experience first-hand the commitment from the firm to make you the best lawyer for the future.

The second part of the programme includes an internship within one of our UK offices. Participants gain real experience in a commercial environment and develop skills needed to succeed as a trainee solicitor at a modern future-facing law firm. A supervisor and buddy will be your main point of contact and will provide high quality work which will give you an accurate insight into the work of a trainee solicitor.

Sponsorship We will sponsor your GDL and LPC for England and Wales qualifying trainees and Diploma in Professional Legal Practice in Scotland.

Vacancies	Approx 65
Trainees	130
Partners	1,000*
Total staff	7,500
	* denotes worldwide figure

Work placement yes

Apply
Online via website

Starting salary
£43,000 (London),
£38,000 (Bristol),
£25,000 (Aberdeen,
Edinburgh and Glasgow),
£27,000 (Sheffield)

Minimum qualifications
ABB at A level and 2.1
degree or equivalent

Sponsorship
GDL/LPC

Offices
London, Bristol, Sheffield,
Aberdeen, Glasgow,
Edinburgh

COHEN DAVIS SOLICITORS
Warlies Park House, Horseshoe Hill, Upshire EN9 3SL
Tel: 020 7183 4123
Email: support@cohendavis.co.uk
Apply to: Mrs Marcia Cohen

Award-winning firm focused on cutting edge social media and internet law. We offer high achievers an exciting opportunity to develop personally and professionally.

V	3[19]
T	1
P	1
TS	4
WP	yes

COLEMANS-CTTS T/A SIMPSON MILLAR
25-29 High Street, Kingston Upon Thames KT1 1LL
Tel: 020 8296 9966
Email: hr@colemans-ctts.co.uk
Apply to: The HR Manager

Colemans-ctts is a progressive and dynamic national law firm. Client relationships and the delivery of high levels of service are the hallmarks of its reputation.

V	0
T	4
P	12
TS	200
WP	no

COLES MILLER
44-46 Parkstone Road, Poole BH15 2PG
Tel: 01202 673011
Email: acormack@coles-miller.co.uk
Apply to: Mr Adrian Cormack

The firm has four offices covering the Bournemouth/Poole conurbation and seeks to provide a wide range of services to both private and commercial clients.

V	3
T	4
P	12
TS	110
WP	yes

COLLAS CRILL
Glategny Court, PO Box 140, Glategny Esplanade, St Peter Port, Guernsey GY1 4EW
Tel: 01481 734278
Email: recruitment@collascrill.com
Apply to: Ms Katherine Mercer

Collas Crill is a leading global offshore firm providing a comprehensive range of services to the international and local finance and business communities, and HNWI.

V	3[19]
T	8
P	33
TS	183
WP	no

COLLINS SOLICITORS
20 Station Road, Watford WD17 1AR
Tel: 01923 223324
Email: collins@collinslaw.co.uk
Apply to: Mrs Lesley Collins

Niche practice specialising in personal injury plus full range of legal services. Situated opposite county court building, adjacent to Watford Junction station, 20 minutes from Euston.

V	0
T	3
P	5
TS	24
WP	no

COLLYER BRISTOW LLP
4 Bedford Row, London WC1R 4TF
Tel: 020 7242 7363
Email: recruitment@collyerbristow.com
Apply to: Mrs Corinne Johnson

Collyer Bristow is based in central London and has 30 partners. The firm has a strong client base in the commercial and private client sectors.

V	4-5
T	8
P	30
TS	140
WP	yes

THE COMMERCIAL LAW PRACTICE
Copper Street, Pulmann Court, Dorchester DT1 1GA
Tel: 01305 544 015
Email: mh@thecommerciallawpractice.com
Apply to: Mrs Marielle Hemingway

The Commercial Law Practice is located in Dorchester specialising in residential and commercial property, business acquisitions, employment law, commercial mediation and other related commercial and corporate work.

V	0
T	2
P	4
TS	11
WP	yes

COMMUNITY LAW CLINIC SOLICITORS
101 Chamberlayne Road, London NW10 3NP
Tel: 020 8960 3200
Email: law@clcsolicitors.co.uk
Apply to: Ms Amrik Bains

Specialists in immigration and social welfare law. Committed to legal aid work dealing with immigration, housing, debt, benefits, welfare benefits employment, family and community care.

V	0
T	2
P	1
TS	24
WP	no

V = Vacancies / **T** = Trainees / **P** = Partners / **TS** = Total Staff / **WP** = Work Placement

Cooley (UK) LLP

Dashwood, 69 Old Broad Street, London EC2M 1QS
Tel: 020 7583 4055
Email: uktrainee@cooley.com
Web: www.cooley.com/uktrainee

The firm Cooley lawyers solve legal issues for entrepreneurs, investors, financial institutions and established companies. Clients partner with Cooley on transformative deals, complex IP and regulatory matters and high-stakes litigation, often where innovation meets the law. Cooley is one of the pre-eminent law firms for technology and life sciences. The firm has 900 lawyers across 13 offices in the US, China and Europe. The firm has received a number of recent accolades; it was named one of *Fortune*'s '100 best places to Work For' in 2015, 2016, 2017 and 2018, as well as being recognised as an elite 'Top-5 Innovative Law Firm' by the *Financial Times*. Cooley opened in London in January 2015 and since has been named London Office of the Year at both the 2017 and 2015 British Legal Awards. Cooley was recognised at the *Legal Week* Innovation Awards for International Law Firm Innovation in 2016 and in 2018 was awarded *The Lawyer*'s International Firm of the Year.

Types of work The UK practice has strengths across many of Cooley's core practice areas, among them corporate/M&A, private equity and venture capital, banking and finance, tax, technology and life sciences transactions, IP, complex high-stakes litigation, international arbitration, insurance and reinsurance, competition, employment, privacy and data protection.

Who should apply To join Cooley you need to be stimulated by solving business and legal challenges. Academic excellence (minimum 2.1 and at least 320 UCAS points or equivalent), great analytical skills and a rigorous approach are essential. You should demonstrate plenty of energy, drive and determination. Your understanding of business and commercial considerations should be of a good standard. You will also be adaptable, capable of thinking on your feet and have developed great communication and interpersonal skills from a variety of situations. Understanding teamwork, evidence of leadership and seeking responsibilities are vital. Interesting achievements and making the most of non-academic and work experience (not necessarily all legal) opportunities will help applicants stand-out.

Training programme The Cooley training experience will revolve around small groups of trainees and really hands-on involvement. We truly believe in learning by doing. Trainees spend four six-month periods in some of the firm's contentious and non-contentious corporate/transactional and litigation areas. Trainees give preferences for seats and there may also be opportunities for client secondments from time to time. The focus is on your development as a truly commercial lawyer. Supplementing your hands-on learning will be a programme designed to increase your knowledge and skill for the work Cooley does. You'll also develop your finance, marketing and commercial understanding. Practice group programmes and firm-wide opportunities will enhance this. Working alongside and learning from some of the best lawyers in their fields will give you a fantastic start to your professional life. A multilevel support network of partners, mentors and a buddy system ensures you have a targeted level of guidance.

When and how to apply The summer placement scheme is the route into being considered for a training place. Apply online by 31 January 2019.

Work placements Two structured two-week placements for eight (two groups of four) students. These will take place in June 2019 and July 2019.

Sponsorship Course fees and a living allowance while studying: £8,000 pa if studying in London, £7,500 outside London.

Vacancies	4
Trainees	8
Partners	28
Total staff	180

Work placement yes

Apply
Online

Starting salary
£46,000

Minimum qualifications
2.1 degree, at least ABB at A level (not including general studies) or equivalent

Sponsorship
GDL/LPC

Offices
Beijing, Boston, Colorado, London, Los Angeles, New York, Palo Alto, Reston, San Diego, San Francisco, Seattle, Shanghai, Washington DC

Covington & Burling LLP

265 Strand, London WC2R 1BH
Tel: 020 7067 2000
Email: graduate@cov.com
Web: www.cov.com/en/careers/lawyers/london-graduate-recruitment-programme
🐦 covingtonllp

The firm Covington & Burling LLP was founded in Washington DC nearly a century ago. Today, the firm has over 1,000 lawyers globally across offices in Beijing, Brussels, Dubai, Frankfurt, Johannesburg, London, Los Angeles, New York, San Francisco, Seoul, Shanghai, Silicon Valley and Washington DC. Covington's London office, overlooking the Royal Courts of Justice, was established 30 years ago. We offer services across a wide range of practice areas, advising clients on their most challenging and complex matters. Most of the work has an international element, and all our practice groups operate across borders. Covington has been rated a Top Ranked Leading Law Firm in *Chambers UK 2018* and appears in *The Lawyer* Top 30 International Law Firm, as well as Legal Business Global 100 surveys. At Covington, you will have an opportunity to work on cutting-edge deals for international and UK corporates such as Microsoft, Astra Zeneca and Facebook, *Fortune 100* businesses and leading technology, life sciences and media companies.

Types of work Corporate advisory (including capital markets, M&A, finance, private equity, venture capital and funds), commercial litigation, data privacy, employment, financial services, insurance coverage disputes, intellectual property, internal investigations and compliance, international arbitration, life sciences, project and finance, tax, technology and media. As a trainee you will receive work assignments designed to develop your skills and will get the support and training to excel in your work. In addition, all our lawyers, including trainees, are encouraged to undertake pro bono work.

Who should apply We are looking for candidates with consistently high academic results (on target for a 2.1 degree or above and with strong A-level results), commercial awareness, strong interpersonal skills and the ability to work well in a team.

Training programme You will do four six-month seats, rotating between departments. All trainees will undertake a seat in corporate and a seat in dispute resolution. We offer optional seats in employment, life sciences, project and finance, technology and media and client secondments may also be available. We aim to distinguish our trainee programme by offering a genuine support network which includes assigning associate buddies and undertaking regular performance reviews. We have an excellent record of retaining trainees on qualification and we aim to recruit trainees who are interested in making a long term commitment to the firm.

When and how to apply Please submit an application form via the online application system, the details of which can be found on our website. Please apply by 12 July 2019.

Work placements Each year we offer up to 10 summer placements on each of our two-week programmes. Participants sit with a senior lawyer and will be given as much hands-on experience as possible. Students will spend each of their two weeks in a different practice area and will be given as much hands-on experience as possible. They will also get involved in a research project, participate in group activities and attend a series of presentations. We also organise a number of social events so that students can have some fun and get to know us.

Sponsorship Successful training contract applicants will receive payment of tuition fees for both the GDL and the LPC, as well as a maintenance grant of £8,000.

Vacancies	8
Trainees	16
Partners	283
Work placement	yes

Training contract deadline
12 July 2019

Apply
Online

Starting salary
1st year – £43,000
2nd year – £47,000
NQ – £95,000

Minimum qualifications
2.1 degree

Sponsorship
GDL/LPC

Offices
Beijing, Brussels, Dubai, Frankfurt, Johannesburg, Los Angeles, New York, San Francisco, Seoul, Shanghai, Silicon Valley, Washington DC

COVINGTON

CONRAD KING & SOLOMON SOLICITORS 836-840 Leeds Road, Bradford BD3 9TX **Tel:** 01274 656 465 **Email:** info@nursolicitors.com **Apply to:** Mr Adam Green	A young and energetic practice with an established reputation for providing excellent client care and specialist advice in civil litigation, education, immigration, business and commercial, property, and wills and probate.	V 2 T 0 P 1 TS 6 WP yes
CORRIES SOLICITORS LTD 1st Floor, Rowntree Wharf, Navigation Road, York YO1 9WE **Tel:** 0845 241 5566 **Email:** sarah.haskins@corries.co.uk **Apply to:** Mrs Kerry Stojanovic	Corries is a modern and progressive law firm, specialising in personal injury claims, asbestos claims, criminal injuries and medical negligence.	V 0 T 2 P 2 TS 47 WP no
COTTERHILL HITCHMAN LLP Atlas House, 4-6 Belwell Lane, Sutton Coldfield B74 4AB **Tel:** 0121 323 1860 **Email:** mail@cotterhillhitchman.co.uk **Apply to:** Ms Saima Zulfiqar	Small niche firm. Mainly commercial, private client, litigation, and employment work.	V 0 T 1 P 3 TS 15 WP no
COVENTRY CITY COUNCIL Legal Services, Council House, Coventry CV1 5RR **Tel:** 024 76833000 **Email:** customer.services@coventry.gov.uk **Apply to:** Legal Services Management Team	Legal Services is an in-house legal team supporting all Coventry City Council services as well as providing support for both local authority and academy schools.	V 0 T 1 P 0 TS 52 WP no
COWANS SOLICITORS LLP 114 South Street, Dorking RH4 2EW **Tel:** 01306 886622 **Email:** enquiries@cowansdorking.co.uk **Apply to:** Miss Sarah Delahunty	General practice including litigation, family and matrimonial, crime, conveyancing, and wills and probate. Committed to legally aided work. No set recruitment schedule for trainees or paralegals.	V 0 T 2 P 2 TS 25 WP no
COWLISHAW & MOUNTFORD 90 High Street, Uttoxeter ST14 7JD **Tel:** 01889 565211 **Apply to:** Mr Paul Hopkins	General practice in a country town with a mix of private and franchised legal aid work.	V 0 T 0 P 1 TS 10 WP no
COZENS-HARDY LLP Castle Chambers, Opie Street, Norwich NR1 3DP **Tel:** 01603 625231 **Email:** celinsdell@cozens-hardy.com **Apply to:** Mrs Caroline Linsdell		V 1[19] T 2 P 13 TS 70 WP no
CRIPPS LLP Number 22, Mount Ephraim, Tunbridge Wells TN4 8AS **Tel:** 01892 515121 **Email:** graduates@cripps.co.uk **Apply to:** Mrs Katie Slade	A key regional law firm serving clients nationally and internationally from offices in Kent and London. Recognised countrywide for commercial, private client and property work.	V 7 T 14 P 51 TS 360 WP yes

V = Vacancies / **T** = Trainees / **P** = Partners / **TS** = Total Staff / **WP** = Work Placement

CROCKETT & CO 260 Harehills Lane, Leeds LS9 7BD **Tel:** 0113 226 0111 **Email:** info@crockettsolicitors.co.uk **Apply to:** Miss H Crockett	Lexcel accredited specialist family law firm dealing in contact, care, divorce, domestic violence and other niche legal work.	V T P TS WP	0 2 2 8 no
CROSSE & CROSSE 14 Southernhay West, Exeter EX1 1PL **Tel:** 01392 258451 **Apply to:** Mr TP Selley	Well established (1915) firm dealing with all main areas of work. Legal aid franchise. Specialises in personal injury, civil and family.	V T P TS WP	0 2 8 56 no
CROWN PROSECUTION SERVICE CPS HQ - Petty France, 102 Petty France, Westminster, London SW1H 9AJ **Tel:** 0151 213 5017 **Email:** strategic.resourcing@cps.gov.uk **Apply to:** Miss Emily Miller	The CPS recruits pupil barristers and trainee solicitors across England and Wales with permanent Crown Prosecutor posts available upon successful qualification.	V T P TS WP	1[19] 30 2315 6051 no
CUMBRIA LAW CENTRE 8 Spencer Street, Carlisle, Cumbria CA1 1BG **Tel:** 01228 515 129 **Email:** reception@comlaw.co.uk **Apply to:** Ms Claire Burton	Cumbria's law centre, free specialist practice in housing, employment, welfare benefits and debt; also human rights and anti-discrimination.	V T P TS WP	0 1 0 13 no
CUNNINGTONS Great Square, Braintree CM7 1UD **Tel:** 013 7632 6868 **Email:** info@cunningtons.co.uk **Apply to:** Mr Aaron Coombs	Cunningtons have over 260 years legal experience with branches nationwide. We offer a complete range of legal services including: residential and commercial conveyancing, family law, wills, trusts, probate, civil litigation and employment.	V T P TS WP	Varies 0 9 60 yes
CURTIS LAW SOLICITORS LLP Witton Chambers, Witton Business Park, Cartmel Road, Blackburn BB2 2TA **Tel:** 01254 297 130 **Email:** info@curtislaw.co.uk **Apply to:** Miss T Riaz	We are a dynamic rapidly growing legal practice with a strong client base and a large spectrum of specialist areas.	V T P TS WP	8 2 4 115 yes
CURTIS MALLET-PREVOST COLT & MOSLE LLP 99 Gresham Street, London EC2V 7NG **Tel:** 020 7710 9800 **Email:** recruitmentlondon@curtis.com **Apply to:** Tuula Davis	US-headquartered firm with 17 offices worldwide. London specialises in international arbitration and corporate/commercial, and provides the ideal balance between friendly local office and varied international work.	V T P TS WP	2[19] 3 7 14 no
CURWENS LLP Crossfield House, Gladbeck Way, Enfield EN2 7HT **Tel:** 020 8363 4444 **Email:** enfield@curwens.co.uk **Apply to:** Ms Lisa Dearman	'Mini-regional' firm covering Hertfordshire and North London. A general practice also having particular strengths in litigation, employment, and company/commercial work.	V T P TS WP	2[19] 5 15 90 no

V = Vacancies / **T** = Trainees / **P** = Partners / **TS** = Total Staff / **WP** = Work Placement

DAC Beachcroft LLP

100 Fetter Lane, London EC4A 1BN
Tel: 020 7242 1011
Email: trainee@dacbeachcroft.com
Web: www.dacbeachcroft.com
🐦 dacbeachcroft

The firm DAC Beachcroft is a leading international legal business with more than 2,300 plus employees and coverage across the UK, Europe, Asia-Pacific, Latin America and North America. Our flexible approach to resourcing enables us to apply the right mix of legal, commercial and process skills to deliver the right outcome at the right price, depending on our clients' individual needs. In addition to this we believe in developing our employees have been awarded with the investors in people gold award. We are a legal business who have extensive knowledge of the markets and sectors in which we operate. We are particularly adept at reducing difficult issues of law and fact to comprehensible and manageable proportions and producing commercial solutions which facilitate our clients business strategies. We have evolved from being a domestic law firm to become a global legal business with a growing footprint in various countries. Our objective is to align ourselves to where our clients need us to be.

Types of work We ensure that all our graduates have the opportunity to grow their client skills early in their career by providing them with access to clients in each part of the business you train within. This might include attending client meetings, participating in tenders and managing their own caseloads.

Who should apply Prospective trainees must typically have:a minimum of 120 UCAS points* (or equivalent), a 2.1 degree classification, and – because we recruit one year in advance – you must be in the final year of your law degree or be completing your GDL currently. *New tariff UCAS points for entry to higher education from 2017

Training programme Our learning and development programme includes four six-month seats across a range of specialised disciplines growing and developing technical knowledge. Alongside we provide a range of activities and opportunities to grow great business and client skills. This is achieved through offering a range of engaging activities, on the job learning and contact and interaction with our clients. We are committed to ensuring that our programme will bring out the best in our trainees, equipping them for a successful career here with us as DAC Beachcroft.

When and how to apply The application process for training contracts commencing in September 2020 is open from the 1 November 2018 until the 31 January 2019. DAC Beachcroft runs a combined application process, with the vacation scheme forming part of the assessment process for training contract places. Successful online applicants will be invited to a half-day assessment centre in order to be selected for a place on the vacation scheme. To find out more, and apply for the 2020 intake once the application window opens, please visit the DAC Beachcroft job site www.dacbeachcroft.com/en/gb/about/careers/where-you-fit-in/trainee-solicitors/becoming-a-trainee-with-us. If you have any questions about the recruitment process, please contact trainee@dacbeachcroft.com.

Work placements A vacation scheme at DAC Beachcroft forms part of the training contract assessment process. During the vacation scheme candidates have the opportunity to experience the typical work our trainees are involved with as well as learn more about our business and clients. There are plenty of opportunities for candidates to meet with colleagues at all levels, as well as existing trainees, to get a true sense of life working at DAC Beachcroft.

Sponsorship We fully fund the LPC with the BPP.

Vacancies	13
Trainees	29
Partners	240
Total staff	2,300

Work placement   yes

Apply
Online

Minimum qualifications
2.1 degree

Sponsorship
LPC

Offices
Bristol, Leeds, London, Manchester, Newcastle, Newport

DACbeachcroft

Proud diversity and inclusion partner of

 aspiringsolicitors

CURZON GREEN SOLICITORS 114-116 Oxford Road, High Wycombe, Buckinghamshire HP11 2DN **Tel:** 01494 451355 **Email:** training@curzongreen.co.uk **Apply to:** Miss Jennifer Sole	Curzon Green Solicitors offer our trainees a supporting environment to develop their careers. Both trainee positions will be based at our Buckinghamshire office in 2019	V 2^{19} T 4 P 3 TS 22 WP yes
CYRIL JONES & CO 17 Egerton Street, Wrexham LL11 1NB **Tel:** 01978 367 830 **Apply to:** Mr Gareth Jones	Small general practice in North Wales, varied workload covering most areas of law, mainly conveyancing, family and probate and PI. Legal aid franchise.	V 0 T 2 P 5 TS 20 WP no
DAKERS MARRIOTT SOLICITORS Quayside Chambers, 353-357 High Street, Rochester ME1 1DA **Tel:** 01634 813 300 **Email:** mail@dakersmarriott.co.uk **Apply to:** Mr Mark Marriott	A city practice in the provinces. We are a very busy practice where quality advice is available.	V 0 T 0 P 3 TS 12 WP no
DARLINGTON BOROUGH COUNCIL Feethams, Darlington, County Durham DL1 5QT **Tel:** 01325 405490 **Email:** luke.swinhoe@darlington.gov.uk **Apply to:** Mr Luke Swinhoe	Local authority. Have previously had trainees but do not have trainee currently as post deleted.	V 0 T 0 P - TS 19 WP no
DARLINGTONS Darlingtons House, 7 Spring Villa Park, Edgware HA8 7EB **Tel:** 020 8951 6666 **Email:** sakers@darlingtons.com **Apply to:** Mr Stephen Akers		V 1 T 2 P 6 TS 42 WP yes
DARWIN GRAY LLP Helmont House, Churchill Way, Cardiff CF10 2HE **Tel:** 029 2082 9100 **Email:** sthompson@darwingray.com **Apply to:** Mr SP Thompson	Darwin Gray is a full service commercial practice specialising in the following areas: commercial property, litigation, employment, commercial, company law, franchising and insolvency.	V 0 T 2 P 7 TS 22 WP no
DAVID & SNAPE Old Castle Offices, South Street, Bridgend CF31 3ED **Tel:** 01656 661115 **Email:** sue.smith@davidandsnape.com **Apply to:** Ms Susan Smith	A busy, friendly and progressive high street firm with membership of several law society panels and a legal services commission franchise.	V 0 T 0 P 4 TS 26 WP no
DAVID GRAY SOLICITORS LLP Old County Court, 56 Westgate Road, Newcastle Upon Tyne NE1 5XU **Tel:** 0191 232 9547 **Email:** recruitment@davidgray.co.uk **Apply to:** Ms Debora Sanderson	Private work and LAA contracted firm. Working within crime, family, immigration, commercial and residential conveyancing, wills/ probate, elderly client care and mental health.	V 0 T 4 P 9 TS 67 WP no

V = Vacancies / **T** = Trainees / **P** = Partners / **TS** = Total Staff / **WP** = Work Placement

Davis Polk & Wardwell London LLP

5 Aldermanbury Square, London EC2V 7HR
Tel: 020 7418 1300
Email: londonrecruiting@davispolk.com
Web: careers.davispolk.com/training-london

The firm Davis Polk is a global law firm. For more than 165 years, Davis Polk has ranked among the premier law firms with practices that are world class across the board. Today, with 10 offices strategically located in key locations around the globe, New York, Northern California, Washington DC, São Paulo, London, Paris, Madrid, Hong Kong, Beijing and Tokyo, Davis Polk remains one of the small handful of firms that leading companies and financial institutions turn to on their most significant and complex legal matters. Davis Polk lawyers collaborate seamlessly across practice groups and geographies to provide our clients with exceptional service. Our extensive cross-border experience coupled with the diversity of our professionals and top local law capabilities allow us to bridge business, cultural, language, legal and regulatory differences across jurisdictions.

Types of work Our London-based team of over 60 lawyers regularly advise on high profile, cross-border capital markets, M&A, and finance and restructuring transactions. Our highly ranked tax, financial regulatory and antitrust lawyers collaborate closely with our corporate and finance teams to provide innovative strategies for our clients. As a globally diverse team many of our lawyers are dual-qualified with extensive language skills and hail from countries around the world.

Who should apply We seek to hire applicants from a variety of backgrounds with outstanding academic and non-academic achievements, personal skills and creativity, and with a demonstrated willingness to take initiative. We strive to find exceptional lawyers who share our commitment to excellence and who will be collaborative and supportive colleagues.

Training programme Trainees will undertake a number of rotations through our corporate, credit and specialist practice areas, providing each trainee with the variety of experiences necessary to lay the foundation for a successful legal career.

Davis Polk trainees will also have the opportunity to experience a six-month secondment to our New York office.

Our training partner mentors each trainee and provides advice and guidance throughout the program.

Starting salary of £55,000 (rising to £60,000 after a year), with a full benefits package, including 25 days' holiday and full LPC sponsorship.

When and how to apply Please visit our website at careers.davispolk.com/training-london for information on how to apply. Please note that we will be recruiting our 2021 intake of trainees directly from our Summer 2019 vacation schemes.

Work placements Please visit our website at careers.davispolk.com/training-london for information on how to apply for a place on Davis Polk's 2019 summer vacation scheme. We will accept applications from 1 December 2018 through to 13 January 2019.

Sponsorship GDL and LPC fees and maintenance grants are paid.

Vacancies	Approx 4
Trainees	7
Partners	8
Total staff	90
Work placement	yes

Apply
Online at
careers.davispolk.com

Starting salary
1st year – £55,000
2nd year – £60,000

Minimum qualifications
2.1 degree or higher

Sponsorship
GDL/LPC

Offices
10 offices across 8 countries

DAVID PHILLIPS & PARTNERS 202 Stanley Road, Bootle L20 3EP **Tel:** 0151 922 5525 **Apply to:** Mrs Susan Christopher	London office deals with high profile criminal cases. Bootle office is a general practice with an emphasis on legal aid work both criminal and civil.	**V** 0 **T** 3 **P** 15 **TS** 75 **WP** yes
DAVIES AND PARTNERS Rowan House, Barnett Way, Barnwood, Gloucester GL4 3RT **Tel:** 01452 612345 **Email:** recruitment@daviesandpartners.com **Apply to:** Ms Suzanne Williams	Regional commercial practice with an emphasis on heavyweight property law, clinical negligence and commercial litigation. Integrated offices in Bristol, Gloucester, Birmingham and London.	**V** 1[19] **T** 9 **P** 12 **TS** 170 **WP** no
DAVIES JOHNSON Old Harbour Office, Guy's Quay, Sutton Harbour, Plymouth PL4 0ES **Tel:** 01752 226020 **Email:** info@daviesjohnson.com **Apply to:** Mr Charles Patterson	Specialist shipping and commercial practice.	**V** 0 **T** 0 **P** 0 **TS** 26 **WP** no
DAVIS & CO St Michaels Rectory, St Michaels Alley, Cornhill, London EC3V 9DS **Tel:** 020 7621 1091 **Email:** trevor.davis@davis-solicitors.com **Apply to:** Mr Trevor Davis	Niche City firm specialising in utilities litigation with blue-chip client base. Candidates should have a good academic background and have an interest in advocacy.	**V** 0 **T** 0 **P** 1 **TS** 2 **WP** no
DAVIS BLANK FURNISS LLP 90 Deansgate, Manchester M3 2QJ **Tel:** 0161 832 3304 **Email:** carole.burleigh@dbf-law.co.uk **Apply to:** Mrs Carole Burleigh	While having a successful corporate and business department, the firm is firmly committed to retaining private client work. Training in a wide range of work.	**V** 2 **T** 4 **P** 10 **TS** 60 **WP** no
DAWSON CORNWELL 15 Red Lion Square, London WC1R 4QT **Tel:** 020 7242 2556 **Email:** mail@dawsoncornwell.com **Apply to:** Ms Helen Kings	A specialist family law firm, described in *Chambers 2018* as "a leader in the field, not just nationally but internationally".	**V** 1[20] **T** 5 **P** 10 **TS** 54 **WP** yes
DAWSON HART The Old Grammar School, Church Street, Uckfield TN22 1BH **Tel:** 01825 762281 **Email:** info@dawson-hart.co.uk **Apply to:** Mr Trevor Mersh	We invest valuable time with our trainees and aim to offer them a career with us, assisting them through all stages up to partnership level.	**V** 0 **T** - **P** 7 **TS** 42 **WP** no
DAYBELLS LLP 43-45 Broadway, Stratford, London E15 4BL **Tel:** 020 8555 4321 **Email:** info@daybells.com **Apply to:** Mr Qaiser Malik	We are an established local practice with specific emphasis on client care. The firm has developed a niche in residential and commercial conveyancing.	**V** 1[20] **T** 1 **P** 3 **TS** 10 **WP** yes

V = Vacancies / **T** = Trainees / **P** = Partners / **TS** = Total Staff / **WP** = Work Placement

Debevoise & Plimpton LLP

65 Gresham Street, London EC2V 7NQ
Tel: 020 7786 9000
Web: www.debevoise.com

The firm Debevoise & Plimpton LLP is a leading international law firm with offices in New York, Washington DC, London, Paris, Frankfurt, Moscow, Hong Kong, Shanghai and Tokyo. The London office works on many of the highest profile and most complex transactions in Europe and worldwide. We do this by virtue of our English and New York law expertise and our close integration with our other offices.

Types of work In developing our practice in London, we have sought to replicate the core strengths of our practice worldwide. Our focus is on private equity, insurance, international disputes and investigations, financial institutions, M&A, finance, capital markets and tax.

Clients include: AIA Group Limited, Alta One Capital, American International Group, Baring Vostok, The Carlyle Group, Clayton, DH Equity Partners, Clayton Dubilier & Rice, Deutsche Bank, Global Infrastructure Partners, HarbourVest Partners, Helios Investment Partners, Interros, Metric Capital, Morgan Stanley, Norilsk Nickel, Oaktree Capital Management, Park Square Capital Partners, Polyus Gold, Rexel, Stone Point Capital, Tishman Speyer, Triton and Uralkali.

Who should apply We look for students whose personal qualities, academic records and other achievements demonstrate exceptional ability, motivation and potential for growth. The training contract is open to both law and non-law graduates. We are looking for individuals who have consistently high levels of achievements both at A level (or equivalent) and at university. Applicants should be expecting to achieve at least a 2.1 in any degree discipline and have a minimum of 360 UCAS points at A level (or equivalent).

Training programme One of Debevoise's basic principles is that each of our associates should become a 'well rounded' lawyer – an effective counsellor, advisor, and advocate – who can combine specific legal knowledge with the ability to deal with a broad range of situations. We believe that lawyers best develop their skills through a combination of formal training and on-the-job experience, in a respectful and collegial environment. The two years are split into four six-month seats and trainees have the opportunity to gain experience in at least three distinct areas of law.

When and how to apply Apply online between 1 October 2018 and 11 November 2018 for spring and summer vacation schemes in 2019, and between 1 June 2019 and 15 July 2019 for training contracts beginning in September 2021. An online application form will be available on our website during these times. Anyone interested in a training contract with Debevoise is strongly encouraged to apply for a vacation scheme place.

Work placements Debevoise offers two-week vacation schemes which run in the spring and summer each year. Applications for 2019 can be made between 1 October 2018 and 11 November 2018.

Sponsorship Full tuition fees are paid for GDL and LPC, together with a maintenance grant of £9,000 per year.

Vacancies	8
Trainees	16
Partners	21
Total staff	213

Work placement yes

Training contract deadline
15 July 2019

Apply
Online

Starting salary
1st year – £50,000
2nd year – £55,000

Minimum qualifications
2.1 degree

Sponsorship
GDL/LPC plus a maintenance grant of £9,000

Offices
New York, Washington DC, London, Paris, Frankfurt, Moscow, Hong Kong, Shanghai, Tokyo

Debevoise
&Plimpton

Dechert LLP

160 Queen Victoria Street, London EC4V 4QQ
Tel: 020 7184 7000
Email: graduate.recruitment@dechert.com
Web: www.dechert.com/careers
f dechertllp **𝕏** dechertllp

The firm Dechert is a global law firm. We deliver deep legal expertise and practical commercial judgment for high-stakes matters in sectors with the greatest complexities, intricacies and regulatory demands.

Types of work Our lawyers in London are active in all Dechert's core practice areas of corporate and securities, financial services and investment management, finance and real estate, white collar defence, complex commercial litigation, international arbitration and intellectual property, as well as financial restructuring, employment, international trade and EU government affairs, EU and UK competition and tax.

Who should apply The first step to securing a training contract is to attend a vacation scheme. We offer places on our spring scheme primarily to all final-year undergraduates (both law and non-law), all graduates and postgraduates, and we offer places on our summer scheme primarily to penultimate-year law undergraduates.

Training programme We recruit up to 10 trainee solicitors each year. We have recruited and continue to recruit excellent trainees from all academic backgrounds. Our commitment to your development is reflected in our highly personalised six-seat rotation system. We believe that by allowing you to experience up to six different practice areas during your two-year training, we can help you learn more and give you a sound base for your future career. We work hard to ensure that each seat is right for you as your experience and interests develop. You can also choose to repeat a seat if you are enjoying the work and want to get to know the practice area better. However, we know that the most important training is that which goes on every day, with your supervisor guiding your work and providing you help and feedback. So, in each seat, you will sit with an experienced lawyer, chosen because of their interest and skill in training. You will receive mid and end-of-seat appraisals, including regular reviews with the partner responsible for your development. Your professional development is monitored on a regular basis by the graduate recruitment and trainee development Team, as well as your personal 'panel' partner, all of whom are available to help with any concerns that you may have from time to time.

When and how to apply Please refer to our website, www.dechert.com/careers for scheme dates, deadlines and the application form.

Work placements In 2019, we will be running two vacation schemes. Our two-week vacation schemes are designed to give you an idea of what it will be like to be a trainee solicitor at Dechert: each week you will sit in a different practice group and you are given real work to do by lawyers. Exactly what you will do will depend on which practice groups you sit in, but your work load will most likely include research, drafting and attending meetings. You will also attend training sessions on a range of topics, such as legal writing and negotiation. Sports and social events are an important part of the vacation schemes as they enable you to get to know each other and our people better.

Sponsorship We pay our future trainees' GDL and LPC fees if they accept the training contract offer before they begin the course. We ask all of our future trainees to complete these courses at BPP. In addition to course/tuition fees, we pay future trainees £10,000 per year when they undertake the full-time GDL or LPC. This is paid in two equal instalments of £5,000 in September and January.

Vacancies	10
Trainees	20
Partners	312
Total staff	2,295

Work placement yes
(see Insider Report on p77)

Apply
Online

Minimum qualifications
2.1 degree

Sponsorship
GDL/LPC

Offices
London

Proud diversity and inclusion partner of

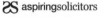

DE MARCO SOLICITORS 1 Generator Hall, Electric Wharf, Sandy Lane, Coventry CV1 4JL **Tel:** 024 7699 8055 **Email:** enquiries@demarcosolicitors.com **Apply to:** Miss Sandra Garlick	De Marco Solicitors is niche *Legal 500* firm specialising in employment and company/commercial law. No current vacancies.	V 0 T 0 P 1 TS 12 WP yes
DEAN MANSON LLP - SOLICITORS 243 Mitcham Road, Tooting, London SW17 9JQ **Tel:** 020 8767 5000 **Email:** info@deanmanson.com **Apply to:** Mr Ejaz Baig	Applications are invited for four prospective trainees under apprentice scheme each with language skills in Polish, Tamil, Arabic and Hindi.	V 4 T 2 P 2 TS 10 WP yes
DEAN SOLICITORS 123 Drake Street, Rochdale, Lancashire OL16 1PZ **Tel:** 01706 661400 **Email:** info@deansolicitors.co.uk **Apply to:** Mr M Din	General practice with LEXCEL accreditation specialising in personal injury, conveyancing and immigration.	V 0 T 2 P 2 TS 9 WP no
DEAN WILSON LLP Ridgeland House, 165 Dyke Road, Brighton BN3 1TL **Tel:** 01273 249200 **Email:** jbh@deanwilson.co.uk **Apply to:** Mr Julian Hunt	An award-winning firm with a national reputation for property, landlord and tenant and employment law; solicitors to various national associations; family, probate.	V 2²⁰ T 2 P 13 TS 76 WP no
DEBENHAMS OTTAWAY LLP Ivy House, 107 St Peters Street, St Albans AL1 3EW **Tel:** 01727 837 161 **Email:** recruitment@debenhamsottaway.co.uk **Apply to:** Mrs Alexandra Langley	Regional practice with specialist teams dealing with private client, family, employment, dispute resolution, commercial and residential property, company commercial and corporate matters.	V 0 T 3 P 11 TS 120 WP no
DEBIDINS 6 Broadway, London W13 0SR **Tel:** 020 8567 6343 **Email:** info@debidins.co.uk **Apply to:** Mr D Debidins	General high street pratice of long-standing with full range of legal service. No legal aid franchise.	V 0 T 0 P 2 TS 4 WP no
DENBY & CO 119 Duke Street, Barrow-In-Furness LA14 1XE **Tel:** 01229 822366 **Email:** info@denbyco.co.uk **Apply to:** Mr John H Denby	Franchised high street general practice. Offices in Barrow and Ulverston. Personal injury, family, crime, conveyancing and probate.	V 1 T 1 P 5 TS 26 WP no
DENTONS One Fleet Place, London EC4M 7WS **Tel:** 020 7320 3751 **Email:** graduaterecruitment@dentons.com **Apply to:** Miss Alexandra Mundy	Global commercial law firm specialising in: banking and finance; corporate; dispute resolution; energy and infrastructure; EU and competition; real estate; tax; TMT.	V 50 T 90 P 2892 TS 10455 WP yes

V = Vacancies / **T** = Trainees / **P** = Partners / **TS** = Total Staff / **WP** = Work Placement

DEREK B FORREST SOLICITORS 71 Hough Lane, Leyland PR25 2SA **Tel:** 01772 424999 **Email:** derek@solicitordirect.com **Apply to:** Mr Derek Forrest	A high street solicitor and estate agent working nationwide over phone and internet. Heavily computerised without secretaries.	**V** 0 **T** 1 **P** 2 **TS** 8 **WP** no
DEVON & CORNWALL CONSTABULARY Middlemoor, Exeter EX2 7HQ **Tel:** 0139 2452863 **Apply to:** Mr Brent Davision	The force's legal services provide legal support for the chief constable of Devon and Cornwall constabulary across a number of disciplines. Mainly litigious work.	**V** 0 **T** 1 **P** 1 **TS** 12 **WP** no
DEVONSHIRES SOLICITORS 30 Finsbury Circus, London EC2M 7DT **Tel:** 020 7628 7576 **Email:** trainee.recruit@devonshires.co.uk **Apply to:** Ms Katy Perry	Leading City firm with an established reputation for delivering a personal and bespoke service to both public and private sector organisations.	**V** 6[20] **T** 12 **P** 35 **TS** 240 **WP** no
DEXTER MONTAGUE LLP 105 Oxford Road, Reading RG1 7UD **Tel:** 0118 939 3999 **Email:** info@dextermontague.co.uk **Apply to:** Mr William Montague	DMP is a medium-sized Thames Valley practice specialising in property, business/commercial, private client, family, and civil litigation, including PI, employment and housing. LSC contracts in family and housing.	**V** 1[20] **T** 1 **P** 4 **TS** 24 **WP** yes
DF LEGAL LLP 62/63 High Street, Tewksbury, Gloucestershire GL20 5BJ **Tel:** 01684 850 750 **Apply to:** Mr JG Daniels	Expanding forward-looking private practice with specialisms in interesting areas of work.	**V** 2 **T** 4 **P** 3 **TS** 24 **WP** yes
DH LAW SOLICITORS LTD 130-132 Uxbridge Road, Hanwell, London W7 3SL **Tel:** 020 8840 8008 **Email:** rheian@dhlaw.org.uk **Apply to:** Ms Rheian Davies	An award-winning firm. We hold legal aid franchises in mental health, housing, family and community care.	**V** 0 **T** 2 **P** 1 **TS** 10 **WP** yes
DLA PIPER UK LLP 3 Noble Street, London EC2V 7EE **Tel:** 08700 111 111 **Email:** graduaterecruitment@dlapiper.com **Apply to:** Graduate Recruitment	DLA Piper is a leading global business law firm. With over 90 offices in more than 40 countries, we provide seamless local and cross-border advice.	**V** Up to 70 **T** 150 **P** 1300 **TS** 8500 **WP** yes
DMA LAW 56 Duke Street, Darlington DL3 7AN **Tel:** 01325 482299 **Email:** enquiries@dma-law.co.uk **Apply to:** Mr John Relton	The firm offers a friendly yet challenging environment. Career development is taken seriously. Donnelly Adamson sets high standards wihin the profession and expects nothing less.	**V** 0 **T** 0 **P** 5 **TS** 34 **WP** no

V = Vacancies / **T** = Trainees / **P** = Partners / **TS** = Total Staff / **WP** = Work Placement

DMH STALLARD LLP Gainsborough House, Pegler Way, Crawley RH11 7FZ **Tel:** 01293 605067 **Email:** recruitment@dmhstallard.com **Apply to:** Graduate Recruitment	DMH Stallard LLP is an innovative and progressive firm that seeks opportunities to stand out from the crowd.	V T P TS WP	0 4 59 259 yes
DOLMANS SOLICITORS One Kingsway, Cardiff CF10 3DS **Tel:** 029 2034 5531 **Email:** philipb@dolmans.co.uk **Apply to:** Ms Clare Hoskins	Specialist public sector and insurance litigation practice. Dynamic business services including corporate finance, commercial, property, sports law, employment and dispute resolution. Established private client department.	V T P TS WP	0 - 9 39 no
DONALD RACE & NEWTON 5/7 Hargreaves Street, Burnley BB11 1EA **Tel:** 01282 864500 **Apply to:** Mr David Rogers	Burnley-based, three-office general practice specialising in crime, family and personal injury with commercial and domestic conveyancing. LSC contract. Please note that we do not currently have any vacancies.	V T P TS WP	0 2 6 47 yes
DORSEY 199 Bishopsgate, London EC2M 3UT **Tel:** 020 7031 3700 **Email:** london@dorsey.com **Apply to:** Ms Roselynne Atkins	The London office has over 30 lawyers and trainees and continues to build on its strengths in corporate law, litigation, corporate tax, property and IP.	V T P TS WP	2 3 14 45 no
DOUGLAS-JONES MERCER 16 Axis Court, Mallard Way, Swansea Vale, Swansea SA7 0AJ **Tel:** 01792 650000 **Email:** bjd@djm.law.co.uk **Apply to:** Mr Jonathan Powell	South Wales practice dealing with private client, and ever growing commercial departments. Offices in Swansea. Clients vary from large companies to private individuals.	V T P TS WP	1 2 6 50 no
DOWSE & CO 23-25 Dalston Lane, London E8 3DF **Tel:** 020 7254 6205 **Email:** mh@dowse.co.uk **Apply to:** Mr Myles Hickey	Small high street legal aid practice specialising in employment, family, housing and PI.	V T P TS WP	0 4 3 14 no
DRUCES LLP Salisbury House, London Wall, London EC2M 5PS **Tel:** 020 7638 9271 **Email:** recruitment@druces.com **Apply to:** Ms Teresa Randles	Druces LLP is an ambitious City firm, embarking on exciting times and change. It is renowned for the openness and approachability of its staff and the close relationships it develops and maintains with clients.	V T P TS WP	2 4 21 86 yes
DRYSDALES SOLICITORS LLP Cumberland House, 24-28 Baxter Avenue, Southend-on-Sea SS2 6HZ **Tel:** 01702 423 400 **Email:** a.murrell@drysdales.net **Apply to:** Mr AD Murrell		V T P TS WP	1 1 3 20 no

V = Vacancies / **T** = Trainees / **P** = Partners / **TS** = Total Staff / **WP** = Work Placement

DWF LLP

1 Scott Place, 2 Hardman Street, Manchester M3 3AA
Tel: 0161 603 5000
Email: trainees@dwf.law
Web: www.dwf.law/graduate
f dwf-llp-graduate-recruitment **🐦** dwf_graduate

The firm We are a global legal business, transforming legal services through our people for our clients. Led by managing partner and CEO Andrew Leaitherland, we have over 26 key locations and over 2,800 people delivering services and solutions that go beyond expectations. We have received recognition for our work by the *Financial Times* who named us as one of Europe's most innovative legal advisers, and we have a range of stand-alone consultative services, technology and products in addtion to the traditional legal offering.

Types of work The business has core strengths in corporate and banking, insurance and litigation, and in-depth industry expertise in eight core sectors, namely energy and industrials; financial services; insurance; public sector; real estate; retail, food and hospitality; technology; and transport and logistics, which underpin its go-to-market strategy. DWF is focused on delivering service excellence to all of its clients in the UK and internationally, which include major household names and FTSE-listed companies such as adidas, Aviva, Babcock, DHL, Royal Bank of Scotland, RSA, Serco, Telefonica, NewRiver Retail, Whitbread and Zurich.

Who should apply We're looking for people who are committed to a career in law, who enjoy working as part of a busy team and respond positively to a challenge. Our trainees need a 2.1 or higher in any degree discipline and AAB at A level (or equivalent)/AAABB at Scottish Higher Level. Commercial acumen, good organisational skills and a fresh way of thinking about client needs are all hallmarks of a DWF team member.

Training programme At DWF we use our values to help define and reinforce our culture and enable us to recruit, retain and develop the highest quality people. This is reflected in our training contract, where our future trainees are made to feel part of the DWF team from the moment of offer. Once within the business, our trainees get a high level of responsibility in terms of legal work and exposure to business delvelopment and CSR. Many DWF trainees also have the opportunity to complete a client secondement.

When and how to apply Applications must be made online via our website www.dwf.law/graduate. Training contract applications will be accepted from October 2018 until 5 July 2019. Apply by 4 January 2019 for the vacation scheme.

Work placements The DWF summer vacation scheme takes place in June, dates of which depend on location. If you are in your penultimate or final year of a law degree, final year of a non-law degree or a graduate of any discipline then you are eligible to apply. Applications are usually open from the start of October until January, and you must make an online application. The business recruits the majority of its trainees through the vacation scheme, so it's a good opportunity to get ahead and see why DWF is the right business for you. The two-week vacation scheme gives you the chance to work with partners, associates and trainees across two different practice groups. You'll work on live legal matters and will be given responsibility right from the start. This is combined with a variety of internal workshops and presentations, helping you understand DWF as a business. You'll also complete a group project that's designed to aid your professional development and provide you with some of the essential skills of a successful commercial lawyer.

Sponsorship DWF sponsors the LPC/Scottish Diploma fees.

Vacancies	Up to 40
Trainees	84
Partners	316
Total staff	2,800+

Work placement yes

Training contract deadline
5 July 2019

Apply
Online

Starting salary
£22,000 - £38,000
(excluding Belfast)

Minimum qualifications
2.1 in any subject and
AAB in A levels/AAABB
in Scottish Highers or
equivalent

Sponsorship
LPC/Scottish Diploma fees

Offices
Manchester, Liverpool,
Leeds, Newcastle, London,
Milton Keynes, Bristol,
Birmingham, Edinburgh,
Glasgow, Belfast, Dublin,
Brussels, Paris, Berlin,
Cologne, Munich, Milan,
Dubai, Chicago, Toronto,
Sydney, Brisbane,
Melbourne, Newcastle (New
South Wales), Singapore

DUNCAN GIBBINS SOLICITORS Forum House, Kings Park, Knowsley L34 1BH **Tel:** 0151 949 5757 **Email:** info@duncangibbins.com **Apply to:** Mr M Dean	We are a specialist claimant personal injury firm operating in the North West but with a nationwide client base. We also have a small wills and probate department.	V 2 T 5 P 2 TS 34 WP no
DUNCAN LEWIS SOLICITORS LTD Spencer House, 29 Grove Hill Road, Harrow HA1 3BN **Tel:** 020 7923 4020 **Email:** darsheetav@duncanlewis.com **Apply to:** Ms Darsheeta Vaghela	Fastest growing legal aid firm; over 20,000 clients each year. Quality committed (12 quality marks) and largest number of training contracts at high-street level.	V 100 T 68 P 33 TS 421 WP yes
DW LAW Suite 2, Marquis House, 68 Great North Road, Hatfield, Hertfordshire AL9 5ER **Tel:** 01707 261177 **Email:** office@dwlaw.co.uk **Apply to:** Mr Francis Domingo	A firm that specialises in criminal defence work that can provide the challenge and satisfaction of achievement in an increasingly demanding environment in criminal litigation.	V 0 T 1 P 2 TS 8 WP yes
EAST HAMPSHIRE DISTRICT COUNCIL Council Offices, Penns Place, Petersfield, Hampshire GU31 4EX **Tel:** 01730 234 069 **Email:** tracy.beavis@easthants.gov.uk **Apply to:** Mr Nick Leach	Legal services department within a local authority providing a wide range of services to the council, councillors and officers.	V 0 T 0 P 0 TS 7 WP no
EATON SMITH LLP 14 High Street, Huddersfield HD1 2HA **Tel:** 01484 821300 **Email:** mail@eatonsmith.co.uk **Apply to:** Mrs Janet Hogg	We provide a complete legal service to both the commercial and private client.	V 0 T - P 7 TS 80 WP no
EB LEGAL Astute House, Wilmslow Road, Cheshire SK9 3HP **Tel:** 01625 544 797 **Email:** info@eblegal.co.uk **Apply to:** Mrs Elizabeth Tselepis-Beesley	We are a relatively new but dynamic firm specialising primarily in personal injury and consumer credit law. We are looking for trainees wishing to specialise in these areas.	V 1 T 1 P 1 TS 5 WP yes
EC3 LEGAL LLP 106 Leadenhall Street, London EC3A 4AA **Tel:** 0203 553 4888 **Email:** info@ec3legal.com **Apply to:** Mrs Gisele Coupe	With the insurance industry as its heartland, the firm's clients comprise insurers, Lloyd's businesses, brokers, MGAs and industry trade bodies.	V 0 T - P 6 TS 24 WP no
EDMONDSON HALL 25 Exeter Road, Newmarket CB8 8AR **Tel:** 01638 560556 **Email:** solicitors@edmondsonhall.com **Apply to:** Mr Mark Edmondson	Leading niche bloodstock and sports law practice. Equine litigation. Vet negligence, sale and purchase disputes etc. Award-winning sports lawyers. Friendly but forward thinking. Smart offices. Partners recognised specialists.	V 0 T 1 P 3 TS 20 WP yes

V = Vacancies / **T** = Trainees / **P** = Partners / **TS** = Total Staff / **WP** = Work Placement

EDWARDS DUTHIE
269-275 Cranbrook Road, Ilford IG1 4TG
Tel: 020 8514 9000
Email: allinfo@edwardsduthie.com
Apply to: Mrs Coral Joyce

A substantial, diverse practice with particular expertise in personal injury, crime and property. Four offices across East London and Essex. Legal aid franchises in all areas.

V	0
T	7
P	12
TS	85
WP	no

EDWIN COE LLP
2 Stone Buildings, Lincoln's Inn, London WC2A 3TH
Tel: 020 7691 4000
Email: recruitment@edwincoe.com
Apply to: Mrs Liz Austin

Ranked as 'UK-200' law firm, Edwin Coe LLP provides high-quality partner led legal advice to a broad spectrum of UK and international clients.

V	4
T	9
P	39
TS	172
WP	yes

ELBORNE MITCHELL LLP
88 Leadenhall Street, London EC3A 3BP
Tel: 020 7320 9000
Email: lawyers@elbornes.com
Apply to: Ms Margaret Martin

The firm is a friendly high flyer, the clients professional or substantial business people, and work is specialised and intellectually challenging.

V	2
T	4
P	8
TS	21
WP	no

ELLIOTT BRIDGMAN LIMITED
66-70 Court Street, Madeley, Telford TF7 5EP
Tel: 01952 684544
Email: info@elliottbridgman.com
Apply to: Mrs Joanne Foulkes

Lexcel accredited private law firm dealing with private client, notary public, probate and conveyancing, children and family matters and mental health law.

V	2
T	-
P	1
TS	21
WP	yes

ELLIS JONES SOLICITORS LLP
Sandbourne House, 302 Charminster Road, Bournemouth BH8 9RU
Tel: 01202 525333
Email: email@ellisjones.co.uk
Apply to: Miss Sabre King

Progressive and expanding partnership in the south of England. Banking litigation, commercial property, residential property, company commercial, personal injury, private client, family and civil litigation.

V	2
T	4
P	12
TS	130
WP	yes

ELLISONS
Headgate Court, Head Street, Colchester CO1 1NP
Tel: 01206 764477
Email: recruitment@ellisonslegal.com
Apply to: Mr Alan Dearsley

V	1 20
T	4
P	17
TS	160
WP	no

EMD LAW LLP
13 Warrior Square, St Leonards-On-Sea, East Sussex TN37 6BA
Tel: 01580890600
Email: lcb@emdlaw.co.uk
Apply to: Mrs Elizabeth Dumbleton

V	0
T	-
P	3
TS	13
WP	no

EMERY JOHNSON ASTILLS
3 & 5 Welford Road, Leicester LE2 7AD
Tel: 0116 2554855
Email: legal@emeryjohnson.com
Apply to: Ms Isabel Wilson

Leicester firm specialising in criminal, family, childcare, conveyancing and private client. Young, dynamic team committed to providing a quality service. Currently recruiting paralegals.

V	2
T	3
P	5
TS	45
WP	yes

V = Vacancies / **T** = Trainees / **P** = Partners / **TS** = Total Staff / **WP** = Work Placement

EMW Law LLP

Seebeck House, One Seebeck Place, Knowlhill, Milton Keynes MK5 8FR
Tel: 0345 070 6000
Email: hr@emwllp.com
Web: www.emwllp.com
🐦 emwlaw

The firm EMW is a progressive and well-established corporate and commercial law firm. We have rapidly gained recognition as a leading law firm offering niche legal services. We work with our clients to provide solutions, which often involves drawing on expertise from a number of our specialist areas and putting together a tailor-made team to ensure we achieve the best possible results. We are also very conscious about the future and are constantly responding to the changing needs of the commercial world by renewing and developing our services. This not only benefits our clients but creates opportunities for existing staff and new recruits. We are not a firm that stands still.

Types of work Recognised as having leading teams in corporate and commercial including banking and finance; and real estate including planning and construction. We also have a strong reputation for employment, dispute resolution, arbitration and property litigation, insolvency, restructuring and asset based lending, intellectual property, technology and wills, trust and probate. We are currently ranked top tier in the *Legal 500* South East region, in our key service areas.

Who should apply Our success is built on our people and we take our trainee solicitor recruitment very seriously. We are looking for candidates who have a 2.1 degree or above, who are approachable, have great communication skills and an appetite for success. However, if you have not achieved a 2.1 degree but still think you have something to offer us please email us telling us why we should still consider you.

Training programme We actively promote a friendly, supportive, practical and business-like approach to your training by offering a comprehensive induction training programme, quarterly trainee seminars, practical workshops with particular emphasis on developing your business development skills and a detailed appraisal at the end of each seat.

We aim to give all trainees the best commercial grounding by giving you the opportunity to complete your training contract by way of six-month seats within corporate finance, real estate and dispute resolution, with the fourth seat allocation to be decided between either employment or commercial contracts. Trainees are given the opportunity to take on responsibility and be involved in a wide range of legal work.

We pride ourselves on our 'open door' policy and encourage coaching and mentoring throughout the training contract. The quality of our training programme was recognised by LawCareers.Net Training and Recruitment Awards by winning the 'Best Trainer' Award in 2013 and winning the 'Best Recruiter' Award in 2014 and 2015. In 2017, Stephen Kay (our training principal) was nominated for Best Training Principal (small trainee intake). We achieved Investors in People Gold Status in June 2015.

Benefits include: BUPA, income protection, death in service benefit together with the following in-house schemes: childcare vouchers, car share, cycle to work and public transport schemes. We aim to recruit our trainees on qualification and encourage their continued development through to associate and partner level; three of our current partners started their career with the firm as trainees.

When and how to apply Please visit careers.emwllp.com and apply by 31 August 2019 for a 2021 training contract.

Vacancies	5
Trainees	10
Partners	34
Total staff	172

Training contract deadline
31 August 2019

Apply
Online

Starting salary
£24,750 minimum

Minimum qualifications
2.1 degree

Offices
Gatwick, London, Milton Keynes

EMSLEYS SOLICITORS LIMITED 6 Colton Mill, Bullerthorpe Lane, Leeds LS15 9JN **Tel:** 0113 2644414 **Email:** corinne.pujara@emsleys.co.uk **Apply to:** Mrs Corinne Pujara	A six director general practice firm with specialised claimant personal injury and property departments.	**V** 1[20] **T** 1 **P** 6 **TS** 120 **WP** no
THE ENDEAVOUR PARTNERSHIP LLP St Mark's Court, Teesdale Business Park, Stockton on Tees TS17 6QW **Tel:** 01642 610300 **Email:** careers@endeavour.law **Apply to:** Ms Sharon Hutchinson	We are a commercially focused law firm, working exclusively with a range of businesses and sectors to provide effective and efficient legal solutions.	**V** 3 **T** 6 **P** 10 **TS** 55 **WP** yes
ENGLAND & CO 7-8 South Quay, Great Yarmouth NR30 2QN **Tel:** 01493 844308 **Email:** pmason@englandandco.co.uk **Apply to:** Mr Peter Mason	A well-established firm providing a wide range of legal services. We are committed to public funding and have Investors in People and Lexcel status.	**V** 0 **T** 0 **P** 6 **TS** 25 **WP** no
ENOCH EVANS LLP St Pauls Chambers, 6-9 Hatherton Road, Walsall WS1 1XS **Tel:** 01922 720333 **Email:** ss@enoch-evans.co.uk **Apply to:** Miss Sukie Shemar	Full service commercial firm serving a cross section of both commercial and private clients with specialist departments covering a wide range of legal services.	**V** Poss[19] **T** 4 **P** 13 **TS** 75 **WP** no
ERIC ROBINSON SOLICITORS 5a St John, Hedge End, Southampton SO30 4AA **Tel:** 01489 788922 **Email:** recruitment@ericrobinson.co.uk **Apply to:** Ms Catherine Maxfield	Six offices in Southampton region. General practice including legal aid, probate, large matrimonial, crime, personal injury and property. Developing commercial department.	**V** 2 **T** 2 **P** 9 **TS** 140 **WP** no
ESSEX LEGAL SERVICES SEAX House, Victoria Road South, Chelmsford CM1 1QH **Tel:** 033301 39993 **Email:** paul.turner@essex.gov.uk **Apply to:** Mr Paul Turner	Local authority wide-ranging practice including child care, employment, prosecutions, land, commercial, insurance and civil litigation.	**V** 0 **T** - **P** - **TS** 120 **WP** no
EVERATT'S LLP First Floor Offices, 17 St. Ann's Road, Harrow, Middlesex HA1 1JU **Tel:** 020 8424 0088 **Email:** mail@everatts.co.uk **Apply to:** Mr Shilan Shah	Small, well-established general practice with commercial and litigation bias, no legal aid work.	**V** 1 **T** 1 **P** 2 **TS** 6 **WP** no
EVERSHEDS SUTHERLAND (INTERNATIONAL) LLP 1 Wood Street, London EC2V 7WS **Tel:** 0845 497 9797 **Email:** gradrec@eversheds-sutherland.com **Apply to:** Graduate Recruitment	Eversheds Sutherland is one of the world's largest full-service law firms operating as one team across Europe, the US, Africa, Asia and the Middle East.	**V** 50 **T** 110 **P** 395 **TS** 3235 **WP** yes

V = Vacancies / **T** = Trainees / **P** = Partners / **TS** = Total Staff / **WP** = Work Placement

	V	T	P	TS	WP

EVERYS
The Laurels, 46 New Street, Honiton EX14 1BY
Tel: 01404 43431
Email: law@everys.co.uk
Apply to: Mrs Jo Garrod

Progressive, well-established practice with offices in London, Exeter, Honiton, Exmouth, Ottery St Mary, Sidmouth, Seaton, Budleigh Salterton and Taunton.

V 0
T 4
P 10
TS 100
WP no

EWINGS & CO
148 High Street, London SE20 7EU
Tel: 020 8778 1126
Email: enquiry@ewings.uk.com
Apply to: Mrs DM Ewings

General high street practice centrally located. Committed to expansion of its private and publicly funded work. Quality mark holders in family and crime.

V 0
T 2
P 3
TS 30
WP no

EXPRESS SOLICITORS
Resolution House, 311-319 Palatine Road, Northenden, Manchester M22 4HH
Tel: 0161 9044 660
Email: recruitment@expresssolicitors.co.uk
Apply to: Mr James Maxey

Top 200 claimant personal injury and clinical negligence firm. Exceptional year on year growth. A land of development and opportunity.

V 5[19]
T 17
P 22
TS 230
WP yes

FARADAYS SOLICITORS
142 Seven Sisters Road, London N7 7NS
Tel: 020 72811001
Email: enquiries@faradayssolicitors.co.uk
Apply to: Mrs Caroline Lewis

Energetic four-partner firm that specialises in criminal law, family law and personal injury. We are established with an excellent reputation.

V Varies
T 1
P 4
TS 20
WP yes

FARLEYS SOLICITORS LLP
22-27 Richmond Terrace, Blackburn BB1 7AF
Tel: 01254 606000
Email: n.molyneux@farleys.com
Apply to: Mr Nicholas Molyneux

We are a large practice offering a full range of work areas based across East Lancashire and Manchester.

V 2[19]
T 6
P 12
TS 170
WP no

FARNFIELDS
The Square, Gillingham SP8 4AX
Tel: 01747 825432
Email: info@farnfields.com
Apply to: Ms Susan Lacey

As a 'high street' practice operating in four locations our core services are property (residential and commercial), private client, family and mediation.

V 0
T 0
P 4
TS 65
WP no

FBC MANBY BOWDLER LLP
George House, St John's Square, Wolverhampton WV2 4BZ
Tel: 01902 578000
Email: hr@fbcmb.co.uk
Apply to: Miss Charlotte Clode

We aim to develop exceptional people who intelligently deliver a stellar service from trainee through to partner.

V 0
T 5
P 29
TS 182
WP no

FEARON & CO
Westminster House, 7 Faraday Road, Guildford, Surrey GU1 1EA
Tel: 01483 540 840
Email: enquiries@fearonlaw.com
Apply to: Mr A J Phillips

Niche firm of solicitors established in 1825 and based just outside Guildford town centre specialising in property, probate and litigation.

V 0
T 1
P 1
TS 6
WP no

V = Vacancies / **T** = Trainees / **P** = Partners / **TS** = Total Staff / **WP** = Work Placement

Faegre Baker Daniels LLP

7 Pilgrim Street, London EC4V 6LB
Tel: 020 7450 4500
Email: stephen.llewellyn@faegrebd.com
Web: www.faegrebd.com
f faegrebd **𝕏** faegrebd

The firm Faegre Baker Daniels LLP offers a full complement of legal services to clients ranging from emerging enterprises to multinational companies. The firm's 750 plus legal and consulting professionals handle complex transactions and litigation matters throughout Europe, the United States and Asia. Faegre Baker Daniels is one of the 75 largest firms in the US.

Types of work In London we focus on advising clients which range from *Fortune 500* companies to high quality emerging companies meeting their legal needs, both domestically and internationally.

Corporate: includes mergers and acquisitions, takeovers, management buy-outs, joint ventures, private equity, financing, flotations (IPOs), fundraisings and corporate reorganisations. We have particular expertise in advising on AIM listings.

Business litigation: general commercial litigation with a growing emphasis on mediation and arbitration, much of which is international.

Commercial: a wide range of contentious and non-contentious commercial and IP matters for a diverse client base. Our expertise also covers franchising, outsourcing, international data privacy, e-commerce and digital media.

Employment: advice on a broad range of employment issues from recruitment to dismissal and also on employers' duties on business sales and reorganisations, share option and incentive plans, global mobility and immigration and termination issues such as redundancy, unfair and wrongful dismissal and restrictive covenants.

Real estate: advice on all aspects of property investments and management, development and finance, as well as corporate real estate issues.

Who should apply We are looking for motivated people not only with strong academics, but who are also team players with good all-round ability, common sense and ambition. In addition, strong communication skills and an appreciation of our clients' commercial interests are essential.

Training programme The London office is split into four main practice groups. We offer training in each of these groups and trainees will assist a number of partners or solicitors within any group. This provides a good breadth of experience and you will quickly become integrated within the firm. Our aim is for trainees to be one of the team and to have responsibility (subject to appropriate supervision) at an early stage. We provide some in-house training, and trainees are encouraged to attend outside lectures and courses where appropriate. Appraisals are undertaken every three months.

When and how to apply Online application form available at www.faegrebd.com/trainee-solicitors-uk-only. Your application should be received by 15 July two years before the commencement of the training contract. Interviews take place during September each year.

Work placements There are a limited number of places available each year. You should apply using our online application form by 31 March 2019.

Sponsorship LPC fees.

Vacancies	2
Trainees	4
Partners	8
Total staff	46
Work placement	yes

Training contract deadline
15 July 2019

Apply to
Online

Starting salary
£38,000 (September 2018)

Minimum qualifications
2.1 degree

Sponsorship
LPC

Offices
Beijing, Boulder, Chicago, Denver, Des Moines, Fort Wayne, Indianapolis, London, Los Angeles, Minneapolis, Shanghai, Silicon Valley, Washington DC

FAEGRE BAKER DANIELS

Remember to cite *The LawCareers.Net Handbook* on your application form if you apply to this firm.

344 THE LAWCAREERS.NET HANDBOOK

Farrer & Co LLP

66 Lincoln's Inn Fields, London WC2A 3LH
Tel: 020 3375 7000
Email: graduaterecruitment@farrer.co.uk
Web: www.farrer.co.uk

The firm Farrer & Co is a successful law firm with a distinguished history and an excellent reputation built up over many years.

The firm provides a full service to clients as well as having outstanding expertise in a number of niche sectors. This is coupled with careful attention to personal service and quality, and a strong emphasis on the human touch based on the goodwill of numerous close client relationships.

We have approximately 450 staff, including 275 lawyers, many of whom are leaders in their fields and some 80 of whom are partners.

Types of work Farrer & Co has expertise in a number of diverse fields including intellectual property, sports, media, matrimonial, heritage, employment, estates work, charity law and financial services. Clients range from national institutions, museums, galleries, schools and universities to high profile individuals and companies such as banks and media organisations.

Who should apply Those applicants who appear eager to break the mould – as shown by their initiative for organisation, leadership, exploration or enterprise. We look for trainees who are highly motivated individuals with keen intellects and engaging and interesting personalities.

Training programme The training programme involves each trainee in probably the widest range of cases, clients and issues possible in a single law firm. This provides a broad foundation of knowledge and experience, with the opportunity to make an informed choice about the area of law in which to specialise. A high degree of involvement in client work is encouraged under the direct supervision of associates and partners. Trainees attend regular internal and external seminars. The training principal reviews trainees' progress at the end of each seat and extensive feedback is given. The firm has a friendly atmosphere and holds regular sporting and social events.

When and how to apply You can apply at any time. The closing date for training contract applications is 31 July 2019. Applications are dealt with online via the firm's website. A covering letter forms part of the online application.

Work placements Farrer & Co runs Easter and summer vacation schemes for those considering a career in law. An allowance of £300 per week will be paid. The dates for the 2019 vacation schemes will be available from the autumn of this year. The deadline is 31 January 2019 for all schemes. Approximately 100 applicants for summer vacation schemes will be invited to one of three open days held at the firm's offices in March 2019, which present a good opportunity to get to know the firm. These will help us make the final selection of successful candidates.

Sponsorship Fees for GDL and LPC and £7,000 grant per year.

Vacancies	10
Trainees	20
Partners	80
Total staff	450
Work placement	yes

Training contract deadline
31 July 2019

Apply to
Graduate Recruitment and Development Adviser

Starting salary
£38,000 (September 2018)

Minimum qualifications
2.1 degree

Sponsorship
GDL/LPC

Offices
London

FARRER&Co

Proud diversity and inclusion partner of

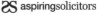 aspiringsolicitors

Remember to cite *The LawCareers.Net Handbook* on your application form if you apply to this firm.

TRAINING CONTRACT DIRECTORY **345**

FELLOWES SOLICITORS LLP 21 Church Hill, Walthamstow, London E17 3AD **Tel:** 020 8520 7392 **Email:** info@fellowes.org **Apply to:** Mrs Judith Stalley	Long-established general high street practice based in East London, covering conveyancing and probate with a franchise in criminal. Recruitment is open - no deadlines.	**V** 1 **T** 1 **P** 4 **TS** 14 **WP** yes
FENTONS 55 Princess Street, Manchester M2 4EW **Tel:** 0161 2386400 **Email:** melanie.ridgewell@fentons.co.uk **Apply to:** Miss Melanie Ridgewell	Personal injury, employment, probate and wills, clinical negligence and serious injury.	**V** 0 **T** 0 **P** 24 **TS** 210 **WP** no
FERDINAND KELLY 96 Broad Street, Birmingham B15 1AU **Tel:** 0121 643 7733 **Email:** info@ferdinandkelly.co.uk **Apply to:** The Recruitment Partner	Niche commercial firm. Specialisms: commercial litigation, commercial property, employment, European law; commercial work generally, sometimes with an international element.	**V** 0 **T** 0 **P** 1 **TS** 5 **WP** no
FIELD SEYMOUR PARKES 1 London Street, Reading RG1 4QW **Tel:** 0118 951 6200 **Email:** lisa.cross@fsp-law.com **Apply to:** Ms Lisa Cross	Dynamic Thames Valley full-service practice with an impressive and growing client base, active in both commercial and private client work areas.	**V** 3 **T** 8 **P** 20 **TS** 110 **WP** yes
FIELDFISHER 2 Swan Lane, London EC4R 3TT **Tel:** 020 7861 4000 **Email:** graduaterecruitment@fieldfisher.com **Apply to:** Mrs Amelia Spinks	Fieldfisher is a European law firm providing commercial solutions across a range of industry sectors.	**V** 18 **T** 28 **P** 223 **TS** 986 **WP** yes
FIELDINGS PORTER Silverwell House, Silverwell Street, Bolton BL1 1PT **Tel:** 01204 387742 **Email:** info@fieldingsporter.co.uk **Apply to:** Mr Fraser Young	Long established general practice dealing with a wide variety of work from high value commercial to PI and legal aid franchises.	**V** 3-4 **T** 5 **P** 11 **TS** 76 **WP** no
FINN GLEDHILL 1-4 Harrison Road, Halifax HX1 2AG **Tel:** 01422 330000 **Email:** barbara.lee@finngledhill.co.uk **Apply to:** The Training Principal	A Yorkshire general practice with two offices, undertaking both commercial and private client work. Has a legal aid franchise.	**V** 0 **T** 0 **P** 6 **TS** 50 **WP** no
FISHER JONES GREENWOOD SOLICITORS Charter Court, Newcomen Way, Colchester Business Park, Colchester CO4 9YA **Tel:** 01206 835300 **Email:** info@fjg.co.uk **Apply to:** Mrs Rebecca Greene	Dynamic, modern, friendly firm undertaking commercial, property, family, litigation, crime, employment, wills and probate, landlord and tenant etc with specialist immigration and human rights department.	**V** 0 **T** 4 **P** 21 **TS** 141 **WP** no

V = Vacancies / **T** = Trainees / **P** = Partners / **TS** = Total Staff / **WP** = Work Placement

FISHER MEREDITH 7th Floor, 322 High Holborn, London WC1V 7PB **Tel:** 020 7091 2700 **Email:** hr@fishermeredith.co.uk **Apply to:** Ms Jo Secker	Fisher Meredith is an award winning London firm with an outstanding reputation for acting on behalf of individuals, businesses and organisations with highly successful results.	V 2^{20} T 6 P 11 TS 41 WP no
FISHERS 4-8 Kilwardby Street, Ashby De La Zouch, Leicestershire LE65 2FU **Tel:** 01530 412167 **Email:** enquiries@fishers-dewes.co.uk **Apply to:** Mr MCA Killin	A long-established practice with strong client base and niche areas in company and commercial, commercial property, taxations and trusts.	V 0 T 1 P 5 TS 38 WP no
FITZ SOLICITORS Chappell House, The Green, Datchet SL3 9EH **Tel:** 01753 592 000 **Email:** info@fitz-legal.com **Apply to:** Mr JF Fitzgerald	A boutique practice offering outstanding service to discerning clients in corporate/commercial, environmental, conveyancing, wills and probate, civil litigation and family.	V 0 T 1 P 1 TS 5 WP no
FLADGATE LLP 16 Great Queen Street, London WC2B 5DG **Tel:** 020 3036 7000 **Email:** trainees@fladgate.com **Apply to:** Ms Hayley Webster	A leading commercial practice - our property, corporate and litigation departments provide wide-ranging legal services to a diverse portfolio of UK and international clients.	V 6 T 12 P 74 TS 261 WP no
FLETCHER DERVISH 582 Green Lanes, London N8 0RP **Tel:** 020 8800 4615 **Email:** law@fletcherdervish.co.uk **Apply to:** Mr D Dervish	Long-established practice committed to high standard of work. Franchised in family, crime, housing, immigration with departments in PI, consumer/ general contract, property and wills/ probate.	V 0 T 3 P 1 TS 20 WP no
FOOT ANSTEY LLP Salt Quay House, 4 North East Quay, Sutton Harbour, Plymouth PL4 0BN **Tel:** 01752 675000 **Email:** contact@footanstey.com **Apply to:** Ms Ina Simon	A leading regional law firm with a strong and supportive team ethos, committed to a comprehensive training and development programme and excellent standards of service.	V 12^{20} T 24 P 49 TS 500 WP yes
FORBES SOLICITORS 73 Northgate, Blackburn BB2 1AA **Tel:** 01254 580000 **Email:** graduate.recruitment@forbessolicitors.co.uk **Apply to:** Mrs Emma Fitzsimmons	Forbes recruits high calibre individuals with strong local connections, who are keen team players. Training is offered in several commercial and private client departments.	V 4 T 10 P 44 TS 320 WP yes
FORD SIMEY LLP The Forum, Barnfield Road, Exeter EX1 1QR **Tel:** 01392 274126 **Email:** info@fordsimey.co.uk **Apply to:** Mr David Williams	General practice with specialist teams dealing with private client, family, personal injury and commercial. Welcomes non-law graduates.	V 0 T 0 P 11 TS 64 WP no

V = Vacancies / **T** = Trainees / **P** = Partners / **TS** = Total Staff / **WP** = Work Placement

Forsters LLP

31 Hill Street, London W1J 5LS
Tel: 020 7863 8333
Web: www.forsters.co.uk

The firm We are a dynamic, successful firm committed to being the best. Based in Mayfair, Forsters was founded in 1998 and has since more than trebled in size. While we are best known for our top-flight real estate and private client practices, we also have thriving corporate and dispute resolution teams. Forsters offers interesting, intellectually challenging work, high quality clients and fantastic people to work with and learn from. We are dedicated to giving outstanding client service in a highly professional, collaborative and supportive environment.

Types of work The firm has a strong reputation for all aspects of commercial and residential real estate work. The real estate groups deal with investment funding, development, planning, construction, landlord and tenant, property taxation and residential investment and development. Forsters is also recognised as having one of the leading private client practices in London with a client base comprising a broad range of individuals and trustees in the UK and offshore. Our corporate practice specialises in company acquisitions and disposals, financings and joint ventures and shareholder arrangements. The dispute resolution group handles and resolves a wide variety of commercial disputes through litigation, arbitration and mediation as well as working alongside the firm's private client group in relation to trust and probate disputes.

Who should apply We recruit graduates from a broad range of backgrounds and welcome both graduate and undergraduate applicants with degrees in any discipline. Our standard criteria are a minimum of ABB at A level or equivalent (excluding general studies) and a 2.1 or higher degree classification (achieved or predicted). Beyond this, we are looking for ambitious, personable and motivated candidates who thrive on responsibility within a team environment.

Training programme A training contract with Forsters consists of six four-month seats. In the first year, this usually involves seats in three of the following groups/departments: commercial real estate, private client, residential property and corporate. In the second year, it may be possible for trainees to spend their final seat in the practice area into which they are going to qualify. As the training contract progresses, increasing responsibility is given; trainees start working on their own files and talking to and meeting with clients. Supervision and guidance is always available but we are keen that our trainees quickly start playing a real role in our teams. In addition to on the job training, there are regular in-house seminars on legal and commercial topics as well as training on our IT and other in-house systems. Our trainees also attend a bespoke Professionals Skills Course, provided by a leading training supplier and designed for Forsters.

When and how to apply All applications should be made online at www.graduates.forsters.co.uk. The closing date for training contracts commencing in September 2021 is 31 July 2019.

Work placements Forsters offers up to 14 vacation scheme places during the summer, each for a two-week period. Please see our website for more details.

Sponsorship We have an exclusive arrangement with The University of Law for the provision of GDL and LPC courses to our future trainees, but we do not mind if you have already completed either course elsewhere. Payment of course fees, plus a maintenance grant of £6,000 per year of study, is offered to future trainees who have yet to complete these courses.

Vacancies	7-9
Trainees	17
Partners	53
Total staff	400 approx
Work placement	yes

Training contract deadline
31 July 2019

Apply
Online

Starting salary
1st year – £40,000
2nd year – £42,000

Minimum qualifications
2.1 degree, ABB at A level or equivalent (excluding general studies)

Sponsorship
GDL/LPC

Offices
London

FORSTERS

Remember to cite *The LawCareers.Net Handbook* on your application form if you apply to this firm.

348 THE LAWCAREERS.NET HANDBOOK

FORRESTERS SOLICITORS LIMITED
117 Duke Street, Barrow In Furness LA14 1XA
Tel: 01229 820 297
Email: mail@forresterssolicitors.co.uk
Apply to: Mrs Emma Scott

V	0
T	-
P	2
TS	15
WP	no

FOSTERS
William House, 19 Bank Plain, Norwich NR2 4FS
Tel: 01603 620508
Email: hbrown@fosters-solicitors.co.uk
Apply to: Mr Iain McClay

Winner of UK Law Firm of the Year (Regional) 2013, and Law Society Excellence Award. Applications ongoing.

V	0
T	3
P	13
TS	130
WP	no

FOUNTAIN SOLICITORS LIMITED
ManderHouse, 36 Bardford Street, Walsall WS1 3QA
Tel: 01922 645 429
Email: info@fountainsolicitors.com
Apply to: Mr Ramzan Sharif

We specialise in immigration, asylum, family, personal injury, public law, leases, social welfare law, criminal law and employment law.

V	1[19]
T	1
P	1
TS	40
WP	yes

FOX WILLIAMS LLP
10 Finsbury Square, London EC2A 1AF
Tel: 020 7628 2000
Email: application@foxwilliams.com
Apply to: Graduate Recruitment Team

We are City lawyers with an uncompromising focus on quality, value and our clients' commercial success.

V	3[20]
T	6
P	34
TS	118
WP	yes

FRANCES LINDSAY & CO
48 Broadway, Maidenhead, Berkshire SL6 1LU
Tel: 01628 634667
Email: info@franceslindsay.co.uk
Apply to: Ms Frances Lindsay

Specialist family law practice. Non-legal aid.

V	0
T	1
P	1
TS	5
WP	no

FRANK BRAZELL & PARTNERS
97 White Lion Street, Islington, London N1 9PF
Tel: 020 7689 8989
Apply to: Mr FW Brazell

We have an experienced team of solicitors. We specialise in all areas of criminal and family work and have an expanding private client department.

V	0
T	3
P	3
TS	28
WP	no

FRANKLINS SOLICITORS LLP
8 Castilian Street, Northampton NN1 1JX
Tel: 01604 828282
Email: emma.mcnally@franklins-sols.co.uk
Apply to: Ms Emma McNally

A well-established firm specialising in corporate commercial services, employment, conveyancing, family, wills, trusts and probate, delivering a high quality service to all our clients.

V	0
T	3
P	14
TS	100
WP	yes

FRASER BROWN
84 Friar Lane, Nottingham NG1 6ED
Tel: 0115 9888 777
Email: info@fraserbrown.com
Apply to: Ms Sarah Poole

V	0
T	2
P	15
TS	107
WP	no

V = Vacancies / **T** = Trainees / **P** = Partners / **TS** = Total Staff / **WP** = Work Placement

Freeths LLP

Cumberland Court, 80 Mount Street, Nottingham NG1 6HH
Tel: 0845 274 6815
Email: carole.wigley@freeths.co.uk
Web: www.freeths.co.uk
🐦 freeths

The firm Freeths is a top 60 national law practice, turning over in excess of £78 million annually, with some 147 partners and 750 staff working in a network of 12 offices throughout England. This means that we have considerable strength, extensive legal knowledge and are able to offer a quick and responsive service across all business areas. In recognition of high levels of employee engagement, we have received awards from Best Companies, Investors in People and *Sunday Times* Best Company. The *Legal 500*'s UK rankings recommended 144 of Freeths' lawyers and named 24 of them as Elite Leading Lawyers.

Types of work Freeths offers a complete commercial service covering the bigger picture of commercial operations and dispute resolution within a variety of sector specialisms. However, while we specialise in commercial advice, we also advise our business clients on their personal affairs including wills, care of the elderly and disabled, clinical negligence, Court of Protection, debt recovery and trust formation, personal injury, and administration and taxation.

Who should apply There is no such thing as a typical Freeths candidate. So if you are a bright and talented individual who will make a real difference to our firm over the coming years then we are interested in your application. We are flexible in our approach to finding the best talent hence we have no minimum criteria and we welcome applications from both law and non-law students and from those who have already graduated or completed either their LPC or GDL.

Training programme At Freeths we "think differently" and this also applies to the flexible graduate programmes we offer. We believe that it is your career therefore you should be the one to choose how it starts. So if you prefer to focus on gaining valuable work experience prior to commencing either your LPC or training contract, then our legal assistant foundation programme could be for you. Equally, if you prefer a more traditional route to qualification then our direct entry route allows you the opportunity to complete your academic qualifications prior to starting your training contract with us.

When and how to apply To apply for one of our training schemes, you will need to complete our online application form which can be found either on our website www.freeths.co.uk/recruitment/graduates or at www.apply4law.com/freeths. If you have any specific access requirements or are unable to complete the online application form please contact carole.wigley@freeths.co.uk.

Sponsorship If you are offered a place on our legal assistant foundation scheme then we provide funding to cover relevant LPC and GDL fees. Loans are available for the direct entry route.

Vacancies	20
Trainees	40
Members	147
Total staff	750
Work placement	no
Training contract deadline	14 July 2019
Apply to	Online
Starting salary	£25,000
Sponsorship	GDL/LPC
Offices	Birmingham, Derby, Leeds, Leicester, Liverpool, London, Manchester, Milton Keynes, Nottingham, Oxford, Sheffield, Stoke-on-Trent

FREETHS

Fried, Frank, Harris, Shriver & Jacobson LLP

41 Lothbury, London EC2R 7HF
Tel: 020 7972 9600
Email: londonhumanresources@friedfrank.com
Web: www.friedfrank.com
🐦 friedfrank

The firm Frank, Harris, Shriver & Jacobson LLP advises the world's leading corporations, investment funds and financial institutions on their most critical legal needs and business opportunities. The firm's approximately 500 lawyers are based in North America and Europe.

Types of work Antitrust and competition; corporate (asset management, corporate governance, finance, mergers and acquisitions, private acquisitions and private equity); international arbitration; international trade and investment; litigation; pro bono; real estate; restructuring and insolvency; tax; and white collar defense, regulatory enforcement and investigations.

Who should apply If you are applying to Fried Frank during your studies, we recommend that you apply in either the penultimate year of your law degree or the final year of a non-law degree. Fried Frank also welcomes graduates and those changing careers. In hiring trainee associates and pupil barristers, we look for energetic, motivated candidates who demonstrate a high level of intellectual ability, curiosity, and creativity, as well as a strong interest in working in a collegial setting.

Training programme Fried Frank offers a dynamic and engaging training programme which provides meaningful work assignments across UK, US and international mandates. Trainees spend six months working with close-knit teams of partners and associates across four departments in a hands-on learning environment. Working closely and socialising with partners, counsel, associates and staff, our trainees leave the programme with a clear understanding of what Fried Frank can offer them as a place to begin their legal careers.

When and how to apply If you are interested in joining an international firm with quality work and training, please apply by completing our application form, located on our firm's careers website. Once complete, please return your form to londonhumanresources@friedfrank.com.

Work placements Fried Frank offers one and three-month internship placements in our litigation department. Interns gain experience within the legal industry, while being exposed to top quality work and clients. Our internship programme details and application form can be found on our careers website. Please note that applications for our internship programme are separate to those for our training contract.

Sponsorship For future trainees of the firm, we sponsor both the GDL and LPC, and provide an annual maintenance grant of £7,000.

Vacancies	2
Trainees	4
Partners	15
Total staff	118

Training contract deadline
30 June 2019

Apply
Online

Starting salary
£45,000

Minimum qualifications
2.1 degree

Sponsorship
GDL/LPC

Offices
London, New York,
Washington DC, Frankfurt

FRIED FRANK

FREEMAN JOHNSON
11 Victoria Road, Darlington DL1 5SP
Tel: 01325 466221
Email: darlington@freemanjohnson.co.uk
Apply to: Mr Kevin Campbell

Offices at Darlington, Durham and Spennymoor. All general private client work. Legal aid franchise in personal injury, matrimony and criminal. Some company commercial.

V	1
T	2
P	8
TS	45
WP	yes

FRESHFIELDS BRUCKHAUS DERINGER LLP
65 Fleet Street, London EC4Y 1HT
Tel: 020 7785 5554
Email: ukgraduates@freshfields.com
Apply to: Graduate Recruitment

We are a leading international law firm providing first-rate legal services to corporations, financial institutions and governments worldwide.

V	80
T	160
P	381
TS	4925
WP	yes

FURLEY PAGE LLP
39 St Margaret's Street, Canterbury CT1 2TX
Tel: 01227 863118
Email: hr@furleypage.co.uk
Apply to: Mrs Karen Cook

One of the leading law firms in Kent and South East, acknowledged for its expertise and client service by *Legal 500* and *Chambers & Partners*.

V	2
T	2
P	18
TS	150
WP	yes

GA SOLICITORS
Gill Akaster House, 25 Lockyer Street, Plymouth PL1 2QW
Tel: 01752 203500
Email: stuart.elford@gasolicitors.com
Apply to: Mr Stuart Elford

We look for those who share our values and deliver a high quality service.

V	2[19]
T	2
P	18
TS	77
WP	no

GABB & CO
32 Monk Street, Abergavenny NP7 5NW
Tel: 01873 852432
Email: abergavenny@gabb.co.uk
Apply to: Mrs Betty Harriot-Pole

V	0
T	0
P	6
TS	36
WP	no

GABY HARDWICKE
33 The Avenue, Eastbourne, East Sussex BN21 3YD
Tel: 01323 435900
Email: ann.townsend@gabyhardwicke.co.uk
Apply to: Ann Townsend

A major Sussex firm with 150 staff servicing private and commercial clients with specialist corporate, property, probate and litigation departments.

V	2[20]
T	2
P	17
TS	150
WP	no

GALBRAITH BRANLEY
18 Friern Park, North Finchley, London N12 9DA
Tel: 020 8446 8474
Email: solicitors@galbraithbranley.com
Apply to: Mr Anthony Branley

Legal aid/private firm undertaking criminal defence and family law work. All prospective trainees start as paralegals.

V	1
T	3
P	1
TS	15
WP	no

GAMLINS LAW
31-37 Russell Road, Rhyl LL18 3DB
Tel: 01745 343500
Email: gamlins@gamlins.co.uk
Apply to: Mrs Kate Sutherland

The largest firm in North Wales specialising in: commercial, property, personal injury/clinical negligence, litigation, matrimonial/family law, private client, crime and regulatory matters.

V	2[19]
T	5
P	11
TS	70
WP	yes

V = Vacancies / **T** = Trainees / **P** = Partners / **TS** = Total Staff / **WP** = Work Placement

Gateley Plc

One Eleven, Edmund Street, Birmingham B3 2HJ
Tel: 0121 234 0000
Email: graduaterecruitmentengland@gateleyuk.com
Web: www.gateleyplc.com
🐦 gateleyplc

The firm Gateley Plc is a leading national, commercial law firm. Operating in eight UK cities and with an office in Dubai, the firm helps clients meet their commercial goals through the delivery of clear and pragmatic legal advice and solutions.

In 2015 Gateley made legal history by becoming the first UK law firm to list on the AIM market of the London stock market.

Types of work Our specialist teams cover all aspects of legal services, including corporate, commercial, banking, real estate, restructuring, technology, construction, employment, pensions, dispute resolution, regulatory, private wealth and family, tax, and shipping and transport, as well as global mobility which encompasses the management of the selection and relocation of employees for international assignments.

Who should apply We accept applications from second-year law students, final- year non-law students and postgraduates.

Training programme We invest heavily in the training and development of our trainees and ask that they complete four six-month training seats. Our preference is that over the course of their training, all of our trainees will complete a seat in at least one corporate discipline, one real estate discipline and one contentious area.

When and how to apply Applicants must apply for training contract opportunities via the careers page on the Gateley Plc website.

Work placements We run two summer vacation schemes which take place from the last week of June and throughout July. We are accepting applications from students to all of our offices.

Sponsorship We will sponsor successful candidates to undertake the GDL and the LPC. We also offer a maintenance grant to successful candidates while they are studying the LPC.

Vacancies	20
Trainees	32
Partners	144
Total staff	868

Training contract deadline
31 January 2019

Apply
Online

Minimum qualifications
2.1 degree

Sponsorship
GDL/LPC

Offices
Birmingham, Nottingham, Leicester, Manchester, Leeds, London, Reading, Guildford

•Gateley Plc

GARDEN HOUSE SOLICITORS	Efficient Lexcel accredited general	V	1
23 London Road, Hertford SG13 7LG	practice in Hertford Town. Personal	T	1
Tel: 01992 422128	injury, private client, dispute	P	1
Email: patricia@ghsolicitors.co.uk	resolution, employment, family.	TS	10
Apply to: Mrs Patricia Ling		WP	yes

GC SOLICITORS	We are a friendly high street practice	V	0
27 Leys Avenue, Letchworth Garden City SG6 3ED	specialising in the areas of personal	T	0
Tel: 01462 483800	injury, crime (including motoring	P	2
Email: admin@gcsols.co.uk	offences and transport/regulatory	TS	17
Apply to: Mr Ben Singh	law), family and childcare.	WP	no

GELDARDS LLP	Geldards LLP is an established	V	6[20]
Dumfries House, Dumfries Place, Cardiff CF10 3ZF	commercial practice with three	T	12
Tel: 029 2039 1777	main offices (Cardiff, Derby and	P	57
Email: recruitment@geldards.com	Nottingham) offering interesting	TS	352
Apply to: HR department	and challenging work in a friendly	WP	no
	atmosphere.		

GEORGE GREEN LLP	George Green LLP is a leading full	V	2
195 High Street, Cradley Heath, West Midlands	service law firm. Our lawyers make	T	4
B64 5HW	a difference by helping our clients	P	15
Tel: 013 8441 0410	succeed.	TS	81
Email: vpalmer@georgegreen.co.uk		WP	no
Apply to: Ms Vanessa Palmer			

GEPP & SONS SOLICITORS LLP	A large and long established Lexcel	V	2[19]
58 New London Road, Chelmsford CM2 0PA	accredited practice in Essex, offering	T	4
Tel: 01245 493939	a full range of legal services to	P	17
Email: training@gepp.co.uk	businesses and private clients.	TS	91
Apply to: Mrs Karen Mollison		WP	no

GHP LEGAL	Leading regional firm, offering	V	0
26-30 Grosvenor Road, Wrexham LL11 1BU	a complete and comprehensive	T	4
Tel: 01978 291456	service, with experts specialising in	P	10
Email: wrexham@ghplegal.com	all aspects of private, commercial	TS	87
Apply to: The Practice Manager	and legal aid work.	WP	yes

GIDE LOYRETTE NOUEL LLP	Gide Loyrette Nouel, an international	V	4
125 Old Broad Street, London EC2N 1AR	firm founded in France, has a	T	4
Tel: 020 7382 5500	highly-renowned, specialist banking	P	6
Email: tcapplications@gide.com	and finance and dispute resolution	TS	46
Apply to: Ms Stephanie Leduc	practice in the City of London.	WP	no

GILBERT STEPHENS LLP	A long-established highly respected	V	1
15-17 Southernhay East, Exeter EX1 1QE	firm offering a comprehensive range	T	-
Tel: 01392 424242	of legal services. The firm also has its	P	12
Email: hr@gilbertstephens.co.uk	own financial services department.	TS	126
Apply to: Ms Sarah Judd		WP	no

V = Vacancies / **T** = Trainees / **P** = Partners / **TS** = Total Staff / **WP** = Work Placement

Gibson, Dunn & Crutcher UK LLP

Telephone House, 2-4 Temple Avenue, London EC4Y 0HB
Tel: 020 7071 4000
Email: graduaterecruitment@gibsondunn.com
Web: www.gibsondunn.com
f gibsondunncareers ✔ gibsondunn

*Law*Careers.Net®
AWARDS 2018
BEST WORK PLACEMENT SCHEME
CITY FIRM

The firm Gibson Dunn is one of the top law firms in the world with a London practice established over 30 years ago. We work on a fully integrated basis with our other offices around the world, offering full-service capabilities on a wide range of business issues to listed companies, large private companies, investment banks, private equity firms, start-up ventures and many other organisations with international operations and ambitions.

Types of work The London office handles all aspects of corporate work including public and private M&A, private equity, finance, capital markets, tax, commercial real estate, and restructuring and insolvency. The office also has an extensive dispute resolution practice, which handles commercial litigation, regulatory investigations, international arbitration, and employment and competition law disputes, and which regularly represents clients in courts in the UK and in jurisdictions such as the British Virgin Islands.

Who should apply We welcome applications for training contracts and summer placement schemes from bright, ambitious individuals. We are particularly seeking those who are capable of taking the initiative, who have strong interpersonal and organisational skills and who can rise to the challenge of working directly with partners and within small, focused teams and having client contact early in their careers. We welcome students and graduates of any discipline.

Training programme During the two-year training contract, trainees will have the opportunity to spend time in a number of different areas. We ask trainees to complete at least one seat in a transactional area of practice and at least one seat in a disputes area of practice. We also expect to be able to offer trainee secondments to one of our international offices and to a client. As a Gibson Dunn trainee, you will work alongside some of the most talented lawyers in Europe, the US and Asia. Based in London, you will become involved in international transactions and cases, working often with our colleagues and clients overseas. You will share a room with a partner or a senior associate and will work with them on their matters, whilst also having the opportunity to work with other lawyers in the firm. You will be encouraged to work on some of the London office's growing number of local and international pro bono activities. We are proud to have a strong and sustained commitment to pro bono work and our trainees are encouraged to get involved with this tradition.

When and how to apply Applicants should complete our online application form, accessed via the careers pages of our website at www.gibsondunn.com/careers/law-students.

Work placements Gibson Dunn's London office is delighted to offer a number of places on our summer placement scheme in July 2019. The summer placement scheme is an excellent opportunity for prospective trainees of the firm to experience a true picture of life at Gibson Dunn, with opportunities to do meaningful work and mix with lawyers and staff socially. Applicants should complete our online application form, accessed via the careers pages of our website at www.gibsondunn.com/careers/law-students. Our summer placement scheme is a key part of the recruitment process at Gibson Dunn and we aim to recruit our future trainees primarily from the scheme. We therefore strongly encourage you to apply for a place on the scheme if you are interested in joining us as a trainee.

Sponsorship We will pay all GDL and LPC fees in full and offer a maintenance grant (currently £8,000) for each year of study.

Vacancies	7-8
Trainees	12
Partners	404
Total staff	2,694

Training contract deadline
31 July 2019

Apply
Online

Minimum qualifications
2.1 degree

Sponsorship
GDL/LPC

Offices
London, Beijing, Brussels, Century City, Dallas, Denver, Dubai, Frankfurt, Hong Kong, Houston, Los Angeles, Munich, New York, Orange County, Palo Alto, Paris, San Francisco, São Paulo, Singapore, Washington DC.

GIBSON DUNN

GILL & CO
Trevian House, 422-426 Ley Street, Ilford, Essex
IG2 7BS
Tel: 020 8554 1011
Email: info@gillsolicitors.com
Apply to: Mrs GK Bhogal

V	1
T	1
P	2
TS	14
WP	no

GILL TURNER TUCKER
Colman House, King Street, Maidstone ME14 1JE
Tel: 01622 759051
Email: trudie.mills@gillturnertucker.com
Apply to: Mrs Trudie Mills

Established in 1949 we are a general practice with an emphasis on commercial and matrimonial work.

V	0
T	1
P	4
TS	27
WP	no

GIRLINGS
16 Rose Lane, Canterbury CT1 2UR
Tel: 01227 768374
Email: judithneenan@girlings.com
Apply to: Mrs Judith Neenan

Candidates initially spend six to nine months as paralegals, and subject to performance, start their training contracts in the September. Contribution toward LPC/SQE may be considered.

V	2 to 20
T	2
P	14
TS	100
WP	yes

GLAISYERS SOLICITORS LLP
One St James's Square, Manchester M2 6DN
Tel: 0161 832 4666
Email: kxc@glaisyers.com
Apply to: Mrs Karen Culliney

Medium-sized practice which provides the wealth of work types that satisfy our clients' needs from minor private client matters up to large commercial transactions.

V	0
T	3
P	11
TS	85
WP	yes

GLANVILLES
West Wing Cams Hall, Cams Hill, Fareham,
Hampshire PO16 8AB
Tel: 01329 282841
Email: fareham@glanvilles.co.uk
Apply to: Miss Mikyla Wollaston

Three offices situated in South Hampshire and the Isle of Wight. Mix of commercial and private client work. Long established.

V	0
T	2
P	13
TS	100
WP	no

GLOVERS SOLICITORS LLP
6 York Steet, London W1U 6QD
Tel: 020 7935 8882
Email: central@glovers.co.uk
Apply to: Mrs Mandy Marson

Property law specialists. Early responsibility encouraged and full involvement in all areas - commercial property, property finance, property litigation, general commercial litigation, construction and employment.

V	2
T	4
P	11
TS	38
WP	no

GLP SOLICITORS
672 Bolton Road, Pendlebury, Swinton,
Manchester M27 8FH
Tel: 0161 793 0901
Email: pendlebury@glplaw.com
Apply to: Mr Sheldon Fagelman

A modern progressive law firm specialising in personal injury, family law and conveyancing.

V	0-1
T	0
P	4
TS	9
WP	no

GOODHAND & FORSYTH
76 Station Road, Redhill, Surrey RH1 1PL
Tel: 01737 773 533
Email: elainebrown@goodhandandforsyth.co.uk
Apply to: Mr Keith Goodhand

V	0
T	0
P	2
TS	31
WP	no

V = Vacancies / **T** = Trainees / **P** = Partners / **TS** = Total Staff / **WP** = Work Placement

Goodman Derrick LLP

10 St Bride Street, London EC4A 4AD
Tel: 020 7404 0606
Email: law@gdlaw.co.uk
Web: www.gdlaw.co.uk
🐦 goodmanderrick

The firm Goodman Derrick LLP is an established London law firm with a broad commercial practice and a particularly strong reputation for high-profile media work. We represent both UK and international clients. Our emphasis is on providing high quality yet practical legal advice tailored to our clients' business needs.

Types of work Our practice is focused on corporate, property and dispute resolution work. We provide a range of services throughout five departments: corporate; property; dispute resolution (including family); private client and employment. Within these departments we have specialists in media, IP/IT, hotels, charities, film finance and collector cars. The firm has an impressive client list acting for many public figures, public and large private companies, large retail chains, property companies, publishers, television companies, broadcasters and independent producers, charities and trade associations. We aim to offer a supportive and stimulating working environment where trainees are given maximum client contact and responsibility from the start.

Who should apply Applicants should ideally have a minimum 2.1 degree (not necessarily law) and a strong academic background. In addition we look for trainees who are confident, motivated and practically-minded to suit our working environment.

Training programme We invest a lot of time and resource in our trainees and our training is aimed at producing solicitors with well-rounded knowledge, skills and abilities. Hands-on experience is supplemented by internal and external training courses.

Trainees undertake four seats of six months each selected from our five departments. Where possible these will include corporate, property and a dispute resolution based seat, as we believe the skills learned in these practice areas are essential for a trainee's development. Trainees gain experience of media work within our dispute resolution and corporate departments.

Trainees are not assigned exclusively to any particular partner, but are treated as part of the department's team from day one, enabling them to experience the breadth of the department's work. Trainees are appropriately supervised and will share a room with a fee earner (usually a partner) to maximise their experience.

Trainees will play an active and essential role working with partners and fee earners on larger cases and transactions, but where possible trainees also run their own files. We like to encourage initiative and responsibility at an early stage. Trainees are also given maximum client contact.

When and how to apply The closing date for training contracts commencing in September 2021 is 30 June 2019. Apply by online application form available on our website www.gdlaw.co.uk.

Sponsorship Funding for the LPC fees at the institution of your choice and a maintenance grant of £4,000 during the LPC.

Vacancies	3
Trainees	8
Partners	35
Total staff	112

Work placement no

Training contract deadline
30 June 2019

Apply
Online

Starting salary
1st year – £34,500
2nd year – £35,500

Minimum qualifications
2.1 degree, A-C at A level

Offices
London

GOODMAN DERRICK LLP

Goodwin Procter (UK) LLP

100 Cheapside, London EC2V 6DY
Tel: 020 7447 4200
Email: hrrecruitinglon@goodwinlaw.com
Web: www.goodwinlaw.com/careers/working-in-london
🐦 goodwinlaw

The firm Goodwin is a global 50 law firm with offices in Boston, Frankfurt, Hong Kong, London, Los Angeles, New York, Paris, San Francisco, Silicon Valley and Washington DC.

Excelling at complex and sophisticated transactional work and precedent-setting, bet-the company litigation, the firm combines in-depth legal knowledge with practical business experience to help clients maximise opportunities, manage risk and move their business forward. The firm hires talented, motivated people committed to excellence, innovation, collaboration and client service and believes that every lawyer and staff member deserves a supportive, meritocratic environment in which people of all backgrounds are given the opportunity to excel and thrive.

Types of work Private equity, private investment funds, finance, real estate industry, technology and life sciences, tax.

Who should apply We welcome applications from candidates at all universities in all degree disciplines.

Candidates need a minimum of a 2.1 degree and AAB at A level (or equivalent).

Unfortunately we are not able to accept applications from students in their first year at undergraduate level.

Training programme Goodwin's London office recruits six trainees each year and offers a variety of training in our core practice areas including tech and life sciences, private equity, private investment funds and real estate.

Our size and continued growth allow us to offer our trainees and associates increased responsibility and meaningful client contact from the outset. We work in small teams, which gives our lawyers the opportunity to work directly with, and be mentored by, senior colleagues, and to develop a network that will be an invaluable part of their future career development.

Goodwin trainees will complete four six-month seats.

When and how to apply You can apply from January 2019 for training contracts commencing September 2021. To apply, please visit our website www.goodwinlaw.com/careers/working-in-london.

Work placements The Goodwin summer vacation scheme provides real insight into what it is like to train and work at Goodwin and gives us a window to get to know students better.

Students will witness first-hand the work we do for our clients by shadowing associates, attending client and business unit meetings, and attending information sessions focussed on the work of each practice area in the London office.

Students will leave our programme with valuable mentors and a large professional and social network.

Sponsorship Full sponsorship of the GDL and LPC fees and £7,000 maintenance grant per year of study.

Vacancies	6
Trainees	9
Partners	23
Total staff	140

Work placement yes

Training contract deadline
31 July 2019

Apply
Online

Minimum qualifications
2.1 degree and AAB at A level (or equivalent)

Sponsorship
GDL/LPC

Offices
London

GOODWIN

Gordons LLP

Riverside West, Whitehall Road, Leeds LS1 4AW
Tel: 0113 227 0100
Email: recruitment@gordonsllp.com
Web: www.gordonsllp.com
🐦 gordonsllp

The firm Gordons is a leading independent Yorkshire firm with offices in Leeds and Bradford. We are a modern, straight-talking, ambitious law firm dedicated to delivering a comprehensive and integrated range of legal services to corporate and individual clients including some of the UK's most successful companies and well-loved brands. We aim to be the law firm of choice in our region, providing a genuine alternative to the national firms.

Types of work As a result of our strong reputation and recognised expertise in both corporate and private work, our client base extends far beyond the Yorkshire region.

A full-service firm, areas of work include commercial property, property litigation, retail, construction, corporate/commercial, insolvency, commercial litigation, intellectual property, employment, personal injury, private client and residential property.

Who should apply Academically our entry standard is a 2.1 degree although we will take a broader view for those that just miss out.

In recruiting trainees we are looking to select our solicitors and indeed partners of the future. We therefore require committed and loyal trainees who are keen to build a successful career in the region and specifically with us. We offer a broad-based training which gives early and increasing responsibility to trainees in a supportive environment. Applicants must therefore be willing to be challenged from day one.

The firm takes pride in its ability to build enduring relationships with clients. It is therefore essential that our trainees have the potential to be at ease with clients, be able to relate well to them in both a business and a social context, and most importantly inspire trust and confidence in the legal advice that they give. So interpersonal skills, a professional yet friendly manner and sound commercial awareness are criteria we use to measure the suitability of applicants.

Training programme The training contract consists of four six-month seats. During the second year of the training contract trainees are able to express their preference of department and we try to accommodate these requests where possible. Trainees spend time at both Leeds and Bradford offices, and are actively encouraged to get involved in marketing, networking, training and other events hosted by the firm and/or clients. The environment is supportive and friendly, with trainees having regular meetings with their supervisors to ensure their progress.

Outside of working hours the firm has frequent activities that trainees can get involved in, both social and in support of our charity of the year.

When and how to apply The deadline for our 2021 intake is 31 July 2019. Application is via our online form which can be found on the trainee section of our website at www.gordonsllp.com/careers/trainee-solicitors.

Sponsorship The firm provides sponsorship towards LPC fees.

Vacancies	4
Trainees	8
Partners	26
Total staff	200

Training contract deadline
31 July 2019

Apply
Online

Starting salary
1st year – £25,000
2nd year – £27,000
(reviewed annually)

Minimum qualifications
2.1 degree

Offices
Leeds, Bradford

GOODMAN RAY 5 Cranwood Street, London EC1V 9AE **Tel:** 020 7608 1227 **Email:** mail@goodmanray.com **Apply to:** Ms Alison Fowler	Family practice. Central London area. No training contracts until further notice.

V 0
T 2
P 5
TS 20
WP no

GOODY BURRETT LLP St Martin House, 63 West Stockwell Street, Colchester CO1 1WD **Tel:** 01206 577676 **Email:** law@goodyburrett.co.uk **Apply to:** Mr BC Johnston	One of the oldest firms in Colchester (over 250 years), offers friendly, relaxed but professional legal services to private clients and companies.

V 120
T 1
P 4
TS 30
WP yes

GORDON DADDS LLP 6 Agar Street, London WC2N 4HN **Tel:** 020 7493 6151 **Email:** recruitment@gordondadds.com **Apply to:** Mr David Ruck	The firm of choice for ambitious individuals, combining the skills needed to address legal issues with the human qualities that make working together a pleasure.

V 6
T 13
P 39
TS 236
WP no

GOSSCHALKS Queens Gardens, Hull HU1 3DZ **Tel:** 01482 324252 **Email:** rjt@gosschalks.co.uk **Apply to:** Mr Richard Taylor	Purpose built city centre offices. Major national clients with emphasis on commercial and licensing work. Many partners recognised as specialists in their own field.

V 3
T 6
P 28
TS 124
WP no

GOTELEE 31-41 Elm Street, Ipswich IP1 2AY **Tel:** 01473 211121 **Email:** mary.canning@gotelee.co.uk **Apply to:** Mrs Mary Canning	A well-established firm with a strong client base covering most areas of commercial private client and litigation work.

V 0
T 1
P 19
TS 122
WP no

GOUGH-THOMAS & SCOTT 8 Willow Street, Ellesmere, Shropshire SY12 0AQ **Tel:** 01691 622413 **Apply to:** Mr MJ Kendall	Offices in Ellesmere and Oswestry, a young go ahead firm in a rural area dealing with general practice.

V 1
T 1
P 4
TS 18
WP no

GRAEME QUAR & CO Orchard House, Furzehall Farm, Fareham PO16 7JH **Tel:** 01329 827 004 **Email:** gquar@quar.co.uk **Apply to:** Mr Graeme Quar	A law firm advising business.

V 0
T 0
P 1
TS 9
WP no

GRAHAM & ROSEN 8 Parliament Street, Hull HU1 2BB **Tel:** 01482 323123 **Email:** hpd@graham-rosen.co.uk **Apply to:** Miss Helen Drewery	General practice including private client, personal injury and matrimonial. Member of network of European lawyers. No vacancies at present.

V 0
T 1
P 6
TS 45
WP no

V = Vacancies / **T** = Trainees / **P** = Partners / **TS** = Total Staff / **WP** = Work Placement

Government Legal Profession

Tel: 0845 300 0793
Email: glstrainees@tmpw.co.uk
Web: www.gov.uk/gls

The firm Government lawyers provide legal advice to the government of the day and represent it in court proceedings. Whether the government is creating new laws, buying goods and services, employing people or defending its decisions in court, it needs significant levels of legal advice on a whole range of complex issues. To carry out this work, the government needs its own lawyers, who understand its business, to provide legal services to a wide client base – including a range of central government departments and other government bodies.

Types of work Fighting tax avoidance. Drafting the gender pay gap regulations. Working on the space industry bill. Supporting the negotiations on the terms of the UK's withdrawal from and new relationship with the EU. Promoting competition for the benefit of consumers. Preventing cyber crime. These are just some examples of the work lawyers have been involved in recently. The diversity of our work reflects the wide range of activities within government. These range across issues of national and international significance and across public and private law, embracing advisory and legislative work, litigation, commercial and a wealth of specialist areas.

Who should apply Departments are looking for people with excellent analytical ability and communication skills. Since our lawyers have the opportunity to work in different legal areas throughout their careers, applicants need to provide evidence of innovative thinking. And because that work has a significant and positive impact upon the lives of millions across the country, you must be passionate about public service.

Training programme Two-year training opportunities are primarily available within the Government Legal Department (GLD), HM Revenue and Customs (HMRC), the National Crime Agency (NCA), and the Competition and Markets Authority (CMA). If your application is successful, you will join one of these departments and the structure of your training period will vary accordingly. A valued member of your legal team, you will be fully involved in a broad range of work. You will have an active role to play in casework. You may liaise with government ministers, senior policy makers and counsel. And you may have the opportunity to participate in the legislative process itself.

When and how to apply Trainees are usually recruited two years in advance. However, a number of places are usually available for those looking to start their training sooner. The recruitment arrangements have previously involved online ability tests and a half-day assessment centre. Please check the website for full details when the legal trainee application process opens in early July.

Work placements Around 30 placements are usually available each year on the diversity summer scheme. This scheme is for undergraduates or graduates from diverse backgrounds which are currently under-represented in the legal profession. Please check the website for further information.

Sponsorship Departments will pay your Legal Practice Course (LPC) or Bar Professional Training Course (BPTC) fees in full provided you have not yet started either course. Where the course has begun, departments will pay your fees for the remainder of the course. If you intend to study the LPC or BPTC on a full-time basis, you may be eligible for a grant of about £5,400-£7,600. Retrospective payments to candidates who have completed their courses cannot be made. Funding for the GDL may be available. If your application is successful, you will need to discuss GDL funding with your department.

Vacancies	Approx 60
Trainees	50-60
Total lawyers	2,000

Work placement yes

Apply
Online

Starting salary
1st year – Around £28,000

Minimum qualifications
2.2 degree

Sponsorship
LPC/BPTC

Offices
Mostly London although there are legal teams in the regions e.g. Bootle, Bristol, Leeds and Manchester

Government
Legal Profession

Gowling WLG (UK) LLP

Two Snowhill, Birmingham B4 6WR
Tel: 0800 096 9610
Email: trainees-uk@gowlingwlg.com
Web: gowlingwlgcareers.co.uk
f gowlingwlgtrainees **𝕏** gowlingtrainees

The firm We're a leading sector-focused international law firm. But we're different. What sets us apart is a growing reputation for client experience, outstanding people and creative energy. You'll find us in Canada, Europe, Middle East, Asia and the UK, focused on key global sectors including real estate, energy, financial services, life sciences, natural resources, infrastructure and technology. We're a firm with momentum, making bold moves in the international legal market, where we've significantly increased our footprint and capability. And we have an appetite for further international growth.

Types of work Our areas of expertise include: real estate, corporate, dispute resolution, banking and finance, employment, pensions, tax, EU trade, competition, public law and regulatory, corporate recovery and insolvency, intellectual property, IT, projects, outsourcing and general commercial.

Who should apply Penultimate-year law students, final-year non-law students and graduates. We welcome applications from exceptional candidates with well-rounded personalities from diverse cultures and different backgrounds. We're not prescriptive when it comes to qualifications, so we don't ask for particular grades at A level or degree. If you are intelligent, talented, willing to learn and work hard, we think you deserve the chance to prove yourself.

Training programme Treated as a lawyer from day one, you'll enjoy early responsibility, international opportunities and exposure to big-ticket work as you learn from legal experts across the globe. Our training contracts consist of four six-month seats and we'll get you started with a full and comprehensive induction, designed to help you settle into life here. Choosing from our broad-ranging practice areas, your programme will typically include a contentious seat, a non-contentious seat, real estate and an optional seat (which could be an international secondment or working for a client). You'll get deeply involved in interesting casework for an exceptional scope of clients, enjoying top tier training in a high performing, hugely encouraging culture. It'll be a continuous learning journey with one-to-one guidance from a partner mentor, a dedicated supervisor, the graduate recruitment team and, of course, the strong support network of legal experts all around you.

When and how to apply The first stage of the selection procedure is an online application form. After we receive your application form, we'll invite you to complete a game based assessment. If successful, you will then be asked to undertake a video interview. Assessment days are the final part of our selection procedure for places on our vacation schemes and for training contract applications.

Work placements We run vacation schemes at our London and Birmingham offices, during spring and summer. You'll experience life at an international law firm first-hand, meet our people and clients, and gain an insight into our work and culture. One of our current trainees will help you settle in and is on hand to answer any queries you may have. You'll have a dedicated supervisor who will ensure you receive quality work, support and constructive feedback. There will also be plenty of social events to help you network and build up professional relationships (while enjoying yourself too, of course).

Sponsorship We cover your Legal Practice Course (LPC) and Graduate Diploma in Law (GDL) fees, as well as providing a maintenance grant for each course.

Vacancies	25
Trainees	50
Partners	593
Total staff	3,171

Work placement yes

Apply
Online at
gowlingwlgcareers.co.uk

Starting salary
Birmingham – £28,000
London – £40,500

Sponsorship
GDL/LPC

Offices
Beijing, Birmingham, Brussels, Calgary, Dubai, Guangzhou, Hamilton, London, Monaco, Montréal, Moscow, Munich, Ottawa, Paris, Singapore, Stuttgart, Toronto, Vancouver, Waterloo

GOWLING WLG

GRAYS

Duncombe Place, Duncombe Place, York YO1 7DY
Tel: 01904 634771
Email: brianmitchell@grayssolicitors.co.uk
Apply to: Mr Brian Mitchell

Matters handled include private client work, landed and settled estates, tax, trusts and probate, charities, property litigation, professional negligence, agricultural, commercial and domestic conveyancing, and landlord and tenant work.

V	0
T	0
P	5
TS	26
WP	no

GREATER MANCHESTER POLICE

Professional Standards Branch - Legal Services, Force Headquarters, Central Park, Northampton Road, Manchester M40 5BP
Apply to: Sian Williams

V	0
T	0
P	-
TS	0
WP	no

GREENBERG TRAURIG LLP

The Shard, Level 8, 32 London Bridge Street, London SE1 9SG
Tel: 020 3349 8700
Email: gradrecruit@gtlaw.com
Apply to: Training Principal

GT is the multidisciplinary London office of international firm Greenberg Traurig and prides itself on its reputation for client focused service and building long-term relationships.

V	4+19
T	10
P	25
TS	105
WP	yes

GREENHOUSE STIRTON & CO

1-2 Faulkner's Alley, Cowcross Street, London EC1M 6DD
Tel: 020 7490 3456
Email: greenhousestirton@mediationlawyers.co.uk
Apply to: Mr M Stirton

Private client firm specialising in court of protection, probate charity and mediation.

V	0
T	0
P	2
TS	3
WP	yes

GREENWOODS GRM LLP

Monkstone House, City Road, Peterborough PEI 1JE
Tel: 01733 887700
Email: rmpreston@greenwoodsgrm.co.uk
Apply to: Mrs Rosa Preston

We are a fast-growing commercial firm based in London, Peterborough and Cambridge, with an excellent reputation built on a regional, national and international client base.

V	3
T	4
P	10
TS	140
WP	yes

GREGORY ABRAMS DAVIDSON LLP

20-24 Matthew Street, Liverpool L2 6RE
Tel: 0151 236 5000
Email: info@gadllp.co.uk
Apply to: The Personnel Manager

Dynamic, forward-thinking practice that has achieved particular recognition for property, commercial, personal injury, family, crime and education law. A friendly yet challenging environment for trainees.

V	0
T	2
P	9
TS	78
WP	yes

GRM LAW

1 Bedford Row, London WC1R 4BZ
Tel: 020 7242 0631
Email: law@grm.co.uk
Apply to: Ms Melissa Butler

Long-established private client, company/commercial and litigation practice with strongly developed Anglo-German, and other connections including Anglo-German trade organisations.

V	0
T	0
P	11
TS	40
WP	no

GROSS & CO

83/84 Guildhall Street, Bury St Edmunds IP33 1LN
Tel: 01284 763333
Email: gdk@gross.co.uk
Apply to: Mr Graeme Kirk

An independent firm providing a quality service throughout the world.

V	0
T	-
P	5
TS	28
WP	no

V = Vacancies / **T** = Trainees / **P** = Partners / **TS** = Total Staff / **WP** = Work Placement

GUILDFORD BOROUGH COUNCIL Millmead House, Millmead, Guildford, Surrey GU2 4BB **Tel:** 01483 505050 **Email:** businesssupportlegal@guildford.gov.uk **Apply to:** Mr Robert Parkin	Local government in-house legal practice dealing primarily with planning, housing, public entertainment and taxi licensing, conveyancing, procurement, contracts and general local government law.	**V** **T** **P** **TS** **WP**	0 2 - 20 no
GUILE NICHOLAS SOLICITORS 43 Lodge Lane, North Finchley, London N12 8JG **Tel:** 020 8492 2290 **Email:** hr@gnlaw.co.uk **Apply to:** HR Department	Specialist firm: family, housing, court of protection, employment, wills/probate, mental health, AVP and general civil litigation. Private and legal aid work.	**V** **T** **P** **TS** **WP**	0 5 5 30 yes
HAINS & LEWIS Penffynnon, Hawthorn Rise, Haverfordwest SA61 2BQ **Tel:** 0834 4080 125 **Email:** law@hainsandlewis.co.uk **Apply to:** Miss V H Hains	General high street/legal aid practice - two branch offices. Five solicitors specialising in family, property, probate, public law, general civil litigation and some crime.	**V** **T** **P** **TS** **WP**	0 2 4 30 no
HALL SMITH WHITTINGHAM 1 Dysart Buildings, Nantwich, Cheshire CW5 5DP **Tel:** 01270 610 300 **Email:** law@hswsolicitors.co.uk **Apply to:** Mrs Kay Master	General practice but known for strength in family, agriculture, private client work. Only candidates with a 2.1 degree are interviewed and preference is given to local candidates.	**V** **T** **P** **TS** **WP**	0 2 5 40 no
HANNE & CO SOLICITORS The Candle Factory, 112 York Road, London SW11 3RS **Tel:** 020 7228 0017 **Email:** info@hanne.co.uk **Apply to:** Mrs Grainne Fahy	Hanne & Co is a full service law firm with an outstanding reputation. We are always looking for ambitious people to join our team.	**V** **T** **P** **TS** **WP**	3^{20} 6 12 60 no
HARBOTTLE & LEWIS LLP Hanover House, 14 Hanover Square, London W1S 1HP **Tel:** 020 7667 5000 **Email:** graduaterecruitment@harbottle.com **Apply to:** Ms Lisa Lacuna	The firm specialises in the media, entertainment, leisure and aviation industries. Regarded by *Legal 500* as a leading firm across all its industry areas.	**V** **T** **P** **TS** **WP**	6 11 42 186 no
HARDING EVANS LLP 2 North Street, Newport, Gwent NP20 1TE **Tel:** 01633 244233 **Email:** thomasn@hevans.com **Apply to:** Miss Nikki Thomas	For our 2019 intake the firm are identifying and recruiting our future trainee solicitors through our internal paralegal pool.	**V** **T** **P** **TS** **WP**	1 3 10 120 yes
HARPER & ODELL 61-63 St John Street, London EC1M 4AN **Tel:** 020 7490 0500 **Email:** law@harperandodell.co.uk **Apply to:** Mr RA Hussein	Long-established, busy central London commercial practice specialising in personal injury, landlord and tenant and contractual claims, property disputes and residential and commercial conveyancing.	**V** **T** **P** **TS** **WP**	TBC 2 2 5 no

V = Vacancies / **T** = Trainees / **P** = Partners / **TS** = Total Staff / **WP** = Work Placement

HARRIS & HARRIS LEGAL SERVICES LLP 14 Market Place, Wells BA5 2RE **Tel:** 01749 674747 **Email:** joshua.eva@harris-harris.co.uk **Apply to:** Mr Joshua Eva	Applications are invited for a training contract, to commence September 2019. We also offer a one year office clerk role for undergraduate law students.	V 1[19] T 1 P 7 TS 50 WP yes
HARRIS WATERS & CO 406-408 High Road, Ilford, Essex IG1 1TW **Tel:** 020 8478 0888 **Email:** roger@harriswaters.com **Apply to:** Mr R Waters	We are an expanding dynamic firm with a growing reputation for our professional yet warm and friendly services in family law, litigation, residential and commercial conveyancing.	V 1 T 1 P 2 TS 11 WP yes
HARRISON CLARK RICKERBYS SOLICITORS 5 Deansway, Worcester WR1 2JG **Tel:** 01905 746 453 **Email:** kware@hcrlaw.com **Apply to:** Miss Kate Ware	Harrison Clark Rickerbys are listed as first tier in the prestigious legal directories *Legal 500* and *Chambers & Partners* and is Lexcel accredited.	V Approx 10 T 20 P 70 TS 460 WP yes
HARROWELLS 1 St Saviourgate, York YO1 8ZQ **Tel:** 01904 558600 **Email:** careers@harrowells.co.uk **Apply to:** Mrs Louise Osborne		V 4 T 7 P 20 TS 135 WP no
HART READE 104 South Street, Eastbourne BN21 4LW **Tel:** 01323 727321 **Email:** info@hartreade.co.uk **Apply to:** Mrs Fiona Gausden	Established and respected high street firm which advises private and business clients on all main areas of law. Lexcel, CQS, ALEP accredited.	V 2 T 1 P 6 TS 60 WP no
HATCHERS SOLICITORS Welsh Bridge, 1 Frankwell, Shrewsbury SY3 8LG **Tel:** 01743 248545 **Email:** mail@hatchers.co.uk **Apply to:** Mr Patrick Gittins	General practice with some specialisms. Broad client base. Three offices in central and North Shropshire. Specialisms: environment, agriculture, debt, PI, crime, family, private client, corporate and employment.	V 0 T 1 P 13 TS 90 WP no
HATTEN WYATT SOLICITORS & ADVOCATES 51/54 Windmill Street, Gravesend DA12 1BD **Tel:** 01474351199 **Email:** recruitment@hatten-wyatt.com **Apply to:** Mr Jasvinder Gill	Well established high street firm with offices throughout Kent.	V 4[20] T 2 P 9 TS 80 WP yes
HAWKSWELL KILVINGTON LTD 17 Navigation Court, Calder Park, Wakefield, West Yorkshire WF2 7BJ **Tel:** 01924258719 **Email:** ltankard@hklegal.co.uk **Apply to:** Mrs Louise Tankard	We are based south of Leeds in a modern business park. We have established a national reputation as a niche construction law practice.	V 1 T 2 P 3 TS 15 WP no

V = Vacancies / **T** = Trainees / **P** = Partners / **TS** = Total Staff / **WP** = Work Placement

HAY & KILNER LAW FIRM
Merchant House, 30 Cloth Market, Newcastle upon Tyne NE1 1EE
Tel: 0191 232 8345
Email: ros.sparrow@hay-kilner.co.uk
Apply to: Recruitment Partner

We are looking for confident and commercially aware individuals with excellent communication skills. We will provide you with a broad training programme.

V	3
T	3
P	24
TS	82
WP	yes

HAYES + STORR
18-19 Market Place, Fakenham, Norfolk NR21 9BH
Tel: 01328 863231
Email: law@hayes-storr.com
Apply to: Mr Alex Findlay

Busy, dynamic and expanding practice with seven offices across North and West Norfolk. We offer a broad range of services to individuals and commercial clients.

V	2
T	2
P	11
TS	90
WP	no

HCB SOLICITORS
1-5 Longley Road, Worsley, Manchester M28 3JB
Tel: 0161 790 1411
Email: reception@hcbgroup.com
Apply to: Ms Margaret McCormack

A well-established general practice with four offices in Greater Manchester covering matrimonial, crime, personal injury, commercial conveyancing and litigation. Legal aid franchise.

V	1
T	3
P	8
TS	52
WP	no

HEALD SOLICITORS LLP
Artemis House, 4 Bramley Road, Milton Keynes MK1 1PT
Tel: 01908 662277
Email: linda.bray@healdlaw.com
Apply to: Mr David Dees

We mainly serve businesses (mostly owner-managed), their owners and key personnel. Commercial property, corporate and commercial, dispute resolution, family and private client departments.

V	1[20]
T	1
P	4
TS	30
WP	yes

HELIX LAW
1 Frederick Terrace, Frederick Place, Brighton BN1 1AX
Tel: 01273 761990
Email: careers@helix-law.com
Apply to: Mr Alex Cook

We are a firm specialising in dispute resolution, litigation and adjudication. We look for hard working ambitious people who deliver.

V	2[20]
T	2
P	4
TS	14
WP	no

HEMPSONS
100 Wood Street, London EC2V 7AN
Tel: 020 7839 0278
Email: erecruitment@hempsons.co.uk
Apply to: The Trainee Solicitor Coordinator

Offices: London, Harrogate, Newcastle and Manchester, offering a full range of legal services to NHS and healthcare clients (both individuals and institutional) and charities.

V	3
T	3
P	46
TS	300
WP	no

HENRY'S SOLICITORS LIMITED
72-74 Wellington Road South, Stockport, Cheshire SK1 3SU
Tel: 0161 477 8558
Email: reception@henrysolicitors.co.uk
Apply to: Mr Kieran Henry

A criminal and prison law specialist company with a fraud contract. We are one of the North West's leading criminal law providers.

V	1
T	3
P	-
TS	25
WP	yes

HEPTONSTALLS
7-13 Gladstone Terrace, Goole DN14 5AH
Tel: 01405 765661
Email: recruitment@heptonstalls.co.uk
Apply to: Ms Sharon Speirs

A friendly general practice firm with a strong emphasis on personal injury and medical negligence work. Applications should be made using the application form.

V	1-2
T	0
P	6
TS	100
WP	no

V = Vacancies / **T** = Trainees / **P** = Partners / **TS** = Total Staff / **WP** = Work Placement

Herbert Smith Freehills LLP

Exchange House, Primrose Street, London EC2A 2EG
Tel: 020 7374 8000
Email: graduatesuk@hsf.com
Web: www.herbertsmithfreehills.com
f hsfgraduatesuk 🐦 hsfgraduatesuk

The firm Look at law differently. We are Herbert Smith Freehills, a leading, full-service, global law firm working on some of the world's biggest cases. With award-winning expertise in multiple fields, our progressive approach sets us apart. Inclusivity is our defining characteristic: here, you will be a part of everything. By combining perspectives and potential from diverse backgrounds, we're able to view and practice law differently. This allows us to break new ground, whether it's a complex international dispute or a billion-pound, cross-border deal. Now, we want to add your expertise to the mix.

Types of work Our work is incredibly varied. We provide top quality tailored legal advice to major corporations, governments and financial institutions as well as various commercial organisations. We advise more FTSE 100 clients than any other UK or US-headquartered firm. Our dispute resolution practice is number one in the UK, Asia and Australia and this includes both our leading international arbitration practice and award-winning in-house advocacy unit. We can therefore offer a complete litigation service and a realistic alternative to the Bar. And that's not all. Our other practice areas include finance, competition, regulation and trade, real estate and employment, pensions and incentives as well as specialist areas like intellectual property and tax.

Who should apply Herbert Smith Freehills is a place where you have both global exposure and a supportive network. You'll focus on technical excellence and a client led approach. If you've got the drive to make the most of the opportunities on offer and the ambition and potential to become a brilliant lawyer, don't compromise. Be a part of everything at Herbert Smith Freehills. The minimum academic qualification required is a 2.1 degree (or equivalent); applications are accepted from students with law and non-law backgrounds and those looking to change careers.

Training programme Herbert Smith Freehills' trainees can be a part of it all. The training contract balances contentious and non-contentious work with pro bono opportunities and real responsibility. Trainees rotate around four six-month seats with the opportunity to go on secondment either to a client or to one of the firm's international offices.

When and how to apply This year, we will only be recruiting our future trainees from our vacation schemes and all candidates will have the opportunity at the end of their vacation scheme to interview for a training contract. These schemes have been specifically designed to build and test the unique skills and knowledge required to succeed here. It's really important that you have this knowledge and these skills in place when you join: it will make you a better lawyer, let you build connections with our team and give you a much stronger start to your career here. It's also a two-way process. The scheme gives you the chance to get to know us and see what life is like at Herbert Smith Freehills before you make a decision about your career. For those who are unable to attend a vacation scheme, please get in touch with Shaunna Morey at shaunna.morey@hsf.com to discuss your individual circumstances, which we will consider on a case-by-case basis.

Work placements Winter vacation scheme 2018 deadline: 15 October 2018. Spring and summer vacation scheme 2019 deadline: 4 January 2019.

Sponsorship Herbert Smith Freehills provides funding and a maintenance allowance for GDL and LPC courses.

Vacancies	60
Trainees	132
Partners	468*
Total staff	4,932*

*denotes worldwide figure

Work placement   yes

Apply
Online at careers.
herbertsmithfreehills.com/
uk/grads

Starting salary
£44,000

Minimum qualifications
2.1 degree

Sponsorship
GDL/LPC

Offices
Throughout Asia, Australia, Europe, the Middle East and the USA

HERBERT SMITH FREEHILLS

Proud diversity and inclusion partner of

∂S aspiringsolicitors

Remember to cite *The LawCareers.Net Handbook* on your application form if you apply to this firm.

Hewitsons LLP

Elgin House, Billing Road, Northampton NN1 5AU
Tel: 0160 423 3233
Email: carolinelewis@hewitsons.com
Web: www.hewitsons.com
🐦 hewitsons

The firm Hewitsons is ranked among the UK's foremost regional law firms with 45 partners and around 100 lawyers based at its main centres in Northampton and Cambridge.

Types of work The firm has a strong reputation in a range of specialisms and a national and international client base, particularly in Europe and across North America. Its areas of noted expertise include corporate and commercial work, technology, employment, competition law, property, construction, planning, environment, insolvency, bioscience, agriculture, tax, trusts and charities.

Who should apply The firm welcomes applications from candidates who have achieved a high standard of academic success, with a minimum of a 2.1 degree, and who are bright, personable, have initiative and enjoy working as part of a team.

Training programme Training contracts are offered at Northampton and Cambridge, with placements in London and Milton Keynes. Trainees complete four placements of six months each in a range of different legal specialisms. During each seat, the trainee is supervised closely by a partner or senior solicitor, and progress is monitored on a day-by-day basis as well as in a formal three-monthly review, carried out mid-seat and at end of seat. The firm provides a comprehensive induction programme specifically tailored for the needs of trainee solicitors. The Professional Skills Course is coupled with an extensive programme of trainee solicitors' seminars provided by specialist in-house lawyers.

When and how to apply Telephone the director of human resources, Caroline Lewis, on 0160 423 3233 or email carolinelewis@hewitsons.com. Applications for training contracts to start in September 2021 should be made between July and August 2019.

Work placements The firm operates a vacation scheme in June, July and August for undergraduates in their first year. A selection process with interview applies. Application is by way of letter and CV to carolinelewis@hewitsons.com.

Vacancies	15
Trainees	15
Partners	45
Total staff	254
Work placement	yes

Training contract deadline
August 2019

Apply to
Caroline Lewis

Starting salary
£23,500

Minimum qualifications
2.1 degree

Offices
Northampton, Cambridge,
Milton Keynes, London

HFW

Friary Court, 65 Crutched Friars, London EC3N 2AE
Tel: 020 7264 8000
Email: grad.recruitment@hfw.com
Web: www.hfw.com
🐦 hfwgrads

The firm We are a sector focused, entrepreneurial law firm. But there's more to us than that. We have a passion for the sectors we work in – whether we are solving complex issues across construction, aviation and shipping, or providing advice across insurance, commodities and energy. We're people who like to get things done. It's this pragmatism, combined with our creative approach, that makes us our clients' go-to commercial advisers.

And we are, unapologetically, absolute experts in what we advise our clients on. So yes, we're different. Our clients say "less traditional" – "progressive", even. We say we're specialist lawyers here to add value to our clients.

Types of work Aviation, commodities, construction, energy, financial institutions, insurance and reinsurance, logistics, mining, ports and terminals, shipping, space, yachts, travel, cruise and leisure.

Who should apply Our trainees share our entrepreneurial spirit and are bright and commercial. We look for individuals who are eager to solve problems in new and practical ways, and who want to build collaborative relationships. Strong communication skills are a must. In addition, as our training contract is truly international we look for individuals who have a global perspective and an interest in completing international work.

Our trainees come from a variety of backgrounds and disciplines and we welcome applications from both law and non-law students and undergraduates and experienced individuals alike.

Training programme Every year we recruit only a small number of trainees – 15 per year split across a September and March intake. This enables us to give every trainee our full attention, and means that your individual contribution makes a real difference. A training contract at HFW consists of four six-month seats – typically three contentious seats and one transactional seat, with at least one seat spent outside of London in an international office. Overall, we aim to provide you with a dynamic, supportive and varied environment in which you are challenged to become the best lawyer you can be and encouraged to contribute to the success of our global business.

When and how to apply Apply online via our website: www.hfw.com/graduate-recruitment. The deadline for vacation scheme applications is 31 January 2019. The deadline for training contract applications is 31 July 2019.

Work placements Our vacation schemes are a key part of our recruitment process for trainees and we consider all of our vacation scheme participants for a training contract. Completing a vacation scheme enables you to experience our work first hand, and also provides you with valuable insight into our industry sectors, our global reach and our culture. Alongside spending time in at least one department of your choice, you can expect to attend presentations, social events and a final round partner interview for a training contract.

Each year we run a one-week spring vacation scheme and various summer vacation schemes (ranging between one and two weeks in duration).

Sponsorship GDL/LPC fees paid and a maintenance grant of £7,000 (£5,500 outside London) is available for each year of study.

Vacancies	15
Trainees	33
Partners	170
Total staff	1,016

Work placement — yes

Training contract deadline
31 July 2019

Apply
Online

Starting salary
1st year – £38,000
2nd year – £40,000

Sponsorship
CPE/GDL/LPC

Offices
Beirut, Brussels, Dubai, Geneva, Hong Kong, Houston, Jakarta, Kuwait, London, Melbourne, Paris, Perth, Piraeus, Riyadh, São Paulo, Shanghai, Singapore, Sydney

HFW

Proud diversity and inclusion
partner of

🅰️ aspiringsolicitors

HER MAJESTY'S COURTS & TRIBUNALS SERVICE
Legal Operations Team, 102 Petty France, London SW1H 9AJ
Tel: 020 3334 2582
Email: benjamin.wood@hmcts.gsi.gov.uk
Apply to: Mr Benjamin Wood

HMCTS employs 1,200 lawyers who are mostly responsible for providing advice to magistrates on matters of law, practice and procedure. Legal roles also exist in other jurisdictions, albeit in smaller numbers.

V	0
T	0
P	0
TS	1200
WP	no

HEREFORDSHIRE DISTRICT COUNCIL
Brockington, 35 Hafod Road, Hereford HR1 1SH
Tel: 01432 260266
Apply to: Ms Erica Hermon

A busy legal practice serving both Herefordshire Council and a range of local public sector organisations.

V	0
T	0
P	0
TS	31
WP	no

HERRINGTON CARMICHAEL LLP
Building 9, Riverside Way, Watchmoor Business Park, Camberley, Surrey GU15 3YL
Tel: 012 7668 6222
Email: anne.walsh@herrington-carmichael.com
Apply to: Mrs Anne Walsh

General practice with offices in Camberley and Wokingham. Specialist commercial and private client departments dealing with most areas of work except crime or legal aid.

V	3-4[20]
T	8
P	13
TS	95
WP	no

HERTFORDSHIRE COUNTY COUNCIL
County Hall, Pegs Lane, Hertford SG13 8DE
Tel: 01992 555510
Email: hertsdirect@hertscc.gov.uk
Apply to: Mr D Simon

V	0
T	3
P	-
TS	-
WP	no

HETHERTONS LLP SOLICITORS
Northern House, 7-9 Rougier Street, York Y01 6HZ
Tel: 01904 625 327
Email: law@hethertons.co.uk
Apply to: The Staff Partner

General legal practice with offices in York and Boroughbridge. Private and publicly funded work and a comprehensive range of legal services.

V	0
T	1
P	3
TS	31
WP	no

HEWITTS
207 Newgate Street, Bishop Auckland DL14 7EL
Tel: 01388 604691
Email: enquiries@hewitts.co.uk
Apply to: Ms Laura Saunders-Jerrom

General legal practice with five offices situated in rural South West Durham and Teeside.

V	0
T	2
P	13
TS	103
WP	no

HEXTALLS LTD
28 Leman Street, London E1 8ER
Tel: 020 7488 1424
Email: janeclark@hextalls.com
Apply to: Ms Emma Bond

Specialises in national and international insurance/reinsurance and other commercial litigation/dispute resolution, shipping, transport/travel and sports and leisure.

V	0
T	0
P	8
TS	30
WP	no

HIBBERTS LLP
144 Nantwich Road, Crewe, Cheshire CW2 6BG
Tel: 01270215117
Email: cjb@hibberts.com
Apply to: Ms Carolyn Brooksbank

Long established and highly regarded practice located in Cheshire and Shropshire. We pride ourselves in providing personal, practical and professional advice to all our clients.

V	1[19]
T	1
P	9
TS	96
WP	yes

V = Vacancies / **T** = Trainees / **P** = Partners / **TS** = Total Staff / **WP** = Work Placement

Higgs & Sons

3 Waterfront Business Park, Brierley Hill DY5 1LX
Tel: 0345 111 5050
Email: beyourself@higgsandsons.co.uk
Web: www.higgsandsons.co.uk
f higgsandsonsgrads **🐦** higgsandsons

The firm Higgs & Sons is one of the largest and most respected law firms in the West Midlands, operating out of offices in Brierley Hill and employing over 200 staff. The firm's headquarters are situated in a modern, purpose designed facility at the prestigious Waterfront Business Park. We are well recognised in the *Legal 500* and *Chambers & Partners* guide to the legal profession.

Higgs & Sons is different from the typical law firm. We successfully combine traditional values with an innovative approach to legal problems which has helped to attract an impressive client base while also staying true to our local community. Clients and staff alike are attracted to Higgs' ability to offer an all round service in a number of areas. We are proud to provide a supportive and friendly working environment within which colleagues can thrive. The opportunity for career progression is clear as almost half of our partners trained with the firm.

Types of work For the business client: corporate and commercial; insolvency; employment; commercial litigation; and commercial property.

For the private client: wills; probate and trusts and tax; employment; personal injury; clinical negligence; conveyancing; dispute resolution; and matrimonial/family.

Who should apply Applications are welcome from law and non-law students who can demonstrate consistently high academic records, a broad range of interpersonal skills and extra-curricular activities and interests. We would like to hear about what you have done to develop your wider skills and awareness. We are looking for people who want to get involved and participate fully in the business.

Training programme A training contract at Higgs is different from those offered by other firms. There is the unique opportunity to undertake six four-month seats in a variety of departments, including a double seat in the department into which you wish to qualify as you approach the end of your training contract. Throughout the training contract you will receive a mix of contentious and non-contentious work and an open door policy means that there is always someone on hand to answer questions and supervise your work. Regular appraisals take place at the end of each seat and a designated partner oversees you throughout the duration of your training contract, acting as a mentor. Participation in BTSS events and an active Higgs social environment ensures an effective work life balance.

Benefits include private medical insurance, contributory pension, life assurance, 25 days' holiday and BTSS membership.

When and how to apply Apply online at www.higgsandsons.co.uk. Please see website for details.

Sponsorship Professional Skills Course, GDL and LPC.

Vacancies	6
Trainees	12
Partners	35
Total staff	227

Training contract deadline
Please see website

Apply
Online

Starting salary
1st year – £23,500
2nd year – £25,000

Minimum qualifications
2.1 preferred

Sponsorship
GDL/LPC

Offices
Brierley Hill

Hill Dickinson LLP

No 1 St Paul's Square, Liverpool L3 9SJ
Tel: 0151 600 8000
Email: recruitment@hilldickinson.com
Web: www.hilldickinson.com
🐦 hd_trainees

The firm We are a leading and award-winning international commercial law firm with more than 840 people, including 175 partners and legal directors. From offices in the UK, mainland Europe and Asia, we deliver advice and strategic guidance spanning the full legal spectrum. We act as a trusted adviser to businesses, organisations and individuals across the globe and from a wide range of market sectors, advising on non-contentious advisory and transactional work through to all forms of commercial litigation and arbitration. We pride ourselves on fostering the strongest client relationships and adding value through innovation.

Types of work As a full-service law firm, we offer the full range of commercial legal services, from employment and property and construction to corporate, commercial and dispute resolution. We have notable strength, experience and presence in a number of market sectors, including marine, transportation and logistics, retail, insurance, health, international trade, education, and banking and financial services.

Who should apply Academically, you'll need at least a 2.1 and ABB or equivalent. We want our trainees to show a commitment to learning throughout their careers. We want trainees with the insight and awareness to understand our clients' demands and what is expected of us as an international law firm, so we want to hear about your business background. You'll need to have experiences that demonstrate your passion for a career in law and the motivation you've got to get there.

Training programme Modest numbers: we recruit to retain, so for 2021, we're taking on up to 10 trainees which means that we'll have the resources and time to give you as much support as you need.

Immediate responsibilities: because of our small intake, there's lots of interesting work to go around and you'll be given challenges from the start.

Choices: you'll work four seats and be able to select preferences from a variety of different areas of law.

A mentor: your mentor (a Hill Dickinson solicitor) will be on hand from day one and throughout your training contract to offer advice, guidance and support.

Office sharing: you'll share an office with a partner, who will help you develop your legal knowledge and be there to support you.

A social scene: our trainees work really hard and as you'd expect, it's not all fun and games. But when they do let their hair down, they get together and do it properly! We organise events and competitions throughout the year and there are plenty of opportunities to get involved in our corporate responsibility activity, too.

When and how to apply Apply via our online form at www.hilldickinson.com/careers which opens 1 November 2018, closing 31 January 2019 for vacation schemes and 31 July 2019 for training contracts.

Work placements We have up to 44 vacation scheme places available in our northern offices and 10 in London. Apply online by 31 January 2019.

Vacancies	10
Trainees	27
Partners	175
Total staff	840

Work placement yes

Training contract deadline
31 July 2019

Apply
Online

Starting salary
1st year – £24,000
2nd year – £26,000
London:
1st year – £32,000
2nd year – £34,000

Minimum qualifications
2.1 degree

Sponsorship
LPC plus maintenance grant

Offices
Liverpool, Manchester, Leeds, London, Piraeus, Singapore, Monaco, Hong Kong

HILL DICKINSON

HILL & ABBOTT Burgundy Court, 64-66 Springfield Road, Chelmsford CM2 6JY **Tel:** 01245 258892 **Email:** cst@hill-abbott.co.uk **Apply to:** Mrs Kerry Huggins	General practice with specialisms in personal injury, family, child care, trusts, commercial and conveyancing.	V 0 T 2 P - TS 40 WP yes
HILLIERS HRW Mindenhall Court, High Street, Stevenage SG1 3UN **Tel:** 01438 346 000 **Email:** admin@hilliershrw.co.uk **Apply to:** Mrs Fiona Nash	Offices at present in Bedfordshire & Hertfordshire. An extremely forward thinking firm in IT and all business matters.	V 0 T 1 P 2 TS 32 WP no
HILLYER MCKEOWN LLP Gorse Stacks House, George Street, Chester, Cheshire CH1 3EQ **Tel:** 01244 318 131 **Email:** enquiries@law.uk.com **Apply to:** Mr Richard Burnett	Hillyer McKeown LLP is a full service commercial and private client firm. The firm's three offices cover Chester, North Wales and the Wirral Pensinula. No vacancies at present.	V 1 T 2 P 12 TS 80 WP no
HINE SOLICITORS 285 Banbury Road, Summertown, Oxford OX2 7JF **Tel:** 01865 514348 **Email:** recruitment@hinesolicitors.com **Apply to:** Abi Wilson	The training contract will have a heavy emphasis on criminal law. Presently training seats are also offered in prison law and conveyancing.	V 10 T 21 P 8 TS 180 WP no
HKH KENWRIGHT & COX Mountsview House, 202-212 High Road, Ilford, Essex IG1 1QB **Tel:** 020 8553 9600 **Email:** admin@hkhsol.com **Apply to:** Mr KS Mian	Specialist criminal and family firm. Handles residential and commercial conveyancing. Serious Fraud Panel members. Private immigration and work permits. Legal aid and private client base.	V 0 T 1 P 2 TS 19 WP yes
HODDERS Po Box 344, 11 Station Road, Harlesden, London NW10 4UD **Tel:** 020 8965 9862 **Apply to:** Ms Nycki Gray-Cooper	A medium-sized five partner law firm with offices in Northwest London, Wembley, Battersea and High Wycombe.	V 0 T 2 P 5 TS 65 WP no
HOLDEN & CO. LLP 32-33 Robertson Street, Hastings TN34 1HT **Tel:** 01424 722422 **Email:** law@holdenandco.co.uk **Apply to:** Mr David Nessling	General high street practice of a legal aid plus private work Lexcel accredited firm.	V 1 T 1 P 4 TS 23 WP no
HOLMES & HILLS Bocking End, Braintree, Essex CM7 9AJ **Tel:** 01376 320 456 **Email:** legaladvice@holmes-hills.co.uk **Apply to:** Mrs Sue Bushell	Holmes & Hills offers a full range of legal assistance from personal, family and property services to comprehensive support for your business.	V 0 T 5 P 9 TS 105 WP no

V = Vacancies / **T** = Trainees / **P** = Partners / **TS** = Total Staff / **WP** = Work Placement

Hodge Jones & Allen LLP

180 North Gower Street, London NW1 2NB
Tel: 020 7874 8300
Email: dwhite@hja.net
Web: www.hja.net
🐦 hodgejonesallen

The firm Hodge Jones & Allen was founded in 1977 and to this day remains committed to providing first-class legal help to both individuals and organisations.

Our philosophy has always been to enable individuals to have access to justice where otherwise they might be denied it and this ethos remains as strong today as it did back then. We strive to right wrongs, achieve justice for all and get the very best result for our clients. People have always been at the heart of our firm.

"We have been on the forefront of the legal sector – changing lives, making headlines and advancing the law, since our inception and hope to continue this for many years to come." – Patrick Allen, senior partner.

Types of work Civil liberties, criminal defence, employment, family, wills and probate, medical negligence, personal injury, dispute resolution, social housing, serious fraud, military claims, industrial disease, property disputes and court of protection.

Who should apply Applications from both law and non-law graduates are welcome. You should be able to demonstrate a consistently high level of academic and personal achievement. We generally expect an upper second class degree.

The firm is looking for people who:
Communicate clearly and effectively;
Have an excellent academic record;
Can demonstrate they are interested and committed to the work the firm does;
Are hard-working and dedicated;
Understand and share the ethos of the firm; and
Have a record of achievement in extracurricular activities

Training programme Trainees have a full induction on joining Hodge Jones & Allen covering the work of the firm's main departments, procedural matters and professional conduct. Training consists of four six-month seats. Formal reviews of progress are held at least once during the seat. The training is well structured and the trainees have the benefit of a mentoring scheme. The firm provides good clerical support so trainees can concentrate on legal work rather than administration. The firm has an excellent IT infrastructure and continues to invest heavily in IT to keep pace with innovation.

When and how to apply Applications are invited by 26 July 2019 for training contracts to begin in September 2020. All recruitment information is available on our website at www.hja.net.

Applications are by application form only, downloaded from our website. Guidance notes, a job description and FAQs can be accessed on our website.

Sponsorship Sponsorship contributions may be considered, but are not generally available.

Vacancies	6-10
Trainees	16
Partners	46
Total staff	216

Training contract deadline
26 July 2019

Apply to
Trainee Solicitor Scheme

Starting salary
1st year – £25,500
2nd year – £27,500

Minimum qualifications
2.1 degree

Offices
London

hodge jones & allen
solicitors

Remember to cite *The LawCareers.Net Handbook* on your application form if you apply to this firm.

374 THE LAWCAREERS.NET HANDBOOK

Hogan Lovells

Atlantic House, Holborn Viaduct, London EC1A 2FG
Tel: 020 7296 2000
Email: graduate.recruitment@hoganlovells.com
Web: www.hoganlovells.com/graduates
f hoganlovellsgradsuk 🐦 @hlgraduatesuk

The firm When you choose Hogan Lovells, you're not just choosing a career in law. You're choosing a career in law with a more progressive international outlook, a clearer focus on innovation and a sharper commercial edge. You're choosing a team with a healthy contempt for boundaries and conventions. One that likes to work in a more collaborative and joined-up way, shaping the business landscape, overcoming unforeseen challenges and creating new opportunities for its clients. In short, when you choose a career with Hogan Lovells, you're choosing to be a global game-changer.

Types of work Something else that makes us stand out as a firm – aside from the unified way we work across the globe – is our exceptional range of practice areas. For the people who work with us, this breadth presents an incredible variety of disciplines to explore, from corporate to finance to government regulatory, and from intellectual property to litigation, arbitration and employment law. It's inspiring stuff. Especially when you realise that, within these specialisms, our expertise – and the clients we work with – extend to virtually every industry sector.

Training programme Each year, we take on around 50 graduates (from law and non-law subjects) as trainee solicitors. Our two-year training contract is split across four six-month seats that cover different practice areas. Together, they offer greater exposure to, and broader understanding of, international law. For their third seat, our trainees also have the chance to apply for an international or client secondment.

When and how to apply The application window for training contracts for non-law students and graduates is open between 17 September 2018 and closes on 31 January 2019. Applications for law students reopen on 1 June 2019 and must be submitted by 31 July 2019.

Work placements For penultimate-year students, final-year students and graduates, we also host summer and winter vacation schemes. These offer you the chance to work alongside partners, associates and our current trainees, and start developing the skills you'll need to be a successful lawyer.

Our summer vacation schemes are open to all penultimate and final-year students, as well as graduates. And we'll accept applications from 17 September 2018 until 6 January 2019.

The winter vacation scheme is specifically for final-year students and graduates. The application window opens 17 September 2018 and closes 31 October 2018.

Sponsorship Maintainance grants are available for GDL and accelerated LPC. GDL is £7,000 outside of London and £8,000 within London. LPC sponsorship is £10,000.

Think globally. Discover your potential. Become a game-changer. Find out more and apply at hoganlovells.com/graduates.

Vacancies	Up to 50
Trainees	120
Partners	800
Total staff	5,000

Work placement yes
(see Insider Report on p79)

Training contract deadline
31 July 2019

Apply
Online at
hoganlovells.com/graduates

Starting salary
Year 1 – £45,000
Year 2 – £50,000

Minimum qualifications
2.1 degree (or equivalent)

Sponsorship
GDL/LPC

Offices
Alicante, Amsterdam, Baltimore, Beijing, Birmingham, Boston, Brussels, Budapest, Colorado Springs, Denver, Dubai, Düsseldorf, Frankfurt, Hamburg, Hanoi, Ho Chi Minh City, Hong Kong, Houston, Jakarta, Johannesburg, London, Los Angeles, Louisville, Luxembourg, Madrid, Mexico City, Miami, Milan, Minneapolis, Monterrey, Moscow, Munich, New York, Northern Virginia, Paris, Perth, Philadelphia, Rio de Janeiro, Riyadh, Rome, San Francisco, São Paulo, Shanghai, Silicon Valley, Singapore, Sydney, Tokyo, Warsaw, Washington DC, Zagreb

Proud diversity and inclusion
partner of

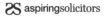

HOOD VORES & ALLWOOD The Priory, Church Street, Dereham NR19 1DW **Tel:** 0845 3724240 **Email:** roger.margand@hoodvoreslaw.co.uk **Apply to:** Mr Roger Margand	Mid-Norfolk medium-sized rural firm able to offer excellent experience, particularly in private client and property work.	V 0 T 1 P 5 TS 25 WP no
HOOPER & WOLLEN Carlton House, 30 The Terrace, Torquay TQ1 1BS **Tel:** 01803 213251 **Email:** lawyers@hooperwollen.co.uk **Apply to:** Mr Clive Meredith	Leading South Devon firm. Departments include trust and probate, conveyancing - domestic and commercial, civil litigation, personal injury, family/child care, LSC franchise and company/commercial.	V 0 T 4 P 11 TS 84 WP no
HORSHAM DISTRICT COUNCIL Parkside, Chart Way, Horsham, West Sussex RH12 1RL **Tel:** 01403 215100 **Email:** legaladmin@horsham.gov.uk **Apply to:** Mr Robert Baxendale	Local authority legal department.	V 1 T 1 P - TS 15 WP no
HORWICH FARRELLY Alexander House, 94-96 Talbot Road, Old Trafford, Manchester M16 OSP **Tel:** 0161 413 1937 **Email:** sarah.halliwell@h-f.co.uk **Apply to:** Miss Sarah Halliwell	Easter and summer vacation schemes available. Horwich Farrelly hire students into paralegal roles. Once probation is completed paralegals are eligible to apply for training contracts.	V 15 T 30 P 35 TS 730 WP yes
HORWOOD & JAMES LLP 7 Temple Square, Aylesbury, Buckinghamshire HP20 2QB **Tel:** 01296 487361 **Email:** enquiries@horwoodjames.co.uk **Apply to:** Miss Jill Swift	Business and private client lawyers, established in Aylesbury, Buckinghamshire, for over 200 years.	V 0 T 1 P 5 TS 28 WP no
HOTCHKISS WARBURTON 34 High Street, Crediton, Devon EX17 3JP **Tel:** 01363 774752 **Email:** enquiries@hotchkiss-warburton.co.uk **Apply to:** Mrs L Stone	Small high street firm specialising in conveyancing, wills and probate.	V 0 T - P 2 TS 6 WP no
HOWARD & OVER 114 Albert Road, Devonport, Plymouth PL2 1AF **Tel:** 01752 556606 **Email:** admin@howard-over.co.uk **Apply to:** Ms Katherine Millman	Offices at Devonport, Plymstock and Ivybridge. General practice with two partners and 10 other fee-earners. The firm has a legal aid franchise in two categories.	V 0 T 0 P 2 TS 32 WP no
HOWARD KENNEDY No1 London Bridge, London SE1 9BG **Tel:** 020 3755 6000 **Email:** trainee.recruitment@howardkennedy.com **Apply to:** Trainee Recruitment	We are a full-service firm, with core real estate, corporate and dispute resolution departments, and further teams in employment, private client and family.	V 10^{20} T 16 P 53 TS 350 WP no

V = Vacancies / **T** = Trainees / **P** = Partners / **TS** = Total Staff / **WP** = Work Placement

Howes Percival LLP

Nene House, 4 Rushmills, Northampton NN4 7YB
Tel: 0160 423 0400
Email: katy.tebbutt@howespercival.com
Web: www.howespercival.com
f howespercivalgrad **𝕏** hpgradrecruit

The firm Howes Percival LLP is a leading commercial law firm with offices in Cambridge, Leicester, Manchester, Milton Keynes, Northampton and Norwich. Our working environment is progressive, focussed but friendly and our corporate structure means that fee earners are rewarded on merit and can progress to associate or partner status quickly.

Types of work The firm is a recognised market leader in corporate and commercial, commercial property, planning, employment, commercial and property litigation, construction, IP/IT, insolvency, regulatory, family and private client, among other things.

The top quality work we do means that we are instructed by major companies. We were shortlisted for Regional Law Firm of the Year 2016 in *The Lawyer* awards which recognised our ambitious strategy for growth in recent years and has seen us modernise and improve every aspect of our business.

Who should apply Well-educated, focused, enthusiastic, commercially aware graduates with a minimum 2.1 degree in any discipline. We welcome confident communicators with strong interpersonal skills who share our desire to be the best.

Training programme Trainees usually complete four six-month seats. They report direct to a partner or director and after three months and again towards the end of each seat will be formally assessed by the fee earner training them. Trainees will be given every assistance by the fee-earners in their department to develop quickly, and will be given responsibility as soon as they are ready.

Staff benefit from a flexible benefits package, including contributory pension and private medical insurance.

When and how to apply The closing date for training applications in 2021 is 19 July 2019. Our application form is online and can be found on the graduate page of our website.

Work placements These are available in June and July. Please apply via the online application form found on the graduate page of our website.

Sponsorship GDL and LPC. Details available upon request.

Vacancies	8
Trainees	14
Partners	43
Total staff	208

Work placement yes
(see Insider Report on p80)

Training contract deadline
19 July 2019

Apply
Online

Minimum qualifications
2.1 degree

Sponsorship
GDL/LPC

Offices
Cambridge, Leicester, Manchester, Milton Keynes, Northampton, Norwich

HOWARTH GOODMAN First Floor, The Lexicon, 10 Mount Street, Manchester M2 5NT **Tel:** 0161 832 5068 **Email:** sb@howarthgoodman.com **Apply to:** Mr Steven Baddiel	Commercial property, employment, landlord and tenant, company, building contract disputes.

V Poss
T 1
P 2
TS 11
WP yes

HOWELL JONES LLP 75 Surbiton Road, Kingston upon Thames, Surrey KT1 2AF **Tel:** 020 8549 5186 **Email:** keith.howell-jones@howell-jones.com **Apply to:** Mr Simon Carter	We offer a broad range of services including company commercial, litigation, personal injury, property, matrimonial and private client.

V 0
T 0
P 14
TS 75
WP no

HRJ FOREMAN LAWS 25 Bancroft, Hitchin, Hertfordshire SG5 1JW **Tel:** 01462 458711 **Email:** simon.cousins@foremanlaws.co.uk **Apply to:** Mr Simon Cousins	Company/commercial and property are our forte - with a practice geared to the business community.

V 0
T 3
P 5
TS 35
WP no

HSR LAW The Law Chambers, 7/8 South Parade, Doncaster, South Yorkshire DN1 2ED **Tel:** 01302 347800 **Email:** richard.allwood@hsrlaw.co.uk **Apply to:** Mr Richard Allwood	Three offices organised in five teams: civil litigation/PI; family (franchised); private client; crime(franchised); business/agriculture; and property and corporate.

V 0
T 1
P 7
TS 42
WP no

HUGH JAMES Hodge House, 114-116 St Mary Street, Cardiff CF10 1DY **Tel:** 029 20224871 **Email:** diane.brooks@hughjames.com **Apply to:** Mrs Diane Brooks	Hugh James, a top 100 and Wales' largest regional law firm.

V 10
T 20
P 64
TS 680
WP yes

HUGHES PADDISON 10 Royal Crescent, Cheltenham GL50 3DA **Tel:** 01242 574244 **Email:** jal@hughes-paddison.co.uk **Apply to:** Miss Jennifer Allen	Medium sized practice providing services across the board including family, private client, residential conveyancing, commercial property, company law, civil litigation, business law and commercial disputes.

V 2
T 4
P 11
TS 60
WP no

HUMPHREYS & CO 14 King Street, Bristol BS1 4EF **Tel:** 0117 929 2662 **Email:** lawyers@humphreys.co.uk **Apply to:** Ms Amanda Weaver	Central Bristol niche practice. Commercial: intellectual property; employment; litigation; company/ commercial; property. Private client: planning, residential property; defamation; professional negligence; asbestos litigation.

V 1-2
T 3
P 4
TS 30
WP yes

HUMPHRIES KIRK LLP Glebe House, North Street, Wareham, Dorset BH20 4AN **Tel:** 01929 552141 **Email:** m.knight@hklaw.eu **Apply to:** Mrs Melanie Knight	Specialised practice offering family, conveyancing, private client, PI, IP, construction, commercial litigation, company/commercial and commercial property work from offices in Dorset, London and Europe.

V 1[19]
T 3
P 20
TS 180
WP yes

V = Vacancies / **T** = Trainees / **P** = Partners / **TS** = Total Staff / **WP** = Work Placement

Irwin Mitchell LLP

Riverside East, 2 Millsands, Sheffield S3 8DT
Tel: 0370 1500 100
Email: graduaterecruitment@irwinmitchell.com
Web: www.irwinmitchell.com
f irwinmitchellsolicitors ✔ irwinmitchell

The firm The firm was founded in 1912 and is the UK's largest full-service law firm, covering business, personal and private wealth clients. We are passionate about delivering excellent levels of service with an expert hand and a human touch, our five core values guiding us at every stage. Our social responsibility programme is fundamental to who we are and consists of four strands woven into the fabric of the group; pro bono, community, people, environment. The Irwin Mitchell independent registered charity has made over £1.8 million of charitable donations. We encourage applications from all backgrounds. We recently won the 2018 award for 'Excellence in Diversity' from the Signature Awards. We are also listed in numerous graduate surveys for most popular graduate recruiter including *The Guardian*, *The Times* and *TargetJobs*.

Types of work As a full-service law firm we provide business services for organisations, personal legal services to individuals, and private wealth services to private clients. For business legal services, the firm offers expertise in banking and finance, commercial litigation, construction, corporate, employment, insolvency, investigations, pensions, planning, real estate and tax. Our typical clients are drawn from a cross-section of growing businesses to large companies, and come from a range of sectors including technology, consumer, financial services, manufacturing, media and entertainment, real estate, and education. For personal legal services, the firm remains one of the leading personal injury and medical negligence litigation practices in the UK. Irwin Mitchell covers all the key injury areas such as asbestos-related disease, serious injury, international travel litigation, medical negligence and product liability. Within the PLS training contract, private wealth offers a wide range of services for private clients including succession planning, tax, reputation protection, family, and probate administration. It also advises business owners and executives on their personal business wealth.

Who should apply We welcome candidates from law and non-law backgrounds as well as career changers. We carry out anonymised application screening ensuring that we test your suitability through our various assessments. We look for candidates who can demonstrate they are able to deal with the complexities of the theory and application of the law within a business setting. Applicants should share the firm's five core values, show evidence of our key competencies (listed on our website) and also display a real motivation for their application to Irwin Mitchell.

Training programme At application stage we'll ask you to choose which stream (business legal services or personal legal services) and which office you would prefer to work in. You will undertake a number of training seats in your chosen stream, gaining practical experience and real responsibility.

When and how to apply To apply for a legal work placement and/or a training contract please complete our online application.

Work placements Our placements are a vital part of our recruitment strategy. A large proportion of our current/future trainee solicitors have undertaken a work placement with the firm therefore we encourage all those interested in joining us to apply for a legal work placement.

Sponsorship If successful, we will meet all the fees associated with your LPC and, if applicable, your GDL if you have not started or completed your studies when offered a training contract. We also provide a maintenance grant.

Vacancies	45
Trainees	98
Partners	255
Total staff	2,900

Work placement yes

Training contract deadline
30 June 2019

Apply
Online

Minimum qualifications
2.1 desired

Sponsorship
GDL/LPC

Offices
Birmingham, Bristol, Cambridge, Chichester, Gatwick, Glasgow, Leeds, London, Manchester, Middlesbrough (consulting office), Newcastle, Sheffield, Southampton

(IM) irwinmitchell
solicitors

Remember to cite *The LawCareers.Net Handbook* on your application form if you apply to this firm.

TRAINING CONTRACT DIRECTORY **379**

HUNT AND COOMBS SOLICITORS
35 Thorpe Road, Peterborough PE3 6AG
Tel: 01733 882800
Email: andrew.cave@hcsolicitors.co.uk
Apply to: Mr Andrew Cave

General practice firm with specialities in family, property, probate, crime and dispute resolution. Has legal aid franchises, Lexcel and IIP. Committed to IT solutions and training.

V	2
T	0
P	8
TS	85
WP	no

HUNTERS
9 New Square, Lincoln's Inn, London WC2A 3QN
Tel: 020 7412 0050
Email: trainingcontracts@hunters-solicitors.co.uk
Apply to: The Training Principal

Traditionally known for private client, charity and matrimonial work. Now a broadly based Lincoln's Inn practice with a significant presence in other fields.

V	1-2
T	4
P	28
TS	71
WP	yes

HUTTONS
16 St Andrew's Crescent, Cardiff CF10 3DD
Tel: 029 20378621
Email: stuart.hutton@huttons-solicitors.co.uk
Apply to: Ms C Strowbridge

We are niche litigation practice covering clinical negligence, commercial litigation, contentious probate, criminal and family law and some non-contentious property, trusts and corporate work.

V	0
T	1
P	3
TS	25
WP	yes

IKIE SOLICITORS LLP
20 Marischal Road, Lewisham, London SE13 5LG
Tel: 020 8463 0808
Email: ikiesolicitors@aol.com
Apply to: Mr A N Ikie

Small firm with services offered in high street general practices. Applicants must have a minimum 2.1 degree.

V	0
T	2
P	2
TS	5
WP	no

INGHAMS
32-38 North Albert Street, Fleetwood FY7 6AW
Tel: 01253 873481
Email: enquiries@inghams-law.co.uk
Apply to: HR Department

A general high street practice, with four offices across the Fylde Coast in Lancashire, undertaking a broad range of legal work, including publicly funded.

V	Poss
T	1
P	7
TS	43
WP	yes

THE JACKSON LEES GROUP
Walker House, Exchange Flags, Liverpool L2 3YL
Tel: 0151 282 1700
Email: recruitment@jacksonlees.co.uk
Apply to: Miss Claire Hardman

Business and property, dispute resolution, personal injury, clinical negligence, court of protection, family, wills/estates. Lexcel. Offices: Liverpool, Manchester, Birkenhead, Heswall, West Kirby.

V	0
T	7
P	-
TS	280
WP	no

JACKSONS LAW FIRM
17 Falcon Court, Preston Farm Industrial Estate, Stockton-on-Tees TS18 3TU
Tel: 01642 356500
Email: recruitment@jacksons-law.com
Apply to: Ms Adrienne Patterson

Jacksons' philosophy is based upon a modern approach to business, incorporating the most up to date information technology and a commercial style management structure.

V	2
T	4
P	11
TS	70
WP	no

JACOBS & REEVES
153 High Street, Poole, Dorset BH15 1AU
Tel: 01202 674425
Email: jsingleton@jacobsreeves.co.uk
Apply to: Ms Janice Singleton

Well-established firm with three offices in Poole and Wimborne. Strong client base covering most areas of general practice, commercial, private client and litigation.

V	0
T	1
P	6
TS	45
WP	no

V = Vacancies / **T** = Trainees / **P** = Partners / **TS** = Total Staff / **WP** = Work Placement

JAMES MURRAY SOLICITORS 41 Merton Road, Bootle, Liverpool L20 7AP **Tel:** 0151 933 3333 **Email:** info@jamesmurray.law.co.uk **Apply to:** Ms J Thomas	We offer training contracts on merit to in-house paralegals usually within one year. Vacancies arise through expansion and CVs received are kept on file.	V 0 T 6 P 4 TS 68 WP no
JAY VADHER & CO 185 Romford Road, London E15 4JF **Tel:** 020 8519 3000 **Apply to:** Mr BND Vadher	High street firm with litigation and conveyancing departments. CLS franchises.	V 1 T 1 P 3 TS 8 WP no
JEFFREY GREEN RUSSELL LIMITED Waverly House, 7-10 Noel Street, London W1F 8GQ **Tel:** 020 7339 7000 **Email:** humanresources@jgrlaw.co.uk **Apply to:** Human Resources Manager	Jeffrey Green Russell is a medium-sized commercial West End practice with a diverse client base specialising in company/commercial, litigation, property, gaming, licensing and leisure, and private client.	V 2 T 4 P 21 TS 76 WP no
JEREMY ROBERTS & CO 51 Park Road, Peterborough PE1 2TH **Tel:** 01733 343943 **Email:** jeremyroberts.co@btconnect.com **Apply to:** Mr J Roberts	A small, friendly, high street solicitors in Peterborough specialising in family, criminal, employment, accident and general litigation with some conveyancing and general work.	V 1 T 0 P 1 TS 8 WP yes
JH POWELL & CO Cathedral Chambers, 2 Amen Alley, Derby DE1 3GT **Tel:** 01332 372211 **Email:** djt@jhpowell.co.uk **Apply to:** Mr David Tomlinson	City centre commercial and private client practice.	V 0 T 2 P 6 TS 20 WP no
JMW SOLICITORS No 1 Byrom Place, Manchester M3 3HG **Tel:** 0161 832 8087 **Apply to:** Mr Richard Powell	Main work areas are personal injury, clinical negligence, commercial property, corporate, insolvency, commercial litigation, intellectual property, employment, family, sports and media, crime and private client.	V Approx 10 T 10 P 35 TS 380 WP no
JNP LEGAL 15 Glebeland Street, Merthyr Tydfil CF47 8AU **Tel:** 01685 350421 **Email:** law@jnplegal.org **Apply to:** Mr Antony Williams	JNP Legal is a forward thinking High Street practice. We have three offices and employ 50 members of staff.	V 1[19] T 4 P 4 TS 48 WP no
JOELSON JD LLP 30 Portland Place, London W1B 1LZ **Tel:** 020 7580 5721 **Email:** training@joelsonlaw.com **Apply to:** Mr Niall McCann	Founded in 1957, we undertake company/commercial, gambling/ liquor licensing, litigation, property, private client, employment, immigration, IP and international work for commercial clients.	V 4[19] T 5 P 14 TS 80 WP no

V = Vacancies / **T** = Trainees / **P** = Partners / **TS** = Total Staff / **WP** = Work Placement

Jones Day

21 Tudor Street, London EC4Y 0DJ
Tel: 020 7039 5959
Email: recruit.london@jonesday.com
Web: www.jonesdaylondon.com
f jonesdaygraduatesuk 𝕏 jonesday

The firm Jones Day is a global law firm with more than 2,500 lawyers in 43 offices across five continents. The firm is distinguished by: a singular tradition of client service; the mutual commitment to, and the seamless collaboration of, a true partnership; formidable legal talent across multiple disciplines and jurisdictions; and shared professional values that focus on client needs. Our 200 London-based lawyers (including around 60 partners and 40 trainees) collaborate with their colleagues from Jones Day practices and offices across the globe to guide clients through their toughest challenges.

Types of work In London's critical financial centre, our lawyers are perfectly placed to address the most demanding and complex global matters: including cross-border M&A; real estate and finance transactions (including banking, capital markets, investment funds, private equity and structured finance); global disputes; and regulatory matters involving the UK, US and other authorities. Additional specialist areas include business restructuring; competition/antitrust; corporate criminal investigations; corporate tax planning; employment and pensions; intellectual property; and projects and infrastructure.

Who should apply We recruit people who are committed to a legal career and want to become partners of the future. Around half our London partners trained with the firm. Successful candidates have either a law or non-law degree; strong intellectual ability; good communication skills; and demonstrate resourcefulness, drive and dedication. 60% of our current trainees are non-law graduates and 35% were graduates or postgraduates when they applied to us.

Training programme The firm operates a distinctive, non-rotational training system, designed to provide flexibility and responsibility from the start. Our trainees work across different practice areas at the same time and are encouraged to assume their own workload. This allows for a high level of client contact, faster development of potential and the opportunity to compare and contrast different disciplines alongside one another. As our trainees do not move to a different department every six months they don't miss the end of deals or trials that they have worked on. Work will vary from small cases which trainees may handle alone (under the supervision of a senior lawyer) to matters where they will assist a partner or an associate solicitor. The firm runs a structured seminar programme to support the practical teaching trainees receive from lawyers with whom they work.

When and how to apply Apply for a placement if you want to train at Jones Day. We expect to recruit our trainees from our placement candidates. All our placement schemes are open to final-year law and non-law students, graduates and postgraduates; our placement schemes are also open to penultimate-year students undertaking a qualifying law degree. Applications open on 1 September 2018. We recruit on a rolling basis, so cannot guarantee availability. Early applications are always advised. Final deadlines are 26 October 2018 (winter scheme); 14 December 2018 (spring scheme) and 10 January 2019 (summer scheme).

Work placements 70 places for two-week placements in winter, spring and summer holidays. Attendees experience work in a truly global law firm and see how our non-rotational training system works in practice by taking on real work from a variety of practice areas. They are also able to meet a range of lawyers at various social events. We pay an allowance of £500 per week.

Sponsorship GDL and LPC fees paid and £10,000 maintenance per year. Fast track LPC for sponsored students from August to end February each year with six-month gap before commencing training.

Vacancies	20
Trainees	40 approx
Partners	60 approx
Total staff	350 approx

Work placement yes
(see Insider Report on p81)

Training contract deadline
10 January 2019

Apply to
Graduate Recruitment
Manager

Starting salary
1st year – £50,000
2nd year – £57,000
NQ – £105,000

Minimum qualifications
2.1 degree (gained or predicted)

Sponsorship
GDL and LPC

Offices
London, Continental
Europe, Asia, United States,
Latin America, Middle East,
Asia Pacific

JOHAR & CO
Beckville House, 66 London Road, Leicester LE2 OQD
Tel: 0116 2543345
Email: info@johars.com
Apply to: Mr DK Johar

Franchised firm with IIP. General high street practice dealing with conveyancing, litigation, matrimonial, PI and immigration; clients both corporate and individual.

V	1
T	3
P	2
TS	25
WP	no

JOHN CHAPMAN AND CO
152-154 Epsom Road, Sutton SM3 9EU
Tel: 020 8337 3801
Apply to: Mr Andrew Larner

Conveyancing, wills and probate, litigation - personal injury, matrimonial, children. There are no vacancies at present.

V	0
T	0
P	4
TS	22
WP	no

JOHN HODGE SOLICITORS
10/11 Morston Court, Aisecome Way, Weston-Super-Mare BS22 8NG
Tel: 01934 410910
Email: jane.banks@johnhodge.co.uk
Apply to: Mrs Jane Banks

Well-established general practice. Training offered in family law, personal injury, conveyancing, dispute resolution and probate.

V	0
T	0
P	4
TS	65
WP	yes

JOHNS & SAGGAR LLP
34-36 Grays Inn Road, London WC1X 8HR
Tel: 020 3490 1475
Email: info@johnsandsaggar.co.uk
Apply to: Mr Khalid Sofi

Our specialist team are able to deal with a wide range of legal services to individuals, businesses and organisations.

V	0
T	0
P	2
TS	13
WP	yes

THE JOHNSON PARTNERSHIP
Cannon Courtyard, Long Row, Nottingham NG1 6JE
Tel: 0115 941 9141
Email: mail@thejohnsonpartnership.co.uk
Apply to: Mr Bill Soughton

Criminal work. Vacancies start as work experience and possibly lead onto training contracts.

V	1-2
T	4
P	13
TS	110
WP	yes

JORDANS
Neil Jordan House, Wellington Road, Dewsbury, West Yorkshire WF13 1HL
Tel: 01924 457 171
Email: recruitment@jordanssolicitors.co.uk
Apply to: Mrs S Taylor

An independent, medium-sized practice serving both the business community and private individuals across a broad range of specialisms.

V	1[20]
T	8
P	4
TS	65
WP	no

JOSEPH HILL & CO
220 - 224, High Road, Tottenham N15 4AJ
Tel: 020 8880 3535
Email: joehillsols@yahoo.co.uk
Apply to: Mr Phaedon Georgiou

Large criminal law practice requires dedicated and ambitious candidates. Successful applicants will gain experience in serious and complex cases and undertake police station accreditation.

V	5[19]
T	3
P	2
TS	12
WP	yes

JOVES SOLICITORS
312 Lewisham Road, London SE13 7PA
Tel: 020 8852 4544
Apply to: Mr AA Ekwekwu

Friendly firm specialising in immigration, employment and civil litigation and contracts.

V	0
T	1
P	-
TS	3
WP	yes

V = Vacancies / T = Trainees / P = Partners / TS = Total Staff / WP = Work Placement

K&L Gates LLP

One New Change, London EC4M 9AF
Tel: 020 7648 9000
Email: traineerecruitment@klgates.com
Web: www.klgates.com
🐦 klgates

The firm K&L Gates LLP is a fully integrated global law firm with lawyers located across five continents. K&L Gates represents leading global corporations, growth and middle-market companies, capital markets participants and entrepreneurs in every major industry group as well as public sector entities, educational institutions, philanthropic organisations and individuals. Our practice is a robust full market practice – cutting edge, complex and dynamic, at once regional, national and international in scope.

Types of work K&L Gates is active in the areas of corporate/M&A, debt capital markets, private equity, restructuring and insolvency, banking and asset finance, structured finance, derivatives, aviation, funds, antitrust, competition and trade regulation, public policy, real estate, planning and environment, intellectual property, media and sport, construction, energy, infrastructure and resources, insurance coverage, regulatory, tax, employment, litigation, international arbitration, investigations, enforcement and white collar crime plus other forms of dispute resolution.

Who should apply The firm welcomes applications from both law and non-law students. The firm also welcomes applications from relevant postgraduates. You should be highly motivated, intellectually curious, with an interest in commercial law and be looking for comprehensive training.

Training programme The firm ensures each trainee is given exceptional opportunities to learn, experience and develop so that they can achieve their maximum potential. Trainees spend six-month seats in four of the areas mentioned above. Each trainee sits with a supervisor and is allocated an individual mentor to ensure all round supervision and training. The firm has a thorough induction scheme and career development programme. High importance is placed on the acquisition of business and professional skills, with considerable emphasis on client contact and early responsibility. The training programme consists of weekly legal education seminars, workshops and a full programme of skills electives. Pro bono and corporate social responsibility activities are also encouraged.

When and how to apply Apply between 1 November 2018 and 31 July 2019 to begin in September 2021.

Work placements The firm's formal summer legal work placement scheme is open to law and non-law students and other relevant postgraduates. Your two weeks with us in July will provide you with broad exposure to opportunities in diverse areas. We aim to give you a seat in at least two departments, and wherever possible we will allocate you to a seat of your choice.

Sponsorship GDL funding: fees paid plus £5,000 maintenance grant.
LPC funding: fees paid plus £7,000 maintenance grant.

Vacancies	TBD
Trainees	17
Partners	53
Total staff	233
Work placement	yes

Training contract deadline
31 July 2019

Apply to
Hayley Atherton

Minimum qualifications
2.1 degree

Sponsorship
GDL/LPC

Offices
Austin, Beijing, Berlin, Boston, Brisbane, Brussels, Charleston, Charlotte, Chicago, Dallas, Doha, Dubai, Fort Worth, Frankfurt, Harrisburg, Hong Kong, Houston, London, Los Angeles, Melbourne, Miami, Milan, Munich, Newark, New York, Orange County, Palo Alto, Paris, Perth, Pittsburgh, Portland, Raleigh, Research Triangle Park, San Francisco, São Paulo, Seattle, Seoul, Shanghai, Singapore, Sydney, Taipei, Tokyo, Warsaw, Washington DC, Wilmington

JUDGE & PRIESTLEY LLP Justin House, 6 West Street, Bromley BR1 1JN **Tel:** 020 8290 7406 **Email:** gcollier@judge-priestley.co.uk **Apply to:** Ms Lucy El-Aawar	J&P are a leading firm in North Kent providing expert, professional and friendly advice to individuals and businesses in every major industry sector.	V 1 T 2 P 11 TS 130 WP no
JW HUGHES & CO Bank House, Lancaster Square, Conwy, Gwynedd LL32 8AD **Tel:** 01492 593442 **Apply to:** Mr DC Roberts	Established and busy general practice with well appointed offices in Conwy and Llandudno. Departmental structure dealing with areas of law in which the firm specialises.	V 0 T 1 P 6 TS 34 WP no
JWK SOLICITORS 19 Northumberland Street, Morecambe LA4 4AZ **Tel:** 01524 416960 **Apply to:** Mr D Harrison	A multi-discipline practice comprising three offices: Morecambe; Lancaster; and Great Eccleston. Supported by IT for the future. Broad commercial private/legal aid client base.	V 0 T 0 P 5 TS 34 WP no
K J COMMONS & CO 2-6 Upper Jane Street, Workington, Cumbria CA14 4AY **Tel:** 01900 604 698 **Email:** helen.mcneil@kjcommons.co.uk **Apply to:** Ms Helen McNeil	Franchised firm in crime, family, PI and clinical negligence. Large criminal practice. Other areas covered - conveyancing and wills. Offices also in Carlisle and Whitehaven.	V Poss T 3 P 2 TS 55 WP no
KAIM TODNER SOLICITORS LTD 11 Bolt Court, London EC4A 3DQ **Tel:** 020 7353 6660 **Email:** recruitment@kaimtodner.com **Apply to:** Ms Edina Balogh		V 0 T 4 P 8 TS 70 WP no
KANGS SOLICITORS 2a Wake Green Road, Birmingham B13 9EZ **Tel:** 0121 449 9888 **Email:** enquiries@kangssolicitors.co.uk **Apply to:** Mr H Kang	Niche criminal firm specialising in white collar crime/serious fraud work. Member of LSC specialist fraud panel.	V 1-2[20] T 1 P 1 TS 10 WP no
KATTEN MUCHIN ROSENMAN UK LLP Paternoster House, 65 St Paul's Churchyard, London EC4M 8AB **Tel:** 020 7776 7620 **Email:** lon.recruiting@kattenlaw.co.uk **Apply to:** Ms Michelle Johnson	Full-service firm with more than 600 lawyers worldwide in 14 offices. Our London office is growing and currently comprises approximately 45 lawyers.	V 2-3 T 4 P 18 TS 66 WP yes
KC LAW CHAMBERS SOLICITORS Unit B2, 62 Beechwood Road, London E8 3DY **Tel:** 020 7254 3353 **Email:** info@kclawchambers.com **Apply to:** Ms Roma Aheer	We are a firm of solicitors based in London, providing a wide range of legal service, with emphasis on personal injury, immigration employment and intellectual property law.	V 2[19] T 0 P 2 TS 5 WP yes

V = Vacancies / **T** = Trainees / **P** = Partners / **TS** = Total Staff / **WP** = Work Placement

Kennedys

25 Fenchurch Avenue, London EC3M 5AD
Tel: 020 7667 9667
Email: hr.admin@kennedyslaw.com
Web: www.kennedyslaw.com
f kennedystrainees

The firm We are a global law firm with expertise in dispute resolution and advisory services. We handle contentious and non-contentious matters for many industries, and provide claims and coverage advice to insurers and self-insureds for all lines of business across the globe.

Types of work Our growing network of offices delivers practical legal solutions to the insurance, corporate and public sectors. We combine our expertise with values built upon being approachable, straightforward, supportive and distinctive.

Our team handles both contentious and non-contentious legal services for many industries including: insurance and reinsurance, aviation, banking and finance, construction and engineering, healthcare, life sciences, public sector, rail, real estate, retail, shipping and international trade, sport and leisure, transport and logistics, and travel and tourism.

Who should apply At Kennedys we aim to recruit the best trainee talent and encourage diversity and an environment built upon different skills and backgrounds, to represent our global firm. Our atmosphere is friendly and supportive and our relationships are built on trust. We are looking for trainees that are collaborative and enthusiastic team players.

Training programme Our two year training contract allows you to develop relevant experience and skills that will set you up in your career as an excellent solicitor. During your training contract, you will complete four six-month seats across our core practice areas of insurance and reinsurance, liability, healthcare and commercial. We also offer exciting secondment opportunities to our Hong Kong office and UK clients.

At Kennedys, we offer training to ensure you are supported throughout your training contract. Throughout your training, you will be given the opportunity to attend in-house and external seminars, whilst having access to a large array of online skills and technical learning via our internal learning management system.

We currently offer training contracts in our Birmingham, Cambridge, Chelmsford, Edinburgh, London, Manchester and Taunton offices.

When and how to apply Applications for our 2019/20 training contracts open on the 1 May 2018 and will close on the 31 December 2018. Applications for our 2019 winter vacation scheme will open on the 1 May 2018 and close on the 30 September 2018.

Work placements In January, we run a one-week vacation scheme in our London office, offering the opportunity to experience what it would be like to work as a trainee at Kennedys in the UK.

During the week, you will be allocated a supervisor who will be responsible for your day-to-day tasks as well as a trainee buddy to support you. We arrange a schedule of activities during the week, to allow you the opportunity to learn more about Kennedys whilst we get to know you too. We ask for feedback from your supervisor after the week has finished, to help with our decisions on making training contract offers. We then offer training contract positions to commence the following year.

Vacancies	20
Trainees	43
Partners	270
Total staff	1,900

Work placement yes
(see Insider Report on p83)

Training contract deadline
31 December 2018

Apply
Online via our website
www.kennedyslaw.com

Starting salary
£36,000 (London)
£26,000 (regional)
£19,000 (Scotland)

Minimum qualifications
2.1 degree, any discipline,
300 UCAS points or
equivalent at A level

Offices
Auckland, Austin, Bangkok,
Basking Ridge, Belfast,
Bermuda, Birmingham,
Bogotá, Brussels,
Buenos Aires, Cambridge,
Chelmsford, Chicago,
Copenhagen, Dubai, Dublin,
Edinburgh, Glasgow,
Hong Kong, Lima,
Lisbon, London, Madrid,
Manchester, Melbourne,
Mexico City, Miami,
Moscow, New York, Paris,
Philadelphia, Santiago,
São Paulo, Sheffield,
Singapore, Sydney, Taunton

Kennedys

KEEBLES LLP Commercial House, Commercial Street, Sheffield S1 2AT **Tel:** 0114 2765555 **Email:** lisa.limb@keebles.com **Apply to:** Mr Giles Searby	One of Yorkshire's leading law firms, hlw Keeble Hawson LLP offers dynamic and commercial legal advice through its offices in Sheffield, Leeds and Doncaster.	V 4 T 8 P 36 TS 280 WP yes
THE KEITH JONES PARTNERSHIP Second Floor, 4 Europa Boulevard, Birkenhead, Merseyside CH41 4PE **Tel:** 0151 650 6830 **Email:** info@kjplaw.co.uk **Apply to:** Mrs Karen Doleman	We are a niche firm who specialise in commercial litigation and general commercial matters.	V 0 T 1 P 3 TS 15 WP yes
KENNARD WELLS SOLICITORS 84a High Street, Epping, Essex CM16 4AE **Tel:** 01992 570505 **Apply to:** Mr Richard Cohen	General family based practice with wide ranged private client work and legal aid franchises.	V 1 T 1 P 5 TS 35 WP no
KESAR & CO SOLICITORS 20 - 25 Market Square, Bromley, Kent BR1 1NA **Tel:** 020 8181 3100 **Email:** recruitment@kesarco.co.uk **Apply to:** Mr Mladen Kesar	Preference may be given to the IAAS accredited candidates.	V 2^{20} T 5 P 1 TS 29 WP yes
KINGSLEY BROOKES Estate Buildings, Railway Street, Huddersfield HD1 1JY **Tel:** 01484 302800 **Email:** practice.manager@kingsleybrookes.co.uk **Apply to:** Mrs Sam Goodall	A specialist criminal litigation firm, set up in 1998 with offices based in Huddersfield.	V 0 T 1 P 2 TS 5 WP no
KINGSLEY SMITH SOLICITORS LLP 81/87/89 High Street, Chatham, Kent ME4 4EE **Tel:** 01634 811118 **Email:** mail@kslaw.co.uk **Apply to:** Mrs Elizabeth Kingsley-Smith	We provide quality legal advice in a full range of legal services to individuals and businesses in the Medway towns and across Kent.	V 0 T 0 P 4 TS 20 WP no
KIRWANS 363 Woodchurch Road, Birkenhead, Merseyside CH42 8PE **Tel:** 0151 608 9078 **Email:** sbirchall@kirwans.co.uk **Apply to:** Mrs Sarah Birchall	Practice covering wills and estates, crime, conveyancing, family, personal injury, general civil, private client, general commercial, housing. LEXEL and Investor in People accreditation.	V 0 T 4 P 5 TS 80 WP no
KITELEYS 7 Stephens Court, 15-17 St Stephens Road, Bournemouth BH2 6LA **Tel:** 01202 299992 **Email:** office@kiteleys.co.uk **Apply to:** Mrs Paula Rose	One of the fastest growing law firms in the South with seven offices across Dorset and Hampshire, each committed to providing the best possible service to a wide range of clients.	V 0 T 2 P 4 TS 50 WP yes

V = Vacancies / **T** = Trainees / **P** = Partners / **TS** = Total Staff / **WP** = Work Placement

Kingsley Napley LLP

Knights Quarter, 14 St Johns Lane, London EC1M 4AJ
Tel: 020 7814 1200
Email: recruitment@kingsleynapley.co.uk
Web: www.kingsleynapley.co.uk
🐦 kingsleynapley

The firm We are a central London law firm advising nationally and internationally based clients covering a wide range of specialist areas from family and criminal to corporate and property work. Our wide range of expertise means that we can provide support for our clients in all areas of their business and private lives. Our reputation is strong, many of our lawyers are leaders in their field and our practice areas are highly ranked by the legal directories. We are known for combining creative solutions with pragmatism and a friendly sensitive approach, where the relationship between lawyer and client is key. We look for exceptional people with a wide range of skills to provide the breadth of service our clients require. In return, we offer a culture of individual responsibility, autonomy and development.

Types of work Criminal litigation, dispute resolution, clinical negligence and PI, employment, family and divorce, immigration, private client, company and commercial, real estate, public law and regulatory and professional discipline.

Who should apply Applications are welcomed from both legal and non-legal graduates who have a strong academic background (achieved a 2.1 degree). A trainee will need to demonstrate commercial awareness, motivation and enthusiasm. To be successful you will need excellent communication skills with the ability to be a creative, practical problem solver. We look for team players who bring something to the table and have a long-term interest in Kingsley Napley and the areas of legal practice it focuses on. Successful short-listed candidates will be asked to attend an assessment centre and partner interview as part of the selection process.

Training programme You will not be a bag carrier as a trainee at Kingsley Napley. By choosing to start your career with us you will be given meaningful and good quality experience working alongside and being supervised by highly experienced lawyers, who are specialists in their legal field. Trainees complete four six-month seats, providing a wide range of practical experience and skills in contentious and non-contentious work. The training programme is broader than most other firms due to the wide ranging areas of law practised here. Individual preference for seats is sought and will be balanced with the firm's needs. Trainees work closely with partners and solicitors in a supportive team structure, and have regular reviews to assist development. The firm maintains a friendly and open environment and it is the firm's policy that each trainee sits with a partner or senior solicitor while working for a department as a whole. The firm gives trainees the chance to meet clients, be responsible for their own work and join in marketing and client development activities.

When and how to apply Individuals are invited to apply from October 2018 with a closing date of 31 May 2019. A link to the online application form can be found on our website. For queries relating to training contracts at Kingsley Napley please email Vicki Tavener at vtavener@kingsleynapley.co.uk.

Work placements Kingsley Napley offer a limited number of one-week legal work placements during March to September each year. Work experience students have an opportunity to experience a number of aspects of life in a law firm, for example: general administration, library research and shadowing our qualified solicitors. To apply, a CV and covering letter should be submitted in the work experience section of our website www.kingsleynapley.co.uk/careers/work-experience.

Vacancies	6
Trainees	13
Partners	53
Total staff	378
Work placement	yes
Training contract deadline	
31 May 2019	
Apply	
Online	
Minimum qualifications	
2.1 degree	
Offices	
London	

Kirkland & Ellis International LLP

30 St Mary Axe, London EC3A 8AF
Tel: 020 7469 2000
Web: ukgraduate.kirkland.com

The firm Kirkland & Ellis International LLP is a leading international law firm with approximately 2,200 lawyers representing global clients.

Types of work Corporate: Kirkland has one of the most active and highly regarded private equity practices encompassing all aspects of this rapidly changing field.
Finance: Kirkland's leading finance practice includes the representation of both borrowers and lenders in a wide variety of transactions.
Investment funds: Kirkland is uniquely positioned to serve its clients in connection with the organisation and operation of private equity, real estate and hedge funds.
Restructuring: Kirkland has earned a distinguished international reputation acting for a varied range of clients in complex corporate restructuring, work-out and bankruptcy planning, negotiation and litigation.
Real estate finance: Lawyers practising in the real estate area at Kirkland have broad experience in real estate secured lending and structured finance, both in the representation of lenders and borrowers.
Financial services regulatory: Kirkland advises clients of the firm that are regulated by the UK Regulator, the US Regulator or both.
Tax: Kirkland has a strong international reputation for providing sophisticated tax counselling and effectively representing clients in tax disputes worldwide.
International arbitration and litigation: Kirkland represents multinational corporations, governments and government-owned entities in international arbitration and litigation cases around the world.
Antitrust and competition: Kirkland's antitrust and competition practice has decades of experience in litigation and transaction clearance.
Technology and IP transactions: Kirkland represents clients in all areas of IP, patent litigation, trademark matters, outsourcing, computer software, licensing, distribution, joint venture agreements, biotechnology, data protection and e-commerce issues.
Capital markets: Kirkland represents issuers, sponsors and underwriters in a wide variety of international securities transactions, with a particular focus on offerings of high-yield and other complex debt securities.

Who should apply Successful candidates will have a strong academic record and be motivated to work hard in a professional, friendly and entrepreneurial team.

Training programme You will be given early responsibility to work on complex multi-jurisdictional matters. On the job training is actively supported by an extensive education programme, carefully tailored to meet your needs. Trainees will have the opportunity to apply for an overseas secondment.

When and how to apply Apply online by 6 January 2019 for spring and summer vacation schemes, and by 14 July 2019 for training contracts beginning in August 2021.

Work placements Two-week vacation schemes across the spring and summer.

Sponsorship Full sponsorship of GDL and LPC fees, plus a maintenance grant of £10,000.

Vacancies	10
Trainees	20
Partners	900*
Total staff	3,978*

* denotes worldwide figure

Work placement yes
(see Insider Report on p85)

Training contract deadline
14 July 2019

Apply to
Emma Ridley

Starting salary
1st year – £50,000
2nd year – £55,000

Minimum qualifications
2.1 degree

Sponsorship
GDL/LPC

Offices
Beijing, Boston, Chicago, Dallas, Hong Kong, Houston, London, Los Angeles, Munich, New York, Palo Alto, San Francisco, Shanghai, Washington DC

KIRKLAND & ELLIS

Proud diversity and inclusion
partner of

 aspiringsolicitors

KITSONS LLP
Minerva House, Orchard Way, Torquay TQ2 7FA
Tel: 01803 202020
Email: recruitment@kitsons-solicitors.co.uk
Apply to: Miss Louise Mason

Established 1826. Serves private and commercial clients. Lexcel, investor in people, CQS, resolution, ELA, SFE, STEP, law society's family panel and alternative dispute resolution accredited.

V	Poss[19]
T	4
P	16
TS	100
WP	no

KOTECHA & CO
40b Station Road, North Harrow, Harrow, Middlesex HA2 7SE
Tel: 020 8426 0014
Email: info@kotechasolicitors.co.uk
Apply to: Ms Nayna Kotecha

Small friendly high street practice carrying out property work, wills and probate, matrimonial, landlord and tenant and personal injury.

V	0
T	1
P	2
TS	5
WP	yes

KUIT STEINART LEVY
3 St Mary's Parsonage, Manchester M3 2RD
Tel: 0161 832 3434
Email: alisonpearse@kuits.com
Apply to: Ms Alison Pearse

This UK200-listed Manchester commercial law firm advises and services businesses, their owners and high-net-worth individuals, including SMEs, financial institutions, property investment companies and PLCs.

V	6
T	13
P	35
TS	185
WP	yes

KUNDERT SOLICITORS LLP
4 The Quadrant, Coventry CV1 2EL
Tel: 024 7622 7741
Email: chris@kundert.co.uk
Apply to: Mr CJD Jones

General practice, two office locations in the centre of Coventry and at the north of the city. Mixed practice of contentious and non-contentious work.

V	0
T	1
P	4
TS	30
WP	yes

LA STEEL
Oxford Villa, 123 Dodworth Road, Barnsley, South Yorkshire S70 2EJ
Tel: 01226 770 909
Email: enquiries@lasteelsolicitors.com
Apply to: Mr LA Steel

Specialists in civil litigation, including personal injury, consumer law and professional and clinical negligence. Referrals solely through satisfied clients. No charge win or lose.

V	0
T	0
P	0
TS	8
WP	yes

LACEYS SOLICITORS LLP
5 Poole Road, Bournemouth BH2 5QL
Tel: 01202 557256
Email: info@laceyssolicitors.co.uk
Apply to: Mr Sam Freeman

A progressive *Legal 500*, Investors in People and Lexcel firm. Strong with both commercial and private clients.

V	2
T	2
P	13
TS	110
WP	no

LADERMAN AND CO
4 The Shrubberies, George Lane, London E18 1BD
Tel: 020 8530 7319
Apply to: Mr Daniel C Laderman

V	Poss
T	2
P	2
TS	13
WP	no

LAMPORT BASSITT
46 The Avenue, Southampton SO17 1AX
Tel: 023 80634931
Email: e-mail@lamportbassitt.co.uk
Apply to: Mr John Newton

The firm does not offer training contracts to external candidates. It recruits candidates as paralegals, and may internally promote these to trainees after one year's employment.

V	0
T	3
P	11
TS	80
WP	no

V = Vacancies / **T** = Trainees / **P** = Partners / **TS** = Total Staff / **WP** = Work Placement

LAND LAW LLP 10-14 Market Street, Altrincham WA14 1QB **Tel:** 0161 928 8383 **Email:** aawprivate@land-law.co.uk **Apply to:** Mr AAF Whyte	Niche commercial property firm.	V T P TS WP	0 3 6 46 no
LANGLEY WELLINGTON LLP SOLICITORS Royal House, 60 Bruton Way, Gloucester GL1 1EP **Tel:** 01452 521286 **Email:** lawyers@langleywellington.co.uk **Apply to:** Miss Helen Stephens	A long-established Gloucester firm, offering a wide range of legal services. Investors in People accredited.	V T P TS WP	0 - 8 70 no
LANGLEYS SOLICITORS LLP Queens House, Micklegate, York YO1 6WG **Tel:** 01904 610886 **Email:** recruitment@langleys.com **Apply to:** Ms Joanne Startup	Based in Lincoln and York, Langleys is a full-service firm providing legal services in insurance law, commercial law, private law and residential conveyancing.	V T P TS WP	5 8 34 335 yes
LANYON BOWDLER SOLICITORS LLP Chapter House North, Abbey Lawn, Abbey Foregate, Shrewsbury SY2 5DE **Tel:** 01743 280280 **Email:** colin.spanner@lblaw.co.uk **Apply to:** Mrs Kay Kelly	General practice. Six Shropshire and Herefordshire offices. Significant private and commercial lines, planning, commercial property and litigation. Specialists in personal injury and clinical negligence.	V T P TS WP	3^{20} 8 26 225 no
LARCOMES LLP 168 London Road, North End, Portsmouth PO2 9DN **Tel:** 023 9244 8100 **Email:** enquiries@larcomes.co.uk **Apply to:** Mr Julian Quartermain		V T P TS WP	1 0 6 40 no
LATHAM & WATKINS 99 Bishopsgate, London EC2M 3XF **Tel:** 020 7710 1000 **Email:** londongraduates@lw.com **Apply to:** Miss Larissa Hope	Latham & Watkins is a leading international law firm with an award-winning London office.	V T P TS WP	24 48 77 600 yes
LATIMER HINKS 5-8 Priestgate, Darlington DL1 1NL **Tel:** 01325 341500 **Apply to:** Mr Paul Saunders	General long-established practice providing legal services for commercial, agricultural and private clients in Durham, Teesside and North Yorkshire.	V T P TS WP	Poss 2 9 51 no
LATIMER LEE 35 Bury New Road, Prestwich, Manchester M25 9JY **Tel:** 0161 798 9000 **Email:** customerservices@latimerlee.com **Apply to:** Mr SR Latimer	Large local firm dedicated in providing exceptional work.	V T P TS WP	0 0 - - yes

V = Vacancies / **T** = Trainees / **P** = Partners / **TS** = Total Staff / **WP** = Work Placement

Lee Bolton Monier-Williams

1 The Sanctuary, Westminster, London SW1P 3JT
Tel: 020 7222 5381
Web: www.lbmw.com

The firm Lee Bolton Monier-Williams is a long established law firm with modern values, based in the heart of Westminster but with a client base spread across the UK and internationally. We act for companies, individuals and businesses across a wide range of sectors with a particular focus on charities, education, real estate, private client and landed estates, wine and spirits, IP and retail.

Types of work Our private client teams advise individuals and businesses on all wealth management and personal matters from wills, trusts and estates to tax planning and family issues.

Our real estate team deal with all aspects of commercial and residential property including development projects, joint ventures, sales and acquisitions, finance, asset management and property disputes.

Our leading EEC (education, ecclesiastical and charity) team acts for numerous well known charities, schools and institutions across a range of highly complex and important projects.

Our corporate and commercial team advises all kinds of business including start-ups, family companies, schools and well known large corporations on all aspects of the commercial life-cycle from incorporation to M&A, compliance, IP and corporate restructuring.

Our employment team advises businesses and individuals on both contentious and non-contentious employment matters including work place disputes, restrictive covenants, dismissals and TUPE.

Our dispute resolution team advise on a range of range of contentious matters including contract and commercial disputes, property disputes, trust and family disputes and IP disputes

Who should apply We are looking for trainees with a good degree (2.1 or above) in law or non-law subjects, who are highly motivated and have first-class communication skills. We expect our trainees to have a genuine interest in the law and what we do, to be professional, enthusiastic and to have a sense of humour.

Training programme Trainees spend six months in our four main departments – private client, dispute resolution, real estate and education and charity.

From the outset our trainees are given responsibility for their own work and have immediate contact with clients and other senior fee earners. Working alongside a senior lawyer or partner, trainees receive mentoring and support throughout the training contract. Trainees play a pivotal role in small teams where expectations are high.

When and how to apply Before 28 February to begin two years later in September. CV and covering letter to susie.hust@lbmw.com. Vacation placements in the spring and summer break form part of the recruitment process, for exact dates please see website.

Sponsorship Contribution towards cost of LPC – £7,000.

Vacancies	2
Trainees	4
Partners	12
Total staff	66

Training contract deadline
28 February 2019

Apply to
Susie Hust

Starting salary
£26,500

Minimum qualifications
2.1 degree, any subject

Sponsorship
LPC

Offices
London

Lee Bolton Monier-William
Solicitors

LAWTONS SOLICITORS
Calverton House, 2 Harpenden Road, St Albans,
Herts AL3 5AB
Tel: 01727 614267
Email: stephenhalloran@lawtonslaw.co.uk
Apply to: Mr Stephen Halloran

Leading criminal defence solicitors covering Bedfordshire, Hertfordshire and London. We seek individuals with good academic records and commitment to criminal work.

V	2[19]
T	2
P	2
TS	25
WP	no

LAYTONS SOLICITORS LLP
2 More London Riverside, London SE1 2AP
Tel: 020 7842 8000
Email: careers@laytons.com
Apply to: Mr John Skelly

Laytons is a commercial law firm whose primary focus is developing dynamic business. Practice areas include: corporate/commercial, IP and data protection, property/construction, dispute resolution and employment.

V	6
T	5
P	29
TS	118
WP	yes

LCF LAW
2 The Embankment, Sovereign Street, Leeds LS1 4BP
Tel: 0113 244 0876
Email: hthornton@lcf.co.uk
Apply to: Mrs Harriet Thornton

LCF Law has offices in Leeds, Bradford, Harrogate and Ilkley - focusing on corporate, disputes, property, personal law. Not all law firms are created equal.

V	2[19]
T	7
P	21
TS	134
WP	no

LEATHES PRIOR
74 The Close, Norwich NR1 4DR
Tel: 01603 610911
Email: lsmith@leathesprior.co.uk
Apply to: Miss Lauren Smith

Specialising in corporate and commercial, employment, regulatory and defence, dispute resolution, mediation, personal injury, sports, franchising, conveyancing, wills, trusts and probate, family and commercial property.

V	1-4
T	7
P	13
TS	100
WP	yes

LEIGH DAY
Priory House, 25 St John's Lane, London EC1M 4LB
Tel: 020 7650 1200
Email: jobs@leighday.co.uk
Apply to: Miss Lucy Taylor

Leigh Day is a specialist law firm operating across personal injury, environment, international, human rights, product liability, clinical negligence, employment and discrimination.

V	8-10[20]
T	20
P	44
TS	420
WP	yes

LENNONS SOLICITORS LTD
Chess Chambers, 2 Broadway Court, Chesham HP5 1EG
Tel: 01494 773377
Email: recruitment@lennonssolicitors.co.uk
Apply to: Ms Teresa Fawcett-Mitchell

General practice specialising in commercial/residential property, commercial work, dispute resolution (including personal injury, professional and medical negligence), employment, matrimonial, civil work, and wills and probate.

V	1[19]
T	2
P	4
TS	42
WP	no

LEO ABSE & COHEN
40 Churchill Way, Cardiff CF10 2SS
Tel: 02920 383252
Email: rosemaryd@leoabse.co.uk
Apply to: Ms Hayley Jones

Established in the 1950s. A progressive and expanding law firm in South Wales offering a comprehensive range of legal services with particular emphasis on litigation.

V	0
T	4
P	13
TS	140
WP	no

LEONARD CANNINGS SOLICITORS LLP
First Floor, Oakwood Court, 62a The Avenue,
Southampton SO17 1XS
Tel: 023 8023 4433
Email: diana.cannings@leonardcannings.co.uk
Apply to: Ms DM Cannings

Specialist litigation practice concentrating on childcare, family, crime, housing and immigration law.

V	2
T	2
P	3
TS	20
WP	no

V = Vacancies / **T** = Trainees / **P** = Partners / **TS** = Total Staff / **WP** = Work Placement

Linklaters LLP

One Silk Street, London EC2Y 8HQ
Email: graduate.recruitment@linklaters.com
Web: careers.linklaters.com
f linklatersgradsuk ✔ linklatersgrads

The firm From a shifting geopolitical landscape to the exponential growth in FinTech, this is a time of unprecedented change. At Linklaters, we're ready. Our people go further to support our clients, with market-leading legal insight and innovation. And we go further for each other, too. We're people you want to work with, generous with our time and ready to help. So no matter what the future holds, with us you'll be one step ahead. Great change is here, and we make sure you're ready.

Types of work Rather than specialise in just one area, we're proud to have best-in-class divisions across the board, in corporate, finance and projects, and dispute resolution. And in practice, they frequently work together to advise clients. As a Linklaters colleague, our breadth of expertise means that, wherever you focus, you'll be involved in the very best work, and benefit from continuous, tailored training from experienced lawyers.

Who should apply Our vision is to be best-in-class, which means winning in our chosen markets. To achieve it, we're looking for people with the right approach. And how you think matters more than what you've specialised in, and where. It's why we recruit a diverse mix of candidates who have studied a wide range of subjects, not just law. If you bring the positive ambition and drive we're looking for, and an enthusiasm for learning, we'll give you the world-class opportunities, training and rewards that you need to succeed.

Training programme The Linklaters training programme offers the knowledge and contacts you need to hit the ground running. Non-law graduates spend a conversion year studying the Graduate Diploma in Law (GDL). And all graduates complete the bespoke, accelerated Legal Practice Course (LPC) before starting training contracts. Then over two years you'll take up four six-month seats (placements) in different practice areas and sometimes abroad, for the breadth and depth of knowledge you need to develop and qualify. And throughout your career, you'll be supported with world-class training, courtesy of the Linklaters Law & Business School.

When and how to apply Full details, including applying for training contracts, vacation schemes and our first-year insight programme, are available at careers.linklaters.com.

Work placements We run vacation schemes and insight programmes. To find out more about these, our training contracts, and how to apply, please visit careers.linklaters.com.

Sponsorship For the GDL and LPC, Linklaters covers all costs and we also offer maintenance grants. You'll find all the details on our website.

Vacancies	100
Trainees	230
Partners	490*
Total staff	5,270*

* denotes worldwide figures

Work placement yes
(see Insider Report on p87)

Apply
Online

Starting salary
£44,000

Minimum qualifications
2.1 degree

Sponsorship
GDL/LPC

Offices
Abu Dhabi, Amsterdam, Antwerp, Bangkok, Beijing, Berlin, Brussels, Dubai, Düsseldorf, Frankfurt, Hamburg, Hong Kong, Lisbon, London, Luxembourg, Madrid, Milan, Moscow, Munich, New York, Paris, Rome, São Paulo, Seoul, Shanghai, Singapore, Stockholm, Tokyo, Warsaw, Washington DC

Linklaters

LESTER ALDRIDGE LLP
Russell House, Oxford Road, Bournemouth BH8 8EX
Tel: 01202 786161
Email: humanresources@la-law.com
Apply to: Emma Starmer | Human Resources

Regional firm, with offices in Bournemouth, Southampton and London. Strong commercial and private client departments offering full range of legal services and several niche areas.

V	8
T	16
P	46
TS	324
WP	yes

LESTER MORRILL
27 Park Square West, Leeds LS1 2PL
Tel: 0113 245 8549
Email: info@lmlaw.co.uk
Apply to: Ms M Clancy (HR Dept)

Specialists in crime, clinical negligence, family, inquests, social welfare, JRs and actions against the police. Lexcel and IIP accredited.

V	0
T	1
P	4
TS	38
WP	no

LEWIS SILKIN
5 Chancery Lane, Clifford's Inn, London EC4A 1BL
Tel: 020 7074 8000
Email: train@lewissilkin.com
Apply to: Trainee Recruitment Team

Commercial firm with a friendly informal style which encourages client contact and personal development. Two key focus areas include global employment and creative industries.

V	Up to 6
T	9
P	58
TS	350
WP	yes

LIGHTFOOTS LLP
1-3 High Street, Thame, Oxfordshire OX9 2BX
Tel: 01844 212 305
Email: lparke@lightfoots.co.uk
Apply to: Ms Lesley Parke

V	0
T	1
P	10
TS	107
WP	no

LODDERS SOLICITORS LLP
Number 10 Elm Court, Arden Street, Stratford-upon-Avon, Warwickshire CV37 6PA
Tel: 01789 293 259
Email: sarah.naffine@lodders.co.uk
Apply to: Mrs Sarah Naffine

At Lodders, our trainees are given a good level of responsibility and exposure to quality work in a variety of areas during their training programme.

V	3
T	6
P	28
TS	130
WP	yes

LONDON SOLICITORS
Unit 3 Fountayne Business Centre, Broad Lane, London N15 4AG
Tel: 020 8808 1285
Email: cemal@thelondonsolicitors.co.uk
Apply to: Mr Cemal Turk

London Solicitors is a solicitors firm with a difference. We have a strong reputation for conveyancing, landlord and tenant, civil litigation, immigration and family matters.

V	3
T	-
P	2
TS	14
WP	yes

LUQMANI THOMPSON & PARTNERS
77-79 High Road, Wood Green, London N22 6BB
Tel: 020 8365 7800
Email: enq@luqmanithompson.com
Apply to: Ms Milla Walker

London-based firm specialising in immigration, human rights and public law including civil actions against the immigration service.

V	0
T	2
P	5
TS	9
WP	no

LYONS DAVIDSON
Victoria House, 51 Victoria Street, Bristol BS1 6AD
Tel: 0117 904 6000
Email: trainingcontracts@lyonsdavidson.co.uk
Apply to: Miss Sarah Wright

Lyons Davidson is a national law practice operating from headquarters in Bristol and offices in Solihull, Leeds, Surrey, Plymouth, Cardiff and London.

V	4-6
T	20
P	36
TS	1200
WP	no

V = Vacancies / **T** = Trainees / **P** = Partners / **TS** = Total Staff / **WP** = Work Placement

Macfarlanes LLP

20 Cursitor Street, London EC4A 1LT
Tel: 020 7831 9222
Email: gradrec@macfarlanes.com
Web: www.macfarlanes.com
𝕏 macfarlanesgrad

The firm Macfarlanes is a distinctive London-based law firm, focused on its clients and on delivering excellence in the international legal market. The firm is known for the quality of its work; not just in dealing with the full range of corporate and commercial matters, but in advising clients on their private affairs as well.

Macfarlanes has made a deliberate choice to remain smaller than many of its peers. The cohesive nature of the firm means that clients benefit from collective experience and close-knit teams. The firm has decided against growth at the expense of quality, against size at the expense of efficiency and agility. So while large enough to advise on the most complex matters, the firm is also small enough to ensure that its people and work are exceptional, without fail.

Types of work Our main practice areas are: commercial, competition, corporate and M&A, derivatives and trading, employment, finance, financial services regulation, investment management, litigation and dispute resolution, pensions, private client, private equity, real estate, restructuring and insolvency and tax.

Who should apply We believe the strongest firm is achieved by choosing a mix of people reflecting different styles so as to meet the needs that we – and our varied range of clients – will have in the future. We look for a rare combination of intellectual curiosity, character and drive. We are looking for ambitious trainees who will thrive on responsibility and challenge and who are ready to begin their careers on day one. We welcome applications from candidates with either a law or non-law background with a 2.1 degree or above.

Training programme Woven into every aspect of life at the firm is an enduring commitment to the development of trainees. Training begins with the Macfarlanes tailored LPC and a week-long induction course at the start of your training contract. During the two-year training contract you'll be working on real cases, doing real work for real clients. As a trainee you will complete four six-month seats in different practice areas including a compulsory corporate and M&A seat. Our seat rotation is designed with trainees in mind – we want to give you enough flexibility to shape your training contract and do seats that interest you. Support and guidance are, of course, vital and you will find your supervisor and principal a valuable source of information and inspiration.

When and how to apply The closing date for training contract applications beginning September 2021 or March 2022 is 31 July 2019. Applications are to be made online via our website.

Work placements For first-year students, we offer an insight day to provide an overview of a City law firm. Applications and further information is available on our website. Our vacation schemes are designed to give you a two-week snapshot as life as a trainee. We offer vacation schemes at Easter and two summer vacation schemes. We welcome applications from students who are in at least their penultimate year of a degree from any degree discipline, with a predicted 2.1 or above. Applications are online via our website with a deadline of 31 January 2019.

Sponsorship CPE/GDL and LPC fees paid and a maintenance allowance of up to £7,000.

Vacancies	30
Trainees	59
Partners	85
Total staff	723

Work placement yes
(see Insider Report on p89)

Training contract deadline
31 July 2019

Apply
Online

Starting salary
£44,000

Minimum qualifications
2.1 degree anticipated or acheived

Sponsorship
GDL/LPC

Offices
London

MACFARLANES

Proud diversity and inclusion partner of

M & S SOLICITORS LIMITED
20 Newton Road, Heather, Leicestershire LE67 2RD
Tel: 01530 266000
Email: rhughes@mslaw.co.uk
Apply to: Mr R Hughes

We are a niche commercial law firm practising in a rural location.

V	0
T	-
P	3
TS	10
WP	no

M OLUBI SOLICITORS
Unit 4, 2 Tunstall Road, London SW9 8BN
Tel: 020 7737 3400
Email: info@olubi.com
Apply to: Mr Moses Olubisose

South London busy and fast expanding solicitors require energetic hard working applicants for work experience, caseworkers/paralegals, training contracts, marketing, admin and support workers.

V	4
T	2
P	1
TS	7
WP	yes

MACHINS SOLICITORS LLP
Victoria Street, Luton LU1 2BS
Tel: 0158 251 4000
Email: barbara.coppin@machins.co.uk
Apply to: Ms Barbara Coppin

Machins offer genuine expertise and commercial aptitude across a broad range of business and individual services. Recognised as one of the region's leading commercial firms.

V	4[20]
T	7
P	12
TS	100
WP	no

MACKARNESS & LUNT
16 High Street, Petersfield GU32 3JJ
Tel: 01730 265111
Email: clairethompson@macklunt.co.uk
Apply to: Mrs Claire Thompson

A general practice firm dealing with residential and commercial conveyancing, litigation, family, probate, wills, LPAs, trusts and other matters.

V	0
T	-
P	3
TS	18
WP	no

MACRAE & CO LLP
59 Lafone Street, London SE1 2LX
Tel: 020 7378 7716
Email: office@macraeco.com
Apply to: Mr JA Turnball

Commercial firm with predominantly international clientele.

V	0
T	0
P	3
TS	7
WP	no

MAGRATH SHELDRICK LLP
22 Chancery Lane, London WC2A 1LS
Tel: 020 7495 3003
Email: ben.sheldrick@magrath.co.uk
Apply to: Mr Ben Sheldrick

Central London niche firm specialising in business immigration and employment law. Top tier in all the main directories.

V	2[19]
T	4
P	8
TS	65
WP	no

MAJOR & CO
51 Quarry Street, Guildford, Surrey GU1 3UA
Tel: 01483 455 771
Email: d_major@majorlaw.co.uk
Apply to: Mr David Major

A friendly and efficient firm dealing with a wide range of private client and small-medium business work.

V	0
T	1
P	1
TS	8
WP	yes

MAKIN DIXON SOLICITORS
Wool Exchange, 10 Hustlergate, Bradford, West Yorkshire BD1 1RE
Tel: 01274 747747
Email: enquiries@makindixon.co.uk
Apply to: Ms J Campbell

We are a team of specialist solicitors focused entirely on family law. We are an ever expanding firm with 10 offices, including offices in Bradford, Skipton, Halifax and Keighley, covering all aspects of family law.

V	0
T	6
P	2
TS	70
WP	no

V = Vacancies / **T** = Trainees / **P** = Partners / **TS** = Total Staff / **WP** = Work Placement

MAKKA SOLICITORS LTD
44 Upper Tooting Road, London SW17 7PD
Tel: 020 8767 9090
Email: makkaltd@hotmail.com
Apply to: Mr F Chaudhary

Our main aim is to help the community and we are looking for like minded staff who wish to do the same.

V	1
T	1
P	3
TS	8
WP	yes

MAKWANA SOLICITORS
Devonshire House, 582 Honeypot Lane, Stanmore, Middlesex HA7 1JS
Tel: 020 8732 5458
Email: info@makwanas.co.uk
Apply to: Miss S Makwana

The firm is a mixed private practice dealing in all types of criminal defence, family and civil litigation work.

V	1
T	0
P	1
TS	2
WP	yes

MALCOLM C FOY & CO LTD
51 Hallgate, Doncaster DN1 3PB
Tel: 01302 340005
Email: info@malcolmcfoy.co.uk
Apply to: Mrs A Pashley

General practice with offices in Doncaster and Rotherham. No criminal work undertaken. Specialising in commercial and civil litigation, matrimonial, personal injury, private client and residential and commercial property conveyancing.

V	1
T	4
P	8
TS	57
WP	yes

MALIK & MALIK
234-236 High Road, Willesden, London NW10 2NX
Tel: 020 8830 3050
Email: malikandmalik@lawyer.com
Apply to: Mr M Nazeer

Malik & Malik was established on 1 June 1998. The firm deals with the following areas of law: crime; immigration and nationality; landlord and tenant; conveyancing; and personal injury.

V	1
T	4
P	2
TS	15
WP	yes

MALIK LEGAL SOLICITORS LTD
579 Cheetham Hill Road, Manchester M8 9JE
Tel: 0161 7956217
Email: info@maliklegal.co.uk
Apply to: Mr Maqbool Malik

Three-partner firm, six solicitors, seven support staff, specialising in administrative law, immigration, crime, human rights, judicial review, company law, personal injury and civil law.

V	4
T	2
P	3
TS	14
WP	yes

MANDER HADLEY SOLICITORS
1 The Quadrant, Coventry CV1 2DW
Tel: 024 76631212
Email: enquiries@manderhadley.co.uk
Apply to: Miss Naomi O'Halloran

Located in Coventry and Kenilworth. Specialising in civil and criminal litigation, family, conveyancing, commercial and company, charities, probate, trusts and wills.

V	0
T	0
P	9
TS	45
WP	no

MAPLES TEESDALE LLP
30 King Street, London EC2V 8EE
Tel: 020 7600 3800
Email: enq@maplesteesdale.co.uk
Apply to: Ms Anastasia Klein

Maples Teesdale are the UK's leading commercial property law specialists, providing innovative, full service and truly partner-led services to UK based and international clients

V	3[20]
T	6
P	18
TS	68
WP	no

MARRIOTT HARRISON LLP
11 Staple Inn, London WC1V 7QH
Tel: 020 7209 2000
Email: liz.arscott@marriottharrison.co.uk
Apply to: Ms Liz Arscott

Leading corporate/media firm based in the City providing specialist services including corporate, banking, restructuring, media, employment, real estate and dispute resolution across various sectors.

V	2-3[20]
T	6
P	19
TS	58
WP	yes

V = Vacancies / **T** = Trainees / **P** = Partners / **TS** = Total Staff / **WP** = Work Placement

Firm	Description	V	T	P	TS	WP
MARTIN CRAY AND CO 177 Edward Street, Brighton BN2 0JB **Tel:** 01273 673226 **Email:** mcray@martincray.co.uk **Apply to:** Mr MW Cray	The firm specialises in personal injury, family, probate, conveyancing and employment.	1	2	2	22	yes
MARTIN MURRAY & ASSOCIATES 152-156 High Street, Yiewsley, West Drayton UB7 7BE **Tel:** 01895 431332 **Email:** info@mmasolicitors.co.uk **Apply to:** Mr A Cosma	Martin Murray & Associates is a franchised firm and is one of the leading criminal practices in the Thames Valley.	0	2	9	70	no
MARTIN SEARLE SOLICITORS 9 Marlborough Place, Brighton BN1 1UB **Tel:** 01273 609911 **Email:** fiona@ms-solicitors.co.uk **Apply to:** Ms Fiona Martin	Niche employment and community care law practice seeking trainee solicitors on a yearly basis. Casework experience and IT skills essential. Recruiting in January.	0	-	2	15	no
MARTIN SHEPHERD SOLICITORS LLP 753 High Road North, Finchley, London N12 8LG **Tel:** 020 8446 4301 **Email:** acd@martinshepherd.co.uk **Apply to:** Ms Antoinette Doyle	A four branch North London general high street practice with a bias towards commercial work.	0	-	6	34	no
MARTIN-KAYE LLP The Foundry, Euston Way, Telford TF3 4LY **Tel:** 01952 272222 **Email:** recruit@martinkaye.co.uk **Apply to:** Mrs Alison Carter	A progressive practice in the expanding new town of Telford dealing with all aspects of commercial, corporate, IP, employment, litigation and property. Agency work undertaken.	Poss	1	6	60	no
MATRIX SOLICITORS Normanton Business Centre, 258 Normanton Road, Derby DE23 6WD **Tel:** 01332 363454 **Apply to:** Mr Shamim Khan	Niche litigation, company/commercial, environmental and energy law and business immigration specialists in the centre of Derby.	0	0	1	7	yes
MAURICE TURNOR GARDNER LLP 15th Floor, Milton House, Milton Street, London EC2Y 9BH **Tel:** 020 7786 8710 **Email:** trainees@mtgllp.com **Apply to:** Mrs Sophie Mazzier	Maurice Turnor Gardner is a boutique private client firm with charity, commercial trust, partnerships, trust dispute resolution and real estate teams.	1-2[20]	4	10	38	yes
MAYO WYNNE BAXTER LLP 3 Bell Lane, Lewes BN7 1JU **Tel:** 01273 223267 **Email:** recruitment@mayowynnebaxter.co.uk **Apply to:** Miss Grace Young	We recruit trainees via a paralegal to trainee initiative, sourcing candidates for the following year. One vacancy remains for 2019.	1[19]	4	31	214	no

V = Vacancies / **T** = Trainees / **P** = Partners / **TS** = Total Staff / **WP** = Work Placement

Mayer Brown International LLP

201 Bishopsgate, London EC2M 3AF
Tel: 020 3130 8621
Email: graduaterecruitment@mayerbrown.com
Web: www.mayerbrownfutures.com
🐦 talk2mayerbrown

The firm Mayer Brown was one of the first law firms to develop a global platform in recognition of the fact that many of its clients increasingly needed integrated, cross-border legal advice. The firm is now one of the world's leading global law firms with offices in major cities across the Americas, Asia, Europe and the Middle East. In Brazil, the firm has an association with Tauil & Chequer Avogados. Through the association, the extensive international expertise of its lawyers and its presence in the leading financial centres around the world, Mayer Brown provides high quality legal advice and client-focused solutions to support many of the world's leading businesses.

Types of work Our lawyers have expertise across a wide range of areas including corporate, finance, real estate, construction, litigation and dispute resolution, employment, pensions, antitrust and competition, insurance and reinsurance, tax, financial services regulatory and intellectual property.

Who should apply We are looking for candidates who not only have a consistently strong academic record including a minimum of a 2.1 degree (predicted or obtained) in any discipline, but also who have a wide range of interests and achievements outside their academic career. Additionally, we would like to see innovative candidates who can demonstrate a drive for results, good verbal and written communication skills, and an ability to analyse, with good judgement and excellent interpersonal skills.

Training programme One of the advantages of joining Mayer Brown are the choices available to you. As a trainee at the firm, you will be able to tailor your training contract across a broad range of seats, including our main practice areas in London (as listed above), and the potential to complete an international secondment. If you don't want to stray too far, you have the option to gain valuable in-house experience by going on secondment to one of the firm's major clients. While Mayer Brown is a global law firm, our London office remains a tightly knit team with an open and inclusive culture. You will be given significant opportunities to assist on matters which may be multidisciplinary, cross-border, complex and high-profile in nature.

When and how to apply The deadline for training contracts commencing in March/September 2021 is 31 July 2019. However we encourage students to apply for a vacation scheme as this is the main pipeline for our training contracts each year; the deadline is 31 January 2019 for schemes in the spring and summer and we welcome applications from penultimate year, finalists and graduates too. Applications are made online via the website.

Work placements We run three vacation schemes each year; one in the spring and two in the summer. You will gain experience in two key practice areas and be involved in seminars and social events including a trip to our Paris office. Our vacation schemes are the main pipeline for our training contracts each year.

Sponsorship The firm will cover the cost of the GDL and LPC and provide a maintenance grant of £7,000 in London and £6,500 elsewhere. The firm asks all LPC students to complete the LPC at BPP Law School in London.

Vacancies	15
Trainees	30
Partners	75
Total staff	approx 460

Work placement yes
(see Insider Report on p91)

Training contract deadline
31 July 2019

Apply
Online

Starting salary
£44,000

Minimum qualifications
2.1 degree or equivalent and AAB at A level or equivalent

Sponsorship
GDL/LPC

Offices
Bangkok, Beijing, Brasilia, Brussels, Charlotte, Chicago, Dubai, Düsseldorf, Frankfurt, Hanoi, Ho Chi Minh City, Hong Kong, Houston, London, Los Angeles, Mexico City, New York, Palo Alto, Paris, Rio de Janeiro, San Francisco, São Paulo, Shanghai, Singapore, Tokyo, Washington DC

MAYER·BROWN

Proud diversity and inclusion
partner of

 aspiringsolicitors

Mcdermott Will & Emery UK LLP

110 Bishopsgate, London EC2N 4AY
Tel: 020 7577 6900
Web: www.mwe.com
🐦 mcdermottlaw

The firm McDermott Will & Emery is a leading international law firm with lawyers located across the United States, Europe and Asia, plus the firm further extends its reach through a strategic alliance with MWE China Law Offices in Shanghai.

McDermott Will & Emery's London office, founded in 1998, brings a full-service legal practice to Europe and complements McDermott's capabilities in France, Germany, Italy and Belgium.

The London office is part of an extensive 20 office international network that provides a unique platform from which McDermott offers legal advice to local and international organisations. The London office represents a wide range of clients, including large commercial, industrial and financial corporations, small and medium-sized businesses, trustees and high-net-worth individuals and families. The firm has around 60 lawyers at present in London, the majority are English-qualified.

Types of work Corporate/transactional, private client, international tax, energy, healthcare, employment, data privacy, finance and real estate.

Who should apply The firm is looking for the brightest, best and most entrepreneurial trainees. Candidates will need to demonstrate commercial awareness and a genuine understanding of the firm.

Training programme The primary focus is to provide a practical foundation for your career with the firm. You will experience four seats over the two-year period and a deliberately small number of trainees mean that the firm is able to provide a degree of flexibility in tailoring seats to the individual. Trainees get regular support and feedback.

The firm provides a comprehensive range of benefits which includes private medical and dental insurance, life assurance, permanent health insurance, pension, season ticket loan, subsidised gym membership, an employee assistance programme and 25 days' holiday.

When and how to apply Candidates must apply online at www.apply4law.com/mwe by 28 June 2019 to begin a training contract in September 2021.

Sponsorship GDL and LPC funding with maintenance grant.

Vacancies	2
Trainees	4
Partners	566*
Total staff	2,167*

*denotes worldwide figure

Training contract deadline
28 June 2019

Apply
Online at
www.apply4law.com/mwe

Starting salary
£43,000

Minimum qualifications
First or high 2.1 degree

Sponsorship
GDL/LPC

Offices
Boston, Brussels, Chicago, Dallas, Düsseldorf, Frankfurt, Houston, London, Los Angeles, Miami, Milan, Munich, New York, Orange County, Paris, San Francisco, Seoul, Silicon Valley, Washington DC, strategic alliance with MWE China Law Offices (Shanghai)

McDermott Will & Emery

MCGUIREWOODS LONDON LLP 11 Pilgrim Street, London EC4V 6RN **Tel:** 020 7632 1600 **Email:** lhr@mcguirewoods.com **Apply to:** Mrs Jane Gritt	The London office of a cross border law firm offering a broad spectrum of legal services within international and domestic corporate matters.	V 1 T 2 P 13 TS 50 WP no
MCHALE & COMPANY 19/21 High Street, Altrincham, Cheshire WA14 1QP **Tel:** 0161 928 3848 **Email:** mch@mchaleandco.co.uk **Apply to:** Mrs Philippa Wright	Established and expanding firm offering specialist advice in the areas of conveyancing (commercial and domestic), financial mis-selling, employment, personal injury, private client and commercial litigation.	V 1 T 4 P 5 TS 40 WP no
MCMILLAN WILLIAMS SOLICITORS MW House, 41 Chipstead Valley Road, Coulsdon CR5 2RB **Tel:** 020 3551 8500 **Email:** dawn.fazackerley@mwsolicitors.co.uk **Apply to:** Miss Dawn Fazackerley	MW Solicitors prides itself on its excellent in-house training, which takes talented individuals from paralegals through to trainee solicitors and beyond.	V Varies T 43 P 60 TS 400 WP yes
MEIKLES 8 North Street, Ferryhill, County Durham DL17 8HX **Tel:** 01740 652811 **Email:** lawrence.petterson@meikles-solicitors.co.uk **Apply to:** Mr L Petterson	High street solicitors with five offices long established throughout South Durham. Significant legal aid practice. Specialising in family, particularly children, criminal, mental health and conveyancing.	V 1[20] T 1 P 9 TS 52 WP yes
MEMERY CRYSTAL LLP 165 Fleet Street, London EC4A 2DY **Tel:** 020 7242 5905 **Email:** helen.seaward@memerycrystal.com **Apply to:** Mrs Helen Seaward	A full-service independent firm specialising in corporate, employment, tax, litigation, IP, property and property litigation. Known for its international sectors including natural resources and retail.	V 4 T 8 P 33 TS 140 WP yes
METCALFE COPEMAN & PETTEFAR 28-32 King Street, Kings Lynn PE30 1HQ **Tel:** 01553 778102 **Email:** alison.muir@mcp-law.co.uk **Apply to:** Miss Alison Muir	A firm with four offices which undertakes some specialist commercial work as well as its general practice, which includes legal aid work.	V 1[19] T 4 P 15 TS 120 WP no
METCALFES SOLICITORS 46-48 Queen Square, Bristol BS1 4LY **Tel:** 011 7929 0451 **Email:** info@metcalfes.co.uk **Apply to:** Ms Justine Tipling	Commercial practice providing quality, cost effective, partner led service to medium sized businesses, together with niche clinical negligence, claimant personal injury and private client practice.	V 0 T 2 P 6 TS 55 WP no
MFG SOLICITORS LLP Adam House, Birmingham Road, Kidderminster, Worcestershire DY10 2SH **Tel:** 01562 820 181 **Email:** denise.clarke@mfgsolicitors.com **Apply to:** Mrs Denise Clarke	Specialising: family, property, wills/probate, litigation. Niche expertise: tax, agriculture, company commercial and employment. On the Law Society's family/children panels and personal injury trust panel.	V 2-4[20] T 6 P 30 TS 140 WP no

V = Vacancies / **T** = Trainees / **P** = Partners / **TS** = Total Staff / **WP** = Work Placement

Michelmores LLP

Woodwater House, Pynes Hill, Exeter EX2 5WR
Tel: 01392 688 688
Email: gradrecruitment@michelmores.com
Web: www.michelmores.com
f michelmorescareers **y** mmcareers

The firm Michelmores is a top 100 full-service law firm with offices in Exeter, Bristol and London, over 440 staff and a turnover in excess of £34m.

At Michelmores we recruit to retain, viewing our trainees as future senior associates and partners of the firm. Retaining trainees is very important to us and we have an excellent track record, retaining 100% of our trainees in 2018.

In 2018 we were also awarded the LawCareers.Net award for 'Best Recruiter - Medium Regional Firm'.

Types of work Antitrust/competition, corporate and finance, financial restructuring, financial services and investment management, intellectual property, litigation and arbitration, finance and investment, private wealth, real estate, agriculture, education, energy, manufacturing, public sector and retail.

Who should apply Michelmores welcomes applications from both law and non-law graduates. Successful candidates will have a strong academic background, be logical thinkers, practical problem solvers and team players. We look for well-rounded individuals who share our ambition and drive and genuinely want to share in our future success as we continue to grow.

We are recruiting London trainees to join in 2019, 2020 and 2021 and Exeter and Bristol trainees for 2021.

Training programme Our structured trainee development programme aims to equip our trainees with the key skills needed to be successful solicitors, on both a technical and personal level. Trainees work closely with their supervisors in each department and are given a high level of client exposure, responsibility and client involvement at a very early stage.

Trainees usually spend six months in each of the firm's main departments – business, real estate and private client. There are also opportunities to have seats in different offices and to undergo secondments.

When and how to apply Please apply for all our vacancies via our online application form on our website. For London 2019 and 2020 training contracts and our Exeter summer vacation scheme, please apply by 31 January 2019.

For 2021 training contracts in Exeter, Bristol and London, please apply by 30 June 2019.

Work placements Our summer vacation scheme runs every July in our Exeter HQ. The scheme is as much about you getting to know Michelmores as a place to work, as it is about us getting to know you. You will have the opportunity to spend time in one department for the week, as we aim to give you a real hands-on insight into one area of law and life as a trainee.

Sponsorship We sponsor trainees to complete the LPC at the University of Law and also offer a £5,000 bursary.

Other benefits at Michelmores include social events, such as our late summer ball and annual firm quiz, the opportunity to work a day a week from home once qualified, an additional day off for your birthday, and a gym and subsidised café at our Exeter HQ.

Vacancies	10
Trainees	16
Partners	66
Total staff	440

Apply
Online

Minimum qualifications
2.1 degree

Sponsorship
LPC

Offices
Exeter, Bristol, London

Michelmores

MIAN & CO The Citadel, 190 Corporation Street, Birmingham B4 6QD **Tel:** 0121 684 8000 **Email:** mians@btinternet.com **Apply to:** Mrs T S Mian	Long-established criminal defence solicitors practice. Offices based directly opposite Birmingham magistrates court. Mainly legally aided work undertaken.	V 0 T 2 P 2 TS 9 WP no
MIDDLETON & UPSALL LLP T/A MIDDLETONS 94 East Street, Warminster BA12 9BG **Tel:** 01985 214 444 **Email:** swhite@mulaw.co.uk **Apply to:** Mr Charles Goodbody		V 0 T - P 4 TS 30 WP no
MIDDLETON SOLICITORS Granite House, 8-10 Stanley Street, Liverpool L1 6AF **Tel:** 0151 236 5599 **Email:** reception@middletonsolicitors.co.uk **Apply to:** Mr Alan Middleton	We are a young city centre based practice. We specialise in various areas of law including sports law, private client, commercial and personal injury.	V 1[19] T 1 P 3 TS 25 WP yes
MIDDLEWEEKS Swan Building, 20 Swan Street, Manchester M4 5JW **Tel:** 0161 839 7255 **Apply to:** Barbara Cohen	A Manchester litigation practice which specialises in criminal litigation and which is highly regarded in that field, particularly in the area of white collar crime.	V 0 T 2 P 2 TS 19 WP yes
MILBANK TWEED HADLEY & MCCLOY 10 Gresham Street, London EC2V 7JD **Tel:** 020 7615 3000 **Email:** lnrecruiting@milbank.com **Apply to:** Mr Robert Girvan, Manager of Professional Development & Legal Recruiting	International firm headquartered in New York with offices in Europe, the US, Asia and South America, advising government entities, corporations and financial institutions.	V 5 T 9 P 28 TS 195 WP yes
MILBURNS SOLICITORS LIMITED 3-5 Main Street, Cockermouth, Cumbria C13 9LE **Tel:** 01900 67363 **Email:** lstorr@milburnssolicitors.co.uk **Apply to:** Mrs Louise Storr	Eight-partner, four-office firm with large client base in West Cumbria. LEXCEL accredited with LSC quality marks in conveyancing and family.	V 1[19] T 2 P 8 TS 50 WP yes
MILLAN SOLICITORS 1368 Leeds Road, Bradford, West Yorkshire BD3 8ND **Tel:** 01274 660 111 **Email:** millansolicitors@gmail.com **Apply to:** Miss GK Millan	Millan Solicitors is a family firm with family values. We are a young, dynamic, expanding firm specialising in civil litigation, immigration and personal injury work.	V 0 T 1 P 1 TS 2 WP yes
MILLER EVANS & CO 1st Floor, Pepper Street, London E14 9RP **Tel:** 020 7987 2515 **Email:** askus@me-solicitors.co.uk **Apply to:** Ms Charlotte Miller	We are a small forward-thinking highly-respected practice at Canary Wharf dealing mainly with property and private client - but also commercial law.	V 1 T 1 P 2 TS 10 WP yes

V = Vacancies / T = Trainees / P = Partners / TS = Total Staff / WP = Work Placement

Mills & Co

Milburn House, Dean Street, Newcastle upon Tyne NE1 1LE
Tel: 0191 233 2222
Email: recruitment@mills-co.com
Web: www.mills-co.com

The firm Mills & Co Solicitors Limited specialises exclusively in shipping and international trade. Based in Newcastle upon Tyne, and currently with a team of 23 lawyers we are the largest specialist in our fields outside London. Newcastle has strong historical roots in shipping and has long been the UK's 'second city' for shipping law and our work is conducted before the same London-based courts and tribunals as the London firms specialising in the same fields. Within shipping and international trade globally, we are ranked alongside the leading London law firms and are compared favourably by clients and legal directories. For academically gifted lawyers wanting to combine the intelletual stimulation of working in some of the most interesting and varied areas of international commercial law with the quality of life advantages of the North East, our traineeships provide a unique opportunity.

Types of work We are a full-service firm in our specialist fields. In shipping we have a significant presence in both 'dry' work (essentially law of contract type work involving all types of contracts used for hiring and insuring ships, carrying cargoes, building and financing new ships, and buying, selling, financing and repairing second-hand ships), as well as 'wet' work (essentially law of tort type work involving collisions between one ship and another ship as well as between ships and other structures, groundings, as well as specialists contracts concerning salvage, towage and other services provided to ships in distress). In international trade we are involved in drafting, advising on and litigating contracts in relation to the international sale of goods.

Who should apply We aim to provide work to the highest standards in the UK and therefore seek trainees who combine high academic achievement (AAB at A level and 2.1 at university level) with an outgoing personality and an international outlook. Languages are an advantage as our lawyers travel to visit the leading shipping markets globally. We are committed to providing the best training possible with the aim that our trainees will stay with us upon qualification and ultimately become partners in the firm. In return we are seeking a genuine interest in shipping law and a clear commitment to remaining in the North East.

Training programme We operate a three-seat system each of about eight months in shipping litigation (shipping contract/tort disputes), commercial (a non-contentious seat including ship sale and purchase, shipbuilding, ship repair and ship finance) and commercial litigation (commodity sale contract disputes). In each seat the trainee sits with a partner specialising in the relevant field. We have a roughly one-to-one ratio between partners and non-partners which allows us to provide detailed supervision of trainees and junior lawyers. Trainees can expect to receive work from most of the partners during their traineeships as we do not operate in teams and aim to ensure that trainees sample all areas of the firm's work.

When and how to apply Apply via our website www.mills-co.com before 29 July 2019 for training contracts commencing in 2021.

Work placements We offer one-week vacation schemes in Spring and Summer 2019 ahead of our 29 July 2019 deadline for 2021 traineeships.

Sponsorship We will pay your GDL and LPC fees.

Vacancies	1
Trainees	2
Partners	13
Total staff	31
Work placement	yes

Training contract deadline
29 July 2019

Apply to
See website

Starting salary
£26,500

Minimum qualifications
AAB At A level, 2.1 degree

Sponsorship
GDL/LPC

Offices
Newcastle upon Tyne

MILLS & Co.
——— SOLICITORS ———

Mills & Reeve LLP

Botanic House, 100 Hills Road, Cambridge CB2 1PH
Tel: 01223 222336
Email: graduate.recruitment@mills-reeve.com
Web: www.mills-reeve.com
🐦 millsandreeve

The firm Mills & Reeve is a major UK law firm and among the 50 largest UK law firms. Our business model is straightforward – the highest quality advice, outstanding client service and value for money. Our highly collaborative culture underpins this model and has created our strong ambition to grow. Increased scale and focus have enabled us to achieve leading positions in our work for substantial and high growth businesses and individuals as well as in the health, higher education and further education sectors, real estate and insurance across the UK.

Our commercial clients include global and UK based businesses, FTSE and AIM listed organisations, private companies and start-ups. We work with firms across the globe (including fellow members of the SCG Legal, a worldwide network of leading law firms) to support our clients' international requirements.

For the 15th year running Mills & Reeve has been listed in *The Sunday Times* Top 100 Best Companies to Work For, which recognises that we put people at the centre of our business.

Types of work Mills & Reeve's services are delivered through firm-wide core groups: corporate and commercial, employment, family, insurance disputes, private client, projects and construction, real estate and regulatory, public and commercial disputes. Further specialist sector teams focus on: charities, education, food and agribusiness, government, health, sport, technology and life sciences.

Who should apply We welcome applications from penultimate-year and final-year law students, final-year non-law students and graduates. Candidates should already have or expect a 2.1 degree or equivalent from either a law or non-law background. You'll have a good balance between academic ability, interpersonal skills, drafting skills, common sense, commercial awareness, confidence and a professional attitude. We look for candidates who have the potential to develop into our solicitors of the future.

Training programme Trainees complete six four-month seats and work alongside a partner or principal associate. Movement between offices is encouraged and supported with an accommodation allowance. Training is supported by a full induction, in-house training programme developed by our team of professional support lawyers and the professional skills course (PSC).

When and how to apply Apply online. Closing dates are 31 July 2019 for training contracts commencing September 2021 and 31 January 2019 for summer placements in 2019.

Work placements Our award-winning summer placement scheme allows you to get a taste of Mills & Reeve and the legal profession before applying for a training contract. We offer two weeks' work experience at one of our offices in Birmingham, Cambridge, Manchester and Norwich. Online applications for two-week placements during the summer must be received by 31 January 2019.

Sponsorship Mills & Reeve will fund the GDL and LPC course fees for future trainees. There is also a maintenance grant during the GDL and LPC.

Vacancies	20
Trainees	39
Partners	122
Total staff	994

Work placement yes
(see Insider Report on p92)

Training contract deadline
31 July 2019

Apply
Online

Starting salary
£26,500

Minimum qualifications
2.1 degree, any discipline

Sponsorship
GDL/LPC

Offices
Birmingham, Cambridge, Leeds, London, Manchester, Norwich

MILLS & REEVE
Achieve more. Together.

Mishcon de Reya LLP

Africa House, 70 Kingsway, London WC2B 6AH
Tel: 020 3321 7000
Email: trainee.recruitment@mishcon.com
Web: www.mishcon.com/graduates
f mishcon ✖ mishcongrads

The firm Based in London with an office in New York, Mishcon de Reya services an international community of clients and provides advice in situations where the constraints of geography often do not apply. The work we undertake is cross-border, multi-jurisdictional and complex. Our clients are dynamic and sophisticated and we reflect that in our belief in challenging the conventional or accepted ways of working. We fiercely guard our clients' interests, recognising the significant nexus between business affairs and personal affairs. Building strong personal connections with our clients and their businesses is important to us. It is for these reasons we say 'It's business. But it's personal'.

Mishcon de Reya has grown rapidly in recent years, showing more than 100% revenue growth since 2010. A central role is played by the academy, the firm's in-house place of learning, development and new thinking, the active and innovative social impact strategy and various diversity initiatives are reflected in its top 30 place in *The Sunday Times* Best Companies to Work For list of 2018.

Types of work We work across six practice areas: corporate, employment, dispute resolution, intellectual property, private or real estate law. The firm also has a number of specialist groups including competition, finance and banking, fraud, immigration, international arbitration and art.

Who should apply Applications are welcome from penultimate-year law and final-year non-law undergraduate students as well as other graduates wishing to commence a training contract in two years' time. The firm recruits from a wide range of universities. Our trainees are typically high-achieving and intelligent individuals with good interpersonal skills and outgoing personalities. Strength of character and ability to think laterally are also important.

Training programme Trainees have the opportunity to gain experience, skills and knowledge from across the firm in four six-month seats involving both contentious and non-contentious work. Because of the relatively few training contracts offered, trainees can be exposed to high-quality work with lots of responsibility early on. Trainees are supported with a wide ranging training and development programme in addition to the Professional Skills Course. Trainee performance is monitored closely and trainees can expect to receive regular feedback in addition to mid-seat and end-of-seat appraisals.

When and how to apply Applicants should submit an online application for vacation schemes via our trainee recruitment website: www.mishcon.com/graduates. Applications open on 1 October and close 15 January 2019. Applicants will be considered for a training contract once they have completed a vacation scheme.

Work placements We run three vacation schemes, one over Easter and two in July. Our schemes have been designed to provide individuals with an insight into the role of a trainee, our culture and our people. As well as being paid on the vacation scheme, those not living within commuting distance of London will be provided with free accommodation. We run a fun vacation scheme with an informative workshop programme covering all practice areas of the firm, combined with individual and group work sessions.

Sponsorship The firm provides full LPC and GDL funding, and a maintenance grant of £7,000 payable in the GDL and LPC year.

Vacancies	12-15
Trainees	30
Partners	124
Total staff	910
Work placement	yes
Training contract deadline	
15 January 2019	
Apply to	
Charlotte Lynch,	
Graduate & Lateral	
Recruitment Manager	
Starting salary	
£42,000	
Minimum qualifications	
2.1 degree or higher	
Sponsorship	
GDL/LPC	
Offices	
London, associated	
office in New York	

Mishcon de Reya

MILLS CHODY LLP 226-228 Kenton Road, Kenton, Harrow, Middlesex HA3 8BZ **Tel:** 020 8909 0400 **Email:** info@millschody.com **Apply to:** Mr Ranjeet Johal	A well-established high street firm specialising predominantly in property, family law, private client and litigation.	V 1-2 T 1 P 4 TS 15 WP no
MILNE MOSER 100 Highgate, Kendal, Cumbria LA9 4HE **Tel:** 01539 729786 **Email:** solicitors@milnemoser.co.uk **Apply to:** Mr D J Emmett	An old-established but progressive general practice and estate agency undertaking all types of contentious and non-contentious work.	V 0 T 0 P 6 TS 27 WP no
MINCOFFS SOLICITORS LLP 5 Osborne Terrace, Jesmond, Newcastle upon Tyne NE2 1SQ **Tel:** 0191 281 6151 **Email:** marketing@mincoffs.co.uk **Apply to:** Ms Michelle Dodds	Mincoffs Solicitors, one of the northeast's major law firms providing a first class legal service to commercial and private clients across the UK.	V 1^{20} T 2 P 10 TS 70 WP yes
MINSTER LAW SOLICITORS Kingfisher House, Calder Park, Wakefield WF2 7UA **Tel:** 0345 356 3000 **Email:** training.contracts@minsterlaw.co.uk **Apply to:** Mrs Amy Thirtle	Minster Law are personal injury specialists with specific expertise in accidents involving a vehicle or on a motorcycle.	V 0 T 5 P - TS 500 WP yes
MLP LAW LLP 7 Market Street, Altrincham, Cheshire WA14 1QE **Tel:** 0161 926 9969 **Email:** lesleys@mlplaw.co.uk **Apply to:** Mrs Lesley Sullivan	Applications are invited from self motivated lawyers of partnership potential. This dynamic and highly accredited practice offers outstanding hands-on training and structured career progression.	V 3^{20} T 2 P 6 TS 22 WP yes
MOHAMMED & CO St John's House, 42 St John's Place, Preston PR1 3XX **Tel:** 01772 888700 **Apply to:** Mr Hanif Mohammed		V 0 T 2 P 1 TS 13 WP yes
MONRO WRIGHT & WASBROUGH LLP 7-8 Great James Street, London WC1N 3DF **Tel:** 020 7404 7001 **Email:** contact@mww-llp.com **Apply to:** Mr Nicholas Barlow	Long established private client firm situated beside Gray's Inn, specialising in litigation, taxation, trusts/estates, charities, commercial and residential property.	V 2^{20} T 3 P 9 TS 35 WP no
MOORE BLATCH LLP Gateway House, Tollgate, Chandlers Ford SO53 3TG **Tel:** 023 8071 8000 **Email:** recruitment@mooreblatch.com **Apply to:** Graduate Recruitment	One of the South's leading full-service law firms advising businesses and private clients. Nearly 300 staff based in London, Lymington, Richmond and Southampton.	V 3^{20} T 6 P 42 TS 270 WP no

V = Vacancies / **T** = Trainees / **P** = Partners / **TS** = Total Staff / **WP** = Work Placement

Morgan, Lewis & Bockius UK LLP

Condor House, 5-10 St Paul's Churchyard, London EC4M 8AL
Tel: 020 3201 5000
Email: londontrainingprogramme@morganlewis.com
Web: www.morganlewis.com

The firm With 30 offices across North America, Asia, Europe and the Middle East, Morgan Lewis provides comprehensive corporate, transactional, regulatory and litigation services to clients of all sizes across all major industries. Founded in 1873, Morgan Lewis comprises more than 2,200 legal professionals.

Types of work Morgan Lewis's London office offers a wide range of business and commercial services, including: competition; corporate; debt and equity capital markets; finance and restructuring; labour and employment including employment litigation and immigration advice; investment management; structured transactions; tax; international commercial dispute, arbitration and white collar matters. Morgan Lewis is also strong in various business sectors, including life sciences, financial services and technology, where the firm's leading regulatory and commercial lawyers provide a real insight into their industries.

Who should apply Morgan Lewis is seeking candidates with a consistently strong academic record, including a minimum of AAB at A level (or equivalent) and a 2.1 (predicted or gained) in their undergraduate degree. We look for a range of prior work experience, volunteering and extra-curricular activities to demonstrate the development of your skills and experience. In particular, we are looking for candidates to show us their commercial awareness, team spirit, resilience and passion for a career in law.

Training programme Morgan Lewis's London training programme is led by an experienced training principal. Our partners and trainee supervisors also have broad experience of working with trainees. Our programme will provide you with consistently high-quality, challenging assignments, working directly with senior lawyers across a range of practices and industry groups on complex and frequently cross-border matters. Through this hands-on and varied experience, you can expect to build a thorough understanding of the firm's business and of working with international, high profile clients. Over two years you will complete four six-month seats with the opportunity to gain experience in at least three distinct areas of law. International secondment opportunities to our Brussels and Dubai offices may also be available. In addition to formal appraisals, the office environment allows regular contact with, and feedback from, the training principal, supervisors and other lawyers. Trainees will have the opportunity to actively participate in all in-house associate training sessions, and to take part in pro bono work and business development activities.

When and how to apply Candidates should apply for a training contract by completing the firm's online application form (via our website). Applications will be accepted from October 2018 for training contracts to commence in 2021. The closing date for applications is 15 July 2019.

Work placements Our summer vacation scheme provides students with the opportunity to learn more about the firm, meet some of our people and gain insight into life at Morgan Lewis. Applications will be accepted from October 2018 for all vacation schemes taking place in 2019. The closing date for applications is 31 January 2019.

Sponsorship We will sponsor students through the GDL and LPC. A maintenance grant of £8,000 will also be provided. The firm does not provide retrospective funding for law school fees or maintenance grants.

Vacancies	8
Trainees	15
Partners	33
Total staff	160

Work placement yes

Training contract deadline
15 July 2019

Apply
Online at
www.morganlewis.com

Starting salary
£47,000

Minimum qualifications
High 2.1 degree plus AAB at A level

Sponsorship
GDL/LPC

Offices
Almaty, Astana, Beijing, Boston, Brussels, Chicago, Century City, Dallas, Dubai, Frankfurt, Hartford, Hong Kong, Houston, London, Los Angeles, Miami, Moscow, New York, Orange County, Paris, Philadelphia, Pittsburgh, Princeton, San Francisco, Shanghai, Silicon Valley, Singapore Tokyo, Washington DC, Wilmington.

Morgan Lewis

Remember to cite *The LawCareers.Net Handbook* on your application form if you apply to this firm.

TRAINING CONTRACT DIRECTORY 409

Morrison & Foerster (UK) LLP

CityPoint, One Ropemaker Street, London EC2Y 9AW
Tel: 020 7920 4000
Email: lmccall@mofo.com
Web: www.mofo.com
f mofollp 𝕐 mofo_londongrad

The firm Morrison & Foerster is a leading global firm with over 1,000 lawyers in key technology and finance centres in the US, Europe and Asia. In Europe we have a team of 120 lawyers in our strategic hubs of London, Berlin and Brussels. We work alongside our colleagues in the US and Asia, drawing on cultural, jurisdictional and market knowledge to deliver the best advice and client service with a global approach. Dynamic technology companies, significant financial investors and financial institutions, leading consumer product companies and other market leaders come to MoFo for our expertise, knowledge, advice, commerciality, transaction support and individually tailored client service. We handle some of the world's largest cross-border transactions and resolve some of the biggest disputes across multiple jurisdictions. Our firm was built on, and continues to succeed, because of the talent of our lawyers and their innovative approach in the practice of law. We practise in a collegial environment where we value teamwork and diverse perspectives and operate as one firm. As our nickname suggests, we take our work seriously but we don't take ourselves too seriously.

Types of work Bankruptcy and restructuring, capital markets, corporate/M&A, data privacy, employment, equity derivatives, financial transactions, funds, investigations, litigation, outsourcing, tax and technology transactions.

Who should apply We're looking for people who are intellectually curious, focused and highly motivated. We want applications from students who can demonstrate a genuine interest in law, have a strong interest in technology and finance and who are excited by the significant responsibility that a training contract at MoFo offers. Our culture sets us apart; we value diversity, have a strong commitment to pro bono and want our future trainees to share this philosophy.

Training programme We offer our trainees the support and training needed to excel in their work. Key elements include our trainee induction, ongoing training through the MoFo academy and significant on-the job training. This combination enables our trainees to develop the necessary skills to deliver exceptional client service on the complex global matters we act on for our clients. The training period consists of four six-month seats with the potential of a seat in one of our Asian offices. There's an active mentoring programme as well as a formal review process four times annually.

When and how to apply Apply via our online application form at careers.mofo.com/law-students. We have six vacancies for 2021; the closing date is 6 January 2019.

Work placements In 2019 we will be running two, two-week vacation schemes on 17 to 28 June 2019 and 1 to 12 July 2019. Our vacation schemes provide prospective trainees a chance to learn about MoFo behind the scenes and to consider whether they want to become a future trainee and an ambassador for our firm. Through our work assignments, summer associates gain a good picture of how much responsibility we give our trainees. It's also an opportunity to get to know our London-based attorneys and staff. We treat our vacation scheme as an extended interview and it is the sole method of selecting our future trainees.

Sponsorship We pay full GDL and LPC course fees at The University of Law for our future trainees. We also offer an £8,000 maintenance grant during the GDL and LPC. If students have already completed the GDL or LPC prior to securing a training contract with us we offer 50% reimbursement of fees.

Vacancies	6
Trainees	9
Partners	19
Total staff	90

Work placement yes
(see Insider Report on p93)

Training contract deadline
6 January 2019

Apply
Online at
careers.mofo.com/law-students

Starting salary
£46,000

Minimum qualifications
2.1 degree

Sponsorship
GDL/LPC

Offices
Beijing, Berlin, Brussels, Denver, Hong Kong, London, Los Angeles, New York, Northern Virginia, Palo Alto, San Diego, San Francisco, Shanghai, Singapore, Tokyo, Washington DC

MORRISON
FOERSTER

MOOSA-DUKE SOLICITORS 11 De Montfort St, Leicester LE1 7GE **Tel:** 01162547456 **Email:** enquiries@moosaduke.com **Apply to:** Mrs Mehmooda Duke	Niche practice specialising in clinical negligence only. LSC franchise for clinical negligence. Law Society clinical negligence panel.	V 1[19] T 2 P 2 TS 11 WP yes
MORGAN JONES & PETT Grey Friars House, 18-20 Prince of Wales Road, Norwich NR1 1LB **Tel:** 01603 877000 **Email:** davidpett@m-j-p.co.uk **Apply to:** Mr DR Pett	Specialist personal injury and clinical negligence firm. Also family and conveyancing departments. Offices in Norwich.	V 0 T 1 P 3 TS 23 WP no
MORRISH SOLICITORS LLP Oxford House, Oxford Row, Leeds LS1 3BE **Tel:** 0113 245 0733 **Email:** paul.scholey@morrishsolicitors.com **Apply to:** Mr Paul Scholey	City centre location close to law courts. Most types of legal work undertaken with particular specialisation in personal injury. Not recruiting trainees at present.	V 0 T 4 P 15 TS 90 WP no
MORRISONS SOLICITORS LLP Clarendon House, Clarendon Road, Redhill RH1 1FB **Tel:** 01737 854 500 **Email:** hr@morrlaw.com **Apply to:** Miss Michela James	A Morrisons Solicitors trainee solicitor benefits from working in a firm with more than 200 years of accumulated knowledge and expertise across some of the most important sectors of UK law.	V 2-4[20] T 4 P 13 TS 140 WP no
MORTONS 110-112 High Street West, Sunderland SR1 1TX **Tel:** 0191 514 4323 **Email:** mortons@mortons-solicitors.com **Apply to:** The Practice Manager		V 0 T 1 P 6 TS 35 WP no
MOSS & CO 17 Lower Clapton Road, London E5 ONS **Tel:** 020 8986 8336 **Email:** narinder.moss@mosslaw.co.uk **Apply to:** Mrs Narinder Moss	A specialist legal aid firm for crime, housing and actions against the police, as well as welfare benefits. Police station accreditation an advantage.	V 1[19] T 2 P 2 TS 10 WP yes
MOWLL & MOWLL Trafalgar House Gordon Road, Whitfield, Dover, Kent CT16 3PN **Tel:** 01304 873344 **Email:** enquiries@mowll.co.uk **Apply to:** Mrs Eileen Sutton	Established 130 years in Dover dealing with commercial property, company law, probate, conveyancing, family and civil litigation including employment.	V 0 T 0 P 5 TS 24 WP no
MUCKLE LLP Time Central, 32 Gallowgate, Newcastle upon Tyne NE1 4BF **Tel:** 0191 211 7879 **Email:** alison.appleby@muckle-llp.com **Apply to:** Alison Appleby	Muckle LLP is a highly successful commercial law firm in Newcastle, focussed around being the number one law firm in the North East for business.	V 4 T 9 P 30 TS 137 WP yes

V = Vacancies / **T** = Trainees / **P** = Partners / **TS** = Total Staff / **WP** = Work Placement

Mundays LLP

Cedar House, 78 Portsmouth Road, Cobham Surrey KT11 1AN
Tel: 01932 590500
Email: enq@mundays.co.uk
Web: www.mundays.co.uk
🐦 mundayslaw

The firm Mundays is one of Surrey's leading law firms, operating from modern offices, with easy access to London and the M25. Many of our lawyers have worked in the City but have chosen to relocate to a firm where we aim to offer a service as good as (if not better than) competitors in London at more economic rates, while enabling our lawyers to achieve a better work/life balance. We offer our diverse range of clients (both corporate and private) comprehensive, responsive and commercial advice, with separate departments working closely together as appropriate.

Types of work The firm is divided into six principal departments: commercial property, residential property and development, corporate and commercial (including employment), dispute resolution, private wealth and family. Within these departments, we have specialisms such as banking and insolvency.

Who should apply Candidates will need to demonstrate their confidence, ability to communicate and personality. They are also required to have three A levels or equivalent (ordinarily ABB or better), have or expect to receive at least a 2.1 degree (applications from law and non-law graduates are welcome), and to demonstrate comparable performance in any postgraduate courses in law. We are looking for well-rounded individuals who are keen to develop their career with us as trainees and beyond.

Training programme Trainees typically spend periods of six months in each of four departments, sharing a room with a partner or senior solicitor so that they can observe exactly how the job is done and have the opportunity to learn from day one. Trainees also have the opportunity to work for other fee earners so that they are exposed to a wide range of specialisms and working styles in their department.

So far as possible, we aim to accommodate the wishes of trainees to gain experience of any particular specialist area in which we practise. Trainees are encouraged to take on responsibility from the beginning of their training through direct experience of dealing with matters and working alongside fee-earners. Progress is closely monitored and training given to reflect the needs of individual trainees.

As a result, we are extremely pleased that Mundays was nominated for the award of Best Trainer - Medium Regional firm at the LawCareers.Net Training and Recruitment Awards from 2012 to 2016 and again in 2018. In addition, our former Training Principal Stephen Morris was proud to be nominated in 2014 and 2018 for the award for Best Training Principal - Small Trainee Intake. These nominations were based on feedback surveys from our current trainees in each year. These nominations acknowledge the high quality of the training on which we pride ourselves.

The Lex 100 also announced Mundays as a winner in the Client Contact category where trainees 'feel like part of the team - rather than a small cog' and also a winner in the Work/Life Balance category. *The Lex 100* 2016/17 survey consisted of anonymous responses gathered from over 3,000 trainees at 173 law firms across the UK.

When and how to apply You can apply from April 2019 for training contracts commencing September 2021.

Vacancies	2
Trainees	4
Partners	26
Total staff	98

Training contract deadline
1 August 2019

Apply
Online

Starting salary
£26,000

Minimum qualifications
2.1 degree, ABB at A level
(or equivalent)

Offices
London, Surrey

MUNDAYS.
Making the law work for you.

MULLIS & PEAKE 8-10 Eastern Road, Romford, Essex RM1 3PJ **Tel:** 01708 762326 **Email:** martyntrenery@mplaw.co.uk **Apply to:** Mr Martyn Trenerry	We specialise in commercial work for business including company, employment and licensing. Private client includes litigation, accident claim, trust and probate, and advice to the elderly.	V T P TS WP	Poss[19] 2 7 56 no
MURRELL ASSOCIATES LIMITED 14 High Cross, Truro, Cornwall TR1 2AJ **Tel:** 01872 226 990 **Email:** info@murrellassociates.co.uk **Apply to:** Mr Chris Wills	Murrell Associates is a specialist team of corporate/commercial lawyers, providing commercial legal services to businesses in the South West and beyond.	V T P TS WP	0 0 3 16 yes
MUSA PATELS 71-73 Bradford Road, Dewsbury WF13 2EG **Tel:** 01924 437800 **Email:** info@musapatels.co.uk **Apply to:** Mr Musa Patel	General practice specialising in criminal law, immigration law, residential and commercial conveyancing.	V T P TS WP	0 0 2 16 no
MUSTOE SHORTER 6-8 Frederick Place, Weymouth DT4 8HQ **Tel:** 01305 752700 **Apply to:** The Staff Partner	Small company with the latest technology with offices in Dorchester and Weymouth dealing with most types of high street business.	V T P TS WP	0 3 7 50 no
MYERSON SOLICITORS LLP Grosvenor House, 20 Barrington Road, Altrincham WA14 1HB **Tel:** 0161 941 4000 **Email:** applications@myerson.co.uk **Apply to:** Miss Jordanna Reynolds	A leading independent firm, representing businesses and individuals in Manchester, Cheshire, the UK, EU and beyond. MLA 2018 Winner: Law Firm of the Year (Medium).	V T P TS WP	3 8 20 93 yes
NANDY & CO 62 Woodgrange Road, Forest Gate, London E7 0QH **Tel:** 020 8536 1800 **Apply to:** Ms Nanda Welivitgodage		V T P TS WP	0 0 - - no
NAPTHENS 7 Winckley Square, Preston PR1 3JD **Tel:** 01772 888444 **Email:** human.resources@napthens.co.uk **Apply to:** Ms Nicola Mason	Departments in commercial property, residential property, family, wills and estate planning, corporate, litigation, employment, rural and licensing. Offices in Preston, Blackburn, Blackpool, Southport, Liverpool, Cumbria.	V T P TS WP	2-4[20] 7 27 229 no
NASH & CO SOLICITORS LLP Beaumont House, Beaumont Park, Plymouth PL4 9BD **Tel:** 01752 664444 **Email:** law@nash.co.uk **Apply to:** Mrs Joanne Arnold	A leading Plymouth commercial and private client law firm specialising in all main areas of legal practice.	V T P TS WP	0 3 12 72 yes

V = Vacancies / **T** = Trainees / **P** = Partners / **TS** = Total Staff / **WP** = Work Placement

NELSONS	Nelsons is one of the largest law	V	0
Pennine House, 8 Stanford Street, Nottingham	firms in the East Midlands, providing	T	6
NG1 7BQ	a full range of legal services to the	P	48
Tel: 0115 958 6262	corporate and private sectors.	TS	193
Email: careers@nelsonslaw.co.uk		WP	no
Apply to: HR Department			

NEWCASTLE UNDER LYME BOROUGH COUNCIL	Local authority.	V	0
Civic Offices, Merrial Street, Newcastle,		T	-
Staffordshire ST5 2AG		P	-
Tel: 01782 717717		TS	2
Email: paul.washington@newcastle-staffs.gov.uk		WP	no
Apply to: Mr Paul R Washington			

NEXUS SOLICITORS	We provide commercial legal services	V	0
Carlton House, 16-18 Albert Square, Manchester	and business advice to SME's, plcs	T	1
M2 5PE	and high net worth individuals. Nexus	P	9
Tel: 0161 819 4900	is a commercial practice established	TS	45
Email: cpugh@nexussolicitors.co.uk	in July 2000.	WP	no
Apply to: Mr Christopher Pugh			

NOBLE SOLICITORS	We are a busy criminal and mental	V	0
26-28 Stuart Street, Luton, Bedfordshire LU1 2SW	health specilaist practice covering	T	0
Tel: 01582 544370	the Bedfordshire and north	P	3
Apply to: Mr Gareth Cotton	Hertfordshire area.	TS	40
		WP	yes

NOCKOLDS	General practice undertaking all	V	4[20]
Market Square, Bishops Stortford CM23 3UZ	types of legal work for a wide variety	T	6
Tel: 01279 755777	of private and commercial clients.	P	13
Email: hrdept@nockolds.co.uk		TS	140
Apply to: Mrs Sue Stevenson		WP	yes

NORTH YORKSHIRE COUNTY COUNCIL	Provides legal advice to North	V	0
County Hall, Northallerton, North Yorkshire DL7 8AD	Yorkshire County Council and other	T	2
Tel: 0845 872 7374	public bodies, expertise in all areas	P	0
Email: legal.services@northyorks.gov.uk	of public sector law. We have the	TS	43
Apply to: Mrs Pauline Smurthwaite	Lexcel standard.	WP	yes

NORTON PESKETT	Medium-sized firm with large private	V	0
148 London Road North, Lowestoft, Suffolk NR32 1HF	client workloads. Branch offices at	T	-
Tel: 01502 533000	Beccles, Gorleston, Great Yarmouth,	P	6
Email: enquire@nortonpeskett.co.uk	Norwich and Halesworth.	TS	118
Apply to: Miss Leanne Griffen		WP	no

OBASEKI	We provide expert advice on	V	1[20]
Unit 1, 222 Kingsland Road, London E2 8AX	property, immigration, family,	T	2
Tel: 020 7739 7549	employment, criminal, commercial	P	3
Email: solicitors@legalpaal.com	and civil law. We offer private service	TS	11
Apply to: Ms Jennifer Obaseki	and legal aid.	WP	yes

V = Vacancies / **T** = Trainees / **P** = Partners / **TS** = Total Staff / **WP** = Work Placement

Norton Rose Fulbright LLP

3 More London Riverside, London SE1 2AQ
Tel: 020 7444 2113
Email: graduate.recruitment@nortonrosefulbright.com
Web: www.nortonrosefulbrightgraduates.com
f nortonrosefulbrightgraduatesuk **𝕪** nlawgrad

The firm Norton Rose Fulbright is a global firm. We provide the world's pre-eminent corporations and financial institutions with a full business law service. We have more than 4,000 lawyers and legal staff in over 50 cities across Europe, the United States, Canada, Latin America, Asia, Australia, Africa, and the Middle East.

Types of work Recognised for our industry focus, we are strong across all the key industry sectors: financial institutions; energy; infrastructure, mining and commodities; transport; technology and innovation; as well as life sciences and healthcare. Wherever we are, we operate in accordance with our global business principles of quality, unity and integrity. We aim to provide the highest possible standard of legal service in each of our offices and to maintain that level of quality at every point of contact.

Training programme There's no progress more vital than what you'll experience on our training contracts. Over two years – broken into four six-month seats – you'll hit all kinds of new firsts with us, big and small. You'll explore new areas, for instance. Each seat will take you through different sectors and practice areas, with at least one seat in each of corporate, banking and litigation. One of your seats will almost certainly be on secondment too – your first encounter with working in a new country, or maybe six months spent working in a client office. As you move from one milestone to the next, you'll have a sizeable team at your back. A partner mentor to turn to and to learn from. A trainee buddy to teach you the ropes. And the whole trainee development team, to keep you on track from day to day.

When and how to apply We offer up to 45 training contracts each year across two intakes. For the March 2021 and September 2021 intakes law and non-law penultimate years, finalists and graduates should apply from 1 October 2018 to 14 July 2019.

Work placements Finding the place you want to spend your career is a moment you'll always remember, and that's exactly the kind of insight we offer on our vacation schemes. Whether you're with us for one week or two, we pack a lot into these three schemes. You'll do real work, for real clients. You'll network with colleagues. You'll present group projects on legal issues. It's a lot of new ground to cover, but if you want to understand what it's really like to work here, nothing else comes close. Pay for the week is £360, and on top of that, you'll leave us knowing for sure that you're on the right path.

Open days and first-year opportunities – Everyone remembers the first day they walked through the doors of their future firm. For many of our lawyers, that happens on our open days and first step programmes. First step caters to first-year undergraduates, while our open days are designed for undergraduates, graduates and career changers of all degree subjects. Either way, it's the opportunity to step through our doors, make a first impression, and use our packed schedule of interactive sessions to discover whether law is right for you. For more information please visit our website www.nortonrosefulbrightgraduates.com.

Sponsorship We cover the cost of GDL and LPC course fees and our maintenance grants are £8,000 for the GDL and £10,000 for the LPC.

Vacancies	Up to 45
Trainees	106
Partners	1,200*
Total staff	4,000*
	*denotes worldwide figure

Work placement yes

Training contract deadline
14 July 2019

Apply
Online

Starting salary
£45,000

Minimum qualifications
AAB at A level and
2.1 degree or equivalent

Sponsorship
GDL/LPC

Offices
Over 50 cities across Europe, the United States, Canada, Latin America, Asia, Australia, Africa, and the Middle East

^NORTON ROSE FULBRIGHT

Proud diversity and inclusion
partner of

ƻƨ aspiringsolicitors

Remember to cite *The LawCareers.Net Handbook* on your application form if you apply to this firm.

Orrick, Herrington & Sutcliffe (UK) LLP

107 Cheapside, London EC2V 6DN
Tel: 020 7862 4600
Email: recruitlondon@orrick.com
Web: www.orrick.com/london/gradrecruitment
f orrick 🐦 orrick

The firm Orrick is a leading international law firm with more than 1,100 lawyers in 25 offices located throughout North America, Europe and Asia. Orrick has earned a global reputation advising both established and emerging companies, banks and international financial institutions. Much of Orrick's client work involves cross-border transactions in the tech, finance and energy sectors, as well as dispute resolution and regulatory investigations. At Orrick you will benefit from its core values of collegiality, integrity, excellence, enthusiasm and respect for individuality.

Who should apply If you set your standards high, have a strong work ethic and are a bright, talented graduate of any discipline looking for a firm offering a broad-based training contract, then Orrick could be for you. Applicants should have at least three A-level passes at grades A and B and a 2.1 degree.

Training programme Orrick is a firm for those looking for a high level of responsibility from day one. We value team players and reward collaboration over competition. We aim to give individuals the opportunity to flourish in a lively and supportive work environment and encourage interaction among lawyers across international offices at every level of experience within the firm. We support learning through a steadfast focus on training and a mentoring programme that will provide trainees with the right foundation for building their legal career and for working with clients. A genuine open door policy means trainees work closely with partners and of counsel as well as associates to gain practical experience in research, drafting, procedural and client-related skills.

Our two-year training programme is made up of six four-month seats with regular appraisals throughout. Our dedicated trainee partner oversees the supervision and management of our trainees. There are regular training sessions on legal and soft skills to enhance your development as a lawyer. Our extensive training programme is provided by in-house experts, clients and specialist professionals. Trainees undertake the Professional Skills Course during their induction programme.

When and how to apply Our training contract and open day applications will open from 12 October 2018, and you can apply online via our website. Our training contract applications will close on 28 June 2019. We will be holding open days in the spring of 2019. Applications for these will close on 8 February 2019.

Work placements We will be holding open days in the spring of 2019 which provide a good opportunity to see the London office of a US law firm in action. Applicants spend the day learning more about the firm and the work on offer in the London office as well as participating in a business game designed to give a flavour of the work of a City lawyer. Further details can be found on our website.

Sponsorship GDL and LPC fees paid plus £7,000 maintenance.

Vacancies	6-8
Trainees	12
Partners	33
Total staff	168

(Figures for London office)

Training contract deadline
28 June 2019

Apply
Online

Starting salary
£40,000 (2018)

Minimum qualifications
As and Bs at A level plus 2.1 degree, any discipline

Sponsorship
GDL/LPC

Offices
Beijing, Brussels, Düsseldorf, Geneva, Hong Kong, Houston, London, Los Angeles, Milan, Moscow, Munich, New York, Orange County, Paris, Portland, Rome, Sacramento, San Francisco, Seattle, Shanghai, Silicon Valley, Taipei, Tokyo, Washington DC, Wheeling (GOC)

Osborne Clarke LLP

One London Wall, London EC2Y 5EB
Tel: 0117 917 3484
Email: trainee.recruitment@osborneclarke.com
Web: www.joinoc.com
f osborneclarketrainee **𝕏** oc_trainee

The firm Osborne Clarke is an award-winning multinational law firm. We've grown rapidly, with 25 global offices and we're proud to say that our influence and impact can be applied almost anywhere. The core sectors we work in all thrive on innovation; digital business, energy, financial services, life sciences, real estate, recruitment and transport. Our sector teams include lawyers from all legal disciplines, effortlessly blending expertise, insight and enthusiasm. Crucially, we think sector-first, organising ourselves around the current affairs and future challenges of the industries we serve, rather than traditional legal practice areas. It helps keep us one step ahead. Like any private practice, legal expertise is at the heart of everything we do. But what makes us distinctive? For a start, you can expect to get involved in truly fascinating work. The variety of our deals and the diversity of our clients provide an exciting and immersive commercial framework. This is a firm where fresh ideas (and the confidence and conviction to see them through) are highly prized, and we're never afraid to take a view. It is also firm with a coherent commercial vision, with a clear direction, supported by a compelling sense of purpose and identity. Put simply, we're going places. And you can put our positive, can-do attitude down to sustained success, in terms of both profile and performance. Finally, there's our culture. When we asked our recent recruits what attracted them to us, they used words like 'friendly', 'inclusive', 'open' and 'fun'. To our clients we are 'approachable', 'proactive', 'understanding' and 'formidable'.

Types of work Main areas of expertise include; banking and finance, business regulation, commercial, corporate, employment and benefits, litigation, pensions, projects, real estate, restructuring and insolvency and tax.

Who should apply? We are looking for candidates who can: communicate effectively; think commercially and practically; solve problems creatively; build effective relationships; and demonstrate initiative. Foreign language skills are also an advantage.

Training programme Our high profile clients expect us to be brilliant, so we put a lot of effort into helping our people be the best they can throughout their careers – not just at the start of it. We foster the brightest and the best, with class-leading training and development programmes, and a unique climate of learning and discovery for everyone. We place value on individuals and respect their needs, motivations and choices. Our workplaces are designed to promote collaboration, often featuring open plan structures that make it easy to fit-in, mix and get involved. You'll also find flexible and imaginative approaches to everyone's work/life needs, with a connected infrastructure that is adaptive and tailored to bringing out the best in people. As a trainee, you'll complete four seats: corporate or banking, real estate or tax, litigation, and one other. In each seat, a senior lawyer will supervise your day-to-day progress and give you regular feedback, so you know how you're doing. They're there to help you up your game. Every three months, you'll have a formal progress review to help you track your development. Our trainees get lots of responsibility. And they find that it's what differentiates their training contracts from others.

Work placements Each of our vacation scheme placements runs for two weeks over the summer and offers a great opportunity for candidates to really get to know the firm. The placement follows a structured programme which allows candidates to spend time in two different departments and get involved in real client work. Beyond work there are plenty of social events organised by our trainees.

Vacancies	20
Trainees	40
Partners	258
Total staff	1,632
Work placement	yes
(see Insider Report on p94)	

Apply
Online via
www.joinoc.com

Starting salary
Bristol – £37,500
London and Thames
Valley – £42,500

Minimum qualifications
2.1 degree, any discipline

Sponsorship
GDL/LPC

Offices
Amsterdam, Barcelona, Berlin, Brescia, Bristol, Brussels, Busto Arsizio, Cologne, Hamburg, London, Madrid, Milan, Munich, New York, Padua, Paris, Reading, Rome, San Francisco, Silicon Valley, Stockholm, Zaragoza

Osborne Clarke

Remember to cite *The LawCareers.Net Handbook* on your application form if you apply to this firm.

Firm	Description	V	T	P	TS	WP
OGLETHORPE STURTON & GILLIBRAND 16 Castle Park, Lancaster LA1 1YG **Tel:** 01524 846846 **Email:** dlgillibrand@osg.co.uk **Apply to:** Mr David Gillibrand	A well-established firm in serving the business and rural community based in North Lancashire and the South Lakes.	1-2	3	8	46	no
OLDHAM MARSH PAGE FLAVELL White House, 19 High Street, Melton Mowbray, Leicester LE13 0TZ **Tel:** 01664 563162 **Apply to:** Mr Neil Pidgeon	General market town practice including financial services, personal injury, matrimonial, crime. Legal aid franchise.	Poss	0	3	30	no
O'MELVENY Warwick Court, 5 Paternoster Square, London EC4M 7DX **Tel:** 020 7088 0000 **Email:** graduate-recruitment@omm.com **Apply to:** Mrs Natalie Beacroft	O'Melveny is an international law firm with over 750 lawyers working across 15 offices in the US, Europe and Asia.	Up to 3	6	7	50	yes
O'NEILL PATIENT SOLICITORS LLP Chester House, 2 Chester Road, Hazel Grove, Stockport, Cheshire SK7 5NT **Tel:** 0844 576 2121 **Email:** enqs@oneillpatient.co.uk **Apply to:** Mr Steven Thomas	An established and successful firm enjoying an enviable reputation for both private client and company/commercial work which also specialises in volume conveyancing and remortgage work.	0	0	10	240	no
OSBORNES SOLICITORS LLP Livery House, 7-9 Pratt Street, London NW1 0AE **Tel:** 020 7485 8811 **Email:** sandrahillard@osbornes.net **Apply to:** Mrs Sandra Hillard	A firm which undertakes all aspects of general practice, carried out to a high professional standard.	4	7	18	110	yes
OSMOND & OSMOND 55/57 Temple Chambers, Temple Avenue, London EC4Y OHP **Tel:** 020 7583 3434 **Email:** p.flaherty@osmondandosmond.co.uk **Apply to:** Mr Paul Flaherty		1[19]	2	2	8	yes
OURY CLARK SOLICITORS 10 John Street, London WC1N 2EB **Tel:** 020 7067 4300 **Email:** hr@ocsolicitors.com **Apply to:** Ms Juliet Oury	We are a London based boutique legal practice specialising in commercial, corporate, commercial property, employment, litigation, GDPR and business immigration. Advising all types of businesses.	1	3	7	21	no
OVER TAYLOR BIGGS 4 Cranmere Court, Lustleigh Close, Exeter EX2 8PW **Tel:** 01392 823 811 **Email:** richard.biggs@otb.uk.com **Apply to:** Mr Christopher Over	We are a dynamic commercial practice with an emphasis on property, corporate and litigation services.	1	1	5	20	no

V = Vacancies / **T** = Trainees / **P** = Partners / **TS** = Total Staff / **WP** = Work Placement

OWEN WHITE Senate House, 62-70 Bath Road, Slough SL1 3SR **Tel:** 01753 876800 **Email:** caryn.beidas@owenwhite.com **Apply to:** Caryn Beidas	We are a top rated regional law firm with specialisms in social housing, real estate, franchising and employment, and have a high trainee retention rate.	V 2 T 5 P 6 TS 40 WP no
OWEN WHITE AND CATLIN 74 Church Road, Ashford, Middlesex TW15 2TP **Tel:** 01784 254188 **Apply to:** Mrs JD Williamson	One of the largest practices covering all aspects of legal work in West London. Progressive and expanding firm and provides a wealth of opportunity for trainees.	V 3 T 0 P 11 TS 130 WP no
OZORAN TURKAN 203 Green Lanes, Islington, London N16 9DJ **Tel:** 020 7354 0802 **Email:** info@ozoranturkan.com or ozoranturkan@aol.com **Apply to:** Ms D Ozoran	Small high street firm; two partners covering family, crime, immigration, conveyancing, wills and probate.	V 2 T 2 P 2 TS 10 WP yes
PAINTERS 29 Church Street, Kidderminster DY10 2AU **Tel:** 01562 822295 **Email:** cdh@painters-solicitors.co.uk **Apply to:** Mr Charles Hobbs	High street practice doing contentious and non-contentious work, commercial and private client, criminal and family, legal aid contracts.	V 0 T 0 P 9 TS 50 WP no
PALMERS 19 Town Square, Basildon, Essex SS14 1BD **Tel:** 01268 240000 **Email:** recruitment@palmerslaw.co.uk **Apply to:** Mrs Gina Newman	Palmers Solicitors is an established law firm in Essex covering the whole spectrum of legal advice for commercial and private clients from its three offices.	V 1 T 1 P 8 TS 100 WP yes
PARAGON LAW LIMITED Finelook Studios, 7B Broad Street, Nottingham NG1 3AJ **Tel:** 0115 964 4123 **Email:** hruk@paragonlaw.co.uk **Apply to:** Miss Marie Stafford	Multiple award winning niche immigration law firm, recognised as a leader in its field of practice by the *Legal 500* and *Chambers & Partners*.	V 1 T - P 5 TS 30 WP yes
PARDOES SOLICITORS LLP West Quay House, Northgate, Bridgwater TA6 3EU **Tel:** 01278 457891 **Email:** hr@pardoes.co.uk **Apply to:** HR Department	Serving the South West, our offices in Bridgwater, Taunton, Yeovil, Dorchester and Bridport provide a broad range of legal services (personal and commercial).	V 1[20] T 1 P 7 TS 76 WP no
PARIS SMITH LLP 1 London Road, Southampton SO15 2AE **Tel:** 023 80482482 **Email:** sarah.giles@parissmith.co.uk **Apply to:** Mrs Sarah Giles	Large regional firm, based in Southampton and Winchester. Established practice with various specialist areas. Recognised as leaders in the South by *Legal 500* and *Chambers*.	V 5 T 10 P 37 TS 200 WP yes

V = Vacancies / **T** = Trainees / **P** = Partners / **TS** = Total Staff / **WP** = Work Placement

PARK WOODFINE HEALD MELLOWS LLP
1 Lurke Street, Bedford MK40 3TN
Tel: 01234 400000
Email: admin@pwhmllp.com
Apply to: The Managing Partner

General firm covering commercial, family, civil litigation, conveyancing, probate and wills, commercial, family, commercial mediation and employment. Well established with three branch offices.

V	0
T	1
P	7
TS	60
WP	no

PARKER BULLEN LLP
45 Castle Street, Salisbury SP10 3SS
Tel: 017 2241 2000
Email: sarah.waller@parkerbullen.com
Apply to: Mrs Sarah Waller

Premier law firm based in Salisbury and Andover. Rapidly growing, dynamic and innovative, offering experience in legal services for both individuals and businesses.

V	2[20]
T	6
P	7
TS	60
WP	yes

PARKER RHODES HICKMOTTS
14 & 22 Moorgate Street, Rotherham, South Yorkshire S60 2DA
Tel: 01709 511100
Email: info@prhsolicitors.co.uk
Apply to: Mrs Fiona Shinner

A general practice high street firm based in Rotherham.

V	0
T	3
P	3
TS	49
WP	no

PATCHELL DAVIES
183 High Street, Blackwood, Gwent NP12 1ZF
Tel: 01495 287 128
Email: law@patchelldavies.co.uk
Apply to: Mr H Patchell

Single office high street practice established 1977 established private client, conveyancing, commercial, family and litigation base.

V	0
T	0
P	2
TS	7
WP	no

PATTERSONS SOLICITORS
31 Harrison Road, Halifax, West Yorkshire HX1 2AF
Tel: 01422 353555
Email: pattersonssolicitors@googlemail.com
Apply to: Mr Brent J Patterson

Firm specialising in legal aid work: crime, benefits, debt, education, housing. Some personal injury.

V	0
T	0
P	1
TS	7
WP	no

PAUL ROBINSON SOLICITORS LLP
The Old Bank, 470/474 London Road, Westcliff SS0 9LD
Tel: 01702 338338
Email: ablack@paulrobinson.co.uk
Apply to: The Partnership Secretary

Established 1983. General practice undertaking all areas of law. Investor in people. Lexcel. CQS.

V	1
T	2
P	9
TS	85
WP	no

PEACOCK & CO
94 High Street, Wimbledon Village, London SW19 5EG
Tel: 020 8944 5290
Email: kim@peacock-law.co.uk
Apply to: Ms Kim Peacock

General practice with offices in the heart of Wimbledon Village and Epsom Surrey.

V	1
T	2
P	8
TS	30
WP	no

PEARSON HINCHLIFFE LLP
Albion House, 31 Queen Street, Oldham OL1 1RD
Tel: 0161 785 3500
Email: joanne.ormston@phsolicitors.co.uk
Apply to: Ms Joanne Ormston

V	2[19]
T	2
P	8
TS	49
WP	no

V = Vacancies / **T** = Trainees / **P** = Partners / **TS** = Total Staff / **WP** = Work Placement

Paul Hastings

8th Floor, Ten Bishops Square, London E1 6EG
Tel: 020 3023 5100
Email: yvettecroucher@paulhastings.com
Web: www.paulhastings.com
f paulhastingsllp **🐦** paul_hastings

The firm With lawyers serving clients from 21 worldwide offices, Paul Hastings provides a wide range of services across Europe, America and Asia. Through a collaborative approach, entrepreneurial spirit and firm commitment to client service excellence, the legal professionals of Paul Hastings deliver innovative solutions to many of the world's top financial institutions and *Fortune 500* companies.

Types of work Paul Hastings' London office focuses on corporate, capital markets, private equity, real estate, real estate finance, corporate and structured finance, leveraged finance, acquisition finance, restructuring, private funds, tax, financial services, technology and cyber security, employment and litigation. The London office has experience in multi-jurisdictional European transactions, working with our offices in Frankfurt, Milan and Paris.

Who should apply We seek undergraduates and postgraduates from both law and non-law backgrounds who combine intellectual ability with enthusiasm, creativity and a demonstrable ability to thrive in a challenging environment.

Training programme We offer an extensive and instructive training programme for our trainees, spending six months in four practice areas, including the opportunity for a secondment to a client.

When and how to apply Online application through Paul Hastings website www.paulhastings.com/office/london/training-contracts. Please apply by 31 July 2019 for training contracts commencing in September 2021.

Work placements Ad hoc work placements offered on application to the London office.

Sponsorship GDL and LPC fees and maintenance offered to successful applicants.

Vacancies	6-8
Trainees	13
Partners	28
Total staff	150
Work placement	yes

Training contract deadline
31 July 2019

Apply
Online

Starting salary
£45,000

Minimum qualifications
2.1 degree

Sponsorship
LPC/GDL and maintenance grant

Offices
Atlanta, Chicago, Houston, Los Angeles, New York, Orange County, Palo Alto, San Diego, San Francisco, São Paulo, Washington, Brussels, Frankfurt, London, Milan, Paris, Beijing, Hong Kong, Seoul, Shanghai, Tokyo

PAUL
HASTINGS

Payne Hicks Beach

10 New Square, Lincoln's Inn, London WC2A 3QG
Tel: 020 7465 4300
Email: recruitment@phb.co.uk
Web: www.phb.co.uk

The firm Payne Hicks Beach is a medium size London law firm with a global reach, a 300 year history at the same location in Lincoln's Inn and a thoroughly 21st century approach to client service. The firm provides solution-led advice and legal services to domestic and international private and commercial clients including individuals, families, businesses and trustees. Much of the firm's work has an international element building on strong links with the USA, Canada, Scandinavia, the Middle East and Far East, the main offshore centres, Switzerland and other European countries. Work is regularly handled in French, Italian, German, Danish and Arabic. The firm consistently 'punches above its weight' in the complexity of the clients it serves and matters it handles, and specialist advisers work in close-knit teams to deliver a seamless service across all its practice areas. Trainees invariably feel part of the team from the moment they arrive.

Types of work The firm's reputation has been built on family and private client work as one of the small number of firms in the UK who provide these services at the highest level. Its commanding position in these areas is complemented by an excellent reputation for contentious trusts and dispute resolution, privacy and media law, company and commercial law, employment, residential and commercial property and citizenship and immigration work. Despite their position in the market, Payne Hicks Beach's lawyers pride themselves on the confidentiality and discretion with which they conduct their work, not least because the firm's clients include many household names, as a result of which the firm is one of London's best kept secrets.

Who should apply Applicants for training contracts should have an excellent academic record (an upper second class degree is a minimum requirement), a high degree of drive and determination, and will need to demonstrate, by reference to their experience or otherwise, an ability to analyse problems accurately, to be creative in finding practical commercial solutions, and communicating these clearly, as well as a flair for building relationships with colleagues and clients alike.

Training programme Trainees usually spend six months in each of four specialist departments, with their preferences being taken into account in this rotation so far as possible. There is only one trainee per department at any one time, so he or she plays a very important role, receiving a high level of responsibility, with real work and supervised client contact from the outset. Trainees are subject to regular assessment, with mid seat reviews and end of seat appraisals, and engage in the required Professional Skills and induction courses, as well as a formal in-house training programme. However, with the firm's team outlook and open door policy they also have constant access to help and support from partners and associates who are acknowledged experts in their fields.

When and how to apply Applications are made online via the firm's online application system AllHires (accessed via the firm's website). This includes a requirement for a formal letter of application, submitted online.

Work placements Due to the confidential nature of the work, and the high profile of the firm's clients, as a matter of policy neither work placements nor summer schemes are offered.

Sponsorship Payne Hicks Beach offers full GDL and LPC funding, and a maintenance grant each year of study. BPP Law School is the firm's preferred provider.

Vacancies	2
Trainees	5
Partners	26
Total staff	146

Training contract deadline
31 July 2019

Apply
Online

Starting salary
Competitive

Minimum qualifications
2.1 degree

Sponsorship
GDL/LPC

Offices
London

PAYNE|HICKS|BEACH

PEMBERTON GREENISH LLP
45 Cadogan Gardens, London SW3 2AQ
Tel: 020 7591 3333
Email: law@pglaw.co.uk
Apply to: Mrs Debbi Jentas

Pemberton Greenish LLP is a central London law firm specialising in real estate, private wealth and corporate.

V	0
T	4
P	14
TS	89
WP	no

PENNINGTONS MANCHES LLP
125 Wood Street, London EC2V 7AW
Tel: 020 7457 3000
Email: traineepost@penningtons.co.uk
Apply to: Ms Jenny Vine

Broad practice with business services, real estate and private individuals divisions and focus on sectors.

V	14-16
T	25
P	113
TS	700
WP	no

PETER BROWN & CO SOLICITORS LLP
1st Floor, Comer House, 19 Station Road, New Barnet, Hertfordshire EN5 1QJ
Tel: 020 8447 3277
Email: info@peterbrown-solicitors.com
Apply to: Ms Vicky Gower

We are based in New Barnet and specialise in commercial and residential property. Nearly all our work is from established clients or recommendations.

V	1
T	0
P	6
TS	20
WP	no

PETERS & PETERS
15 Fetter Lane, London EC4A 1BW
Tel: 020 7822 7777
Email: jbeckwith@petersandpeters.com
Apply to: Ms Julie Beckwith

Recognised as market leader in business crime, international and domestic commercial fraud, encompassing commercial/civil litigation, criminal cartels, extradition, economic sanctions and regulatory work.

V	2
T	2
P	10
TS	75
WP	yes

PHILCOX GRAY LTD
73-75 Newington Causeway, London SE1 6BD
Tel: 020 3207 2074
Email: postroom@philcoxgray.co.uk
Apply to: Ms Margaret Sullivan

High street social welfare practice with specialists in child law, family, housing and mediation. Offices in Elephant and Castle and Brixton.

V	0
T	1
P	4
TS	23
WP	yes

PHILLIPS
6 Wood Street, Mansfield, Nottinghamshire NG18 1QA
Tel: 01623 658556
Email: enquiries@phillips-solicitors.co.uk
Apply to: Mr Mark Marriott

Growing practice with contracts in criminal and family law. Aims to serve working class people with high quality and a smile.

V	0
T	2
P	2
TS	9
WP	no

PICKERINGS SOLICITORS
Etchell House, Etchell Court, Bonehill Road, Tamworth, Staffs B78 3HQ
Tel: 01827 317070
Email: recruitment@pickerings-solicitors.com
Apply to: Ms Sue Hatton

Specialist advice for businesses and individuals throughout the Midlands. LEXCEL & CQS and in the *Legal 500* of leading law firms.

V	1
T	1
P	4
TS	57
WP	no

PINSENT MASONS LLP
30 Crown Place, London EC2A 4ES
Tel: 0141 567 8776
Email: graduate@pinsentmasons.com
Apply to: Graduate Recruitment

Pinsent Masons is a global 100 law firm, specialising particularly in the energy, infrastructure, financial services, real estate and advanced manufacturing and technology sectors.

V	68
T	140
P	430
TS	3000
WP	yes

V = Vacancies / **T** = Trainees / **P** = Partners / **TS** = Total Staff / **WP** = Work Placement

PITMANS LLP
The Anchorage, 34 Bridge Street, Reading RG1 2LU
Tel: 0345 222 9222
Email: psmith@pitmans.com
Apply to: Mr Phil Smith

Commerical practice primarily serving large and medium-sized corporate clients in property, dispute resolution, commercial, corporate, pensions, employment and niche areas.

V	8
T	15
P	36
TS	210
WP	no

PJE SOLICITORS
115 Broadway, Treforest, Pontypridd, Rhondda Cynon Taff CF37 1BE
Tel: 01443 408647
Email: info@pjesolicitors.co.uk
Apply to: Mr Mark David Leyshon

Well-established firm. Strong litigation, employment, matrimonial and conveyancing client base. Aim to expand. 20 minutes from Cardiff. General practice serving valleys and city.

V	0
T	1
P	2
TS	10
WP	no

PLEXUS LAW
30-36 Monument Street, London EC3R 8NB
Tel: 0844 245 4000
Email: info@plexuslaw.co.uk
Apply to: Mr Jonathan Kay

Highly regarded specialist litigation practice and ABS, providing innovative solutions to the insurance, travel and other related industries. Recently merged with specialist insurance firm Greenwoods.

V	0
T	50
P	117
TS	1800
WP	no

POPE & CO
71 High Street, Sittingbourne ME10 4AW
Tel: 01795 474 004
Email: admin@popeandco.co.uk
Apply to: Mr Daniel Milan

Two-partner practice engaging in full range of legal services including family, crime, litigation, conveyancing and probate.

V	0
T	1
P	2
TS	12
WP	yes

PORTER DODSON
Central House, Church Street, Yeovil, Somerset BA20 1HH
Tel: 01935 424581
Email: info@porterdodson.co.uk
Apply to: Ms Deborah Carrington

Expanding general practice working in specialist teams covering commercial (contentious and non-contentious) litigation, private client and property. Five offices in Somerset and Dorset.

V	Poss
T	3
P	22
TS	120
WP	no

PORTNER
7/10 Chandos Street, London W1G 9DQ
Tel: 020 7616 5300
Email: info@portner.co.uk
Apply to: Mr Mitchell Griver

Deals primarily with complex and interesting work providing a personalised service to substantial clients. Niche is commercial property.

V	1
T	1
P	4
TS	29
WP	no

POTHECARY WITHAM WELD
70 St George's Square, London SW1V 3RD
Tel: 020 7821 8211
Email: traineeapplication@pwwsolicitors.co.uk
Apply to: Training Administrator

Main areas are charities and individuals. Work covered includes company and commercial, residential and business property, trusts, wills, probate, civil litigation, employment and education.

V	1[19]
T	2
P	4
TS	28
WP	no

POWELL & CO
Verbruggen's House, No 1 Street, Royal Arsenal Riverside, London SE18 6GH
Tel: 020 8854 9131
Email: info@powell-solicitors.co.uk
Apply to: Ms Ruth Powell

Small, but highly regarded niche clinical negligence firm. We also have PI, family and housing. Law Society panel members, LSC franchise.

V	0
T	1
P	2
TS	14
WP	no

V = Vacancies / **T** = Trainees / **P** = Partners / **TS** = Total Staff / **WP** = Work Placement

POWELL SPENCER & PARTNERS 290 Kilburn High Road, London NW6 2DD **Tel:** 020 7604 5600 **Email:** patriciaemmanuel@psplaw.co.uk **Apply to:** Ms Patricia Emmanuel	We are a legal aid practice specialising in crime, family law, personal injury, clinical negligence and immigration. Not currently recruiting.	V 0 T 1 P 2 TS 44 WP no
PREMIER SOLICITORS LLP Premier House, Lurke Street, Bedford MK40 3HU **Tel:** 01234 358080 **Email:** info@premiersolicitors.co.uk **Apply to:** The Recruitment Partner	Main areas are wills, probate, trusts, tax planning, Court of Protection, commercial property, conveyancing, litigation, company commercial, immigration, family, employment and notary services.	V 20 T 15 P 8 TS 100 WP yes
PRETTYS Elm House, 25 Elm Street, Ipswich IP1 2AD **Tel:** 014 7323 2121 **Email:** lbloomfield@prettys.co.uk **Apply to:** Miss Lisa Bloomfield	A large practice in East Anglia, Prettys has a substantial commercial division, and an established private client base.	V 3-4 T 6 P 6 TS 75 WP yes
PUNCH ROBSON 35 Albert Road, Albert Road, Middlesbrough TS1 1NU **Tel:** 01642 230700 **Email:** mhealy@punchrobson.co.uk **Apply to:** Mrs M Healy	We are an ambitious, good quality firm acting for many local commercial property and private clients. We also have family and mental health specialist practitioners.	V 1-2[19] T 2 P 7 TS 53 WP yes
PWC 1 Embankment Place, London WC2N 6DX **Tel:** 0808 100 1500 **Email:** notapplicable@uk.pwc.com **Apply to:** Online	You will develop into a commercial business lawyer through experience of working in multi-disciplinary teams with PwC, to offer complete, rounded solutions for clients.	V 25 T 25 P 35 TS 320 WP yes
QUALITY SOLICITORS J A HUGHES Centenary House, King Square, Barry Vale of Glamorgan CF62 8HB **Tel:** 01446 411000 **Email:** timhackett@jahughes.com **Apply to:** Mr TG Hackett	We are a high street practice founded in 1888. A forward looking firm, covering a wide spectrum of law.	V 1 T 6 P 6 TS 30 WP yes
QUALITY SOLICITORS JOHN BARKERS 2 Town Hall Street, Grimsby DN31 1HN **Tel:** 01472 268888 **Apply to:** Ms Kerry Chinn	General practice, but with emphasis on commercial and commercial property matters. The office is located centrally in Grimsby in its commercial hub.	V Poss T 0 P 2 TS 6 WP yes
QUALITYSOLICITORS BRADBURY ROBERTS & RABY Wadsworth House, Laneham Street, Scunthorpe, North Lincolnshire DN15 6PB **Tel:** 01724 854000 **Email:** clareslatter@qualitysolicitors.com **Apply to:** Mrs Clare Slatter	Medium-sized firm in town centre, handling personal injury, commercial, employment, conveyancing, probate, matrimonial and family. Family legal aid franchise. LEXCEL accredited.	V 1[19] T 6 P 4 TS 49 WP no

V = Vacancies / **T** = Trainees / **P** = Partners / **TS** = Total Staff / **WP** = Work Placement

QUALITYSOLICITORS DAVISONS
Sycamore House, 54 Calthorpe Road, Birmingham B15 1TH
Tel: 0121 685 1234
Email: g.davison@qsdavisons.com
Apply to: Mr G Davison

Practice specialising mainly in conveyancing with family, employment, private client, litigation and commercial work throughout six offices in the West Midlands area.

V	0
T	11
P	7
TS	150
WP	no

QUALITYSOLICITORS HOWLETT CLARKE LLP
96 Church Street, Brighton BN1 1UJ
Tel: 01273 327 272
Email: eloisefb@howlettclarke.co.uk
Apply to: Ms Eloise Freeman-Brown

We are a long-established general practice of over 240 years, providing a full range of legal services to the business community and to private individuals.

V	220
T	4
P	3
TS	45
WP	no

QUALITYSOLICITORS LARGE & GIBSON
Kent House, 49 Kent Road, Portsmouth PO5 3EJ
Tel: 023 9229 6296
Email: reception@largeandgibson.co.uk
Apply to: Mr Richard Wootton

Criminal, civil litigation, family, commercial and residential conveyancing, company, wills and probate, company, personal injury and employment.

V	0
T	0
P	2
TS	20
WP	no

QUALITYSOLICITORS LAWSON & THOMPSON
30 Front Street, Newbiggin-by-the-Sea, Northumberland NE64 6PL
Tel: 01670 856060
Apply to: Mr TJR Barker

High street practice with good local client base. Applications invited from ambitious, hardworking individuals with a good sense of humour who are prepared to be team players.

V	0
T	0
P	6
TS	30
WP	no

QUALITYSOLICITORS MIRZA
216 Hoe Street, Walthamstow, London E17 3AY
Tel: 020 8520 4416
Email: k.elahi@mirzasolicitors.co.uk
Apply to: Mr Khalid Elahi

V	2
T	2
P	4
TS	18
WP	yes

QUALITYSOLICITORS TRUEMANS
Eden House, 38 St Aldates, Oxford OX1 1BN
Tel: 01865 722 383
Email: info@truemans.org.uk
Apply to: Mr M Trueman

Oxford city centre firm with excellent reputation. Higher court advocacy is a speciality. Full provision of high street services offered.

V	0
T	1
P	3
TS	18
WP	no

QUALITYSOLICITORS TURNERLAW
Oakfield House, 93 Preston New Road, Blackburn BB2 6AY
Tel: 01254 688400
Email: law@turnerlaw.co.uk
Apply to: Mr P Garner

General practice including personal injury, family, commercial and crime.

V	0
T	3
P	3
TS	25
WP	no

RADCLIFFESLEBRASSEUR
85 Fleet Street, London EC4Y 1AE
Tel: 020 7222 7040
Email: gradrec@rlb-law.com
Apply to: Mrs Erika Ely

A friendly, medium-sized, full service firm ranked in the legal directories, with particular emphasis on healthcare, private clients, growing businesses and property.

V	4
T	8
P	40
TS	170
WP	no

V = Vacancies / **T** = Trainees / **P** = Partners / **TS** = Total Staff / **WP** = Work Placement

RAI SOLICITORS	An established sole practitioner firm	V	0
19 Stoke Road, Slough SL2 5AP	providing a wide range of legal services	T	1
Tel: 01753 576 800	with emphasis on conveyancing,	P	-
Email: info@raisolicitors.com	immigration and family law.	TS	3
Apply to: Mr ZS Rai		WP	yes

RAJ LAW SOLICITORS	We are based in South West London.	V	0
169 Tooting High Street, Tooting Broadway,	We provide services in relation to	T	2
London SW17 0SY	criminal defence, immigration and	P	2
Tel: 020 3133 0000	asylum, civil litigation and family law.	TS	8
Email: info@rajlaw.co.uk		WP	no
Apply to: Mr Raj Boodhoo			

RALLI LTD	Ralli applies law exceptionally	V	0
Jackson House, Sibson Road, Sale M33 7RR	across its broad range of specialist	T	0
Tel: 0161 832 6131	practices. It relies on talented people	P	5
Email: lisa.harris@ralli.co.uk	with exceptional skills to achieve this.	TS	45
Apply to: Mrs Lisa Harris		WP	no

RATCLIFFE & BIBBY SOLICITORS	A three-office firm based in Lancaster,	V	0
69-71 Church Street, Lancaster LA1 3ET	Carnforth and Morecombe provide	T	2
Tel: 01524 39039	a wide variety of services including	P	5
Email: sarah.carr@rblegal.co.uk	conveyancing, personal injury,	TS	45
Apply to: Miss S Carr	employment, family and probate.	WP	yes

RATNA & CO	We are a small firm specialising in	V	Poss
169a High Street North, London E6 1JB	immigration, property, family and	T	1
Tel: 020 8470 8818	wills with some employment work.	P	2
Email: ratna@ratna.co.uk		TS	7
Apply to: Mr Majid Shafiq		WP	no

RAWAL & CO	Established high street firm holding	V	1
310 Ballards Lane, North Finchley, London N12	SQM's in crime, housing, and family.	T	1
0EY	Applications from law graduates for	P	1
Tel: 020 8445 0303	traineeship.	TS	7
Email: solicitors@rawalaw.co.uk		WP	yes
Apply to: Ms Linda Burchill			

RAWLINS DAVY PLC	Well-established local firm with	V	0
Rowland House, Hinton Road, Bournemouth BH1	offices in central Bournemouth,	T	2
2EG	who have in recent years expanded	P	8
Tel: 01202 558844	to create a highly focused team of	TS	45
Email: enquiries@rawlinsdavy.com	principally general commercial and	WP	no
Apply to: Mr E John Kennar	commercial property lawyers.		

RAWLISON BUTLER LLP	Leading law firm which delivers a full	V	0
Griffin House, 135 High Street, Crawley RH10 1DQ	range of quality commercial services,	T	1
Tel: 01293 527744	as well as providing expert guidance	P	14
Email: info@rawlisonbutler.com	to the private client.	TS	74
Apply to: Ms Jo Graver		WP	no

V = Vacancies / **T** = Trainees / **P** = Partners / **TS** = Total Staff / **WP** = Work Placement

Reed Smith

The Broadgate Tower, 20 Primrose Street, London EC2A 2RS
Tel: 020 3116 3000
Email: graduate.recruitment@reedsmith.com
Web: www.reedsmith.com
f reedsmithgraduatesuk 𝕏 reedsmithllp

The firm Reed Smith is a global law firm, with more than 1,800 lawyers in 28 offices throughout Europe, the Middle East, Asia and the United States. Our offices benefit from an international framework, but each one retains key elements of the local business culture. London is currently the largest office with over 650 people and is based in The Broadgate Tower, which boasts fantastic views of the city.

Types of work We are particularly well known for our work advising leading companies in the areas of energy and natural resources, financial services, shipping, entertainment and media, and health and life sciences. We provide litigation and other dispute resolution services in multijurisdictional and high-stake matters deliver regulatory counsel, and execute the full range of strategic domestic andcross-border transactions.

Who should apply We are looking for individuals with the drive and potential to become a world-class business lawyer. We want 'players' rather than 'onlookers' with a strong intellect, initiative, the ability to thrive in a challenging profession and the personal qualities to build strong relationships with colleagues and clients.

Training programme Given the range of work undertaken in the London office, trainees get the chance to have a varied training contract and develop a wide range of skills. We offer a four-seat programme, and there are also opportunities for secondments to clients and our overseas offices.

We have developed a new version of the Legal Practice Course (LPC) that fully integrates legal and business learning and leads to a unique Master's qualification, the LLM Legal Commercial Practice. Our bespoke programme was the first of its kind and allows students to study commercial and legal aspects in parallel so that they complete the course before entering the training contract with us.

We have vacancies for training contracts commencing in August 2021 and February 2022.

When and how to apply By 30 June 2019, for training contracts commencing in August 2021 and February 2022. Apply online via our website.

Work placements Our summer vacation scheme allows delegates to spend two weeks in the firm, sitting in two different groups of their choice. In addition to shadowing associates and partners in the team, delegates participate in bespoke training sessions and practical exercises to build their skills and knowledge.

They also enjoy a number of social events arranged for the group. Each year we offer places to applicants who will, on arrival, have completed at least two years of undergraduate study.

Sponsorship We pay for course fees and provide financial assistance for the LPC and GDL.

Vacancies	25
Trainees	50
Partners	649
Total staff	2,939

Work placement   yes
(see Insider Report on p95)

Training contract deadline
30 June 2019

Apply to
Grace Ambrose

Starting salary
£43,000

Minimum qualifications
2.1 degree

Sponsorship
CPE/GDL/LPC

Offices
Abu Dhabi, Athens, Austin, Beijing, Century City, Chicago, Dubai, Frankfurt, Hong Kong, Houston, Kazakhstan, Leeds, London, Los Angeles, Munich, Miami, New York, Paris, Philadelphia, Pittsburgh, Princeton, Richmond, San Francisco, Shanghai, Silicon Valley, Singapore, Tysons, Washington DC, Wilmington

ReedSmith

Proud diversity and inclusion
partner of

READ DUNN CONNELL 30, Park Road, Bingley BD23 3NR **Tel:** 01274723858 **Email:** robert@rdcsolicitors.co.uk **Apply to:** Mr Robert Anderson	Offices in Bradford, Bingley and Ilkley. Well-established firm dealing in commercial; employment; matrimonial; dispute resolution and PI; residential and commercial property; trusts; probate; tax planning.	V 0 T 1 P 4 TS 23 WP no
REENA GHAI SOLICITORS Stable Cottage, 42 High Street, Cranford, Middlesex TW5 9RU **Tel:** 020 8759 9959 **Email:** contact@ghaiandco.com **Apply to:** Ms Reena Ghai	Franchised legal aid department specialising in crime, family and welfare benefits.	V 0-1 T 2 P 1 TS 6 WP no
REES PAGE 8/12 Waterloo Road, Wolverhampton WV1 4BL **Tel:** 01902 577777 **Email:** alund@reespage.co.uk **Apply to:** Mr Andrew Lund	West Midlands practice supplying legal services to corporate and private clients. We are dedicated practitioners with a friendly philosophy to training and trainees.	V 0 T 0 P 8 TS 46 WP no
REST HARROW & CO SOLICITORS 238 Merton Road, London SW19 1EQ **Apply to:** Mr M Ivan-Perera	High street firm providing wide range of legal services with emphasis on commercial law and conveyancing.	V 0 T 1 P 2 TS 3 WP yes
REYNOLDS COLMAN BRADLEY LLP Bury House, Bury Street, London EC3A 5AR **Tel:** 020 7220 4700 **Email:** john.bradley@rcbllp.com **Apply to:** Mr John Bradley	Specialist professional negligence, insurance, commercial and construction litigation practice based in the heart of the city in both London and Bristol.	V 2 T 1 P 4 TS 26 WP yes
RIAZ SOLICITORS 280 Manningham Lane, Bedford BD8 7BU **Tel:** 01274 488110 **Apply to:** Mr M Riaz	We are specialists in criminal defence, personal injury and immigration work.	V 0 T 1 P - TS - WP yes
RIPPON PATEL & FRENCH LLP 37 Harley Street, London W1G 8QG **Tel:** 020 7323 0404 **Email:** rpfsols@aol.com **Apply to:** Mr A Patel		V 1 T 1 P 2 TS 6 WP yes
RIX & KAY SOLICITORS LLP The Courtyard, The Office Village, Uckfield, East Sussex TN22 1SL **Tel:** 01825 744462 **Email:** jennyreardon@rixandkay.co.uk **Apply to:** Ms Jenny Reardon	Rix & Kay Solicitors are a leading practice in the South East with 14 recommendations in the *Legal 500* for its specialist departments.	V 1[19] T 2 P 22 TS 125 WP yes

V = Vacancies / **T** = Trainees / **P** = Partners / **TS** = Total Staff / **WP** = Work Placement

RJR SOLICITORS
18 Melville Street, Ryde, Isle of Wight PO33 2AP
Tel: 01983 562 201
Email: virgil.philpott@rjr.co.uk
Apply to: Mr Virgil Philpott

High street firm with three offices on the Isle of Wight. Established for over 100 years.

V	0
T	0
P	5
TS	45
WP	no

RN WILLIAMS & CO
53 Waterloo Road, Wolverhampton WV1 4QQ
Tel: 01902 429051
Email: cr@rnwilliams.com
Apply to: Miss Charlotte Richards

V	1^{19}
T	1
P	3
TS	19
WP	no

ROBERT LIZAR
159 Princess Road, Moss Side, Manchester M14 4RE
Tel: 0161 226 2319
Email: rlizar@robertlizar.com
Apply to: Ms Patricia Graham

Legal aid work in crime, actions against police, family, mental health, civil liberties.

V	Poss
T	0
P	6
TS	22
WP	no

ROBERT MEATON AND CO SOLICITORS
Victoria Buildings, Albert Square, 1 Princess Street, Manchester M2 4DF
Tel: 0845 634 9955
Email: info@rmandco.co.uk
Apply to: Mr Andrew Davies

General commercial practice that undertakes commercial and residential property, PI, employment, debt collection, commerical litigation, financial mis-selling, professional negligence and business matters.

V	1
T	1
P	2
TS	13
WP	no

ROBERTS JACKSON SOLICITORS
Sandfield House, Water Lane, Wilmslow SK9 5AR
Tel: 01625546073
Email: recruitment@robertsjackson.co.uk
Apply to: Mrs Sophie Weids

Award-winning niche industrial disease practice offering graduate training scheme for LLB, GDL, LPC and BPTC graduates. Excellent training provided. Training contracts only offered internally.

V	6
T	21
P	9
TS	220
WP	yes

ROBINSONS
10-11 St James Court, Derby DE1 1BT
Tel: 01332 291431
Email: rob.styles@robinsons-solicitors.co.uk
Apply to: Mr Rob Styles

A commercial practice but with some retail elements in Derby and Ilkeston.

V	0
T	0
P	7
TS	61
WP	no

ROBSON & CO
147 High Street, Hythe, Kent CT21 5JN
Tel: 01303 264581
Email: post@robson-co.co.uk
Apply to: Mr Malcolm Dearden

Friendly and supportive small practice dealing in a range of non-contentious and contentious services including family law in pretty Cinque Port Town.

V	0
T	0
P	2
TS	8
WP	no

THE ROLAND PARTNERSHIP
St Mark's House 52 St Mark's Road, Saltney, Chester CH4 8DQ
Tel: 01244 659404
Email: anne.hall@therolandpartnership.co.uk
Apply to: Mrs Anne Hall

Specialist solicitors based in Chester, leading firm in medical negligence, serious injury and personal injury, also conveyancing. LSC quality marked.

V	0
T	0
P	2
TS	20
WP	no

V = Vacancies / **T** = Trainees / **P** = Partners / **TS** = Total Staff / **WP** = Work Placement

ROLLITS	Recommended by leading law	V	2-3
Wilberforce Court, High Street, Hull HU1 1YJ	directories for corporate and	T	5
Tel: 01482 323239	commercial work, charity law,	P	21
Email: ed.jenneson@rollits.com	planning and environmental law,	TS	118
Apply to: Mr Edward Jenneson	employment, commercial property,	WP	yes
	intellectual property work and social		
	housing.		

RONALD FLETCHER BAKER LLP		V	3
77a Baker Street, London W1U 6RF		T	5
Tel: 020 7613 1402		P	9
Email: recruitment@rfblegal.co.uk		TS	40
Apply to: Mr Rudi Ramdarshan		WP	no

RONALDSONS	The firm serves the community	V	1
45 Dereham Road, Norwich NR2 4HY	of Norwich and its surrounds by	T	1
Tel: 01603 621113	providing family law and residential	P	1
Email: mail@ronaldsons.com	conveyancing services.	TS	10
Apply to: Mr Richard Ronaldson		WP	no

ROOKS RIDER	Long-established London firm	V	0
Challoner House, 19 Clerkenwell Close, London	servicing UK and international	T	-
EC1R ORR	businesses and private clients	P	7
Tel: 020 7689 7000	specialising in tax.	TS	37
Email: lawyers@rooksrider.co.uk		WP	no
Apply to: Ms Lindsey Hemingway			

ROPES & GRAY INTERNATIONAL LLP	Ropes & Gray is one of the world's	V	7
60 Ludgate Hill, London EC4M 7AW	premier firms. Our London office has	T	15
Tel: 020 3201 1500	been developed to meet the needs of	P	25
Email: londonhr@ropesgray.com	the firm's sophisticated clients.	TS	204
Apply to: Miss Katy McAteer		WP	yes

ROSLING KING LLP	Commercial firm, successfully	V	4[20]
10 Old Bailey, London EC4M 7NG	competes with large City firms,	T	10
Tel: 020 7246 8000	specialising in real estate, banking,	P	14
Email: recruitment@rkllp.com	insurance and reinsurance, corporate,	TS	85
Apply to: Mr James Walton	restructuring and insolvency, dispute	WP	no
	resolution, construction, employment		
	and general commercial.		

ROYDS WITHY KING	An ambitious, collaborative and	V	12
5-6 Northumberland Buildings, Queen Square,	engaged law firm with offices in Bath,	T	22
Bath BA1 2JE	Oxford, London and Wiltshire. We're	P	67
Tel: 01225 425731	seeking driven, client-centric trainees	TS	484
Email: careers@roydswithyking.com	to grow their careers.	WP	yes
Apply to: Miss Claire Fennell			

ROYTHORNES SOLICITORS	A highly successful commercial	V	6[20]
Enterprise Way, Pinchbeck, Spalding, Lincolnshire	firm, specialising in agriculture,	T	6
PEII 3YR	land development and food. With	P	26
Tel: 01775 842500	recognised experts in all departments	TS	194
Email: traineerecruitment@roythornes.co.uk	including litigation, private client and	WP	yes
Apply to: Mrs Gillian Nash-Kennell	corporate teams.		

V = Vacancies / **T** = Trainees / **P** = Partners / **TS** = Total Staff / **WP** = Work Placement

RPC

Tower Bridge House, St Katharine's Way, London E1W 1AA
Tel: 020 3060 6000
Web: www.rpc.co.uk/strikinglyreal
🐦 lifeinalawfirm

The firm At RPC, you can be you. In an environment that's real. Strikingly real. Do you want a career in a firm that values personality as much as professionalism? For us, business success comes from building real relationships and thinking creatively to achieve the best solutions. So, if you value character over conformity, the unique over the uniform, and ambition over apathy, let's talk.

Types of work Banking and finance, commercial litigation, corporate, corporate insurance, competition, construction and projects, corporate finance, dispute resolution, employment, energy, transport, infrastructure, restructuring and insolvency, insurance and reinsurance, intellectual property, IT, media, personal injury, professional negligence, pensions and benefits, real estate, regulatory, tax, technology, outsourcing, international trade and arbitration.

Who should apply Although proven academic ability is important (we require a 2.1 degree or above, not necessarily in law) we value personality, energy, creative thinking, business sense, loyalty and diversity just as highly.

Training programme As a trainee, we believe you'll deliver your best if you're free to be you. And that means being able to ask questions openly, being supported to develop your strengths, and having the right opportunities to grow. Our offices are non-hierarchical and open plan. This means from day one you'll be sitting next to a partner. Whether you're handling complex insurance claims, resolving large-scale global disputes, or providing commercial advice and transactional support, your opinions will be listened to and respected. We believe personal growth comes from being challenged. You'll be given real responsibility throughout your training, but you'll never be left to fend for yourself. Our training is award-winning. You'll have a supervising partner and associate to help you day to day, a mentor to show you the ropes, and a dedicated trainee development team to support you.

When and how to apply Apply online at www.rpc.co.uk/strikinglyreal by 28 June 2019 for a 2021 London training contract. We have two training contract opportunities in our Bristol office, welcoming applications from both a law and non-law background, to start in September 2020 and 2021. The deadline for applications for the Bristol training contract is 15 March 2019.

Work placements We'll show you the real RPC during our summer schemes. And be warned, it's pretty striking. You'll be welcomed into our London office and given an opportunity to spend time getting to experience life in a creative law firm for yourself. It's also our chance to get to know you and understand what you may be able to offer us. During these two weeks, you'll be fully integrated into our teams, giving you a fantastic insight into whether a career at RPC is right for you. Recruitment for our summer schemes usually takes place in January and February. Apply now by visiting www.rpc.co.uk/strikinglyreal. The deadline for applications is the 18 January 2019.

We also run a number of workshops and insight days which provide a great snapshot of RPC. Further details can be found online.

Sponsorship GDL funding: fees paid plus up to £7,000 maintenance. LPC funding: fees paid plus up to £7,000 maintenance.

Vacancies	12
Trainees	24
Partners	79
Total staff	800

Work placement yes
(see Insider Report on p97)

Training contract deadline
28 June 2019

Apply
www.rpc.co.uk/strikinglyreal

Starting salary
£38,000 (London)
£35,000 (Bristol)

Minimum qualifications
2.1 degree

Sponsorship
GDL/LPC

Offices
London, Bristol, Hong Kong,
Singapore

Russell-Cooke LLP

2 Putney Hill, London SW15 6AB
Tel: 020 8789 9111
Email: graduate.recruitment@russell-cooke.co.uk
Web: www.russell-cooke.co.uk
🐦 russellcooke

The firm Russell-Cooke is a top 100 law firm based in London. Our work is diverse, ranging from professional regulation to corporate and commercial, real estate, insolvency, commercial and regulatory litigation, family and children law, employment and immigration, fraud and crime, personal injury and medical negligence, residential property, charities, French property, trust and estates disputes, private client, trusts and tax.

Our expertise is highly rated, with many of our lawyers known as leaders in their fields. We are known as the lawyers' lawyer as a significant amount of our work is received from professional bodies and other lawyers.

Trainees are a fundamental part of our firm. We will give you significant responsibility from the early stages of your career with plenty of client contact. While benefitting from a friendly and professional support network, you will need to be ready to thrive on the challenges that real-life legal work throws at you.

Who should apply In most cases, trainees will need at least two A grades and one B grade at A level (excluding general studies) and an upper second-class degree to be considered. As well as academic grades, intellectual rigour, adaptability and the ability under pressure to handle a diverse range of people and issues efficiently are vital attributes for the role.

Training programme As a trainee you will undertake four six-month seats. Due to the diverse nature of the work we do, there are a variety of seats on offer and we do try to accommodate preferences where possible. As we select a small cohort of trainees to join us each year, you will have ample opportunity to manage your own caseload and deal directly with clients. Each of our trainees is assigned a supervisor to help guide them through the process; ensuring support is available when needed. As a Russell-Cooke trainee, you can expect to receive in-house and external training to develop your skills and knowledge.

When and how to apply Apply online before 30 June 2019 for training contracts beginning in September 2021. Go to www.russell-cooke.co.uk/trainees.

Sponsorship We provide our trainees with capped sponsorship of up to £10,000 per candidate for LPC fees. We also offer an interest-free loan of up to £5,000 repayable out of a trainee's salary over a two-year period.

Vacancies	9
Trainees	20
Partners	62
Total staff	343

Training contract deadline
30 June 2019

Apply
Online at
www.russell-cooke.co.uk/
trainees

Starting salary
£36,500

Minimum qualifications
2.1 degree and AAB grades at A level (excluding general studies)

Offices
Central London, Kingston-upon-Thames, Putney

RUSSELL-COOKE
SOLICITORS

RUSSELL & RUSSELL
Churchill House, Wood Street, Bolton BL1 1EE
Tel: 01204 399299
Email: info@russellrussell.co.uk
Apply to: Mrs Emma Hughes

Long-established regional firm undertaking private and commercial client services. Bolton head office with branches throughout the north west.

V	0
T	2
P	26
TS	200
WP	no

RUSSELLS
Yalding House, 152-156 Great Portland Street, London W1W 5QA
Tel: 020 7439 8692
Email: media@russells.co.uk
Apply to: Mr Mark Sinnott

V	0
T	4
P	10
TS	45
WP	no

SA LAW
Gladstone Place, 36-38 Upper Marlborough Road, St Albans, Hertfordshire AL1 3UU
Tel: 01727 798000
Email: info@salaw.com
Apply to: Mrs Samantha Walsh

SA Law is one of the most dynamic legal practices in the South East offering specialist commercial services supported by leading private client expertise.

V	2[19]
T	6
P	15
TS	90
WP	no

SAMUEL PHILLIPS LAW FIRM
Gibb Chambers, 52 Westgate Road, Newcastle upon Tyne NE1 5XU
Tel: 0191 232 8451
Email: jennygoldstein@samuelphillips.co.uk
Apply to: Ms Jennifer Goldstein

We are a specialist firm offering private client, commercial/civil litigation, family, employment and commercial and residential property.

V	1
T	1
P	4
TS	44
WP	yes

SAMUELS SOLICITORS LLP
18 Alexandra Road, Barnstaple, Devon EX32 8BA
Tel: 01271 343457
Email: mail@samuels-solicitors.co.uk
Apply to: Mr Jan Samuel

A well-established firm with a strong client base covering most areas of commercial, private client and litigation work.

V	0
T	1
P	3
TS	16
WP	no

SAS DANIELS LLP
30 Greek Street, Stockport SK3 8AD
Tel: 0161 475 7676
Email: recruitment@sasdaniels.co.uk
Apply to: Ms Chris Swerling

During the placement, students get insight into life as a trainee, the firm's vision and values, meet management and work in several work types.

V	4
T	6
P	20
TS	150
WP	yes

SAVAS & SAVAGE SOLICITORS LIMITED
20 Stanney Lane, Ellesmere Port CH65 9AD
Tel: 0151 357 2375
Email: sav@savasandsavage.co.uk
Apply to: Mr Savas Argirou

Three training contracts spread between Ellesmere Port and Nantwich branches.

V	4[19]
T	3
P	3
TS	25
WP	yes

SB SOLICITORS
228a Whitechapel Road, London, London E1 1BJ
Tel: 020 7539 1900
Email: sb_solicitor@yahoo.co.uk
Apply to: Mr S Bhuwanee

Growing two-partner practice dealing with housing law, conveyancing (residential and commercial), litigation and construction work.

V	0
T	0
P	2
TS	4
WP	no

V = Vacancies / **T** = Trainees / **P** = Partners / **TS** = Total Staff / **WP** = Work Placement

SCAIFF LLP 23 Foregate Street, Worcester WR1 1UW **Tel:** 01905 27505 **Email:** mail@scaiff.co.uk **Apply to:** Mrs Dawn Hodgkins	General practice with emphasis on company commercial and litigation particularly personal injury and medical negligence.	V 0 T – P 3 TS 21 WP no
SCHILLINGS INTERNATIONAL 41 Bedford Square, London WC1B 3HX **Tel:** 020 7034 9000 **Email:** enquiries@schillings.co.uk **Apply to:** Mrs Lindsey Watts	With over 30 years experience, Schillings assist prominent individuals and businesses wherever they are in the world; whatever their reputation and privacy issues.	V 0 T 0 P 9 TS 62 WP no
SCHOFIELD SWEENEY LLP Church Bank House, Church Bank, Bradford BD1 4DY **Tel:** 01274 306000 **Email:** trainingcontracts@schofieldsweeney.co.uk **Apply to:** Mr Adrian Ballam	An ambitious and progressive commercial law firm with friendly staff that works with a diverse range of businesses, entrepreneurs and public sector organisations.	V 3[20] T 7 P 31 TS 161 WP yes
SCOTT ROWE SOLICITORS Chard Street, Axminster, Devon EX13 5DS **Tel:** 01297 32345 **Email:** kevin.bull@scottrowe.co.uk **Apply to:** Mr Kevin Bull	Well-established West Country firm offering full range of legal services, seeks talented and hardworking trainees. The firm is Lexcel and Investors in People accredited for over 10 years.	V 1[19] T 1 P 3 TS 26 WP no
SEDDONS 5 Portman Square, London W1H 6NT **Tel:** 020 7725 8000 **Email:** trainingcontracts@seddons.co.uk **Apply to:** Mr Simon Jacobs	We advise our UK and international clients on real estate, family law, wealth management, disputes, corporate law, employment and more.	V 2 T 6 P 32 TS 116 WP no
SENTINEL SOLICITORS 204 Seven Sisters Road, Finsbury Park, London N4 3NX **Tel:** 020 7100 3100 **Email:** sajid@sentinelsolicitors.co.uk **Apply to:** Mr Sajid Sheikh	Sentinel Solicitors is an award winning law firm that specialises in immigration and human rights. It offers training and work placement opportunities to law students.	V 2[19] T 1 P 3 TS 6 WP yes
SERGEANT & COLLINS 25 Oswald Road, Scunthorpe DN15 7PS **Tel:** 01724 864215 **Email:** sergeantcollins@tiscali.co.uk **Apply to:** Mr P Wright	Traditional high street practice dealing with conveyancing, probate, family work, crime and general business matters.	V 0 T 1 P 2 TS 15 WP no
THE SETHI PARTNERSHIP SOLICITORS The Barn House, 38 Meadow Way, Eastcote, Ruislip HA4 8TB **Tel:** 020 8866 6464 **Email:** ritu@sethi.co.uk **Apply to:** Mrs Ritu Sethi	General practice - specialising in property work, crime, matrimonial, litigation, immigration, civil litigation, wills and probate.	V 1 T 1 P 3 TS 25 WP yes

V = Vacancies / **T** = Trainees / **P** = Partners / **TS** = Total Staff / **WP** = Work Placement

Shakespeare Martineau LLP

One Colmore Square, Birmingham B4 6AA
Tel: 03300 240 333
Email: training.contracts@shma.co.uk
Web: www.shma.co.uk
🐦 shmalaw

The firm Shakespeare Martineau is a leading law firm that combines creativity, commerciality and clarity. We work with blue-chip companies, leading organisations, high street brands and individuals across the country. We pride ourselves on protecting and growing businesses and personal wealth. Our approach goes beyond just legal solutions: clients trust us to advise on what's possible, what's prudent, and what's coming around the corner.

Types of work Working with businesses of all sizes, we deliver a broad range of specialist legal services and have particular expertise across sectors including; energy, education, healthcare, banking and financial services, investment funds and advanced manufacturing. Our training contracts are varied and seats can be taken in a number of different specialisms across our four key groups: private capital (family and private client), real estate, litigation and corporate and commercial

Who should apply We look for bright trainees who want to fulfil their ambition with us. You'll need a strong academic background: a 2.1 or above in any degree subject. We expect you to share our enthusiasm for our business. But we want more than that too. Show us what sets you apart. You'll be a great candidate to us if you can demonstrate that you have an enterprising spirit together with talent, originality and determination. And when you show us, show us differently. Showcase practical know-how, your personality, efforts and attainments.

We accept both law and non-law graduates. Law students can apply anytime from the penultimate year of your degree, giving you time to complete your Legal Practice Course (LPC) before joining us. Non-law students should apply any time from the final year of your degree, giving you time to complete your Graduate Diploma in Law (GDL) and then your LPC before joining us.

Training programme Our in depth training is set in the real world, with real caseloads and responsibilities. This is first-class, hands on training you can trust to develop your career. As a trainee you will spend two years experiencing at least three areas of the law. This will involve having four six-month stints, called seats, in our various teams. You will also benefit from the Professional Skills Course, which we supplement with a structured training programme from our training academy to heighten your skillset.

Our training contract exposes trainees to a combination of contentious and non-contentious work, tailored to individual strengths, preferences and business needs. Trainees also receive regular support and feedback through our buddy and mentoring schemes.

When and how to apply Apply via our online application form at www.shma.co.uk by 30 June 2019 for training contracts commencing in 2020 or 2021.

We offer training contracts in three locations: East Midlands (with stints in seats at our Leicester and Nottingham offices), West Midlands (with stints in our Birmingham, Solihull and Stratford upon Avon offices) and London.

Vacancies	8
Trainees	15
Partners	141
Total staff	710

Training contract deadline
30 June 2019

Apply
Online

Minimum qualifications
2.1 degree

Offices
Birmingham,
Leicester, London,
Milton Keynes,
Nottingham, Sheffield,
Solihull, Stratford upon
Avon

✦ SHAKESPEAREMARTINEAU

SEWELL MULLINGS LOGIE LLP 7 Dollar Street, Cirencester GL7 2AS **Tel:** 01285 650000 **Email:** jbb@sml-law.co.uk **Apply to:** Mr John Bartholomew	The largest practice in Cirencester providing excellent and varied training. We offer a full range of legal services and have a well established client base.	V 1[20] T 3 P 7 TS 42 WP no
SHACKLOCKS LLP St Peters House, Bridge Street, Mansfield NG18 1AL **Tel:** 01623 626141 **Email:** clarem@shacklocks.co.uk **Apply to:** Mrs Clare McShane	Successful applicants will work as paralegals for up to 12 months with the opportunity of a training contract thereafter for the right candidates.	V 2-4[19] T 3 P 4 TS 43 WP no
SHARPE PRITCHARD LLP Elm Yard, 10-16 Elm Street, London WC1X 0BJ **Tel:** 020 7405 4600 **Email:** tnottage@sharpepritchard.co.uk **Apply to:** Ms Tracey Nottage	Sharpe Pritchard specialise in public sector work including commercial, procurement, infrastructure, construction, administrative, dispute resolution, ICT and data, real estate, planning and parliamentary.	V 3 or 4 T 7 P 24 TS 77 WP yes
SHEARMAN & STERLING (LONDON) LLP 9 Appold Street, London EC2A 2AP **Tel:** 020 7655 5000 **Email:** graduates@shearman.com **Apply to:** Mr Paul Gascoyne	One of New York's oldest firms, our London office, established in 1972 has become a leading practice covering all aspects of international commercial law.	V Approx 15 T 30 P 35 TS 300 WP yes
SHEIKH & CO 208 Seven Sisters Road, London N4 3NX **Tel:** 020 7263 5588 **Apply to:** Mr SA Sheikh	General practice with 80% legal aid work. The firm expanded very rapidly within a year.	V 2 T 4 P 3 TS 35 WP yes
SHERRARDS SOLICITORS LLP 45 Grosvenor Road, St Albans, Hertfordshire AL1 3AW **Tel:** 01727 832830 **Email:** careers@sherrards.com **Apply to:** Mrs Joanne Perry	A progressive firm with a strong bias towards commercial work and litigation, while retaining experienced private client departments.	V 1 T 4 P 15 TS 90 WP no
SHORT RICHARDSON & FORTH LLP 4 Mosley Street, Newcastle-upon-Tyne NE1 1DE **Tel:** 0191 232 0283 **Email:** lb@srflegal.co.uk **Apply to:** Mrs Lisa Berg	We are a commercial law firm based in Newcastle upon Tyne. Practice areas: employment, property, private client, commercial litigation and insolvency, and regulation/financial crime.	V 1 T 1 P 8 TS 23 WP no
SHRANKS Ruskin House, 40/41 Museum Street, London WC1A 1LT **Tel:** 020 7831 6677 **Email:** shrank@shranks.co.uk **Apply to:** Mr Jeremy P Ticktum	Landlord and tenant, commercial property, company/commercial, residential conveyancing, personal injury, employment, general litigation, wills, trusts and probate.	V 0 T 1 P 2 TS 9 WP no

V = Vacancies / **T** = Trainees / **P** = Partners / **TS** = Total Staff / **WP** = Work Placement

Shoosmiths

The Lakes, Bedford Road, Northampton NN4 7SH
Tel: 03700 863075
Email: joinus@shoosmiths.co.uk
Web: www.shoosmiths.co.uk
f shoosmithsgraduates **y** shoosmithsgrads

The firm Growing steadily, with offices across the UK, Shoosmiths is a progressive, forward-thinking law firm, with a real spirit of enterprise. We really value our people, giving them the freedom, recognition and support to succeed; while clients find us open, accessible and easy to work with. This year we were named National/Regional Law Firm of the Year at the Legal Business Awards and we've recently been named Law Firm of the Year at the British Legal Awards, along with being the first top 100 law firm to achieve the Investors in People Gold Standard, shows we are committed to providing the top quality service our clients love, and which our people love to deliver. And we accepted the award for the Best Trainer by LawCareers.Net for four years in a row!

Types of work Shoosmiths is a full-service law firm offering you experience in a variety of areas, including commercial, corporate, employment, real estate, intellectual property, banking, planning, and dispute resolution. Through our Access Legal consumer brand, we also offer private client, personal injury, clinical negligence, and conveyancing.

Who should apply You should be open-minded and innovative with a can-do attitude. You'll be trained in a non-hierarchal, agile, open plan environment. As a trainee, you will value a social life outside the office. Work wise, you will care about the quality of service you give to clients, and will want to make a real and direct contribution to the firm's success. You'll need to demonstrate your desire to train to be an expert in law and the ability to work consistently and collaboratively, for the benefit of you, the firm and your clients.

Training programme There is nothing like diving straight in and having a go, we expect you to relish the opportunity to get experience of real cases and deals from the start. In our opinion, it is the best way to learn. We allocate no more than one trainee to each team, which means trainees enjoy high levels of involvement with the team, and are given good quality work and contact with clients.

Over two years, you will complete four six-month placements, one of which could be an external secondment to a client's in-house legal team, providing an invaluable insight from the client's perspective. Secondments are seen as a valuable opportunity for relationship building with clients and to help the personal development of our solicitors and trainees.

Our trainees take an active part in corporate responsibility from their very first week and develop their personal brand profile and written communication style by contributing to the Shoosmiths careers blog and social media.

When and how to apply Please apply online at www.shoosmiths.co.uk/graduates. Please check our website for locations we are currently recruiting to.

Work placements We offer placements of one week to help you get a real insight into the life of a trainee. You will get early exposure to clients and case files, and will be supported by an expert solicitor. Placements provide invaluable experience, allowing you to choose the right firm for you, and can even fast track you to a place on the assessment day for a training contract.

Sponsorship We are happy to offer you financial assistance in relation to your forthcoming GDL and/or LPC (or equivalent). We do not specify a particular provider for your postgraduate studies.

Vacancies	22
Trainees	42
Partners	190
Total staff	1,630

Work placement yes
(see Insider Report on p99)

Training contract deadline
30 June 2019

Apply
Online

Starting salary
£27,000-£28,000

Minimum qualifications
Any degree

Sponsorship
GDL/LPC

Offices
Belfast, Birmingham, Edinburgh, Leeds, London, Milton Keynes, Manchester, Northampton, Nottingham, Solent, Reading

SHCOSMITHS

Proud diversity and inclusion
partner of

2S aspiringsolicitors

SHULMANS LLP 10 Wellington Place, Leeds LS1 4AP **Tel:** 0113 245 2833 **Email:** training@shulmans.co.uk **Apply to:** Mr Neil Towse	Shulmans LLP is a full service UK 200 corporate law firm based in a single site office in Leeds delivering high quality advice to businesses.	V T P TS WP	3 8 23 214 no
SIDLEY AUSTIN LLP Woolgate Exchange, 25 Basinghall Street, London EC2V 5HA **Tel:** 020 7776 9633 **Email:** graduaterecruitment@sidley.com **Apply to:** Ms Nicole Katz	Sidley Austin LLP is one of the world's largest law firms, with approximately 1,900 lawyers in 20 offices across the globe.	V T P TS WP	12 22 43 270 yes
SILLS & BETTERIDGE LLP 46 Silver Street, Lincoln LN2 1ED **Tel:** 01522 542211 **Email:** recruitment@sillslegal.co.uk **Apply to:** Miss Leanne Davies	A broadly-based, medium sized practice acting for a range of private and business clients and taking publicly funded work. Excellent reputation.	V T P TS WP	2^{20} 6 43 265 yes
SILVERDALE SOLICITORS Silverdale House, 404 Cheetham Hill Road, Manchester M8 9LE **Tel:** 0161 740 0333 **Email:** enquiries@silverdalelaw.co.uk **Apply to:** Mr M J Amin	Broad-based general practice undertaking contentious and non-contentious work. Busy practice with substantial growth over past 12 months including a third office in Manchester city centre.	V T P TS WP	0 2 4 25 yes
SIMKINS LLP Lynton House, 7-12 Tavistock Square, London WC1H 9LT **Tel:** 020 78745600 **Email:** trainingcontractregistrations@simkins.com **Apply to:** Trainee Recruitment	West End commercial law firm providing a wide range of legal services with a particular focus on the media, entertainment, marketing and leisure industries.	V T P TS WP	2 4 20 45 yes
SINTONS LLP The Cube, Barrack Road, Newcastle upon Tyne NE4 6DB **Tel:** 0191 226 7878 **Email:** louise.dack@sintons.co.uk **Apply to:** Mrs Louise Dack	Leading firm with three main practice groups: commercial; private client; and personal injury. Approachable, forward thinking, supportive and committed to continued career development.	V T P TS WP	3 5 26 200 yes
SJP LAW 5 Parliament Street, Hull HU1 2AZ **Tel:** 01482 324591 **Email:** kcu@sjplaw.co.uk **Apply to:** Ms Kirsty Cuckson	Providing a full range of commercial services to medium-sized owner managed businesses; also dealing with complex personal injury/clinical negligence litigation.	V T P TS WP	2 2 5 50 yes
SKADDEN, ARPS, SLATE, MEAGHER & FLOM (UK) LLP 40 Bank Street, Canary Wharf, London E14 5DS **Tel:** 020 7519 7000 **Email:** graduate.hiring@skadden.com **Apply to:** Mr Aidan Connor	Skadden is an award winning global law firm with 25 international offices and approximately 2,000 lawyers. Voted Best US Law Firm in London (*Legal Business*).	V T P TS WP	Approx 10 20 31 250 yes

V = Vacancies / **T** = Trainees / **P** = Partners / **TS** = Total Staff / **WP** = Work Placement

Simmons & Simmons

CityPoint, One Ropemaker Street, London EC2Y 9SS
Tel: 020 7628 2020
Email: recruitment@simmons-simmons.com
Web: www.simmons-simmons.com/graduates
f simmonsgraduates

The firm Scratch the surface of Simmons & Simmons and you'll discover a leading law firm of over 1,600 people, offering legal advice across Europe, the Middle East and Asia. We work with our clients across four key sectors and provide a range of services to help them navigate all kinds of legal challenges, from buying and selling national chain stores to patenting the latest technology. We work in the areas that matter the most to everyone's future, from healthcare and life sciences to technology, media and telecommunications. So whatever you do, wherever you go, you'll see developments we've been involved in. All you need to do is look, and you'll uncover the world of law and the world of Simmons & Simmons.

Types of work We view the world through the lens of our key sectors: asset management and investment funds, financial institutions, healthcare and life sciences, and technology, media and telecommunications. These priority sector teams are drawn from the core practice areas of: corporate and commercial; competition and regulatory; dispute resolution; employment, pensions and incentives; financial markets; information, communications and technology; intellectual property; international projects and construction; real estate and tax.

Who should apply We're looking for perceptive, ambitious future lawyers. You see the finer detail – the intricate legal framework that powers and shapes our everyday – and you've got the drive to be part of it. We are looking for students who are on course for at least a 2.1 in any degree subject. That said, academic performance isn't everything; that's why we look for raw talent and potential throughout our assessment process.

Training programme Our training contracts are offered in both London and Bristol, and either way, you'll spend two years discovering the innovation we're known for. As well as moving through four six-month seats across our sectors, you'll also benefit from the compass programme; our unique and progressive trainee skills academy that offers a combination of practical learning, mentoring and online tools. Our teams will teach you everything they know about the world of law, and you'll find your niche in the process, qualifying into your choice of practice area.

Work placements Get right to the heart of life as a trainee lawyer on our vacation schemes. Over one or two weeks in either Bristol or London, you'll experience the work, the reach and the day-to-day buzz of our international firm. In short, it's the chance for us to get to know each other on a deeper level. That's why it's also the most popular route to a training contract with us, with many vacation schemers returning as trainees.

We run a winter vacation scheme in London and summer vacation schemes in both London and Bristol. We also run a spring insight scheme in London for first-year students of all disciplines, as well as penultimate-year non-law students.

Sponsorship We will cover your full tuition fees for law school and offer a maintenance grant of £7,000 for the GDL and £7,500 for the LPC.

Vacancies	25+
Trainees	60
Partners	280+*
Total staff	1,600+*

*denotes worldwide figure

Work placement yes

Apply
Online at www.simmons-simmons.com/graduates

Starting salary
London:
1st year – £44,000
2nd year – £48,000
Bristol:
1st year – £38,000
2nd year – £39,000

Minimum qualifications
2.1 degree (or equivalent)

Sponsorship
GDL/LPC

Offices
Amsterdam, Beijing, Bristol, Brussels, Doha, Dubai, Dublin, Düsseldorf, Frankfurt, Hong Kong, Jeddah*, Lisbon*, London, Luxembourg, Madrid, Milan, Munich, Paris, Riyadh*, Shanghai, Singapore,
*Associated offices

Simmons & Simmons

Proud diversity and inclusion partner of

 aspiringsolicitors

SLATER & GORDON (UK) LLP 58 Mosley Street, Manchester M3 2BU **Tel:** 0161 3833964 **Email:** recruitment@slatergordon.co.uk **Apply to:** Miss Louise Myers	Slater & Gordon Lawyers is an international, award-winning law firm committed to becoming the largest provider of personal legal services in the UK.	V 53 T 36 P 86 TS 3500 WP no
SLATER GORDON SOLUTIONS LEGAL LTD Slater Gordon Solutions, Dempster Building, Atlantic Way, Brunswick Business Park, Liverpool L3 4UU **Apply to:** Mr Aaron Leigh		V 1 T 10 P 5 TS 1150 WP no
SLAUGHTER AND MAY One Bunhill Row, London EC1Y 8YY **Tel:** 0207 090 4454 **Email:** trainee.recruit@slaughterandmay.com **Apply to:** Mrs Janine Arnold	A leading international law firm whose main activities are in the field of corporate, commercial and financing law.	V 80-85 T 152 P 112 TS 1200 WP yes
SMITH LLEWELYN PARTNERSHIP 18 Princess Way, Swansea SA1 3LW **Tel:** 01792 464444 **Email:** enquiries@smithllewelyn.com **Apply to:** Mr Julian Thomas	South Wales' leading medical negligence, pharmaceutical product liability and personal injury firm; community legal service franchise in all areas committed to the victim.	V 1 T 2 P 4 TS 40 WP yes
SMITH PARTNERSHIP Norman House, Friar Gate, Derby DE1 1NU **Tel:** 01332 225 225 **Email:** recruitment@smithpartnership.co.uk **Apply to:** Mr Bally Atwal	Smith Partnership is a young dynamic firm with offices throughout the East Midlands, work areas include commercial, criminal and private client services.	V 4 T 8 P 28 TS 250 WP no
SO LEGAL LIMITED 55 South Street, Eastbourne, East Sussex BN21 4UT **Tel:** 01323 407555 **Email:** jobs@solegal.co.uk **Apply to:** Mr Hamed Ovaisi	An opportunity to train with a technology driven and modern firm. Candidates will have the LPC and a law degree and ideally be local.	V 5^{20} T 2 P 2 TS 22 WP yes
SONN MACMILLAN WALKER 12 Widegate Street, London E1 7HP **Tel:** 020 7377 8889 **Email:** emacmillan@smw-law.co.uk **Apply to:** Mr Euan Macmillan	Specialist criminal defence firm, mainly legal aid work. Members of the Serious Fraud Panel. Applications accepted for work placements all year round.	V 2^{20} T 4 P 3 TS 25 WP yes
SOOKIAS & SOOKIAS 5th Floor, 15 Brook's Mews, London W1K 4DS **Tel:** 020 7465 8000 **Email:** info@sookias.co.uk **Apply to:** Ms Barbara Lewin	Small West End solicitors specialising in commercial work including immigration, litigation, tax and company matters.	V 0 T 0 P 4 TS 20 WP no

V = Vacancies / **T** = Trainees / **P** = Partners / **TS** = Total Staff / **WP** = Work Placement

SOUTHERNS Mackenzie House, 68 Bank Parade, Burnley BB11 1UB **Tel:** 01282 422711 **Email:** ncronin@southernslaw.info **Apply to:** Mrs Jan Cook	General high street practice. Offices also in Nelson, Colne and Blackpool.	**V** 0 **T** 0 **P** 6 **TS** 63 **WP** no	
THE SPEAKEASY 166 Richmond Road, Cardiff CF24 3BX **Tel:** 029 2045 3111 **Email:** info@speakeasy.cymru **Apply to:** Mr Warren Palmer	Not-for-profit legal advice centre providing free legal advice and representation regarding debt, benefits and housing.	**V** 0 **T** - **P** - **TS** 14 **WP** no	
SPEARING WAITE LLP 34 Pocklingtons Walk, Leicester LE1 6BU **Tel:** 0116 262 4225 **Email:** info@spearingwaite.com **Apply to:** Miss Sarah Moore	One of the largest firms in Leicester specialising in commercial property, corporate, intellectual property, dispute resolution, employment and private client.	**V** 2-4[20] **T** 6 **P** 22 **TS** 98 **WP** no	
SPELTHORNE BOROUGH COUNCIL Council Offices, Knowle Green, Staines upon Thames TW18 1XB **Tel:** 01784 446229 **Email:** legal@spelthorne.gov.uk **Apply to:** Mr Michael Graham	Small local government team in a Surrey district council. Procurement, litigation, property, planning and licensing. We welcome summer placements for interesting candidates.	**V** 0 **T** 2 **P** 0 **TS** 12 **WP** yes	
SPENCE & HORNE 343 Mare Street, Hackney, London E8 1HY **Tel:** 020 8985 2277 **Email:** 202@spencehorne.co.uk **Apply to:** Miss Angela Spence	Small practice specialising in immigration, family, property, housing and probate, offering advice for family housing with limited advice in some areas of civil litigation and compromise agreements.	**V** 0 **T** - **P** 1 **TS** 4 **WP** yes	
SRI KANTH & CO 557 High Road, Wembley, Middlesex HA0 2DW **Tel:** 020 8795 0648 **Email:** info@srikanthsolicitors.co.uk **Apply to:** Mr S Srikanthalingam		**V** 2 **T** 2 **P** 2 **TS** 11 **WP** yes	
STEELE RAYMOND LLP Richmond Point, 43 Richmond Hill, Bournemouth BH2 6LR **Tel:** 01202 204510 **Email:** jenniferrogerson@steeleraymond.co.uk **Apply to:** Ms Jennifer Rogerson	A modern and expanding firm with a wide range of clients providing predominantly business and commercial law advice.	**V** 2-3 **T** 5 **P** 14 **TS** 80 **WP** no	
STEELES LAW SOLICITORS LTD Lawrence House, 5 St Andrews Hill, Norwich NR2 1AD **Tel:** 01603 598 000 **Email:** hr@steeleslaw.co.uk **Apply to:** Human Resources Department	Full service firm with a modern approach and exceptional work-life balance. Providing trainee solicitors with hands on experience from the start.	**V** 0 **T** 4 **P** 4 **TS** 50 **WP** no	

V = Vacancies / **T** = Trainees / **P** = Partners / **TS** = Total Staff / **WP** = Work Placement

Squire Patton Boggs (UK) LLP

7 Devonshire Square, London EC2M 4YH
Tel: 020 7655 1000
Email: careers@squirepb.com
Web: www.squirepattonboggs.com
f squirepattonboggscareers **🐦** spb_careers

The firm We are a global law firm with 47 offices in 20 countries. Our team of 2,600 includes more than 1,500 lawyers. Recognised as having one of the broadest global footprints in the legal industry, we provide access to new knowledge, new markets and new expertise.

We support private and public sector clients across extensive global practice areas. Our teams have well-established local and regional positions across North America, Europe, Asia Pacific, the Middle East and Latin America. Collectively, we cover 140 jurisdictions and speak more than 40 languages.

In the UK, we operate from offices in Birmingham, Leeds, London and Manchester, working with a diverse mix of global clients. Many of these are among the biggest names and brands in the world: FTSE and *Fortune* 100 companies, emerging and fast-growth businesses, financial institutions, and regional and national governments.

Training programme We offer a unique training contract, tailored to individual trainee needs. We provide a comprehensive induction programme at an external campus, followed by tailored department training for each seat and tailored skills training through various seminars and workshops.

The programme comprises six four-month seats during the training contract. The key to the training contract is "involvement and responsibility", which is achieved through the choice and number of seats that can be undertaken during the programme, including secondments to clients and our overseas offices. Trainees benefit from two-tier supervision and challenging work.

When and how to apply Apply online at www.squirepattonboggs.com.

Work placements We run a two-week summer placement scheme and a one-week winter placement scheme that provide students with genuine experience as to what life is like as a trainee solicitor.

Penultimate-year law students, final-year non-law students and all postgraduate students are eligible to apply for the summer placement scheme. Students in their final year or above (law and non-law) are eligible to apply for the winter placement scheme.

All students who are successful in getting onto a placement scheme will automatically be considered for a training contract.

Vacancies	25
Trainees	47
Partners	494
Total staff	3,000
Work placement	yes
Apply	
Online	
Offices	
47 offices across 20 countries	

Stephenson Harwood LLP

1 Finsbury Circus, London EC2M 7SH
Tel: 020 7809 2812
Email: graduate.recruitment@shlegal.com
Web: www.shlegal.com/graduate

The firm Stephenson Harwood is a law firm of over 1,000 people worldwide, including more than 170 partners. Our people are committed to achieving the goals of our clients – listed and private companies, institutions and individuals. We assemble teams of bright thinkers to match our clients' needs and give the right advice from the right person at the right time. Dedicating the highest calibre of legal talent to overcome the most complex issues, we deliver pragmatic, expert advice that is set squarely in the real world. Our headquarters are in London, with nine offices across Asia, Europe and the Middle East. In addition we have forged close ties with other high-quality law firms. This diverse mix of expertise and culture results in a combination of deep local insight and the capability to provide a seamless international service.

Types of work Commercial litigation; corporate; employment and pensions; finance; marine and international trade; and real estate.

Who should apply Firstly we look for a quick intellect. As well as ideally at least a 2.1 in any discipline plus 320 UCAS points or equivalent, you'll need strong analytical skills, sound judgement, imagination and meticulous attention to detail. Also vital are the communication skills to be persuasive and build rapport, plenty of drive and determination, plus a keen interest in business.

Training programme Here at Stephenson Harwood, we take on just 20 trainees per year. There's a lot to look forward to as a trainee at Stephenson Harwood: top quality global work across a range of sectors, an environment that balances cutting edge work with a respectful, friendly culture, and the chance to prove yourself on an international secondment. Our training is not only structured and practical but highly personalised, so you'll have everything you need to develop along a career path that's absolutely right for you. Following a week's intensive induction and a comprehensive post induction programme you'll complete four seats – each six months long – across different practice areas. We also encourage our trainees to apply to gain international experience in our Hong Kong, Singapore, Seoul, Dubai or Paris offices.

When and how to apply Applications for training contracts commencing 2021 are open from 1 October 2018 until 31 July 2019. Please apply online at www.shlegal.com/graduate.

Work placements Our winter, spring and summer placement schemes will give you a real taste of life at the firm. We'll make sure you're involved in quality work and will try to help you experience any areas of law you're particularly interested in. Typically you'll spend one or two weeks in our offices, sitting with qualified lawyers and tackling some case work. You'll also benefit from an organised programme of interactive sessions, talks and social events. What's more, we'll pay you £360 a week.

Sponsorship We pay fees for GDL and LPC at BPP Law School in London and offer maintenance awards of up to £6,000 if you're still studying.

Vacancies	20
Trainees	40
Partners	170+
Total staff	1,000+

Work placement yes
(see Insider Report on p101)

Training contract deadline
31 July 2019

Apply
Online via
www.shlegal.com/graduate

Starting salary
£40,000

Minimum qualifications
2.1 degree

Sponsorship
GDL/LPC

Offices
London, Hong Kong, Paris, Piraeus, Singapore, Shanghai, Dubai, Beijing, Seoul, Myanmar

STEPHENSON HARWOOD

Proud diversity and inclusion
partner of

 aspiringsolicitors

Stevens & Bolton LLP

Wey House, Farnham Road, Guildford GU1 4YD
Tel: 01483 302264
Email: traineerecruitment@stevens-bolton.com
Web: www.stevens-bolton.com

The firm Stevens & Bolton LLP is recognised as a leading national law firm, offering a full range of commercial legal services. We are recommended in 24 specialist practice areas by leading legal directories and have received widespread awards recognition. Over the years we have been named and shortlisted for Best Recruiter and Best Trainer – Medium Regional Law Firm at the LawCareers.Net Training & Recruitment Awards. Based in Guildford, our single office approach ensures excellent communication and efficient co-ordination of our resources. We provide legal services both nationally and internationally, with unswerving focus on quality. From the outset, our trainees get first class experience of the business world. We advise a number of the top 100 and other UK FTSE companies, as well as many other substantial international groups, owner managed businesses and SMEs. As such, the work we carry out is both interesting and challenging. We are committed to being a responsible business. We participate in a wide range of charity and community initiatives, and have full regard to the importance of minimising our impact on the environment. We also organise social events over the year and there are a number of sports teams, including netball and football as well as a firm choir.

Who should apply We welcome applications from candidates with either a law or non-law background, with at least 340 UCAS points and at least one A at A level, who have achieved (or expect to achieve) a 2.1 degree or higher (unless there are exceptional circumstances). Essential qualities include: very good communication skills, being a team player, adaptability, being able to manage competing deadlines and projects, drive and ambition, intelligence, attention to detail, business interest and enthusiasm to be a lawyer and to work for Stevens & Bolton.

Training programme Our trainees have genuine responsibility and experience of dealing with clients – and are made to feel part of the team from day one. As a trainee you will have the chance to spend six months in four of the key business areas we specialise in, namely M&A and other corporate work, insolvency and banking/finance, commercial, private wealth and family, real estate, IP, dispute resolution and employment, pensions and immigration. There may also be an opportunity for trainees to undertake a client secondment. We are dedicated to encouraging continuous professional development, delivered in a variety of ways to give our trainees the best chance to become rounded, assured and respected professionals. Training in technical and business skills and early exposure to stimulating work with a variety of clients is instrumental in providing a solid foundation. Our unique combination of factors – supervision when you need it, support from colleagues and the opportunity to embrace early responsibility as soon as you are ready – creates a compelling proposition at the outset of your career.

When and how to apply Applications should be made by completing our online application form available from our website from 1 December to 1 June each year.

Work placements We run two programmes each year in the summer of one-week duration. Applications are accepted between 1 December and 31 January.

Sponsorship We pay the fees for the CPE/GDL and LPC and a maintenance grant for each course of study. Any future trainees who are yet to take their LPC or the GDL are usually required to attend The University of Law Guildford. Please see the firm's website for further details.

Vacancies	5
Trainees	10
Partners	42
Total staff	227

Work placement yes

Training contract deadline
1 June 2019

Apply to
Online via
www.stevens-bolton.com

Starting salary
£34,000

Minimum qualifications
2.1 degree in a law or non-law degree, 340 UCAS points for A levels

Sponsorship
GDL/LPC plus maintenance grant

Offices
Guildford

STEVENS&BOLTON

STEPHEN RIMMER LLP
28 Hyde Gardens, Eastbourne BN21 4PX
Tel: 01323 644222
Email: ah@stephenrimmer.com
Apply to: Mr Alan Hobden

V	1 [19]
T	2
P	11
TS	92
WP	no

STEPHENS SCOWN
Curzon House, Southernhay West, Exeter EX1 1RS
Tel: 01392 210700
Email: graduaterecruitment@stephens-scown.
co.uk
Apply to: Miss Emma King

A law firm with a regional focus, but the benefits of a big city rival. We have band one *Chambers* rankings across four practice areas.

V	8
T	23
P	55
TS	300
WP	yes

STEPHENSONS
24 Lord Street, Leigh, Lancashire WN7 1AB
Tel: 01942 777777
Email: careers@stephensons.co.uk
Apply to: Mrs Janine Turner

North West regional full service practice. Serving small and medium sized businesses, public sector organisations, bulk referrals from banks and insurance companies, private individuals and LSC work.

V	5
T	18
P	26
TS	325
WP	yes

STONE KING
13 Queen Square, Bath BA1 2HJ
Tel: 01225 337599
Email: tassyvincent@stoneking.co.uk
Apply to: Mrs Tassy Vincent

We know our firm can only succeed with the right people. Our industry focus, including our leading reputation in the charity and education sectors, enables us to provide tailored advice specific to our clients needs.

V	4
T	12
P	42
TS	200
WP	yes

STONE ROWE BREWER
Stone House, 12/13 Church Street, Twickenham, Middlesex TW1 3NJ
Tel: 020 8891 6141
Email: info@srb.co.uk
Apply to: Mr John Andrews

General practice covering personal injury, commercial litigation, employment, family and conveyancing. Members of the Personal Injury Panel and the Employment Lawyers Association.

V	1-2
T	4
P	5
TS	50
WP	no

STORRAR COWDRY
25 White Friars, Chester CH1 1NZ
Tel: 01244 400567
Email: all@storrarcowdry.co.uk
Apply to: Mrs D Storrar

City centre general practice with good quality work. No criminal law.

V	0
T	1
P	7
TS	24
WP	no

STOWE FAMILY LAW LLP
The Old Court House, Raglan Street, Harrogate HG1 1LT
Tel: 01423532600
Email: enquiries@stowefamilylaw.co.uk
Apply to: Ms Morna Bunce

Stowe Family Law is the UK's largest specialist family law firm, with family lawyers and divorce solicitors across a number of UK offices.

V	Varies
T	2
P	30
TS	100
WP	yes

STS SOLICITORS
1st Floor, 159 Brent Street, Hendon, London NW4 4DH
Tel: 020 7112 8355
Email: info@sts-solicitors.com
Apply to: Mrs Husniye Sera Bazen

V	2
T	0
P	1
TS	5
WP	yes

V = Vacancies / **T** = Trainees / **P** = Partners / **TS** = Total Staff / **WP** = Work Placement

Sullivan & Cromwell LLP

1 New Fetter Lane, London EC4A 1AN
Tel: 020 7959 8900
Email: traineesolicitors@sullcrom.com
Web: careers.sullcrom.com/uk-trainee-solicitors
🐦 sullcrom

The firm Sullivan & Cromwell provides the highest quality legal advice and representation to clients worldwide. The results we achieve have set us apart for more than 130 years and serve as a model for the modern practice of law. At S&C, there is no such thing as second best. Meritocracy, responsibility and opportunity foster the success of each new employee. S&C has more than 875 lawyers across an international network of 13 offices on four continents. We maintain a unified firm culture worldwide and provide our clients with highly integrated advice on a global basis. The London office, established in 1972, is S&C's largest office excepting its New York City headquarters. There are approximately 80 English, US and dual-qualified lawyers working in the office across a number of practice areas.

Types of work S&C London is perhaps unique in the scale, complexity and significance of the work carried out in an office of its size. Our practice areas include: M&A and private equity; capital markets; finance (credit, leveraged and acquisition); restructuring; project finance; competition law and tax.

Who should apply We seek trainees who have an excellent prior academic record along with strong academic credentials, including a projected or achieved first or upper second class honours degree, or the equivalent. You should possess genuine intellectual curiosity, integrity, strong interpersonal skills, commercial awareness and an ambition to succeed at one of the world's leading law firms. We expect most of our applicants to be penultimate-year law students and final-year non-law students. Graduates and post-graduates are also eligible.

Training programme We offer our trainees the opportunity to do superior work, meet exceptional people and grow in a supportive culture. We aim to distinguish our trainee programme by offering genuine mentoring from partners and senior lawyers who will take a keen interest in your career development.

When and how to apply To apply for the 2019 summer vacation scheme, apply by CV (including a full classification and percentage breakdown of all academic results) and a covering letter. We will be accepting applications for our 2019 summer vacation scheme from 1 November 2018 through 11 January 2019. To apply for a training contract starting in 2021, apply by CV (including a full classification and percentage breakdown of all academic results) and a covering letter. We will be accepting applications for our 2021 trainee intake from 1 May through 12 July 2019.

Work placements Two two-week summer placements. Remuneration £500 per week.

Sponsorship Full sponsorship of GDL and LPC fees, plus a maintenance grant.

Vacancies	4-6
Trainees	9
Partners	19
Total staff	140

Work placement yes
(see Insider Report on p103)

Training contract deadline
12 July 2019

Apply to
traineesolicitors@sullcrom.com

Sponsorship
GDL/LPC

Offices
Beijing, Brussels, Frankfurt, Hong Kong, London, Los Angeles, Melbourne, New York, Palo Alto, Paris, Sydney, Tokyo, Washington DC

SULLIVAN & CROMWELL LLP

Remember to cite *The LawCareers.Net Handbook* on your application form if you apply to this firm.

TRAINING CONTRACT DIRECTORY **447**

STUART MILLER SOLICITORS 247 High Road, Wood Green, London N22 8HF **Tel:** 020 8888 5225 **Email:** recruitment@stuartmillersolicitors.co.uk **Apply to:** HR Manager	We specialise in defending fraud, cybercrime and criminal cases. Highly commended at the Law Society's Excellence Awards.	V T P TS WP	1 0 2 32 yes
SURREY LAW CENTRE Jacobs Yard, Woodlands Road, Guildford, Surrey GU1 1RL **Tel:** 01483 215000 **Apply to:** Ms Laura Melbourne	We are a law centre that provides clientcentric services to those with domestic abuse, employment, housing or family issues.	V T P TS WP	0 2 0 9 yes
SWEETMAN BURKE & SINKER 158-160 The Broadway, West Ealing, London W13 0TL **Tel:** 020 8840 2572 **Email:** reception@sbs-law.co.uk **Apply to:** Mr Jonathan Koffman	No vacancies at present.	V T P TS WP	Poss 1 3 16 yes
SWITALSKIS SOLICITORS LLP 19 Cheapside, Wakefield WF1 2SD **Tel:** 01924 882 000 **Email:** ruth.coneron@switalskis.com **Apply to:** Mrs RJ Coneron		V T P TS WP	0 4 12 250 no
SYSTECH SOLICITORS LIMITED Chapter House, 18-20 Crucifix Lane, London SE1 3JW **Tel:** 0151 707 1019 **Email:** jayne.bryson@systech-solicitors.com **Apply to:** Mr R A Farrell	We are a niche practice, providing specialist contentious and non-contentious legal services to global clients across all construction and engineering sectors.	V T P TS WP	0 0 0 25 no
TALBOT & CO 148 High Street, Burton-On-Trent, Staffordshire DE14 1JY **Tel:** 01283 564716 **Email:** tombramall@talbotco.co.uk **Apply to:** Mr TJ Bramall	Long-established *Legal 500* firm with extensive high-quality private client base. Particular expertise in wills, tax, trusts, estates and probate. Also property, litigation, matrimonial and charities.	V T P TS WP	1 1 1 20 yes
TALBOT WALKER LLP 16 Bridge Street, Andover, Hampshire SP10 1BJ **Tel:** 01264 363354 **Email:** employment@talbotwalker.co.uk **Apply to:** Miss Sonia Adlem	Three-member general practice.	V T P TS WP	1 1 3 14 no
TALLENTS SOLICITORS 3 Middlegate, Newark NG24 1AQ **Tel:** 01636 671881 **Email:** roy.westerby@tallents.co.uk **Apply to:** The Practice Manager	Offices in Newark, Mansfield and Southwell.	V T P TS WP	0 0 5 51 no

V = Vacancies / **T** = Trainees / **P** = Partners / **TS** = Total Staff / **WP** = Work Placement

TASSELLS 20 West Street, Faversham, Kent ME13 7JF **Tel:** 01795 533337 **Email:** law@tassells-solicitors.co.uk **Apply to:** Mr James Matthews	Broad based general practice, undertaking all the usual non-contentious and contentious work.	V 1 T 1 P 7 TS 21 WP yes
TAYLOR & EMMET LLP 20 Arundel Gate, Sheffield S1 2PP **Tel:** 0114 218 4000 **Email:** HR@tayloremmet.co.uk **Apply to:** HR Department	Taylor&Emmet have a long and proud tradition of recruiting and developing trainees, many of whom have subsequently qualified with us and become partners.	V 2 T 2 P 21 TS 210 WP yes
TAYLOR ROSE TTKW 13-15 Moorgate, London EC2R 6AD **Tel:** 020 3450 4444 **Email:** info@taylor-rose.co.uk **Apply to:** R Reeve	We are a top 200 multi-disciplined law firm with 250 experts operating from six offices, representing clients from everyday cases to the most complex issue.	V 1-2 T 2 P 13 TS 250 WP no
TAYLOR VINTERS LLP Merlin Place, Milton Road, Cambridge CB4 0DP **Tel:** 01223 225148 **Email:** recruitment@taylorvinters.com **Apply to:** Mrs Alix Balfe-Skinner	Taylor Vinters is an international law firm supporting the businesses which drive the innovation economy and the entrepreneurs and private wealth that underpin them.	V 6^{20} T 11 P 25 TS 170 WP yes
TAYLOR WALTON LLP 28-44 Alma Street, Luton LU1 2PL **Tel:** 01582 731161 **Email:** jim.wrigglesworth@taylorwalton.co.uk **Apply to:** Mr Jim Wrigglesworth	Progressive and substantial practice, providing specialist advice to commercial and private clients.	V 4 T 7 P 28 TS 160 WP yes
TAYLOR WESSING 5 New Street Square, London EC4A 3TW **Tel:** 020 7300 7000 **Email:** graduate@taylorwessing.com **Apply to:** Ms Sarah Harte	Taylor Wessing is a leading international law firm with a single-minded, forward-thinking approach to serving clients. By thinking creatively and being proactive, we identify ways to help them achieve their ambitions and deliver innovative solutions.	V Up to 35 T 45 P 400 TS 1800 WP yes
TEACHER STERN LLP 37-41 Bedford Row, London WC1R 4JH **Tel:** 020 7242 3191 **Email:** recruitment@teacherstern.com **Apply to:** Mr James Baker	Long-established commercial practice with a focus on transactional and contentious property, general commercial litigation,commercial and corporate work, employment and private client.	V 3 T 10 P 30 TS 121 WP yes
TEES Tees House, 95 London Road, Bishop's Stortford CM23 3GW **Tel:** 0800 0131165 **Email:** letitia.glaister@teeslaw.com **Apply to:** Miss Letty Glaister	Important regional practice offering a full range of legal services to clients from individuals to public companies, encompassing private clients, agricultural, insurance and commercial concerns.	V 3 T 6 P 21 TS 240 WP yes

V = Vacancies / **T** = Trainees / **P** = Partners / **TS** = Total Staff / **WP** = Work Placement

TEMPLE HEELIS LLP 1 Kent View, Kendal, Cumbria LA9 4DZ **Tel:** 01539 723757 **Email:** lwilliams@templeheelis.co.uk **Apply to:** Mr John Osborne	A progressive provincial practice specialising in civil litigation, including personal injury, wills, tax planning, probate, employment, family and conveyancing.	V 0 T 1 P 6 TS 30 WP no
TERRELLS LLP 61 Lincoln Road, Peterborough PE1 2SE **Tel:** 01733 896 789 **Email:** enquiries@terrells.co.uk **Apply to:** Mr Roger Terrell	Modern high street firm practice (no crime) specialising in family law. Accredited with LEXCEL and Investors in People quality marks.	V 1 T 3 P 2 TS 18 WP no
TERRY JONES SOLICITORS Abbey House, Abbey Foregate, Shrewsbury SY2 6BH **Tel:** 01743 285888 **Email:** recruitment@terry-jones.co.uk **Apply to:** Mr Anthony Iles	We are Lexcel accredited, progressive and pride ourselves in providing professional, practical and cost effective advice and assistance.	V Poss T 9 P 4 TS 120 WP no
THACKRAY WILLIAMS LLP Kings House, 32-40 Widmore Road, Bromley BR1 1RY **Tel:** 020 8290 0440 **Email:** jane.macleod@thackraywilliams.com **Apply to:** Ms Jane MacLeod	The largest firm in the Bromley and North Kent region. A vibrant and progressive general practice with a growing commercial side.	V 3[20] T 7 P 18 TS 140 WP no
THALIWAL & CO SOLICITORS 298 Welford Road, Leicester LE2 6EG **Tel:** 0116 274 5252 **Email:** enquiries@thaliwalsolicitors.co.uk **Apply to:** Mr R Thaliwal	Our mental health law team advise and represent clients in mental health review tribunals, hospital managers meetings and our specialist immigration law team provides advice and assistance in both the East and West Midlands.	V 0 T 0 P 1 TS 11 WP yes
THOMPSON SMITH AND PUXON Stable 6, Stable Road, Colchester CO2 7GL **Tel:** 01206 574431 **Email:** recruitment@tsplegal.com **Apply to:** Mr Sean Stuttaford	Commercial, private client and family work, with niche practices in personal injury and clinical negligence.	V Poss T 1 P 11 TS 75 WP no
THOMPSONS SOLICITORS Congress House, Great Russell Street, London WC1B 3LW **Tel:** 020 7290 0000 **Email:** enquiries@thompsons.law.co.uk **Apply to:** The HR Department	Thompsons Solicitors is the most experienced trade union, employment rights and claimant personal injury practice in the UK.	V 0 T 0 P 50 TS 888 WP no
THOMSON WEBB & CORFIELD 16 Union Road, Cambridge CB2 1HE **Tel:** 01223 578086 **Email:** pcarr@twclaw.co.uk **Apply to:** Ms Pippa Carr	Progressive Cambridge firm with expanding commercial and corporate teams, handling private and public company clients. Private client departments, including trusts, family and crime.	V 1[19] T 2 P 9 TS 39 WP no

V = Vacancies / **T** = Trainees / **P** = Partners / **TS** = Total Staff / **WP** = Work Placement

Thomas Cooper LLP

Ibex House, 42-47 Minories, London EC3N 1HA
Tel: 020 7481 8851
Email: recruitment@thomascooperlaw.com
Web: www.thomascooperlaw.com
f thomascooperlawllp 𝕐 thomascooperllp

The firm Thomas Cooper LLP was funded in 1825 and specialises in international maritime, trade and finance law. We take a pragmatic approach, providing clear advice that helps clients navigate through the complexity of international commerce. We regularly advise on all aspects of maritime law from high profile casualties and major maritime losses to fatal accident and personal injury claims. We also represent our clients' interests in day to day commercial disputes arising under shipping contracts.

Who should apply We do not require our trainees to have a specific knowledge of maritime law, but we do expect solid academics, a willingness and intellectual flexibility to solve practical as well as legal problems and the enthusiasm and personality to succeed in an established, fast paced and professional market. We have a reputation for punching above our weight. Our trainee retention rate is one of the best in the legal sector.

Training programme We are recognised as a leading international law firm and have overseas offices in Paris, Piraeus, Singapore and Madrid. We also provide training seats in a few of our overseas offices. Many of the trainees who have undertaken international seats have enjoyed the experience and we support you every step of the way, assisting you with a place to live, an interesting and challenging workload and the excitement of living and working in a new jurisdiction. Similarly in London training at Thomas Cooper means training as part of a team. We seek to retain all successful candidates and expect trainees to work with senior members of staff and partners as well as with associates and other trainees.

Thomas Cooper LLP's training is hands-on from day one. Each of your seats will be overseen by a partner or senior solicitor. Throughout your qualifying period you will be allocated a supervising partner who will oversee your assessments and act as a point of reference as you move through the firm. You will be expected to interact professionally with our clients, counsel, experts and others and to contribute to the substantive and practical requirements of each case. We are specialist litigators and deal with a variety of commercial arbitration disputes as well as general litigation. Maritime law can be challenging both academically and practically and the type of roles you will be involved in may include: drafting instructions to counsel, assisting in taking witness statements, reviewing disclosure and collating evidence, obtaining further information, and providing advice to clients and to others on the running of the case, and the next step that needs to be taken. You will assist the lead partner by taking a note of conferences with experts and counsel, participating in mediations and preparing cases for arbitration or court.

When and how to apply If you have any questions or would like further information please contact us: recruitment@thomascooperlaw.com. For full details of our application process please visit www.thomascooperlaw.com/careers.

Vacancies	Up to 3
Trainees	6-7
Partners	32
Total staff	96
Work placement	no

Apply
Online

Starting salary
1st year – £34,000
2nd year – £37,500
(based on 2017 salaries)

Minimum qualifications
2.1 degree

Offices
London, Madrid, Paris, Piraeus, Singapore

T H O M A S
C O O P E R

Thomson Snell & Passmore LLP

3 Lonsdale Gardens, Tunbridge Wells, Kent TN1 1NX
Tel: 01892 510000
Email: recruitment@ts-p.co.uk
Web: www.ts-p.co.uk

The firm Thomson Snell & Passmore has a reputation for providing high quality, intelligent advice. We provide a comprehensive legal service and build long-term relationships by encouraging a culture of respect, understanding and excellence. It's a common sense approach that's surprisingly uncommon.

Our offices are located in the centre of Tunbridge Wells and in the Thames Gateway. The firm attracts clients locally, nationally, and internationally.

Types of work We possess a strength and depth of expertise that only a handful of firms in the South East can claim. You will work with a wide range of clients, local and national. Our services are: corporate and commercial; employment; commercial property; dispute resolution; private client; family; residential conveyancing; clinical negligence; and personal injury.

Who should apply We appoint people on the basis of intellectual ability, commercial acumen, enthusiasm, drive, initiative, and strong interpersonal and team-working skills.

Training programme Thomson Snell & Passmore has a reputation for offering excellent training and opportunities. Trainee solicitors are the firm's future assistants, associates and partners. We find out what your personal and professional aspirations are and provide you with the development opportunities you need to achieve them.

A comprehensive induction programme will help you adjust to your career in business and law. We do our very best to allocate seats in your preferred practice areas. Each of the four six-month seats will give you a thorough grounding and exposure to a variety of areas of law. You will have a dedicated trainee supervisor, regular coaching and three-monthly reviews that give you the opportunity to talk through your progress, development needs and future path. Our commitment to bespoke training and development will enable you to move your career in the direction you want it to go.

When and how to apply Apply by 31 July 2019 to begin September 2021. Applicants should apply by the firm's own application form available via our website. A 2.1 degree in any discipline is the minimum required.

Work placements Our structured and inspiring programme will give you a flavour of what to expect from a career in the law and help you make choices for the future.

The firm offers two placements over the Easter period and eight placements over the summer period. Applicants should apply by the firm's own application form available via the website.

Sponsorship Grant and interest-free loan available for the LPC.

Vacancies	6
Trainees	12
Partners	41
Total staff	235

Work placement   yes

Training contract deadline
31 July 2019

Apply
Online

Starting salary
Competitive market rate for a South East regional firm

Minimum qualifications
2.1 degree, any discipline

Sponsorship
LPC

Offices
Tunbridge Wells,
Thames Gateway

Thomson Snell & Passmore

Thrings

6 Drakes Meadow, Penny Lane, Swindon SN3 3LL
Tel: 01793 410800
Email: recruitment@thrings.com
Web: www.thrings.com
f thringslaw 𝕏 thringslaw

The firm South-West leading light Thrings is a major player along the M4 corridor. We are a vibrant, expanding law firm with a diverse client base, offering excellent career prospects to ambitious trainees. We operate from offices in Bristol, Bath, Swindon, London and Romsey. Current trainees feel that the firm offers plenty of 'scope for career development' and gives them 'excellent levels of responsibility' as well as a 'wide range of work', all of which combine to make them feel that they are in the thick of it.

Types of work As a client-focused business, collaboration is a key part of how we work; employees frequently work together across the firm and share expertise and knowledge to best serve our clients needs. We are a full serviced law firm offering clients tailored specialist advice across a wide spectrum of service lines. Our sector expertise and industry knowledge is focused around a small group of discrete areas where we can offer clients strength in depth and a reputation that goes beyond our geographical reach. Agriculture, banking and finance, retail, health and care, private client, and a growing International expertise all give trainees an opportunity to work with a wide array of clients with a variety of challenging and stimulating needs.

Who should apply You're a bright and proactive individual, with a real commercial awareness, who is keen to develop and learn through their training contract. We're looking for people who are enthusiastic, able to think independently, but above all dedicated to a career in law and making a difference for their clients through effective client relationships. Ideally you would hold a 2.1 degree, have already completed your LPC or have a course underway; you may have even completed the GDL/CPE (if applicable). We are open to applicants who have a 2.2 degree if you have paralegal experience. What you need to demonstrate is that you grasp facts well, and can work out effective solutions quickly. If you think that you fit the bill, we're keen to hear from you.

Training programme We operate a structured two-year training contract split into four six-month seats. You can expect to gain experience within at least three different practice areas, with a balance of contentious and non contentious work types. You are likely to work in a number of our offices, which means you'll benefit from working in different environments with different colleagues. You will gain hands-on experience and responsibility from day one and you will get exposure to partners, associates and solicitors alike to help you to develop the skills, setting you up for a great career in law. You will get to work with a diverse client base with support from a dedicated supervisor who will hold regular 1:1's, providing you with feedback to help you gain the exposure and skills you need to be a successful Thrings solicitor. You will get the opportunity to attend training courses and events that are relevant to your career.

Not everything we do at Thrings is legal; we have regular social events and make sure that all of our employees get a work/life balance, including organised events and charity days to support the local communities we live in. We're proud to say we have 'just because days', and we give everyone an extra day off for their birthday. We offer a real career path for someone who is passionate and driven. Additionally, we offer a competitive salary and benefits package.

When and how to apply Apply via our website www.thrings.com for training contracts in 2020.

Vacancies	7
Trainees	16
Partners	58
Total staff	224

Training contract deadline
28 February 2019

Apply
Online

Starting salary
£27,000

Minimum qualifications
2.1 degree or 2.2 degree with paralegal experience

Offices
Swindon, Bath, Bristol, London, Romsey

THRINGS
SOLICITORS

THORNE SEGAR LTD 3 Bancks Street, Minehead, Somerset TA24 5DE **Tel:** 01643 703234 **Email:** clare.cash-davis@thornesegar.co.uk **Apply to:** Mr Matthew Stevens	A progressive company with a clearly planned future, specialising in private client, family and residential conveyance work.	V T P TS WP	1 - 2 27 yes
THORPE & CO 17 Valley Bridge Parade, Scarborough YO11 2JX **Tel:** 01723 364321 **Email:** info@thorpeandco.com **Apply to:** The Recruitment Contact	General practice with three offices including domestic conveyancing, probate, family, personal injury and criminal work.	V T P TS WP	0 1 8 55 no
TILLY BAILEY & IRVINE LLP York Chambers, York Road, Hartlepool TS26 9DP **Tel:** 01429 264101 **Email:** ntaylor@tbilaw.co.uk **Apply to:** Mr Neil Taylor	Tilly Bailey & Irvine is one of the UK's longest established law firms with offices in Hartlepool, Wynyard, Barnard Castle and Stockton.	V T P TS WP	TBC[20] 1 13 146 no
TIM JOHNSON / LAW 117 Temple Chambers, 3-7 Temple Avenue, London EC4Y 0HP **Tel:** 020 7036 9120 **Email:** recruitment@timjohnson-law.co.uk **Apply to:** Mr Tim Johnson	Tim Johnson / Law is a niche firm of solicitors based in the City of London specialising in UK employment and international labour law.	V T P TS WP	1 1 1 8 yes
TINKLIN SPRINGALL 9-11 Rectory Road, Beckenham BR3 1JB **Tel:** 020 8402 7222 **Email:** ics@tinklinspringall.co.uk **Apply to:** Mr Ian Springall	Training covers conveyancing, litigation, probate and general matters.	V T P TS WP	2[19] 4 7 50 no
TINN CRIDDLE & CO 6 High Street, Alford, Lincolnshire LN13 9DX **Tel:** 01507 462882 **Apply to:** Mr Geoffrey Allen	Small, three-office, country practice.	V T P TS WP	0 1 4 10 no
TINSDILLS Hays House, 25 Albion Street, Hanley, Stoke on Trent ST1 1QF **Tel:** 01782 262031 **Email:** lawyers@tinsdills.co.uk **Apply to:** Mrs Jane Massey	The firm has four offices located in North Staffordshire and South Cheshire. The firm is innovative and proactive acting for private, corporate and institutional clients.	V T P TS WP	TBC[19] 9 11 97 no
TLT LLP One Redcliff Street, Bristol BS1 6TP **Tel:** 0333 006 0703 **Email:** graduate@tltsolicitors.com **Apply to:** Ms Jade Montagna	Described by industry commentators as 'the firm to watch', TLT remains one of the fastest growing law firms in the UK.	V T P TS WP	Up to 15 35 110 1020 yes

V = Vacancies / **T** = Trainees / **P** = Partners / **TS** = Total Staff / **WP** = Work Placement

TMJ LEGAL SERVICES LTD Foster House, 99 Raby Road, Hartlepool TS24 8DT **Tel:** 01429 235616 **Email:** legal@tmjlegal.co.uk **Apply to:** Mr KI Morgan	General practice specialising in private client, personal injury and matrimonial/children work.	V Poss T 1 P 3 TS 35 WP yes
TOLLERS SOLICITORS 1 Waterside Way, Bedford Road, Northampton NN4 7XD **Tel:** 01604 258558 **Email:** sarah.finlayson@tollers.co.uk **Apply to:** Mrs Sarah Finlayson	Tollers was founded in 1877, although we may have a long history, our 140 staff take a modern approach to providing high-quality legal services.	V 4 T 4 P 18 TS 140 WP no
TOUSSAINTS First Floor, 150 Soho Road, Birmingham B21 9LN **Tel:** 0121 523 5050 **Apply to:** Miss Mary Toussaint	Busy high street office undertaking residential, commercial property, litigation, civil, crime and family work.	V 0 T 0 P 1 TS 1 WP yes
TOZERS LLP Broadwalk House, Southernhay West, Exeter, Devon EX1 1UA **Tel:** 01392 207020 **Email:** enquiries@tozers.co.uk **Apply to:** Mrs Fiona Grafton-Smith	One of the oldest and largest firms in Devon, we act for clients locally and nationally in a range of specialisations at our three offices.	V Poss T 2 P 20 TS 120 WP yes
TRAVERS SMITH LLP 10 Snow Hill, London EC1A 2AL **Tel:** 020 7295 3000 **Email:** graduate.recruitment@traverssmith.com **Apply to:** Ms Germaine VanGeyzel	Travers Smith is an award-winning independent City law firm with a reputation for enterprising thinking and uncompromising quality in all of its chosen fields.	V 25 T 48 P 83 TS 660 WP yes
TRETHOWANS LLP The Pavilion, Botleigh Grange Business Park, Hedge End Southampton SO30 2AF **Tel:** 023 8032 1000 **Email:** recruitment@trethowans.com **Apply to:** Mrs Kate Ellis	Leading law firm based in the south, advising businesses and individual clients throughout the UK with a team of over 230 people including 40 partners.	V 3-4 T 6 P 40 TS 235 WP no
TROWERS & HAMLINS LLP 3 Bunhill Row, London EC1Y 8YZ **Tel:** 020 7423 8000 **Email:** avithlani@trowers.com **Apply to:** Mr Anup Vithlani	From nine offices in the UK, Middle East and Far East, we offer a comprehensive and joined-up service to clients across the globe.	V 23 T 46 P 157 TS 894 WP yes
TV EDWARDS SOLICITORS 35-37 Mile End Road, London E1 4TP **Tel:** 020 3440 8000 **Email:** enquiries@tvedwards.com **Apply to:** Ms Christine Woolfenden	With offices across London, TV Edwards LLP is a leading predominantly publicly-funded firm offering an extensive range of legal services.	V 0 T 9 P 13 TS 120 WP yes

V = Vacancies / **T** = Trainees / **P** = Partners / **TS** = Total Staff / **WP** = Work Placement

Vinson & Elkins RLLP

20 Fenchurch Street, 24th Floor, London EC3M 3BY
Tel: 020 7065 6000
Web: www.velaw.com
🐦 vecareers

The firm Vinson & Elkins is a leading US-based international law firm with more than 650 lawyers located in 15 cities across the globe. Over four decades ago, we became one of the first US law firms to establish a practice in London. Since then, we have built a dynamic office, undertaking work that has gained the respect of clients around the world. Over the years, V&E has amassed a wealth of experience working on projects for clients in almost every country on the map. We are accustomed to working not only in well-defined markets, but also in less familiar and more challenging environments, under developing local regimes or those with evolving communications and infrastructure. We know how to adapt to local customs, cultures and laws, enabling us to handle matters quickly and effectively. We work in tandem with our clients, travelling wherever and whenever we are needed. We know what it takes to make deals work and to win cases. This knowledge enables us to offer creative solutions for our clients engaged in leading-edge projects around the world.

Types of work Our clients are predominantly in the energy, finance and infrastructure sectors and the London office specialises in M&A, private equity, construction, project development and finance, international arbitration and litigation, corporate and structured finance and tax.

Who should apply We are looking to recruit ambitious individuals with exceptional academic results, sound commercial awareness and rounded personalities. The ability to think laterally and creatively is essential, as is a need for common sense and a willingness to take the initiative.

Training programme The firm operates a non-rotational training system and trainees work in all practice areas throughout their two years. The training is designed to provide variety, flexibility and responsibility from the start. V&E won the LawCareers.Net 'Best Recruiter – US Firm in the City' in 2017 and 'Best Trainer – Medium City Firm' award in 2010. V&E won 'Best Training Principal – Small Trainee Intake in 2018 and was also nominated for 'Best Recruiter – US Firm in the City'. While being based in London our trainees can expect to undertake overseas secondments and international travel during the course of their two years.

When and how to apply The deadline for applications is 31 July 2019 to begin training in 2021. Applications should be made by way of our online application form, available from our website. Please note, we give preference to those students who have previously completed a summer vacation placement with us.

Work placements We view vacation placements as an important part of our recruitment process and have been nominated on multiple occasions in the category 'Best Work Placement Scheme – City Firm' and 'Best Recruiter – US Firm in the City' (and won this category in 2017). For Summer 2019 placements apply by 31 January 2019. Applications should be made by way of our application form, available from our website. We are hosting an open day at our London office on 20 March 2019 for first-year law degree students or non-law students in their penultimate year. Applications can be made by emailing graduaterecruitment@velaw.com before 8 February 2019. Please include your name, contact details and your current stage of education. Please also confirm that you have achieved our minimum academic requirements of at least AAB at A level or equivalent. Open day places will be allocated after the closing date.

Sponsorship LPC and GDL fees paid plus a maintenance grant of up to £8,000.

Vacancies	5
Trainees	8
Partners	16
Total staff	100

Work placement yes
(see Insider Report on p104)

Training contract deadline
31 July 2019

Apply to
Andrew Nealon

Starting salary
1st year – £50,000
2nd year – £55,000
NQ salary – £120,000

Minimum qualifications
2.1 degree, AAB at A level
(or equivalent)

Sponsorship
GDL/LPC

Offices
Austin, Beijing, Dallas, Dubai, Hong Kong, Houston, London, Moscow, New York, Richmond, Riyadh, San Francisco, Taipei, Tokyo, Washington DC

Vinson&Elkins RLLP

Firm	Description	V	T	P	TS	WP
TWM SOLICITORS LLP 65 Woodbridge Road, Guildford, Surrey GU1 4RD **Tel:** 01483 752700 **Email:** jobs@twmsolicitors.com **Apply to:** Ms Rita Hilla	A growing and ambitious regional practice seeking trainees with motivation and energy, who can demonstrate a genuine commitment to a career in law.	0	8	32	220	no
VINCENT SYKES 4 West Street, Oundle, Peterborough PE8 4EF **Tel:** 01832 272971 **Email:** danielb@vincentsykes.co.uk **Apply to:** Mr Daniel Berry	Solicitors in small town of Oundle, near Peterborough. Undertake general work with a bias to non-contentious work.	0	1	1	6	no
VINCENT SYKES & HIGHAM LLP Montague House, 1 Chancery Lane, Thrapston, Northamptonshire NN14 4LN **Tel:** 01832 732 161 **Email:** rhona.rowland@vshlaw.co.uk **Apply to:** Mrs Rhona Rowland	Well-established East Midlands firm, specialists in company/commercial work.	0	-	5	26	no
VODAFONE GROUP SERVICES Vodafone House, The Connection, Newbury, Berkshire RG14 2FN **Tel:** 01635 33251 **Email:** legaltraining@vodafone.com **Apply to:** Mr Nick Woodrow	Vodafone is the world's leading mobile telecommunications community. Vodafone's Group legal function (based in Newbury, Paddington, Luxembourg and Düsseldorf) supports Vodafone's global initiatives.	0	2	0	110	yes
VWV (VEALE WASBROUGH VIZARDS) Narrow Quay House, Narrow Quay, Bristol BS1 4QA **Tel:** 0117 925 2020 **Email:** careers@vwv.co.uk **Apply to:** Mrs Ellen Marsh	We act nationally for clients in education and charities, healthcare, private wealth, family-owned business and public sectors. We also offer a dedicated service to individuals.	8-10	18	72	411	yes
VYMAN SOLICITORS LTD Vyman House, 104 College Road, Harrow, Middlesex HA1 1BQ **Tel:** 020 8427 9080 **Email:** anup.vyas@vyman.co.uk **Apply to:** Mr Anup Vyas	Niche commercial practice which provides proactive legal advice and support to its commercial clientele ranging from pharmaceutical and property companies to bar and restaurant businesses.	2	1	4	24	yes
W BROOK & CO 2a Doncaster Road, Goldthorpe, Rotherham, South Yorks S63 9HQ **Tel:** 01709 898697 **Email:** wbrook@walterbrook.wanadoo.co.uk **Apply to:** Mr W Brook	General practice including crime, family law/care, personal injury, domestic conveyancing. Franchised firm.	1-9	1	2	20	no
W H MATTHEWS & CO 11-13 Grove Road, Sutton, Surrey SM1 1DS **Tel:** 020 8642 6677 **Email:** sutton@whmatthews.com **Apply to:** Mr Charles Howard	General practice although very strong private client base. Established in 1881. Seven out of the 12 partners were trainees with the firm.	0	1	12	49	no

V = Vacancies / T = Trainees / P = Partners / TS = Total Staff / WP = Work Placement

Walker Morris LLP

Kings Court, 12 King Street, Leeds LS1 2HL
Tel: 0113 283 2500
Email: hellograduates@walkermorris.co.uk
Web: www.graduate.walkermorris.co.uk
🐦 wmgraduate

The firm Walker Morris LLP are a large, commercial practice based in Leeds. We are a well respected law firm and one of the highest recruiters of trainee solicitors in Leeds with fantastic retention rates. 45% of our partners trained with the firm.

Types of work Company commercial; corporate; intellectual property and trademarks; energy, infrastructure and government; projects; renewables and energy; corporate tax; commercial real estate; planning and environmental; CDR; insolvency; sports; employment; construction; regulatory services.

We offer a full range of services to commercial clients, both nationally and internationally.

Who should apply Second-year law students and final-year non-law students with excellent A-level grades and ideally a 2.1 degree. Applications are also welcome from candidates who are currently on or have completed the GDL/ LPC. We are looking for bright, commercially minded and practical individuals who can get on with clients and team members. They must show a sense of humour and fun when the pressure is on and adopt a commonsense approach to clients' problems.

Training programme Our two-year training programme incorporates six four-month seats with the opportunity to choose your seats in the second year. Trainees sit in an office with either a partner or an associate and receive a formal appraisal at the end of each seat. We provide a structured induction programme in your first week. The Professional Skills Course is provided and IT training/workshops are also given. Formal training including lectures, workshops, seminars, and skills programmes. There is also potential for secondments outside the firm.

When and how to apply We are recruiting 15 trainees for our 2021 intake. The closing date is 31 July 2019 and applicants should complete our online application form.

Work placements We offer a one-week structured vacation scheme. Schemes take place in April and June, with 48 places available. The closing date is 31 December 2018 and applicants should complete our online application form.

Sponsorship We will pay LPC and GDL fees plus £5,000 maintenance fees to students who we have offered a training contract. We are in partnership with BPP Law School – BPP are based in nine city centre locations and you can decide which one you attend.

We offer a £3,000 travel bursary to future trainees. The successful applicants will have demostrated a desire to undertake charitable work and/or develop their commercial skills either in the UK or abroad.

Vacancies	15
Trainees	33
Partners	46
Total staff	450

Work placement yes
(see Insider Report on p105)

Training contract deadline
31 July 2019

Apply to
Andrew Northage,
Graduate Recruitment
Partner

Starting salary
£27,000

Minimum qualifications
Ideally a 2.1 degree

Sponsorship
GDL/LPC

Offices
Leeds

WAINWRIGHT & CUMMINS 57-61 Atlantic Road, London SW9 8PU **Tel:** 020 7737 9330 **Email:** andrew.wainwright@wainwrightcummins.co.uk **Apply to:** Mr AJ Wainwright	We look for individuals with a commitment to working in the publically funded area and who have practical experience of working with similar firms.	V 0 T 4 P 4 TS 35 WP yes
WAKE SMITH SOLICITORS No1 Velocity, 2 Tenter Street, Sheffield S1 4BY **Tel:** 011 4266 6660 **Email:** jo.barnett@wake-smith.com **Apply to:** Mrs Jo Barnett	General practice serving both commercial and private clients.	V 1 T 2 P 19 TS 98 WP yes
WALL JAMES CHAPPELL 15-23 Hagley Road, Stourbridge, West Midlands DY8 1QW **Tel:** 01384 371 622 **Email:** post@wjclaw.co.uk **Apply to:** Mrs S Griffiths	Well-established West Midlands firm offering full range of legal services, seeks talented and hard working trainee.	V 1 T 2 P 7 TS 35 WP no
WALLACE LLP One Portland Place, London W1B 1PN **Tel:** 020 7636 4422 **Email:** trainees@wallace.co.uk **Apply to:** Mrs Tricia Davenport	A commercial law practice respected for its reassuringly straightforward approach. We are a progressive and innovative firm with a portfolio of domestic and international clients.	V 2¹⁹ T 2 P 17 TS 60 WP no
WALLACE ROBINSON & MORGAN 4 Drury Lane, Solihull B91 3BD **Tel:** 0121 705 7571 **Email:** enquiries@wallacerobinson.co.uk **Apply to:** Mr R P Hughes	The firm anticipates two vacancies in 2020.	V 0 T 3 P 6 TS 41 WP no
WALLER & HART SOLICITORS LIMITED Hazelberry, 29 Basset Road, Camborne, Cornwall TR14 8SH **Tel:** 01209 714064 **Email:** solicitors@wallerandhart.co.uk **Apply to:** Mr Peter Clive Hart	Our office is based in Camborne, Cornwall (for over 40 years). We provide a wide range of legal services, specialising in commercial and private clients.	V 1 T - P 2 TS 14 WP no
WALTER WILSON RICHMOND 360B Station Road, Harrow, Middlesex HA1 2DE **Tel:** 020 8427 8484 **Email:** wwr@walterwilson.co.uk **Apply to:** Mr VM Manek	Young forward-looking practice offering training in landlord/tenant, residential and commercial conveyancing, civil litigation, family law, employment, legal aid, probate and inheritance disputes.	V 0 T 2 P 1 TS 7 WP yes
WALTERS & PLASKITT 2 Westport Road, Burslem, Stoke-on-Trent ST6 4AW **Tel:** 01782 819611 **Apply to:** Mr S Leech	General high street practice with an emphasis on crime, family law and litigation. Action against the police, personal injury, legal aid and private clients.	V Poss T 1 P 4 TS 60 WP yes

V = Vacancies / **T** = Trainees / **P** = Partners / **TS** = Total Staff / **WP** = Work Placement

WANNOP & FOX York Road Chambers, York Road, Bognor Regis PO21 1LT **Tel:** 01243 864001 **Email:** info@wannopfox.com **Apply to:** Mr Chris Gambs	Medium-sized mixed practice, largely private client but with some commercial property and general company/commercial work. Franchise in family and crime. No current vacancies.	V 0 T 4 P 6 TS 52 WP no
WANSBROUGHS Northgate House, Devizes SN10 1JX **Tel:** 01380 733 300 **Email:** mail@wansbroughs.com **Apply to:** Ms Anna Wensley Stock	Commercial practice conducting work usually associated with larger practices. Areas include commercial, corporate, commercial and private property, complex tax, trusts, estates, family and insurance litigation.	V 2-3[19] T 4 P 16 TS 90 WP no
WARD GETHIN ARCHER 10 Tuesday Market Place, King's Lynn PE30 1JT **Tel:** 01553 660033 **Email:** sarah.scott@wardgethinarcher.co.uk **Apply to:** Ms Sarah Scott	Residential and commercial property, private client, employment, civil, personal injury and family. Additional offices in Dereham, Ely, Heacham, Swaffham, Chatteris and Watton.	V 1[20] T 1 P 16 TS 149 WP no
WARD HADAWAY Sandgate House, 102 Quayside, Newcastle upon Tyne NE1 3DX **Tel:** 0191 204 4003 **Email:** joinus@wardhadaway.com **Apply to:** Graduate Recruitment Team	Ward Hadaway is a full service commercial law firm with offices in Newcastle, Leeds and Manchester. We are a Northern law firm for national business.	V 10-15 T 26 P 85 TS 450 WP yes
WARNER GOODMAN LLP Portland Chambers, 66 West Street, Fareham PO16 0JR **Tel:** 01329 288121 **Email:** recruitment@warnergoodman.co.uk **Apply to:** Ms Alice Gordon	A well-established medium-sized regional firm. Offices in Southampton, Fareham, Portsmouth and Chandler's Ford. Legal aid franchise; member of specialist panels.	V 2-4 T 7 P 17 TS 160 WP no
WARNERS SOLICITORS Bank House, Bank Street, Tonbridge TN9 1BL **Tel:** 01732 770660 **Email:** recruitment@warners-solicitors.co.uk **Apply to:** Mrs Sally Hardwick	Warners is a modern and innovative law firm built on a strong heritage, providing expert advice to both businesses and individuals.	V 2[20] T 2 P 22 TS 111 WP no
WATKINS SOLICITORS 192 North Street, Bedminster, Bristol BS3 1JF **Tel:** 0117 939 0350 **Email:** bw@watkinssolicitors.co.uk **Apply to:** Ms BJ Watkins	Progressive law firm specialising in family, education, wills, probate and public law. Firm offers informal, unpaid work experience of two weeks waiting list for placement.	V 0 T 2 P 3 TS 32 WP yes
WATSON BURTON LLP 1 St James' Gate, Newcastle NE99 1YQ **Tel:** 0191 244 4444 **Email:** graduates@watsonburton.com **Apply to:** Miss Claire Pringle	Watson Burton is a leading law firm with a well-earned reputation for helping our clients succeed and providing first-class legal advice.	V 3[20] T 10 P 14 TS 110 WP yes

V = Vacancies / **T** = Trainees / **P** = Partners / **TS** = Total Staff / **WP** = Work Placement

Watson Farley & Williams LLP

15 Appold Street, London EC2A 2HB
Tel: 020 7814 8000
Email: uktrainees@wfw.com
Web: www.wfw.com/trainee

The firm WFW was founded in 1982 in the City of London. It has since grown rapidly to over 150 partners with a total staff of over 700. We are a distinctive law firm with a leading market position in international finance and investment, maritime and energy. We also specialise in natural resources, transport, real estate and technology. We have offices in Athens, Bangkok, Dubai, Frankfurt, Hamburg, Hong Kong, London, Madrid, Milan, Munich, New York, Paris, Rome and Singapore. The firm is able to provide an integrated, multi-jurisdictional service between offices and worldwide through an extensive network of specialist correspondence lawyers. In each of our offices our lawyers have expertise in the laws of the local jurisdiction and a knowledge and understanding of local business customs and culture.

Types of work The firm is divided into five practice groups: corporate, finance, energy and projects, litigation and real estate. The groups and our offices work together to support our international client base.

Who should apply Each year we recruit 18 trainees. Although there is no typical WFW trainee, there are certain qualifications, skills and traits that we look for. You will need a 2.1 or above – or predicted if you haven't yet graduated. We also ask for at least ABB from A-level results, or their equivalent, if you have taken other qualifications. As well as academic achievement, we particularly value applicants with clear initiative, drive and commercial awareness.

Training programme Our two-year training contract differs from many other firms. With us you will gain valuable insight from six four-month seats, one overseas in either Athens, Bangkok, Dubai, Hamburg, Paris or Singapore. In each you'll join a team led by a partner and see complex and high value transactions first hand. Your training contract will be hands-on, with as much experience of clients and real, high-profile work as possible. You'll also benefit from plenty of exposure to senior lawyers, many acknowledged leaders in their field. The firm has a reputation for challenging work. Yours will be no exception as we believe that only total immersion can provide you with the experience you require. We give you early responsibility but we also offer plenty of support and feedback.

When and how to apply All applications for training contracts should be made via our website www.wfw.com/trainee before 15 July 2019.

Work placements Our vacation scheme is the best way to familiarise yourself with WFW. The two-week placements are at our London office. They give us a chance to get to know you, and you a chance to experience the firm in more depth.

To appreciate first-hand the kind of work trainees undertake day to day, you will work with solicitors in one of our core practice groups for the whole period. To complement this focus on one area, you will also participate in a variety of training and social events designed to give you a general overview of the firm.

Applications must be received before 14 January 2019.

Sponsorship Full payment of fees for the GDL and LPC as applicable depending on the point of offer. We also provide a maintenance grant of £6,500/£5,500 depending on location.

Vacancies	18
Trainees	36
Partners	157
Total staff	700+

Work placement yes
(see Insider Report on p107)

Training contract deadline
15 July 2019

Apply
Online at
www.wfw.com/trainee

Starting salary
£43,000

Minimum qualifications
ABB at A level or equivalent and 2.1 degree any discipline

Sponsorship
GDL/LPC

Offices
Athens, Bangkok, Dubai, Frankfurt, Hamburg, Hong Kong, London, Madrid, Milan, Munich, New York, Paris, Rome, Singapore

WATSON FARLEY
&
WILLIAMS

WATSON LEGAL Office B, The Dutch Barn, Main Road, Ford End CM3 1LN **Tel:** 01279 466910 **Email:** recruitment@watson-legal.com **Apply to:** Ms Sarah Watson	We believe in delivering a strong client-focused service. We pride ourselves on our professional, friendly and conciliatory approach. We provide a different approach to training, with a truly hands on experience in a supportive working environment.	V 1[19] T 0 P 1 TS 2 WP yes
WATSON WATSON SOLICITORS Mercury House, Shrewsbury Business Park, Shrewsbury, Shropshire SY2 6LG **Tel:** 01743 770 400 **Email:** jenny@watsonwatson.com **Apply to:** Ms Jenny Watson	Watson Watson Solicitors - niche firm based in Shrewsbury, Shropshire with a nationwide client base. Our core areas are corporate, commercial, property and tax law.	V 2 T 5 P 2 TS 20 WP yes
WEDLAKE BELL LLP 71 Queen Victoria Street, London EC4V 4AY **Tel:** 020 7395 3000 **Email:** recruitment@wedlakebell.com **Apply to:** Graduate Recruitment Department	Wedlake Bell provides a full service to UK and international corporate and private clients.	V 8 T 12 P 60 TS 250 WP yes
WEIGHTMANS LLP 100 Old Hall Street, Liverpool L3 9QJ **Tel:** 0345 073 9900 **Email:** graduate.recruitment@weightmans.com **Apply to:** Mrs Denise Wright	Weightmans is a top 45 national law firm with offices in Birmingham, Glasgow, Leeds, Leicester, Liverpool, London and Manchester.	V Up to 18 T 33 P 188 TS 1277 WP yes
WEIL, GOTSHAL & MANGES (LONDON) LLP 110 Fetter Lane, London EC4A 1AY **Tel:** 020 7903 1000 **Email:** graduate.recruitment@weil.com **Apply to:** Mrs Lisa Powell	International law firm, with over 1,200 lawyers worldwide and a reputation for providing first-class US and European legal advice.	V 15 T 26 P 33 TS 297 WP yes
WELLERS LAW GROUP LLP Tenison House, Tweedy Road, Bromley BR1 3NF **Tel:** 020 8464 4242 **Email:** hr@wellerslawgroup.com **Apply to:** Ms Deena Bowman	Registered office Bromley. Additional offices, London, East Horsley and Great Bookham, Surrey, Sevenoaks. Commercial and private client firm with additional specialites of charity law and parish and town councils. Established over 100 years.	V 1[20] T 1 P 3 TS 85 WP no
WENDY HOPKINS FAMILY LAW PRACTICE 13 Windsor Place, Cardiff CF10 3BY **Tel:** 029 2034 2233 **Email:** enquiries@wendyhopkins.co.uk **Apply to:** Miss S E Wyburn	The first and largest purely family law firm in Wales, with expanding offices in Cardiff. Private family work, mainly high-value cases.	V 1 T 1 P 4 TS 27 WP no
WH DARBYSHIRE & SON 252 Lytham Road, Blackpool FY1 6EX **Tel:** 01253 346646 **Apply to:** Miss Lynn S Williams	Two offices, 252 Lytham Road Blackpool and 51 Commonside, Ansdell. Main areas of expertise, personal injury, benefits, probate, domestic, commercial conveyancing, crime and matrimonial. Legal aid franchise.	V 0 T 1 P 5 TS 13 WP no

V = Vacancies / **T** = Trainees / **P** = Partners / **TS** = Total Staff / **WP** = Work Placement

White & Case

5 Old Broad Street, London EC2N 1DW
Tel: 020 7532 2899
Email: londontrainee@whitecase.com
Web: www.whitecasetrainee.com
f whitecase **🐦** whitecase

The firm White & Case is a global law firm with nearly 2,000 lawyers worldwide. We've built an enviable network of 44 offices in 30 countries. That investment is the foundation for our client work in 160 countries today. Complex client projects, nuanced local market knowledge and global capabilities define who we are. Many White & Case clients are multinational organisations with complex needs that require the involvement of multiple offices. As part of our training contract, we offer every trainee a guaranteed six-month overseas seat.

Types of work As a White & Case lawyer, you'll work on fast-paced cutting-edge cross-border projects from the outset of your career. In London, our key areas of work include: bank finance (including regulatory compliance); financial restructuring and insolvency; capital markets (high yield and securitisation); dispute resolution (including antitrust, commercial litigation, intellectual property, international arbitration, trade, white collar and construction and engineering); energy, infrastructure, project and asset finance (EIPAF); corporate (including M&A, private equity, employment, compensation and benefits, investment funds, real estate and tax).

Who should apply White & Case is looking to recruit ambitious trainees who have a desire to gain hands-on practical experience from day one and a willingness to take charge of their own career. We value globally-minded citizens of the world who are eager to work across borders and cultures, and who are intrigued by solving problems within multiple legal systems. They should have an understanding of international commercial issues and an interest in working on big-ticket, cross-border work. We recruit both law and non-law students and owing to the nature of our work, language skills are of interest.

Training programme The training contract consists of four six-month seats, one of which is guaranteed to be spent in one of our overseas offices, including Abu Dhabi, Beijing, Dubai, Frankfurt, Geneva, Hong Kong, Moscow, New York, Paris, Prague, Singapore, Stockholm, and Tokyo. The remaining three seats can be spent in any one of the firm's practice groups in London. Receiving a high level of partner and senior associate contact from day one, our trainees can be confident that they will receive high-quality, stimulating and rewarding work. Trainees work in small, focused teams, so their colleagues trust them to perform tasks accurately and efficiently. White & Case is a "high-stretch, high- support" workplace that celebrates individual excellence and team success. We actively encourage our trainees to take early responsibility, and there is a strong emphasis on practical training, with plenty of support and feedback.

When and how to apply Apply online by 6 November 2018 for our winter vacation scheme and by 31 January 2019 for our spring and summer vacation schemes. Apply for a training contract by 31 July 2019. We hold open days on 14 and 28 November 2018, and also a first year two-day insight scheme on 15-16 May 2019. Please visit our website for more information.

Work placements We offer two-week vacation scheme placements over the winter, spring and summer holidays. A vacation scheme provides a great way to experience first-hand what life is like as a White & Case trainee. Playing an active part in the life of the London office you will receive real work from a dedicated supervisor, attend interactive, informative sessions and be given plenty of opportunities to network at social events.

Vacancies	50
Trainees	79
Partners	101
Total staff	828 (London)

Work placement yes

Training contract deadline
31 July 2019

Apply to
Christina Churchman

Starting salary
1st year – £46,000
2nd year – £50,000

Minimum qualifications
2.1 degree and AAB

Sponsorship
GDL/LPC

Offices
Abu Dhabi, Astana, Beijing, Berlin, Boston, Bratislava, Brussels, Cairo, Doha, Dubai, Düsseldorf, Frankfurt, Geneva, Hamburg, Helsinki, Hong Kong, Istanbul, Jakarta*, Johannesburg, London, Los Angeles, Madrid, Melbourne, Mexico City, Miami, Milan, Moscow, New York, Paris, Prague, Riyadh*, São Paulo, Seoul, Silicon Valley, Shanghai, Singapore, Stockholm, Sydney, Tokyo, Warsaw, Washington DC
*Associated firm

WHITE & CASE

Proud diversity and inclusion partner of

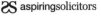 aspiringsolicitors

WH LAW LTD
Priory House, 2 Priory Road, Dudley, West
Midlands DY1 1HH
Tel: 0845 1265900
Email: mrogers@whlaw.co.uk
Apply to: Mr M Rogers

Progressive firm committed to
providing a quality legal service
specialising in employment, health
and safety, environment, PI and
clinical negligence. No current
vacancies.

V	0
T	1
P	3
TS	10
WP	no

WHITE & BLACK LIMITED
Home Park, Bladon, Woodstock OX20 1FX
Tel: 0800 035 2656
Email: applications@wablegal.com
Apply to: Mrs Victoria Wright

We are specialist technology and
corporate lawyers based in London
and Oxford. We advise businesses
across the globe on technology law,
corporate deals & disputes.

V	2
T	2
P	10
TS	20
WP	no

WHITE & CO
51 Alexandra Street, Southend-on-Sea SS1 1BW
Tel: 01702 340340
Email: alison@whitesolicitors.co.uk
Apply to: Miss AM White

Niche family law/wills and probate
practice providing advice and
representation in both publicly and
privately funded work including
public law care proceedings.

V	1[19]
T	-
P	2
TS	12
WP	yes

WHITEHEAD MONCKTON
72 King Street, Maidstone ME14 1BL
Tel: 01622 698000
Email: joanneforbes@whitehead-monckton.co.uk
Apply to: Mrs Joanne Forbes

Whitehead Monckton is one of
the largest law firms in Kent, with
offices in Canterbury, Maidstone,
Tenterden and London. Providing a
comprehensive range of services.

V	Varies[20]
T	2
P	11
TS	118
WP	no

THE WILKES PARTNERSHIP
41 Church Street, Birmingham B3 2RT
Tel: 0121 710 5916
Email: khackett@wilkes.co.uk
Apply to: Mrs Kate Hackett

One of the leading second tier
firms in Birmingham offering a full
range of corporate support services
continuing to expand in all areas.

V	4
T	8
P	21
TS	160
WP	no

WILKIN CHAPMAN LLP
Cartergate House, 26 Chantry Lane, Grimsby
DN31 2LJ
Tel: 01472 262626
Email: hr.officers@wilkinchapman.co.uk
Apply to: Mrs Angela English

Leading Lincolnshire and East
Yorkshire law firm offering a wide
range of legal services to private,
corporate and publicly-funded
clients.

V	5[20]
T	7
P	45
TS	378
WP	yes

WILKINSON & BUTLER
Peppercorn House, 8 Huntingdon Street, St Neots
PE19 1BH
Tel: 01480 219229
Apply to: Mr Dawson

An old-established market town
general practice handling all types
of matters for private clients,
commercial clients and legal aid.

V	0
T	0
P	4
TS	20
WP	no

WILKINSON WOODWARD LIMITED
11 Fountain Street, Halifax HX1 1LU
Tel: 01422 339600
Email: msc@wilkinsonwoodward.co.uk
Apply to: Mrs Maureen Cawthorn

General practice with legal aid
franchises. Clients vary from large
companies to private individuals.

V	1-2
T	2
P	8
TS	92
WP	no

V = Vacancies / **T** = Trainees / **P** = Partners / **TS** = Total Staff / **WP** = Work Placement

Wilsons Solicitors LLP

Alexandra House, St Johns Street, Salisbury, Wiltshire SP1 2SB
Tel: 01722 412412
Email: jo.ratcliffe@wilsonsllp.com
Web: www.wilsonsllp.com
🐦 wilsonsllpcom

The firm Ranked as one of the top private client and charity law firms in the country, our almost 300-year heritage, combined with lawyers who are recognised leaders in their fields, enables Wilsons to provide a unique combination of skills and experience to our clients. Our lawyers are dedicated to ensuring a detailed understanding of their clients' interests and a seamless working relationship across the different specialities of the practice.

Types of work Private client: We act for clients with business interests, landed and inherited wealth, foreign domiciliaries, UK and offshore trustees and non-resident individuals with links to the UK. Services include tax planning, estate and succession planning, asset structuring, UK and offshore trust information and advice, wills and trusts and estate administration and probates and intestacies valued at up to £50m. Family: The team's expertise ranges from pre-nuptial agreements and civil partnerships to divorce, children's arrangements and surrogacy law. Charity: Wilsons has one of the most highly ranked teams in the UK. We advise on the complete range of legal needs and have a particular specialism in contentious and non-contentious legacy work. The constitutional and governance team has considerable expertise in advising military charities and the charitable care sector. Agriculture: Wilsons' rural team has a practice centred on the needs of rural business and landowners. These include complex sales and purchases, development options for landowners, grants and diversification advice and property litigation, including landlord and tenant, partnership matters, boundary, title and rights of way disputes. Commercial: The commercial team specialises in employment, commercial property and corporate work. Corporate work focuses on commercial tax and asset planning, transactions and refinancing. Property: Our clients have substantial commercial, agricultural and residential property interests and the firm advises on purchasing, letting and sales. Litigation and dispute resolution: Wilsons has one of the largest teams outside London. We advise clients on a wide range of contentious matters to provide an efficient and effective means of dispute resolution. In addition to its expertise in agricultural and probate disputes, the firm has specialists who can advise on all aspects of commercial dispute claims and reputation management.

Who should apply We aim to employ the highest quality people; our reputation relies on this. We look for applicants with a 2.1 degree. We place considerable emphasis on teamwork and applicants must be able to demonstrate effective verbal and written communication skills.

Training programme The number of solicitors that have trained, qualified and remained with us is a testament to our trainee programme. If you show willingness and aptitude you will be given responsibility from an early stage.

When and how to apply The deadline for applications for a training contract is 30 June 2019 to commence a training contract in September 2021. Application forms can be obtained from our website.

Work placement Each year in June/July we run a work placement scheme in Salisbury for second-year law students or third-year non-law students onwards. There are five places available on our placement scheme. We make a contribution towards costs. The closing date for applications for a placement in 2019 is 31 March 2019.

Sponsorship We provide an interest-free loan of up to £4,500 for the LPC. Further details are available on application.

Vacancies	4
Trainees	8
Partners	31
Total staff	164
Work placement	yes
Training contract deadline	
30 June 2019	
Apply to	
Mrs Jo Ratcliffe	
Starting salary	
Above market rate	
Offices	
London, Salisbury	

Wilsons
Solicitors

Winckworth Sherwood

Minerva House, 5 Montague Close, London SE1 9BB
Tel: 020 7593 5000
Email: trainees@wslaw.co.uk
Web: www.traineehub.wslaw.co.uk
f winckworthsherwood **𝕏** ws_law

The firm Winckworth Sherwood LLP is a dynamic law firm providing a wide range of legal services to a diverse range of businesses, not-for-profit organisations and private individuals.

Types of work Corporate and commercial: We advise on corporate, mergers and acquisitions, partnerships and JVs, commercial arrangements, outsourcing and procurement, corporate finance and capital markets, funds and IP, IT contracts and data protection.
Employment and partnership: We provide contentious and non-contentious advice covering financial, insurance, retail, hotel, media, publishing, real estate and educational establishments. We also advise senior executives and on partnership disputes, as well as specialist non-contentious partnership advice.
Infrastructure projects: We specialise in private legislation promoting projects of major strategic importance. We also advise central and local government bodies, developers and operators on infrastructure planning, development, constructions, procurement, structuring and finance.
Not for profit: We advise a large number of educational and affordable housing operators, charitable and religious organisations and cultural and leisure service providers, delivering a full range of legal expertise.
Private wealth and tax: We advise high-net worth individuals, family offices, senior executives, private trustees and executors on a full range of private legal matters, including complex residential property solutions, tax and succession issues, pre-marital advice, divorce and family.
Real estate and planning: We work for some of the leading national residential and commercial developers, national house builders, investors and fund managers. This includes commercial real estate and regeneration, planning, development, corporate finance, funds, tax, construction, asset management and property litigation capability.

Who should apply We require a strong academic record both at school and university, but we also look for attributes which demonstrate the potential for making a positive contribution to the firm such as drive and enthusiasm, resilience, team working, excellent communications skills and an analytical and logical approach.

Training programme As a trainee you will rotate though four departments in six-month placements or seats. The purpose of each seat is to give you a solid grounding in that area of the law. We encourage substantial client contact from the start and you will be involved in all phases of a matter. As a trainee you will usually sit with a partner or senior solicitor and may be given the opportunity to manage your own files, subject to suitable supervision. We have a well developed in-house continuing educational programme. As well as legal training, we also provide business skills such as presentation skills, time management and networking.

When and how to apply Apply online at www.traineehub.wslaw.co.uk by 30 June 2019 for a 2021 training contract.

Work placements As part of the trainee recruitment process our summer placement programme runs every year for two weeks in July. Applications should be made online between November and February of each year. We also have a trainee open day in July (as an alternative to the work placement) for potential trainees which forms part of the interview process.

Sponsorship With some conditions, we provide financial assistance for course fees for trainees attending the Legal Practice Course.

Vacancies	8
Trainees	15
Partners	62
Total staff	344

Work placement   yes

Training contract deadline
30 June 2019

Apply
Online

Minimum qualifications
2.1 degree

Sponsorship
LPC

Offices
London, Oxford,
Manchester

Winston & Strawn London LLP

CityPoint, One Ropemaker Street, London EC2Y 9AW
Tel: 020 7011 8700
Email: trainingapplication@winston.com
Web: www.winston.com
🐦 winstonlaw

The firm For more than 160 years, Winston & Strawn LLP has served as a trusted adviser and advocate for clients across virtually every industry. In that time, the firm has built a law practice with tremendous breadth and global reach. We are proud of the many accolades we have received over the years – a tribute to our lawyers' creativity, flexibility, depth of experience, and commitment.

Winston's London office serves high-profile, multinational clients on a distinctly international level. When it comes to our employees, our goal is to maximise individual potential with professional development opportunities, emphasise the firm's culture, and contribute positively to the community. Winston has approximately 1,000 lawyers in a number of practice areas across 16 offices.

Types of work Winston's London office provides high-quality legal services in a diverse range of areas including cross-border corporate and finance, project and transportation finance, private equity and venture capital, litigation, international arbitration, contentious regulatory, and EU antitrust/competition services.

Who should apply We seek well-rounded, commercially aware, imaginative people with a genuine intellectual curiosity and with strong academics (including an expected or achieved first or upper second-class honours degree) who will work hard for our clients, interact well with others in a close-knit team, and make meaningful contributions to our continued growth and success in London, as well as globally. We seek ambitious individuals looking to build a long term career at the firm and want all of our trainees to stay with the firm upon qualification and continue to develop as associates with a view to ultimately become a partner.

Training programme Our trainees are asked to carry out real legal work from day one, interact directly with clients, and contribute to all aspects of firm life. Trainees have our full attention and support throughout their training contract and sit with a partner or a senior associate for each of the four seats.

When and how to apply To secure a training contract you should first apply for our summer vacation scheme. To apply for the 2019 summer vacation scheme (which normally takes place in July each year), please apply by CV and a covering letter. We will be accepting applications from 15 October 2018 to 15 January 2019. Please include a full classification and percentage breakdown of all academic results in your CV.

Work placements A two-week summer placement. Remuneration £400 per week.

Sponsorship Full sponsorship of GDL and LPC fees, plus a maintenance grant (not retrospective).

Vacancies	2
Trainees	5
Partners	14
Total staff	58
Work placement	yes

Apply
Online

Minimum qualifications
2.1 degree

Sponsorship
GDL/LPC

Offices
Brussels, Charlotte, Chicago, Dallas, Dubai, Hong Kong, Houston, London, Los Angeles, Moscow, New York, Paris, San Francisco, Shanghai, Silicon Valley, Washington DC

WINSTON
& STRAWN

WILLANS LLP 28 Imperial Square, Cheltenham GL50 1RH **Tel:** 01242 514000 **Email:** law@willans.co.uk **Apply to:** Ms Bridget Redmond	Practice dealing with a wide spectrum of commercial and private client work (not including criminal law) from town centre offices.	V 0 T - P 14 TS 70 WP no
WILSON & BIRD Ideal House, Exchange Street, Aylesbury HP20 1QY **Tel:** 01296 436766 **Apply to:** Mrs J Majek	High street mixed practice. Private client. Varied workload and experience.	V 1 T 0 P 1 TS 6 WP no
WILSON BROWNE SOLICITORS 4 Grange Park Court, Roman Way, Northampton NN4 5EA **Tel:** 01604 876697 **Email:** enquiries@wilsonbrowne.co.uk **Apply to:** Mr John Whitehouse	General practice with offices in Northamptonshire and Leicester offering a wide range of client services including company/ commercial, residential conveyancing, private client, civil litigation and family.	V 0 T 4 P 16 TS 118 WP no
WILSON SOLICITORS LLP 697 High Road, Tottenham, London N17 8AD **Tel:** 020 8808 7535 **Email:** info@wilsonllp.co.uk **Apply to:** Mr Matthew Davies	Large legal aid practice specialising in immigration law, public law, community care, and family law. We recruit caseworkers who progress to trainee solicitors.	V 5 T 15 P 12 TS 70 WP no
WILSONS SOLICITORS Ease House, 52 High Street, Oxford OX33 1 XT **Tel:** 01865 874 497 **Email:** info@wilsonssolicitors.co.uk **Apply to:** Mr Howard Wilson	We are a legal aid firm in civil and crime with an emphasis on advocacy.	V 2 T 2 P 1 TS 5 WP yes
WLL SOLICITORS Berkeley Square House, Berkeley Square, London W1J 6BD **Tel:** 020 7887 1959 **Email:** info@wllsolicitors.com **Apply to:** The Practice Manager	Niche litigation practice specialising in bankruptcy. Applicants must be highly motivated, relish a high level of responsibility, be team players, have initiative and a 2.1 degree, preferably in law.	V 2 T 1 P 1 TS 7 WP yes
WOMBLE BOND DICKINSON 4 More London Riverside, London SE1 2AU **Tel:** 0845 415 0000 **Email:** joanne.smallwood@bonddickinson.com **Apply to:** Joanne Smallwood	Womble Bond Dickinson, a UK Top 20 law firm, with over 420 partners and 1,000 lawyers based across 18 US cities and eight UK cities.	V Up to 25 T 56 P 123 TS 1200 WP yes
WOODFINES LLP 16 St Cuthberts Street, Bedford MK40 3JG **Tel:** 01234 270600 **Email:** kjobbling@woodfines.co.uk **Apply to:** Mrs Karen Jobbling	A dynamic and expanding regional practice offering a comprehensive range of legal services. We see recruitment and training as the core of our development plan.	V 3^{20} T 6 P 22 TS 140 WP yes

V = Vacancies / **T** = Trainees / **P** = Partners / **TS** = Total Staff / **WP** = Work Placement

Withers LLP

20 Old Bailey, London EC4M 7AN
Tel: 020 7597 6000
Email: recruitment@withersworldwide.com
Web: www.withersworldwide.com
f withersworld **𝕏** withersrecruits

Law *Careers.Net*
AWARDS 2018

BEST TRAINING PRINCIPAL

The firm Withers LLP is an international law firm dedicated to the business, personal and philanthropic interests of successful people, their families, their businesses and their advisers. Our mission is to offer a truly integrated legal service to people with sophisticated global wealth, management and business needs. The firm has been recognised for its great working environment having been consistently listed in *The Sunday Times* 100 Best Companies To Work For (2012-2016). In 2015 the firm won 'Best Training for vacation scheme and training contract' at the AllAboutLaw awards. Furthermore, the firm won LawCareers.Net's 'Best Training Principal' award in 2014, 2015, 2017 and 2018.

Types of work The wealth of today's high-net worth individuals has increased in multiples and many are institutions in their own right. Our global expertise ensures our ability to respond to these changing legal needs and offer integrated solutions to the international legal and tax needs of our clients. With 167 partners and over 1,000 people we have unparalleled expertise in commercial and tax law, trusts, estate planning, litigation, IP, charities, employment, reputation management, family law and other legal issues facing high-net worth individuals.

Withers' reputation in commercial law along with its status as the largest private client team in Europe sets it apart from other City firms. Work is often international due to the complexity of our client base which includes some of the wealthiest global citizens. We have acted for 51% of the UK *Sunday Times* 'Rich List' and a significant number from the US '*Forbes*' and Asian '*Hurun*' rich lists. Trainees who speak a relevant language may have the opportunity to complete a seat in one of our offices abroad.

Who should apply Each year we look for a diverse mix of trainees who are excited by the prospect of working with leaders in their field (who are often in the public eye as spokespersons for the profession). Trainees should have a high degree of determination, great attention to detail and be able to demonstrate business acumen and entrepreneurial flair.

Training programme Trainees spend six months in four different departments. Teams are small (files are typically handled by one senior fee earner and a trainee) so the client will know your name. Buddy and mentor systems as well as on the job training ensure trainees are fully supported from the outset.

When and how to apply Apply online by 31 July 2019 to begin training in September 2021. Interviews usually take place between May and August.

Work placements We run two-week placements at Easter and over the summer in London. Apply online by 31 January 2019 for places in 2019.

Sponsorship Fees plus £5,000 maintenance for both the GDL and LPC are paid.

Vacancies	11
Trainees	22
Partners	167
Total staff	1,100
Work placement	yes
(see Insider Report on p109)	

Training contract deadline
31 July 2019

Apply
Online

Starting salary
1st year – £38,000
2nd year – £40,000

Minimum qualifications
2.1 degree, AAB at A level

Sponsorship
GDL/LPC

Offices
London, Milan, Geneva, Padua, San Francisco, New York, New Haven (Connecticut), Greenwich (USA), Hong Kong, The British Virgin Islands (BVI), Singapore, Sydney, San Francisco, Rancho Santa Fe, Los Angeles, San Diego, Tokyo (Withers Japan, Zeirishi Houjin)

withersworldwide

Proud diversity and inclusion partner of

🎗 aspiringsolicitors

Remember to cite *The LawCareers.Net Handbook* on your application form if you apply to this firm.

WORTLEY BYERS LLP Cathedral Place, Brentwood CM14 4ES **Tel:** 01277 268368 **Email:** aelliss@wortleybyers.co.uk **Apply to:** Mrs Anne Elliss	Wortley Byers is based in Brentwood, Essex. Specialist areas include business law, taxation, employment and litigation, intellectual property law, insolvancy, commercial property and planning.	V 0 T 0 P 11 TS 60 WP no
WRIGHT HASSALL LLP Olympus Avenue, Leamington Spa CV34 6BF **Tel:** 01926 886688 **Email:** humanresources@wrighthassall.co.uk **Apply to:** Human Resources Team	A leading full service commercial law firm, the largest in Warwickshire, with all the services that you would expect from a City or global firm.	V 4 T 8 P 35 TS 280 WP yes
WRIGLEY CLAYDON 29-33 Union Street, Oldham OL1 1HH **Tel:** 0161 624 6811 **Email:** info@wrigleyclaydon.com **Apply to:** Mr John Mann	Medium general practice.	V 1 T 0 P 5 TS 26 WP no
WRIGLEYS SOLICITORS LLP 19 Cookridge Street, Leeds LS2 3AG **Tel:** 0113 244 6100 **Email:** sue.greaves@wrigleys.co.uk **Apply to:** Miss Sue Greaves	A specialist firm which concentrates on the financial affairs, property and assets of private individuals, charities, foundations, trustees and pension schemes.	V 2 T 4 P 27 TS 200 WP no
YORKLAW LTD T/AS BURN & COMPANY Ebor House, LondonEbor Business Park, Millfield Lane, Nether Poppleton, York YO26 6QY **Tel:** 01904 655442 **Email:** enquiries@burn-company.co.uk **Apply to:** Mr Michael Creamer		V 0 T 0 P 5 TS 20 WP no
ZYDA LAW 60 Cygnet Court, Timothy's Bridge Road, Stratford-upon-Avon CV37 9NW **Tel:** 01789 413 949 **Email:** secretary@zydalaw.com **Apply to:** Secretary	Recruiting one trainee solicitor for an award-winning, boutique planning and environmental law firm with expertise in energy and infrastructure development.	V 1 T 2 P 1 TS 5 WP yes

V = Vacancies / **T** = Trainees / **P** = Partners / **TS** = Total Staff / **WP** = Work Placement

Barristers

The Bar Council

The Bar Council represents barristers in England and Wales. It promotes the Bar's high-quality specialist advocacy and advisory services in support of fair access to justice for all; the highest standards of ethics, equality and diversity across the profession; and the development of business opportunities for barristers at home and abroad.

The Bar Council exists to act in the interests of the Bar on all matters relating to the profession and supports barristers from the beginning of their careers, through their development as a barrister and even after they draw their time at the Bar to a close.

As the overarching body giving a united voice to the barristers' profession, the Bar Council has been at the forefront of many campaigns to defend the rule of law, promote access to justice and give its backing to the legal services sector.

Barristers can turn to the Bar Council for help at any point in their careers and on a range of issues, whether that be on wellbeing, developing their practice, help on ethical or practice matters or to seek mentoring from other barristers to help make the next step in their careers.

It is also the Approved Regulator of the Bar of England and Wales, discharging its regulatory functions through the independent Bar Standards Board (BSB) (see page 475).

The profession
Barristers exists to serve the public. As specialist, independent advocates, barristers help people to uphold their legal rights and obligations, acting often on behalf of the most vulnerable members of society. The Bar makes a vital contribution to the efficient operation of criminal, family and civil courts. It provides a pool from which a significant proportion of judges are drawn, on whose independence the rule of law and our democratic way of life depend.

There are over 16,000 barristers in England and Wales, the majority of whom operate independently under the 'cab rank' rule, which requires barristers to accept work, otherwise known as instructions, in any field in which they practise on being offered a proper fee. This duty exists regardless of the barrister's views of the client or the case, which means barristers may have to take on a client or case despite their preference not to do so. The cab rank rule, which governs only barristers, is regarded as a fundamental element of the rule of law in this country. It accounts, at least in part, for the high regard in which the Bar of England and Wales is held both at home and abroad.

Many barristers are involved in pro bono work as members of the Bar Pro Bono Unit or the Free Representation Unit (see page 65).

Approximately 3,000 barristers are employed or in-house. Employed barristers practise in-house within a wide range of organisations and sectors, varying from business and government to social and health services.

Joining the barristers' profession
Contrary to public perception, the barristers' profession is not a career path reserved for the privileged few. The Bar Council is committed to fair access and meritocracy at the Bar, and encourages applications from all those with talent, irrespective of background to ensure that the Bar continues to become a more diverse and socially representative profession.

The Bar Council leads the way in making the barristers' profession open to those who have the skills and ability to pursue a career at the Bar and works closely with other organisations to ensure fair access to the Bar.

The award-winning Bar Placement Week, now in its 10th year, is one Bar Council initiative aimed at giving an insight into the profession for those talented sixth form students who have shown an interest in following a career path at the Bar. The scheme places students in chambers for a week to get a first-hand taste of what it means to be a barrister.

In 2018, the Bar Council launched the 'I am the Bar' social mobility campaign aimed at showing anyone considering entering the profession that people from all walks of life can make it at the Bar. Eleven social mobility advocates – barristers from non-traditional backgrounds – shared their often-difficult journeys to becoming barristers. The aim of the campaign is to inspire others to do the same.

The Bar Council is also the principal sponsor of the annual Young Citizens Bar Mock Trials competition. In its 26-year history, the competition has given over 50,000 state-educated students the opportunity to take part in mock trials held in real criminal courts and gain valuable coaching from real barristers and judges.

As well as attending law fairs at universities with a high proportion of students from non-traditional backgrounds, the Bar Council runs the Pupillage Fair. This recruitment event is the only one run by the Bar and is the largest in the country, with over 50 chambers and 700 students attending.

The Bar Council also runs the Bar e-mentoring scheme which pairs barristers with students who meet social mobility criteria and who are interested in joining the Bar.

Starting out
Students, pupils and junior barristers will be particularly interested in the work of the Bar Council's Young Barristers' Committee (YBC), which represents and promotes the interests of barristers of up to seven years in practice. The promotes and supports young barristers through a number of initiatives such as its annual workshop, the International

Weekend, the Young Bar Dinner, and its dedicated Young Bar Hub and Toolkit (https://youngbarhub.com/).

Beyond the YBC's activities, the Bar Council also operates the confidential Pupils' Helpline to support pupil barristers during the final step on their journey to the Bar.

Providing vital support to barristers on managing their wellbeing or dealing with mental health has been a major aspect of the Bar Council's work in recent years. That extends to pupils and students facing challenges on their career journey to the Bar. The Wellbeing at the Bar initiative and website, which is run by the Bar Council and backed by other organisations, now provides useful guides and resources for students. The whole Wellbeing at the Bar programme is designed to support barristers at all different stages in their careers, including those early years.

Career development
The Bar Council offers a wide range of training courses to support barristers throughout their careers, as well as mentoring services for barristers, such as for those seeking to become silks (Queen's Counsel) and those returning to work following a break for parental leave. The Bar Council also runs a variety of events and conferences to encourage continuing professional development throughout a barrister's career.

For 2018, the Bar Council has introduced a number of courses on 'soft skills', such as how to network for barristers. These modules are aimed at helping barristers grow their practice and learn skills which they may not have learned during their formal qualifications.

A regular Bar Council Training & Events newsletter is sent to all barristers every fortnight to enable the profession to keep abreast of new training opportunities.

International opportunities

The Bar Council promotes the Bar overseas and facilitates introductions and networking opportunities at a wide range of events. It has also sought to encourage and assist barristers, as well as chambers, to think of international work as increasingly important.

Always supporting barristers

Throughout a barrister's career, the Bar Council is there to provide support and services specifically for the Bar.

The Bar Council provides an Ethical Enquiries Service which includes a helpline and a website devoted solely to ethics and practice guides which help barristers meet their obligations in the regulator's (Bar Standards Board's) handbook, and provide best practice on a range of topics including IT, anti-money laundering and even how to deal with enquiries from the media. The Ethical Enquiries helpline provides confidential guidance on ethical problems that barristers may face in the course of their work and is managed by a specially trained team.

The Bar Council also operates a confidential Equality and Diversity Helpline, and the Pupils' Helpline advising barristers (including pupils), clerks and practice managers on regulatory and statutory equality duties, as well as on best practice.

As well as practice-focused support, the Bar Council provides access to a wide range of services such as accountancy, financial planning, insurance and healthcare, many of which are tailored to barristers' needs and often at a competitive rate. In addition, discounts on goods, including barristers' court attire, stationary and laptops, to name a few, are negotiated by the Bar Council with suppliers so that barristers can benefit from reduced prices. Students who pay the student Bar Representation Fee (BRF) of £24 per year can access these services. If you would like to pay the student BRF or talk to someone about the benefits, please contact our member services team on 020 7611 1329 or email: memberservices@barcouncil.org.uk

BarTalk

In addition to the information provided on the Bar Council's website (www.barcouncil.org.uk), the Bar Council provides regular updates about the work it is doing on behalf of the Bar through its fortnightly e-newsletter, BarTalk. To subscribe to BarTalk, email bartalk@barcouncil.org.uk.

Voice of the Bar

Without the Bar Council the barristers' profession's collective voice would not be heard in Whitehall, Westminster, the institutions of the European Union or on the international stage on issues affecting the Bar and the delivery of justice. It has led on major campaigns which go to the heart of the justice system in England and Wales, as well as in other jurisdictions, such as protecting the independence of the judiciary, challenging the introduction of increases in court and employment tribunal fees, cuts to legal aid and international human rights and rule of law violations.

More information

For more information on a career at the Bar, please visit: www.barcouncil.org.uk/careers. If you have any further questions you can email careers@barcouncil.org.uk.

Follow the Bar Council

Twitter: @TheBarCouncil
Facebook: @TheBarCouncil
Linkedin: General Council of the Bar of England and Wales
Youtube: The Bar Council of England and Wales
Instagram: TheBarCouncil
Website: www.barcouncil.org.uk

This information is supplied by the Bar Council.

The Bar Standards Board

The Bar Standards Board (BSB) regulates barristers and specialised legal services businesses in England and Wales in the public interest. It is responsible for:

- setting the education and training requirements for becoming a barrister;
- setting continuing training requirements to ensure that barristers' skills are maintained throughout their careers;
- setting standards of conduct for barristers;
- authorising organisations that focus on advocacy, litigation and specialist legal advice;
- monitoring the service provided by barristers and the organisations it authorises to assure quality; and
- handling complaints against barristers and the organisations that it authorises, and taking disciplinary or other action where appropriate.

Training to become a barrister is changing
We are working to change the training and qualification process to become a barrister in England and Wales. In this article we describe the current process of qualification as well as providing more information about how the process is likely to change.

The current system for qualifying as a barrister in England and Wales
In this section, we explain the current education and training system for barristers in England and Wales.

The Professional Statement for Barristers (www.barstandardsboard.org.uk/media/1787559/bsb_professional_statement_and_competences_2016.pdf) describes the knowledge, skills and attributes that all barristers should have on their first day of practice.

The BSB sets the education and training requirements that must be completed to qualify as a barrister, as well as the process of transferring to the Bar from practice abroad or as a solicitor practising in England and Wales.

The three components of training are termed academic, vocational and work-based learning.

The academic component
Either an undergraduate law degree (2.2 minimum) or an undergraduate degree in another subject (2.2 minimum) and a conversion course commonly known as the Graduate Diploma in Law (GDL). To satisfy the academic component, the law degree or conversion course must contain the seven foundations of legal knowledge subjects.

The vocational component
The Bar Professional Training Course (BPTC), which can be completed full time over one year, or part time over two. One of the requirements for entry to the BPTC is a pass on the Bar Course Aptitude Test (BCAT). The BCAT tests students' critical thinking skills and the result of the test gives an indication of the likelihood of success on the BPTC.

Another requirement for entry to the BPTC is joining one of the four Inns of Court. Students must undertake qualifying sessions, provided by the Inns, in order to be called to the Bar by their Inn on successful completion of the BPTC.

The work-based learning component
This is commonly known as pupillage and is the final component in qualifying for practice at the Bar, during which practical training under the supervision of an experienced barrister is gained. It is a one-year training period (or part-time equivalent) spent in an approved training organisation (ie, either barristers' chambers or another approved legal environment). It is divided into two parts: a non-practising six months (known as the 'first six') and six months in which the pupil can offer reserved legal services with provisional authorisation (known as the 'second six').

Pupillage providers must advertise all pupillage vacancies on www. pupillagegateway.com, which is a service provided by the Bar Council. The Pupillage Gateway offers a common timetable for the application process. Through a financial award or earnings, all pupils must receive no less than £1,000 per month from their training organisation, plus reasonable travel expenses where applicable.

More information on the three current components of qualification is available at: www.barstandardsboard.org.uk/qualifying-as-a-barrister/current-requirements.

How the system is set to change

Future Bar Training (FBT) is our programme of regulatory change focusing on education and training for the Bar. We are aiming to make it more flexible, more accessible and more affordable, while at the same time sustaining the high standards expected of everyone who becomes a practising barrister. The earliest that some of the changes might start is 2019, so you should keep an eye on our FBT webpages for up-to-date information about the changes and their precise timing.

The BSB has decided that it will authorise a limited number of future training routes for students to qualify as barristers. The future system for training for the Bar will retain the three components of training within the current system: academic, vocational and work-based learning.

To satisfy the academic component, a candidate's law degree or conversion course must contain the seven foundations of legal knowledge subjects.

There are more significant changes planned for the vocational and work-based learning components. In particular, by changing our rules to allow a limited number of new training routes

to be authorised it may be possible to undertake each component of training in new and more flexible ways as opposed to having to complete them in the strict sequence required under the current rules. We have also completed a Curriculum and Assessments Review that will lead to a number of significant changes being made to the way in which prospective barristers are taught and assessed in future.

The BSB has also agreed that the Inns of Court will continue to hold an essential role in the training and qualification of barristers and that student membership of an Inn and a minimum number of qualifying sessions will remain. A number of changes are being made to the rules governing pupillage or other forms of work-based learning in relation to its length, supervision arrangements and increasing the minimum award paid to pupils.

One of the priorities of the FBT programme is to ensure that nobody is disadvantaged as a result of any changes made to how barristers will qualify either now or in the future. The BSB is committed to making sure that there is a robust transition process. For the immediate future, the current BPTC will remain.

To read more about the FBT programme, visit http://bit.ly/2MaPEKd.

To read the policy decisions that the BSB released about Future Bar Training in 2018, please visit www.barstandardsboard.org.uk/media-centre/press-releases-and-news/bsb-agrees-further-key-elements-for-the-future-of-bar-training/ and www.barstandardsboard.org.uk/media-centre/press-releases-and-news/bsb-agrees-approach-on-the-role-of-the-inns-of-court-in-the-future-of-bar-training/.

To stay up to date with changes and the FBT programme, follow the BSB on Twitter @barstandards.

The Young Barristers' Committee

The Young Barristers' Committee (YBC) is part of the Bar Council of England & Wales, representing barristers in all areas of practice who are in their first seven years at the Bar.

Its main terms of reference are to advise the representative committees of the Bar Council on all matters of concern to young barristers; to liaise with the BSB on such matters as necessary; and to take such steps as seem likely to promote the interests of the Young Bar, having regard to the interests of the Bar as a whole.

In fact, the YBC was established in 1954, and although it started as an "experiment for a period of one year in the first instance", it continues to flourish as one of the Bar Council's principal representative committees. The breadth of the work that it covers is surpassed only by the Bar Council itself, and it counts among its former chairs the current Master of the Rolls, Sir Terence Etherton, Lord Justice McCombe, Mr Justice Lavender, and the Recorder of London, HHJ Hilliard QC.

What do we do?

The aim of the YBC is to represent the Young Bar and ensure its voice is heard, and to ensure that adequate support and provision is made for young barristers. We do this through making representations both internally in the Bar Council, and externally, to; government, the judiciary, the Bar Standards Board (BSB), the Inns of Court and others involved in training and regulating barristers, and those with whom barristers may interact in their working lives. This work includes responding to consultation papers that are issued by various organisations, attending meetings and providing the invaluable perspective of the Young Bar, and putting on or assisting with events which often feature young barristers. Some of our members are elected, while others are co-opted to ensure that our membership is diverse and includes representatives from each of the circuits and from all areas of practice.

Young Bar Hub and social media

The main source of information for young barristers, provided by the YBC, is the Young Bar Hub at www.youngbarhub.com. The site contains the Young Bar Toolkit: an online information resource with advice and guidance on practice management, finances and wellbeing. There is information for self-employed and employed barristers, and pupils. The site also features the Young Bar Blog, which includes a 'day in the life' series, with snapshots of the experiences and 'typical days' of members or former members of the committee. There are also articles and information about forthcoming events and activities that the YBC is hosting or supporting.

We have a dedicated Twitter account (@YoungBarristers) to ensure that up-to-date information on training, events and other issues of interest to young barristers is available and easily accessible.

Court reform and technology

The YBC has been heavily involved in the Bar Council's work on court reform for several years. This includes the 'online court' proposed in Lord Justice Briggs' Review of the Civil Courts and Lord Justice Jackson's proposals for fixed recoverable costs in certain civil claims. The YBC has contributed to Bar Council responses to the relevant consultations and attended meetings at the Ministry of Justice and with the senior judiciary in order to ensure that the Young Bar's perspective is taken into account. We have made clear the potential issues concerning access to justice, open justice and the right to a fair trial arising out of such proposals, as well as highlighting the potential adverse effects on young barristers.

In connection with the above, this year has also seen a renewed focus on both the positive and potentially negative aspects of technology on barristers' professional lives, including the link to our work on wellbeing. YBC have also investigated some of the Legal Tech opportunities which might be of interest to the Bar.

Remuneration

The cuts to legal aid brought in by the Legal Aid, Sentencing and Punishment of Offenders Act 2012 (LASPO) reduced the availability of public funding for almost all civil and family work. The impact of the act, plus past increases to court fees in the civil courts and the employment tribunal, has disproportionately affected the work available to those at the junior end of the Bar. There has also been an increase in the number of paid "McKenzie Friends", particularly in the family courts. The YBC has previously contributed towards the Bar Council's policy work in highlighting these issues, and responding to the judicial consultation on paid McKenzie Friends.

Remuneration for criminal work is also an area that continues to receive intense focus. The YBC's work is ongoing work with regard to reducing delays in payment and non-payment for appearances in the magistrates' courts, and has been involved in discussions surrounding the revised Advocates Graduated Fee Scheme for defence remuneration in the Crown Court, as well as the need for additional investment in the criminal justice system.

Education and training

The YBC's work on education and training has principally involved responding to consultations sent out by the BSB in relation to Future Training for the Bar, forming part of a working group alongside the Bar Council's Education and Training Committee. The YBC has been a strong supporter of the Bar Council and Inns of Court proposals to introduce a two-part BPTC, which will aim to reduce costs and improve standards, and it is hoped that the Inns will soon be authorised to deliver such a course.

Responding to concerns that stereotypes about the Bar are off-putting to potential applicants from non-traditional backgrounds, the YBC is currently involved in supporting the Bar Council's new 'I am the Bar' campaign, which aims to highlight examples of social mobility and different paths into the profession. Several YBC members are 'social mobility advocates' who have had their stories featured, and Twitter engagement around this issue is also high.

The YBC is also involved in Bar Placement Week, which is now celebrating its 10th anniversary, where 60 students from around the country come to London to experience a week of working with barristers, and receive advocacy training and talks from those in practice.

Wellbeing at the Bar

The YBC has continued to be closely involved with the Bar Council's Wellbeing at the Bar Working Group, which has developed a series of online resources to help barristers manage their wellbeing; support others in chambers; and provide guidance and assistance to those supporting someone in difficulties. The Wellbeing at the Bar website (www.wellbeingatthebar.org.uk/) is a fantastic resource on such matters and a student section will be added soon. There are also dedicated pages on wellbeing in the Young Bar Toolkit.

Young Bar Annual Workshop

This year the YBC held its third annual workshop, entitled 'The 21st Century advocate'. The workshop was designed to focus on practical assistance with life at the modern Bar, looking at areas such as marketing, wellbeing and Legal Tech, alongside more traditional training in advocacy and practice development issues in each of criminal, civil and family practice. Our keynote speaker was the Vice Chair of the Bar, Richard Atkins QC. There was also a plenary session entitled 'Justice in the 21st Century' which featured The Secret Barrister, Penelope Gibbs (Transform Justice), John van der Luit-Drummond (*Legal 500*), Dana Denis-Smith (First 100 Years) and Robert Buckland QC MP (solicitor general for England & Wales). You can see our review of the day here: https://youngbarhub. com/2018/04/24/21st-century-advocate/.

Annual Bar and Young Bar Conference
On Saturday 24 November, for the fourth year running the Young Bar Conference will take place alongside the Bar's Annual Conference. This allows young barristers to get the best of both worlds: sessions that are 'badged' as having a Young Bar focus, in addition to the main keynote addresses and sessions, as well as a chance to meet other barristers from all parts of the profession across all seniorities. The theme for this year's conference is 'All Bar None: Access, Development & Diversification'. Keynote speakers include Lord Sumption (UK Supreme Court), Jeremy Wright QC MP (attorney general for England & Wales) and Baroness Chakrabarti (shadow attorney General). The Young Bar Keynote Speaker is Leslie Thomas QC (co-head, Garden Court Chambers) and this will be followed by an open forum with a Q&A of the leaders of the profession. See the Bar Council website for more details. Pupils and students are welcome to attend, and can do so at a heavily reduced rate: https://thebarcouncil. sym-online.com/registrationforms/ abc2017251712590925911/done/.

International work
Building on the YBC's previous international work, we have continued to be involved with the European Young Bar Association and have maintained contacts with the American Bar Association's Young Lawyers Division, the International Bar Association and the International Association of Young Lawyers.

This includes co-hosting International Weekend in September and welcoming young lawyers from Europe, the US and across the globe to London for a series of networking and educational events. This year also sees the incoming leg of the biennial Anglo Dutch Exchange, which is now over 50 years old and features a week of legal and social activities for our Dutch colleagues. The YBC also administers the Bar Council's International Grant programme, which provides financial support for young barristers in any area of law who wish to attend an international event relevant to their practice.

Contact us
If there is anything on which you would like further guidance or support, please do have a look at www.youngbarhub.com, follow us on Twitter (@YoungBarristers) or contact our policy analyst, Onyeka Onyekwelu, on 020 7611 1323 or at YBC@barcouncil.org.uk.

Richard Hoyle is the chair of the YBC for 2018 and a barrister at Essex Court Chambers. You can follow him on Twitter: @barrickster.

Becoming a barrister

Barristers provide a specialist service in litigation and advocacy, and undertake advisory work. They prepare and present cases for trial, taking on a wide range of cases and clients (but often specialising in one practice area). Barristers also provide an independent advisory service on legal disputes or problems. Most legislation can be interpreted in numerous ways and barristers advise on how it may pertain to a particular case.

Generally, barristers work in private practice and are self-employed. However, they do not operate entirely in isolation: most of them pool their resources to form a 'set' of chambers, which enables them to share many of the costs involved in running a business. Each member of a set is known as a 'tenant' and has a say in the way in which the set is organised.

Pupillage
Pupillage is essentially an apprenticeship whereby pupils observe a set at work and then practise under supervision. It is the final stage of training to be a barrister, where you put into practice everything you have learnt so far. Although you will be 'called to the Bar' on passing the Bar Professional Training Course (BPTC), pupillage is essential for all those wishing to go into practice.

Structure
Pupillage usually takes a year to complete, with the year divided into two six-month periods known as 'sixes'. Each six is spent in a set of chambers (although a small number of places are available in companies and other institutions), under the guidance and supervision of a 'pupil supervisor' – a junior barrister of at least five years' experience. It is not unheard of for each six to be spent in different chambers and/or with a different pupil supervisor.

Content
To qualify as a barrister, pupils are required by the Bar Council to obtain sufficient practical experience of advocacy, conferences and negotiation, as well as legal research and the preparation of drafts and opinions.

The first six is spent shadowing and assisting the pupil supervisor. This involves attending court and case conferences, undertaking research, doing background reading and drafting documents. Thus, a pupil gains insight into how a case is prepared and argued, how a competent practitioner responds to developments as they occur and how pre-arranged tactics can be changed.

The second six sees a pupil take his or her first steps as a professional practitioner. Pupils are permitted to undertake their own cases for clients, under supervision. Inevitably, much of this work involves straightforward cases, but there is always the chance that an important or groundbreaking case may arise.

How to apply
The online application system for pupillages is the Pupillage Gateway (www.pupillagegateway.com).. Most chambers are part of the centralised system (Pupillage Gateway providers), but some are not (non-Pupillage Gateway providers). Available pupillages at both types of chambers are listed on the system, but non-members will have varying deadlines and methods of application, and you will have to check chambers' individual websites for details.

The Pupillage Gateway opens for applications in January and closes in February. First and second round interview offers are sent out, and interviews conducted, throughout February, March and April. Offers are then made through the Gateway in early May. This timing should ensure that candidates will know whether they have secured pupillage before deciding to pay the expensive fees to enrol on the BPTC.

As a rule of thumb, you should apply for pupillage at least a year before you wish to start – that is, in January 2019 for a pupillage beginning in 2020. You can apply to up to 12 Gateway chambers (but as many non-Gateway chambers as you like). There is no longer a clearing function.

Tenancy

On satisfactory completion of pupillage, a pupil will ideally be offered a tenancy at the set in which he or she has trained. However, a quick comparison of the figures concerning the ratio of pupillages to tenancies reveals that this does not necessarily happen. Inevitably, chambers cannot expand indefinitely and sometimes even the most gifted pupil is turned away. In such cases, pupils must work hard to secure a tenancy by any means possible (eg, by undertaking a third or even fourth six or, as a last resort, becoming a 'squatter' (a non-member who uses a set as a base)).

Career timetable: barristers

First-year law and second-year non-law students

The key to this year is thinking ahead. Focus on getting top grades, do your homework on the Bar and get involved in activities that will look good on your CV (mooting and debating are essential, but examples such as Duke of Edinburgh awards or captaining a sports team are also great).

Research and apply for work experience (be it a mini-pupillage or a non-formal placement) in chambers for your summer holiday. Try to arrange a few stints in different chambers to get an overview of the various work areas, unless you are unusually keen to specialise in one particular work area. For an alternative way to pick up much-needed experience, see our "Free Representation Unit" section. Remember that without work experience, any application for pupillage is unlikely to be taken seriously. Work experience will not only give you a stronger CV, but should also help you to decide whether the Bar really is for you.

Join one of the four Inns of Court, which are non-academic societies that provide activities and support for barristers, pupils and students. You must join an Inn before 31 May of the year in which you intend to commence the Bar Professional Training Course (BPTC), but it is a case of the earlier, the better in terms of getting involved with the activities and using the facilities (eg, library and common rooms).

Second-year law and final-year non-law students

Autumn term, winter holidays and spring term

Attend relevant careers events, including careers fairs, presentations and talks, and pupillage fairs. Look into funding possibilities for postgraduate training (eg, local education authority grants and inn scholarships). Keep applying for mini-pupillages.

Non-law degree students will need to apply for a place on the conversion course, known as the Graduate Diploma in Law or GDL. If you intend to study full time, you should apply through the Central Applications Board (www.lawcabs.ac.uk) from September onwards in your final year at university. There is not a closing date for applications; rather, applications are dealt with as they are submitted and institutions are notified weekly of new submissions. Applications for part-time courses must be made directly to the provider.

Summer holidays

Find out about pupillage applications. Look at the different BPTC providers and check their application details. Gain further work experience.

Final-year law and GDL students

Autumn term

Hot on the heels of your mini-pupillages, start making applications for pupillage. Finalise your funding options and be clear about the closing dates for funding applications. For more on funding, see "Financing the vocational courses".

The BPTC is a highly expensive course which does not open up any other career options than the Bar itself, so it is sensible to secure pupillage before deciding to enrol. The centralised BPTC application system – the Bar Student Application Service – usually opens in early December and stays open until the start of the academic year the following September. Find out more and apply at www.barsas.com.

Spring term

Attend pupillage fairs, including the Bar Council's Pupillage Fair on 27 October 2018 and the National Pupillage Fair on 1 December 2018.

Applications for pupillage are made through the centralised Pupillage Gateway (www.

pupillagegateway.com). Most chambers are part of the centralised system (Pupillage Gateway providers), but some are not (non-Pupillage Gateway providers). Available pupillages at both types of chambers are listed on the system, but non-members will have varying deadlines and methods of application, and you will have to check chambers' individual websites for details.

The Pupillage Gateway opens for applications in January and stays open for about a month. As a rule of thumb, you should apply for pupillage at least a year before you wish to start – that is, in January 2019 for a pupillage beginning in 2020. You can apply to up to 12 portal chambers (and as many non-portal chambers as you like). For more on how to apply, see "Becoming a barrister".

Summer term
Pupillage offers via the centralised system will be made in early May. If necessary, obtain a 'certificate of academic standing' from the Bar Standards Board (BSB).

BPTC
If you were unsuccessful in your pupillage applications last year, apply again this year, in the same way as above.

Once you have successfully completed the BPTC, you will have to undertake 12 qualifying sessions (previously known as 'dining') before being called to the Bar by your inn.

Pupillage
Pupillage is one year spent in an authorised training organisation (either a barristers' chambers or another approved legal environment), usually split into two six-month periods referred to as 'sixes'.

First six
Without practising, you will observe and assist your pupil supervisor and other barristers in chambers. The intention is that you share your supervisor's daily professional life.

Second six
During these six months, you will be entitled to supply legal services and exercise rights of audience as a barrister. You may have cases and your own clients, which you will represent in court. This is when you start to build up your reputation as a barrister. At the end of the second six, you must submit a certificate to the BSB certifying that the second six has been satisfactorily completed. Provided that certain training conditions are met, you will be granted a full qualification certificate. Congratulations – you're a barrister!

Clerks

Budding barristers: take heed! Clerks are the people who can make or break your career, furnish you with work or leave you twiddling your thumbs. You need them on your side. They wield formidable power and are an important source of knowledge and support.

The barrister-clerk relationship is as old as the profession itself and is an integral part of the whole process. Broadly speaking, the job of a clerk is to run the day-to-day business of chambers and organise barristers' caseloads. At the junior end of the job, a clerk will prepare papers, carry documents to and from court and perform other administrative tasks. As a clerk becomes more senior, he or she will manage diaries, liaise between solicitors, clients and barristers, and bring business into the chambers.

Declan Redmond is CEO/director of clerking at Keating Chambers, joining them in 2014. Previously, he was senior clerk and chief executive at Wilberforce Chambers. He has held many senior positions in the Institute of Barristers' Clerks (IBC), including chairman from 2005 to 2008, and currently serves as one of the body's vice presidents. With these credentials, it makes sense to listen to what he has to say.

Declan was encouraged to become a clerk by the husband of his college student liaison officer, who was himself a clerk. Declan joined Wilberforce in 1982 and stayed there for 31 years, becoming first junior in 1992, then deputy senior clerk in 1996, senior clerk and chief executive in 1998. Now at Keating, he has risen to the position of CEO and director of clerking.

Declan outlines what his role entails: "These days, I do much more strategic work, which means that I develop and implement business plans that have been agreed with members of chambers. Operations-wise, I have overall responsibility for all the clerks and administration staff (including the finance and administration manager, marketing manager, receptionist and housekeepers). Importantly, I also manage client relationships, which involves a lot of marketing. There is no typical day, which I really like. There are so many different things that can happen – if an important injunction comes in, it can change the way you work during that day. One phone call can change everything. But it's that variety which keeps you going."

The IBC was set up to protect clerks within the profession and to facilitate the exchange of views. Declan says: "It allows us all to get together and find out what's happening in the different sections of the Bar (eg, criminal and chancery). In addition, the Bar Council needs to know what the clerks are thinking, so representatives are often invited to join Bar Council committees." The IBC is also concerned with the education and professional development of its members – it has been involved in developing both the BTEC Advanced Award in Chambers Administration for junior clerks and the two-year ILM Level 5 Diploma in Leadership and Management for more senior clerks.

In terms of clerking, Declan has one very clear message for wannabe barristers: "As clerks, we build the practice of a new tenant up from nothing, calling on our own contacts and those of chambers that have built up over the years. Managing client relations is key to the job – the way that a clerk answers the phone, offering a quality service to solicitors and professional clients alike, is vital. If it all works in tandem and you've got a good clerks team with a good reputation, that will bring work in. We go out to solicitors' offices (even as far as the Cayman Islands, sometimes!) – particularly so when we have a new tenant starting. That person has no contacts, so we go out and talk about the junior end of chambers. We're basically saying, 'Look, this wonderful new person has started,' and asking the solicitor to trust us to recommend the right person for the job. Of course, you hope that after a short while, the new tenant will build his or her own practice. It's always a bit annoying if you've made an introduction and then you don't hear from that client again – that's when you have to start asking questions!"

And it's not just introductions to clients – the clerks also act as a bridge between new tenants and QCs: "Although senior members of chambers may know you as a pupil, they don't really know how good you are when you start. We provide that link. If a QC wants a junior brought in, they will trust the clerk's judgement to suggest the right person." Clerks also negotiate client fees, with senior clerks dealing with the more complicated trials, "although we will bring junior clerks in early to help negotiate, as there's nothing like experience".

Declan kindly explains the oft-mentioned 'cab rank rule': "When you go to get a cab from a taxi rank, provided that certain conditions are met (ie, you are going to pay and the destination is agreed on), that cab has to take you. In the world of barristers, if a solicitor phones up and asks for a particular barrister, and that person is available and certain conditions are met (eg, the pay is adequate and the specialism matches), then the barrister should take the case."

One feature of the job that Declan particularly enjoys is guiding someone's career from the very beginning: "You are dealing with over 60 barristers who are all specialists, all highly intelligent, all highly trained, and your job is to help them go from being an unknown to being the top QC in the country (hopefully!). That is the goal as a clerk – you start with a promising pupil, take them as a new tenant, grow them into a QC and, ultimately, maybe get them to the bench. You have nearly as much invested in their career progression as the barrister. Clerks are very much part of the organisation; there's no sense of 'us and them' any more (or there shouldn't be!). It's gone from being something of a gentlemen's club to a fully fledged professional business now."

Declan has some final advice for pupils and new tenants: "Seek the advice of the clerks. We are always happy to help. For example, we hold a lunch for the mini-pupils and keep in touch with pupils before and during pupillage. Once a person is a tenant, we have regular six-monthly reviews to discuss how things are going. Fantastic academics are not everything; if you don't know how to talk to clients or can't deal with staff, you're not going to succeed. A senior clerk will have seen 30 or 40 people come through chambers and will have a wealth of knowledge to share. Don't forget – they are the people who will be running your business for the next 20 to 30 years."

Types of chambers

There are many different kinds of chambers and where you train has a significant influence on your career, as the style, size and clientele of each will vary. Consider the following broad categories to establish which type of set might best match your career goals and working style.

Central London
Commercial sets
Just as the solicitors' profession has a 'magic circle' of law firms, so too does London's commercial Bar. While the precise composition of this elite group may be up for debate, Brick Court Chambers, Essex Court Chambers, One Essex Court, Fountain Court and Blackstone Chambers would all qualify for inclusion. What is beyond doubt is that there are many highly successful barristers' chambers in Central London - a large proportion of them concentrated in and around the four Inns of Court.

Barristers tend to be very familiar with their peers and rivals, as they regularly compete with them for work or square off across the courtroom. Even within a specialist area, sets will have a particular reputation, or their size and style will mark them out from others. A good example is construction law, which has two acknowledged frontrunners: Keating Chambers and Atkin Chambers. Keating is bigger and probably acts for construction companies more often in disputes. Atkin is smaller; its reputation is more closely associated with representing parties in dispute with construction companies, and some suggest that it has more of an academic bent than Keating. As you get closer to making a decision about your pupillage applications, insight like this becomes important.

There are multiple areas of specialisation, even within the commercial Bar itself: commercial contract disputes, banking and finance, shipping and international trade, tax, intellectual property, professional negligence... the list goes on. Some of the top commercial sets pay pupils handsomely (a few of them up to £60,000) and usually allow some funds to be accessed during law school. Your academic and other credentials will need to be impeccable to pass muster here: look at the biographies of junior members of a set for guidance on what its recruiters are looking for.

For a profile of a barrister who is part of a commercial set, see Adam Smith of Maitland Chambers in the "Property" chapter, p528.

Public law sets
Public law can take many forms, from conflicts over EU legislation to planning appeals, from individuals' entitlement to community care to international extradition. While the same is also true of the commercial Bar, it sometimes surprises pupils how little time they spend in court compared to their peers in common law or crime sets. Check each set's website to see what its pupillage programme entails and the size of the pupillage award; the best will match the awards of the top commercial sets.

For a profile of a barrister who is part of a public law set, see Jennifer Macleod of Brick Court Chambers in the "Public" chapter, p530.

Common law sets
If you are seeking a wide-ranging pupillage with ample court time and a chance to earn your own fees during the second six, then the common law Bar will suit you well. You can cut your advocacy teeth on simple 'infant settlements' (approving a compensation award to a minor); 'winders' (securing a winding-up order in an insolvency case); charging orders and fast-track personal injury claims. Personal injury is a staple at common law sets, but beyond this you will be exposed to a multitude of legal problems, including some small commercial disputes. Confidence, flexibility and an all-zone Oyster card are essential. Your schedule will become unpredictable and you must be ready at all

times to charm and impress the instructing solicitors who send you work during the early years of your career. Pupillage awards vary hugely; however, the very top players will match those paid by commercial sets.

For a profile of a barrister who is part of a common law set, see Muhammed Haque of Crown Office Chambers in the "Common law" chapter, p498.

Crime sets

Motoring offences, juvenile misdemeanours, gruesome murders, child abuse, terrorism, white-collar fraud, regulatory breaches – London's crime sets handle just about every kind of violation you might imagine. Check on the orientation and reputation of the sets you are hoping to apply to, and look at the biographies of juniors and seniors. You may spot an emphasis on defence or a focus on a particular type of crime. Some, for example, specialise in terrorism and extradition; others are boosting their regulatory practices, perhaps in specific sectors such as sport, professional discipline or health and safety. Pupillage involves a baptism of fire, early advocacy and court visits across the capital and beyond. Those motivated primarily by money should look elsewhere.

Regional Bar: supersets and beyond

According to Bar Council statistics, just over half of all chambers in England and Wales are located outside London, and just over one-third of all barristers in private practice work from within them. The main concentrations are in larger cities such as Birmingham, Manchester, Bristol, Leeds and Liverpool. Speak to any regional barrister and they will extol the virtues of a tight-knit professional community in which barristers know not only instructing solicitors, but also medical professionals, social workers and senior police officers. All shades of legal practice can be found in the regions, although sets and individual barristers are less likely to specialise to quite the same degree as in the capital. You may earn less in the regions; however, factor in the cost of living and a regional pupillage could make financial sense. Pupillage awards range from £12,000 to £30,000.

The Birmingham Bar is home to the barrister superset. Here, two chambers in particular – No5 and St Philips – have reshaped the market by drawing together barristers from many of the smaller sets. No5, with more than 250 barristers, also has 'annexes' in London and Bristol.

Public sector pupillages

Both the Crown Prosecution Service (CPS) and the Government Legal Service (GLS) offer pupillages leading to permanent roles with fixed salaries, holiday and sickness pay, pensions and all the usual employment protection rights. The CPS has lately tried to keep more of its prosecution advocacy in-house, as opposed to sending briefs to barristers in local chambers. Meanwhile, the GLS offers a rich training programme shared with solicitor hopefuls and a remarkably interesting career path that takes its lawyers from one government department to another over the course of a single career. The GLS is highly recommended for those who love politics, law and the idea of becoming a civil servant as well as an officer of the court.

Reality check: Competition for pupillage is fierce, so over and above getting exemplary grades, you need to show a commitment to joining the Bar. Mooting at university and doing mini-pupillages at chambers which interest you is a great way to demonstrate that you're keen as well as learning more about the different types of atmosphere in different sets.

LawCareers.Net ™

INFORMATION • JOBS • EVENTS

EVERYTHING YOU NEED TO BECOME A LAWYER

Launching a career in law requires high-quality information.

The LawCareers.Net website and Handbook are comprehensive, independent and authoritative resources.

They provide information, advice, news and features, and offer the only comprehensive list of graduate opportunities in law, including over 5,000 training contracts and 390 pupillages.

Sign up to *LawCareers.Net* ™

Bar practice areas

Admiralty and shipping

Shipping law is one of the oldest and most developed branches of commercial law. It falls into two areas: 'dry' shipping involves contractual issues, such as bill of lading and charterparty disputes, whereas 'wet' shipping involves disputes over the ship itself (eg, collision and salvage). Although the shipping industry is by its nature international, London remains the pre-eminent venue for dispute resolution.

Robert Thomas QC gained experience of both the solicitors' and barristers' professions through various placements and mini-pupillages, before deciding which to pursue. "What ultimately attracted me to the Bar was advocacy – the chance to argue on my feet and make decisions," he explains. "I was also drawn by the independence that comes with the role."

After graduating from the University of Cambridge, Robert completed pupillage at what was then known as 2 Essex Court – now Quadrant Chambers. Still at Quadrant and a home-grown QC, Robert has developed a thriving practice in which shipping law forms an important part: "Traditionally, commercial work was always shipping, insurance and commodities, and those three elements – the international sale, transport and insuring of goods – are still a mainstay of much commercial work at the Bar, although there are so many more aspects to take into account these days. Quadrant has been preeminent in those areas for as long as I can remember, and like all junior barristers starting out, expertise and access to the set's client base was passed down to me by my senior colleagues. As I think most barristers will tell you, there is always a degree of chance in how your practice develops, as much depends firstly on the chambers you join and then which clients you really get on with, and who uses you again. I'm lucky enough to be instructed by several mainstream, high-quality firms who choose to come back to me."

'Wet work'

Many different types of case fall under the shipping umbrella. "The variety is huge," says Robert. "You get everything from 'wet work' – which in shipping means work related to collisions and salvage, and now makes up just a very small part of maritime cases – to disputes about damaged cargo; contractual disputes arising out of charterparty agreements for the hiring of ships; and cases resulting from piracy. For an example of the latter, I'm currently working on a case in which a vessel was hijacked and later released by pirates, which has created very interesting legal consequences."

Disputes in the offshore oil and gas industry also come under Robert's shipping portfolio. And if the variety within this area still does not seem enough, high-end cases can extend far beyond shipping matters. "A good example of that diversity is a long-running case that I was involved in a couple of years ago, in which the main issues were of much wider importance and had very little to do with shipping at all," explains Robert. "We were trying to lift the corporate veil – to get behind the corporate structure of a shipping company to the person pulling the strings behind the scenes. The case involved a former Soviet republic and the layers that an individual had put in place to shield himself from the limelight while making a lot of money. Another case, *Prest v Petrodel*, went to the Supreme Court raising the same issues and just got in front of us in the queue, so unfortunately we did not have the chance to fight our corner in court – and the Supreme Court came to the wrong answer from our point of view. Nonetheless, it shows how issues much broader than disputes purely concerned with shipping can arise."

The variety is one of the most appealing aspects of the job. "The disputes in which I act are very rarely the same and that also goes for the people with whom I work," says Robert. "In shipping, there are almost never bland

For more chambers that work in this practice area, please use the "Pupillage index" starting on p537.

Name: **Robert Thomas QC**
Chambers: **Quadrant Chambers**
University: **University of Cambridge**
Undergraduate degree: **Law**

clients – there is usually an interesting story behind each one. And the fact that this area is so international in scope means that you work with people from all over the world. In fact, our only UK-based clients are usually insurers – only one or two of the big commodity houses base themselves in the United Kingdom and all the other players are foreign. This leads to an interesting range of viewpoints, as people with different backgrounds and experiences are bound to see things differently."

❝ The disputes in which I act are very rarely the same and that also goes for the people with whom I work – in shipping, there are almost never bland clients ❞

However, there is no doubt that life at the Bar is hard work. "Anyone entering the profession should be aware that there will be periods where you really have to roll your sleeves up," warns Robert. "However, this balances out, as during quieter periods you don't need to hang around chambers when you don't need to, because you are your own boss."

Plain sailing?
While Brexit has certainly rocked the boat for the UK economy, Robert does not predict adverse consequences for the shipping Bar: "I think London's pre-eminence in shipping law is unlikely to be affected by Brexit. The only area that I see being immediately affected is the jurisdictional rules – also known as the Brussels Regulations – which are part of European legislation that has long-since superseded common law in most respects. It seems to me that the regulations will have to be put aside now that Britain is to no longer be part of the European Union. However, most of our client base is not based in the European Union either – as an example, we frequently

work with Turkish, Chinese and Russian organisations. This means that we roll with the global markets. Volatility breeds disputes, as you can imagine when people are making a lot of money one minute and losing a lot of money the next, so the uncertainty around the world at the moment means that the commercial Bar is not a bad place to be."

To be successful in this area of law, Robert is keen to emphasise the importance of strong analytical skills. "Most disputes turn on one or two key issues and it is vital to be able to cut through everything else to identify them," he explains. "You also need to approach matters with an open mind, especially considering the international client base – everyone probably comes to things with a few preconceptions, but it is important to be able to put those aside and deal with the facts on the ground as you find them. Good communication skills are also crucial – it sounds obvious, but being able to clearly convey what can be complex and difficult ideas is a real talent. Bear in mind that you will often have to communicate ideas to lawyers and clients in other countries, who are not from the same legal tradition as you. There is a tightrope between not talking down to people and explaining things clearly so that they can understand the issues of the case and why you think that their case is a good or bad one. This also transfers to court – you have to be aware of your audience; if the judge is not receptive to your point, you need to put it in a different way or gracefully move on, instead of ploughing on regardless."

Finally, Robert advises that determination and perseverance will help those harbouring ambitions of becoming barristers themselves to succeed: "There are plenty of people saying that the Bar is a very tough place to build a career, but the key for budding barristers is not to be put off. The Bar is a very competitive environment, but in my view it is also an extremely meritocratic profession, which is something that we don't emphasise enough."

Chancery

Chancery work is split into two areas: traditional and commercial. Traditional chancery includes trusts, probate, real property and tax, while commercial chancery covers a wide range of finance and business disputes. Chancery work often has an international dimension, relating to asset tracing, cross-border insolvency and offshore trusts. Chancery barristers present cases before tribunals all the way up to Supreme Court level and draft a wide range of documentation.

As a student of English literature at the University of York, James MacDougald may well have wandered the labyrinthine pathways of *The Waste Land* or *War and Peace* and attempted to interpret the antiquated verse of *The Canterbury Tales*. He could even have struggled through the anarchic ramblings of *Finnegan's Wake* or sought to find a foothold in the footnotes of *Infinite Jest*. Indeed, such heavyweight literary challenges to the intellect would have been fine preparation for life at the chancery Bar.

"It is very cerebral work," he explains. "Trust law, for example, is extremely complex and the doctrines can seem abstract and artificial, although most of them derive from quite basic principles of ownership and obligations of good faith. You spend a lot of time reading and researching case law, both very ancient and very recent, and trying to analyse difficult concepts. These are often exercises in pure thought, like solving a mathematical problem."

Grappling with knotty problems

This is what attracted James to the profession in the first place and is still what he enjoys most about his work at the chancery Bar today. He also points out that chancery is a great testing ground for those keen to grapple with these intellectual challenges early on in their careers.

"One of the good things about practising in this area, I always tell mini-pupils, is that you actually get asked to advise on quite complex matters at an early stage in your career," he explains. "This may be because a trust or estate has little money in it and therefore cannot justify the expense of a senior barrister, but nonetheless there could be some very knotty problems to resolve. It's quite a steep learning curve in that respect."

At Ten Old Square, where barristers specialise in traditional and commercial chancery work, pupils sit with a different supervisor every three months and will discuss cases, research various points of law and help them draft documents and letters – meaning that they are involved in all areas of their supervisor's practice. In their second six, there may well be the opportunity to look after their own cases and, if instructions come in that the clerks feel are appropriate for them to deal with, some pupils could find themselves on their feet in the county court or High Court.

James points out, however, that if young barristers hope to spend lots of time in the courtroom, chancery may not be the best option. "I go to court about once a fortnight on average," he calculates. "You do get periods where you're in court more often, but chancery work tends to be a lot more advice based."

> ❝ One of the good things about practising in this area is that you actually get asked to advise on quite complex matters at an early stage in your career ❞

In another word of warning, he also reveals that a "traditional chancery" practice can involve quite a lot of complex tax law: "I think

For more chambers that work in this practice area, please use the "Pupillage index" starting on p537.

Name: **James MacDougald**
Chambers: **Ten Old Square**
University: **University of York**
Undergraduate degree: **English literature**

applicants should be aware – particularly if they want a "private client" trusts and inheritance practice – that a very big part of that is advising on capital taxes. The tax law is an entirely statutory code, albeit one that is interpreted by judges. Practising in tax involves close, attentive reading of the statutes and, although it doesn't dominate every case, it's nearly always a factor in trust and estate problems. If you find that a real turn-off, you may want to think twice about working in these areas."

Skills to get you through
Those who relish the prospect of getting to grips with the legislative fine print will need a lively analytical mind and impeccable attention to detail. Professional confidence is also vital because, as we have heard, young chancery barristers will need to stand behind their advice from an early stage. Indeed, this is a quality that James considers crucial throughout a barrister's career: "There's an awful lot of work that involves you giving advice for which you will ultimately have to take responsibility. At first, that can be quite a startling realisation: when you first qualify and suddenly realise that the buck stops with you. In the early years it can be hard to believe that senior, experienced solicitors really want your advice, but they do, so you need to have confidence in your view."

While James agrees that the traditional routes of preparing for the Bar, such as mooting and pro bono work, are always a good idea and provide invaluable advocacy experience, he suggests that it is also vital to get a proper handle on what chancery work actually involves. This can be gained, he suggests, by watching hearings in the High Court's Chancery Division (most courts are open to the public) and through the careful selection of mini-pupillages.

"With mini-pupillages, it's not about sheer volume," he advises. "Once you've

worked out what you are interested in, do perhaps one or two more in that area to satisfy yourself. At the stage of applying for pupillage, your academic background cannot be changed, so the best preparation is to make sure your know exactly what interests you and why, have a detailed grasp of the sort of work that goes on in that area and be able to demonstrate that interest."

Furthermore, at interview it is important to show your familiarity with the chambers you are applying to. "You should research not just the chambers' overall prospectus, but the individual barristers' profiles as well," he suggests. "In the end, we're not a firm; we're just an association of self-employed individuals and we all have different practices that share common themes. Looking at what individuals do will give you a better idea of the work the group does overall. Most chambers will set out their stall quite broadly, but when you scratch the surface you'll see that the practices of individuals can be quite different in different sets."

Civil

Civil law involves relations between persons and organisations. It encompasses a very broad range of legal issues, including those relating to contract, tort, probate and trusts. More specifically, civil law covers disputes that range from employment to professional negligence, and from education to property.

It was not the Bar, but a career in academia that initially beckoned to Andrew Scott after finishing his law degree at the University of Oxford. He stayed on to teach law and research topics in multi-jurisdictional commercial litigation, but soon came to realise that "it is just much more fun arguing cases for real than reading about them". Mind made up, he left Oxford for a similarly intellectual, but more hands-on vocation.

Andrew was called to the Bar in 2010 and is currently a tenant of Blackstone Chambers, a leading commercial set in Temple, the heart of the City of London's legal district where the Inns of Court are based. He has developed a broad civil disputes practice that covers a range of different areas of law. "About 90% of my practice is commercial cases, typically with a cross-border or international element, which could either be foreign parties or legal issues, or foreign legal proceedings taking place alongside those in England and Wales that require coordination," he explains. "At the commercial Bar in London, it is very rare nowadays to encounter any sizable commercial litigation that does not involve a foreign element." Within that 90%, Andrew's cases vary across banking, restructuring and fraud work. The remaining 10% changes from year to year: "At the moment, a large proportion is made up of competition cases."

Life as a litigator
His workload can be split into two broad categories – litigation and advice. "Most of my practice is litigation work – it might start out as advisory, but usually it turns into proceedings of some kind," he explains. "Often in a commercial case, proceedings will begin with a flurry of interim applications or an injunction – possibly a jurisdiction challenge. If a case doesn't settle after that early skirmishing, the parties will dig in and prepare for trial. At any time, I will have a number of cases at different stages of the journey from advisory work to trial preparation."

Much commercial litigation is resolved out of court, but Andrew still gets plenty of opportunities to conduct trial advocacy in certain types of case. "Trials between sophisticated entities, provided they don't involve fraud allegations, will typically settle because it is rarely in the interests of two businesses to incur the costs of a public trial," he observes. "But when you are fighting cases between individuals, or where there are serious allegations of fraud, settlement is less common because the whole point of the litigation in many such cases is for one party to have their day in court and prove that they are right."

As Andrew has grown more senior, opportunities to be 'on his feet' in court have become more frequent. One particular case stands out as a milestone in this particular regard: "In April I successfully applied for a freezing order to restrain a share dividend worth some $95 million, which had been proposed by a Middle Eastern company that my client was litigating against. The litigation was particularly complicated and had a number of moving parts, and it was the first sizeable injunction that I obtained unled – that is, without the supervision of a more senior barrister. The injunction also turned out to be critical to the outcome of the case, which settled soon afterwards. It reflected the career stage that I have now reached, where I am doing more cases on my own and conducting my own advocacy."

The power of persuasion
Advocacy, clearly, is the cornerstone of the job, as well as one of its most enjoyable aspects. "It is ultimately the reason that we do this," he

For more chambers that work in this practice area, please use the "Pupillage index" starting on p537.

Name: **Andrew Scott**
Chambers: **Blackstone Chambers**
University: **University of Oxford**
Degree: **Law**

enthuses. "Whether it is written or in court, all of our work as barristers is done with the intent to persuade someone – be that a client, a judge or even someone on your own team."

Rivalling advocacy in its appeal is the sheer unpredictability from one moment the next: "That is what made me want to stop being an academic and come to the Bar in the first place. It isn't part of a barrister's job to look for problems – they come to us."

There is another side to an unpredictable workload, though, and giving up any semblance of control over his time during certain periods can be a source of frustration: "If you are working on a case and some important development happens that needs to be addressed urgently, it just has to be done. For example, during the preparation for the injunction that I obtained earlier this year I had no time for anything beyond the work, even though the case itself was a significant highlight of my last year, as I mentioned. And particularly in the very early stages of my career, I was surprised by the unpredictability of the working pattern. During that first couple of years when you are trying to build your practice and make contacts, you have very little control over your diary. The cost of being self-employed is that there are times when you must be fully focused on the job."

Public funding crisis
Turning his thoughts to issues facing the wider barristers' profession, Andrew highlights different areas of concern that "very much depend on the area of the Bar that you are targeting for your career. There is a public funding crisis at the Bar which primarily affects practitioners in criminal and family law, but I think it is also beginning to affect the courts, because the consequence of having inadequate representation due a lack of funding to provide barristers is that judges have to take on more work, which puts added pressure on the system. It

may sound dramatic, but I'm not sure how someone who wants to be a criminal or family barrister would achieve that now without some alternative form of income, at least in the early years of your practice. The crisis in that area of the Bar is systemic because it impacts on how we deliver justice."

Meanwhile, "in the corner of the Bar where I practise, the challenges are very different," he continues. "Our issues arise from the need to retain London's status as an attractive centre for international dispute resolution. That is critical because, as I have said, most of the commercial work that we see nowadays is international, and that work provides revenue for solicitors, barristers and a whole host of other industries which spin out of litigation. London is not the only place where this kind of work is done – there are centres around the world, such as in Singapore or the Middle East, that are competing for it. We practitioners must try to ensure that London remains an attractive place for people to come and have their disputes resolved."

Finally, Andrew offers his advice on the four essential skills and attributes that you will need to succeed at the Bar: "The first you could describe as 'shot selection'. Clients take for granted that you will be on top of the law and the facts of the case – what they are really looking for is to take all that material and extract the critical points that are going to win the case, whether they are points of law or factual detail. The next two are more obvious – hard work and endurance are essential, and it is important to put in the hours necessary to crunch through the material. You also need to be willing to work in teams with solicitors – the reality is that the vast majority of litigation is working in small groups within a much larger team." It is certainly instructive that even among self-employed barristers, the nature of a career in the legal profession is highly collaborative.

Commercial

The commercial Bar covers a broad range of practice areas, including banking and financial services, sale of goods and shipping, insolvency, professional negligence and civil fraud, insurance/reinsurance and oil and gas law. Barristers also handle matters for commercial clients that overlap with discrete areas of law such as employment, intellectual property and competition. Although advocacy is an important skill for commercial barristers, there is also a heavy emphasis throughout pupillage on developing a full understanding of commercial law principles and honing one's drafting skills.

With luck and hard work, aspiring commercial barristers will have the chance to participate in high-profile disputes involving oligarchs or the collapse of big business and see news of their cases splashed over the financial press. However, commercial barrister Rajesh Pillai stresses the importance for junior barristers of balancing such opportunities against the need to earn their stripes in their own, smaller matters. "It's still the case that you will do small trials – small insurance actions, fights with utility providers, disputed bills – on your own in the county court," he explains. "It's exciting running your own case, and it's a very important training ground. This is where you develop the habit of making strategic decisions yourself and being at the sharp end of the law."

Nor is the work of a commercial junior removed from the stuff of everyday life. As Rajesh points out: "Everyday legal problems are not the widely reported one-offs, such as the super-injunctions or claims against big banks. They can be about relatively small debts, personal investment advice, fights with utility providers, disputes about the quality of work undertaken – these are the aspects of the law which most people see."

Any doubt that this is a worthwhile apprenticeship can be laid to rest with a glance at Rajesh's own career trajectory. An established figure on the international arbitration circuit, from Paris to Singapore, Rajesh also recently acted as part of the counsel team before the Supreme Court in Eclipse Film Partners, No 35, appearing for one aspect of the case as sole advocate. The case involved Her Majesty's Revenue and Customs taking on a tax avoidance scheme used by various high-profile individuals and the team successfully had the various appeals dismissed. "Commercial law can sometimes be a case of pushing around money between rich people and this can seem unwholesome," Rajesh says wryly. "But in this case the result ended up saving UK taxpayers £1 billion."

❝ Written skills are imperative – in particular the ability to distil complex ideas and present them simply ❞

Little acorns

An analytical mind and the ability to articulate and argue clearly and succinctly are vital to success at the commercial Bar. Not every aspect of the job is glamorous: starting out, you can expect a lot of document analysis and drafting of court documents. "Written skills are imperative – in particular the ability to distil complex ideas and present them simply. It was a crucial aspect of my pupillage," he recalls. "This is something you can practise – work on it and polish it. As a junior, your input to a case will be of most worth here."

Prospective commercial barristers also need to develop a business brain and to understand the commercial implications of every matter. In terms of practical steps, Rajesh advises keeping a weather eye on current affairs, particularly issues where commerce, law and politics intersect. "When I was studying in New York and then as an intern at the WTO

For more chambers that work in this practice area, please use the "Pupillage index" starting on p537.

Name: **Rajesh Pillai**
Chambers: **3 Verulam Buildings**
University: **University of Oxford**
Undergraduate degree: **English**

Appellate Body in Geneva, I really got an insight into how the WTO can affect trading standards, which in turn may impact government policy," he explains. "Look at the whole debate over plain packaging for cigarettes: this is politics, state welfare and law all colliding."

Commercial barristers have strong earning potential and pupillages are highly sought after. So, prospective legal eagles need to ensure that their marks are as good as possible because when it comes to getting a pupillage, they will be competing against the best. In order to emphasise commitment, having some moots or advocacy experience on your CV can help to demonstrate your level of interest, while mini-pupillages can give you a feel for the different types of work on offer – the more you can do, the better. "Even if you go somewhere and you don't like it, that teaches you something," Rajesh points out. "You need to understand where your own interests lie. You need to know why a particular area of practice is interesting to you and why you want to do it."

Interesting times
The Bar has changed substantially during Rajesh's career and, given the recent political upheaval, further transformations are inevitable. He explains that at the top sets everything has shifted onto a bigger scale, which affects the mix of work that juniors can expect. For instance, the counsel teams for some parties to the *Berezovsky* litigation involved two silks and three to four juniors; the upcoming *RBS Rights Issue* case is due to take six months and has involved up to 13 barristers from 3 Verulam Buildings alone. This alters things in two main ways for juniors: "It means that on a big case you're less likely to be making your own decisions and seeing things through from start to finish," Rajesh says. "It also means that you're less likely to be involved in developing strategy."

This is why he is so keen to emphasise the importance when starting out of mixing led work on these big cases with a few lower-value hearings, which might include banking, insolvency and small insurance matters, and which are typically heard at county courts. "It gives you the chance to read up on law and articulate your own arguments," he explains. "It's also good to be in front of different tribunals, it teaches you about the rough and tumble of court life." Aspiring commercial barristers should consider which sets will assist them in getting a variety of opportunities.

In terms of further changes down the road, Rajesh believes that the limitation on funding for courts and the judiciary is definitely an issue, especially for the commercial sector. Separately, solicitors are trying to do a lot more themselves, with bigger firms looking to use solicitor advocates in certain instances.

That said, in addition to court work, international arbitration is on the rise, meaning that commercial barristers can expect to spend a lot more time travelling and broadening their exposure to different tribunals and systems of law. Rajesh recalls a recent Indian arbitration in which he was instructed, which involved a number of witnesses and various accusations of fraud and deceit. "The Dubai-based team actively sought out an English counsel team to handle that side of things," he says, "because the English Bar has a reputation for excellence as advocates – on paper, in oral argument and cross-examination."

Whether this is for you comes down to the fine line between feeling the pressure and thriving on it. "You do have to enjoy it," Rajesh says. "When you're being asked questions by a judge and you have your opponent waiting to trip you up – if you concentrate on the pressure you're under, you'd be a bit of a wreck. But if you relish the challenge, and are prepared to put in the hours learning your craft, the commercial Bar could well be the place for you."

Common law

The common law Bar remains an attractive option for those who believe that variety is the spice of life. Typically, common law chambers are multi-disciplinary and are divided into practice groups so that members can develop and maintain specialisations. Areas of practice can include actions against the police, employment disputes, discrimination law, landlord and tenant, personal injury, professional negligence, family law and criminal law.

Although Muhammed Haque QC gave some initial consideration to a career in the solicitors' profession after graduating from university, he realised that "my heart always lay at the Bar". His mind made up, Muhammed completed a postgraduate law conversion – his original degree being in engineering, economics and management – and progressed onto Bar school before gaining a pupillage at Atkin Chambers.

Atkin specialises in construction law, so pupillage there was a "natural segue" from Muhammed's degree and from there his career has gone from strength to strength. Now a Silk – a barrister awarded the prestigious appointment of Queen's Counsel – Muhammed is a specialist in commercial and common law litigation. "I have a mixed, broad practice which is based solidly around the principles of contract and tort," he explains. "I work on commercial disputes ranging from the straightforward to the very high value, which involve the interpretation of contractual terms and the deconstruction of the factual matrices which surround the formation of a contract. Tortious liability cases are often professional negligence cases and they involve going right back to the first principles you learn at university."

Advisory work and conferences now take up a lot of Muhammed's time – the amount of court work he does has lessened since taking Silk. "I'm now in court once a month or so, whereas it used to be around three times a month on average," he explains. "A lot of preparation and research precedes each appearance. For each day in court, I spend about a week preparing."

Master of your fate

The most appealing aspect of the Bar for Muhammed personally is "without any doubt at all, the independence that it gives you. I enjoy being, by and large, the master of my own time and that I work without a boss. There is no one telling me how to manage my case in terms of strategy or tactics – all of that is my own. Every barrister has a different approach and this is one of the main reasons that clients choose to instruct a particular barrister."

In addition to this, the cases themselves are endlessly interesting: "The instructions I receive are for cases which are at the very pinnacle of the legal world and every single case I act on is difficult."

If forced to pinpoint a negative aspect to life as a barrister, Muhammed would highlight the difficulty inherent in building up strong client relationships within the strictly limited timeframes that barristers are often afforded: "It's not a huge downside, but we come into proceedings quite late on, when a lot of the work has already been done by solicitors, and this means that we often don't have sufficient contact with the client at the start in order to find out what they want and what really motivates them – this is something that we instead have to pick up on as we go. This is in contrast to solicitors, who may have spent six months with the client beforehand, during which time they have built up a very good relationship – not being able to do that can be frustrating. A lot of the time, particularly in the case of academic pieces of work, I receive instructions and never actually meet the client."

For more chambers that work in this practice area, please use the "Pupillage index" starting on p537.

Name: **Muhammed Haque QC**
Chambers: **Crown Office Chambers**
University: **University of Oxford**
Undergraduate degree: **Engineering, economics and management**

Muhammed is also one of the many barristers who can't help but worry occasionally over the general uncertainty surrounding work at the Bar: "The thing about our profession is that tomorrow you could be instructed on an amazing piece of work that keeps you busy for six months – or not. Whether you're at one year's call or 20 years in Silk, you're always waiting for the next piece of work to come in and you don't know what it is going to be. This means that you need to be quite a sanguine person and manage your time well."

A changing profession
Taking a step back, Muhammed describes a period of flux in the profession: "The Bar is going through huge change at the moment. It is largely cost driven and sensibly so, because although it is not quite a race to the bottom, there has been a widespread perception for some years that legal fees are too high. The consequence of that is that people are being squeezed all through the system, which means that with large numbers of meritorious cases, there is simply not the finance to bring them to court. Access to justice may become more and more of an issue over the next couple of years or so. Much will depend on the reforms put in place by Lord Justice Jackson. There is a move toward fixed fees in quite a lot of areas and a wider shift to fixed fees across all areas is almost certainly going to happen now. I support that in principle – I don't think there is anything wrong with parties knowing exactly what they will be liable for at the end of a dispute. There is also nothing wrong with the amount of money eventually recovered being broadly proportionate to the issues involved. The real question is what consequence this will have on the Bar, as much of the solicitors' profession has been working with fixed fees for some years. It will require a large number of barristers to adapt very quickly and for the level at which fixed fees are set to be sufficiently robust."

Muhammed has a couple of good pieces of advice for those with an ambition to succeed as a barrister: "Anyone considering the Bar has to have a determination and belief in their ability to do the job. There will be high points and low points in every junior lawyer's career, but that is part of life and it is important to be realistic about it. Don't forget why you're there and be absolutely resolute in your determination to continue in the profession. The second thing to appreciate is that this career is not all about the law. Being a barrister is a being an adviser, a sounding board – someone who is easy to talk to. Being a great barrister is about understanding the client and what they want from the case, not simply about being able to apply the law to the facts with which you are presented. That is how you are best able to persuade a judge of your client's case – ultimately you are trying to put the judge in your client's shoes and persuade him or her that your client's actions – or inactions – were reasonable. The law is the guide, not the goal."

Finally, Muhammed offers some advice which won't help you win cases, but is nonetheless very important for getting the most out of this career: "Being a barrister can be a lonely profession, but it can also be a sociable profession. I didn't appreciate that a lot of a barrister's time is spent alone, either on the road, in court or in your room in chambers, where you do all your preparation. This means that it is incumbent on you to make the effort to meet other people around chambers and get to know them, and the same goes for court staff and solicitors. But once you appreciate that, you realise that chambers actually has a very social atmosphere and people are always popping in and out of each other's rooms to talk. You get out what you put in."

Competition

Competition and regulatory work involves a mixture of commercial, public and European law. The general competition law prohibitions under EU and domestic law apply to all types of industry, and work in this area also involves a range of sector-specific regulation (eg, in the telecoms, energy and financial services sectors). It also includes merger control under EU law and the Enterprise Act 2002. The work involves a mix of regulatory and court proceedings, with claims for damages for breaches of competition law taking on a higher profile in recent years. Related areas are state aid and the rules on public sector and utility procurement.

Deciding to pursue law at university was more of a "Why not?" than a "That's for me!" moment for Laura Elizabeth John, but a stint as a civil servant confirmed to her that she was on the right path: "My decision to study law was based on no more sophisticated a reason than I was told at school that I'd be a good lawyer and that it meant I could do whatever A levels I wanted! After university, I decided to instead spend 18 months in the civil service, working on putting a bill through Parliament as a policy officer. I realised that I enjoyed law in practice and I reconnected with some of the reasons why I went for it in the first place, so I decided to go back to it." She knew from the outset that the Bar would be a more natural fit: "I preferred the idea of being self-employed. I also like the fact that it is a very meritocratic profession; you do stand or fall on your merits."

Laura competed her pupillage at Monckton, which she describes as being "unqualifiedly positive". The insistence that pupils leave chambers every day at 6:00pm was appreciated, as was the continual assessment process, avoiding stressful pressure points through the year and "allowing us to show how we perform under ordinary conditions, as well as offering a more accurate reflection of what day-to-day practice is like".

High value and multi-party

Although competition law is relatively broad in scope, Laura's work focuses mostly on high-value, multi-party damages claims. "The sorts of issue that arise are often the same as any you would find in any large multi-party litigation – for example, to do with jurisdiction and conflicts of law – as well as more specific issues about whether competition law has been breached," she explains. "Evaluating damages is also very complex, so I work a lot with expert economists and accountants to work out what the world would have looked like if the bad behaviour hadn't occurred. You also become an expert on a really diverse range of issues as you try to get under the skin of a particular industry – for example, I've done cases on lightbulbs, pharmaceutical products and heavy-duty electrical equipment used in power substations. I have had to understand how all those products are manufactured, the supply chain, and the economics of the industries as a whole, in order to work with the witnesses and our experts on the detail of the arguments. That sort of variety is a huge challenge and very stimulating."

Laura goes on to explain what else competition law might encompass: "Many of my colleagues work with the regulators, either at the stage of investigating potential breaches or of handling appeals in the Competition Tribunal or the European courts. There is a whole range of transactional work too; mergers, obviously, but there may also be two companies that want to sign a contract and they need to know whether the terms comply with competition law. Sometimes that sort of work ends up in litigation. For example, I am working on a case about the terms for licensing intellectual property in the telecoms sector, where Company A has sued Company B for infringing its patents, and Company B has alleged that A was in breach of competition law because it had an obligation to give a licence for use on fair, reasonable and non-discriminatory terms."

For more chambers that work in this practice area, please use the "Pupillage index" starting on p537.

Name: **Laura Elizabeth John**
Chambers: **Monckton Chambers**
University: **University of Oxford**
Undergraduate degree: **Law**

French blocking

A fan of the variety offered by the practice area – "I think that's crucial in keeping your interest and motivation in any job" – Laura was privileged to have played a role in the first competition case to be heard by the Supreme Court. Another highlight was a case that went to the Court of Appeal on a procedural point that had been "knocking about for at least 10 years, known as the 'French blocking statute'". She details what occurred: "One of the defendants was resisting disclosure on the basis that it was a French company and French law said that it would commit a criminal offence if it gave disclosure in foreign proceedings. The point went to the Court of Appeal for the first time in our case, and the court confirmed that disclosure is a matter for the English courts and at the discretion of the judge. The judge had exercised his discretion in our favour, which the Court of Appeal upheld, so it was a hands-down win for us and great to get clarity on the point."

As most barristers will tell you, one downside is that your time is no longer entirely your own. "You take on professional and ethical obligations to your clients that you never entirely escape; if someone has an emergency and needs to phone you at 10:00pm, you have to take that call," reflects Laura. "Life outside work can be impacted – which is not to say that you can't have a life, but regularity and predictability are not there in the same way as if you were employed. You regularly have to cancel dinners, drinks and weekends away because matters have to be dealt with in a specific timeframe. It does get easier the more senior you are, but for the first couple of years you have to put your nose to the grindstone and just get on with it."

Justice for all

Laura flags up two recent initiatives which are designed to broaden the scope of who can bring a competition-related action: "The first is a fast-track procedure that aims to move cases through the Competition Appeal Tribunal more quickly and with a costs cap in place. It could be a crucial development, as one of the big problems with competition law claims is cost – getting a case to trial will normally cost millions, if not tens of millions, of pounds, so only the big players can afford to do it. The fast-track procedure should make it more straightforward for smaller players to do something about anti-competitive behaviour." The second is a new procedure to allow for collective actions, similar to those found in the United States: "One feature of competition cases is that the bad behaviour normally occurs at the top of the supply chain – someone overcharges for a small component of a product, with the inflated price being passed down through the supply chain and eventually to the customer at the bottom, who may not even know they've been overcharged. The original overcharger may make millions in illegal profit, but each individual consumer may only have been overcharged pennies and they are unlikely to bring a claim to recover that amount. Collective action is addressing the problem that it is uneconomic for consumers to bring an action, by allowing them to share legal costs."

In Laura's view, the best way to learn more about competition law is to speak to those who are already doing it: "For an area this niche, I don't think you are automatically expected to have studied it – most of us come from a generalist background and then learn on the job. Rather, do a mini-pupillage or come along to drinks evenings at chambers that do this sort of work and talk to the junior barristers." And that applies more generally too: "It is fundamental that you understand the actual job before you apply; the fact that you enjoy studying law and find it interesting is not enough. Practising at the Bar is not like being an academic at all, so you do need to get a feel for the day-to-day job."

Construction

Contentious construction work involves the resolution of disputes by way of litigation, mediation, adjudication or arbitration. Non-contentious work involves drafting and negotiating contracts and advising on projects, insurance, health and safety, environmental matters and insolvency. Clients range from industry associations, insurers, contractors, architects, engineers, public authorities and government bodies to major companies and partnerships.

Law was initially more of an academic interest than a burning vocation for Michael Tetstall; it was only when studying at UCL that he finally decided this was where his future lay. Once that decision was made, however, it wasn't hard to decide which branch of the profession to pursue.

"The chance to be an advocate appealed to me," he explains. "That was definitely something that I wanted; but also the chance to spend more time focusing on law rather than the huge volume of work that goes into running a case as a solicitor. Getting into the gritty legal problems – that was probably what I enjoyed most while studying undergraduate law. Then, as I looked at what was involved in the two careers a little bit more, the idea of being self-employed and being able to manage my own practice with a degree of autonomy also seemed attractive."

Michael's first experience of construction law was while working as a legal assistant at a law firm before securing pupillage at Hardwicke. And when two of his three pupil supervisors had construction-focused practices, this reinforced his desire to explore the area further.

Starting in the shadows
As a pupil, Michael's early days were spent shadowing and learning from his supervisors, assisting where possible with research and small pieces of work here and there. As time passed and he became more experienced, he was asked to provide more substantive assistance, such as writing first drafts of documents and preparing research notes. He found this a valuable learning experience which exposed him to some interesting matters.

"I was involved with one of my supervisors on a claim for a demolition contractor against an employer in a big commercial premises," he recalls. "There was a range of claims and both the facts and the law involved contained a high level of interest and complexity. It was great to be involved over an extended period to see it through from its relatively early stages to a conclusion – to experience first hand client conferences, going through the documents and assisting with some of the work for my supervisor. Just to see how a large, complex, multi-party claim comes together and how that is translated into litigation was very useful."

Complexity at all levels
Since taking tenancy, Michael has developed his own practice. He does a significant amount of construction work of his own, alongside acting as a junior to more senior members of chambers on higher-value cases. His practice involves advising clients as well as appearing in court as an advocate. Outside court, he is also frequently instructed as an advocate in alternative dispute resolution processes such as adjudication and mediation.

"Construction law at the Bar is quite varied," he explains. "From small contractor/employer disputes or domestic disputes between homeowners and contractors to the bigger stuff – large contractors with a number of subcontractors below them and a multinational developer as an employer. Ultimately, the sky's the limit with construction claims and the more senior

For more chambers that work in this practice area, please use the "Pupillage index" starting on p537.

Name: **Michael Tetstall**
Chambers: **Hardwicke Chambers**
University: **University College London**
Undergraduate degree: **Law**

you become, the higher the value of the cases you work on and, in theory, the more complex. However, things don't always work like that and you can end up with some low-value matters at the junior end which can still present quite difficult, thorny issues."

ᴳᴳ Ultimately, the sky's the limit with construction claims and the more senior you become, the higher the value of the cases you work on and, in theory, the more complex 🥟🥟

It is those thorny issues which attracted Michael in the first place and they remain one of the things he enjoys most about the area. "There is a lot of law in it, which I really like," he says. "It doesn't just involve disputes that are entirely decided on the facts; there are a significant number of both factual and legal disputes, and I find that really interesting as a barrister. I also feel that I am constantly learning. You work with experts in a lot of different fields that you may not have come across before and you have to come to understand those fields with their assistance – whether it be different methods for pouring concrete or forensic accountancy. You are working with a diverse team of people and learning a lot as you do so, which is really rewarding."

He suggests that any budding lawyers thinking of practising in the area can get a feel for the sort of work that they might be doing by visiting a hearing at the Technology and Construction Court, a specialist group of courts within the Queen's Bench Division of the High Court of Justice; although he warns that some of the jargon might be a little technical. He also suggests that a number of different chambers (including Hardwicke) publish online construction

newsletters, which provide information in a more accessible form.

Mini adventures

By far the best way to gain experience, he believes, is to do mini-pupillages – not just to bolster a CV, but to understand more about the profession. "Mini-pupillage is really important," he states. "People sometimes think of them purely as a requirement for an application form, but I think it's easy to overlook the fact that at their heart they are about gaining an insight into the law, into different areas of law at a different chambers, and that is a vital aspect. You need to do mini-pupillages for your own benefit, to help you work out what appeals to you, the area in which you want to work and the sort of set in which you'll feel comfortable."

Beyond that, Michael has some advice regarding the level of commitment needed for a career at the Bar: "In terms of overall advice, it is important to be determined and, if you decide that the Bar is for you, to stick at it and show that you have a real, genuine interest in getting there. You should be under no illusion: getting pupillage isn't an easy process and practice at the Bar isn't easy either, so you need to have that genuine desire to do it."

Crime

At the criminal Bar you may be called on to act for either the defence or the prosecution. Specialist criminal law chambers offer expertise in all areas, including child abuse, drug offences, fraud, human rights, mental illness, violent and sexual crime, and white collar crime. As might be expected, criminal barristers spend more time in court than those in almost any other sector of the Bar. The international aspect of criminal law includes human rights, terrorism, war crimes, organised crime, drug trafficking and money laundering. Practitioners in international criminal law regularly appear before foreign tribunals and international courts.

In her own words, Helen Law was "one of those very sad people who at the age of 14 decided I wanted to be a barrister, specifically a criminal barrister", so there was no agonising on a 'what to do with my life' level for her teenaged self, at least. Later, she did a couple of placements at solicitors' firms, but as was fairly clear from the start, they most served to confirm that the Bar was her calling. Although, as Helen points out: "The end point was clear, but the route is always a little unpredictable when you're talking about the Bar."

After graduating in law from the University of Birmingham, doing a master's in public international law and working as a research assistant at the Law Commission for a year, Helen completed the Bar course and secured pupillage – or 'traineeship' as it is termed at this set – at Matrix Chambers, whose barristers cover a wide range of practice areas including crime. "My traineeship was certainly challenging, as you are put under a level of personal scrutiny which I don't think you get in many other job interviews, but I found it utterly fascinating," she recalls of the experience. "My first trainee supervisor was Julian Knowles, who at the time was a junior on a very high-profile murder trial at the Old Bailey. This meant that only a week after I started, I was in court every day for three months – the experience was incredibly interesting and I learnt a lot from day one."

'White collar' crime

In the present, Helen is a successful crime barrister. "I do everything related to criminal justice, which also incorporates criminal law in a public law context – for example, challenging decisions not to prosecute," she explains. "I also perform advisory work during the investigatory stages of criminal cases. For example, in a fraud investigation, I would advise a corporate or individual client about how the case may unfold. And of course I do trial and appellate work, both here and in Strasbourg. The core of my practice is traditionally known as 'white collar' crime, which involves fraud, corruption and money laundering. However, I'm also involved in other areas – I'm currently working on a corruption trial, but am also doing an appeal case concerning drug smuggling and have an immigration offence trial coming up, too."

The workload varies from case to case, particularly in terms of paperwork: "I did a case a few years ago where there were over 100 lever arch files of used and unused evidence, all of which had to be read. In comparison, the case I'm doing at the moment involves fewer than 10 lever arch files of evidence. Reading through the case files is the start of the process with every case – from there you figure out a case strategy which will inform what you do in the months leading up to the trial. There will usually be a lot of preliminary legal research and correspondence, such as disclosure applications. This means that a lot of my work is outside the court room. When a case does finally go to court, I'm often in court for anywhere between one week and three months, as financial crime trials tend to go on longer than some other types of criminal case."

For more chambers that work in this practice area, please use the "Pupillage index" starting on p537.

Name: **Helen Law**
Chambers: **Matrix Chambers**
University: **University of Birmingham**
Undergraduate degree: **Law**

Of all the interesting cases that Helen has worked on so far, one particularly stands out in her memory – partly because it was so nerve wracking: "At five years' call, I prosecuted one of the cases in the parliamentary expenses scandal on my own, which was a daunting, but fantastic experience."

More generally, there are several reasons why Helen enjoys the career of a crime barrister so much. "I'm lucky in that I have a highly varied criminal practice, so no two weeks are the same, and I work in a supportive chambers with some fantastic practitioners in this, and other fields," she explains. "Crime is also a great area to work in for other reasons – it can be intellectually stimulating, but there is also a very human side to the work and you need good people skills to be successful. Your clients will be from all walks of life and they need to be able to trust you. For a period in their lives, you will be a very important person to them because in their mind at least you may be the only thing standing between them and a very unfavourable outcome."

If there is a downside to life at the Bar, it is its unpredictability. Helen admits: "The intensity at which you have to work sometimes is totally out of your control – you can be cruising along, having a normal week when something blows up on a case, and whatever plans you had for the weekend with your family are out the window. But you learn strategies for dealing with it and get better at predicting the types of thing which might blow up."

Cuts and the justice gap
Taking stock of the state of the criminal Bar, Helen identifies one major concern above all others which urgently needs to be addressed: "The most pressing issue is the cuts to legal aid, which have made it incredibly difficult for parts of the justice system to function properly. More people are unrepresented, which slows down the system. Barristers doing legal aid crime have less and less time

to spend on each case, as they are having to take on more and more cases to make ends meet. I think if any area should have its standards rigorously maintained, it's crime, as the consequences are so serious. People go to prison, or dangerous people walk, so to lower the standards of the system is totally unacceptable. It is disappointing that the successive cuts to legal aid fail to recognise the importance of that. If the state does not provide for properly funded representation and a fully resourced criminal justice system, the verdicts produced, guilty or innocent, are not reliable. That is damaging not just to defendants, but also and equally to victims and society at large. I say that as someone who has a mixed practice who is fortunate enough not to be financially dependent on criminal legal aid work."

On a similarly sober note, Helen observes how the cuts have unfortunately made life much more difficult for those trying to establish themselves at the Bar: "If you're at the junior end of the criminal Bar in London, it can be difficult to make ends meet and I know people who have quit because of it." That said, if you can make it through those early years, Helen cannot think of a more interesting, challenging and varied way to earn a living.

For those undaunted, Helen has some worthwhile advice for maximising the chances of success: "It is important to understand what criminal practice involves – this is one area of the Bar that is often portrayed on television, but not necessarily accurately. On a personal level, you need to be resilient and have good stamina, as criminal law is not for the faint hearted. Very good interpersonal skills are also essential – you need to be able to talk to people from all backgrounds. So much of what a barrister does rests on understanding people and having some insight into how what you are saying to, for example, a jury, is going to be received."

Employment

A popular misconception is that this area of law is just about employment contracts. In fact, employment lawyers handle a variety of issues, including unfair dismissal, discrimination, redundancy, equal pay and whistleblowing claims, as well as High Court claims arising out of the employment relationship. There has been a big increase in employment law cases in recent years, due to a combination of new European legislation, government policies and employees' increased awareness of their work-related rights.

The unique offerings of the Bar appealed to Kathleen Donnelly from an early age. "I was attracted by the independence and advocacy – the two essentials which define the barrister's role – and the decision was always pretty clear for me," she explains. After her law degree, Kathleen also spent a year working as a research assistant at the Law Commission, and then studied for a master's in law, to get herself into a strong position to obtain pupillage.

After a year of pupillage at another set where she found she was not a particularly good fit, Kathleen completed a 'third six' at Henderson Chambers, where she really found her feet and went on to gain tenancy. "We have a wide range of practice areas at Henderson and junior barristers are encouraged to gain exposure to different kinds of work before gravitating towards the areas that really interest them," she explains. "These also tend to be the areas that a barrister is particularly good at and where they make more effort to build opportunities by attending talks and networking events."

Broad practice
Employment law was one of the areas that got Kathleen hooked as a junior. "I began doing employment work as part of my broader junior practice," she says, "but it really suited me and now around 50% of my practice is comprised of employment work, with the rest made up of significant civil and commercial litigation work."

In her employment practice, Kathleen acts for both companies and individuals at employment tribunals and in the High Court: "The most straightforward type of employment claim is unfair dismissal, and these are the types of case a junior barrister will usually start with. However, my practice now tends to be a mix of whistleblowing, discrimination and employee competition claims." Indeed, Kathleen believes that the introduction of the two-year service requirement for unfair dismissal claims has caused some cases to be presented in more complex ways, as discrimination or whistleblowing cases, which do not have this service requirement. She finds that her employee competition cases are some of the most interesting and exciting, and these are fought in the High Court.

Cross-examination key
Employment is an ideal area for those who love advocacy because outcomes so often rest on cross-examination. "It is almost never simply a dispute over, for example, the interpretation of a contract – in employment cases there is usually a fundamental dispute about the facts, as well as legal argument about what the law is and how it applies to the facts as may be found by the tribunal," Kathleen explains. "Most cases have interesting underlying facts and in order to present the case well, you really have to get to grips with someone else's workplace and experiences." There is a real sense of obligation to do one's best for the client in matters which can be very serious indeed for all those concerned, for example, when there are allegations of sexual harassment. As a barrister, there is a good deal of job satisfaction both for this reason, and also the need to be familiar and able to work with a complex area of law: "I also have to

For more chambers that work in this practice area, please use the "Pupillage index" starting on p537.

Name: **Kathleen Donnelly**
Chambers: **Henderson Chambers**
University: **University of Oxford**
Undergraduate degree: **Law**

keep myself up to date at all times – much employment law derives from Europe and can change very quickly."

If there is a downside to the role, it is its unpredictability. "Cases tend not to be spread evenly throughout the year, so there are times where I have far too much to do, but barristers tend to prefer to be overworked than too quiet" says Kathleen.

The introduction of employment fees pushed through by the Ministry of Justice as part of the government's cost-cutting austerity programme is posing a problem for employment barristers starting out in this field. "I believe that the introduction of employment tribunal fees has restricted access to justice, while I also think that it has negatively impacted on junior barristers starting out in this area because there are fewer straightforward, one-day unfair dismissal cases going before tribunals," Kathleen explains. "This is fine for the established barristers taking on the lengthier discrimination and whistleblowing cases, but the fees have made it harder for junior barristers to get a foothold in this area. The statistics are clear: unless you assume that all the cases that are now not being brought before tribunals were spurious, there are undoubtedly meritorious cases that are now not being heard." Since we interviewed Kathleen, the Supreme Court has in fact ruled that the government's imposition of employment tribunal fees was unlawful.

Open minded on Brexit

A hot topic on everyone's minds, not least employment barristers', is Brexit. However, Kathleen remains open minded. "There will be a period of some uncertainty, but we will have to make further UK employment legislation or use common law to fill the gaps," she argues. "Also, many of the laws that derive from Europe have had very positive effects for individuals and I think

that it would be very hard to take some of those protections away. However, there will be a period of uncertainty, which for lawyers usually means challenge and opportunity."

The proportionality of legal costs is more of an issue in employment tribunal claims than in other civil litigation, because the usual rule of costs following the event does not apply. "In employment cases, normally the successful party does not recover their fees from the other side, so even if someone has a very good claim, it is very important to manage the cost of winning it," explains Kathleen. Some clients instruct barristers on a direct access basis as a way of managing their legal costs, as this can be a way to keep legal costs down.

Forging a career at the Bar is as tough as it has ever been, but Kathleen has some valuable advice for those steeled for the challenge: "To be a barrister, you need resilience because it is almost certainly not going to be an easy route, but remember that lots of barristers who are now enjoying successful careers did not have a straightforward start to their career, so don't give up at the first hurdle. It is also important to know that in this career you need management skills because you are in effect running your own business – you need to manage your own finances and the development of your own practice; it is not enough just to be a good lawyer. If it suits your character, then there are undoubtedly a great many benefits to life as a barrister, and at the employment Bar. I personally also value the real sense of self determination about the way I carry out my work and the direction in which I choose to take my practice. If you are driven to succeed at the Bar and enjoy the challenge of interesting advocacy, then I encourage you to try to establish a practice which includes employment law."

EU and international

Barristers specialising in this area may appear before the International Court of Justice, the European Court of Human Rights, international tribunals (ICSID, ICC and LCIA), domestic courts and other international tribunals. Matters that may be under dispute include the interpretation of treaties, state responsibility, international investment law, the environment and human rights.

Having studied public international law at undergraduate and postgraduate level and taught the subject for several years at Oxford, Jessica Wells decided that it was time to put her expertise into practice and train as a barrister. "I couldn't see myself in a big City firm," she explains. "It was mainly the independence and variety of the Bar that appealed to me."

Jessica completed her pupillage at Essex Court Chambers – an experience which she describes as "rigorous, but very fair. The chambers were very supportive; we knew exactly what we had to do and when decisions were being taken." Now a tenant at Essex Court, Jessica has developed several areas of expertise, as is the case for many barristers – but it was Essex Court's strength in public international law which attracted her to apply there, and this area forms a significant part of her practice today.

From the start, Jessica was fortunate to be brought into several international cases with senior members of the chambers – including the opportunity to address the International Court of Justice while she was still a pupil: "That was an amazing experience, which I could never have expected to come along so early in my career."

In 2013 Jessica had the privilege of being appointed to the Foreign and Commonwealth Office's newly formed public international law panel of counsel, from which the UK government selects barristers to instruct in international cases. As such, she receives a lot of her work from the government, which has resulted in what she identifies as her undoubted career highlight to date: "I was really fortunate to be part of a team of counsel representing the UK in a case that was brought against it by the Marshall Islands, alleging that the UK and other states were in breach of their obligations relating to nuclear disarmament. We had a hearing in the International Court of Justice (ICJ) in March 2016 – the opportunity to represent your own state in the ICJ is pretty special."

Wide-ranging work

Public international law is unlike some other areas of the Bar in terms of the amount of time spent in court. "For example, barristers practising in personal injury will be in court a lot of the time," Jessica explains. In public international law, on the other hand, the scale and complexity of cases mean that "there's less court work – there is a lot of paperwork, a lot of research, a lot of preparation for hearings." The practice area is also incredibly varied, involving work both at home and abroad: "I work on international law cases in the domestic courts – they seem to come up more and more frequently now, as well as hearings in international tribunals, like the International Court of Justice. There's a whole range of work; international issues can come up in all kinds of cases –for example, it could be a divorce case where someone claims immunity. They crop up in unlikely places."

Public international law also differs from normal commercial casework in that it is less likely to be affected by the issue of rising legal costs. Inevitably, though, recent political upheaval will come to affect this area over the next few years: "I think there are likely to be issues around what happens with human rights arguments. It's not immediately affected by Brexit, but there are obviously

For more chambers that work in this practice area, please use the "Pupillage index" starting on p537.

Name: **Jessica Wells**
Chambers: **Essex Court**
University: **University of Oxford**
Undergraduate degree: **Law**

discussions about whether we should withdraw from the European Convention on Human Rights, and if that happens, it will have a huge impact on domestic cases."

While Brexit is all but inescapable for anyone that follows the news, Jessica has not yet had to confront its impact in her work. However, she predicts that it will have significant repercussions for the the legal profession in general: "A lot of the work that we do in my chambers is international in the sense that it involves parties from other states and how we represent them, and what legal services we can offer to the outside world. That's all going to take some resolution, so the Bar Council will be doing lots of work around that – but thankfully I've managed to avoid it, mostly."

££ You need confidence, an interest in the law and an interest in presenting arguments well ??

While Jessica cites the importance of many public international cases as one of the most rewarding aspects of her job, she readily admits that it can feel like a downside at times. "The great thing about these cases is that they often involve really big issues that have important political consequences, which makes them really exciting and interesting to be involved in, and you learn a lot about the process of government and issues which really matter, like nuclear disarmament," she explains. "The flip side of that is that it makes them quite stressful to deal with – particularly if you're acting for a government. For instance, different departments may have different policy objectives and pressures and the case you're working on may have implications in other areas so that has to be factored into decision

making. It can be stressful, but most exciting things are quite stressful as well."

Making your case
Jessica emphasises the importance of a strong academic record for those hoping to forge a career at the Bar. "Although getting a first isn't necessarily a prerequisite, if you want to be a barrister, a good degree opens a lot of doors," she advises. "It's worth a bit of pain during your studies to put yourself in the best position that you can, because intellectual ability is the main criterion that everyone is looking for." She also identifies some hallmarks of a successful barrister: "You need confidence, an interest in the law and an interest in presenting arguments well," she explains. "A lot of it is about how you communicate, orally but also in writing – being able to make a clear case."

Jessica is keen to emphasise the latter point as something to bear in mind when applying for a pupillage: "Remember that the application form is an example of your advocacy skills. Someone is going to be reading that form quite quickly and you want to make sure that you've argued your best case for why you should be taken on. You want your application to be clear, concise and readable – it's one of the key skills that we're looking for."

To those with a specific interest in public international law, Jessica is encouraging: "My advice is to go for it – there's lots of work out there for juniors who are interested in that area. Research the chambers that specialise in it, try to do a mini-pupillage to get a feel for what the work involves and keep up to date with current affairs, so you know what international issues are out there." While the job comes with its own set of responsibilities and challenges, she has no regrets about her career choice: "I can't think of a job I'd rather do – it's certainly fulfilled the expectations I had."

Family

Family law barristers deal with all legal matters relating to marriage, separation, divorce and cohabitation, as well as issues relating to children, including contact arrangements, care and placement orders, adoption and surrogacy. Family law also encompasses financial negotiations on divorce, inheritance issues, pre-nuptial agreements and disputes between cohabitants. Some cases involve substantial assets and complex financial arrangements, or high-profile disputes between well-known personalities.

About two years after finishing his degree at Oxford, Andy Campbell had something of an epiphany. "I was working in the City and wasn't really enjoying what I was doing," he recalls. "I wanted to do something more fulfilling and challenging. I don't know if I had developed unrealistic expectations of the level of glamour involved from watching films and television like *Kavanagh QC*, but I thought law might fit the bill."

He set about doing a number of mini-pupillages in different sets to experience different practice areas and quickly identified family law as an area in which he would like to specialise. He focused on Queen Elizabeth Building and a number of other family-led sets when applying for pupillage. "Having done a number of mini-pupillages in different areas, I found family law to be the most interesting and engaging," he explains. "It has a mixture of lots of different types of law to keep you on your toes, but the most important thing is that it's not just retrospective. It isn't simply looking at what has happened in the past; it also looks at what might happen in the future and how you can potentially improve things for people. That really appeals to me and a lot of other people who choose the area."

Tough, but enjoyable

While Andy was justified in his expectation that pupillage would be hard work, he emphasises that it was also very enjoyable. During his first six months he was shadowing other members of chambers – predominantly his pupil supervisor – helping them with the matters on which they were working. However, plenty of support was available if he was ever unsure of how best to proceed. "Everyone's door is always open," he says. "Whether you're a pupil or a leading silk, you can go and speak to anyone and get as much help and support as you need."

The support was still there in his second six, but the stakes were raised slightly as Andy started to take on cases of his own. This is also when he realised that he had made the right choice about his future career. "I was prepared for the first six months, because having done my mini-pupillages I didn't find it too hard to imagine what it would be like to shadow others. But when you get your own cases, you can't really prepare for that and hence it has its own pressure attached. Thankfully, I enjoyed it and that was the acid test. If you do a case, finish it and come back thinking that you want to do another, that's definitely a good sign."

As a tenant, Andy finds his time is reasonably evenly divided between chambers and court. Typically he will be in court two or three days a week, working on a varied caseload encompassing everything from financial matters, sorting out the division of money and other assets on divorce, to cases involving children and residence issues. Of course, those court appearances also produce a lot of paperwork – preparing notes, skeleton arguments, position statements, asset schedules and other related documents. That said, he also points out that there is no such thing as a typical week at the family Bar. "There can be a lot of sitting around and waiting to be called, so that involves speaking to clients – reassuring them and advising them while at court," he says. "Then you also get other

For more chambers that work in this practice area, please use the "Pupillage index" starting on p537.

Name: **Andy Campbell**
Chambers: **Queen Elizabeth Building**
University: **University of Oxford**
Undergraduate degree: **Philosophy, politics and economics**

drafting work: doing witness statements, preparing questionnaires for the other side or analysing bank statements. Every week is different. Some weeks are filled with just one case; others you are sat in chambers doing a witness statement that takes three days; or you might find yourself doing five days in court on five different cases. There is no consistency other than the lack of consistency, really."

❝ If you do a case, finish it and come back thinking that you want to do another, that's definitely a good sign ❞

Complexity from the start

As in other areas, the scale of the cases that a family barrister works on tends to increase as they get more senior. However, there are times when more junior members of chambers – even pupils – can find themselves working on more challenging briefs. "Some of the cases I had when I was a pupil were more complex than a number of the cases I'm doing now," suggests Andy. "The reason is that as a pupil you are the cheapest person in chambers, so if someone wants a barrister but doesn't have a lot of money, a pupil may well be their only option. On the whole, my cases are now more complex; but the most complex cases in pupillage were more difficult than the simplest ones I get now."

The cuts to legal aid made in 2013 are one reason why junior barristers are increasingly a first port of call, and the ramifications do not stop there. Not only have they seen a reduction in the amount of work that reaches the Bar (although Andy suggests that the profession is starting to come to terms with the need to restructure practices to adapt to that loss), but the subsequent increase

in the number of litigants in person has also put a strain on the system – something again which the profession and the government are now trying to accommodate.

"There is a drive to make family law less impenetrable for litigants in person," he explains. "So if somebody goes to court, they are not immediately thrust into a dispute with another lawyer and potentially their former partner. There are now more ways to resolve disputes in a better, more efficient manner – including an increase in alternative dispute resolution. The hope is that more people can come to terms before going to court – not least because of the long delays facing the court system as a result of the fact there are more cases, taking longer to resolve due to the lack of proper representation."

Family barristers need a range of skills depending on the work they are handling at the time. As they may be faced with extremely sensitive situations involving feuding partners or children, the ability to pour oil on troubled waters is paramount. It is also useful to be able to read people and how they might react to different legal approaches in court. Andy further points out that some financial savvy is handy when dealing with matrimonial finance work: "It's definitely useful to have a good head for numbers and to have an understanding of how things which impact on people when they get divorced, like pensions and tax on dividends, work."

Housing/landlord and tenant

Housing/landlord and tenant law embraces all aspects of residential and commercial tenancies and covers issues as diverse as anti-social behaviour, disrepair, human rights, possession claims, succession and assignment. Clients might include local authorities, registered providers of social housing, private landlords and, of course, tenants.

Although he enjoyed the study of history and chemistry at school, Simon Atkinson realised pretty quickly during his undergraduate degree in Melbourne, Australia that the sedentary seclusion of the historian or lab-bound labours of a research chemist would not hold his attention for long outside academia. He still wanted to feed his passion for reading and analytical thinking, but was also keen to flex his argumentation muscles, and the Bar seemed like the perfect place to do so.

A born traveller (his father worked for a multinational oil company and travelled extensively during Simon's youth), the native New Zealander decided that he would rather return to the United Kingdom, where he had spent some of his childhood, to further his legal ambitions. He undertook a two-year law degree at Trinity College, Cambridge.

"The opportunities for practising law in London are very good," he explains. "The quality and diversity of work are second to none. Also, [the Australian state of] Victoria, where I then lived, has a fused profession; realistically you have to spend five or six years as a solicitor before going to the Bar and that really didn't interest me. The prospect of going straight to the Bar when my law degree was over seemed much more appealing, which was another reason for coming over."

Law of the land
A confirmed interest in land law which first emerged during his legal studies, combined with a desire to avoid being pigeonholed into a particular area too early in his career, guided Simon to apply to Wilberforce, as the set undertakes a wide variety of chancery and general commercial work. As his practice has since developed, however, property has featured increasingly prominently, to the point where it "now forms the backbone of my work".

"A large part of that is landlord and tenant work – both commercial and residential," explains Simon. "I really enjoy it, because with property work you get into court more frequently, and you are less commonly led by a QC on cases than in other areas. It's pretty safe to say that there are more opportunities for a young barrister working in property to be given more autonomy – advising, pleading and advocacy – than in many other areas of chancery and commercial law."

At six years' call, Simon now finds himself in court on average once, sometimes twice, a week. The rest of his time is spent drafting papers and skeleton arguments, preparing for and attending conferences, advising, reading and researching points of law, and attending to other paperwork. He also spends quite a bit of his time on the road as many of his court appearances are outside London. "I travel quite a lot for court appearances – property work gets me out into the various county courts across England and Wales. This is because claims are usually heard in the county court nearest to the location of the property in dispute. I enjoy travelling on the train and getting out of chambers for a day!"

"I'm never bored in this job," he adds. "There are cases you enjoy more than others and some more tedious exercises that you have to do. But no two cases are alike. You can go from lots of little cases all at once, which is basically what I'm doing at the moment, to a period when you're involved in a single big piece of litigation. You go through cycles."

For more chambers that work in this practice area, please use the "Pupillage index" starting on p537.

Name: **Simon Atkinson**
Chambers: **Wilberforce Chambers**
University: **Melbourne University**
Undergraduate degree: **History and chemistry**

Pupil rotation

Pupils at Wilberforce rotate through pupil supervisors every two to three months so that they can experience the different areas of law in which the set practises. Simon points out that it is rare for pupils in the second six months of pupillage to spend much, if any, time on their feet, with the expectation that pupils are there to learn from their supervisors. That said, there is still plenty of live, paper-based work for them to get stuck into.

"I think I was on my feet only perhaps once or twice while I was still a pupil," he recalls, "but you are given a variety of work – both what we call 'dead cases' – cases which your supervisor has previously worked on but are now finished – and live work. In my first week of pupillage I was charged with doing a first draft of an application for specific disclosure in a live matter. There is a great sense of responsibility that is put on you, because you are trusted to get the work right, but you are always given sufficient time to do so. I found that the level of responsibility increases as the year progresses. So even though you may not be on your feet, you will be working on live matters with your pupil supervisor."

Those keen to secure pupillage at a set specialising in landlord and tenant, or property law more generally, should be able to demonstrate an awareness of how recent political and economic developments might affect the area. "Property law, and landlord and tenant law in particular, is readily affected by wider economic issues – for example, the global financial crisis and Brexit. These issues can have a big impact on how the property market is developing," Simon points out. "When I first started out in practice in 2011, commercial leases were coming up for their five or 10-year rent reviews in a very different set of financial circumstances from those in which the leases had been originally agreed. There was therefore a lot of court litigation – mainly by tenants seeking to prevent their landlords increasing the rents payable under the lease."

He continues: "It is definitely worth prospective members of the property Bar keeping an eye on wider economic, political and social developments, because they have a very real impact on how people deal with their property interests."

❝ It's pretty safe to say that there are more opportunities for a young barrister working in property to be given more autonomy – advising, pleading and advocacy – than in many other areas of chancery and commercial law ❞

As a final piece of advice, Simon warns that when he first came to the Bar he underestimated the sheer amount of hard work involved and the strength needed to deal with it. "You need stamina," he insists. "Obviously, people will tell you that you need to have good academic grades and advocacy skills, both written and oral; this is absolutely true. But it's equally important to be aware that, if you've got a two or three-day trial or you're in court back to back on various matters, you will frequently be working late and getting up early; you'll be thinking about the case for days in advance, potentially; and it is very physically and mentally draining. It is very rewarding, but it is a taxing job. Because you're self-employed, you need to have the drive and determination to put in the hours and the hard work necessary to make sure that you are prepared when you stand up on your feet. So I would say that one of the most underrated strengths at the Bar, particularly in an advocacy-heavy area like landlord and tenant, is stamina."

Human rights

Human rights law is essential for a fair and civilised society where all are protected, including the vulnerable, and is a popular choice for students and practitioners. University law faculties are increasingly offering human rights modules as part of their law degrees and more firms and chambers are boasting specialisms in the field. The introduction of the Human Rights Act 1998 made the European Convention on Human Rights (ECHR) directly enforceable in the national courts.

Aiming for the Bar was a carefully considered choice for human rights lawyer Fiona Scolding. Believing that she had the right qualities to excel as a barrister, including an affinity for working alone and the ability to shoulder responsibility, Fiona remembers why she pursued the career path: "I knew I wanted to represent people in court and I liked the thought of being the front person for an idea. I like being a speechmaker."

A gradual shift
Fiona explains how she did very little human rights work during her pupillage at a common law set, although there were some elements that touched upon the subject, such as actions against the police, and clinical negligence or injury. "Since I was a pupil before the Human Rights Act came into place, nobody really talked about human rights back then," she says. "It was something that happened in Europe, but you didn't use it in your domestic practice on a day-to-day basis."

After moving to become a tenant elsewhere, Fiona found there was a gradual shift into working within the area of human rights as she took on cases related to housing, education or children – all of which had a human rights component. When the Human Rights Act came into force in 1998, it encompassed areas of the law in which she had already operated, so it was only natural to add it to her practice.

Set of principles
Discussing her career in the field, Fiona questions the very definition of her job title. "What is a human rights barrister?" she asks. "You've got human rights cases that deal with property law, criminal law and family law to name a few. Human rights are just a set of principles that you can apply to pretty much any area of practice."

With that in mind, Fiona now specialises in social welfare law, with particular focus on representing children, vulnerable adults and people with disabilities. "As part of my role as counsel to the Independent Inquiry into Child Sexual Abuse, I am spending a lot of time at the moment investigating various institutions," she says, explaining that a current project she is working on looks at the way the Church of England dealt with allegations of child sexual abuse over a 40-year period.

Within her practice, Fiona brings claims against the government, but also represents it in cases involving policies regarding children and vulnerable adults. This requires her to be familiar with human rights constitutional law, both within the UK and internationally: "I say whether these policies are compliant with not only domestic legislation, but also international conventions on the rights of the child and disabled person."

Fiona's work also takes her to the Court of Protection where she is involved in making decisions about the livelihood of vulnerable adults. Questions such as where a person should live, what medical treatment they should receive, and whether or not they can get married all encompass fundamental questions about a person's autonomy and dignity.

For more chambers that work in this practice area, please use the "Pupillage index" starting on p537.

Name: **Fiona Scolding**
Chambers: **Landmark Chambers**
University: **University of Cambridge**
Degree: **History**

Working within such a challenging and high-stakes practice, Fiona describes a piece of work that she is particularly proud of: "I represented a series of foster carers – from grandparents and great aunts to various family relatives – who were not being paid adequately for the work they were doing. These people were not famous or important in any way other than to the children whose lives they transform. I fought to win them adequate remuneration for their work and the recognition that they should be treated equally to other foster carers who were doing the same job."

ff You've got human rights cases that deal with property law, criminal law and family law to name a few. Human rights are just a set of principles that you can apply to pretty much any area of practice 𝅘

Lots to fight for
There is no denying that the legal aid side of the profession is currently going through a tumultuous period, and you don't have to look far to see the news of barrister strikes and the underfunded legal aid system. Fiona admits that money has been tight for the past decade. "The criminal justice system is at breaking point," she says. "There have been so many cuts and morale is low at times, so it's not necessarily the happiest time to enter the profession from a student's point of view. But it is certainly an interesting time to enter the profession because there is lots to fight for."

Listing the advantages of becoming a human rights barrister, Fiona talks about the flexibility of the job, as well as the

independence and opportunity to think for yourself. "The thing I most enjoy is meeting people, finding out about their lives and trying to make them better. It's a privilege to become involved with a person's life during a time of crisis and do what I can to help."

For students aspiring to make a difference by pursuing a career at the human rights Bar, it's worth noting that salary doesn't make it onto Fiona's list of career attractions. "I certainly wouldn't say that you should do it just for the money, because unless you're one of a small number of people practising in a small number of areas, the pay isn't going to balance," she concedes. "It also can be difficult at times because you are alone without a team around you, and you have to do things by yourself."

For those still set on the career path, Fiona has these words of encouragement: "The job is intellectually challenging in a way that many jobs aren't, and I find myself challenged every day, even now. Every day is different. Why wouldn't you want to do it?"

Immigration

Immigration lawyers deal with all legal matters relating to immigration and nationality. The work ranges from asylum and human rights claims through applications by family members and students to advising businesses on securing immigration status for their employees. There is a significant and increasing European law element, and many cases raise important human rights issues. The law is rapidly developing, in terms of both statute law and jurisprudence, and procedural timeframes are tight. There is a good deal of overlap with social welfare, mental health, prison law, criminal law and civil actions.

Many people are inspired to follow their future careers by their experiences at university and Michelle Knorr is no exception. Her journey towards the immigration Bar began with a course on international law during her undergraduate degree in politics and international relations at Brown University in the United States.

"It was my first introduction to legal reasoning and legal argument, and I really enjoyed it," she recalls. "It is quite a unique type of activity, not like other forms of study. I was very interested in the subject – we were looking at things like the legality of the war in Iraq, and our tutor was a negotiator for Palestine. He was involved in negotiating peace agreements and was fascinating to listen to. It showed me a side of the law that I thought was really interesting – that's what gave me the idea of pursuing law."

Michelle set about bolstering her academic knowledge of the subject and garnering valuable wider experience before taking the plunge into practice. She completed a master's in international human rights law at the University of Essex and a stint working in international development before doing the GDL at BPP and the BVC at the Inns of Court

School of Law. After that, Michelle spent at year as an immigration caseworker at Wilson Solicitors in Tottenham, with the instruction of barristers among her duties.

Pupil life

This experience gave her first-hand insight into what life might be like in chambers – although that didn't mean she wasn't still a little wary of beginning her pupillage. "I was terrified when I started," she admits. "I was having nightmares about having to carry people's bags. You hear so many horror stories about being treated badly and I'm not somebody who has much appreciation for hierarchy, so I think I was a bit nervous about that aspect of it. I knew it was going to be hard work – I was quite up for that – but I was scared of the formality of chambers."

As it turned out, she had nothing to worry about: her colleagues at Doughty Street Chambers were "incredibly supportive" and the cases she was given to handle "fascinating". During the first six months of pupillage, much of the work revolves around the caseload of your pupil supervisor. Pupils may draw up initial draft arguments for them and accompany them to conferences and to court. During the second six, young barristers begin to get on their feet in court. At Doughty Street, pupils are kept busy. "We give them a lot of really interesting work on cutting-edge cases" says Michelle. "Once on your feet, the majority of the court work is crime, which is important because it gets you into the courtroom and trains you to be a good advocate. There are loads of magistrates' court briefs and you are running all over the place. You also continue to work with other members of chambers on their civil briefs, often on very high-profile cases. I did quite a lot of immigration as well, largely because I already had an immigration background. So there were solicitors who were willing to brief me and the immigration team felt that it was safe to brief me on

For more chambers that work in this practice area, please use the "Pupillage index" starting on p537.

Name: **Michelle Knorr**
Chambers: **Doughty Street Chambers**
University: **Brown University**
Undergraduate degree: **Politics and international relations**

immigration cases. Unless you have a background in immigration or your pupil supervisor is an immigration practitioner, you wouldn't do many substantive immigration cases as a pupil, but you might do bail hearings or case management hearings – procedural hearings rather than substantive hearings. You can also do pro bono work for Bail for Immigration Detainees or the Asylum Support Appeals Project."

> **❝ I really enjoy meeting my clients: they are amazing people from all over the world ❞**

Today, the main areas of Michelle's practice include asylum, human rights, deportation, family migration and EU law applications. Other immigration lawyers can specialise in business immigration, but there is quite a lot of crossover, with some covering several different areas. A lot of time is spent in court or at tribunals, and you also do a lot of High Court judicial review work.

"In many areas of civil law, you don't actually get to do a lot of advocacy, but in immigration you do," continues Michelle. "You do a lot of tribunal work. If it's on legal aid, it can be quite badly paid now – there are fixed fees, which are very low – but it's really important work and you can balance it out with other work. As you get more senior, you will spend more time drafting grounds for judicial review or drafting skeleton arguments for the Court of Appeal. So you might spend slightly more time out of court once you are a few years in practice. But at the beginning, you can be in court more often than not."

Location for vocation
Michelle readily admits that most barristers who work in immigration have a vocation for the area, and it is the people whom

she works for and with that make it all worthwhile for her. "Not many people fall into immigration work," she says. "It's not the best-paid area – the real rewards are achieving something for your client and working in a legally complex and challenging specialism. So you definitely have really committed lawyers – people who are, in some respects, activist lawyers – and I really enjoy that. I also really enjoy meeting my clients: they are amazing people from all over the world. They have been through so many experiences, many of which are horrific. You hear stories about their managing to flee across continents; you hear about people who've been exceptionally brave and stood up to dictators. You really meet some very inspiring people, the vast majority of whom I feel quite honoured to represent."

She also acknowledges that because of the close relationships that can develop between immigration barristers and their clients, you have to have to steel yourself for the possibility of defeat – something which can be hard to deal with. "I know a number of people who have left immigration work because they couldn't cope with it," says Michelle. "I'm thinking of one good friend in particular, who just found it too upsetting. She won 99.9% of the cases, but it was the others that she couldn't handle. I think you have to have an attitude whereby you know that you are doing your job the absolute best that you can, and you have to accept that the world is as it is – it is not always fair, and that's why a lot of your clients are in the position they are in the first place."

Intellectual property

IP work can be divided into two main areas: hard and soft intellectual property. 'Hard' intellectual property relates to patents, while 'soft' intellectual property covers trademarks, copyright, design rights and passing off. IP barristers advise on issues that range from commercial exploitation to infringement disputes and agreements that deal either exclusively with IP rights or with IP rights in the wider context of larger commercial transactions.

Science and technology might be an unusual platform from which to embark on a career at the Bar, but that was the case for Chris Hall, who began his career in physics. The switch to the Bar did not come for some time. "After I left university, I worked as a private physics tutor for a couple of years before joining BT as an IT project manager," he explains. "After a while, I found that advocating the technical ideas of others was more enjoyable than doing the programming myself, and I began to earn a reputation as someone who could sell a new project to the bosses." Chris was really getting into the advocacy, and at the same time was missing the aspects of self-employment he had enjoyed as a private tutor: "With advocacy, self-employment, and my science and technology experience, a career at the IP Bar made sense."

Pupillage: "tough, challenging, but rewarding"

Chris secured pupillage at 11 South Square. He is candid about how tough the process really is: "From my own experience and from talking to others at various chambers, pupillage is a uniformly tough experience. You cannot escape the reality that pupillage feels like a year-long interview which you can fail at any moment. If I had one tip, I would emphasise that your supervisor is interested primarily in seeing how you would do things if you were in their shoes. This is likely, for example, to involve you doing a piece of work that your supervisor has already done in the past. That can feel like a waste of time,

but of course it isn't because you're trying to prove that you can reach the same standard. Finally, don't lose sight of how brilliant being a barrister is – it is well worth the challenge."

Now a qualified barrister, Chris handles a varied IP caseload. "Most IP barristers start out as general practitioners working across the four key areas – copyright, trademarks, patents and designs," he explains. "It is common for people with science backgrounds to specialise in pharmaceutical or technology patents, but many IP barristers retain wide practices, as the IP Bar is such a specialised area anyway." He also emphasises that IP barristers are regularly involved in many wider cases, such as IT, media or commercial contractual disputes, "where there is an IP angle".

IP law focuses on the granular detail, so Chris's physics background has stood him in good stead. "Most IP sets will tell you that a science, maths or engineering degree is advantageous, if not strictly necessary, because one key skill that IP barristers need is the ability to understand how things work," he explains. This is the case particularly for patents and designs, which usually involve looking at the specific detail of a tangible thing and asking how it works, why it is a certain shape and so on. There are also more specialised niches within IP, so Chris suggests that "you are unlikely to be able to understand complex pharmaceutical patents without some training in chemistry, for example. It is true that a science education lends itself to IP. Nevertheless, a PhD in biochemistry is neither necessary nor sufficient; what really matters is the ability to master new concepts quickly."

Advocacy opportunities

In IP, there are lots of opportunities to go to court. "The IP Bar is unique in that although it is commercial, there are many fixed-cost and low-cost tribunals, affording junior barristers plenty of opportunity to get out there and argue cases. This experience can be difficult to get

For more chambers that work in this practice area, please use the "Pupillage index" starting on p537.

Name: **Chris Hall**
Chambers: **11 South Square**
University: **Imperial College London**
Undergraduate degree: **Physics**

elsewhere at the commercial Bar," Chris explains. "Junior IP practitioners regularly appear in tribunals at the UK Intellectual Property Office, and in the new, bespoke Intellectual Property Enterprise Court."

In terms of litigation, there is an even split between instructions on the side of defendant or claimant. As for where instructions come from, "because IP is quite a small area you regularly see the same faces – there are not that many solicitors who regularly practise in IP, so you build strong relationships with instructing solicitors and there are also many regular clients," Chris continues.

And the cases themselves involve a wide range of products, as Chris outlines: "On my desk I have two snack food products that are sold under very similar names; two scrubbing brushes with similar designs; two letter boxes that function in the same unusual way, and more. One of the satisfying things about IP cases is that a lot of the litigation concerns tangible objects – you can examine them, and see how they work and what they look like."

The job also brings Chris into contact with all kinds of interesting people: "In patent cases, you work with expert witnesses who teach you about very specific areas of technology. This means that in every case you learn something new from a world expert in their field – and you get paid for it! There are some colourful characters too. The first trial I was in concerned the design of caravan covers, and one of the witnesses was an avid caravan enthusiast. In his evidence he described the perils of towing his caravan all over Northwest England in various states of Cumbrian weather with the caravan covers flapping around in the wind and rain. The judge described him as 'engaging and direct'; he was more like a stand-up comedian. In IP, it is more than purely commercial litigation – you regularly get the small family business with a big idea, or sometimes the mad inventor squaring off against the corporations trying to stop him."

However, these 'David v Goliath' situations don't always end in victory for the underdog. "It is very often the case that when a defendant loses, they lose everything," explains Chris. "It's quite a responsibility for a junior barrister to bear. You see a lot of clients – both claimants and defendants – suffer because of something that perhaps could have been avoided with a bit of legal advice early in the day."

There is much afoot in the wider world of IP and Brexit will undoubtedly have a significant effect, as Chris explains: "A lot of IP law is harmonised across the European Union, and there are many rights which are EU-wide, for example the EU trademark and the EU registered design. The scope and practice involving these rights regularly changes with the jurisprudence emerging from 28 member states. There is also a planned introduction of a unitary patent which will be valid across the European Union. In tandem, the Unified Patent Court is being introduced in 2018 to resolve disputes related to those patents."

No need to rush

Chris has some advice to share for those hoping to achieve the necessary standards. "It is very useful to have some experience in the real world," he begins. "As a junior barrister at the IP Bar, you will often be representing small businesses in relatively low-value cases. The case fits your level of experience, but you will usually be dealing with the person at the top of the small business – the chief executive or sole director. This creates a mismatch in terms of experience, and you have to earn the trust of the client despite your lack of experience. It helps to be able to speak to clients on their level and to demonstrate that you understand their commercial world. This gives clients much more confidence in your ability. So I would positively encourage people to get some experience before coming to the Bar."

Media

Media and entertainment barristers have clients in a variety of sectors, including theatre, film, music, publishing, broadcasting, sport and advertising. They advise and represent clients in court and before other tribunals on matters that might include defamation, privacy and confidentiality, contract disputes, advertising standards, sponsorship, intellectual property and restraint of trade.

Three main factors drew Ashton Chantrielle to a life at the Bar: "First, being at the Bar is a great way to specialise in a particular field. Being a solicitor can make things a little more uncertain if you want to specialise, whereas at the Bar you specialise immediately." Second, Ashton was attracted to the independence that comes with being a barrister. "You're part of a chambers," she explains, "but you're self-employed. You work for yourself and have full responsibility over all your cases." Finally, Ashton was enticed by the oral advocacy which comes with the role, which most solicitors don't get the opportunity to do.

Picking the right chambers
After making the decision to pursue a career as a barrister, Ashton gained pupillage at 8 New Square. Although she admits that her time as a pupil was a "steep learning curve," she mostly looks back with fondness. This may be down to Ashton's chambers, which she cites as one of the things that she likes most about her job. "It's actually very important that you pick a chambers that you like," she advises. "Especially if you're in a smaller chambers, you will see these people every day for – if you're lucky – the rest of your career. I feel very lucky to be in the kind of environment I'm in, which means I enjoy going to work in the morning and I enjoy being there."

Clearly smitten with 8 New Square, Ashton describes the day she gained tenancy there

as the highlight of her career. "You spend a lot of time working hard to become a tenant," she explains. "You're competing against people constantly and you have to prove to a lot of people that you have what it takes. So after a year of being on constant trial, to get tenancy is just one of the most amazing feelings."

Surviving the shift from pupil to tenant
Was she intimidated by the switch from pupil to tenant? "It is daunting," she admits. "When you're a pupil you shadow another barrister and that is how you learn to draft documents, how to act in court, strategy, how to run a case. Your work is always checked. When you become tenant it changes quite dramatically because all of a sudden you're on your own – you have to take ownership and responsibility for your cases and try not to mess up!"

That said, Ashton says there are two things that get you through. The first is knowing that someone believes in you, which means that you have to believe in yourself. "They think that you can do it and they have all the experience," she explains. "The second thing is that you can always go and ask a question if you're not sure. You're never in a position where you think 'I'm genuinely alone here' – you always have people around who can help you if you need it and you learn pretty quickly, so the thought is more daunting than the actual experience."

Bridging different interests
Since becoming a tenant, Ashton has built up an extensive client list, including several in the media and entertainment industry. Due to the overlap between the two areas of law, Ashton specialises in IP law, an interest which stemmed from her background in chemistry. "I always considered myself a scientist above everything else, but I didn't want to be a scientist," she reflects. "So I thought about how I could combine the two and IP is a combination of science and law – I wanted to bridge those two

For more chambers that work in this practice area, please use the "Pupillage index" starting on p537.

Name: **Ashton Chantrielle**
Firm: **8 New Square**
University: **University of Bristol**
Undergraduate degree: **Chemistry and law**

together. Being a scientist is quite a different job – you can end up working on one specific area of science for a very long time. I wanted to dip in and out of different types of subject matter and not be stuck on one."

❝ If you're working on a big trial, there's a lot of paperwork that goes into that – a lot of documents, statements, pleadings and arguments – so you do end up in the office probably more than you do in court than if, for example, you did criminal law ❞

"The most important difference between IP and media and other areas of law is that they're quite paperwork-based," Ashton explains. "If you're working on a big trial, there's a lot of paperwork that goes into that – a lot of documents, statements, pleadings and arguments – so you do end up in the office probably more than you do in court than if, for example, you did criminal law." However, IP and media are unique in that the different courts enable junior barristers to be on their feet right from the outset, which for Ashton creates a nice balance: "You get to do both sides of the job quite nicely."

In terms of succeeding in her field of law, Ashton stresses that you must have a serious interest in media and IP, as well as the ability to tackle technical cases. More broadly, Ashton advises that anyone considering becoming a barrister should have a thick skin. "It's not for the faint hearted," she warns. "You need to know that it can be a bumpy ride."

Looming uncertainty
When asked about the key issues facing the profession over the next five years, Ashton

laughs. "The obvious answer is Brexit," she exclaims. "There's a lot of uncertainty around what it's going to bring and how it's going to affect the law – especially IP law, which involves a lot of European rights. There have been a lot of questions from clients," she continues, "but there are no answers at the moment. And when it's your job to give an answer and you don't have one, it's quite difficult!"

"Media and IP are such broad subjects," Ashton explains. "They cover a lot of things, even things you wouldn't expect – like breaches of confidence. That's part of the reason why Brexit is making everything so uncertain, it covers so many different rights."

Expert advice
Ashton's main piece of advice for budding barristers is to do your research. "You should research not only your chambers," she urges, "but also the area of law you're going into. Every chambers will want someone who wants to be there and who makes an effort in getting to know what they do." In addition, she advises those going for pupillage to ensure that their application is up to scratch. "It's the first thing we get," she explains, "so care needs to be taken when preparing it."

Although certain aspects of becoming a barrister may seem daunting, Ashton felt fully prepared throughout the process. "What's good about the Bar is that you're actually quite well informed, so I knew a lot before I applied. It's a well-documented industry." And the best thing? "You can always ask!"

Personal injury

Personal injury (PI) law falls under the law of tort. It involves civil claims brought to obtain compensation for injuries so as to put the injured person back in the position that they would have been in had they not been injured. The subject matter varies considerably, and can range from controversial, high-profile disaster cases through to road traffic accidents and health and safety cases. A related, specialised practice area of PI law is clinical negligence, which involves injuries suffered during medical procedures.

Theo Barclay's passion for the legal profession was first ignited during his studies as a history undergraduate at Oxford. "During my second year I studied some legal history and from that point I thought that becoming a barrister was the way forward – principally because I wanted to be on my feet in court, arguing cases," he recalls. An enjoyable work experience placement with a commercial solicitors' firm failed to change Theo's mind, while a couple of mini-pupillages confirmed that the Bar was where he wanted to be.

After Bar school, Theo completed pupillage at XXIV Old Buildings in Lincoln's Inn before moving to Hailsham Chambers, another commercial set, where he has built up a varied common law practice. "I essentially do a bit of everything," he explains. "Having done a commercial pupillage and then a third six months at Hailsham concentrating mainly on clinical negligence, personal injury and professional negligence matters, I now have a wide variety of different sources of work. It really depends on what comes in at any given moment, but I generally have one or two bigger commercial cases rumbling along in the background, on which I'm a junior, complemented by the day-to-day paperwork of a common lawyer. My favourite part of the job, however, is representing clients in two or three trials a week. The majority of these are personal injury cases."

Advocacy opportunities

Regular court appearances are one of the main draws of PI work, in Theo's view: "That's the brilliant thing about having personal injury as part of your practice – even if you are only two years into your career, you're in court all the time. That has really helped me improve as an advocate. Choosing a practice area that gets you into court is something that I would recommend to everyone. Court advocacy is something that a lot of commercial barristers don't get to do that often, despite being the reason most of us decided to do the job in the first place. There is such a contrast between helping out on a big project and running the show, even on a case which is lower value. It is more interesting on a day-to-day basis when you are in control. As a tennis player might say – the match is 'on your racket'. Personal injury is one of the few areas where you can take the lead in your own cases at only a couple of years' call."

> ** Choosing a practice area that gets you into court is something that I would recommend to everyone **

Some of the most interesting PI cases for barristers at Theo's level of seniority concern fundamental dishonesty: "The general rule is that you cannot as a defendant recover your costs from a claimant, but that rule can be put aside if the claimant has been fundamentally dishonest. However, proving dishonesty in court is very difficult to do, so cases where you think the claimant has been dishonest are an exciting challenge for an advocate. In that situation, it is very important for your client not only to win the case, but also to convince the judge that there has been foul play, and to award the defendant their costs. This requires very careful cross examination in the hostile

For more chambers that work in this practice area, please use the "Pupillage index" starting on p537.

Name: **Theo Barclay**
Chambers: **Hailsham Chambers**
University: **University of Oxford**
Undergraduate degree: **Modern history**

environment that becomes inevitable if you are to accuse someone of lying. Winning these cases is hugely satisfying."

PI work is clearly weighty and consequential in its own right, its suitability for junior barristers honing their advocacy skills notwithstanding. Theo never loses sight of what such cases mean to his clients: "What you're doing matters so much to the people you are representing, whether you are the defendant and are representing a doctor or employer who has been accused of doing something negligent, or you are the claimant and are representing someone who has gone through an awful period in which they have suffered a great deal, and now seeks compensation for substantial losses."

Infinite variety
The unique way of life at the Bar is perhaps the greatest attraction of the job for Theo: "The combination of a university-like way of life – looking things up in the library, thinking hard and meeting tight deadlines – and the intensity of the courtroom is one of the profession's great attractions. The infinite variety is something that I really enjoy. Also, it cannot be overstated how great it is to be in charge of your own time as a self-employed person. Even if you end up working as hard – or harder – than your contemporaries in other professions, there is something wonderful about retaining ultimate control. This does, of course, come with pressure because you have to take responsibility for everything you do. There is a looming nervousness about making a mistake, but that also keeps you invested in the quality of your work."

The Bar – particularly the junior Bar – as we know it is likely to be facing a period of profound change in the near future. "There will be attempts over the next few years to change the costs rules in order to limit the volume of litigation, especially in the PI sector, although the government's intentions have not yet

been fully fleshed out," Theo explains. "It is important to remember that we are working in a market like any other, and any rule changes have a huge impact. It will be important for prospective pupils to keep an eye on the proposals as they develop. The question of online courts is also something that everyone aiming for pupillage needs to consider. If they are introduced in any form, it will fundamentally change the nature of the profession – and therefore the experience of any early-years practitioner. For my part, I think there will be real difficulties in running an online court for PI claims, because so much depends on what an individual says in the witness box – in practice, this can be very different to what has been put in the evidence bundle before."

Nonetheless Theo remains keen to encourage aspiring barristers with the right qualities to pursue their ambitions: "Advocacy lies at the heart of the profession – you need to be someone who likes to stand up and make an unpopular argument under difficult circumstances, before facing tough questions. Academic success is very important as well – you are applying for a job heavily based around research, and the more relevant experience, the better. If you can tick those two boxes there is no reason not to go for it, at which point you will need the third essential quality for getting pupillage – determination. Everyone comes to the Bar through different paths, but there is no barrister who has got there without hard work and a stubborn refusal to give up."

And to that end, Theo signs off with some practical advice: "I would encourage any reader to make full use of the help available at the Inns of Court. When I was starting out, I wish I had educated myself more about what they have to offer. There are so many resources at the Inns to help applicants, including people who can offer invaluable practical advice. It would be remiss not to take every opportunity they offer."

Planning/environment

Planning law regulates the way in which property owners use and develop their property in the interests of the wider community. Local planning authorities are required to follow a legal and policy framework in their decision making. Planning law is often interwoven with other branches of the law, such as environmental, local government and judicial review. Clients might include landowners, developers, local authorities, public and private utilities, government departments, amenity groups and individuals.

In 2012, the year Alexander Greaves was called to the Bar, *Rolling Stone* magazine updated its list of the 500 Greatest Albums of All Time. Nestled at number 258 was the 1968 offering *The Kinks Are The Village Green Preservation Society* – the London band's sixth studio album and one of their most acclaimed works. The album not only cemented a place in music history that year, but also inadvertently held a clue to Alexander's path towards the planning Bar.

"It was not entirely accidental that I ended up in planning law or that I did my pupillage at Frances Taylor Building (FTB)," recalls Alexander. "During my law conversion course, I decided I wanted to go into public law and looked at various different areas. It was then I developed an interest in village green law – a slightly esoteric discipline related to planning law. It was while researching it further that I came across FTB, as they've done quite a lot of work in the area."

He obtained pupillage at FTB and, found that the work he was doing was unlike anything he had experienced during his postgraduate legal education. While he points out that no prior knowledge of the subject is expected of young barristers, the learning curve during his first few months of pupillage was pretty steep.

Three-way split

Pupillage at FTB is split between three supervisors, with pupils spending four months with each and the level of responsibility increasing as experience is gained. "Certainly for the first four months I was pretty much just following my supervisor," recalls Alexander, "accompanying them to inquiries, court, conferences or on site visits. I would also do written work for them in chambers, whether researching points of law or doing first drafts of opinions and skeleton arguments. After the first four months, you are encouraged to start doing more of that sort of work for other members of chambers, which helps broaden your experience. In the second six, you are encouraged take on some work of your own while continuing to do work for other members of chambers."

While much of the work Alexander found himself doing in his own right during this time bore little resemblance to his planning caseload today, it gave him the chance to build confidence dealing with matters on his own and to familiarise himself with the workings of the court. He was also fortunate enough to have the opportunity to act as a junior for another member of chambers on a week-long village green inquiry.

"I'm not sure how many cases I did, but it gives you experience; and although you have the assistance of your supervisors, who are there for guidance if you need it, at the end of the day you are the one on your feet, arguing in court. The nature of the job is such that there isn't a lot of pure planning work at pupil level, although I did do some, so a lot of what I was doing was small county court work, which dropped off once I got tenancy."

Variety is the spice of life

One of the things that Alexander likes most about the planning Bar is that his workload is quite varied and he finds his time split between advisory work, inquiry work and court work. The advisory work consists of

For more chambers that work in this practice area, please use the "Pupillage index" starting on p537.

Name: **Alexander Greaves**
Chambers: **Francis Taylor Building**
University: **University of Manchester**
Undergraduate degree: **History**

looking at papers and advising local planning authorities on decisions they may take, advising prospective developers on potential projects or advising people either who want to object to planning permission or who have other queries about land use.

> **❝ From appearing at a planning inquiry to appearing at the High Court, or even in criminal court dealing with prosecutions following enforcement action – flexibility is the key thing ❞**

A planning inquiry is an appeal against a decision of a local planning authority and is presided over by planning inspectors, who make decisions on behalf of the secretary of state. They can vary in length, although Alexander suggests that a rise in the number of informal hearings (which rarely involve barristers) to clear up minor disputes means there are currently fewer one-or-two day inquiries and most last between one and two weeks. These take place up and down the country, depending on where the land to which they relate happens to be. As such, Alexander often finds himself travelling long distances and staying for the duration of the inquiry, and while he very much enjoys the change of scene, he also warns that "they can quite often be in the middle of nowhere".

He also highlights the differences between inquiries and court proceedings: "It is quite different from court advocacy, in that it is common practice to sit down in these inquiries. It is procedurally more informal than a lot of courts and there is not quite such strict adherence to the rules of evidence as in other areas. The only caveat to that would perhaps be for enforcement inquiries where, because

evidence generally relates to evidence of fact, it is given under oath."

Adapt to survive
The difference between court-based planning work and the more informal environment planning inquiries means that lawyers need to be able to adjust to different tribunals and working conditions. "Being able to adapt to different environments is key," explains Alexander. "From appearing at a planning inquiry to appearing at the High Court, or even in criminal court dealing with prosecutions following enforcement action – flexibility is the key thing."

In addition, Alexander suggests that a general understanding of politics and government policy in the area is very useful and may well be worth cultivating for those attending a pupillage interview at a planning set. "It plays such an important role in the development and application of planning law," he claims. "Policy is so fundamental that having an understanding of current government thinking is vital. National policy and planning practice guidance is available online; you don't need to read through it all, but it's good to have a general understanding of the overriding themes. Quite a lot can be gleaned from the newspapers; affordable housing in London and concerns over fracking are both things that have been in the news quite a lot recently."

"You can also sit in on planning inquiries," he offers. "They happen in council offices up and down the country and are advertised on council websites. Documents are made available to the public either online or at the inquiry venue. It would definitely help you show an interest in planning at interview, where they are interested in why you want to go to a particular chambers, rather than why you just want to be a barrister. It helps to demonstrate that you've looked what that chambers does and show some understanding of the key issues around their areas of specialty."

Professional negligence

Barristers involved in this field deal with claims against professionals such as architects, accountants, solicitors and financial advisers who have allegedly failed to provide services to the level of care and skill which a member of that profession would be expected to demonstrate. Clinical negligence is a type of professional liability that involves disputes between patients and healthcare providers (usually doctors), centring on quality of care. Defendant professionals will usually have indemnity insurance against such claims.

Starting off on a law course at Merton College, Oxford, Shail Patel wasn't sure he'd made the right choice. After a term he tried to switch his field of study to English literature, but as it happens the old stereotype of the sanctimonious English don sometimes rings true, and ultimately things didn't work out. "I think they were happy to see me leave!" he laughs. "So it was down to carrying on with law at Merton or doing English somewhere else – which didn't seem like a great option – so I decided to stick with law, and I'm glad I did in the end, because I started to get the hang of it a little better." As the course progressed, he also started to enjoy it more, and after attending several law fairs and speaking to barristers, he grew ever more enticed by the "intellectual aspects" of the law. So despite the initial diversion, academia's loss proved to be the legal profession's gain.

After the comparatively easy-going university years, plus a stint at Harvard where he obtained an LLM (and sightseeing in the United States also featured prominently), Shail describes his pupillage at Fountain Court Chambers as "a fairly tough experience – suddenly having to show up at 8:30am in a suit every day, after two years of being a student, was quite a challenge." But the experience was nonetheless "very interesting and stimulating" and put him in good stead to thereafter take a tenancy at 4 New Square, where professional negligence briefs are a mainstay of the set's practice.

Always a story unfolding

A subset of commercial litigation, professional negligence typically comprises only a part of a barrister's caseload, alongside contractual disputes, construction work and instructions involving financial services providers and insurers, among other things. But having dipped a toe in English literature while an undergraduate, Shail enthuses over the narrative thrill and personal side of professional negligence cases: "Unlike some commercial litigation, there's always a story – whether it's some transaction or litigation that's gone wrong, or some fraud that accountants have failed to uncover – there's usually some human interest behind it all. With certain types of commercial litigation you're basically just staring at a contract all day – which is a different intellectual challenge, but not something you can really talk about at a dinner party! Professional negligence work often involves some element of human interest and human or business endeavour."

> ❝ Unlike some commercial litigation, there's always a story – whether it's some transaction or litigation that's gone wrong, or some fraud that accountants have failed to uncover – there's usually some human interest behind it all ❞

As a practice area, it offers both range and depth. "One interesting thing is that you're tasked with mastering someone else's professional discipline. Whether it's an accountant, surveyor, architect or insurance

For more chambers that work in this practice area, please use the "Pupillage index" starting on p537.

Name: **Shail Patel**
Chambers: **4 New Square**
University: **University of Oxford**
Degree: **Law**

broker, you need to have a mastery of how they should be doing their job and what principles they should be applying in practising their business," he notes. In terms of trends, he cites the unfailing presence of "some scheme out there that everyone thinks is a good idea at the time but ultimately goes wrong and gives rise to litigation". Of late he has kept busy with liability cases triggered from the aftermath of the dotcom bust and the global financial crisis that followed. "We're seeing a huge amount of failed film, technology and other investments and tax mitigation schemes, ideas from the early 2000s to 2009 – before the government began to shut down this sort of thing – leading to a lot of large-scale litigation rumbling through the courts."

New challenges ahead
With the modern-day prevalence of electronic communication and technology – and the promise of further innovation on that front – professional negligence practitioners will have ample new challenges to tackle in future. Shail points to the rise of online financial fraud and artificial intelligence (AI) as opening a thought-provoking debate on who exactly is liable for tech-related misdeeds and to what extent, which will ultimately be resolved by the courts. "It is only a matter of time before AI and robo-asset management give rise to litigation, people claiming they received bad investment advice from a robot and the like; it'll be a big thing in the future."

Doing the detective work
The adrenaline rush of going to trial is definitely a highlight of the job, but Shail underscores the value of a level-headed and measured approach. "At the commercial Bar we don't get to court as much as the criminal barristers. In some ways everything we do is preparing for court, whether it happens or not – and often it doesn't – but when it does, and it comes off in a way that you know is because of how you've steered the ship

until that day – that's a rewarding thing." He likens the less emotionally charged days of case preparation to "forensic detective work, putting the story together and understanding the nuances – ultimately you have to satisfy yourself that you've picked up on every relevant fact of the case; sometimes you'll find something that no one else has found and it's critical." And when and if the case ultimately comes before the court, the pay-off can be all too sweet: "To cross-examine an expert or a witness accused of dishonesty in a way that leads to them giving an answer that they don't even know is fatal to their side's case – that's when you feel like you're really adding value and can feel like you know what you're doing – until then it's just educated guesswork!"

Be clear and cordial
When asked about what it takes for a budding barrister with an interest in professional negligence to succeed, Shail pinpoints the simple yet potent quality that has proved so useful to him amid all that sleuthing, case building and courtroom advocacy: clarity of thought. "It's not something you can just 'do', but something you can focus on achieving – to always express yourself in as clear and logical a way as possible." He also has some sage advice which perhaps goes overlooked too often: "Try to make a positive impression on everyone you meet. I say this from two perspectives: I'm involved in our pupillage recruitment process and I went through it myself a long time ago. It's not just about leaving a good impression on the barristers that interview you, but also the ones you meet on mini-pupillages, or at recruitment events. It also includes staff involved in recruitment and even the receptionist at a chambers you visit. You don't have to tell them how great you are, but rather be professional, in a way that leaves those people with the feeling that you are a person they would want to share a working environment with in the future."

Property

Property lawyers act for a variety of domestic and international clients – including property investors and developers, farmers, governments, landowners and public sector bodies – on a wide range of transactions and disputes, involving everything from offices and housing to retail developments and industrial units. The common legal issues arising for commercial property lawyers include acquisitions and disposals of land, investments, landlord and tenant matters, developments and contracts, and environmental law and associated liabilities.

Like his namesake, the father of modern economics, Adam Smith took a measured and well-thought out approach to his future career: "I was always interested in law and had done some work experience at school. I went on to do several mini-pupillages, which definitely encouraged me towards the Bar. I liked the idea of being self-employed, as it would give me more direct control over my career. I also thought that, as a litigation solicitor, it might be frustrating to get to know a case well, and then, potentially, have to refer it on to someone else to provide advice on the key issues. I was also drawn to the day-to-day nature of the work: the advocacy, providing advice on merits and tactics, and preparing pleadings and skeleton arguments – it all appealed."

Pupillage at 9 Old Square offered Adam solid insight into the realities of the profession, especially by virtue of having four separate pupil supervisors, all with different practices: "It was useful to see how my pupil supervisors worked and presented things, and, although it was an intense time, they made it as stress-free as it could be." He joined as a tenant at the end of 2002 and the set merged with Maitland soon thereafter.

Property matters
Today, property is a large part of what Adam's practice is about. He describes a handful of the varied cases he has dealt with recently: "My Gibraltar-based client had provided finance to two BVI companies backed by a number of charges over English properties; the borrowers defaulted, and there was an underlying dispute over the terms of the loan agreements and whether they had been varied. It was a commercial dispute, but the focus of the trial was the alleged release of a major part of the security and whether the client had bound itself to that in return for a part-payment. There were technical points about mortgages and a large amount of disputed evidence. Another involved a wealthy family that owned a large portfolio of commercial and residential properties on a fairly informal basis; they had fallen into disagreement with each other and the ownership of the properties was in dispute – it was in large part a fight over who had said what."

Acting as junior to an eminent silk in the House of Lords was a career highlight for Adam, especially as the case concerned "issues that were of some significance to a lot of property owners; the committee, unsurprisingly, quickly got to the heart of the issues and asked some very probing questions." A notable arbitration relating to a metal-producing business, post-Soviet break-up, also stands out: "Our client had been involved in the management of the business. There had been a management buy-out, with external investment, and the dispute was between the external investor and our client. The ultimate investor was a well-known oligarch with all the financial and political cards in his favour. But we achieved a good result for the client, so that was very satisfying."

Pros and cons of self-employment
Referring back to one of his original reasons for choosing the Bar, Adam cites the freedom of self-employment as one of the best features of the job: "Although it may sometimes be illusory, if a gap in your diary opens up (for example, a case has just settled) and you want to take advantage of that by getting away, you are able to do it –

For more chambers that work in this practice area, please use the "Pupillage index" starting on p537.

Name: **Adam Smith**
Chambers: **Maitland Chambers**
University: **University of Oxford**
Undergraduate degree: **Classics**

there's no checking in with the boss. When you're involved with a case and something needs to be done, obviously that has to happen; but, to a certain extent, when you take a case it's your decision to do so." The ability to make a real difference through your work and the keen intellectual challenges are other draw-cards: "Very many cases throw up interesting problems, so there's nearly always something to think about. It's also satisfying to see what we do having a direct impact – if you win a case for an individual, for whom it has been the last throw of the dice, it's personally very significant."

There is no denying, however, that this career can be all-consuming at times. "That can be good and is part of the excitement of it – we are very invested in it; but, at the same time, your personal life can suffer as a result," he admits. "I've had to work through holidays and frequently cancel plans. There is often a lack of predictability, so that all of a sudden something needs to be done urgently, such as seeking an interim injunction. You can also be under a lot of pressure, particularly close to and during trial. As you get more experienced, you become more comfortable with being in that position and working out how to juggle things."

Adam reflects on how life at the Bar is evolving, both in his own field and elsewhere: "Commercial property work is unlikely to change much in the next few years, other than (in terms of its volume and the nature of disputes and issues which arise) as a result of general economic forces; the biggest upheaval is occurring at the criminal Bar, with major structural changes to publicly funded work. One change that has already occurred generally at the Bar is increased specialism. Less and less you see people with a general common law practice – clients appear to be increasingly keen to be advised and represented by a barrister who is a specialist in the relevant field."

Commitment is key

So what makes for an excellent property barrister? According to Adam, it is broadly the same set of skills you would mark as essential in any civil area of law: "Commitment to the job is essential; the most successful barristers make themselves available to clients and are constantly looking for the best angle to achieve the client's objectives. Analytical ability and knowledge of the law are key. There is often a large amount of information involved, so you need to be able to distil that into the far smaller amount of critically relevant information. You need advocacy skills, both oral and written; a lot of work goes into written as well as oral advocacy. If you can get a judge on your side even before the hearing has started with a good skeleton argument, a significant proportion of the hard work is done. You also need good people skills – the ability to get on with both professional and lay clients, to be pleasant and easy to work with, and to inspire confidence."

Adam suggests that the first steps on the path are to do well in whatever undergraduate degree you have chosen – "proving your analytical ability and ability to sift information is possible in all or nearly all degrees" – and to complete perhaps five or six mini-pupillages in the practice areas that you are interested in. "In addition, you need to show an interest in advocacy, so debating or mooting as a law student, or other public speaking, is particularly important."

His final tips include joining an Inn as soon as you've decided that the Bar is for you, because it is "a great opportunity to meet people, do some mooting and explore funding options through Inn scholarships". He also suggests trying a vacation scheme with a solicitors' firm, as a way of "understanding the day to day work of a litigation solicitor and the pressures that they can work under and demonstrating that you've made a well thought-out decision to join the Bar as opposed to qualifying as a solicitor".

Public

The public law Bar spans the full range of administrative, public and constitutional law. Specific areas within the field include civil liberties and human rights, commercial judicial review, community and healthcare law, disciplinary proceedings and the internal administration of public bodies, education law, housing law, planning law, prison law, and social services and social security law. Public law work has a European influence, with a steady stream of cases being referred to the European Court of Justice for preliminary rulings and other cases raising the issue of the application of the European Convention on Human Rights.

Drawn to the Bar by an early interest in advocacy – "I went into law with a view to becoming a barrister; I never had any intention of becoming a solicitor" – Jennifer MacLeod took some time out after university to see the world, living in the United States and South Africa and working for the UN and various NGOs, before returning to pupillage at Brick Court. She describes her time as a pupil: "It was very challenging, initially because of the difference between learning law at university and practising it; they are a gulf apart. Learning to be an advocate took a huge amount of teaching from my pupil supervisors and I found it quite exhausting! But it was also enjoyable and as you start to see yourself improve, there is a thrilling feeling of being able to do something that you couldn't do six months prior."

Now a barrister of four years' call, Jennifer has a public law practice that is incredibly varied – reflecting the nature of a practice area that "encompasses anything to do with the exercise of state power against individuals, be they corporations or people, and whether a state should be constrained in the exercise of that power, with a variety of human rights and international issues involved". She explains some of the things that attracted her to this field: "If you're at university and interested in the principles of how a state governs, then you

will find public law a fascinating area to work in – I certainly do! You are at the edge of politics, law and policy, and part of shaping where things go."

Going public

Jennifer offers examples of the huge variety of both client and subject matter that is a feature of her caseload: "At one point, I was working for a multinational tobacco manufacturer challenging the government's decision to bring in plain packaging; for domestic violence victims in Georgia who were claiming that the state had failed to protect them; for UK welfare beneficiaries who wanted to prove that the government policy of excluding them from certain benefits was unlawful; and for Southern Rail when they were trying to stop the trade unions from striking. I'm currently working for the government on a case against pharmaceutical companies including Pfizer in relation to what's known as 'excessive pricing' of epilepsy drugs. It can be so completely different from one day to the next, you never get bored. And you're also often working on things that you can chat about to anyone – they're important issues in the public domain." She adds that you may find yourself in court less than barristers practising in other areas, "but you're also often working in the public eye, which is both exciting and stressful!"

Reflecting back on one of her seminal career moments, Jennifer says: "I am most proud of my work on the domestic violence case in Georgia, working in collaboration with the European Human Rights Advocacy Centre. We were successful in changing the law completely on domestic violence; the government brought in an entirely new regime, worked with NGOs to develop it and gave compensation to past victims. This relatively small case made a very real practical difference to lots of people's lives."

Both international and domestic work is a feature: "Because my practice entails a lot of

For more chambers that work in this practice area, please use the "Pupillage index" starting on p537.

Name: **Jennifer MacLeod**
Chambers: **Brick Court Chambers**
University: **University of Cambridge**
Undergraduate degree: **Law**

human rights litigation, much of my work is international, but that's not to say that everyone in public law will experience that. For example, I'm also acting for an individual who wants to change the UK law on assisted suicide; which is based in human rights principles but is a domestic public law challenge."

Brexit uncertainty
Public law is one of the practice areas that will be hardest hit by the United Kingdom's exit from the European Union, relying as it does on EU law principles and the presence of a supranational body. Jennifer elaborates: "In this area, Brexit will have particularly large repercussions because significant areas of public law are based on EU principles, and the way we challenge or constrain what the government can do is often based on EU law. The fact that the state is not supreme in the legal system, because the EU legal system supersedes it, is important. When we lose that, it will have an enormous impact on how you challenge what the state does – or if you can at all. One of the purposes of Brexit was to free the state from such constraints, so the repercussions in this area are enormous."

Also linked to Brexit is the future of human rights laws: "There has been much debate on the extent of human rights protections and whether we need the Human Rights Act; for now, we are all watching closely what will happen."

If an interest in the development of the law is your thing, then public could be your career nirvana. "There is a particular focus on legal, rather than factual, disputes, so you have to have a cerebral interest in that," advises Jennifer. "There is not a huge amount of cross-examination or the drama of performing in front of a jury, so if that's what you're looking for, you might want to think about a different area! Public law is very similar to the mooting you will do at university, so if you've enjoyed that, this could be for you."

In addition, being one of the less traditional areas of law means that public attracts a diverse range of practitioners, as Jennifer explains: "People come from all sorts of background, including other sectors, state schools and a wide range of universities, so you definitely shouldn't be put off because of your background. The most important thing is to be as clear as you can be with your analysis and try to get the best grades you possibly can."

❝ If you're interested in the principles of how a state governs, then you will find public law a fascinating area – you're working at the edge of politics, law and policy ❞

Jennifer is keen to pass on some advice about the job that she wished someone had mentioned to her – not that it would have changed her mind about pursuing this is a career, just that to be forewarned is forearmed. "I wish I had been told that it is someone else's job to show that you're doing a bad job, all the time!" she laughs. "It's worth thinking about that before you start; this is not a career free from stress. You are also on a very public stage and things don't always go the way you want. You have to grow a bit of a thick skin."

A final heartening reflection on the nature of the Bar: "One thing I didn't expect was being part of such a great community of people – across chambers and the profession, people are actually in the main very kind and supportive, as well as interesting and smart. I work with amazing colleagues – many of whom have become wonderful friends – and I'm not sure that I expected that. It was a very pleasant surprise."

Revenue

Tax barristers advise and litigate on all aspects of commercial and personal tax issues. Corporate and business tax matters may involve company or group reconstructions, transfer pricing and the use of losses and capital allowances. Tax planning for individuals can encompass capital gains, inheritance and income tax. Typical cases might concern advising on (or acting in disputes concerning) the sale of a family company or the creation and operation of trusts. Barristers also specialise in value added tax and other indirect taxes, including customs duties, excise duties, landfill tax and stamp duties. The work may involve detailed consideration of EU law.

An interest in a highly analytic practice is part of what led Thomas Chacko to a career at the tax Bar: "Tax is a very technical and law-heavy area, both in terms of the legislation and the rapidly evolving case law. We focus more on complex statutory interpretation than most other areas of the Bar, so being alert to language is important."

Despite not knowing much about tax when applying for pupillage, Thomas knew he wanted "to do something technical, and to be in court regularly but not all the time, so I applied to sets that did specialist, commercial or chancery work". He found Pump Court a pleasant place to work and was impressed by "the type of work and the atmosphere in chambers". Following a 12-month pupillage, Thomas was happy to be taken on as a tenant. "We are a collegiate set and pop in and out of each other's rooms all the time," he comments. "That's essential, because the law is fast paced and voluminous, and you need to be able to bang on doors and ask questions of the more experienced members of chambers."

Advice heavy
One key feature of the tax Bar is that the balance between litigating and advising is traditionally more heavily weighted towards the latter, as Thomas explains. "As well as my own pieces of advice, I do devilling for senior members, where you basically provide them with a first draft. That's a great chance to gain exposure to more complex areas of law. Some of our advice is given with a view to litigation, while others focus on how to go about something correctly. Because tax law is complicated and it is possible to fall into traps quite easily, a lot of advance planning is required – VAT, for example, is quite counterintuitive."

This is not to say that tax barristers never get the chance to stand up and put their case to a judge. "We certainly do more advice than most, but there is still a fair amount of litigation," Thomas confirms. "You may find yourself as junior or second junior on a big meaty dispute, where you spend months going through documents, drafting and getting everything ready. Litigation has a long lead time, so a matter might be on your desk for nine months before you get to court." The smaller disputes, which are run without a leader, "are no less difficult – things can still be confusing and messy even when there is little money at stake".

Thomas describes a case of his own involving an academic who wanted his pension to be paid out, but first had to prove that he had not been careless in not having paid national insurance on time: "Often it's about creating an impression. I thought he had a good case, but it largely depended on whether we could project the right 'feel': would the judge think that this is a decent person or is he or she just trying it on? I was pleased that we gave the right impression and succeeded."

Furthermore, it's not just about the minutiae of the tax statutes: "Many cases are more about whether a contract existed or whether procedures were followed correctly. A lot of developments in trust law and restitution

For more chambers that work in this practice area, please use the "Pupillage index" starting on p537.

Name: **Thomas Chacko**
Chambers: **Pump Court Tax Chambers**
University: **University of Cambridge**
Undergraduate degree: **Science**

law have come out of tax litigation, because tax is one of the few areas where it might really matter exactly when a right comes into existence, for example." The variety of subject matter is one of the best bits of the job: "You get a new set of papers, open them and have often not come across the area of tax you are asked to advise on. Then, over the next few days, you start to understand what's going on. Tax is so varied – no one "knows" the tax legislation in this country, there's far too much of it – that you are always working through new questions. That can be unnerving at times."

Thomas has noted a definite shift in the contentious landscape. "Everyone is fighting more – both the Revenue and defendants – and the cases go on for longer. Matters used to be argued technically and informally, and there wasn't as much interest in the factual background. That is no longer the case; a few years ago I did a 29-day trial with dozens of files and 15 witnesses that was a real fight over the evidence. It could have been a Commercial Court dispute, but it was being heard in the Tax Tribunal. Even though, by and large, I prefer having a practice where I'm working on papers, I do also like the fact that I'm in court at least once a month – it's an ideal balance."

Be your own boss
Managing that balance is one of the most enjoyable aspects of a barrister's career. "Because you are self-employed, it's your own business and you decide how and when you work," explains Thomas. "There is no one looking over your shoulder. That can be tricky at times, especially when you have three deadlines approaching at the same time." And although it is something you are aware of before you start, the reality of being your own boss can still come as a shock: "I was surprised by how much the way you run things is your own responsibility. No one tells you what to do each day or when to do it. You have to take that on yourself."

Thomas warns that for the specialist Bar in particular, hard graft is required. "You have to put the work in," he cautions. "Bear in mind that there are only around 30 or 40 people each year who go to the commercial and specialist Bar – that's a tiny amount – and thus getting pupillage is extremely competitive. If you are still at university it is worth doing as well as you can academically."

With one eye on your exemplary grades, the other should be on trying to get a sense of what life at the Bar is all about. "Even in really specialist areas such as tax, you are still an advocate, so being able to demonstrate that you have had some general advocacy experience shows that you are genuinely interested in standing on your feet and having an argument," explains Thomas. "We don't expect you to have studied tax before you get here – there is often not the opportunity to do so – but putting some effort into finding out what this career might involve is a good idea."

ff The law is fast paced and voluminous, and you need to be able to bang on doors and ask questions of the more experienced members of chambers ??

LawCareers.Net™

Delivering your future in law

Our newsletter, LCN Weekly, is packed with news, profiles, opinion and advice about becoming a lawyer.

Sign up to *LawCareers.Net*™

Pupillage directory

How to use the pupillage index and directory

Barristers' index

These tables are designed to allow you to shortlist sets of chambers by particular criteria. Further information about each set is contained within the pupillage directory.

The tables detail:
* the main location of the set;
* the number of annual pupillages at the set;
* the number of tenants and tenancies offered in the past three years;
* whether mini-pupillages are available;
* whether the set uses the Pupillage Gateway application system; and
* 19 specialisation work areas.

It should be noted that the information has been provided by the chambers themselves and has generally not been verified by us. We do not, therefore, claim that the information is fully accurate and comprehensive, only that it can be used as a starting point for shortlisting appropriate sets. Furthermore, although we have attempted to contact every recruiting chambers, some have not returned information and are therefore absent.

Barristers' directory

The directory contains contact information and a brief practice description for all chambers that have provided information. It is therefore an essential reference guide to chambers that offer pupillages and mini-pupillages.

The basic entry includes an application address, telephone number, email address, the applications procedure (Pupillage Gateway or own system) and a brief description of the set, together with the number of pupillages per year, the number of tenants, the number of new tenants in the last three years and whether the set offers mini-pupillages. Those chambers that have a more detailed directory entry appear in bold in the regional indexes.

These resources should be used in conjunction with the section on the Bar practice areas, which features in-depth interviews with numerous barristers who are keen to pass on their advice about making it in the legal profession.

Pupillage index

Barristers' index

	Location	Pupillages funded	Tenancies in the last three years	Number of tenants	Mini-pupillages offered	Apply through Pupillage Gateway
Albion Chambers	Bristol	0	3	66	✔	✔
Amethyst Chambers	London	0	2	5	✔	✔
Angel Chambers	Swansea	2	1	33	✔	✔
Apex Chambers	Cardiff	2	4	23	✔	✔
Arden Chambers	London	2	4	33	✔	✔
Atkin Chambers	London	2	3	45	✔	
Atlantic Chambers	Liverpool	1	3	56	✔	✔
Bank House Chambers	Sheffield	1	4	40	✔	✔
2 Bedford Row	London	4	4	78	✔	✔
7 Bedford Row	London	2	4	84	✔	
25 Bedford Row	London	3	6	69		✔
36 Bedford Row	London	2	3	103	✔	✔
42 Bedford Row	London	1	3	100	✔	✔
29 Bedford Row Chambers	London	2	3	58	✔	✔
Blackstone Chambers	London	4	10	108	✔	✔
4 Breams Buildings	London	4	6	67	✔	✔
One Brick Court	London	Up to 2	1	18	✔	✔
4 Brick Court	London	0	6	36	✔	✔
Brick Court Chambers	London	Normally 4	6	87	✔	✔
Broadway House Chambers	Bradford	2	6	59	✔	
Carmelite Chambers	London	3	6	57	✔	
1 Chancery Lane	London	2	2	44	✔	
Charter Chambers	London	0	8	54	✔	
Chartlands Chambers	Northampton	1	2	13	✔	
Citadel Chambers	Birmingham	2	5	56	✔	
Cloisters	London	2	6	51	✔	✔
College Chambers	Southampton	2	4	27	✔	
Coram Chambers	London	2	4	66	✔	
Cornerstone Barristers	London	2	5	50	✔	✔
Cornwall Street Chambers	Birmingham	Up to 2	2	67		
12CP Barristers	Southampton	1-2	4	28	✔	✔
Criminal Defence Solicitors	London	1	2	3	✔	✔
Crown Office Chambers	London	Up to 3	8	98	✔	
One Crown Office Row	London	2	6	68	✔	✔
Crown Office Row Chambers	Brighton	2	3	47	✔	
Crown Prosecution Service	London	30	60	600		
Deans Court Chambers	Manchester	2	7	75	✔	✔
Dere Street Chambers	Newcastle upon Tyne	Up to 4	6	90	✔	✔
Devereux	London	2	4	51	✔	✔
Doughty Street Chambers	London	2	5	125	✔	✔
2 Dr Johnson's Buildings	London	Up to 2	5	46	✔	

Chancery	Civil	Commercial	Common	Construction	Crime	Employment	EU	Family	Human rights	IP	Landlord/tenant	Personal injury	Planning	Prof negligence	Public	Revenue	Shipping	TMT
	•	•	•		•	•		•				•			•			
•	•		•		•	•		•			•	•		•				
					•													
	•								•	•	•		•		•			
		•		•										•	•			•
•	•		•		•	•		•			•	•		•	•			
•	•		•		•	•		•			•	•		•	•	•		
			•		•				•						•			
	•	•	•		•	•		•				•		•	•			
					•				•									
•			•		•	•		•			•	•		•	•			
	•	•			•	•		•				•		•	•			
								•										
•	•			•		•	•	•		•			•	•			•	•
					•													
	•		•					•							•			•
•		•					•		•	•				•	•		•	•
•	•	•		•	•	•		•			•		•	•	•			•
					•													
•	•	•	•	•		•		•			•		•	•	•			•
		•			•	•		•										
	•		•					•				•		•				
					•													
•	•	•			•	•		•				•		•	•	•		•
	•	•			•	•		•			•	•	•	•				
								•	•									
	•		•			•		•			•	•		•	•	•		
•	•	•	•		•	•		•			•	•		•				•
		•			•	•						•	•					
•	•	•	•	•							•		•					
•	•	•			•	•		•			•	•		•	•	•		
	•		•		•	•		•			•	•		•			•	
•	•	•	•	•	•			•			•		•		•			•
	•	•			•	•		•		•		•	•					
					•													
•	•		•		•	•		•			•	•	•	•				•
	•	•			•	•						•		•	•			•
					•			•				•			•		•	
•					•						•			•	•			•
	•				•			•										•

Barristers' index

	Location	Pupillages funded	Tenancies in the last three years	Number of tenants	Mini-pupillages offered	Apply through Pupillage Gateway
Three Dr Johnson's Buildings	London	0	1	33	✔	
Drystone chambers	London	Up to 2	5	63		✔
East Anglian Chambers	Ipswich	Up to 2	4	43	✔	
Enterprise Chambers	London	1	3	49	✔	✔
Erskine Chambers	London	Up to 2	1	30	✔	
39 Essex Chambers	London	Up to 3	7	128	✔	✔
One Essex Court	London	5	11	110	✔	✔
5 Essex Court	London	Up to 2	4	40	✔	✔
Essex Court Chambers	London	Up to 4	7	90	✔	✔
23 Essex Street	London	1	9	103	✔	
Exchange Chambers	Liverpool	1-2	5	156	✔	
Falcon Chambers	London	Up to 2	4	39	✔	
Farrar's Building	London	2	4	45	✔	✔
Farringdon Chambers	London	2	2	31	✔	
Fenners Chambers	Cambridge	Up to 2	2	50	✔	
Field Court Chambers	London	Up to 2	3	60	✔	
187 Fleet Street	London	2	6	73	✔	✔
Foundry Chambers	London	2	7	54	✔	
Fountain Court Chambers	London	Up to 4	7	81	✔	✔
Francis Taylor Building	London	2	6	56	✔	
1 Garden Court	London	2	5	74	✔	✔
Garden Court Chambers	London	4	27	182	✔	✔
Goldsmith Chambers	London	2	8	73	✔	✔
9 Gough Square	London	Up to 2	4	74	✔	
Gough Square Chambers	London	0	2	26	✔	✔
4-5 Gray's Inn Square	London	1	4	33	✔	
1 Gray's Inn Square	London	2	7	73	✔	✔
Gray's Inn Tax Chambers	London	1		9	✔	✔
GT Stewart Solicitors	London	1	1	15	✔	
Guildford Chambers	Guildford	1	5	23	✔	
Guildhall Chambers	Bristol	2	8	84	✔	✔
Hailsham Chambers	London	2	7	49	✔	✔
2 Harcourt Buildings	London	2	4	39	✔	✔
Harcourt Chambers	London	1-2	4	54	✔	✔
Hardwicke	London	2	12	84	✔	✔
1 Hare Court	London	2	5	42	✔	
2 Hare Court	London	2	8	56		✔
3 Hare Court	London	2	4	35	✔	✔
7 Harrington Street Chambers	Liverpool	1	5	90	✔	✔
Henderson Chambers	London	2	5	48	✔	✔
1 High Pavement	Nottingham	1	2	43	✔	

Chancery	Civil	Commercial	Common	Construction	Crime	Employment	EU	Family	Human rights	IP	Landlord/tenant	Personal injury	Planning	Prof negligence	Public	Revenue	Shipping	TMT
•	•		•			•		•			•	•		•	•			
					•													
•	•	•	•		•	•		•			•	•		•		•		
•		•									•			•				
•																		
		•	•	•		•	•		•			•	•	•	•			•
•	•	•						•		•				•		•		•
		•				•			•			•		•	•			
•	•	•				•		•			•			•	•	•	•	•
					•													
•	•	•	•		•	•	•	•	•	•	•	•	•	•		•		
•	•										•			•				
•	•	•	•		•	•		•	•		•	•		•		•		•
					•													
•	•	•	•		•	•	•	•	•		•	•		•		•		•
•	•	•	•		•	•	•	•	•		•	•		•				•
					•													
					•										•			
		•				•								•				
	•		•		•	•		•	•		•	•	•	•	•			•
	•		•			•		•			•	•		•				
	•	•	•		•	•		•			•	•		•				
	•	•			•									•				
•	•	•			•	•		•			•	•		•	•	•	•	•
•	•	•	•		•	•		•	•		•	•		•	•	•		•
															•			
	•				•	•		•	•		•	•		•	•			
•	•	•			•	•		•			•	•		•	•			
•	•	•			•	•		•			•	•		•	•			
•	•	•	•		•						•			•				
								•										
•		•		•		•	•		•		•	•		•				
								•										
					•													
	•	•	•			•	•		•		•			•				
	•				•			•						•				
	•	•	•		•		•	•			•	•		•		•		•

Barristers' index

	Location	Pupillages funded	Tenancies in the last three years	Number of tenants	Mini-pupillages offered	Apply through Pupillage Gateway
Hogarth Chambers	London	1	2	21	✔	
Invictus Chambers	London	2	5	19	✔	✔
Iscoed Chambers	Swansea	1	5	35	✔	✔
One ITL	London	2	4	26	✔	✔
KBG Chambers	Plymouth	1	3	35	✔	
KBW	Leeds	1	4	38	✔	✔
11KBW	London	2-4	6	59	✔	✔
6KBW College Hill	London	2	3	47	✔	
KCH Garden Square Barristers	Nottingham	Up to 2	22	60	✔	
Keating Chambers	London	3	4	64	✔	✔
Kenworthy's Chambers	Manchester	1-2	4	65	✔	✔
1 King's Bench Walk	London	2	6	57	✔	
2 King's Bench Walk	London	2	4	73	✔	✔
2 King's Bench Walk	London	1	1	10	✔	
4 King's Bench Walk	London	2	6	54	✔	✔
5 King's Bench Walk	London	3	7	48	✔	✔
7 King's Bench Walk	London	Up to 4	6	62	✔	✔
9 King's Bench Walk	London	1	10	26	✔	
12 King's Bench Walk	London	2-3	8	86	✔	✔
Kings Chambers	Manchester	Up to 3	5	111	✔	
Lamb Building	London	Up to 3	4	54	✔	
Landmark Chambers	London	2	7	88	✔	✔
Lincoln House Chambers	Manchester	1-2	5	67	✔	
Linenhall Chambers	Chester	1	1	70	✔	
Littleton Chambers	London	2	3	53		✔
Maidstone Chambers	Maidstone	1-2	2	15	✔	
Maitland Chambers	London	Up to 3	5	70	✔	✔
Malins Chambers	London	1	1	6		
Matrix Chambers	London	2	5	91		
1 MCB	London	0	7	51	✔	
Monckton Chambers	London	2	5	60	✔	✔
15 New Bridge Street	London	2	3	46		
New Court Chambers	London	2	6	34	✔	✔
New Park Court Chambers	Leeds	3	3	61	✔	✔
3 New Square	London	1	1	20	✔	✔
4 New Square	London	Up to 2	5	80	✔	
8 New Square	London	1	1	29	✔	✔
New Square Chambers	London	1	3	40	✔	
New Walk Chambers	Leicester	Up to 3	7	22		
No5 Chambers	Birmingham	Up to 3	53	256	✔	
Northampton Chambers	Northampton	1-2	4	14	✔	

Chancery	Civil	Commercial	Common	Construction	Crime	Employment	EU	Family	Human rights	IP	Landlord/tenant	Personal injury	Planning	Prof negligence	Public	Revenue	Shipping	TMT
•		•								•								•
•	•	•	•		•	•		•			•	•		•				
•	•	•	•		•	•		•			•	•	•	•				
	•				•	•		•				•		•				
	•	•	•		•	•		•			•	•		•				
	•	•				•	•	•					•					
•	•	•	•	•	•	•	•	•	•		•	•	•	•				
		•		•		•							•	•			•	•
•	•	•	•		•	•		•	•	•	•	•	•	•	•	•		
							•											
	•		•		•			•			•	•		•				
•		•	•	•				•			•	•		•				
			•		•			•										
	•	•				•									•		•	
					•													
	•		•		•						•	•		•				
•	•	•	•	•	•	•		•		•	•	•	•	•	•			
•	•	•	•		•	•		•		•	•	•	•	•	•			
•	•	•					•		•		•	•		•	•			
	•	•				•					•			•				
	•	•	•		•	•		•			•	•		•				
•	•	•		•		•	•				•	•		•				•
•	•	•					•				•			•				•
	•		•		•	•					•	•		•	•	•		•
	•	•	•		•	•	•	•							•	•		•
	•	•		•	•	•		•			•	•		•	•	•	•	•
					•			•						•	•	•	•	
		•					•											
•	•	•	•		•	•		•			•	•		•				•
							•											
•	•		•								•			•	•			•
							•											•
•	•	•			•	•		•			•	•	•	•	•	•		
•	•	•	•	•	•	•	•	•			•	•	•	•	•	•		
	•				•			•										•

Barristers' index

	Location	Pupillages funded	Tenancies in the last three years	Number of tenants	Mini-pupillages offered	Apply through Pupillage Gateway
Old Court Chambers	Middlesbrough	0-1	1	19		
Ten Old Square	London	1	2	26	✔	✔
15 Old Square	London	1	1	11	✔	
Old Square Chambers	London	2	6	79	✔	✔
Old Square Chambers (Bristol)	Bristol	0	6	79	✔	✔
Oriel Chambers	Liverpool	Up to 2	3	53	✔	
Outer Temple Chambers	London	4	9	88	✔	✔
Five Paper	London	2	3	40	✔	✔
4 Paper Buildings	London	3	6	79	✔	
5 Paper Buildings	London	2	6	46	✔	✔
9 Park Place	Cardiff	2	6	60	✔	
30 Park Place	Cardiff	1	18	67	✔	✔
Park Square Barristers	Leeds	2	6	125	✔	
Parklane Plowden Chambers	Leeds	Up to 4	7	91	✔	
3PB	London	3	26	170	✔	✔
4 Pump Court	London	2	6	66	✔	
5 Pump Court	London	2	3	49	✔	✔
6 Pump Court	London	0	5	40	✔	✔
Pump Court Chambers	London	2	5	92	✔	✔
1 Pump Court Chambers	London	2	5	75	✔	✔
Pump Court Tax Chambers	London	1-2	2	35	✔	
QEB Hollis Whiteman	London	4	3	65	✔	
Quadrant Chambers	London	3	3	65	✔	✔
Queen Elizabeth Building	London	2	5	34	✔	✔
Queen Square Chambers	Bristol	2	6	39	✔	
Radcliffe Chambers	London	2	3	59	✔	
Three Raymond Buildings	London	Up to 3	5	52		
5RB	London	Up to 2	3	28	✔	✔
Red Lion Chambers	London	3	7	98	✔	
Regency Barristers Chambers	Peterborough	0	1	14		
Selborne Chambers	London	1	3	30	✔	
Serjeants' Inn Chambers	London	0	4	61	✔	✔
Serle Court	London	Up to 3	7	68	✔	✔
South Square	London	Up to 3	5	44	✔	
11 South Square	London	1	2	17	✔	✔
5 St Andrew's Hill	London	2	6	62	✔	✔
St Ives Chambers	Birmingham	Up to 3	12	74	✔	
9 St John Street Chambers	Manchester	2	7	96	✔	✔
18 St John Street Chambers	Manchester	Up to 4	6	74	✔	✔
St John's Buildings	Manchester	1	10	156	✔	
St John's Chambers	Bristol	2	7	83	✔	

Chancery	Civil	Commercial	Common	Construction	Crime	Employment	EU	Family	Human rights	IP	Landlord/tenant	Personal injury	Planning	Prof negligence	Public	Revenue	Shipping	TMT
	•	•	•		•	•		•			•	•	•	•	•			
•		•									•			•		•		
																•		
						•						•	•	•				
•	•	•	•	•	•	•		•			•		•	•				
•	•	•				•		•			•					•		
					•				•					•				
•	•	•	•	•	•	•		•			•		•	•				
•	•	•	•	•	•	•		•			•		•	•				
•	•	•	•		•	•		•			•		•	•				
•	•	•	•	•	•			•			•		•	•				
•	•	•	•	•	•	•	•	•			•	•	•	•	•			•
	•	•	•	•		•		•			•			•				•
	•	•	•		•	•		•			•		•	•				
	•	•	•	•	•	•		•			•		•	•				
•	•	•	•	•	•	•		•			•			•				
					•										•			
	•		•			•	•							•			•	
•	•	•			•	•		•			•	•		•				
•	•	•					•					•		•	•		•	•
	•								•	•				•				•
					•													
	•					•		•				•	•	•				
•	•	•			•			•			•			•	•			
•	•	•												•				
•	•	•												•				
																		•
	•				•			•							•			
•	•	•	•		•	•		•	•		•	•	•					
•	•	•		•	•			•	•		•	•		•				
•	•	•	•		•			•			•	•		•		•		
	•	•			•	•		•			•	•	•	•	•			
•	•	•	•	•	•			•		•		•	•	•	•	•		

Barristers' index

	Location	Pupillages funded	Tenancies in the last three years	Number of tenants	Mini-pupillages offered	Apply through Pupillage Gateway
St Mary's Chambers	Nottingham	2	4	32	✔	✔
St Paul's Chambers	Leeds	0	4	44	✔	
St Philips Chambers	Birmingham	Up to 2	20	175	✔	
Staple Inn Chambers	London	1	5	25	✔	
Three Stone	London	1	3	30	✔	
4 Stone Buildings	London	2	5	36	✔	✔
5 Stone Buildings	London	1	3	37	✔	✔
9 Stone Buildings	London	1	2	25	✔	
Stone Chambers	London	1	5	26	✔	
Stour Chambers	Canterbury	1	2	16	✔	
Sussex Chambers	Eastbourne	1	1	12	✔	
Tanfield Chambers	London	3	6	65	✔	
Fourteen	London	1	3	34	✔	✔
Temple Court Chambers	London	1	6	18		
Temple Garden Chambers	London	2	6	70	✔	✔
3 Temple Gardens	London	Up to 2	7	52	✔	✔
2TG	London	3-4	7	61	✔	✔
Thomas More Chambers	London	1	4	43	✔	✔
Trinity Chambers	Newcastle upon Tyne	1-2	10	71	✔	✔
Trinity Chambers	Essex	0	4	23	✔	
Unity Street Chambers	Bristol	1	1	13	✔	
3 Verulam Buildings	London	Up to 4	8	80	✔	✔
Westgate Chambers	Lewes	Up to 2	3	49	✔	
Wilberforce Chambers	London	2	6	70	✔	✔
15 Winckley Square	Preston	2	5	50	✔	✔
XXIV Old Buildings	London	3	4	45	✔	

Chancery	Civil	Commercial	Common	Construction	Crime	Employment	EU	Family	Human rights	IP	Landlord/tenant	Personal injury	Planning	Prof negligence	Public	Revenue	Shipping	TMT
								•										
•	•	•		•	•	•		•		•	•	•	•	•	•	•		
•	•	•	•	•	•	•		•		•	•	•	•	•	•			
		•	•		•	•		•			•			•				
•	•	•									•			•		•		
•							•				•							
•											•			•		•		
•	•					•					•			•	•			
		•				•											•	
	•		•					•			•			•				
	•	•			•			•			•	•		•	•			
	•			•		•		•			•	•						
								•										
	•					•		•			•		•					
	•	•							•			•		•	•			
•	•	•	•		•	•		•		•	•	•	•	•	•			•
•	•	•	•		•			•	•		•	•	•	•	•			
	•							•			•			•				
•	•		•		•	•		•		•		•		•	•			
	•		•											•				•
	•				•	•		•			•	•						
•	•	•								•			•	•		•		•
	•				•	•		•			•	•						
•	•	•		•										•				

Pupillage directory

ALBION CHAMBERS Broad Street, Bristol BS1 1DR **Tel:** 0117 927 2144 **Email:** pupillage@albionchambers.co.uk Apply through Pupillage Gateway	A large, friendly, Western Circuit set with five silks and 61 juniors covering crime, family, employment, PI and other common law areas.	PF 0 T 66 T_{L3Y} 3 MP yes
AMETHYST CHAMBERS 1st Floor, 41 East Street, London BR1 1QQ **Tel:** 0208 466 6673 **Email:** info@amethystchambers.com Apply through Pupillage Gateway		PF 0 T 5 T_{L3Y} 2 MP yes
ANGEL CHAMBERS Ethos Building, Kings Road, Swansea SA1 8AS **Tel:** 01792 464623 **Email:** clerks@angelchambers.co.uk Apply through Pupillage Gateway	Busy common law set specialising in crime, family and civil law.	PF 2 T 33 T_{L3Y} 1 MP yes
APEX CHAMBERS Harlech House, 20 Cathedral Road, Cardiff CF11 9LJ **Tel:** 029 2023 2032 **Email:** clerks@apexchambers.net Apply through Pupillage Gateway		PF 2 T 23 T_{L3Y} 4 MP yes
ATLANTIC CHAMBERS 4-6 Cook Street, Liverpool L2 9QU **Tel:** 0151 236 4421 **Email:** julie@atlanticchambers.co.uk Apply through Pupillage Gateway	Atlantic Chambers have one 12-month common law pupillage available.	PF 1 T 56 T_{L3Y} 3 MP yes
BANK HOUSE CHAMBERS Old Bank House, 3 Hartshead, Sheffield S1 2EL **Tel:** 0114 275 1223 **Email:** w.digby@bankhousechambers.co.uk Apply through Pupillage Gateway	General common law set specialising in crime, family, civil, employment, personal injury and housing.	PF 1 T 40 T_{L3Y} 4 MP yes
2 BEDFORD ROW Chambers of William Clegg QC, London WC1R 4BU **Tel:** 020 7440 8888 **Email:** loakley@2bedfordrow.co.uk Apply through Pupillage Gateway	Criminal set specialising in general, regulatory crime and fraud. Tenants defend and prosecute at all levels.	PF 4 T 78 T_{L3Y} 4 MP yes
7 BEDFORD ROW Chambers of Collingwood Thompson QC, London WC1R 4BS **Tel:** 020 7242 3555 **Email:** pupillage@7br.co.uk **Apply to:** Helen Compton	A leading common law set practising a mix of civil and criminal work both in London and on the Midland Circuit.	PF 2 T 84 T_{L3Y} 4 MP yes

PF = Pupillages funded / T = Tenants / T_{L3Y} = Tenancies in last 3 years / MP = Mini-pupillages offered

Arden Chambers

20 Bloomsbury Square, London WC1A 2NS
Tel: 020 7242 4244
Email: pupillage@ardenchambers.com
Web: www.ardenchambers.com
f ardenchambers 𝕐 ardenchambers

Description of Chambers Arden Chambers dominates social housing law. We are responsible for all the major publications in this area (eg, *Encyclopedia of Housing Law*; *Journal of Housing Law*; *Housing Law Reports*; *Manual of Housing Law*; *Homelessness and Allocations*) and are habitually ranked as the leading set in both *Chambers & Partners* and the *Legal 500*. Our members are consistently found in the higher courts dealing with social housing cases (both for landlords and occupiers).

We are also active (and very well regarded) in related areas. Local government and public law forms a large part of our practice and, again, we produce some of the leading texts (*Encyclopedia of Local Government Finance*; *Judicial Review*). Many members also have significant landlord and tenant/property/ planning law practices. We are particularly well-known for our long-leasehold work, with members responsible for two of the leading works (leasehold disputes; leasehold valuation tribunals). A former member of chambers is now the senior president of the First-tier Tribunal (Property Chamber). Other members are active in both the Housing Law Practitioners Association and the Property Bar Association.

The focus on producing authoritative works stems from our history. We were established by Andrew Arden QC and six other current members in 1993 in order to provide a specialist centre of practice for housing and local government law, based on the publications which Andrew authored or edited.

Areas of work Housing, local government, landlord and tenant, leasehold property, property, planning and public law.

Who should apply Those with an interest in our practice areas who are also prepared to devote part of their professional efforts to maintaining our portfolio of publications.

Pupillage programme We offer two pupillages annually for 12 months. Each pupil is allocated a co-ordinator for the whole period.

When and how to apply Please see the chambers' website regarding applying for pupillage (www.ardenchambers.com).

Mini-pupillages Limited number available during each year. Please apply using the application form on our website (www.ardenchambers.com) and send it to mini.pupillage@ardenchambers.com.

Sponsorship/funding Up to £10,000 award for first six months, guaranteed earnings of £10,000 for second six months, subject to clawback (presently subject to review).

Pupillages funded	2
Tenants	33
Tenancies in last 3 yrs	4
Mini-pupillages	yes

Apply to
Check website for details

Applications contact
Mrs Anita Heartfield

Remuneration for pupillage
Up to £10,000 award in first six, guaranteed earnings of £10,000 for second six, subject to clawback (presently subject to review)

arden
chambers

Atkin Chambers

1 Atkin Building, Gray's Inn, London WC1R 5AT
Tel: 020 7404 0102
Email: clerks@atkinchambers.com
Web: www.atkinchambers.com
🐦 atkinchambers

Description of Chambers Atkin Chambers is a leading commercial set specialising in construction, energy and technology disputes, and related professional negligence claims. As well as leading in the domestic field, its barristers have significant international practices spanning Europe, the Middle East, Asia-Pacific, Africa and the Caribbean. Chambers is consistently ranked as one of London's leading sets in the legal directories.

Areas of work Atkin Chambers is a leader in its field: construction law. Its barristers are regularly instructed to advise and act as advocates in relation to some of the largest and most complex international and domestic disputes in their field of expertise. Members of Atkin Chambers have been involved in many of the most high-profile domestic disputes in the fields of construction, technology, power, energy, computers and telecommunications of recent years, both in court and arbitration. Examples include the Panama Canal, the Shard, Wembley Stadium, the upgrade of London Underground, Heathrow T5, and the Grenfell Tower Inquiry, as well as major oil and gas and renewable energy projects. Members are also regularly involved in high-value construction, energy and infrastructure projects around the globe and regularly appear at international arbitrations seated in locations such as the Gulf States, Hong Kong and Singapore. Significant opportunities for international travel and practise exist at the junior end of chambers.

Who should apply Applicants for pupillage should have a first-class degree or a good 2.1. Postgraduate qualifications are viewed favourably but are not essential. Applications from non-law graduates are welcomed. Pre-existing knowledge of construction law is not required.

Pupillage programme Atkin Chambers takes recruitment to pupillage and tenancy extremely seriously. The market-leading pupillage award of £72,500 reflects this. The pupillage year is highly structured and provides all of the Bar Council's training requirements along with the additional training chambers considers is necessary for successful entry into the high-quality commercial work of its practice. Chambers provides its own advocacy training and assessment in addition to that provided by the Inns of Court. Full and up-to-date details of may be viewed on chambers' website.

Atkin Chambers operates under its equality and diversity policy in accordance with the Bar Standard Board's equality and diversity code.

When and how to apply Applications for the year starting in October 2020 open on Saturday 29 September 2018 and close at midnight on Wednesday 12 December 2018. Applications should be made by sending a CV, a covering letter of no more than two pages in length and two references (of which at least one should be academic) to pupillage@atkinchambers.com.

Mini-pupillages Up to 10 mini-pupillages are offered each year. Details and application dates are on chambers' website.

Sponsorship/funding Two fully-funded pupillages of £72,500 per pupil for 12 months. A drawdown of up to £25,000 is available during the BPTC year.

Pupillages funded	2
Tenants	45
Tenancies in last 3 yrs	3
Mini-pupillages	yes
Apply via website	
Remuneration for pupillage	£72,500
Minimum qualifications	2.1 degree

Atkin
Chambers
Barristers

29 Bedford Row Chambers

29 Bedford Row, London WC1R 4HE
Tel: 020 7404 1044
Email: clerks@29br.co.uk
Web: www.29br.co.uk
🐦 29bedfordrow

Description of Chambers Routinely ranked as one of the top chambers for family law by the major guides to the legal profession, we can justifiably lay claim to being the most modern and dynamic of the top specialist family law sets. Our record of recruitment from amongst our own pupils is second-to-none, and our pupils – both those who are recruited, and those who are not – comment on the thoroughness of the training they receive here, and the friendliness of the set as a place in which to complete their training. As an organisation, our belief, and experience, is that the source of our ongoing success is in our pupils and junior members. The level of our pupillage award and our commitment to the pupillage programme is a testament to the strength of that belief.

Chambers & Partners describes us as a "formidable specialist family set offering strength at every level in proceedings relating to relationship breakdown and children" and continues "it is renowned for its expertise in handling enormous financial disputes for high net worth and high-profile figures". *Legal 500* is in a similar vein, saying we "continue to display strength in depth across the board of big-brained lawyers who can translate complex legal issues into practical, real-world advice". Recent cases involving members of chambers include the Supreme Court appeals in *Mills v Mills* [2017] EWCA Civ 129 (judgment not yet handed down), *Sharland v Sharland* [2015] UKSC 60, and *Vince v Wyatt* [2015] UKSC 15, the Court of Appeal appeals in *Sharp v Sharp* [2017] EWCA Civ 408, *Hart v Hart* [2018] EWCA Civ 1058 and [2017] EWCA Civ 1306 and *Bezeliansky v Bezelianskaya* [2016] EWCA Civ 76.

Areas of work At 29BR we offer specialist knowledge at every level of seniority, and in every aspect of family law. Work is largely based in London and the South East, but all members practice nationwide with many practitioners practicing regularly in Manchester, Birmingham, Bristol and the other main regional centres. We boast a strong team of top-flight matrimonial finance practitioners, dealing with domestic and international cases. We have expertise in all aspects of the law relating to children; including child abduction and adoption. In public law cases we act for parents, local authorities and guardians. We also specialise in work arising out of the Civil Partnership Act 2004, TLATA and the Inheritance Act.

Who should apply If you are interested in pursuing a career at the Bar specialising in family law and practising at the highest level, then 29BR is the ideal choice for you. Applicants should generally have at least an upper second-class degree.

Pupillage programme Up to two 12-month pupillages are available annually with awards of up to £35,000. Pupillage will normally be spent with three pupil supervisors and all pupils are encouraged to attend court with other members of chambers in order to gain first-hand experience in all our fields of expertise. Pupils can expect to be in court (and earning) on a regular basis during their second six.

When and how to apply Chambers is a member of the Bar Council's Pupillage Gateway. Applications should be submitted in accordance with the Pupillage Gateway timetable.

Mini-pupillages We offer mini-pupillages. Mini pupils can expect to attend Court, attend conferences and read paperwork whilst shadowing a number of different barristers. To apply please complete the application form on our website.

Pupillages funded	2
Tenants	58
Tenancies in last 3 yrs	3
Mini-pupillages	yes
Apply through Pupillage Gateway	
Remuneration for pupillage	£35,000
Minimum qualifications	2.1 degree

29
BEDFORD ROW
CHAMBERS

Blackstone Chambers

Blackstone House, Temple, London EC4Y 9BW
Tel: 020 7583 1770
Email: pupillage@blackstonechambers.com
Web: www.blackstonechambers.com

Description of Chambers Chambers occupies large and modern premises in the Temple.

Areas of work Blackstone Chambers' formidable strengths lie in its principal areas of practice: commercial, employment, EU, public law, human rights and public international law. The commercial law work includes financial/business law, international trade, conflicts, sport, media and entertainment, intellectual property and professional negligence. Public law incorporates judicial review, acting both for and against central and local government agencies and other regulatory authorities. It also covers all areas affected by the impact of human rights and other aspects of administrative law. All aspects of employment law, including discrimination, are covered by chambers' extensive employment law practice, and chambers' EU work permeates practices across the board. Chambers recognises the increasingly important role which mediation has to play in dispute resolution.

Who should apply Chambers looks for articulate and intelligent applicants who are able to work under pressure and demonstrate high intellectual ability. Successful candidates usually have a 2.1 honours degree at least, although not necessarily in law.

Pupillage programme Chambers offers four 12-month pupillages to those wishing to practise full time at the Bar, normally commencing in September each year. Pupillage is divided into four sections and every effort is made to ensure pupils receive a broad training. The environment is a friendly one; pupils attend an induction week introducing them to the chambers' working environment. Chambers prefers to recruit new tenants from pupils wherever possible. Chambers is a member of the Pupillage Gateway.

When and how to apply Pupillage applications should be made via the Pupillage Gateway. Please refer to the Gateway for dates.

Mini-pupillages Assessed mini-pupillages are an essential part of our pupillage recruitment process and no pupillage will be offered at Blackstone Chambers unless the applicant has undertaken an assessed mini-pupillage. Applications for mini-pupillage are accepted from 1 September 2018 until the Pupillage Gateway opens in 2019. Any applicant for pupillage through the Gateway who has not already made an application for mini pupillage direct will be treated as an applicant for both mini-pupillage and pupillage. We strongly recommend that applications be made early in our mini-pupillage application window. Applications are preferred in the year before pupillage commences.

Sponsorship/funding Awards of £65,000 per annum are available. A partial draw-down of up to £18,500 is available in the BPTC year. As chambers insists on an assessed mini-pupillage as part of the overall pupillage recruitment process, financial assistance is offered either in respect of out of pocket travelling or accommodation expenses incurred in attending the mini-pupillage, up to a maximum of £250 per pupil.

Pupillages funded	4
Tenants	108
Tenancies in last 3 yrs	10
Mini-pupillages	yes
Apply through Pupillage Gateway	
Remuneration for pupillage	£65,000
Minimum qualifications	2.1 degree

25 BEDFORD ROW
25 Bedford Row, London WC1R 4HD
Tel: 020 7067 1500
Email: clerks@25bedfordrow.com
Apply through Pupillage Gateway

We are a leading criminal set specialising in defence work. We pride ourselves on maintaining the highest standards of professionalism, integrity and commitment.

PF 3
T 69
T$_{L3Y}$ 6
MP no

---

36 BEDFORD ROW
36 Bedford Row, London WC1R 4JH
Tel: 020 7421 8000
Apply through Pupillage Gateway

36 Bedford Row will be offering two specialist pupillages: one crime and one civil. The pupillages will be offered through Pupillage Gateway.

PF 2
T 103
T$_{L3Y}$ 3
MP yes

---

42 BEDFORD ROW
Bedford Row, London WC1R 4LL
Tel: 020 7831 0222
Email: clerks@42br.com
Apply through Pupillage Gateway

PF 1
T 100
T$_{L3Y}$ 3
MP yes

---

4 BREAMS BUILDINGS
Chancery Lane, London EC4A 1HP
Tel: 020 7092 1900
Email: clerks@4bb.co.uk
Apply through Pupillage Gateway

4BB is a criminal set. Members prosecute and defend across the whole range of criminal cases, including murder, fraud, terrorist cases, and serious sexual offences.

PF 4
T 67
T$_{L3Y}$ 6
MP yes

ONE BRICK COURT
Chambers of Sir Edward Garnier QC, Temple, London EC4Y 9BY
Tel: 020 7353 8845
Email: clerks@onebrickcourt.com
Apply through Pupillage Gateway

Leading specialists in media, communications and information law, including defamation, privacy, breach of confidence, data protection, reporting restrictions, contempt, FOI, harassment and other media-related work.

PF Up to 2
T 18
T$_{L3Y}$ 1
MP yes

---

4 BRICK COURT
Ground Floor, Temple, London EC4Y 9AD
Tel: 020 7832 3200
Email: clerks@4bc.co.uk
Apply through Pupillage Gateway

Chambers is a leading set in all aspects of family law, with particular regard to child protection issues. Regularly instructed on behalf of local authorities, guardians and parents.

PF 0
T 36
T$_{L3Y}$ 6
MP yes

BRICK COURT CHAMBERS
7-8 Essex Street, London WC2R 3LD
Tel: 020 7379 3550
Email: lyana.peniston@brickcourt.co.uk
Apply through Pupillage Gateway

Brick Court Chambers is a leading set with particular expertise in commercial, EU, competition and public law. We normally offer four pupillages each year.

PF Normally 4
T 87
T$_{L3Y}$ 6
MP yes

BROADWAY HOUSE CHAMBERS
9 Bank Street, Bradford BD1 1TW
Tel: 01274 722560
Email: jos@broadwayhouse.co.uk
Apply to: Miss Joanne O'Shea

A progressive common law set of chambers with premises in both the centre of Leeds and Bradford.

PF 2
T 59
T$_{L3Y}$ 6
MP yes

PF = Pupillages funded / **T** = Tenants / **T**$_{L3Y}$ = Tenancies in last 3 years / **MP** = Mini-pupillages offered

CARMELITE CHAMBERS 9 Carmelite Street, London EC4Y 0DR **Tel:** 020 7936 6300 **Email:** pupillage@carmelitechambers.co.uk **Apply to:** Miss Orla O'Sullivan	An established set specialising in defence work. Pupils will have the opportunity both to learn and to put that learning into practice as advocates.	PF 3 T 57 T_{L3Y} 6 MP yes

PF 3
T 57
T_{L3Y} 6
MP yes

CARMELITE CHAMBERS
9 Carmelite Street, London EC4Y 0DR
Tel: 020 7936 6300
Email: pupillage@carmelitechambers.co.uk
Apply to: Miss Orla O'Sullivan

An established set specialising in defence work. Pupils will have the opportunity both to learn and to put that learning into practice as advocates.

PF 3
T 57
T$_{L3Y}$ 6
MP yes

---

1 CHANCERY LANE
1 Chancery Lane, London WC2A 1LF
Tel: 020 7092 2900
Email: jfensham@1chancerylane.com
Apply to: Ms Jenny Fensham

Personal injury, professional negligence and clinical negligence practice offering pupils an opportunity to develop wide-ranging litigation skills. Also property, travel and human rights.

PF 2
T 44
T$_{L3Y}$ 2
MP yes

CHARTER CHAMBERS
33 John Street, London WC1N 2AT
Tel: 020 7618 4400
Email: clerks@charterchambers.com

Work: mainly criminal (prosecution and defence), public, prison law, immigration, family, employment. Second six pupils conduct a substantial amount of work in their own right.

PF 0
T 54
T$_{L3Y}$ 8
MP yes

CHARTLANDS CHAMBERS
3 St Giles Terrace, Northampton NN1 2BN
Tel: 01604 603322
Email: enquiries@chartlands-chambers.co.uk
Apply to: Mr Andrew Davies

Common law chambers. Principal field: family law. Also: immigration and general civil litigation.

PF 1
T 13
T$_{L3Y}$ 2
MP yes

CITADEL CHAMBERS
190 Corporation Street, Birmingham B4 6QD
Tel: 0121 233 8500
Email: clerks@citadelchambers.com
Apply to: The Pupillage Committee Secretary

Chambers is a large criminal set. Chambers also undertakes some licensing, common law and other specialist work. Pupillages are focussed completely on crime.

PF 2
T 56
T$_{L3Y}$ 5
MP yes

CLOISTERS
1 Pump Court, Temple, London EC4Y 7AA
Tel: 020 7827 4000
Email: pupillage@cloisters.com
Apply through Pupillage Gateway

Informal, award-winning chambers at the cutting edge of employment, PI, clinical negligence, human rights, public law, commercial, media and sports law.

PF 2
T 51
T$_{L3Y}$ 6
MP yes

COLLEGE CHAMBERS
19 Carlton Crescent, Southampton SO15 2ET
Tel: 023 8023 0338
Email: nmaton@college-chambers.co.uk
Apply to: Mr Neil Maton

Established set of chambers with wide work base. Emphasis on all forms of civil and family litigation.

PF 2
T 27
T$_{L3Y}$ 4
MP yes

CORAM CHAMBERS
9-11 Fulwood Place, London WC1V 6HG
Tel: 020 7092 3700
Email: clerks@coramchambers.co.uk
Apply to: Mrs Gillian Maguire

Members of Coram Chambers act in leading cases in children's disputes in both public and private law and matrimonial finance.

PF 2
T 66
T$_{L3Y}$ 4
MP yes

PF = Pupillages funded / **T** = Tenants / T$_{L3Y}$ = Tenancies in last 3 years / **MP** = Mini-pupillages offered

CORNERSTONE BARRISTERS
2-3 Gray's Inn Square, London WC1R 5JH
Tel: 020 7242 4986
Email: cornerstone@cornerstonebarristers.com
Apply through Pupillage Gateway

Cornerstone, a well established, leading set with a friendly, flexible approach, is committed to the care and provision of an excellent legal service to our clients.

PF	2
T	50
TL3Y	5
MP	yes

CORNWALL STREET CHAMBERS
85-87 Cornwall Street, Birmingham B3 3BY
Tel: 0121 233 7500
Email: clerks@cornwallstreet.co.uk
Apply to: Mr Timothy Clarke

Principally crime, family and common law with specialists in other fields. Annexes in Oxford and Shrewsbury.

PF	Up to 2
T	67
TL3Y	2
MP	no

12CP BARRISTERS
20 Carlton Crescent, Southampton SO15 2ET
Tel: 023 8032 0320
Email: clerks@12cp.co.uk
Apply through Pupillage Gateway

A medium-sized, multi-disciplinary set which prides itself on being friendly, approachable and providing a high quality service. Application deadline is noon on 1 February 2019.

PF	1-2
T	28
TL3Y	4
MP	yes

CRIMINAL DEFENCE SOLICITORS
11-15 St Mary at Hill, Lower Ground, London EC3R 8EE
Tel: 020 7353 7000
Email: pupillagecommittee@criminaldefence.co.uk
Apply through Pupillage Gateway

Criminal Defence Solicitors is a friendly and expanding firm. We are a predominantly legal aid practice specialising in criminal law.

PF	1
T	3
TL3Y	2
MP	yes

CROWN OFFICE ROW CHAMBERS
Blenheim House, 119 Church Street, Brighton BN1 1UD
Tel: 01273 625625
Email: clerks@1cor.com
Apply to: The Pupillage Committee

A long-established, busy set committed to expansion in Sussex. Up to two 12-month pupillages available each year.

PF	2
T	47
TL3Y	3
MP	yes

CROWN PROSECUTION SERVICE
CPS HQ - Petty France, 102 Petty France, Westminster, London SW1H 9AJ
Tel: 020 3357 0899
Email: strategic.resourcing@cps.gsi.gov.uk
Apply to: Mr Martin McKay-Smith

The CPS offers positions throughout England & Wales for pupil barristers and trainee solicitors. Permanent Crown Prosecutor opportunities are available upon successful qualification.

PF	30
T	600
TL3Y	60
MP	no

DEANS COURT CHAMBERS
24 St John Street, Manchester M3 4DF
Tel: 0161 214 6000
Email: clerks@deanscourt.co.uk
Apply through Pupillage Gateway

A leading set of chambers on the Northern Circuit. 11 silks. Excellent facilities. Well-funded pupillages with a view to a tenancy.

PF	2
T	75
TL3Y	7
MP	yes

DERE STREET CHAMBERS
33 Broad Chare, Newcastle upon Tyne NE1 3DQ
Tel: 03443351551
Email: clerks@derestreet.co.uk
Apply through Pupillage Gateway

A broad-based pupillage with experience of differing areas of chambers' practice. Chambers has premises in both York and Newcastle.

PF	Up to 4
T	90
TL3Y	6
MP	yes

PF = Pupillages funded / T = Tenants / TL3Y = Tenancies in last 3 years / MP = Mini-pupillages offered

Crown Office Chambers

2 Crown Office Row, Temple, London EC4Y 7HJ
Tel: 020 7797 8100
Email: clerks@crownofficechambers.com
Web: www.crownofficechambers.com

Description of Chambers Crown Office Chambers is one of the foremost sets of chambers specialising in civil common law work. Formed by the merger of One Paper Buildings and Two Crown Office Row, both long established sets with many leading and highly-regarded practitioners, we are now a set of 96 members, including 23 silks. We have high-calibre teams of counsel in a number of areas of work, ranging from county court disputes to large and complex litigation, and have state-of-the-art facilities.

Areas of work A wide range of common law and commercial work, with particular specialisms in construction, commercial contracts, insurance and reinsurance, personal injury, health and safety, product liability, professional negligence and clinical negligence.

Who should apply The members of Crown Office Chambers pride themselves on their professionalism, an astute and business-orientated awareness of the practical needs of solicitors and clients, combined with an approachable and 'unstuffy' attitude to their work. We look for the same in our pupils, all of whom are regarded as having strong tenancy potential. Pupils are welcomed as an integral part of chambers from the moment they arrive, and are expected to display the motivation, dedication and intelligence which are the hallmarks of a first-class barrister. Academically, we look for a first or upper second-class honours degree (not necessarily in law), and a flair for the oral and written presentation of complex legal arguments. You will be expected to work hard and to show strong commitment to your work, but in a friendly and relaxed chambers' environment.

Pupillage programme Pupils sit with two pupil supervisors in their first six months, and one in their second, but are likely to work with a number of different members of chambers practising in different fields of work over the course of the year. They appear in court regularly during their second six, generally handling applications and small trials in the county courts, affording ample opportunity to develop advocacy skills. Chambers also organises a series of advocacy training sessions.

When and how to apply Apply by midnight on 6 February 2019, to begin October 2020 on chambers' application form, downloadable from the chambers' website at www.crownofficechambers.com.

Mini-pupillages Limited number of mini-pupillages available in selected weeks throughout the year. Online form downloadable from chambers' website.

Sponsorship/funding Up to three pupillages offered per year, each with an award of £65,000 (£55,000 plus £10,000 guaranteed earnings in your second six), part of which may be forwarded during the BPTC year.

Pupillages funded	Up to 3
Tenants	96
Tenancies in last 3 yrs	5
Mini-pupillages	yes
Apply via website	
Remuneration for pupillage	£65,000 (£55,000 plus £10,000 guaranteed earnings)
Minimum qualifications	2.1 degree or equivalent

One Crown Office Row

Temple, London EC4Y 7HH
Tel: 020 7797 7500
Email: mail@1cor.com
Web: www.1cor.com
🐦 1crownofficerow

Description of Chambers This is a long-established and leading civil set of 70 members including 25 silks. 1 Crown Office Row is recognised as one of the leading sets in the UK, particularly in the fields of civil and public law. Indicators of excellence are the high number of members on the Attorney General's panels, the growing number of QCs and the high number of former members now in the senior judiciary. We run the highly acclaimed UK Human Rights Blog and the podcast series Law Pod UK.

Areas of work Our members practise in a wide range of specialisms and have been recognised as leading practitioners in areas including: clinical negligence, personal injury, professional negligence, professional discipline, inquests, public inquiries, public and administrative law, mediation, human rights, environmental law, costs, employment and equality, immigration and asylum, tax, and cyber. We also have many members with successful practices in multi-party actions, technology and construction and sports law. In the last few years, our instruction has included the Paterson litigation, Grenfell Tower inquiry and Windrush compensation scheme, amongst other top flight cases. *Chambers & Partners* has described the set as follows: "Its top-flight performers amass between them an enviable bank of knowledge of medical and regulatory issues, all of which is seasoned with efficient case management and excellent responsiveness. It also proves surprisingly versatile. Experts in environment, personal injury, civil liberties and general public law abound at an outfit that forms a whole that is very much greater than the sum of its parts."

Who should apply Candidates should have a keen interest in the areas of work in which members practise. Academic prowess is important, with a normal requirement of a first or upper second-class degree. A sound grounding in legal principle is expected. Chambers retains a strong reputation for the advocacy skills of its members and demonstration of an aptitude for advocacy is helpful. This may be shown in a number of ways, for instance mooting, debating and work in the voluntary legal services sector. Work at the Bar demands high levels of commitment and we look for signs that applicants have that quality by examining, for example, whether they have done mini-pupillages or in some other way established that the Bar, with all its challenges and hurdles, is for them.

Pupillage programme We offer up to two 12-month pupillages. Each pupillage is split between three pupil supervisors. Pupils can expect to gain a wide experience of court and paperwork and have opportunities to help and accompany other members of chambers (including silks) on interesting cases.

When and how to apply Chambers is a member of the centralised pupillage application system, Pupillage Gateway: www.pupillagegateway.com. Full details of the selection process are at www.1cor.com.

Mini-pupillages We offer places for 15 mini-pupils during June and July each year with applications closing at the end of February. Applications should be addressed to Owain Thomas QC. We also run an assessed mini-pupillage scheme aimed at students from less advantaged backgrounds. Full details are at www.1cor.com.

Sponsorship/funding Each pupil receives an annual award of £55,000 paid as a £27,500 grant in the first six months and as £27,500 of guaranteed earnings in the second six. We also fund all necessary training courses for pupils. Pupils may draw down up to 20% of the award in advance to assist in funding their BPTC.

Pupillages funded	2
Tenants	68
Tenancies in last 3 yrs	6
Mini-pupillages	yes
Apply through Pupillage Gateway	
Remuneration for pupillage	£55,000
Minimum qualifications	2.1 degree

1 CROWN OFFICE ROW

DEVEREUX Queen Elizabeth Building, Temple, London EC4Y 9BS **Tel:** 020 7353 7534 **Email:** pupillage@devchambers.co.uk Apply through Pupillage Gateway	Devereux is one of the UK's top civil and commercial sets leading in commercial, employment, personal injury/clinical negligence, insurance, professional negligence, tax and telecommunications law.	PF 2 T 51 TL3Y 4 MP yes
DOUGHTY STREET CHAMBERS 53-54 Doughty Street, London WC1N 2LS **Tel:** 020 7404 1313 **Email:** enquiries@doughtystreet.co.uk Apply through Pupillage Gateway	While at the forefront of many cutting-edge domestic and international human rights cases, we operate across a whole range of different areas of law.	PF 2 T 125 TL3Y 5 MP yes
2 DR JOHNSON'S BUILDINGS Temple, London EC4Y 7AY **Tel:** 020 7936 2613 **Email:** pupillage@2drj.com **Apply to:** Mr Daniel Benjamin	A medium-sized busy and friendly set. 70% crime, 30% family and civil. Up to two funded 12-month pupillages.	PF Up to 2 T 46 TL3Y 5 MP yes
THREE DR JOHNSON'S BUILDINGS Temple, London EC4Y 7BA **Tel:** 020 7353 4854 **Email:** clerks@3djb.co.uk **Apply to:** Ms Lisa Peacock	We are a well established family and civil law set, providing a first-class professional service. Chambers does not plan to offer a pupillage in the forthcoming year.	PF 0 T 33 TL3Y 1 MP yes
DRYSTONE CHAMBERS 35 Bedford Row, Holborn, London WC1R 4JH **Tel:** 020 7404 1881 **Email:** pupillage@drystone.com Apply through Pupillage Gateway	Pupils receive expert training and supervision in general crime, regulatory and extradition law in this leading criminal law set.	PF Up to 2 T 63 TL3Y 5 MP no
EAST ANGLIAN CHAMBERS 5 Museum Street, Ipswich IP1 1HQ **Tel:** 01473 214481 **Email:** ymay@ealaw.co.uk **Apply to:** Mrs Yvonne May	East Anglian Chambers based at three sites, Ipswich, Norwich and Chelmsford, offering a wide range of opportunities.	PF Up to 2 T 43 TL3Y 4 MP yes
ERSKINE CHAMBERS 33 Chancery Lane, London WC2A 1EN **Tel:** 020 7242 5532 **Email:** clerks@erskinechambers.com **Apply to:** Mr Matthew Parfitt	Erskine Chambers specialises in company law, insolvency and related fields. Our policy is one of expansion and we aim to recruit tenants from our pupils.	PF Up to 2 T 30 TL3Y 1 MP yes
39 ESSEX CHAMBERS 81 Chancery Lane, London WC2A 1DD **Tel:** 020 7832 1111 **Email:** clerks@39essex.com Apply through Pupillage Gateway	Long established civil set with 128 members, including 43 QCs. Chambers has several members on each of the Attorney General's A, B and C panels for civil litigation. Chambers prides itself on its friendly and professional atmosphere.	PF Up to 3 T 128 TL3Y 7 MP yes

PF = Pupillages funded / T = Tenants / TL3Y = Tenancies in last 3 years / MP = Mini-pupillages offered

Enterprise Chambers

9 Old Square, Lincoln's Inn, London WC2A 3SR
Tel: 020 7405 9471
Email: london@enterprisechambers.com
Web: www.enterprisechambers.com

Description of Chambers Enterprise Chambers is ranked amongst the leading sets at the chancery commercial bar. Chambers has a strong bias towards litigation and all of its barristers tend to have a firmly court-centred practice. It is a long-established but forward thinking set, with 28 members in London (former members including Lord Millett, Lord Cross, Lord Justice Balcombe and Mr Justice Mann) and equally thriving branches in Leeds, Newcastle and Bristol. Chambers values the ability of its members to approach problems in a manner which is both intellectually rigorous and practically grounded and it prides itself on its down-to-earth and client-friendly reputation.

Areas of work Insolvency and company, including: all aspects of the insolvency of companies, partnerships and individuals; directors' duties; fraudulent and wrongful trading and other misconduct; international and cross-border insolvency; and shareholders' disputes. Property, including: both real property law and landlord and tenant practice. The former covers issues arising from the sale of land, land registration, mortgages, easements, adverse possession and property fraud, amongst others. The latter covers issues arising from leases of all types, whether business, agricultural or social housing tenancies. Commercial, including: general contractual disputes and issues arising from the sale of goods, banking, guarantees, consumer credit, business finance, carriage of goods, civil fraud, professional negligence, regulatory matters, and private international law. Equitable remedies, covering: injunctions (including freezing injunctions and search orders), specific performance, and issues arising from constructive trusts, fiduciary duties, fraud and tracing, restitution, estoppel, rectification and rescission.

Who should apply Applications are invited from candidates with a minimum 2.1 degree or equivalent. We seek the best candidates regardless of their background. We always aim to recruit our starter junior tenants from our pupils and have been delighted to maintain a 100% retention rate for our pupils over at least the last eight years, and to then support them in developing thriving junior practices. We therefore look to offer pupillage to those candidates who have the potential to succeed as tenants in chambers.

Pupillage programme Chambers offers one 12-month pupillage in London each year (recruitment for our Leeds, Newcastle and Bristol branches is conducted separately). Pupils have a minimum of four supervisors and are encouraged to work for other members of chambers to give them the best exposure to all areas of chambers' practice. Our goal is to make pupillage as stimulating and enjoyable as possible and to prepare pupils for a successful practice at the Bar. To that end, pupils in their second six are offered real advocacy experience in court, at an appropriate level, with the support of chambers.

When and how to apply Through the Pupillage Gateway. Further information about the selection process is available on our website.

Mini-pupillages Please see our website to apply for mini-pupillage.

Sponsorship/funding The pupillage award is currently £55,000, including £5,000 of guaranteed earnings. A proportion of this as agreed with chambers may be drawn down in advance. The award may be subject to review and applicants are referred to the Pupillage Gateway for confirmation of the amount.

Pupillages funded	1
Tenants	49
Tenancies in last 3 yrs	3
Mini-pupillages	yes
Apply through Pupillage Gateway	
Remuneration for pupillage	£55,000 (subject to review)
Minimum qualifications	2.1 degree or equivalent

ONE ESSEX COURT
One Essex Court, Temple, London EC4Y 9AR
Tel: 020 7583 2000
Email: clerks@oeclaw.co.uk
Apply through Pupillage Gateway

One Essex Court ordinarily offers four commercial and one intellectual property pupillage.

PF	5
T	110
T_{L3Y}	11
MP	yes

5 ESSEX COURT
5 Essex Court, Temple, London EC4Y 9AH
Tel: 020 7410 2000
Email: clerks@5essexcourt.co.uk
Apply through Pupillage Gateway

Legal Cheek's Best Chambers for Training 2018. Leading chambers specialising in public law, human rights, police law, personal injury and employment.

PF	Up to 2
T	40
T_{L3Y}	4
MP	yes

ESSEX COURT CHAMBERS
24 Lincoln's Inn Fields, London WC2A 3EG
Tel: 020 7813 8000
Email: pupillage@essexcourt.net
Apply through Pupillage Gateway

Our members offer advisory and advocacy expertise on disputes relating to all aspects of business and commerce, both domestic and international.

PF	Up to 4
T	90
T_{L3Y}	7
MP	yes

23 ESSEX STREET
23 Essex Street, London WC2R 3AA
Tel: 020 7413 0353
Email: clerks@23ES.com
Apply to: Ms Kate Lumsdon

23 Essex Street is a modern, innovative, approachable set of barristers, with a leading reputation in the fields of crime, fraud and a range of regulatory and disciplinary matters.

PF	1
T	103
T_{L3Y}	9
MP	yes

EXCHANGE CHAMBERS
One Derby Square, Liverpool L2 9XX
Tel: 0845 300 7747
Email: campbell@exchangechambers.co.uk
Apply to: Miss Chantal Campbell

Exchange Chambers is a leading set with offices in Manchester, Liverpool and Leeds.

PF	1-2
T	156
T_{L3Y}	5
MP	yes

FARRAR'S BUILDING
Temple, London EC4Y 7BD
Tel: 020 7583 9241
Email: chambers@farrarsbuilding.co.uk
Apply through Pupillage Gateway

Farrar's Building is a leading set of chambers situated in the heart of the Temple, specialising in personal injury, employment, company and commercial work.

PF	2
T	45
T_{L3Y}	4
MP	yes

FARRINGDON CHAMBERS
Gemini House, 180 Bermondsey Street, London SE1 3TQ
Tel: 020 7089 5700
Email: recruitment@farringdon-law.co.uk
Apply to: Miss Molly Pinkus

PF	2
T	31
T_{L3Y}	2
MP	yes

FENNERS CHAMBERS
3 Madingley Road, Cambridge CB3 OEE
Tel: 01223 368761
Email: pupillage@fennerschambers.com
Apply to: Miss Caroline Allison

Fenners is a common law set offering a varied and well-rounded pupillage affording pupils the opportunity to experience different areas of law prior to specialisation.

PF	Up to 2
T	50
T_{L3Y}	2
MP	yes

PF = Pupillages funded / **T** = Tenants / **T_{L3Y}** = Tenancies in last 3 years / **MP** = Mini-pupillages offered

Falcon Chambers

Falcon Court, London EC4Y 1AA
Tel: 020 7353 2484
Email: pupillage@falcon-chambers.com
Web: www.falcon-chambers.com
🐦 falconchambers1

Description of Chambers Falcon Chambers is recognised by the legal directories, solicitors and clients as the leading property chambers. Many of the major practitioner texts relating to property law are written by our members. We place a lot of importance on being a friendly, closely integrated group of colleagues. Many former members of chambers have become judges, including the former President of The Supreme Court Lord Neuberger of Abbotsbury, Lord Justice Lewison and Mr Justice Morgan.

Areas of work Members of chambers are heavily involved in litigation in the real property, landlord and tenant and property-related fields, including cases involving insolvency, trusts, banking, revenue, professional negligence, environmental and treasury work. We are involved in both contentious and non-contentious work.

Who should apply Applications are welcome from all who have or expect to achieve a 2.1 or first in their degree, including students who have not yet completed a first degree, or non-law students who have not yet completed a GDL. The successful applicant will absorb complex information and identify essential points and practical solutions quickly; communicate clearly, concisely and persuasively, both orally and in writing; and remain calm, objective and confident while working under pressure.

Pupillage programme Our current policy is to offer up to two pupillages each year, each of which is for 12 months. Pupils are allocated to a different pupil supervisor every three months in order to see a range of work and practices. We aim to give our pupils a good grounding in advocacy, in addition to the courses offered by the Inns, by providing structured advocacy training throughout the year. Few of our applicants will have studied our speciality in any depth, and therefore we provide an intensive course in landlord and tenant law at Falcon Chambers usually held in the last week of September, immediately prior to the commencement of pupillage.

When and how to apply Falcon Chambers does not receive applications through the Pupillage Gateway. Applications should be made on chambers' application form which is available from the website from the beginning of December 2018 for pupillages starting in October 2020. The closing date is 4 January 2019 and interviews are held in January and February. More details are available on our website.

Mini-pupillages Our mini-pupillages are not assessed, and there is no requirement that you come to chambers on a mini-pupillage before you apply for a pupillage. We do, however, encourage interested students to visit us for a few days to experience life at Falcon Chambers. We find that those who do so invariably apply to us for pupillage. The programme lasts for three days (usually Tuesday to Thursday), during which time we try to ensure that you will spend some time in court, sit in on a conference with clients and also sample some paperwork. We hold three mini-pupillage sessions each year, full details along with dates, when to apply and the application form are all available on our website.

Sponsorship/funding Our pupillage award is up to £65,000 per pupil (for those starting in October 2020), of which up to £22,000 is available for drawdown during the BPTC year. In addition, in their second six months, pupils can expect to earn some additional income from their own work. Successful pupils who become junior tenants are usually fully employed doing their own work shortly after being taken on.

Pupillages funded	Up to 2
Tenants	39
Tenancies in last 3 yrs	4
Mini-pupillages	yes

Apply via website

Remuneration for pupillage
Up to £65,000

Minimum qualifications
2.1 degree

Falcon Chambers

Francis Taylor Building

Inner Temple, London EC4Y 7BY
Tel: 020 7353 8415
Email: clerks@ftbchambers.co.uk
Web: www.ftbchambers.co.uk
🐦 ftb_pupillage

Description of Chambers Francis Taylor Building's (FTB) reputation for excellence is long-standing and we are consistently featured in the legal directories for our expertise and leading role in planning, land valuation, infrastructure, environmental, public law, licensing and regulatory law. Members of chambers undertake specialist advisory work and regularly appear in courts at all levels in this country and abroad, including specialist tribunals and public inquiries. From head of chambers to the most junior tenant, the workload is wide and varied. There are 24 Queen's Counsel in chambers and most junior tenants find themselves working on cases as junior to a silk on a fairly regular basis.

Areas of work As part of our specialist practice, chambers also undertakes work connected with transport and works schemes, utilities, highways, energy, rating, religious liberty and ecclesiastical, heritage and conservation, common land and village greens, education, minerals, statutory nuisance and regulation, health and safety, compulsory purchase and compensation, easements and covenants, mediation, advertisements, employment and consumer law among other areas of related work.

Who should apply Prospective pupils should demonstrate a high intellectual ability and have a degree of at least upper second level. They should have an interest in the fields, in which chambers practises.

Pupillage programme Three pupil supervisors – four months each.

What will you do as a pupil? The first six months – Pupils usually sit in their pupil-supervisors' rooms and experience all aspects of their professional lives. During the first six months pupils read their pupil-supervisors' instructions and papers, research relevant law, attempt their own draft pleadings and opinions for discussion, and attend with them at court and in conference with solicitors and lay clients. Chambers have an in house training programme for pupils which includes seminars in practice areas and advocacy exercises. The second six months – Pupils are expected to undertake a certain amount of written work for, and attend at court with, other members of chambers as well as their pupil-supervisors. In recent years second-six pupils have also been briefed to appear in a variety of courts and tribunals, including the High Court, County Court and planning inquiries. Pro bono work for FRU, Law For All, the Bar Pro Bono Unit and others is actively encouraged.

What are the prospects of tenancy? Since 2012, chambers has recruited 10 junior tenants. There can, of course, be no guarantee that a new tenant will be recruited from each new year's intake. Chambers recognises its responsibility to those who are not offered a tenancy and does its best to ensure that suitable positions are found elsewhere. In recent years, some of its former pupils have obtained tenancies in other chambers; others have joined major firms of solicitors or worked as lawyers in central and local government.

When and how to apply Apply by 31 January 2019 to begin October 2020. Chambers' application form available on the website or by application to Ms Saira Kabir Sheikh QC.

Mini-pupillages Apply to Mr Charles Streeten.

Sponsorship/funding Two awards of not less than £60,000. A drawdown of up to £15,000 available for BPTC.

Pupillages funded	2
Tenants	56
Tenancies in last 3 yrs	6
Mini-pupillages	yes
Apply via website	
Remuneration for pupillage	Not less than £60,000
Minimum qualifications	2.1 degree

ftb
Francis Taylor Building

FIELD COURT CHAMBERS 5 Field Court, Gray's Inn, London WC1R 5EF **Tel:** 020 7405 6114 **Email:** pupillage16@fieldcourt.co.uk **Apply to:** The Training and Pupillage Committee	Chambers is an established, highly regarded and friendly set with three broad practice areas: civil, family and public. Members are recommended in UK *Legal 500*.

PF Up to 2
T 60
T_{L3Y} 3
MP yes

187 FLEET STREET 187 Fleet Street, London EC4A 2AT **Tel:** 020 7430 7430 **Email:** chambers@187fleetstreet.com Apply through Pupillage Gateway	A high-profile chambers whose members defend and prosecute in all areas of criminal and regulatory law (especially serious crime and corporate fraud).

PF 2
T 73
T_{L3Y} 6
MP yes

FOUNDRY CHAMBERS Quality House, 5-9 Quality Court, Chancery Lane, London WC2A 1HP **Tel:** 020 7400 1800 **Email:** clerks@foundrychambers.com **Apply to:** Miss Natalie McNamee	Criminal defence and prosecution (inc CPS, SFO, HMRC); fraud and financial regulation; local authority; business regulation; extradition; immigration; professional discipline; tax litigation.

PF 2
T 54
T_{L3Y} 7
MP yes

FOUNTAIN COURT CHAMBERS Temple, London EC4Y 9DH **Tel:** 020 7583 3335 **Email:** lucy@fountaincourt.co.uk Apply through Pupillage Gateway	A leading set of chambers specialising in commercial work. Up to four pupillages offered through the Pupillage Gateway. Mini-pupillages are available, though not a requirement for 2019 Gateway round.

PF Up to 4
T 81
T_{L3Y} 7
MP yes

1 GARDEN COURT Ground Floor, Temple, London EC4Y 9BJ **Tel:** 020 7797 7900 **Email:** clerks@1gc.com Apply through Pupillage Gateway	1 Garden Court is one of the foremost family law chambers in London and are consistently recognised as leading specialists in the legal directories.

PF 2
T 74
T_{L3Y} 5
MP yes

GARDEN COURT CHAMBERS 57-60 Lincoln's Inn Fields, London WC2A 3LJ **Tel:** 020 7993 7600 **Email:** info@gclaw.co.uk Apply through Pupillage Gateway	A civil liberties chambers specialising in human rights; family; immigration; crime; housing and civil including employment; gypsy/traveller; inquests; prison; and claims against the police/public authorities.

PF 4
T 182
T_{L3Y} 27
MP yes

GOLDSMITH CHAMBERS Chambers of Anthony Metzer QC, Goldsmith Building, Temple, London EC4Y 7BL **Tel:** 020 7353 6802 **Email:** v.wilson@goldsmithchambers.com Apply through Pupillage Gateway	Argent Chambers has merged with Goldsmith Chambers as of 6 May.

PF 2
T 73
T_{L3Y} 8
MP yes

GOUGH SQUARE CHAMBERS 6-7 Gough Square, London EC4A 3DE **Tel:** 020 7353 0924 **Email:** gsc@goughsq.co.uk Apply through Pupillage Gateway	Gough Square Chambers is a small and friendly set that has developed a leading reputation in consumer, regulatory and financial work.

PF 0
T 26
T_{L3Y} 2
MP yes

PF = Pupillages funded / T = Tenants / T_{L3Y} = Tenancies in last 3 years / MP = Mini-pupillages offered

9 Gough Square

The Chambers of Andrew Ritchie QC, 9 Gough Square, London EC4A 3DG
Tel: 020 7832 0500
Email: pupillage@9goughsquare.co.uk
Web: www.9goughsquare.co.uk
🐦 9goughsquare

Description of Chambers 9 Gough Square is a leading common law set of chambers known for its core strengths in advocacy, drafting and advisory work. Clients include solicitors, local government, central government, corporate bodies and individuals. Tenants practise in all areas of work for the first three years after recruitment, which provides enviable advocacy experience and develops an interesting and varied practice.

Areas of work Members of chambers work and specialise in a wide variety of areas. The largest group in chambers practises in personal injury and clinical negligence work and its members are ranked in the leading Bar directories. Members of chambers also represent parties at inquests. There is a strong criminal team with work in fraud, sexual offences and general crime, and a growing regulatory team working with professional bodies and individuals. 9 Gough Square has long been known for its police work, accepting instructions from the Metropolitan Police and other constabularies in a variety of civil and quasi-criminal cases. The family team undertakes public and private law work, regularly appearing in High Court and Court of Appeal cases. Court of Protection work permits cross-over between the family and civil disciplines. The commercial and property team is routinely involved in cases of all levels of complexity, acting for businesses, creditors, debtors, landlords and other individuals. Its members cover the full spectrum of disputes from cases relating to commercial leases and construction contracts to consumer credit and insolvency matters. As a common law set, members of chambers, and particularly junior tenants, frequently encounter and tackle a wide variety of other areas of work, including employment, public and costs work.

Who should apply We look for candidates of high intellectual ability, usually evidenced by at least a 2.1 degree or equivalent, who can also demonstrate a commitment to the Bar and a flair for advocacy, combined with common sense and sound judgement. If words such as highly-motivated, robust and a real team player apply to you, then we would like to hear from you. 9 Gough Square operates and observes a robust equality and diversity policy. For many years we have been at the forefront of E&D issues at the Bar.

Pupillage programme We offer up to two pupillages of 12 months' duration. All pupillages are funded. We strive to ensure that a pupil sees as broad an array of work as possible, and particularly in our main practice areas. Before a pupil starts on his or her feet, he or she will have sat with a pupil supervisor in each of civil, criminal and family work. The pupillage programme includes regular feedback and assessed exercises.

When and how to apply The application window will open on 17 December 2018. On that date, details about how to apply and the application form and guidance will be published on the website www.9goughsquare.co.uk/pupillage.html. The application system is online and applications are only accepted through the dedicated chambers application system. The deadline by which applications must be received will be 17 February 2019. 9 Gough Square is not a member of the Pupillage Gateway.

Mini-pupillages 9 Gough Square accepts applications for mini-pupillage via its website. There is usually one application window each year, during the early summer. For further details please see www.9goughsquare.co.uk/mini-pupillage.html.

Pupillages funded	Up to 2
Tenants	74
Tenancies in last 3 yrs	4
Mini-pupillages	yes

Apply via website

Remuneration for pupillage
£50,000

Minimum qualifications
Usually 2.1 or equivalent

4-5 GRAY'S INN SQUARE Gray's Inn, London WC1R 5AH **Tel:** 020 7404 5252 **Email:** clerks@4-5.co.uk	A modern set of chambers that specialises in public law and human rights, planning and environmental law, commercial, sports, intellectual property, education and employment.	PF 1 T 33 T_{L3Y} 4 MP yes
1 GRAY'S INN SQUARE (Chambers of Stephen Harvey QC), Gray's Inn, London WC1R 5AA **Tel:** 020 7405 0001 **Email:** pupillage@1gis.co.uk Apply through Pupillage Gateway	Chambers is an established common law set with over 70 members inlcuding a number of silks, leading juniors and members of the judiciary.	PF 2 T 73 T_{L3Y} 7 MP yes
GRAY'S INN TAX CHAMBERS 36 Queen Street, London EC4R 1BN **Tel:** 020 7242 2642 **Email:** pupillage@taxbar.com Apply through Pupillage Gateway	A leading set of chambers specialising in revenue law (domestic, European and international). Members undertake all aspects of tax litigation and advice.	PF 1 T 9 T_{L3Y} 0 MP yes
GT STEWART SOLICITORS 2A Melbourne Grove, East Dulwich, London SE22 8PL **Tel:** 020 8299 6000 **Email:** r.manek@gtstewart.co.uk **Apply to:** Mr Ronnie Manek	GT Stewart is established as one of the leading firms in London for publicly funded work and regularly receives referrals from other firms and agencies.	PF 1 T 15 T_{L3Y} 1 MP yes
GUILDFORD CHAMBERS Stoke House, Leapale Lane, Guildford GU1 4LY **Tel:** 01483 539131 **Email:** clerks@guildfordchambers.com **Apply to:** The Pupillage Committee	Family and civil law set serving the South East.	PF 1 T 23 T_{L3Y} 5 MP yes
GUILDHALL CHAMBERS 23 Broad Street, Bristol BS1 2HG **Tel:** 0117 930 9000 **Email:** info@guildhallchambers.co.uk Apply through Pupillage Gateway	Friendly progressive set in the centre of Bristol, situated in two large premises and offering pupils modern IT facilities and thorough training.	PF 2 T 84 T_{L3Y} 8 MP yes
2 HARCOURT BUILDINGS 1st Floor Left, 2 Harcourt Buildings, Temple, London EC4Y 9DB **Tel:** 020 7353 2112 **Email:** clerks@2hb.co.uk Apply through Pupillage Gateway	A leading criminal chambers, defending and prosecuting in London and on the Western and South Eastern Circuits.	PF 2 T 39 T_{L3Y} 4 MP yes
HARCOURT CHAMBERS Temple, London EC4Y 9DB **Tel:** 0844 561 7135 **Email:** clerks@harcourtchambers.law.co.uk Apply through Pupillage Gateway	Awarded Family Set of the Year in *Chambers'* UK Bar Awards 2017; members practice in London and a wide geographical area and include six silks.	PF 1-2 T 54 T_{L3Y} 4 MP yes

PF = Pupillages funded / **T** = Tenants / **T**_{L3Y} = Tenancies in last 3 years / **MP** = Mini-pupillages offered

Hailsham Chambers

4 Paper Buildings, Ground Floor, Temple, London EC4Y 7EX
Tel: 020 7643 5000
Email: clerks@hailshamchambers.com
Web: www.hailshamchambers.com
🐦 hailsham_chamb

Description of Chambers Hailsham Chambers is a top tier civil law set. We win awards for our excellence and we are recognised by the legal directories as a leading set in our three main practice areas. We strive to provide the highest standards of advocacy, advice and service, with a committed open door policy and friendly atmosphere within chambers. We are proud of our history, which includes a number of former law lords, but we are innovative and forward-thinking.

Areas of work At Hailsham Chambers we excel in our key areas of professional negligence, medical law, costs, regulatory and disciplinary, personal injury and commercial law. We have leading practitioners and experts In all these fields and are recognised by the legal directories as a leading set for professional and medical negligence, professional disciplinary and costs disputes. We have strong and long-established relationships with all of the leading insurers and national and City firms working in our areas of practice.

Who should apply We wish to recruit two pupils to start in September 2020. You will be a motivated, ambitious candidate who can meet the following criteria: intellectual ability and curiosity – usually a minimum 2.1 degree is required but special circumstances will be considered, persuasive communication in both oral and written advocacy, personal qualities which will allow you to succeed at the Bar and interest in chambers and in our areas of practice.

We are passionate about encouraging applications from a diverse pool of candidates. We place emphasis on our problem question because we aim to recruit candidates who sparkle with ability.

Pupillage programme We provide 12-months' intensive, high-quality training in a relaxed atmosphere with three supervisors, covering at least two areas of chambers' specialisation. You will also have a mentor, who is a recent junior tenant, who can discuss pupillage confidentially with you. We also tailor a thorough advocacy training and assessment programme to give our pupils the best chance at tenancy. Our retention rate is excellent and all seven pupils in the last three years have become tenants.

When and how to apply For 12-month pupillage commencing September 2020, please apply through the Pupillage Gateway.

Mini-pupillages We encourage you to apply for a mini-pupillage although it is not assessed and does not form part of our pupillage decision making process. Hailsham Chambers offers mini-pupillages throughout the year to those who are over 18 years old. Please see more information on our website.

Sponsorship/funding We will offer two 12-month pupillages commencing in September 2020. Each of our 12-month pupillages has an award of £50,000 including £5,000 guaranteed earnings.

Pupillages funded	2
Tenants	49
Tenancies in last 3 yrs	7
Mini-pupillages	yes
Apply through Pupillage Gateway	
Remuneration for pupillage	£50,000 including £5,000 guaranteed earnings
Minimum qualifications	2.1 degree

Hardwicke

New Square, Lincoln's Inn, London WC2A 3SB
Tel: 020 7242 2523
Email: enquiries@hardwicke.co.uk
Web: www.hardwicke.co.uk
🐦 hardwickelaw

Description of Chambers Hardwicke specialises in commercial, construction, insurance and property law and has expertise in professional negligence, insolvency and personal injury work. We are a successful, innovative set with a reputation for high quality legal expertise, excellent administration and an approachable, business-focused style. This is consistently recognised in *Chambers & Partners* and *Legal 500*.

Who should apply We are looking for candidates of the highest calibre with the potential to become successful barristers. Academic achievement forms a significant part of our considerations, but is not the only criterion. We look at three core skill sets that we think are essential in a good barrister: legal, interpersonal and business/client care skills. When selecting pupils, we are looking for applicants who show the potential to excel in all of these areas.

Pupillage programme We offer up to two 12-month pupillages each year both with a view to tenancy. Our policy is therefore only to offer pupillage to those candidates whom we consider have the potential to become tenants with us. We look for pupils with exceptional intellectual ability, excellent communication skills and a genuine interest in our areas of work. You will need to be confident and able to work both on your own and with others, demonstrating not only legal, analytical ability but also commercial good sense. We put a great deal of effort into providing you with the support and training necessary to succeed in an extremely competitive environment. From day one you will be part of our team and included in chambers events and introduced to clients. We have an open door policy and ensure our pupils feel they are able to approach any member of chambers for guidance and advice.

Our 12-month pupillages are split into three periods of four months. During each period, you will be assigned a pupil supervisor and other members of chambers with whom you will work. You will share the daily professional life of your pupil supervisor, producing pleadings and opinions on their cases, attending conferences and receiving regular feedback. Advocacy is a key component of a Hardwicke pupillage. We will provide you with in-house advocacy training, supervised by our members, many of whom are advocacy trainers at the Inns and/or part-time judges. During your second six months, you can expect to find yourself in court two to three days a week.

When and how to apply We are a member of Pupillage Gateway. You can also find details on our website on how to apply.

Mini-pupillages We offer up to 12 mini-pupillages per year (three per quarter). Applicants should complete our application form on the recruitment pages of our website. Please visit Hardwicke's website for closing dates and details about eligibility.

Sponsorship/funding We offer up to two pupillages each year with an award of £55,000 split as an award of £40,000 and guaranteed earnings of £15,000. Up to £15,000 of the award may be drawn down during your BPTC year. We will fund attendance at the Bar Council's compulsory courses. We also have a guaranteed earnings scheme for our first and second year tenants to give financial security to those just starting out.

Pupillages funded	2
Tenants	86
Tenancies in last 3 yrs	12
Mini-pupillages	yes

Applications contact
Allison Longely

Remuneration for pupillage
£55,000

Hardwicke

1 Hare Court

Temple, London EC4Y 7BE
Tel: 020 7797 7070
Email: clerks@1hc.com
Web: www.1hc.com

Areas of work 1 Hare Court was the first set of chambers to specialise in family law and we now have 13 silks and 28 juniors. The majority of chambers' work is in the area of matrimonial finance, while some members of chambers are involved in child law disputes. Former members of chambers include two previous presidents of the Family Division, two Lords Justice of Appeal and four High Court judges of the Family Division. Current members of chambers have acted in almost all the landmark matrimonial finance cases, including *White*, *Miller/McFarlane*, *McCartney*, *Radmacher v Granatino*, *Prest*, *Whyatt v Vince*, *Sharland*, *Owens* and *Waggett*. Chambers' clients tend to be high-net worth individuals from the worlds of commerce, entertainment, finance and sport.

We expect that applicants will have a strong academic record. 1 Hare Court has a long-standing tradition of contributing to legal works. *Rayden on Divorce*, the principal practitioners' textbook, was renamed *Rayden & Jackson* as a tribute to the former head of chambers Joseph Jackson QC, who edited the work for many years. Members of chambers continue to edit *Rayden & Jackson*, as well as many other leading books, and we regularly contribute articles to the specialist press. Candidates who demonstrate the potential to carry on this strong intellectual tradition will impress.

A pupillage at 1 Hare Court offers training in advocacy, advice and drafting in every aspect of family work, particularly matrimonial finance. Our strong reputation and the quality of training available means that those pupils who are not taken on stand a good prospect of finding a professional opportunity elsewhere, frequently in other specialist chambers.

Who should apply Candidates should be able to show that they have a flair for advocacy, presentational and analytical skills and the ability to develop sound judgement, as well as having a strong academic record. Given the emphasis on financial work, some aptitude and interest in commercial/financial matters is desirable. However, chambers' work remains rooted in human problems and a sympathetic but perceptive response to those problems is essential.

When and how to apply We recruit pupils once a year. Applications for pupillages commencing in October 2020 open and close in accordance with the Pupillage Gateway timetable. Applications should be sent with a full CV and handwritten covering letter (marked pupillage application) to the chambers administrator. References may be helpful. Those invited for an interview are likely to be interviewed on a Saturday in April 2019. Chambers is not a member of Pupillage Gateway but keeps to the timetable for the communication and acceptance of offers. For more information see the chambers' website.

Mini-pupillages These are available during term time only. Applicants must be at least at undergraduate level and have some interest in family law. Applications are accepted twice a year and should be sent with a full CV and handwritten covering letter marked for the attention of Thomas Harvey. For mini-pupillages between February – July 2019, please apply between 1-31 January 2019. For mini-pupillages between October 2019 – January 2020, please apply between 1-31 July 2019. Ordinarily applications will not be considered outside of these application periods.

Sponsorship/funding Two fully-funded pupillages.

Pupillages funded	2
Tenants	42
Tenancies in last 3 yrs	5
Mini-pupillages	yes
Apply by CV	
Remuneration for pupillage	£35,000 per pupillage plus earnings in second six
Minimum qualifications	2.1 degree

1 HARE COURT

Henderson Chambers

2 Harcourt Buildings, Temple, London EC4Y 9DB
Tel: 020 7583 9020
Email: clerks@hendersonchambers.co.uk
Web: www.hendersonpupillage.co.uk
🐦 henderson_bar

Description of Chambers Henderson Chambers is a leading commercial/common law chambers with acknowledged expertise in all of its principal areas of practice. Members and pupils are frequently involved in high-profile commercial and common law litigation.

Areas of work Henderson Chambers has unrivalled expertise in product liability (which covers a wide range of commercial work including sale of goods and insurance disputes, multi-party pharmaceutical and medical device claims and regulatory and enforcement proceedings) and is consistently rated as the leading set in this area. Chambers is also widely recognised for the excellence of its health and safety work.

Over the last few decades chambers has been involved in many of the major commercial and landmark international group actions.

In addition, members are noted for their expertise and experience in areas including: banking and finance, consumer credit, employment law, regulatory and disciplinary proceedings, public law and judicial review, personal injury, property law, and technology and construction. Several members of chambers are treasury counsel (civil). Many of them are currently engaged in the Grenfell Tower inquiry, the VW emissions litigation and the Post Office group action.

Who should apply Chambers looks for individuals who can demonstrate a first-class intellect whether via the traditional route of an outstanding higher education record or via proof of success in other professions, in business or in employment. It is a friendly and sociable set which works hard, both at servicing the needs of clients, as well as engendering a nurturing and supportive professional environment. Chambers is looking for potential tenants who can help it meet those twin objectives.

Pupillage programme Pupillages are for 12 months, usually with four different pupil supervisors for three months each. Pupils have the opportunity to spend four weeks at Griffiths & Partners in the Turks and Caicos Islands in order to experience practice in another jurisdiction at first hand. Pupils will attend court regularly (on their own cases) during their second six months.

When and how to apply We are part of the Pupillage Gateway and abide by its timetable. Queries about pupillage should be addressed to Helen Ghalem.

Mini-pupillages Chambers offers unassessed mini-pupillages. Our online application system operates to fixed application periods. Visit our pupillage website at www.hendersonpupillage.co.uk for details of how to apply. We also recognise that for those who live outside the capital, it can be expensive to stay in London. We offer up to 15 bursaries every year of £200 each to candidates who are likely to have difficulty meeting the costs of attending a mini-pupillage with us.

Sponsorship/funding Chambers offers up to two funded 12-month pupillages a year. Our pupils receive a minimum remuneration of £70,000. This consists of a guaranteed award of £70,000, plus any additional earnings during the second six months. A drawdown of up to £10,000 is available during the year before pupillage commences.

Pupillages funded	2
Tenants	48
Tenancies in last 3 yrs	6
Mini-pupillages	yes

Apply through Pupillage Gateway

Remuneration for pupillage
£70,000 award plus any additional earnings in the second six

HENDERSON CHAMBERS

2 HARE COURT
Temple, London EC4Y 7BH
Tel: 020 7353 5324
Email: clerks@2harecourt.com
Apply through Pupillage Gateway

We are recognised as a leading criminal set, with an even mix of prosecution and defence work. We offer up to two fully-funded 12-month pupillages per year.

PF	2
T	56
T$_{L3Y}$	8
MP	no

---

3 HARE COURT
Temple, London EC4Y 7BJ
Tel: 020 7415 7800
Email: clerks@3harecourt.com
Apply through Pupillage Gateway

Commercial/common law set which undertakes consitutional, human rights and criminal appeals in the Privy Council. We offer two funded 12-month pupillages each year.

PF	2
T	35
T$_{L3Y}$	4
MP	yes

---

7 HARRINGTON STREET CHAMBERS
7 Harrington Street, Liverpool L2 9YH
Tel: 0151 242 0707
Email: claireb@7hs.co.uk
Apply through Pupillage Gateway

Applications to chambers are through the Pupillage Gateway portal.

PF	1
T	90
T$_{L3Y}$	5
MP	yes

---

1 HIGH PAVEMENT
Lace Market, Nottingham NG1 1HF
Tel: 0115 941 8218
Email: clerks@1highpavement.co.uk
Apply to: Mr Avik Mukherjee

Specialist criminal chambers for the East Midlands.

PF	1
T	43
T$_{L3Y}$	2
MP	yes

HOGARTH CHAMBERS
Lincoln's Inn, 5 New Square, London WC2A 3RJ
Tel: 020 7404 0404
Email: lpavlovsky@hogarthchambers.com
Apply to: Ms Briget Harrison

We are one of the leading intellectual property law sets. Chambers' specialisms include media and entertainment, IT, privacy and chancery law.

PF	1
T	21
T$_{L3Y}$	2
MP	yes

INVICTUS CHAMBERS
1 Mitre Court Buildings, Temple, London EC4Y 7BS
Tel: 03301194300
Email: join@invictuschambers.org
Apply through Pupillage Gateway

PF	2
T	19
T$_{L3Y}$	5
MP	yes

ISCOED CHAMBERS
86 St Helen's Road, Swansea SA1 4BQ
Tel: 01792 652988
Email: clerks@iscoedchambers.co.uk
Apply through Pupillage Gateway

Iscoed Chambers is a long-established common law set based in Swansea.

PF	1
T	35
T$_{L3Y}$	5
MP	yes

ONE ITL
Fleet House, 8-12 New Bridge Street, London EC4V 6AL
Tel: 020 7427 4400
Email: clerks@1itl.com
Apply through Pupillage Gateway

Specialist criminal law chambers prosecuting and defending the full range of criminal work. Also court martial and prison law.

PF	2
T	26
T$_{L3Y}$	4
MP	yes

PF = Pupillages funded / T = Tenants / T$_{L3Y}$ = Tenancies in last 3 years / MP = Mini-pupillages offered

KBG CHAMBERS 115 North Hill, Plymouth PL4 8JY **Tel:** 01752 221551 **Email:** clerks@kbgchambers.co.uk **Apply to:** Mr Thomas Challacombe	General common law set covering all of the West Country, predominantly Devon and Cornwall.	PF 1 T 35 T∟₃ʏ 3 MP yes
KBW The Engine House, 1 Foundry Square, Leeds LS11 5DL **Tel:** 0113 297 1200 **Email:** clerks@kbwchambers.com Apply through Pupillage Gateway	Applications for pupillage must be made through the Pupillage Gateway.	PF 1 T 38 T∟₃ʏ 4 MP yes
11KBW 11 King's Bench Walk, Temple, London EC4Y 7EQ **Tel:** 020 7632 8500 **Email:** claire.halas@11kbw.com Apply through Pupillage Gateway	This leading employment set also specialises in public and commercial law. Two to four funded pupillages are usually offered each year.	PF 2-4 T 59 T∟₃ʏ 6 MP yes
6KBW COLLEGE HILL 21 College Hill, London EC4R 2RP **Tel:** 020 3301 0910 **Email:** pupillage@6kbw.com **Apply to:** The Pupillage Secretary	Leading set in criminal law and related fields, including public law, extradition, corporate crime and investigations, inquests and regulatory law.	PF 2 T 47 T∟₃ʏ 3 MP yes
KCH GARDEN SQUARE BARRISTERS 1 Oxford Street, Nottingham NG1 5BH **Tel:** 0115 9418851 **Email:** clerks@kchgardensquare.co.uk **Apply to:** Mrs Moira Ashton-Walsh	Family/civil pupillage. Mixed common law set based in Nottingham and Leicester. Innovative and forward thinking. Barmark, *Legal 500 and Chambers & Partners* rated.	PF Up to 2 T 60 T∟₃ʏ 22 MP yes
KEATING CHAMBERS 15 Essex Street, London WC2R 3AA **Tel:** 020 7544 2600 **Email:** clerks@keatingchambers.com Apply through Pupillage Gateway	Keating Chambers is an award-winning, commercial set specialising in complex domestic and international construction, engineering, energy, international arbitration, procurement, technology and related professional negligence disputes.	PF 3 T 64 T∟₃ʏ 4 MP yes
KENWORTHY'S CHAMBERS Arlington House, Bloom Street, Salford, Manchester M3 6AJ **Tel:** 0161 832 4036 **Email:** maria@kenworthysbarristers.co.uk Apply through Pupillage Gateway	Kenworthy's are a forward thinking set striving for access to justice; with professionalism and excellence as the driving force to everything we do.	PF 1-2 T 65 T∟₃ʏ 4 MP yes
1 KING'S BENCH WALK Temple, London EC4Y 7DB **Tel:** 020 7936 1500 **Email:** pupillage@1kbw.co.uk **Apply to:** Ms Nichola Bentley	1 King's Bench Walk has a pre-eminent reputation in family law, both nationally and internationally.	PF 2 T 57 T∟₃ʏ 6 MP yes

PF = Pupillages funded / **T** = Tenants / **T**∟₃ʏ = Tenancies in last 3 years / **MP** = Mini-pupillages offered

7 King's Bench Walk

Temple, London EC4Y 7DS
Tel: 020 7910 8300
Email: pupillage@7kbw.co.uk
Web: www.7kbw.co.uk

Description of Chambers 7 KBW is a top commercial chambers, with a reputation for excellence, intellectual rigour and providing practical, commercial advice. Its members practise across the full breadth of commercial law and are ranked highly in the leading legal directories. Members appear regularly in the Commercial Court, the Court of Appeal, the Supreme Court, the Privy Council and in arbitrations. They also appear in court and arbitrations in a significant number of other jurisdictions including Singapore, Bermuda, the Bahamas, the Cayman Islands, Dubai and Hong Kong.

Areas of work 7KBW's practice areas are exclusively commercial and cover the following: all aspects of insurance and reinsurance, shipping and transport, professional negligence, civil fraud, international trade and commodities, energy, oil and gas, agency, injunctions and arrests, shipbuilding, sale of goods, banking and financial services, aviation, construction and private international law. Most of 7KBW's work has an international dimension.

Who should apply Candidates with strong analytical and intellectual abilities. 7KBW does not typically interview candidates who do not have a first or a good upper second-class degree. 7KBW offers up to four pupillages per year.

Pupillage programme Pupils are allocated a pupillage supervisor for the first two to three months and will change pupillage supervisor more frequently thereafter. A large component of pupillage is assisting in the preparation of trials and applications and attending court with the pupil supervisor. It will also involve drafting statements of case, researching the law, advices and attending conferences. Whatever the nature of the pupil supervisor's work, a pupil can expect to be fully involved in it. 7KBW also organises advocacy exercises and pleading seminars for its pupils.

When and how to apply Applications should be made via the Pupillage Gateway 2019 season for pupillages commencing in September 2020. Deferred pupillages commencing in September 2021 will also be available but will only be offered in exceptional circumstances.

Mini-pupillages Two-day mini-pupillages are available. Mini-pupillages do not include any formal assessments and completon of a mini-pupillage is not a prerequisite for applying for pupillage, but it is strongly encouraged. For information about how and when to apply, please refer to the website at https://7kbw.co.uk/pupillage/mini-pupillage.

Sponsorship/funding Pupillages are fully funded, with awards of £65,000 for 12 months. 7KBW is willing to advance up to £25,000 of the award on an interest-free basis for use during the BPTC year, on condition that any advance will be repaid if the pupil does not pass the BPTC exams or complete his or her pupillage.

Pupillages funded	Up to 4
Tenants	62
Tenancies in last 3 yrs	6
Mini-pupillages	yes
Apply through Pupillage Gateway	
Remuneration for pupillage	£65,000
Minimum qualifications	Good 2.1 degree

2 KING'S BENCH WALK Ground Floor, Temple, London EC4Y 7DE **Tel:** 020 7353 1746 **Email:** clerks@2kbw.com Apply through Pupillage Gateway	General common-law chambers, primarily based on the Western Circuit. We have chambers in both London and at 3 Guildhall Walk, Portsmouth PO1 2RY.	PF 2 T 73 T$_{L3Y}$ 4 MP yes
2 KING'S BENCH WALK Chambers of Michael Cogan, Lower Ground Floor, Temple, London EC4Y 7DE **Tel:** 020 7583 0695 **Email:** admin@2kbw.net **Apply to:** Mr Barry Henderson	Multi-racial set. Of particular concern to all practitioners are those areas of law which deal with the liberty and rights of the individual.	PF 1 T 10 T$_{L3Y}$ 1 MP yes
4 KING'S BENCH WALK Second Floor, Temple, London EC4Y 7DL **Tel:** 020 7822 7000 **Email:** clerks@4kbw.co.uk Apply through Pupillage Gateway	4KBW is a dedicated common law set situated in Temple, London. Chambers specialises in civil, criminal, family and immigration work.	PF 2 T 54 T$_{L3Y}$ 6 MP yes
5 KING'S BENCH WALK Chambers of Sarah Forshaw QC & Mark Heywood QC, Temple, London EC4Y 7DN **Tel:** 020 7353 5638 **Email:** clerks@5kbw.co.uk Apply through Pupillage Gateway	Applications through Pupillage Gateway only.	PF 3 T 48 T$_{L3Y}$ 7 MP yes
9 KING'S BENCH WALK Chambers of Shabeena Azhar & Jonathan Mole, Temple, London EC4Y 7DX **Tel:** 020 7353 9564 **Email:** pupillage@9kbw.com **Apply to:** Mrs Christine Eadie	9 KBW offers one criminal pupillage a year. We always recruit a pupil who we think has what it takes to become a tenant.	PF 1 T 26 T$_{L3Y}$ 10 MP yes
12 KING'S BENCH WALK Temple, London EC4Y 7EL **Tel:** 020 7583 0811 **Email:** chambers@12kbw.co.uk Apply through Pupillage Gateway	Chambers covers all contentious civil common law work (except matrimonial). Specialists in personal injury including cross-border claims, clinical negligence and employment. Friendly atmosphere.	PF 2-3 T 86 T$_{L3Y}$ 8 MP yes
KINGS CHAMBERS 36 Young Street, Manchester M3 3FT **Tel:** 0345 034 3444 **Email:** clerks@kingschambers.com **Apply to:** Ms Debra Andrés	One of the largest and most successful sets outside London, specialising in common law, chancery and commercial, and planning and public law.	PF Up to 3 T 111 T$_{L3Y}$ 5 MP yes
LAMB BUILDING Temple, London EC4Y 7AS **Tel:** 020 7797 7788 **Email:** clerks@lambbuilding.co.uk **Apply to:** Daniel Darnbrough	Chambers offer a 12-month pupillage with specified pupillage supervisors and a 'link' junior tenant. Pupillage supervisors are available in crime, family and immigration.	PF Up to 3 T 54 T$_{L3Y}$ 4 MP yes

PF = Pupillages funded / **T** = Tenants / T$_{L3Y}$ = Tenancies in last 3 years / **MP** = Mini-pupillages offered

Landmark Chambers

180 Fleet Street, London EC4A 2HG
Tel: 020 7430 1221
Email: pupillage@landmarkchambers.co.uk
Web: www.landmarkchambers.co.uk
🐦 landmark_lc

Description of Chambers Landmark is ranked as the number one planning and environmental chambers in the UK by the top legal directories. We are consistently regarded as one of the leading sets in our other main areas of work and in the last two years we have won Real Estate Set of the Year and Planning/Environmental Set of the Year at the *Chambers UK* Bar Awards. Members have been involved in some of the most significant cases and inquiries in recent years, including Crossrail and HS2, the third runway for Heathrow, the Supreme Court property case *Day v Hosebay Ltd* and the recent infringement of LGBTQ+ rights case *Jones v AG Trinidad & Tobago*.

Areas of work Landmark is the UK's leading specialist chambers in planning and infrastructure, environmental, property, public and international law.

Pupillage programme During your four seats of pupillage, we will encourage you to work for a cross-section of members and we will arrange for our silks to act as your satellite supervisors on more complex cases. This will allow you to see a wide variety of work and take advantage of Landmark's unique position as a leading specialist set, with significant overlap between its private and public law practices. In your second six months you will also be offered opportunities to appear in court of your own accord, usually in the County Court or First-Tier Tribunal.

We are committed to providing our pupils with high-quality and constructive training. To that end, you will receive regular feedback from your supervisors and, at the end of the first and third seats, you will be invited to participate in formal feedback sessions with the chair and secretaries of our pupillage committee. Finally, our pupils participate in, and receive feedback in relation to, three written and one oral advocacy assessments during their pupillage year.

When and how to apply Chambers runs a split recruitment process, the first phase of which is designed for candidates who have a particular interest in developing a significant property law practice. The second phase of the process is designed for applicants who are able to demonstrate that they have a strong interest in developing a significant practice in at least one of Landmark's areas of expertise. Landmark is currently in the process of reviewing its recruitment timetables and processes. Further information will be made available through our website in October 2018.

Mini-pupillages Landmark runs a comprehensive mini-pupillage programme from Chambers' offices in London, taking up to 60 students per annum for a period of three to five days' duration.

Landmark Chambers believes that it's important to ensure that students from all backgrounds are able to undertake their mini-pupillage at minimal expense to themselves and, in doing so, improve social mobility at, and access to, the Bar. We therefore offer all mini-pupils a maximum reimbursement of £100 for reasonable travel and lunch expenses. Additionally, Landmark operates a discretionary accommodation funding scheme for students visiting from outside of London.

To find out more about pupillage, mini-pupillage, Landmark's open evenings, property moot competition and judicial review moot competition, please visit www.landmarkchambers.co.uk/pupillage-recruitment.

Pupillages funded	Up to 2
Tenants	89
Tenancies in last 3 yrs	7
Mini-pupillages	yes

Apply to
Landmark Chambers'
recruitment portal and
Pupillage Gateway

Remuneration for pupillage
£65,000, of which £25,000
may be taken as an early
drawdown

⌐Landmark
Chambers ⌐

Littleton Chambers

3 King's Bench Walk North, London EC4Y 7HR
Tel: 020 7797 8600
Email: fschneider@littletonchambers.co.uk
Web: www.littletonchambers.com
🐦 littleton1

Description of Chambers Littleton is acknowledged as being a top-class set in each of its main practice areas. Its success is based upon both the desire to maintain high professional standards and a willingness to embrace change. It prides itself on the skills of its tenants, not only as advocates and advisers on the law, but also for their analytical and practical skills.

Areas of work Littleton Chambers specialises in commercial litigation, employment law, professional negligence, sports law, mediation and arbitration.

Who should apply Applications are invited from candidates with a minimum 2.1 degree or equivalent. Littleton takes a considerable amount of care in choosing our pupils and prefers to recruit its tenants from persons who have completed a full 12-month pupillage with chambers. We endeavour to take on pupils who not only have excellent academic skills, but who show a flair for advocacy, have the ability to understand practical commercial issues, and importantly, have the interpersonal skills to provide the qualities that are expected of the modern-day Bar. We operate an equal opportunities policy which is designed to support diversity in our pupillage recruitment process.

Pupillage programme Chambers generally offers pupillage to two people each year. During the 12-month pupillage, you will have the benefit of four pupil supervisors in succession. Your pupil supervisors will provide support and guidance to you throughout, ensuring that you understand not only the nuts and bolts of a barrister's work, but also the ethical constraints which are such a distinctive feature of chambers' professional life. After six months pupillage you will be entitled to take on your own work. Your pupil supervisor will provide assistance in the preparation of briefs to ensure that your client receives the best possible service from you.

When and how to apply Littleton is a member of the Pupillage Gateway. Offers are made in accordance with their timetable and where appropriate, in the academic year before bar finals.

Mini-pupillages An assessed mini-pupillage forms part of our pupillage application process and mini-pupillages are not offered outside of this process.

Sponsorship/funding We believe that fair remuneration is important. Our pupils receive a £67,500 pupillage award and they keep all second six earnings. It is possible to draw down some of this funding during the year of bar finals.

Pupillages funded	2
Tenants	53
Tenancies in last 3 yrs	3

Apply through Pupillage Gateway

Remuneration for pupillage
£67,500

Minimum qualifications
2.1 degree

LITTLETON

Maitland Chambers

7 Stone Buildings, Lincoln's Inn, London WC2A 3SZ
Tel: 020 7406 1200
Email: pupillage@maitlandchambers.com
Web: www.maitlandchambers.com

Description of Chambers We are a leading set of chambers in commercial chancery litigation ranked at the top of our field in the legal directories. Our appeal to you at the start of your career is the combination of the high-quality instructions we receive, the breadth of our work (from major international litigation to domestic contractual and property disputes) and the volume of advocacy that we do. The majority of our work is done in London, though we frequently advise and appear for clients in other parts of the UK; and much of our work has an international aspect, involving acting for clients and appearing in court overseas.

Areas of work We undertake a full range of commercial chancery work, which is essentially concerned with business, finance and property. Our core areas of practice include commercial litigation, banking, financial services and regulation, civil fraud, insolvency and restructuring, media law, pensions, professional negligence, real property, charity law, trusts and tax. Most of what we do is concerned with dispute resolution (advising, drafting court documents and appearing as advocates); but we also do some non-contentious work in the private client field.

Who should apply Our typical recruit has a first-class mind and a sense of commercial practicality, and will enjoy and be stimulated by the challenge of oral and written advocacy. Academically we look for a first or 2.1 degree. You must have an aptitude for and general enjoyment of complex legal argument (demonstrated by mooting). Not all of our barristers have law degrees: of our ten most junior tenants, the majority read subjects other than law and we recognise that training in other academic disciplines can be a good preparation for a legal career. We encourage applications from people from all sections of society, regardless of gender, race, disability, sexual orientation, religion, belief or age.

Pupillage programme We offer up to three 12-month pupillages. You will sit with different barristers during your time in chambers and so have the opportunity to see a wide range of practices; however, you will spend your first three months with one supervisor, so that you can find your feet and establish a point of contact. At regular intervals during your pupillage you will participate in advocacy exercises that take the form of mock hearings, which are prepared in advance from a set of papers, just as in practice. Senior members of chambers act as the tribunal, probing your argument during the 'hearing' and then providing detailed feedback afterwards. There is no limit to the number of tenancy offers we can make in each year; as a general rule, if you are of the requisite standard, you will be offered tenancy.

When and how to apply In 2018 Maitland Chambers joined the Pupillage Gateway (for pupillages commencing in 2020). Please refer to the Gateway for relevant dates and deadlines.

Mini-pupillages Applications are considered three times a year; please see our website for current deadlines and details of how to apply.

Sponsorship/funding A pupillage award (£65,000 for pupillage starting in October 2020) is offered to all pupils in chambers. Up to £20,000 of the award may be drawn down in advance for BPTC fees or during the BPTC year. We operate a cashflow assistance scheme during the early stages of practice.

Pupillages funded	Up to 3
Tenants	70
Tenancies in last 3 yrs	4
Mini-pupillages	yes

Applications contact
Ms Valerie Piper

Remuneration for pupillage
£65,000

Minimum qualifications
2.1 degree

Matrix Chambers

Griffin Building, Gray's Inn, London WC1R 5LN
Tel: 020 7404 3447
Email: matrix@matrixlaw.co.uk
Web: www.matrixlaw.co.uk
🐦 matrixchambers

Description of Chambers Matrix is a barristers' chambers located in London, Geneva and Brussels. We are a collection of lawyers specialising in a wide range of practice areas throughout the UK and internationally. Described as "professional and forward thinking", we are an approachable set that are proud of our record of innovation. Our core values govern the way we work and outline our commitment to operating within an environment where diversity, accessibility and client care are widely championed.

Areas of work We have a multi-disciplinary approach with several members recognised as leading practitioners in *Chambers & Partners* and *Legal 500*. Matrix acts for private and public clients and has particular expertise in over 29 international and domestic areas of law including commercial, competition, crime, data protection, defamation, discrimination, education, employment, environmental, extradition, fraud, freedom of information, human rights, immigration, nationality and asylum, international arbitration, local government, public and administrative law, media, mutual assistance, prison, social welfare, and sports law. Matrix has a strong international presence, acting in more than 114 countries for governments, international corporations, legal firms and individuals. We have offices in Geneva and Brussels, and a dedicated brand for our international work, known as 'Matrix International'.

Who should apply Matrix welcomes applications from exceptional candidates from all backgrounds. For further details, please see our traineeship brochure on the 'recruitment' page of our website.

Pupillage programme Matrix offers up to two traineeships, both starting 1 October for 12 months. The 12-month training period is split roughly into quarters. The training committee tends to choose who will supervise in the first quarter while trainees are finding their feet, but trainees are consulted throughout on which areas of law they would be interested in covering. It is expected that trainees will experience the wide range of work covered at Matrix with seats in varied practice areas throughout the year. There is a scheduled programme of training that takes place throughout the year and includes internal and external training, written and advocacy exercises and secondments. Matrix trainees do not generally take on oral advocacy in their own right until the last quarter.

When and how to apply Please check our website for information on how to apply for a traineeship.

Mini-pupillages We currently do not offer mini-pupillages, but for up-to-date information and details on opportunities available and how to apply please visit the 'recruitment' section of our website at www.matrixlaw.co.uk/recruitment.

Sponsorship/funding Matrix offers up to two 12-month training places with an award of £40,000 and an additional £10,000 contribution during the BPTC year for applicants who are yet to undertake Bar finals. Any applicants who have already completed the BPTC year will still be entitled to the additional £10,000 contribution in the year prior to commencing traineeship.

Pupillages funded	2
Tenants	91
Tenancies in last 3 yrs	5

Apply to
Check website for
application details

Remuneration for pupillage
£40,000 with an additional
£10,000 contribution during
the BPTC year

Monckton Chambers

1-2 Raymond Buildings, Gray's Inn, London WC1R 5NR
Tel: 020 7405 7211
Email: chambers@monckton.com
Web: www.moncton.com
🐦 moncktonlaw

Description of Chambers Monckton Chambers specialises in public and commercial law and the interface between the two.

Areas of work We are recognised as a leading set within our specialisms, which include: competition and regulatory; public; sports; tax; and technology, media and communications. Our work is carried out in areas of the law that are rapidly growing and fast moving. It is exceptionally demanding, but also highly rewarding.

Who should apply We are looking for candidates of the highest intellectual calibre. Most successful candidates for pupillage will have a first class honours degree (although it need not be in law) or a graduate degree in law.

We do not, however, expect candidates to have any experience or expertise in the specialised areas in which we practice, merely an interest and enthusiasm for the work that we do. We welcome applications from candidates who have degrees in subjects other than law and are taking (or have taken) the GDL.

It is not only intellectual skills that we are looking for; we are seeking candidates with the personal skills to win the trust of clients and judges alike. Monckton Chambers is a dynamic place to work. Members actively engage in speaking at conferences and seminars, in London and internationally, and in contributing to a variety of publications, ranging from our own marketing materials, to specialist journals and practitioner texts. We are looking for junior tenants who will bring real energy to chambers.

When and how to apply Monckton Chambers is a member of the Bar Council Pupillage Gateway and all applications should be made in accordance with that scheme. We invite applications from pupils in the year preceding the October in which pupillage is due to start. We are, however, in exceptional circumstances willing to consider applications for deferral.

Mini-pupillages We operate a mini-pupillage scheme. This is intended for people who are in their final year at, or have already graduated from, university, and who are interested in our areas of legal practice. Details of how to apply can be found on our website.

Pupillages funded	2
Tenants	60
Tenancies in last 3 yrs	5
Mini-pupillages	yes

Applications contact
Wendy Holmes

Remuneration for pupillage
£65,000 for 12 months

LINCOLN HOUSE CHAMBERS
Tower 12, The Avenue North, 18-22 Bridge Street,
Manchester M3 3BZ
Tel: 0161 832 5701
Email: pupillage@lincolnhousechambers.com
Apply to: Mr Daniel Thomas

A nationally prominent set of criminal chambers with a fast expanding civil base. Chambers has a modern and progressive approach to all aspects of work.

PF	1-2
T	67
T$_{L3Y}$	5
MP	yes

LINENHALL CHAMBERS
1 Stanley Place, Chester CH1 2LU
Tel: 01244 348 282
Email: clerks@linenhallchambers.co.uk
Apply to: The Pupillage Committee

Busy, large, provincial set undertaking work of a wide description. Members are divided into criminal, civil and family teams (with some overlapping).

PF	1
T	70
T$_{L3Y}$	1
MP	yes

MAIDSTONE CHAMBERS
51 Earl Street, Maidstone ME14 1PD
Tel: 01622 688592
Email: clerks@maidstonechambers.co.uk
Apply to: Ms Alexia Zimbler

Friendly set looking to develop future tenants for an expanding workload. Most of our work is in Kent plus occasionally in London, Essex and Sussex.

PF	1-2
T	15
T$_{L3Y}$	2
MP	yes

MALINS CHAMBERS
115 Temple Chambers, 3-7 Temple Avenue,
London EC4Y ODA
Tel: 020 7353 8868
Email: malins@btinternet.com
Apply to: Mr Julian Malins QC

We are a small set specialising in international work. We take one pupil a year and we advertise the vacancy on the Bar Council website.

PF	1
T	6
T$_{L3Y}$	1
MP	no

---

1 MCB
Third Floor, 15 New Bridge Street, London EC4V 6AU
Tel: 020 7452 8900
Email: clerks@1mcb.com
Apply to: Ms Julie Clarke

Chambers has expanded from its radical beginnings to a progressive and friendly set. Strong specialist teams in criminal defence, housing, immigration, family and employment.

PF	0
T	51
T$_{L3Y}$	7
MP	yes

---

15 NEW BRIDGE STREET
15 New Bridge Street, London EC4V 6AU
Tel: 020 7842 1900
Email: clerks@15nbs.com
Apply to: Ms Keeley Holland

15 New Bridge Street offers expert representation in criminal, regulatory and immigration law. We combine the highest standards of service with an approachable manner.

PF	2
T	46
T$_{L3Y}$	3
MP	no

NEW COURT CHAMBERS
Temple, London EC4Y 9BE
Tel: 020 3582 7123
Email: clerks@newcourtchambers.com
Apply through Pupillage Gateway

New Court Chambers is a specialist family set with particular expertise in public law care, private law children, financial relief and Court of Protection.

PF	2
T	34
T$_{L3Y}$	6
MP	yes

NEW PARK COURT CHAMBERS
16 Park Place, Leeds LS1 2SJ
Tel: 0113 243 3277
Email: clerks@npc-l.co.uk
Apply through Pupillage Gateway

One of the most prestigious sets outside London, based in Leeds and Newcastle. Specialising in serious crime, regulatory law, professional misconduct, civil, and family work.

PF	3
T	61
T$_{L3Y}$	3
MP	yes

PF = Pupillages funded / **T** = Tenants / **T**$_{L3Y}$ = Tenancies in last 3 years / **MP** = Mini-pupillages offered

4 New Square

Lincoln's Inn, London WC2A 3RJ
Tel: 020 7822 2000
Email: pupillage@4newsquare. com
Web: www.4newsquare.com
🐦 4newsquare

Description of Chambers 4 New Square is a leading commercial and civil set of barristers comprising of 80 members, of whom 25 are Queen's Counsel. Its members are recognised as leading practitioners in a wide range of fields including commercial law, professional liability, international arbitration, insurance and reinsurance, commercial chancery, construction and engineering, public law, financial services, costs and sports law.

In recent years individual members of 4 New Square have consistently been included as leading practitioners in the two main legal directories (*Legal 500* and *Chambers & Partners*) and 4 New Square has been named as the top set for professional negligence at the *Chambers UK* Bar Awards in 2015 and 2016. *Jackson & Powell on Professional Liability* (the main text in this area) is written and edited by current and former members of chambers.

Chambers attracts a large amount of junior advocacy work which reflects the emphasis on developing pupils and junior tenants into experienced advocates to equip them for a successful career at the Bar.

When and how to apply 4 New Square is not part of the Pupillage Gateway scheme. Pupillage applications should be made in accordance with the details on our website www.4newsquare.com.

Mini-pupillages We strongly encourage students to apply for a mini-pupillage with us as we believe that they allow prospective applicants to get a real understanding of the work done in chambers. Mini-pupils also have the opportunity to meet members of chambers and get a feel for the working environment.

Mini-pupillages last for two days and, save in exceptional circumstances, take place in specific weeks in May, July, November and December of each year. Mini-pupillages do not involve formal assessment but we do record feedback on your likely suitability for pupillage in chambers. Mini-pupillage application details can be found on our website www.4newsquare.com.

Sponsorship/funding The total annual award is £65,000, comprising a £55,000 award (of which £5,000 is paid immediately upon acceptance of the offer and a further £15,000 can be drawn down during the BPTC year) and guaranteed earnings in the second six months of £10,000. Pupils are allowed to keep any earnings from their second six months, including any earned in excess of the £10,000 guarantee. New tenants have a guaranteed income of £240,000 (net of chambers' expenses), in addition to their pupillage awards, over the first three years of practice.

Pupillages funded	Up to 2
Tenants	80
Tenancies in last 3 yrs	5
Mini-pupillages	yes

Applications contact
Ms Ella Igbiaye

Remuneration for pupillage
£65,000

Minimum qualifications
Good 2.1 degree

NEW SQUARE

New Square Chambers

Lincoln's Inn, London WC2A 3SW
Tel: 020 7419 8000
Email: pupillage@newsquarechambers.co.uk
Web: www.newsquarechambers.co.uk
🐦 newsqchambers

Description of Chambers New Square Chambers offers a concentration of experience in chancery and commercial work and related international matters. We have 40 members, five silks and 35 juniors.

Areas of work New Square Chambers undertakes a full range of commercial and chancery work including: charities; civil fraud; company law (including directors' disqualification proceedings and shareholders' disputes); highways and rights of way; insolvency; intellectual property; landlord and tenant; partnership law; pensions; probate, administration of estates, wills and intestacy and family provision; professional negligence; property law; revenue; trusts; settlements and taxation. A considerable amount of our work has an international element. Several members of chambers have established practices in overseas jurisdictions, including Antigua, the Bahamas, Bermuda, the British Virgin Islands, the Caymans, the Channel Islands, Gibraltar, Hong Kong and Singapore, and before the Privy Council. Our members' international practices span the full range of chambers' work, including trusts, land, insolvency and public law, in litigious and non-contentious contexts. The editors of *Lewin on Trusts*, *Theobald on Wills*, *Shareholders' Rights*, *Williams Mortimer and Sunnucks – Executors Administrators and Probate*, and the *Law of Freedom of Information* are all members of chambers.

Pupillage programme At New Square Chambers, we aim to recruit bright and enthusiastic pupils with a proven academic background. Consequently, applicants will usually have a first or good upper second degree, although this need not be in law. Despite our size we are an informal and friendly set, and encourage our pupils to take an active part in the life of chambers. Pupils undertake four seats of three months, each with a different pupil supervisor, in order to experience the full range of chambers' work. In addition, pupils are given the opportunity to learn something of the practices of other members of chambers during their pupillage.

When and how to apply Chambers offers one 12-month pupillage, terminable after six months on either side, which carries with it an award of £65,000. Chambers is not a member of the Pupillage Gateway and applications for pupillage commencing in 2019 should be made on our application form which is available at www.newsquarechambers.co.uk. The closing date is 18 January 2019. Applications should be submitted via email in accordance with chambers' pupillage policy which may also be found on our website.

Mini-pupillages A limited number of mini-pupillages are available, usually lasting for three days. Applicants must have at least completed the second year of their law degree or, if they are not yet studying law, the third year of their degree. As with pupillage applicants, we require applicants for minipupillage to be of at least a high 2.1 or first-class standard. Applications may only be made by email to minipupillage@newsquarechambers.co.uk between 1 August and 30 September in any given year and must be made in the manner prescribed in our mini-pupillage policy which can be found in Appendix I to the chambers' Pupillage Policy (2003). Applications not made in the prescribed manner may not receive a response. Please refer to our website for further details or telephone Ms Kristina Lukacova in chambers on 020 7419 8000.

Pupillages funded	1
Tenants	40
Tenancies in last 3 yrs	3
Mini-pupillages	yes

Applications contact
Mr Jeff Hardman

Remuneration for pupillage
£65,000 for 12 months

Minimum qualifications
2.1 degree

3 NEW SQUARE Lincoln's Inn, London WC2A 3RS **Tel:** 020 7405 1111 **Email:** clerks@3newsquare.co.uk Apply through Pupillage Gateway	A specialist intellectual property chambers which is regularly recommended as a leading set for patent, trademark, copyright, media and entertainment law.	PF T T_{L3Y} MP	1 20 1 yes
8 NEW SQUARE 8 New Square, Lincoln's Inn, London WC2A 3QP **Tel:** 020 7405 4321 **Email:** clerks@8newsquare.co.uk Apply through Pupillage Gateway	The largest specialist intellectual property, media and IT chambers in the UK, covering a broad range of work from technical patent to high profile media.	PF T T_{L3Y} MP	1 29 1 yes
NEW WALK CHAMBERS 27 New Walk, Leicester LE1 6TE **Tel:** 0116 255 9144 **Email:** clerks@newwalkchambers.co.uk **Apply to:** The Management Committee	Chambers continues to enjoy a strong work base coupled with expertise in its specialist areas.	PF T T_{L3Y} MP	Up to 3 22 7 no
NO5 CHAMBERS Steelhouse Lane, Birmingham B4 6DR **Tel:** 0845 210 5555 **Email:** pupillage2016@no5.com **Apply to:** Ms Shirley Titmarsh	One of the largest and most dynamic sets of chambers in the country offering unparalled training opportunities to succesful pupillage candidates.	PF T T_{L3Y} MP	Up to 3 256 53 yes
NORTHAMPTON CHAMBERS 22 Albion Place, Northampton NN1 1UD **Tel:** 01604 636271 **Email:** clerks@northampton-chambers.co.uk **Apply to:** The Pupillage Committee	Small, well-established, friendly set. Mainly criminal and family work for local solicitors. Good quality work for junior tenants.	PF T T_{L3Y} MP	1-2 14 4 yes
OLD COURT CHAMBERS Newham House, 96-98 Borough Road, Middlesbrough TS12HJ **Tel:** 01642 23 25 23 **Email:** clerks@oldcourtchambers.net **Apply to:** Mr Stephen Constantine		PF T T_{L3Y} MP	0-1 19 1 no
15 OLD SQUARE Lincoln's Inn, London WC2A 3UE **Tel:** 020 7242 2744 **Email:** taxchambers@15oldsquare.co.uk **Apply to:** Ms Amanda Hardy QC	Chambers specialises in revenue law.	PF T T_{L3Y} MP	1 11 1 yes
OLD SQUARE CHAMBERS (BRISTOL) 3 Orchard Court, St Augustines Yard, Bristol BS1 5DP **Tel:** 0117 930 5100 **Email:** clerks@oldsquare.co.uk Apply through Pupillage Gateway	The defining quality of Old Square Chambers is excellence. This is the standard we set for ourselves in the delivery of services to our clients, and the criterion by which we assess prospective tenants and pupils.	PF T T_{L3Y} MP	0 79 6 yes

PF = Pupillages funded / **T** = Tenants / **T**$_{L3Y}$ = Tenancies in last 3 years / **MP** = Mini-pupillages offered

XXIV Old Buildings

24 Old Buildings, Lincoln's Inn, London WC2A 3UP
Tel: 020 7691 2424
Email: clerks@xxiv.co.uk
Web: www.xxiv.co.uk
🐦 xxivpupillage

Description of Chambers XXIV Old Buildings is a leading commercial chancery chambers of 45 members with broad domestic expertise and pre-eminence in international work.

Areas of work The barristers at XXIV Old Buildings specialise in a variety of commercial chancery areas with a particular emphasis on trusts and estates and commercial litigation. Areas in which members regularly take instructions include arbitration; aviation; charities; civil fraud, asset tracing and recovery; company; construction; financial services; insolvency; international and offshore; partnership; pensions; professional negligence; real estate litigation and trusts, probate and estates.

XXIV Old Buildings is known for its pre-eminence in international and offshore work, both contentious and advisory. With offices in both London and Geneva, the barristers at XXIV Old Buildings regularly appear in courts and tribunals in offshore centres including the British Virgin Islands, the Cayman Islands, Bermuda, Jersey, the Isle of Man, the DIFC, the Bahamas, Gibraltar, Hong Kong and Malaysia.

Who should apply Each year we are looking for up to three pupils with a first or 2.1 degree, though not necessarily in law, who have an enthusiasm for the type of work we do, sound judgement and the application required to succeed in a very competitive and intellectually demanding environment.

Pupillage programme We like to recruit our junior members from those who have undertaken pupillage with us. We are therefore careful that our pupils acquire all the skills necessary to make them successful commercial chancery barristers. During a 12-month pupillage, a pupil will have, on average, four pupil supervisors with whom they will spend the majority of their time.

When and how to apply Please see our website www.xxiv.co.uk for details of the closing date and application details for pupillages commencing in October 2020. The deadline for applications is Monday 26 November 2018. Keep up to date with our dedicated twitter feed www.twitter.com/xxivpupillage.

Mini-pupillages Chambers offers mini-pupillages throughout the year. Each lasts on average three days. Our website also contains guidance on mini-pupillage applications.

Sponsorship/funding Up to a quarter of the pupillage the award may (upon application) be drawn down during the BPTC.

Pupillages funded	3
Tenants	45
Tenancies in last 3 yrs	4

Mini-pupillages   yes

Applications contact
Mr Edward Cumming QC

Remuneration for pupillage
Up to £65,000 each

Minimum qualifications
2.1 degree

Ten Old Square

10 Old Square, Lincoln's Inn, London WC2A 3SU
Tel: 020 7405 0758
Email: pupillage@tenoldsquare.com
Web: www.tenoldsquare.com
f tenoldsquare **y** tenoldsquare

Description of Chambers Chambers is a leading commercial Chancery set which enjoys the highest reputation in the specialist areas of: private client work, including the administration of estates, capital taxation, charities, trusts and settlements, family provision, probate, court of protection and matrimonial finance; partnership; property litigation, including conveyancing, real property disputes, landlord and tenant, mortgages and securities, development contracts and manorial rights; company and insolvency; commercial litigation; financial services; banking; local government; and professional negligence.

Areas of work Private client, partnership and LLPs, property and commercial chancery.

Who should apply We are looking for a potential tenant. Candidates should have a real enthusiasm for our areas of practice, be of proven high academic ability and possess excellent powers of analysis, reasoning and presentation. In addition, the successful candidate will demonstrate sound judgement and be highly motivated. Our specific selection criteria are set out in our pupillage policy, available on our website.

Pupillage programme The pupillage is structured so that our pupil can see the full range of chambers' work. Our pupil will have two pupil supervisors throughout the 12 months and will sit with two other members of chambers, under the supervision of their supervisor. It is also likely that, throughout the pupillage, our pupil will undertake work for other members of chambers. Monitoring of a pupil's progress takes place at the end of work through discussion with their pupil supervisor and through monthly written reviews, rather than by way of formal assessment.

When and how to apply Chambers uses the Pupillage Gateway. Shortlisted candidates will be invited for interview, will spend a day in chambers and will be asked to prepare a piece of written work.

We offer one 12-month pupillage.

Mini-pupillages Apply by application form, available on the website or from the clerks' room. Deadlines are 7 January, 15 July and 15 October.

Sponsorship/funding £60,000, with the option of drawing down up to a quarter in the year prior to pupillage.

Pupillages funded	1
Tenants	26
Tenancies in last 3 yrs	2
Mini-pupillages	yes

Apply through Pupillage Gateway

Remuneration for pupillage
£60,000

Old Square Chambers

10-11 Bedford Row, London WC1R 4BU
Tel: 020 7269 0300
Email: clerks@oldsquare.co.uk
Web: www.oldsquare.co.uk
🐦 oldsqchambers

Description of Chambers The defining quality of Old Square Chambers is excellence. This is the standard we set for ourselves in the delivery of services to our clients, and the criterion by which we assess prospective tenants and pupils. Many of our members hold part-time judicial positions, sit on specialist panels, act as mediators, and edit or contribute to leading practitioner texts. We are a highly specialised, forward thinking set, committed to expansion. Our objective is to select a small number of pupils with the aim of recruiting our tenants from them. Chambers operates an equality and diversity policy which fully complies with the Bar Standards Board's requirements. We are committed to ensuring all of our recruitment and selection processes are fair and that protected characteristics are safeguarded. We are based in Bedford Row but also operate from premises in Bristol.

Areas of work Our work is balanced between claimant and defendant or respondent, and includes the protection of individual rights. We work on behalf of trade unions, commercial organisations, the NHS and local and central government. In employment we cover all the relevant areas including: discrimination, collective action, individual rights, restraint of trade and human rights. We also have a thriving practice in the field of professional regulatory and disciplinary work, especially in the healthcare sector. In personal injury we have an excellent profile spanning all types of litigation. Particular areas of strength include catastrophic injury, disaster and multi-party litigation. In clinical law we have a number of expert practitioners encompassing all disputes affecting and involving the medical, dental, pharmaceutical and nursing professions. In product liability and health and safety compliance we engage in civil and criminal litigation of varying complexity as well as public inquiry work. In environmental law we represent corporate and individual defendants. Case experience includes prosecutions of major pollution incidents, permit breaches, marine regulation prosecutions, the release of hazardous or noxious substances and the escape of controlled waste. We also undertake human rights and public law work where it relates to our main fields of practice. Much of our work involves the use of European jurisprudence.

Who should apply We assess candidates on a number of criteria. These may change from year to year but generally include: intellectual ability (measured by academic or other achievement), potential as an advocate, interest in chambers' fields of practice, ability to cope with hard work and pressure, and interpersonal skills.

Pupillage programme Pupils are offered generous funding. Pupils will experience a wide variety of court and paperwork. There is also the opportunity to work closely with silks on complex and sometimes high profile cases.

When and how to apply As per Pupillage Gateway.

Mini-pupillages Apply online via our website.

Sponsorship/funding 2020 award will be £50,000, comprising of an award of £40,000 and guaranteed minimum earnings of £10,000, which may be exceeded depending on earnings in the second six. A draw down system facility is available for BPTC on application.

Pupillages funded	2
Tenants	79
Tenancies in last 3 yrs	6
Mini-pupillages	yes

Apply through Pupillage Gateway

Remuneration for pupillage
£50,000 including £10,000 guaranteed earnings

Minimum qualifications
2.1 degree preferred

ORIEL CHAMBERS 14 Water Street, Liverpool L2 8TD **Tel:** 0151 236 7191 **Email:** clerks@orielchambers.co.uk **Apply to:** Ms Tina Moss	We are a prominent, busy, friendly set who offer the successful applicant an excellent grounding in all of chambers' practice areas.	PF Up to 2 T 53 TL3Y 3 MP yes
OUTER TEMPLE CHAMBERS 222 Strand, London WC2R 1BA **Tel:** 020 7353 6381 **Email:** pupillage@outertemple.com Apply through Pupillage Gateway	Mixed common-law chambers. 12-month pupillages (Sep 2020) come with an award of £60,000; one 18-month 'FRUpillage' (2019) via direct application. IIP platinum accredited.	PF 4 T 88 TL3Y 9 MP yes
FIVE PAPER Ground Floor, 5 Paper Buildings, Temple, London EC4Y 7HB **Tel:** 020 7815 3200 **Email:** pupillage@fivepaper.com Apply through Pupillage Gateway	Leading set in *Chambers & Partners* and the *Legal 500*. Five specialist practice groups: property, commercial, employment, family and business immigration and regulatory.	PF 2 T 40 TL3Y 3 MP yes
4 PAPER BUILDINGS First Floor, Temple, London EC4Y 7EX **Tel:** 020 7427 5200 **Email:** pupillage@4pb.com **Apply to:** The Pupillage Committee	4 Paper Buildings is an exclusive specialist family law set and has a reputation as one of the friendliest sets in which to undertake pupillage.	PF 3 T 79 TL3Y 6 MP yes
5 PAPER BUILDINGS 5 Paper Buildings, Temple, London EC4Y 7HB **Tel:** 020 7583 6117 **Email:** clerks@5pb.co.uk Apply through Pupillage Gateway	A leading criminal set with 11 QCs, specialising in criminal law, fraud, consumer law, professional discipline and regulatory, health and safety and international crime.	PF 2 T 46 TL3Y 6 MP yes
9 PARK PLACE 9 Park Place, Cardiff CF10 3DP **Tel:** 029 2038 2731 **Email:** pupillage@9parkplace.co.uk **Apply to:** Mr Matthew Barry	9 Park Place is a leading set offering a wide spectrum of legal specialisation. Chambers offers two funded pupillages each year.	PF 2 T 60 TL3Y 6 MP yes
30 PARK PLACE Cardiff CF10 3BS **Tel:** 029 2039 8421 **Email:** pupcom@30parkplace.co.uk Apply through Pupillage Gateway	A mutli-disciplinary chambers highly ranked in the major legal directories; offering expert legal advice and representation, across a wide range of practice areas.	PF 1 T 67 TL3Y 18 MP yes
PARK SQUARE BARRISTERS 6 Park Square, Leeds LS1 2LW **Tel:** 0113 245 9763 **Email:** pupillages@psqb.co.uk **Apply to:** Mr Simon Clegg	PSQB is the largest multi-disciplinary chambers on the NE Circuit. We offer exceptional training, resources and support in pupillage.	PF 2 T 125 TL3Y 6 MP yes

PF = Pupillages funded / **T** = Tenants / TL3Y = Tenancies in last 3 years / **MP** = Mini-pupillages offered

4 Pump Court

Temple, London EC4Y 7AN
Tel: 020 7842 5555
Email: chambers@4pumpcourt.com
Web: www.4pumpcourt.com
🐦 4pumpcourt

Description of Chambers 4 Pump Court is a leading set of commercial barristers' chambers, with a reputation for excellence in advocacy. We pride ourselves on our reputation as an approachable, supportive, and friendly place to work.

Areas of work The work of chambers covers virtually every aspect of commercial law, with particular expertise in construction and engineering; international arbitration; energy; insurance and reinsurance; technology and telecommunications; shipping; banking; and professional negligence. We are ranked highly in the legal directories in all our areas of specialism.

Who should apply We look to recruit bright, independent-minded candidates with excellent academic qualifications (minimum 2.1). They will be articulate and confident, and have the ability to get on with people and to demonstrate common sense and sound judgment. We are committed to equal opportunities and diversity, and select candidates for pupillage and tenancy solely on merit.

Pupillage programme Our pupils have three pupil supervisors (two in the first six, one in the second six) so they experience as broad a range of our work as possible. In the second six months they undertake a significant case load of their own. We place great emphasis on the development of advocacy skills and are committed to giving our pupils as much court experience as we can.

When and how to apply Applications for pupillage must be made on our standard application form, which can be downloaded from our website, and submitted by 4pm on Friday, 11 January 2019 by email to pupillage@4pumpcourt.com or by post.

Mini-pupillages Limited places available throughout the year upon application by completing the application form available to download from our website and return to minipupillage@4pumpcourt.com.

Sponsorship/funding Two funded pupillages with awards of £70,000, of which up to £15,000 may be advanced during the Bar Professional Training Course. Any fees earned in the second six months are in addition to the award.

Pupillages funded	2
Tenants	66
Tenancies in last 3 yrs	6

Mini-pupillages   yes

Apply
pupillage@4pumpcourt.com

Remuneration for pupillage
£70,000 plus earnings in
second six (October 2020)

Minimum qualifications
2.1 degree

Pump Court

Pump Court Tax Chambers

16 Bedford Row, London WC1R 4EF
Tel: 020 7414 8080
Email: pupils@pumptax.com
Web: www.pumptax.com
🐦 pumptax

Description of Chambers Pump Court Tax Chambers is the largest set specialising in tax law (35 members, 13 silks).

Areas of work Members of chambers undertake litigation and provide advice in relation to all areas of tax law, both personal and corporate. Members appear in courts at all levels from the tax tribunals to the Supreme Court and the CJEU.

Who should apply Anyone interested in practising in an area of law requiring an analytical mind and a grasp of other areas of law, especially trust law and European law. Tax advice provides intellectually stimulating challenges, while tax litigation (which is an increasing part of our work) often involves novel points of law, as well as complex statutory interpretation and factual analysis. Many recent developments in the law of restitution have been tested in tax cases.

Pupillage programme Chambers offers 12-month pupillages. Pupils generally spend their first 10 weeks with one pupil supervisor followed by four to six weeks with three other supervisors. They also spend time with silks and senior juniors. This allows them to see a wide variety of work and also gives members at different levels of seniority the opportunity to give them feedback.

When and how to apply Chambers keeps its membership of the Pupillage Gateway under review and has chosen not to participate in the Pupillage Gateway for pupillages starting in October 2020. Details of the application process are available on our website.

Mini-pupillages We welcome applications for mini-pupillages. Mini-pupillages of three days' duration are available throughout the year. Please apply by CV and covering letter, marked for the attention of the mini-pupillage secretary, by post or email. Further details (including details of deadlines for applications) are available on our website.

Sponsorship/funding Pupils are typically awarded £60,000, £12,000 of which can be drawn down during Bar school.

Pupillages funded	1-2
Tenants	35
Tenancies in last 3 yrs	2
Mini-pupillages	yes
Apply by CV	
Remuneration for pupillage	
Typically £60,000	
Minimum qualifications	
Generally, a 2.1 degree	

PUMP COURT
TAX CHAMBERS

PARKLANE PLOWDEN CHAMBERS 19 Westgate, Leeds LS1 2RD **Tel:** 0113 228 500 **Email:** pupillagecivil@parklaneplowden.co.uk **Apply to:** Mr Andrew Sugarman	We are likely to offer up to 3-4 pupillages across our civil and family practice areas to commence October 2020.	PF Up to 4 T 91 T_{L3Y} 7 MP yes

3PB Chambers of Nigel Lickley QC, 3 Paper Buildings, Temple, London EC4Y 7EU **Tel:** 020 7583 8055 **Email:** pupillage@3pb.co.uk Apply through Pupillage Gateway	Based in London, Winchester, Bournemouth, Oxford and Bristol, we invest a great deal of time and money in pupillage. We regard it as essential to the long term future of our chambers. Candidates with potential are supported and trained to the highest possible level.	PF 3 T 170 T_{L3Y} 26 MP yes

| 5 PUMP COURT
Ground Floor, Temple, London EC4Y 7AP
Tel: 020 7353 2532
Email: clerks@5pumpcourt.com
Apply through Pupillage Gateway | Chambers is looking for one pupil who has a genuine interest in a common law pupillage and one who wishes to specialise in criminal law. | PF 2
T   49
T_{L3Y} 3
MP yes |

| 6 PUMP COURT
First Floor, Temple, London EC4Y 7AR
Tel: 020 7797 8400
Email: clerks@6pumpcourt.co.uk
Apply through Pupillage Gateway | Chambers' work is divided between four specialist groups: criminal law, planning and environmental law, civil litigation and family law. Chambers also has an annexe in Maidstone. | PF 0
T   40
T_{L3Y} 5
MP yes |

| PUMP COURT CHAMBERS
3 Pump Court, Temple, London EC4Y 7AJ
Tel: 020 7353 0711
Email: j.lee@pumpcourtchambers.com
Apply through Pupillage Gateway | Large common law chambers based in London and on the Western Circuit, specialising in civil, criminal, family and international work. | PF 2
T   92
T_{L3Y} 5
MP yes |

| 1 PUMP COURT CHAMBERS
Elm Court, Temple, London EC4Y 7AH
Tel: 020 7842 7070
Email: agi@1pumpcourt.co.uk
Apply through Pupillage Gateway | Chambers is committed to removing inequality and promoting diversity and justice. We provide a specialist first class representation, particularly to publicly funded and unfunded clients. | PF 2
T   75
T_{L3Y} 5
MP yes |

| QEB HOLLIS WHITEMAN
1-2 Laurence Pountney Hill, London EC4R 0EU
Tel: 020 7933 8855
Email: pupillage@qebhw.co.uk
Apply to: Mr Tom Kark QC | First-class set specialising in criminal law, professional disciplinary regulation, inquests and Inquiries, with an extensive in-house advocacy training programme. | PF 4
T   65
T_{L3Y} 3
MP yes |

| QUEEN SQUARE CHAMBERS
56 Queen Square, Bristol BS1 4PR
Tel: 0117 921 1966
Email: pupillage@qs-c.co.uk
Apply to: Mr James Bromige | Chambers is located in Bristol and our members are instructed in cases nationwide, with a particular focus on the Western and Wales and Chester Circuits. | PF 2
T   39
T_{L3Y} 6
MP yes |

PF = Pupillages funded / T = Tenants / T_{L3Y} = Tenancies in last 3 years / MP = Mini-pupillages offered

Quadrant Chambers

Chambers of Luke Parsons QC, Quadrant House, 10 Fleet Street, London EC4Y 1AU
Tel: 020 7583 4444
Email: pupillage@quadrantchambers.com
Web: www.quadrantchambers.com

Description of Chambers We are a leading set of barristers specialising in commercial law. We act as advocates in court, arbitrations and inquiries, and provide specialist legal advice to clients from around the world in a wide range of industry areas. A number of us also act as arbitrators and mediators. Many of us are qualified to practise in other jurisdictions, including Australia, the BVI, California, Germany, Hong Kong, New York and South Africa. Distinguished former members of Quadrant Chambers have gone on to chair high-profile public enquiries, and to sit as judges in the High Court (QBD, Commercial, Administrative and Admiralty Courts), DIFC Courts, European General Court, Court of Appeal, House of Lords, Privy Council and UK Supreme Court.

Areas of work We hold a pre-eminent international position as a commercial disputes set with the majority of our work involving international clients. We have a reputation for excellence, or are market leaders, in our areas of focus: energy, international arbitration, shipping, banking and finance, commodities and international trade, fraud, insolvency, insurance and reinsurance, and aviation.

Who should apply We look for candidates with a very strong academic background. Successful applicants will generally have (or be predicted) a first class degree, and they must have/be predicted at least a high 2.1 to apply. Candidates must have excellent analytical abilities, outstanding written and oral communication skills and the ability to perform under pressure. They must also be able to demonstrate that they have the commitment, energy and robustness to succeed in the competitive world of the Commercial Bar. Successful candidates often read law for their first degree, and an increasing number also have postgraduate law degrees. However, these are not pre-requisites. We welcome applications from candidates who have studied any serious academic subject at university.

Pupillage programme We offer up to three pupillages of 12 months' duration each year. We aim to develop in our pupils the skills, knowledge and sound judgment they will need to become successful commercial barristers. During their first and second six months, pupils sit with up to three pupil supervisors and are exposed to a wide range of high quality commercial work. Tenancy decisions are made at the end of June. Pupils also undertake advocacy and written assessments throughout their pupillage.

When and how to apply Quadrant Chambers uses the Pupillage Gateway to manage its applications. Thereafter our process involves a series of interviews. Please see our website for further details.

Mini-pupillages Mini-pupillages are available in March/April, July, September and December of each year. Places are limited. Please see our website for details.

Sponsorship/funding Pupils receive an award of £65,000, part of which may be advanced during the BPTC year. Pupils also have the opportunity to do fee-earning work during their second six.

Pupillages funded	3
Tenants	65
Tenancies in last 3 yrs	3
Mini-pupillages	yes
Apply through Pupillage Gateway	
Remuneration for pupillage	£65,000 (earnings not included)
Minimum qualifications	2.1 degree

Queen Elizabeth Building

Chambers of Tim Amos QC, Queen Elizabeth Building, Temple, London EC4Y 9BS
Tel: 020 7797 7837
Email: clerks@qeb.co.uk
Web: www.qeb.co.uk

Description of Chambers QEB is a leading set of family law chambers, particularly well-known for dealing with the financial consequences of divorce, but with immense experience in all aspects of family law including: jurisdictional disputes, foreign divorces, pre-marital agreements, civil partnerships, injunctions both financial and domestic, private law child work, child abduction, Inheritance Act claims and disputes between former cohabitees. In addition some members practise in general common law with particular emphasis on personal injury and professional negligence work.

QEB has been established for well over 100 years and is consistently rated as one of the top-ranking sets for family law. Many members of chambers are listed as leaders in their field in the annual publications *Chambers & Partners* and *Legal 500*.

Members of QEB have been involved in many of the most important cases of legal principle, including: *White, Sorrell, Miller, Spencer, Marano, Robson, Schofield, Jones, Z v Z* (No.2), *Petrodel v Prest, Mittal, Cooper-Hohn, AB v JJB* (EMR Modification), *Arif v Anwar, Broomfield, A v B* (Art.19 and Seisin B 11a) and *Fields*. Many members of chambers have continued into high judicial office. Currently, Lord Wilson sits in the Supreme Court, while Lord Justice Moylan sits in the Court of Appeal.

Who should apply The practice of family law is infinitely varied and clients come from all walks of life. International and conflict of laws issues arise increasingly often. An ability to deal not only with complex financial disputes, often involving commercial issues, but also with child-related or other emotionally fraught and sensitive situations, is essential. We are looking for applicants with a strong academic record (minimum 2.1 law or non-law degree save in exceptional circumstances), good legal and analytical skills, and an ability to communicate sensitively with a wide range of people at a critical time in their lives.

Pupillage programme QEB offers two pupillages each year. A pupillage at QEB offers top-quality training and very good financial support in a busy, friendly environment. A 12-month pupillage involves three pupil supervisors, but pupils are also encouraged to work with other tenants at all levels to gain a broad experience of our work. All our pupils are automatically considered candidates for tenancy and new tenants are only recruited from QEB pupils. Our reputation is such that where a pupil is not taken on, he or she is usually well placed elsewhere.

When and how to apply Chambers is a part of the Pupillage Gateway system. Applicants should apply in early 2019 season for a pupillage beginning in September 2020. Please consult the Pupillage Gateway website for details of the timetable.

Mini-pupillages Applications for mini-pupillages are to be made by application form. Please consult our website at www.qeb.co.uk for full details.

Sponsorship/funding Chambers offers a pupillage award of £35,000 pa minimum, plus earnings in the second six and from devilling. Pupils do not pay chambers' expenses or clerks' fees. Chambers also funds the compulsory inn advocacy and practice management training courses.

Pupillages funded	2
Tenants	34
Tenancies in last 3 yrs	4
Mini-pupillages	yes

Apply through Pupillage Gateway

Remuneration for pupillage
£35,000 minimum (plus earnings in second six from devilling)

Minimum qualifications
2.1 degree, save in exceptional circumstances

Remember to cite *The LawCareers.Net Handbook* on your application form if you apply to this chambers.

PUPILLAGE DIRECTORY 593

Serle Court

6 New Square, Lincoln's Inn, London WC2A 3QS
Tel: 020 7242 6105
Email: pupillage@serlecourt.co.uk
Web: www.serlecourt.co.uk
🐦 serle_court

Description of Chambers Acknowledged as "one of the very best commercial chancery sets, and one of the few that genuinely competes in both traditional chancery and commercial litigation", Serle Court "offers a variety of skill sets that others can't provide, and houses some of the biggest names at the Bar" – *Chambers & Partners*.

Serle Court is one of the leading commercial chancery sets with 67 barristers including 25 silks. Widely recognised as a leading set, Serle Court is recommended in 11 different areas of practice by the legal directories. Serle Court has a stimulating and inclusive work environment and a forward looking approach.

Areas of work Litigation, arbitration, mediation and advisory services across the full range of chancery and commercial practice areas including: civil fraud, commercial litigation, company, insolvency, offshore, partnership and LLP, trusts and probate, and property.

Who should apply Chambers is interested in well-rounded candidates from any background. Chambers looks for highly motivated individuals with outstanding intellectual ability, combined with a practical approach, sound judgment, an ability to develop good client relationships and the potential to become excellent advocates. Serle Court has a reputation for "consistent high quality" and for having members who are "highly intelligent, user-friendly, approachable and supportive" and seeks the same qualities in pupils. Chambers generally requires a degree classification of a good 2.1 as a minimum. Serle Court is committed to equality and diversity and encourages and welcomes applications from women, people of minority ethnic origin and people with disabilities, as well as candidates from other groups which are under-represented in the legal sector.

Pupillage programme Pupils sit with four pupil supervisors in order to experience a broad range of work. Chambers aims to recruit up to three pupils each year. Serle Court offers an excellent preparation for successful practice, a genuinely friendly and supportive environment, the opportunity to learn from some of the leading barristers in their field and a real prospect of tenancy.

When and how to apply Chambers now participates in the online pupillage applications scheme Pupillage Gateway. Applications must be made through the Pupillage Gateway.

Mini-pupillages About 30 available each year. The application form is available at www.serlecourt.co.uk/join-us/mini-pupillage.

Sponsorship/funding Serle Court offers awards of £65,000 for 12 months, of which up to £22,000 can be drawn down during the BPTC year. Chambers also provides an income guarantee worth up to £120,000 over the first two years of practice.

Pupillages funded	Up to 3
Tenants	67
Tenancies in last 3 yrs	7
Mini-pupillages	yes

Apply through Pupillage Gateway

Remuneration for pupillage
£65,000

Minimum qualifications
Good 2.1 degree

serle court

RADCLIFFE CHAMBERS
11 New Square, Lincoln's Inn, London WC2A 3QB
Tel: 020 7831 0081
Email: clerks@radcliffechambers.com
Apply to: Pupillage Committee

Described by *Legal 500* as 'a go-to set' for traditional chancery and commercial work, and shortlisted for best training in the 2018 *Legal Cheek* Awards.

PF 2
T 59
T$_{L3Y}$ 3
MP yes

THREE RAYMOND BUILDINGS
Gray's Inn, London WC1R 5BH
Tel: 020 7400 6400
Email: pupillage@3rblaw.com
Apply to: Mrs Donna Garner

Leading set with a national and international reputation. Expertise in crime, fraud, extradition, public law, licensing/regulatory law, health and safety, professional discipline, police law.

PF Up to 3
T 52
T$_{L3Y}$ 5
MP no

5RB
5 Gray's Inn Square, Gray's Inn, London WC1R 5AH
Tel: 020 7242 2902
Email: pupillage@5rb.com
Apply through Pupillage Gateway

Chambers is particularly well known for expertise in all areas of media and communications law.

PF Up to 2
T 28
T$_{L3Y}$ 3
MP yes

RED LION CHAMBERS
18 Red Lion Court, London EC4A 3EB
Tel: 020 7520 6000
Email: clerks@18rlc.co.uk
Apply to: Miss Genevieve Reed

We are a leading set specialising in criminal and regulatory law. Members undertake work of the highest quality for both the prosecution and defence.

PF 3
T 98
T$_{L3Y}$ 7
MP yes

REGENCY BARRISTERS CHAMBERS
45 Priestgate, Peterborough PE1 1LB
Tel: 01733 315 215
Email: clerks@regencychambers.law.co.uk
Apply to: Mr Nigel Sleight

Family law and civil litigation chambers.

PF 0
T 14
T$_{L3Y}$ 1
MP no

SELBORNE CHAMBERS
10 Essex Street, London WC2R 3AA
Tel: 020 7420 9500
Email: pupillage@selbornechambers.co.uk
Apply to: The Pupillage Secretary

Chambers usually offers one 12-month pupillage.

PF 1
T 30
T$_{L3Y}$ 3
MP yes

SERJEANTS' INN CHAMBERS
85 Fleet Street, London EC4Y 1AE
Tel: 020 7427 5000
Email: jfarrell@serjeantsinn.com
Apply through Pupillage Gateway

Serjeants' Inn Chambers is a busy, progressive and friendly set of chambers. Our principal practice areas include medical, police, regulatory and disciplinary and employment law.

PF 0
T 61
T$_{L3Y}$ 4
MP yes

---

11 SOUTH SQUARE
Gray's Inn, London WC1R 5EY
Tel: 020 7405 1222
Email: clerks@11southsquare.com
Apply through Pupillage Gateway

11 South Square is a leading set of barristers chambers specialising in intellectual property law as well as information technology and media and entertainment work.

PF 1
T 17
T$_{L3Y}$ 2
MP yes

PF = Pupillages funded / **T** = Tenants / **T**L3Y = Tenancies in last 3 years / **MP** = Mini-pupillages offered

South Square

3-4 South Square, Gray's Inn, London WC1R 5HP
Tel: 020 7696 9900
Email: pupillage@southsquare.com
Web: www.southsquare.com

Description of Chambers South Square is a highly respected and successful commercial set involved in complex and high-profile international and domestic commercial litigation. Members are recognised as leaders in their fields in all the key legal directories and have acted in some of the most important commercial cases of the last decade – including Lehman Brothers, MF Global, Madoff, Northern Rock, Formula One and the LIBOR litigation. *Chambers UK* Bar Guide describes South Square as having "members with unrivalled talent" and "excellent in everything they do".

Areas of work South Square's work is mainly focussed on financial and banking issues. We are the market leader for restructuring and insolvency, and widely recognised for our work in banking and finance litigation. Members also specialise in commercial litigation, company law and civil fraud related disputes. South Square's work has a significant international focus and members regularly appear in the courts and tribunals of international jurisdictions, notably the Cayman Islands, British Virgin Islands, Bermuda, Dubai, Hong Kogn and Singapore.

Who should apply Chambers look to recruit up to three high calibre pupils with a strong academic record and the potential to become an outstanding commercial barrister. The minimum academic qualification is a 2.1 degree. Pupils are selected from a broad range of backgrounds and experience, whether recent university graduates or those seeking a second career at the Bar. A number of members have degrees in law, some have taken non-law degrees and then sat the CPE/GDL, and others have started their career in another sector before becoming a barrister.

Pupillage programme Pupils are welcomed into all areas of chambers' life and are provided with a structured programme designed to train and equip them for practice in a dynamic and challenging environment. Pupils sit with a number of supervisors for periods of six to eight weeks to experience a range of practices and work. Pupillage is not run as a competition between pupils and chambers' approach is to recruit all pupils as tenants who meet the required standard.

When and how to apply The deadline for pupillages commencing in October 2020 is 7 January 2019.

Mini-pupillages Chambers also offers five-day mini-pupillages carrying an award of up to £750, and two-day unfunded mini-pupillages. See the chambers' website for further details www.southsquare.com/pupillage.

Sponsorship/funding Pupils receiving awards of £65,000 per annum (reviewable annually). £20,000 of the pupillage award may be paid in advance for living expenses during the BPTC. As a junior tenant you would receive a number of benefits including; subsidised travel and conference fees, no rent during your first 15 months of tenancy and no receipts charge for the first six months, subsidised membership of key professional associations for the first two years and assistance and training in financial planning and business development.

Pupillages funded	Up to 3
Tenants	44
Tenancies in last 3 yrs	5
Mini-pupillages	yes

Applications contact
The Pupillage Administrator

Remuneration for pupillage
£65,000 (reviewable annually)

Minimum qualifications
2.1 degree

5 Stone Buildings

Lincoln's Inn, London WC2A 3XT
Tel: 020 7242 6201
Email: clerks@5sblaw.com
Web: www.5sblaw.com
🐦 5sblaw

Description of Chambers 5 Stone Buildings is one of the outstanding sets of Chancery chambers with many distinguished present and former members, including a number of current and former law lords. We have 37 members, of whom seven are silks. Chambers is consistently ranked highly in the legal directories and the vast majority of our members are recommended practitioners. When compared to the largest chancery sets, chambers is relatively small. We believe that our size and ethos enables us to ensure that pupils and young tenants are trained and clerked properly and are well prepared for the problems and opportunities which practice will throw at them. All members of chambers, however senior, are always willing to assist other members, however junior, and to provide advice and guidance when requested. Generous terms are offered to junior tenants in their first years of practice, including heavily subsidised rent and an income guarantee.

Areas of work Members' work covers a wide span of civil law with an emphasis on chancery work, from specialist wills, trust and probate, pension and revenue work through to real property and professional negligence. Chambers is instructed by a wide range of solicitors, from the largest City firms to sole practitioners outside London. Many members have practices involving work from the major offshore financial centres.

Who should apply Applicants should normally have at least a 2.1 degree. Our policy is only to offer pupillages to candidates whom we believe to be potential tenants. We welcome applications from law and non-law graduates alike.

Pupillage programme We aim to offer one 12-month pupillage each year and to recruit tenants from our pupils. Pupils will normally sit with at least three pupil supervisors during that period with a view to experiencing a wide range of work. Pupils are given regular feedback as to how they might improve or refine their work.

When and how to apply Chambers is a member of Pupillage Gateway. Please consult our website for information about the selection criteria and process.

Mini-pupillages We offer a limited number of mini-pupillages each year for periods of two days. Details and a timetable for applications can be found on our website at www.5sblaw.com.

Sponsorship/funding Up to £60,000 per pupillage, £15,000 of which can be drawn down during the BPTC year.

Pupillages funded	1
Tenants	37
Tenancies in last 3 yrs	3
Mini-pupillages	yes
Applications contact	Chambers' Administrator
Remuneration for pupillage	Up to £60,000
Minimum qualifications	2.1 degree

5 Stone Buildings

St John's Chambers

101 Victoria Street, Bristol BS1 6PU
Tel: 0117 923 4700
Email: officemanager@stjohnschambers.co.uk
Web: www.stjohnschambers.co.uk
🐦 stjohnschambers

Description of Chambers St John's Chambers in Bristol is one of the largest and most prestigious barristers' sets in the South West, offering specialist advice and services in civil law. We were recently voted 'Regional Set of the Year 2018' by *Legal 500* UK Bar.

We are recognised nationally as providing first-class legal advice and representation in the 14 core practice areas: agriculture and rural affairs, clinical negligence, commercial, construction and engineering, Court of Protection, employment, family and divorce, inquests and public inquiries, personal injury, professional negligence, public and administrative law, real estate, wills and trusts, and tax.

Areas of work Agriculture and rural affairs, clinical negligence, commercial, construction and engineering, Court of Protection, employment, family and divorce, inquests and public inquiries, personal injury, professional negligence, public and administrative law, real estate, tax, wills and trusts.

Who should apply St John's Chambers will be recruiting outside of the Pupillage Gateway. We look to recruit top quality applicants with the ability to analyse information quickly and to present arguments succinctly and persuasively. The successful applicant will have strong academic credentials (subject to any extenuating circumstances) together with experience of mooting, public speaking debating or presentations and a desire to excel. We also welcome interest from suitably qualified professionals who are changing careers. While pupillage can offer experience across practice groups, market forces generally require specialisation as the norm once tenancy has been offered. Pupils are therefore expected to focus on key areas during pupillage.

Pupillage programme Each year, the pupillage committee, with the heads of each practice group, defines the pupillage requirements for the following year. As a pupil at St John's Chambers, your pupillage will cover all necessary aspects of your specialist area(s).

When and how to apply Application dates and details will be found on the website from January 2019. Should you have any general enquiries about pupillage then please do not hesitate to contact Isabelle Mills at isabelle.mills@stjohnschambers.co.uk.

Mini-pupillages Mini-pupillages (non-assessed) are an opportunity to experience life at the independent Bar. Applications for mini-pupillage are considered on a quarterly basis. The ideal time to apply is: i) if you are studying law and you are a second-year student or ii) you are in your third year or studying the BPTC, but we will consider applications before then, especially from non-law candidates. Please see our website for details. Student visits are not available.

Sponsorship/funding We offer two funded pupillages with awards each of £35,000 in the first 12 months. Exceptionally three pupillages will be offered depending on recruitment needs. In general terms, funded pupillage means that chambers will guarantee a pupil's income each month for the 12-month period of pupillage. This is subject to a clawback to the extent of any fees actually received during the second six months of pupillage.

Pupillages funded	2
Tenants	83
Tenancies in last 3 yrs	7
Mini-pupillages	yes

Apply to
Check website for details

Remuneration for pupillage
£35,000

Minimum qualifications
2.1 and would consider 2.2 degree with extenuating circumstances

St John's
CHAMBERS

5 ST ANDREW'S HILL 5 St Andrew's Hill, London EC4V 5BZ **Tel:** 020 7332 5400 **Email:** clerks@5sah.co.uk Apply through Pupillage Gateway	A leading criminal set with an excellent reputation in financial and white collar crime. Chambers prides itself on a friendly, diverse and relaxed working atmosphere.	PF 2 T 62 TL3Y 6 MP yes
ST IVES CHAMBERS Chambers of Jeremy Weston QC, 1-3 Whittall Street, Birmingham B4 6DH **Tel:** 0121 236 0863 **Email:** pupillage@stiveschambers.co.uk **Apply to:** Mr Timothy Bowe	St Ives Chambers is an expanding general common law set with a strong local and national reputation across all practice areas.	PF Up to 3 T 74 TL3Y 12 MP yes
9 ST JOHN STREET CHAMBERS 9 St John Street, Manchester M3 4DN **Tel:** 0161 955 9000 **Email:** ruth.bailey@9sjs.com Apply through Pupillage Gateway	Recognised as one of the leading sets of barristers, we have many members of chambers who are acknowledged leaders in their particular field of expertise.	PF 2 T 96 TL3Y 7 MP yes
18 ST JOHN STREET CHAMBERS 18-20 St John Street, Manchester M3 4EA **Tel:** 0161 278 1800 **Email:** pupils@18sjs.com Apply through Pupillage Gateway	Chambers was founded in 1973 and has developed into a strong mixed set practising in the principal specialist groups: crime, civil, family and business/property.	PF Up to 4 T 74 TL3Y 6 MP yes
ST JOHN'S BUILDINGS 24-28a St John Street, Manchester M3 4DJ **Tel:** 0161 214 1500 **Email:** clerk@stjohnsbuildings.co.uk **Apply to:** Mr Mike Fry	A leading Manchester/Preston/Chester common law set with a strong reputation and acknowledged collegial culture. Family, PI/clinical negligence, crime, employment, commercial and public/admin law. Modern, efficient and friendly.	PF 1 T 156 TL3Y 10 MP yes
ST MARY'S CHAMBERS 26-28 High Pavement, Nottingham NG1 1HN **Tel:** 0115 950 3503 **Email:** clerks@stmarysflc.co.uk Apply through Pupillage Gateway	A well established specialist family law set practising throughout the East Midlands and beyond. Further expansion is expected.	PF 2 T 32 TL3Y 4 MP yes
ST PAUL'S CHAMBERS St Paul's House, 23 Park Square, Leeds LS1 2ND **Tel:** 0113 245 5866 **Email:** clerks@stpaulschambers.com **Apply to:** Secretary of Pupillage Committee	Founded in 1982, St Paul's Chambers now comprises 39 tenants working in complementary areas of expertise, in order to provide a consistent service across a broad range of legal fields.	PF 0 T 44 TL3Y 4 MP yes
ST PHILIPS CHAMBERS 55 Temple Row, Birmingham B2 5LS **Tel:** 0121 246 7000 **Email:** pupillage@st-philips.com **Apply to:** Ms Emily Smith	We are one of the largest regional and national sets in the country with offices in Birmingham, Leeds and London.	PF Up to 2 T 175 TL3Y 20 MP yes

PF = Pupillages funded / **T** = Tenants / **TL3Y** = Tenancies in last 3 years / **MP** = Mini-pupillages offered

STAPLE INN CHAMBERS Second Floor, 7 Staple Inn, London WC1V 7QH **Tel:** 020 7242 5240 **Email:** pupillage@stapleinn.co.uk **Apply to:** The Pupillage Secretary	Application window for pupillage commencing October 2019 will be advertised on Chambers' website. There will be no announcement before the Pupillage Gateway window closes.	PF 1 T 25 T_{L3Y} 5 MP yes

THREE STONE Ground Floor, Lincoln's Inn, London WC2A 3XL **Tel:** 020 7242 4937 **Email:** clerks@3sb.law.co.uk **Apply to:** Ms Constance McDonnell	A chancery and commercial set specialising in financial and property litigation and advice.	PF 1 T 30 T_{L3Y} 3 MP yes

4 STONE BUILDINGS Lincoln's Inn, London WC2A 3XT **Tel:** 020 7242 5524 **Email:** pupillage@4stonebuildings.com Apply through Pupillage Gateway	4 Stone Buildings specialise in litigation and advisory work in the fields of company law, commercial law, financial services regulation, insolvency and international trusts.	PF 2 T 36 T_{L3Y} 5 MP yes

9 STONE BUILDINGS Lincoln's Inn, London WC2A 3NN **Tel:** 020 7404 5055 **Email:** clerks@9stonebuildings.com **Apply to:** Mr Philip Brown	Rooted in commercial chancery practice, chambers undertakes advocacy, drafting and advice in a range of property, insolvency, private client and commercial matters, domestically and overseas.	PF 1 T 25 T_{L3Y} 2 MP yes

STONE CHAMBERS 4 Field Court, Gray's Inn, London WC1R 5EF **Tel:** 020 7440 6900 **Email:** pupillage@stonechambers.com **Apply to:** Mr Henry Ellis	Stone Chambers is a leading commercial and shipping set based in London and Singapore, specialising in international commercial litigation and arbitration. Accepts direct pupillage applications.	PF 1 T 26 T_{L3Y} 5 MP yes

STOUR CHAMBERS Mill Studio, 17a Stour Street, Canterbury CT1 2NR **Tel:** 01227 764899 **Email:** clerks@stourchambers.co.uk **Apply to:** Pupillage Coordinator	Chambers' specialisations are: family law and general civil law. Applications must be made on chambers' application form.	PF 1 T 16 T_{L3Y} 2 MP yes

SUSSEX CHAMBERS 5 Chiswick Place, Eastbourne BN21 4NH **Tel:** 01323 642102 **Email:** clerks@sussexchambers.co.uk **Apply to:** Miss Rebecca Upton	Criminal, family and general common law set.	PF 1 T 12 T_{L3Y} 1 MP yes

TANFIELD CHAMBERS 2-5 Warwick Court, London WC1R 5DJ **Tel:** 020 7421 5300 **Email:** clerks@tanfieldchambers.co.uk	Tanfield is a leading property law set and a 'force to be reckoned with' across all aspects of commercial and residential real estate litigation and ADR.	PF 3 T 65 T_{L3Y} 6 MP yes

PF = Pupillages funded / **T** = Tenants / **T**_{L3Y} = Tenancies in last 3 years / **MP** = Mini-pupillages offered

FOURTEEN 14 Gray's Inn Square, Gray's Inn, London WC1R 5JP **Tel:** 020 7242 0858 **Email:** clerks@fourteen.co.uk Apply through Pupillage Gateway	A leading family law set, with practice teams in children law, family finance, the Court of Protection and international family law.	PF 1 T 34 T∟₃ʏ 3 MP yes
TEMPLE COURT CHAMBERS Hamilton House, One Temple Avenue, London EC4Y OHA **Tel:** 020 7353 7888 **Email:** clerks@templecourt.co.uk **Apply to:** Ms Chris-Ann Campbell		PF 1 T 18 T∟₃ʏ 6 MP no
TEMPLE GARDEN CHAMBERS 1 Harcourt Buildings, Temple, London EC4Y 9DA **Tel:** 020 7583 1315 **Email:** clerks@tgchambers.com Apply through Pupillage Gateway	Leading general common and public law set instructed by a wide range of solicitors including those representing government departments, insurance companies and trade unions.	PF 2 T 70 T∟₃ʏ 6 MP yes
3 TEMPLE GARDENS Chambers of John Coffey QC, Temple, London EC4Y 9AU **Tel:** 020 7353 3102 **Email:** clerks@3tg.co.uk Apply through Pupillage Gateway	Chambers is well-established, specialising in all areas of criminal law. Chambers has achieved accreditation to Barmark as issued by the General Council of the Bar.	PF Up to 2 T 52 T∟₃ʏ 7 MP yes
2TG Chambers of Neil Moody QC, Temple, London EC4Y 9AY **Tel:** 020 7822 1200 **Email:** kpoulton@2tg.co.uk Apply through Pupillage Gateway	2tg is a common law and commercial chambers. We specialise in banking, clinical negligence, employment, insurance, personal injury and professional negligence.	PF 3-4 T 61 T∟₃ʏ 7 MP yes
THOMAS MORE CHAMBERS 7 Lincoln's Inn Fields, London WC2A 3BP **Tel:** 020 7404 7000 **Email:** clerks@thomasmore.co.uk Apply through Pupillage Gateway	A successful and established common law set with an excellent reputation. We offer a broad and challenging pupillage covering a comprehensive cross-section of our work.	PF 1 T 43 T∟₃ʏ 4 MP yes
TRINITY CHAMBERS The Custom House, Quayside, Newcastle upon Tyne NE1 3DE **Tel:** 0191 232 1927 **Email:** info@trinitychambers.co.uk Apply through Pupillage Gateway	Busy provincial set with sites in Newcastle and Middlesbrough with significant specialisations including those indicated. Chambers has Barmark and Investors in People accreditation.	PF 1-2 T 71 T∟₃ʏ 10 MP yes
TRINITY CHAMBERS Highfield House, Moulsham Street, Chelmsford, Essex CM2 9AF **Tel:** 01245 605040 **Email:** clerks@trinitychambers.law.co.uk	Trinity Chambers is a busy and dynamic set focused in Chelmsford. Members specialise predominantly in family and civil law.	PF 0 T 23 T∟₃ʏ 4 MP yes

PF = Pupillages funded / T = Tenants / T∟₃ʏ = Tenancies in last 3 years / MP = Mini-pupillages offered

3 Verulam Buildings

Gray's Inn, London WC1R 5NT
Tel: 020 7831 8441
Email: chambers@3vb.com
Web: www.3vb.com

Description of Chambers 3 Verulam Buildings is one of London's largest and most highly regarded commercial sets of chambers, its members regularly involved in the leading cases of the day. Recent examples include the RBS Rights Issue Litigation, *Tchenguiz v Grant Thornton*, *Yukos v The Russian Federation*, *Terra Firma v Citigroup* and *VTB Capital v Nutritek*. Over 70% of 3VB's barristers are ranked in one or more legal directories, and both its silks and juniors are frequently nominated for and awarded industry accolades for their achievements. 3VB prides itself on its professional expertise and the outstanding opportunities afforded to all tenants to build leading commercial practices. It is a forward-looking set providing a diverse, friendly and informal atmosphere with excellent practice managers, spacious premises and first-class facilities.

Areas of work 3VB's members are recognised as leading practitioners in a variety of the fields that make up international commercial practice: banking, financial services, commercial and contractual disputes, civil fraud, international arbitration, energy, construction, insolvency, insurance, technology, IT and telecoms, media and professional negligence.

Who should apply Commercial practice is demanding and 3VB seeks the brightest and the best. The characteristics we seek in our recruits are a high level of intellectual and analytical ability, very strong oral and written advocacy skills and the temperament and determination to succeed at the competitive commercial Bar. We aim to nurture those qualities during pupillage and in the early years of practice. As a general guide an applicant will be unlikely to reach the first round of interviews without a good 2.1 in their undergraduate studies (as well as a good record on the GDL where applicable). Many successful applicants have a first or a Master's degree, or both.

Pupillage programme Pupils sit with four pupil supervisors for three months each over the year. 3VB's pupil supervisors are high achievers at various levels of seniority, and pupils have the opportunity to work with many other members of chambers as well as their supervisors. So, pupils are exposed to a range of cases and to top-quality expertise from which to learn their skills, all in an encouraging and supportive environment, to ensure as far as we can that they perform to the best of their ability during their pupillage year. During the practising six months, pupils are given the opportunity to undertake advocacy on their own account, in order to start building up experience and earnings. Tenancy at 3VB is offered to all pupils who make the grade.

When and how to apply 3VB offers up to four twelve-month pupillages per year (including deferred pupillages). 3VB is a member of the Pupillage Gateway and, save for established practitioners and other applicants who have obtained dispensation from the BSB from the requirement to undertake pupillage, we invite all applicants to make their application via the Pupillage Gateway website.

Mini-pupillages Two-day mini-pupillages are an essential part of chambers' selection procedure and it is strongly encouraged that prospective applicants for pupillage apply for a mini-pupillage; please visit the 3VB website for further information – www.3vb.com/pupillage/mini-pupillage.

Sponsorship/funding The pupillage award is currently £65,000 per annum, not including second-six earnings. Up to £20,000 of this award can be drawn down during the year prior to pupillage.

Pupillages funded	Up to 4
Tenants	80
Tenancies in last 3 yrs	8
Mini-pupillages	yes
Apply through Pupillage Gateway	
Remuneration for pupillage	£65,000 for 12 months

Wilberforce Chambers

8 New Square, Lincoln's Inn, London WC2A 3QP
Tel: 020 7306 0102
Email: pupillage@wilberforce.co.uk
Web: www.wilberforce.co.uk
🐦 wilberforcech

Description of Chambers We are one of the leading commercial chancery and business law sets of chambers in the UK, comprising of 70 specialist barristers, including 33 QCs. Our barristers are involved in some of the most intellectually challenging and legally significant matters undertaken by the Bar today.

Areas of work Our principal areas of practice include arbitration, banking and financial services, civil fraud and investigations, commercial litigation, company, insolvency and restructuring, information technology, media and entertainment, pensions, professional liability, property, trusts, tax, probate and estates.

Who should apply You should possess high intellectual ability, excellent communication skills and a strong motivation to do commercial chancery work. You need to be mature and confident, have the ability to work with others and analyse legal problems clearly, demonstrating commercial and practical good sense. We have a minimum requirement of a 2.1 degree in law or another subject, and we have a track record of taking on GDL students, as well as undergraduate law students, as pupils and as tenants.

Pupillage programme We offer two 12-month pupillages. We provide an excellent pupillage and operate a well-structured programme aimed at providing you with a broad experience of commercial chancery practice. You will sit with different pupil supervisors with whom you will be able to develop your skills.

A key feature of pupillage programme is that our pupils are not in competition with one another for a tenancy. We assess each pupil solely on their own abilities and performance, with a view to taking on both pupils as tenants at the end of their time with us.

When and how to apply Pupillage applications should be made via the Pupillage Gateway. Please refer to the Gateway for all relevant dates.

Mini-pupillages We run four mini-pupillage weeks with two weeks held in December, one at Easter and one in July. Please visit our website for an application form and further information on when to apply. See website for details of application dates.

Sponsorship/funding A pupillage award of £65,000 (for pupillage starting in October 2020) is offered to all pupils. The award is payable in monthly instalments and up to £20,000 of the award may be drawn down during the BPTC year. We fund attendance at the compulsory courses which pupils are required to undertake by the Bar Council. We also provide an interest free loan to assist with cash flow during the early stages of practice.

Pupillages funded	2
Tenants	70
Tenancies in last 3 yrs	6
Mini-pupillages	yes

Apply via website

Remuneration for pupillage
£65,000

Minimum qualifications
2.1 degree

Wilberforce
CHAMBERS

UNITY STREET CHAMBERS 5 Unity Street, Bristol BS1 5HH **Tel:** 0117 906 9789 **Email:** chambers@unitystreetchambers.com **Apply to:** The Pupillage Secretary	Applications should be made by way of covering letter and CV. Pupils are taken on with a view to tenancy. Mini-pupillages are also offered.	PF 1 T 13 T_{L3Y} 1 MP yes
WESTGATE CHAMBERS 64 High Street, Lewes BN7 1XG **Tel:** 01273 480 510 **Email:** clerks@westgate-chambers.co.uk **Apply to:** Mr Christopher Prior	Chambers' principal areas of work are criminal, family and civil. Pupils will receive advocacy training throughout pupillage.	PF Up to 2 T 49 T_{L3Y} 3 MP yes
15 WINCKLEY SQUARE Preston PR1 3JJ **Tel:** 01772 252828 **Email:** paulm@15wsq.co.uk Apply through Pupillage Gateway		PF 2 T 50 T_{L3Y} 5 MP yes

PF = Pupillages funded / **T** = Tenants / T_{L3Y} = Tenancies in last 3 years / **MP** = Mini-pupillages offered

Useful information

Glossary

ABS Alternative business structures were brought in by the Legal Services Act in October 2011 and are licensed by the Solicitors Regulation Authority. ABSs enable lawyers to form partnerships with non-lawyers and allow companies to invest in law firms and provide legal services. See also 'Tesco law'.

ADR Alternative dispute resolution, which comprises various methods for resolving problems without going to court.

Advocacy The act of arguing or pleading in favour of something either orally or in writing. A key skill for lawyers.

Affidavit A written statement, the truth of which must be sworn before an officer of the court.

Annulment A legal decree stating that a marriage was never valid.

Appeal A request to a supervisory court, usually composed of a panel of judges, to overturn the legal ruling of a lower court.

Arbitration A method of alternative dispute resolution whereby the disputing parties agree to submit their differences to the judgment of an impartial person or group.

Articles of incorporation A document that must be filed in order for a company to incorporate. Among other things, it must include the name and address of the corporation, its general purpose, and the number and type of shares of stock to be issued.

Assistant/associate solicitor Next step on the career ladder after the two-year training period.

Associated office (Usually overseas) office with which a firm has an arrangement to share work and to second trainees.

Bad faith Dishonesty or fraud in a transaction, such as entering into an agreement with no intention of honouring its terms.

Bail The money that a defendant pays as a guarantee that he or she will show up in court at a later date.

Bankruptcy Another term for insolvency.

The Bar Term used to refer to the barristers' branch of the legal profession.

Bar Council Official body representing barristers in England and Wales.

Bar Standards Board Independent board responsible for regulating barristers in England and Wales.

Barrister A lawyer who has been called to the Bar and who appears in court to argue a client's case.

Beneficiary Person named in a will or insurance policy to receive money or property; person who receives benefits from a trust.

Black-letter law The principles of law which are generally known and free from doubt or dispute.

Board of directors The group of people elected by a corporation's shareholders to make major business decisions for the company.

Bolt-on A department (or even an entire smaller firm) that joins an existing firm. Generally, the larger firm will not have practised in the specialist area in which the newcomers excel.

Bond A document through which one party promises to pay another within a specified amount of time.

Boutique Small niche firm offering specialist advice on one or a few specific areas of law.

BPTC The Bar Professional Training Course, the vocational stage between degree and pupillage. It replaced the BVC in September 2010.

Brief Details of a client's case, prepared by a solicitor and given to the barrister who argues it in court.

Burden of proof The duty of a party in a case to convince the judge or jury that enough facts exist to prove the allegations in question.

BVC The Bar Vocational Course, which was replaced by the BPTC in September 2010.

Call to the Bar A formal ceremony following completion of the BPTC during which you are given the title of barrister (although you must complete pupillage before you can practise).

Case law The law created by judges when deciding individual cases. Also known as 'common law'.

Caveat emptor Latin for 'buyer beware', this principle gives the buyer full responsibility for determining the quality of the goods in question.

Chambers Offices of a group of barristers.

Chinese walls Procedures enforced within firms to restrict access to certain information and so avoid any awkward conflicts of interest.

CILEx The Chartered Institute of Legal Executives is the professional body that represents trainee and practising chartered legal executives. See also 'Legal executive'.

Citizens Advice Previously the Citizens Advice Bureau. A charity service offering legal and financial advice to the public.

The City The commercial and financial area in the centre of London.

Claimant Formerly 'plaintiff'. The person or body that initiates a lawsuit.

Codicil A supplement to a will.

Collateral An asset that a borrower agrees to give up if he or she fails to repay a loan.

Common law The law created by judges when deciding individual cases. Also known as 'case law'.

Contentious Legal situation where a dispute has arisen.

Contingency fee A fee arrangement in which the lawyer is paid out of any damages that are awarded.

Contract An agreement between two or more parties in which an offer is made and accepted, and each party benefits.

Copyright A person's right to prevent others from copying works that he or she has written, authored or otherwise created.

Corporate finance Area of law that involves, among other things, advising clients on mergers and acquisitions, takeovers and stock exchange flotations.

Corporation An independent entity created to conduct a business.

Counsel Barrister(s) acting for one of the parties in a legal action.

CPE Common Professional Exam, a conversion course for non-law graduates. More often referred to as the GDL.

CPS The Crown Prosecution Service is responsible for prosecuting criminal cases investigated by the police in England and Wales. Employs solicitors and barristers.

Creditor An individual (or institution) to whom money is owed.

Damages The financial compensation awarded to someone who suffered an injury or was harmed by another's wrongful act.

Debtor Person who owes money.

Decision The judgment rendered by a court.

Deed A written legal document that describes a property and outlines its boundaries.

Defamation Publication of a statement that injures a person's reputation. Libel and slander are defamation.

Defendant In criminal cases, the person accused of the crime. In civil matters, the person or organisation that is being sued.

Devilling Doing paperwork for other members of chambers.

Due diligence Investigation carried out to establish an accurate picture of a company's finances and market position.

Due process The concept that laws and legal proceedings must be fair.

ECHR The European Convention on Human Rights 1950 protects human rights within the member states of the Council of Europe; the European Court of Human Rights is an international judicial body responsible for upholding the convention.

Encumbrance Any claim or restriction on a property's title.

Equity partner A partner at a firm who owns a share of the business (and is liable for its failures).

Glossary

Equivalent means Introduced in 2014 by the SRA, this allows anyone to apply to qualify as a solicitor provided that (i) their skills and legal work experience are equivalent to that which a qualifying solicitor would have attained following a training contract, and (ii) they have completed the LPC.

Escrow Money or documents, such as a deed or title, held by a third party until the conditions of an agreement are met.

Estate All the property that a person owns.

Evidence The various testimony and documents presented in court to prove an alleged fact.

Ex parte Latin term meaning 'by or for one party'. Refers to situations in which only one party appears before a judge.

Executor Person named in a will to oversee and manage an estate.

Expert witness A witness with a specialised knowledge of a subject who is allowed to discuss an event in court even though he or she was not present.

Fee earner A lawyer at a firm for whose time the firm charges.

First six The first six months of pupillage. During this stage the pupil will train under a barrister, but will not have rights of audience.

Force majeure When parties to a commercial agreement are excused from performance of the contract due to events that are beyond their control.

Franchise A business relationship in which an owner (the franchisor) licenses others (the franchisees) to operate outlets.

FTSE The Financial Times Stock Exchange. The FTSE 100 is an index of the top 100 companies in the country, based on share value and turnover.

GDL Graduate Diploma in Law, a conversion course for non-law students. See also 'CPE'.

GLS The Government Legal Service provides legal services across the spectrum of the government's activities. Employs solicitors and barristers.

Good faith To act honestly and without deception.

Human Rights Act 1998 Statute that requires public authorities to act in a way that is compatible with the rights guaranteed by the ECHR. It requires the courts to read and give effect to primary legislation in a way that is compatible with the convention rights.

Hung jury A jury that is unable to reach a verdict.

In camera Latin for 'in chambers'. Refers to a hearing or inspection of documents that takes place in private, often in a judge's chambers.

In-house Refers to a lawyer who works within a company (not a law firm) as a salaried employee.

Inns of Court Collective name for the four legal societies in London that have the exclusive right of admission to the Bar.

Interlocutory order Temporary order issued during the course of litigation. Typically cannot be appealed because it is not final.

Intestate To die without a will.

IPO Initial public offering is the first sale of stock by a listed company to the public.

Jackson reforms Civil costs reforms recommended in a report by Lord Justice Jackson that came into force on 1 April 2013. See also 'LASPO'.

JLD Part of the Law Society, the Junior Lawyers Division is a group for students, trainees and newly qualified solicitors.

Judgment A court's official decision on the matter before it.

Jurisdiction A court's authority to hear a dispute.

LASPO The Legal Aid, Sentencing and Punishment of Offenders Act 2012 introduced wide-ranging changes to the legal aid system and reformed the use of conditional fee agreements. Highly controversial.

Law clinic A free legal advice centre, usually staffed by volunteer lawyers and students.

Law Commission An independent body set up in 1965 to keep the law of England and Wales under review and to recommend reform where needed.

Law Society Official body representing solicitors in England and Wales.

Lawyer Umbrella term used to refer to both barristers and solicitors.

LDP Legal disciplinary practices – introduced by the Legal Services Act – allow the eight different types of 'official' lawyer, known as authorised persons (ie, solicitor, barrister, legal executive, licensed conveyancer, trademark attorney, patent attorney, notary and costs lawyer), to go into partnership. They also permit firms to have up to 25% of their partnership made up of non-lawyers.

Legal aid The provision of assistance, advice or representation to people who are otherwise unable to afford legal representation.

Legal apprentice An individual who joins a law firm straight from school, rather than going to university, to work in a role similar to that of a paralegal.

Legal executive A qualified legal professional who specialises in a particular area of law and often performs work that is similar to that of a solicitor. See also 'CILEx'.

Legal Services Act 2007 A law that has opened up the legal market by allowing lawyers to form new business structures and permitting corporations to move into the legal services market. See also 'ABS'.

Legal Services Board The independent body responsible for overseeing the regulation of lawyers in England and Wales.

LETR The Legal Education and Training Review report was published in June 2013, setting out 26 key recommendations for change, particularly in regard to quality, accessibility and flexibility.

Liability Legal responsibility, duty or obligation.

Libel Defamatory written statements or materials.

LLB Letters written after someone's name, showing that he or she has the degree of bachelor of laws.

LLC A limited liability company is a business structure that is a hybrid of a partnership and a corporation.

LLD Letters written after someone's name, showing that he or she has a doctorate in law.

LLM Letters written after someone's name, showing that he or she has the degree of master of laws.

LLP A limited liability partnership is essentially a hybrid between a general and limited partnership. An LLP protects partners from personal liability for the negligent acts of the other partners.

Lockstep A system by which partners' pay is decided by time served as partner in predictable sequence. Pay rises in a series of steps (eg, after one, three, five, seven and 10 years).

LPC The Legal Practice Course is the vocational stage between degree and training contract.

M&A Mergers and acquisitions. A merger occurs where two or more companies join as one. An acquisition is the takeover of one company by another.

Magic circle Term used to refer to the top five UK law firms: Allen & Overy, Clifford Chance, Freshfields Bruckhaus Deringer, Linklaters and Slaughter and May.

MDP Multi-disciplinary partnership. A combination firm offering the full range of professional services, particularly law and accountancy functions.

Mediation A method of alternative dispute resolution in which a neutral third party helps to resolve a dispute.

Mini-pupillage Work experience within a set of chambers.

Ministry of Justice The body responsible for prisons, judges and courts, and probation.

Moot A mock trial, designed to test advocacy skills.

Negligence A failure to exercise the degree of care that a reasonable person would have used in the circumstances.

Niche firm/chambers Firm or set that specialises in a certain area of law.

Non-contentious Legal situation where there is no dispute.

Notary An official authorised to certify, for example, deeds, contracts or copies of documents.

Glossary

No win, no fee An agreement whereby a solicitor acting in a claim is entitled to be paid his or her fee only if he or she wins. Such payment is usually made by the loser or his or her insurance company. Also known as a 'conditional fee'.

Paralegal A non-lawyer who does legal work which often resembles that of a solicitor.

Partnership An association of two or more people who agree to share in the profits and losses of a business venture.

Patent A document issued to an inventor, detailing ownership, rights and the nature of the invention.

Period of recognised training Introduced in 2014 by the SRA to replace the term 'training contract' (although most firms still refer to it in this way), it refers to the two-year pre-qualification training period for a solicitor, normally spent in a law firm.

Perjury The crime of knowingly making a false statement while under oath in court.

Piercing the corporate veil The concept through which a corporation's shareholders, who are usually protected from liability for the corporation's activities, may be held responsible for certain actions.

Pleadings The allegations by each party of its claims and defences.

Power of attorney The authority to act legally for another person.

Precedent A previously decided case that is considered binding in the court where it was issued and in all lower courts in the same jurisdiction.

Prima facie Latin for 'at first sight', meaning that a matter appears to be self-evident on first examination.

Pro bono The giving of free legal advice and services.

Profits per partner A firm's total profit divided by the number of partners at the firm.

PSC Professional Skills Course, which must be passed while training to qualify as a solicitor.

Punitive damages Money awarded to a victim that is intended to punish a defendant and stop the person or business from repeating the type of conduct that caused the injury in question.

Pupil barrister A trainee barrister who is effectively practising, but is not yet fully qualified. Also known as a 'pupil'.

Pupillage The training period before qualifying as a barrister.

Pupil supervisor A barrister who oversees an individual's training during pupillage.

QC Queen's Counsel, a barrister who has been appointed counsel to Her Majesty on the advice of the lord chancellor. Also known as a 'silk'.

Qualifying sessions Run by the four Inns of Court, students must complete 12 qualifying sessions before they can be called to the Bar. Sessions can include dinners, workshops, moots and residential weekends. Formerly called 'dining'.

Receivership The appointment by a court of a receiver to take custody of the property, business, rents and profits of a party to a lawsuit pending a final decision.

Salaried partner Unlike an equity partner, a salaried partner is still an employee of a firm, though with enhanced status, influence and responsibilities.

Seats Periods of training during a training contract. Normally six months long each.

Second six The second six months of pupillage. The pupil continues to train under a barrister, but has rights of audience in all courts.

Secondment Placement with a law firm's client or to an overseas office.

Settlement The resolution or compromise by the parties in a civil case.

SIF The Solicitors Indemnity Fund, covering liability for claims made against its members.

Silk Another term for QC.

Slander Defamatory oral statements.

Solicitor A lawyer who provides clients with skilled advice and representation. Mostly works in private practice.

Sponsorship The payment of GDL and/or LPC fees by a firm to individuals who have been offered a training contract.

SQE The Solicitors Qualifying Exam is due to come into force in 2020 and will replace the GDL and LPC. It will need to be passed by all prospective solicitors (whether coming through the university, equivalent means or apprenticeship route) in order to qualify.

Square Mile London's financial centre, as defined by London's old medieval walls.

Squatter A barrister who remains in chambers after pupillage, but not as a tenant.

SRA The Solicitors Regulation Authority is the body in charge of setting and maintaining standards for solicitors.

Stare decisis Latin for 'to stand by that which is decided'. Refers to the principle of adhering to precedent when deciding a case.

Subpoena An order compelling a person to appear to testify or produce documents.

Tenant A barrister based in a particular set of chambers after pupillage.

Tesco law Euphemistic term for both the Legal Services Act and ABSs, which allow companies (eg, supermarkets or banks) to provide legal services. See also 'ABS'.

Title Ownership of property.

Tort A civil wrong that results in an injury to a person or property.

Trademark A word, name or symbol used to identify products sold or services provided by a business.

Training contract The two-year pre-qualification training period for a solicitor. See also 'period of recognised training'.

Transaction A deal arranged by two sets of lawyers.

Tribunal A court or forum established to settle certain types of dispute.

Trust A legal obligation with respect to property given by one person (donor) to another (trustee).

Vacation scheme Paid, formal work experience within a law firm. Also known as a 'work placement scheme'.

White-collar crime Term referring to financial crimes, such as fraud or insider dealing, committed primarily by persons at management level.

White-shoe firm A traditional, long-established US firm.

Work placement scheme Paid, formal work experience within a law firm, usually for one or two weeks. Also known as a 'vacation scheme'.

Useful addresses

Association of Graduate Careers Advisory Services
Unit R8D, Riverside Building, Sheafbank Business Park, Prospect Road, Sheffield S2 3EN
Tel: 0114 251 5750
Email: info@agcas.org.uk
Web: www.agcas.org.uk

Association of Costs Lawyers
Herringbone House, Lion Road, Palgrave, Diss, Norfolk IP22 1AL
Tel: 0203 174 0967
Web: www.associationofcostslawyers.co.uk
Email: enquiries@costlawyer.co.uk

Association of Taxation Technicians
1st Floor, Artillery House, 11-19 Artillery Row, London SW1P 1RT
Tel: 020 7340 0551
Email: info@att.org.uk
Web: www.att.org.uk

Association of Women Solicitors London
74A Seven Sisters Road, London N7 6AE
Tel: 07760 272809
Email: awslondon1@gmail.com
Web: www.awslondon.co.uk

Bar Association for Commerce, Finance and Industry
BACFI, PO Box 4352, Edlesborough, Dunstable Beds LU6 9EF
Tel: 01525 222244
Email: secretary@bacfi.org
Web: www.bacfi.org

Bar Council
289-293 High Holborn, London WC1V 7HZ
Tel: 020 7242 0082
Email: contactus@barcouncil.org.uk
Web: www.barcouncil.org.uk

Bar Standards Board
289-293 High Holborn, London WC1V 7HZ
Tel: 020 7611 1444
Email: contactus@barstandardsboard.org.uk
Web: www.barstandardsboard.org.uk

Black Solicitors Network
608 Holloway Road, London, N19 3PH
Email: enquiries@blacksolicitorsnetwork.org
Web: www.blacksolicitorsnetwork.co.uk

British Institute of Verbatim Reporters
Mary Sorene, 73 Alicia Gardens, Kenton, Harrow, Middlesex HA3 8JD
Tel: 020 8907 8249
Email: sec@bivr.org.uk
Web: www.bivr.org.uk

Career Development Loans
Tel: 0800 100 900
Web: www.gov.uk/career-development-loans

Central Applications Board
Ground Floor, Suite 2, River House, Broadford Business Park, Shalford, Surrey GU4 8EP
Email: applications@lawcabs.ac.uk
Web: www.lawcabs.ac.uk

Central Law Training Ltd
Wrens Court, 52-54 Victoria Road, Sutton Coldfield, Birmingham B72 1SX
Tel: 0121 362 7705
Email: registrar@clt.co.uk
Web: www.clt.co.uk

Chartered Institute of Legal Executives (CILEx)
Kempston Manor, Kempston, Bedfordshire MK42 7AB
Tel: 01234 841000
Email: info@cilex.org.uk
Web: www.cilex.org.uk

Chartered Institute of Patent Attorneys
2nd Floor Halton House, 20-23 Holborn, London EC1N 2JD
Tel: 020 7405 9450
Email: mail@cipa.org.uk
Web: www.cipa.org.uk

Chartered Institute of Taxation
1st Floor, Artillery House, 11-19 Artillery Row,
London SW1P 1RT
Tel: 020 7340 0550
Email: comms@tax.org.uk
Web: www.tax.org.uk

The Directory of Social Change
352 Holloway Road, London N7 6PA
Tel: 0207 697 4200
Email: cs@dsc.org.uk
Web: www.dsc.org.uk

Citizens Advice
3rd Floor North, 200 Aldersgate Street, London
EC1A 4HD
Tel: 03454 040 506
Web: www.citizensadvice.org.uk

Local Government Association
18 Smith Square, Westminster, London SW1P 3HZ
Tel: 020 7664 3000
Email: info@local.gov.uk
Web: www.local.gov.uk

Commercial Bar Association
3 Verulam Buildings, Gray's Inn, London WC1R 5NT
Tel: 020 7404 2022
Email: admin@combar.com
Web: www.combar.com

Employment Law Bar Association
Tel: 01895 256 972
Email: admin@elba.org.uk
Web: www.elba.org.uk

Council for Licensed Conveyancers
WeWork, 131 Finsbury Pavement, London
EC2A 1NT
Tel: 020 3859 0904
Email: clc@clc-uk.org
Web: www.clc-uk.org

European Commission
Europe House, 32 Smith Square, London
SW1P 3EU
Tel: 020 7973 1992
Email: comm-rep-london@ec.europa.eu
Web: http://ec.europa.eu/unitedkingdom

Criminal Bar Association
Suite 23, 30 St Dunstan's St, Canterbury CT2 8HG
Tel: 01304 849149
Email: aaron.dolan@criminalbar.com
Web: www.criminalbar.com

The Faculty of Advocates
Parliament Square, Edinburgh EH1 1RF
Tel: 0131 226 5071
Email: info@advocates.org.uk
Web: www.advocates.org.uk

The Crown Office
25 Chambers Street, Edinburgh EH1 1LA
Tel: 03000203000
Email: enquirypoint@copfs.gsi.gov.uk
Web: www.copfs.gov.uk

Family Law Bar Association
PO Box 857, Haywards Heath RH16 9PR
Tel: 0207 427 5591
Email: admin@flba.co.uk
Web: www.flba.co.uk

Crown Prosecution Service
Rose Court, 2 Southwark Bridge, London SE1 9HS
Tel: 020 3357 0899
Email: enquiries@cps.gov.uk
Web: www.cps.gov.uk

Free Representation Unit
5th Floor Kingsbourne House, 229-231 High
Holborn, London, WC1V 7DA
Tel: 020 7611 9555
Web: www.thefru.org.uk

Useful addresses

Government Legal Department
One Kemble Street, London WC2B 4TS
Tel: 020 7210 3000
Email: thetreasurysolicitor@governmentlegal.gov.uk
Web: www.gov.uk/government/organisations/
government-legal-department

Gray's Inn
Treasury Office, 8 South Square, London WC1R 5ET
Tel: 020 7458 7800
Web: www.graysinn.org.uk

Inner Temple
Treasury Office, Inner Temple, London EC4Y 7HL
Tel: 020 7797 8250
Email: enquiries@innertemple.org.uk
Web: www.innertemple.org.uk

Lincoln's Inn
Treasury Office, Lincoln's Inn, London WC2A 3TL
Tel: 020 7405 1393
Email: mail@lincolnsinn.org.uk
Web: www.lincolnsinn.org.uk

Middle Temple
Treasury Office, Ashley Building, Middle Temple
Lane, London EC4Y 9AT
Tel: 020 7427 4800
General enquiry: education@middletemple.org.uk
Email: members@middletemple.org.
Web: www.middletemple.org.uk

Institute of Barristers' Clerks
Queen Elizabeth Building, Temple, London,
EC4Y 9BS
Tel: 020 3763 8999
Email: admin@ibc.org.uk
Web: www.ibc.org.uk

Career Development Institute (CDI)
Ground Floor, Copthall House, 1 New Road,
Stourbridge, West Midlands DY8 1PH
Tel: 01384 376464
Email: hq@thecdi.net
Web: www.thecdi.net

**Institute of Chartered Accountants in England
and Wales (ICAEW)**
Chartered Accountants Hall, Moorgate Place
London EC2R 6EA
Tel: 020 7920 8100
Email: generalenquiries@icaew.com
Web: www.icaew.com

**Institute of Chartered Secretaries &
Administrators**
Saffron House, 6-10 Kirby Street, London
EC1N 8TS
Tel: 020 7580 4741
Email: info@icsa.org.uk
Web: www.icsa.org.uk

Institute of Legal Finance & Management
2nd Floor, Marlowe House, 109 Station Road,
Sidcup, Kent DA15 7ET
Tel: 020 8302 2867
Email: info@ilfm.org.uk
Web: www.ilfm.org.uk

Institute of Paralegals
Suite 1, 3rd Floor, 11-12 St James's Square,
London SW1Y 4LB
Tel: 020 3034 1487
Email: office@theiop.org
Web: www.theiop.org

Institute of Trademark Attorneys
ITMA Office, 5th Floor Outer Temple, 222-225
Strand, London WC2R 1BA
Tel: 020 7101 6090
Email: tm@citma.org.uk
Web: www.citma.org.uk

Intellectual Property Bar Association
Web: www.ipba.co.uk

Junior Lawyers Division
113 Chancery Lane, London WC2A 1PL
Email: juniorlawyers@lawsociety.org.uk
Web: http://communities.lawsociety.org.uk/junior-
lawyers

Law Centres Network
Floor 1, Tavis House, 1-6 Tavistock Square,
London WC1H 9NA
Tel: 020 3637 1330
Email: info@lawcentres.org.uk
Web: www.lawcentres.org.uk

National Association of Licensed Paralegals
Lincoln House, 1-3 Brixton Road, London
SW9 6DE
Tel: 0845 8627000
Email: info@nationalparalegals.co.uk
Web: www.nationalparalegals.co.uk

The Law Commission
1st Floor, Tower, 52 Queen Anne's Gate, London
SW1H 9AG
Tel: 020 3334 0200
Email: enquiries@lawcommission.gsi.gov.uk
Web: www.lawcom.gov.uk

Pupillage Gateway
The Bar Council, 289-293 High Holborn London
WC1V 7HZ
Tel: 020 7611 1321
Email: pupillagegateway@barcouncil.org.uk
Web: www.pupillagegateway.com

Law Society
113 Chancery Lane, London WC2A 1PL
Tel: 020 7242 1222
Web: www.lawsociety.org.uk

Personal Injuries Bar Association
Devereux Chambers, Devereux Court, London
WC2R 3JH
Email: weir@devchambers.co.uk
Web: www.piba.org.uk

Law Society of Northern Ireland
96 Victoria Street, Belfast BT1 3GN
Tel: 028 9023 1614
Email: enquiry@lawsoc-ni.org
Web: www.lawsoc-ni.org

Planning and Environmental Bar Association
4a Woodside Business Park, Whitley Wood Lane,
Reading, RG2 8LW
Tel: 0118 987 3345
Email: peba@peba.org.uk
Web: www.peba.org.uk

Law Society of Scotland
Atria One, 144 Morrison Street, Edinburgh
EH3 8EX
Tel: 0131 226 7411
Email: lawscot@lawscot.org.uk
Web: www.lawscot.org.uk

Property Bar Association
5 Quernmore Road, London N4 4QU
Web: www.propertybar.org.uk

Legal Aid Practitioners Group
12 Baylis Road, London SE1 7AA
Tel: 020 7833 7431
Web: www.lapg.co.uk

Revenue Bar Association
Temple Tax Chambers, 3 Temple Gardens, London
EC4Y 9AU
Tel: 020 7353 7884
Email: rba@templetax.com
Web: www.revenue-bar.org

The Magistrates Association
10A Flagstaff House, St George Wharf, London
SW8 2LE
Tel: 020 7387 2353
Email: information@magistrates-association.org.uk
Web: www.magistrates-association.org.uk

Society of Asian Lawyers
Web: www.societyofasianlawyers.co.uk

Useful addresses

Solicitors Regulation Authority
The Cube, 199 Wharfside Street, Birmingham
B1 1RN
Tel: 0370 606 2555
Email: contactcentre@sra.org.uk
Web: www.sra.org.uk

Universities and Colleges Admission Service (UCAS)
Rosehill, New Barn Lane, Cheltenham,
Gloucestershire, GL52 3LZ
Tel: 0371 468 0468
Web: www.ucas.com

Technology & Construction Bar Association
Web: www.tecbar.org